THE
TRANSFORMATION
OF
RUSSIAN
SOCIETY

**ASPECTS OF
SOCIAL CHANGE
SINCE 1861**

Edited by Cyril E. Black

HARVARD UNIVERSITY PRESS
CAMBRIDGE • MASSACHUSETTS
1960

Distributed in Great Britain by Oxford University Press, London

Library of Congress Catalog Card Number: 60–13286

Printed in the United States of America

PREFACE

The papers in this volume were originally presented at a conference held at Arden House, in Harriman, New York, on April 25–27, 1958, under the auspices of the Joint Committee on Slavic Studies of the American Council of Learned Societies and the Social Science Research Council. The steering committee which planned the program and procedures drew heavily on the experience of two earlier conferences held under the same auspices, the results of which have been published in Abram Bergson, ed., *Soviet Economic Growth: Conditions and Perspectives* (Evanston, Ill., 1953), and Ernest J. Simmons, ed., *Continuity and Change in Russian and Soviet Thought* (Cambridge, Mass., 1955).

The papers were prepared and circulated in advance, so that the conference sessions could be devoted primarily to discussion, and have subsequently been revised in a number of cases. The selection of the topics and participants was based in the main on research already completed or in progress. This volume therefore reflects in considerable measure the scope and variety, as well as the limitations, of the work on modern Russia that is being done in the United States. In addition, it was fortunately possible to include three European scholars, whose interests are closely related to this general subject. The summary and review at the end of each section was prepared by the session chairmen on the basis of the papers as originally presented at the conference. Needless to say, the views expressed in this volume are those of the individual authors.

At a later stage, when there is freer access to Russia and when theories of social change have been more fully developed, it will no doubt be possible to make a more comprehensive and systematic study of this subject. As the reader will readily see, this volume makes no claim to treating all aspects of Russian society, nor does it approach the subject on the basis of a strictly defined theory as to how societies are structured and how they change. The purpose of the present effort is to raise questions rather than to settle them, and to interest scholars in a somewhat different approach to the study of modern Russia from that which has traditionally been adopted. To this end, scholars in economics, education, history, literature, philosophy, political science, and sociology have pooled their knowledge and points of view, and it is hoped that as a by-product of this common effort work in each discipline will be stimulated by that in the others.

In addition to the participants whose work is presented here, a number of other scholars took part in the conference discussions. At each of the five conference sessions — the chapters in Part One of this volume were distributed as background papers — the deliberations were initiated by a discussion leader: Geroid T. Robinson of Columbia University for law, politics, and social change; Henry L. Roberts of Columbia University for social stratification; Ernest J. Simmons of Columbia University for education, scholarship, and religion; Philip E. Mosely of the Council on Foreign Relations for family, youth, and human welfare; and Nathan Leites of the RAND Corporation for personal and social values. The conference was also attended by Robert F. Byrnes of Indiana University, Hedley Donovan of *Time Inc.*, Dana B. Durand of the United States government, William B. Edgerton of Indiana University, Charles Jelavich of the University of California at Berkeley, William H. E. Johnson of the University of Pittsburgh, Kurt L. London of the United States government, Robert H. McNeal of the University of Alberta, Harry Schwartz of the *New York Times,* and Sergius Yakobson of the Library of Congress.

It is a pleasant duty, on the occasion of the publication of the conference papers, to thank those whose special efforts contributed to the success of this venture. The Joint Committee on Slavic Studies, under the chairmanship of William B. Edgerton, deserves the principal credit for the initiation and support of the conference and of this volume; the members of the conference steering committee — Alex Inkeles, Philip E. Mosely, Henry L. Roberts, Nicholas S. Timasheff, and the editor — established the general policies which guided the planning of the conference, and many others were consulted from time to time; Pendleton Herring and Bryce Wood of the Social Science Research Council, and Frederick H. Burkhardt of the American Council of Learned Societies, gave this enterprise the benefit of the long experience of their organizations in support of American scholarship; and Robert H. McNeal earned the indebtedness of his fellow participants for his efficient handling of the administrative details of the conference. Thanks are also due to many others who read individual sections of the manuscript and assisted the authors with advice and criticism.

Funds for the support of the conference and of this volume were made available from the program for Slavic and East European Studies administered by the Subcommittee on Grants of the Joint Committee on Slavic Studies, and supplementary publication grants were made by the American Council of Learned Societies, the Russian Institute of Columbia University, and the Russian Research Center of Harvard University. The editor also wishes to express his thanks to the Center of International Studies of Princeton University for making available its support and facilities in the preparation of this manuscript for publication and in the drafting of the introductory and concluding chapters.

March 1960   Cyril E. Black

CONTENTS

PART FOUR • EDUCATION, SCHOLARSHIP, AND RELIGION

PART FIVE • FAMILY, YOUTH, AND HUMAN WELFARE

PART SIX • PERSONAL AND SOCIAL VALUES

PART SEVEN • CONCLUSION

CONTENTS

INTRODUCTION

INTRODUCTION

CYRIL E. BLACK

I

The growing interest in Russia on the part of American scholars since the Second World War has been centered primarily on political history and structure, economic development, and trends of thought. Although contemporary Soviet society is now the subject of intensive study, little attention has been devoted to the broader problems of social change that have been raised by the transformation of Russia during the past century from a predominantly agrarian to a predominantly industrial way of life. As has been pointed out recently in an appraisal of American historical scholarship relating to Russia, "Political developments and foreign policy are often discussed without reference to the social and economic forces which form an inseparable part of any national scene. These forces are particularly important for an understanding of Russia, because it is specifically these aspects that are so different from those familiar to American historians. Many of the limitations of American historical work on Russia may be explained by its two-dimensional approach." [1]

This neglect of social change in Russia as a subject for scholarship has perhaps been magnified by the great interest in contemporary Soviet institutions. It is natural that the revolution of 1917 should have exerted a powerful attraction for students of Russia, but the result has been a focusing of interest in the latest developments and a tendency to treat events before and since the revolution in separate compartments. The valuable work that has been done by anthropologists, economists, political scientists, and sociologists has been preoccupied to such an extent with the even more limited period since the inauguration of the five-year plans that there has been little opportunity to study social change over a longer time-span. Much systematic research has been done in these disciplines, but their perspective is restricted primarily to the structure of society in a relatively short period of development. [2] The historians, for their part, have as a rule not ventured much beyond 1917 except in studying ideology and foreign policy. The types of source material on which historians are accustomed to rely are not readily available for much of the Soviet period,

[1] John S. Curtiss, in Harold H. Fisher, ed., *American Research on Russia* (Bloomington, 1959), 33.
[2] See especially the chapters by Gregory Grossman on economics, John A. Armstrong on political science, and Arthur S. Barron on social relations in Fisher, 34–65, 77–102.

and only recently have professional historians turned their attention to the problems raised by the inclusion of the Soviet period into the long stream of Russian history. It should be noted in passing, however, that American historians have not been alone in this relative neglect of Soviet history. A similar lack of interest has been characteristic of historians in Europe; and even in the Soviet Union — although for somewhat different reasons — historians have concentrated their attention on the prerevolutionary era.

It must also be recognized that it is not an easy matter to define the scope of social history, or to find a satisfactory theoretical basis for describing social change. What is involved is more a way of looking at things than a separate subject matter. Certain characteristic problems are no doubt of particular interest to social historians — the changing relations of individuals and groups, and the evolution of such institutions as education, medical care, and transportation, for example — but this is the lesser part of the story. In a larger sense, all political, economic, technological, and intellectual developments have their social effects, and social history, is concerned with the responses of individuals and groups to these developments.

One may limit the subject by concentrating on social change in a single society, such as Russia, over the period of a century in which the impact of the technological revolution is clearly apparent. Yet even within such limits one is confronted with the problem of finding appropriate categories for the presentation and interpretation of a vast array of materials in a most complex and ever-changing interrelationship. The shortcomings of our methodology being what they are, one must start by treating those aspects of social change which have already been investigated in some detail. As the study of social change develops in the various disciplines concerned, it will eventually be possible to provide a more comprehensive picture of the adaptation of Russian society to the most dynamic forces that human society has encountered.

II

The selection of 1861 as a point of departure is of necessity somewhat arbitrary, but the role that this date has played in the history of Russian periodization deserves some attention. The doctrine that 1861 marks the dividing line between "feudalism" and "capitalism" is today a cornerstone of the Soviet periodization of Russian history, second in importance only to 1917 in modern times, although this consensus was reached only after lengthy controversies. The traditional periodization of Russian history emphasized the three successive states which had Kiev, Moscow, and St. Petersburg as their capitals, and some historians also stressed the significance of the transitional era of Mongol rule from the mid-thirteenth to the mid-fifteenth centuries) between the Kievan and the Muscovite periods. These and other non-Soviet variants were in agreement, however, that Russian history from the reign of Peter the Great to the revolution of 1917 should be treated as a single period, and that the era of reforms starting in 1861, however significant, was not of sufficient importance to serve as a principal division of Russian history.

The first generation of Soviet historians experimented rather indecisively with various alternatives to this traditional scheme, burdened as they were by a rather ambiguous theoretical heritage. Marx and Engels had originally characterized Tsarist society as "semi-Asiatic" as distinct from the "feudal" and later "capitalist" societies of Europe, on the one hand, and the "Asiatic" societies of India and China, on the other. Plekhanov accepted this approach, as did Lenin until the world war, with its two significant implications: first, that tsarism was not the same thing as feudalism or capitalism, and, second, that "semi-Asiatic" tsarism had to be replaced by a bourgeois society before conditions would be appropriate for a socialist revolution. This relatively clear-cut doctrine was somewhat confused by later speculations of Marx and Engels as to possible interactions of European and Russian revolutionary situations, and then the dramatic events of war and revolution placed these abstractions in an entirely new light. Lenin needed to justify his revolution as part of the inexorable logic of history, and before long Stalin found it desirable to portray the Soviet Union as being in the forefront of a universal historical trend. They therefore ignored or deliberately misrepresented the main current of Marxist (and earlier Leninist) theory, and generalized as universally applicable the successive stages of feudalism, capitalism, and socialism which had originally been postulated for Europe alone.

This adjustment of theory to circumstance during the 1920's naturally led to considerable confusion in Soviet historical circles, and it was not until the 1930's that the problem of periodization was systematically discussed. It was at this time that the decision was taken to regard the millennium of Russian history ending in 1861 as the "feudal" period. Despite extensive debates in recent years, no very satisfactory consensus has been reached as to the subdivision of this long period into more manageable subperiods, but in any event 1861 has stood firm.[3] The period from 1861 to 1917 is now regarded as that of "capitalism," and this in turn is now divided into subperiods of "premonopolistic capitalism" (1861–1890) and "imperialism" (1890–1917). The period of "socialism" (since 1917), on the other hand, is currently considered to comprise two general subperiods: "the transitional period from capitalism to socialism" (1917–1937), and "the period of the completion of the construction of socialism and of the gradual transition to communism" (since 1937).[4]

[3] See Leo Yaresh, "The Problem of Periodization," in C. E. Black, ed., *Rewriting Russian History: Soviet Interpretations of Russia's Past* (New York, 1956), 32–77.
[4] The table of contents of *Istoriia SSSR: Epokha sotsializma* (Moscow, 1958), 767–772, offers a convenient synopsis of the latest system of periodization.

European and American historians have, more frequently than not, adhered to the traditional pre-Soviet interpretation, although increasing attention has been paid in recent years to the contrast between the apparent stability of the era of Nicholas I and the restless change which marked the reigns of Alexander II and his successors. Since there are few natural "periods" in history, apart from the rise and fall of well-defined political and economic systems, a scheme of periodization must depend to a very considerable degree on the purposes which it is meant to serve. The traditional periodization of Russian history was based on political considerations and was further subdivided into the reigns of the sovereigns, if these were long or important, or of a series of rulers, if they were short and insignificant. This system, like the "presidential synthesis" in American history, has the advantage of clearly defined political periods along with the disadvantage that these are better adapted to a discussion of political events than to one of social and economic trends. In the case of Russia, the main periods were in fact sufficiently broad to provide ample scope for interpretation. With regard to the last prerevolutionary period, however, embracing the eighteenth, nineteenth, and early twentieth centuries, the disadvantages of a purely political periodization are more impressive. The nineteeth century in particular was an era of very rapid change in all aspects of Russian life — marked by unprecedented intellectual activity, the dissolution of a long-established economic system, and a general reconstruction of political and social institutions — and it lost a good deal by being treated as part of a longer period held together principally by the rule of the Romanov family. There has been, at the same time, a tendency to distort Russian history somewhat by trying to fit it into the European mold. For Europe, and the Americas as well, the century starting with the French Revolution and Napoleon and ending with the First World War makes a manageable and coherent period. Russia developed on a rather different schedule, however, and this raises the question of an alternative periodization.

The Soviet system of periodization, in contrast to the traditional, is based primarily on economic considerations, although political factors are also taken into account. This system is also influenced by the demands of the Communist Party, as already suggested. These demands have not been particularly controversial as they relate to recent history, for the period since 1917 must now clearly be designated as one of "socialism" and must be preceded by one of "capitalism." The question of the boundary between "capitalism" and "feudalism" is somewhat more problematical, although 1861 is probably the most reasonable of the various available alternatives. It is only with the thousand-year period of "feudalism" that Soviet historians have found Leninism-Stalinism to be a real obstacle to a scholarly consideration of the problems of interpretation, but the controversies which this debate has aroused do not concern us here.

The significance of 1861 for Russian social history is that it marks a convenient point of division between the predominantly agrarian and the predominantly industrial eras in Russia. These two eras, defined essentially as two stages of knowledge and technology and only secondarily as forms of production, are widely used as a basis for periodizing history. Indeed, in many countries the transition from one stage to the other has been marked by political upheavals which facilitate periodization, although rarely have the issues been as well defined as in the case of the French Revolution. In Russia this transition was somewhat muted because it took place without a political upheaval, as the result of an orderly decision by state authorities, and within one of the traditionally defined "periods." This is no reason, however, to neglect its significance for social history.

It is of course clear that the reform of 1861 marked neither the end of special restrictions on the peasants nor the beginning of the rapid growth of heavy industry. A significant proportion of peasants remained under serious limitations until the end of the century. Industrialization had been under way since the eighteenth century or even earlier, but heavy industry did not expand rapidly until the 1880's. Yet it would be too much to expect of history to have such great events turn on a single year, and the significance of 1861 is that it was the year in which the state took the decision to emancipate the serfs. This decision inaugurated a new era in Russian social history.

To place this emphasis on 1861 is not to underestimate the importance of 1917. Both years mark important political decisions of which the social and economic consequences were not immediately apparent, and the latter is unquestionably the more important year of decision in the perspective of the entire sweep of Russian history. Yet in terms of a social history that seeks to assess the impact on Russia of dynamic changes resulting from the application of a new technology, 1861 was the more important date. This particular process of change was well under way by 1917, however much its course may have been affected by the dramatic events of that year.

III

A satisfactory interpretation of social change in Russia since 1861 would require a firmer basis in theory and a much broader foundation of research than are now available. Despite the significant advances in social theory in recent decades, and the very elaborate research on certain aspects of Soviet society, this field of study is still young. There are nevertheless several types of questions to which one may legitimately seek the answers at this stage. One of these concerns continuity and change. While this may at first glance appear to be a rather unsophisticated approach to social history, since it is clear that every social process has continuity at the same time that change is taking place, it is nevertheless a convenient device for sorting out certain distinctive trends. It is particularly useful as a means of finding out how profoundly a society is affected by the revolution in technology. Are some aspects of a society changed more than others? To what extent is the impact on certain obvious aspects such as health, education, and per-capita production matched in the fields of political institutions and values? Are there some aspects of human activity that remain relatively unaffected?

This problem is important because the study of modernization has been so much under the influence of the Western prototype that there has been a tendency to assume that the Western pattern will be reproduced all over the world in almost all its aspects. Indeed, modernization is frequently thought of as a process by which non-Western societies are transformed along Western lines. If, on the other hand, it should turn out that significant aspects of a society remain relatively unchanged by the technological revolution, one must anticipate no less cultural variety in the modern world of several generations hence than exists today. It is a question of the extent to which historically formed traditions survive modernization. The answer to this question will not be known until the process has gone a good deal further in several societies with distinctly different traditions from those of the West, but every study of social change should seek to make its contribution to the answer.

The question of continuity and change within a given society is thus closely related to that of the comparability of societies. A good deal of thought is now being devoted to the relative stages of development in different societies, and in a few specialized fields, such as economic growth and population changes, it is possible to demonstrate statistically the relative "maturity" of societies that have undergone the technological revolution relatively early or relatively late. Due to the lack of reliable statistics, however, only a few aspects of human activity are susceptible to such periodization in historical depth. While statistics may never be available for most societies except in the most recent period, there is a great deal that can be learned about the nature of social change from a comparison of different societies. At the most elementary level, it should be possible to identify those aspects of modernization which are truly universal: the acceptance of change, urbanization, the applicability of the exact sciences, and the mechanization of production, for example; and those which appear to be relatively unaffected, such as language, the nature of authority, and what the cultural anthropologists call "national character." Our knowledge of social change within each society would be enhanced by the understanding of this process which the comparative study of societies would contribute.

Russia is particularly appropriate for study from this point of view, since the question of Russia's relation to Europe has been a central theme both of Russian intellectual history and of European comment about Russia. If it were possible to compare Russian traditional values and national character with those of European societies, on the one hand, and with those of one or more Asian societies, on the other, we would know a good deal more than we do now about the relation between the universal and the particular. At the same time, the study of social change in Russia is complicated by the fact that the country which we customarily refer to as "Russia" is in fact a conglomerate of many peoples of which the Russians, as distinct from the Ukrainian, Belorussian, and non-Slavic minority peoples, comprise little more than one half the population. Of the non-Russian nationalities, some are very close to the Russians in historical experience and national character. Others, however, vary greatly in both the nature of their traditional values and institutions and the degree to which they have been affected by modern technology. To this extent, Russia is in itself a laboratory of comparative social change. Indeed, there is scarcely a generalization that one can make about Russian society that would not have to be modified with respect to one or another of its component peoples if only our knowledge were more complete. It is, in fact, a measure of the inadequacies of our knowledge that in discussing Russian society we cannot yet grapple satisfactorily with these various subsocieties and must discuss Russia as though it were more homogeneous than it actually is.

Although the study of social change has not advanced very far, much valuable work has been done on social structure. An understanding of social structure is fundamental to the study of social change, since the latter involves the comparison of the structure of a given society at two or more different stages in its growth. In approaching the structure of Russian society, one may thus draw on the extensive body of concepts based on analyses of European and American social structure. While exercising appropriate caution in applying these concepts to a somewhat different type of society, one nevertheless has a useful guide in describing Russian political and economic institutions, the composition and relationship of social strata, the organization of family, religion, education, and social services, and the prevailing values and norms. Not only can Western concepts serve as tools of analysis, but they can also be tested and refined in the course of study of non-Western societies. As for social change, it can at least be described in those areas in which the necessary preliminary research has been done. One may also speculate on the causes and mechanisms of change, although this will have to be done without much assistance as yet from the theorists.

PART ONE

SOCIETY AND CHANGE

SOME PRINCIPAL CHARACTERISTICS
OF INDUSTRIAL SOCIETIES

TALCOTT PARSONS

I

The task of this chapter is to attempt to delineate, in the light of general sociological theory and of comparative and historical empirical knowledge, some of the principal features of the structure of that still small, but increasing, group of societies which can be called "industrial." Naturally this will include consideration of some of the principal sociological conditions which seem to be necessary for the development of such a society, but the emphasis here will not be on the process of development but rather on structural characteristics as such. These two problems are by no means identical.

These structural characteristics are both economic and noneconomic. The economic ones concern the characteristics of an industrial economy, in the sense in which the economist would use this term. To analyze this is not my task here, and I shall therefore attempt to outline only a few of its main highlights. Some discussion of it is necessary, however, because it provides the essential points of reference for the classification and analysis of the important noneconomic factors with which my main discussion will be concerned. It is precisely those aspects of the same society of which an industrial economy is a part, but which are not and, I think, cannot be adequately dealt with in technical economic analysis, that will be outlined here. After making one preliminary point, I shall proceed to a very broad outline of the essentials of an industrial economy, and in the course of that discussion introduce a classification of the main noneconomic factors with which I think it is essential to deal.

The point which needs to be made before taking up the problem of the industrial economy is that, certainly by contrast with all previous types of society and hence its own immediate historical antecedents, an industrial society must at some time have given special emphasis to the development of the economy, and hence have accorded to the economy a place of special prominence in the structure of the society. An industrial society therefore either is or has been one in which economic considerations have had a certain primacy over others. This in turn means that, relative to concerns "internal" to the society, such as its values, religion, personality interests, or its own integration, such a society must have been characterized by a pronounced orientation toward mastery of the external environment of the system. This emphasis is difficult to identify within a cultural complex, but it stands out sharply in contrasts such as that between modern Western society and India and China. Economic emphasis is not, however, the only type of orientation to situational mastery. There is also political emphasis on power position in a system of politically organized societies, or "states." By contrast with concern for power position, the economic emphasis, externally, is on mastery of the physical environment and economic advantage through trade with other societies.

It is essential to distinguish, however, between this question of economic versus political primacy in the pattern of mastery of the situation external to the society in question and that of the role of political agency in the development and management of an economy, industrial or otherwise. Internally political agency may be of the very first importance in the latter context, and externally it may also be an agency of first importance in securing and maintaining control of basic resources, and in influencing the character and terms of trade. I shall argue below that the main differentiation of type, at least in the early stages of industrialism, is between that type which does and that which does not rely most heavily on political agency in the developmental and industrial-management contexts. The Soviet Union is the paradigmatic example of such reliance, whereas the United States approaches the extreme in the other direction in the present phase. In an earlier phase, Great Britain was an even purer type.

II

In dealing with the main features of an industrial economy I shall adopt Alfred Marshall's pattern of classification and attempt to fill in the main rubrics with broad empirical-typological characterizations.[1] The first essential distinction is that between consumption and production. For anything approaching the industrial level there is implied, in the relation between them, a highly elaborated division of labor in the conventional economic sense. This in turn implies a high degree of specialization of producing units both at the stage of the completion and distribution of products, and at earlier stages in the production sequence. For the household consumer, because such consumers are the source of labor supply at all levels, this also implies that consumer goods for any one household are drawn from many producing units. Hence there must be some structure of markets, both a consumer-goods market and a labor

[1] The version of the Marshallian classification used here, and the way I shall employ it to indicate the main points of articulation with the noneconomic structures of the same society, have been developed in Talcott Parsons and Neil J. Smelser, *Economy and Society: A Study in the Integration of Economic and Social Theory* (Glencoe, 1956). There are a few modifications of this treatment.

market. Such a market system must be mediated either by money or by some functional equivalent, an "accounting" system.

The famous dictum of Adam Smith, that the division of labor depends on the extent of the market, is very relevant here. The products of the same producing unit must somehow, in a large number of cases, reach very large numbers of consuming units. There is, however, one very important qualification to be made. This is that the proportion of total production going to household consumers may vary greatly, as a function of rates of new investment and of nonhousehold consumption. Both the latter, particularly investment in the capitalization of heavy industry and consumption by government, especially for armaments, may be much more concentrated than is household consumption and may allow greater concentration of industrial units.

On the whole, however, relatively extended consumer markets have developed prior to and independently of industrial organization, though this is a quantitative matter. More crucial for present purposes is the organization of the factors of production in the economist's sense. For any given productive purpose the supplies of the factors of production should not be fixed, but should be capable of mobilization. From the point of view of the economy as a system, then, there should be flexible, economically sensitive mechanisms of allocation of the factors. These factors are, according to Marshall, land, labor, capital, and organization. Let me discuss each of these in turn.

Through most of economic tradition land has been treated as a natural resource, the supply of which is, for purposes of economic analysis, treated as given. The essential point is that the total quantity of such resources available to the economy is not a function of its price. What is open to the operation of "economic forces" is only the allocation of this fixed quantity of resources. Acquisition of such resources abroad by market procedures would, I presume, be treated as capital investment from the point of view of the economy in question. The point is that such resources were, like capital goods in the ordinary sense, acquirable by committing a portion of the product of economic activity, for the economy as a whole, not only for the individual unit.

There are, however, other sets of components, which behave, from the point of view of the economy as a whole, like land in the physical-resource sense. These components should, for analytical purposes, be classified with land. They comprise the main interests of the sociologist, consisting of cultural resources and institutional structures. The cultural category in turn breaks down into two components of particular significance for economic analysis, namely technological knowledge and commitment to cultural values. The first is not particularly problematical from the present point of view. Empirically so far as knowledge is produced by economic organization as such it becomes a form of capital, but generally it seems safe to say that the more fundamental framework of the "state of the arts" is the outcome of noneconomic processes and interests and should be treated as a given for economic purposes. This may be treated as an empirical problem. It also seems correct to say that technological development becomes a product of productive processes rather than a given factor far more in the later than in the earlier stages of industrial development.

With reference both to technological knowledge and to natural resources it is quite clear that relatively high levels are necessary for an industrial economy, simply because the latter is, by comparison with other types, characterized by high levels of productivity. There is, however, the one crucial difference between the two: usable knowledge is "produced" by two processes which, though economic factors play a part, are predominantly noneconomic, namely research and education.

The second cultural component I have referred to as value-commitments. Empirically it influences the economy through the channel of human services, including those of "enterpreneurs." But it should be considered a given from the point of view of the functioning of the economy.[2] It is therefore essential to divide the motivation of human services in production into two components, that element which, psychologically, we would call internalized values and that which we would think of as responsive to such economic sanctions as rewards. It is the first component which is here at issue. In industrial terms it may be called high motivation for achievement in directions which can be utilized for economic production.[3] This factor therefore articulates with the value system of the society and the mechanisms of its institutionalization.

In empirical terms "labor" usually means to the economist the concrete activities of an individual human being in a productive context, including all the factors which determine these activities. In the present analytical sense, however, it must refer to one set of components determining such activities, namely, given the individual's value-commitments, those which determine what portion of his energies will become available for particular productive purposes. It is this component the supply of which can, under certain conditions, be treated as a function of economic sanctions, that is, of its price. Clearly "wages" constitute a prime determinant of the allocation of a given labor supply among economic uses, and is often an important factor in attracting people, or portions of their energies, into the labor force. An industrial society from this point of view requires both an adequate labor force in terms of magnitude and a

---

[2] This is the element which Marshall referred to as "activities," as distinguished from "wants," in his analysis of the relation between consumption and the motivation to produce. See Talcott Parsons, *The Structure of Social Action* (2nd ed., Glencoe, 1949), ch. 4.

[3] I mean achievement here in essentially the sense used by David C. McClelland, and others, in *The Achievement Motive* (New York, 1953).

flexible or mobile labor force. The levels of skill of that force I should treat mainly as a given for purposes of economic analysis, namely the "internalization" of technological culture through educational processes.

The factor of capital is from the point of view of the production process a special one because it is not, in the same sense, independent. Capitalization is essentially the diversion of the product of past production to form an instrumentality of future production. To be built up from a preindustrial level, an industrial economy clearly requires a very large capital investment, either from internal sources or from outside. The production of capital goods as such, however, presents no special problems from the present point of view; it is simply part of the general production process.

There is, however, common to capital and to consumer goods a crucial problem — that of the basis on which they can be used, controlled, and exchanged. This involves the whole complex of the institution of property. This in turn is closely involved with the institutionalization of money and processes of exchange through contract.

The quantity of labor in an analytical sense is not a given from the point of view of the processes of the economy. But the institutional framework within which labor services become available for production is a given. Hence the degree and kinds of flexibility or mobility of the labor force will be determined by institutional patterns which are economic givens. The same applies to the institution of property in its relations to both capital and consumer goods and to money and the whole range of financial instruments. None of the quantities of these are necessarily given independently of economic processes, but the institutional framework within which their allocation takes place and their quantities vary is a noneconomic given factor. Here again the industrial economy requires not only high capitalization, but flexibility in the market structures so that the quantities devoted to production can be large, and flexibly allocated, relative to other competing claims upon them.

The factor of organization in Marshall's sense must, like labor and capital, be broken down into an economic factor and a given noneconomic component or aspect. The given factor concerns the institutional framework within which the combination of the factors of production takes place. This concerns the institutional structure of the collectivities or "organizations" within which productive processes are carried out. In the strict analytical sense this is what I shall call a "political" area of institutionalization, distinguishing this analytical sense from that of "government" which I shall treat as political organization at the level of the total society considered as a system.

In this sense an industrial economy requires the appropriate institutional framework for the establishment of "firms" which can operate in terms of a clear primacy of economic (that is, productive) functions, as measured in market or administrative terms, and which, internally, allow a high degree of control over the factors as well as access to supplies of them from outside.

From this institutional component of organization it is necessary to distinguish the "entrepreneurial" component. This is a flexible, allocable resource which can be attracted into certain fields of production by economic opportunity. This latter factor is cognate with political leadership in the concrete sense rather than, as in the former case, with the institutional pattern of leadership.

The factors of the social system which must be treated as givens from the point of view of economic analysis will be treated under two main headings in the following pages: (1) commitments to values; and (2) the structure of institutional systems, on the level first of the general character of normative institutions, particularly that of law. It will then be studied in more detail with respect to a primarily "economic" context (relating to labor and capital as factors) comprising contract, property, and occupation, and a primarily "political" complex (relating to organization as a factor) and comprising what I shall call leadership, authority, and "regulation." Technological knowledge and the attendant skills must be omitted because of limitations of space.

There is, however, one further major subject which is too vital to omit which is also primarily noneconomic in orientation, though it may be "harnessed" to productive goals — namely, political organization at the societal, or governmental, level. This does not relate specifically to any one factor of production, but is most closely connected with organization. It is significant above all in two ways: as presenting first, through administrative mechanisms, a set of alternatives to the mechanisms of the market, and secondly alternatives to independent entrepreneurship. In connection with the latter it may be a particularly important instrumentality of new and rapid development.

III

As I noted at the beginning of this chapter, the relevance of value-commitments is in part relative to the stage of development of a society. In general, however, industrialization is possible only through a very substantial relative accentuation of stress on the problems of orientation of a society to external exigencies, whether the main focus of this orientation be economical or political. Therefore, as a first step it may be said that industrialization implies either a strong emphasis in this direction built into the longer-run institutionalized value-system, or a shift in the direction of greater emphasis in the relatively recent background. At the same time, industrialization is related to the level of structural differentiation of the society. Hence one would not expect that societies below a given level of such differentiation would respond readily even to outside stimulus in this respect, whatever their values.

It can also be stated as a generalization that, whatever the causal factors, spontaneous development of a major orientation of values from within a society is always expressed in the character of its religious tradition, which therefore constitutes an important index of its values. From this point of view, the Judaeo-Christian tradition has from early times tended, with certain periods of "recession," to be highly activistic in relation to the external environment. By contrast, the great civilizations of the Orient, notably China and India, have had a quite different character. But there have been a number of different phases in the development of the West from this point of view; the one most directly relevant as underlying the development of industrialism is certainly that associated with what Max Weber called "ascetic Protestantism," in northwestern Europe and North America in the two centuries immediately preceding the Industrial Revolution.[4]

The essential point here is that the institutionalization of a system of values, when internalized in the personalities of individuals, can motivate sufficient "drive" in the field of economic production to carry through the immense labor of industrialization. It can also "legitimize" the institutional arrangements and political structures associated with this process, which often involve quite radical changes from previous states of affairs.

The requisite system of values need not, however, arise spontaneously within the society. It may become institutionalized through processes which are analogous to the internalization of adult culture by children — namely, by what anthropologists would call "diffusion." This is likely to be the main process in cases of societies which have been industrialized at a late period after important models already were in existence and impinged on them in important ways. Here, however, the relative "hospitality" of the value system of the society undergoing industrialization is a factor of the first importance. In the case of Japan there seem to have been important elements favoring such reception, whereas in China such elements were much less prominent and hence a more radical change was necessitated.[5] At the very least, however, it would have taken very much longer for Japan to develop an industrial type of organization had not both the model and the economic and political pressure of the West existed. Quite clearly this influence of the external model is the most crucial factor at present in the widespread attempts at industrial develop-

[4] A recent contribution, N. J. Smelser, "The British Cotton Textile Industry, 1780–1840" (Harvard University, unpublished dissertation, 1958), has assembled evidence that there was a marked revival of Puritanism in the north of England in the later eighteenth century.

[5] Robert N. Bellah, *Tokugawa Religion* (Glencoe, 1957).

ment in the underdeveloped societies, whether their industrialization is proceeding under Communist or "democratic" auspices.

Let me return for a moment to the role of these internalized and institutionalized values. The essential point at the motivational level is the urge to achievement in occupational roles devoted to productive tasks. These tasks may manifest a wide variety of technical content, and also of course be located over a wide organizational range in terms of technical and organizational status and responsibility. But there are above all two major characteristics that define the core of the motivational problem: people must be motivated to serve the goal of production beyond the levels previously treated as normal, desirable, or necessary in the society, and they must perform such tasks to a much higher degree than before in organizations specifically differentiated from other, nonproductive, functional contexts (labor must be "alienable").

Most preindustrial societies have not had the cultural or structural basis for a value system which would motivate this type of activity over a wide range. For example, the main models of the good life have tended very widely to be "aristocratic" and to treat active mastery of the situation as altogether inferior to religious or style-of-life interests which stood in sharp contrast with such mastery; or, if it was valued, it has been mainly in a political context with a military emphasis above all. In either case economic production has tended to be treated as a definitely inferior function, fit only for persons of low if not servile status. The second great uniformity in preindustrial societies is the fusion of most productive functions with others in nexuses of relations with primarily noneconomic significance, or at best only very partial economic significance. Peasant agriculture may serve as a type case of this latter phenomenon.

In this connection it should be made quite clear that internalized values constitute a quite different component of motivational systems from the "economic rationality" which the main tradition of economics has tended to emphasize. The expression of an internalized value is not primarily dependent on any specific level of reward for its motivation. This was Weber's fundamental point as against the economic-utilitarian interpretations of "capitalism." Market mechanisms, and with them monetary rewards, have played an enormously important allocative function in the development of industrial societies. But this is quite a different matter from the reward-function of money income being held to account for the main directions and intensity levels of the deeper motivational "drives" underlying high production.[6]

Similar considerations apply to the importance of values in legitimizing institutionalized norms. This is above all the case with the mobility of the factors of production, but also applies to the consumption side of the

[6] This point has recently been cogently stated in David C. McClelland, *Community Development and the Nature of Human Motivation*, mimeographed (1957).

economy. The barriers to the mobilization of resources in the interest of production have been so fundamental as to involve the value level at many points. This is evident from the strong strain of *moral* indignation which has generally been aroused by large-scale attempts to increase the range of such mobility. It is a gross error to suppose that the predominant question of economic development where it involves major structural change in the society is that of finding more efficient ways of producing more goods. However true it may have been the first time industrialism appeared, today this statement is surely incorrect. The principal barrier to development is resistance to changing the values and institutionalized norms which form the main structural framework of the society.

Where the primary process of value change involves borrowing from a model external to the society, I suggest that ideology tends to serve functions analogous to those of religious movements in changing internal values. Industrialization is a process directly involving the economic and only secondarily, though vitally, the political sector of the social structure. The standards set for it are also taken from societies with cultural traditions, particularly at the religious level, which are foreign to the society undergoing industrialization. The necessary changes in the structure of the society are then "justified" in terms of a system of beliefs which are held with high emotional intensity and are indeed, in their sociological characteristics and functions, far removed from "technical" considerations of economic efficiency and political effectiveness. The function of these ideologies is not to define technologies of economic organization, but to legitimize change in values and in institutional structure.

Seen in this perspective, a remarkable thing has happened in the world in the last generation or so. In spite of the immense range of variation in values and other elements of culture, as in social structure, there has come to be an almost world-wide consensus on the evaluation of high, industrial-level, economic productivity. Ideology is the main expression of this at high cultural levels. Essentially it means the general acceptance of the industrial models of Western society as providing at least *one* essential part of the "good society." The intense emotionalism accompanying the assertions of ideology and the clear ambivalence involved, such as intense anticolonialism, at the same time indicate serious strains which, in many cases, are occasioned largely by the incompleteness of the institutionalization of the new values and norms. The broad ideological division between the "capitalistic" and the "socialistic" models of the industrial society reflects the ways in which the role of government is differentially conceived, which will be further discussed later.[7]

[7] I have discussed various of these problems further in a paper, "Some Reflections on the Institutional Framework of Economic Development," in *The Challenge of Development* (Jerusalem, 1958). It is there pointed out that in the "underdeveloped

IV

The legal system. In the modern Western world the essential institutional prerequisites of industrialization, with respect notably to markets and to the mobility and organization of the factors of production, are rooted in legal systems the main outlines of which antedate the Industrial Revolution, namely, modern Roman Law and English Common Law.

The essential fact about these bodies of law is that, far more than any other legal systems, they have institutionalized principles over wide areas of the field of human relations that are congruent with the institutional requirements of industrial organization of the economy. In Islamic, Chinese, or Hindu legal systems there is nothing comparable to this. Of course there are important differences between the Roman and Common Law systems, but broadly they are comparable in the relevant respects.

Perhaps it may be said that the most important general characteristic of these Western legal systems is that they have institutionalized firm patterns of rights and obligations which, within politically organized units of society, have cut across the lines drawn by the traditional "primary" bases of social solidarity, and hence have become in certain respects independent of them. The most important such lines of primary solidarity would be kinship, including its temporal dimension in lineage terms, the "feudal" types of political allegiance, and the solidarity of the smaller units of territorial community. Ethnic solidarities may be regarded in certain senses as extensions of kinship.

Against such bases of solidarity these legal systems have embodied principles of universalism and of specificity. By universalism I mean that rules have been formulated and held to apply to categories of persons or collectivities on the basis of generally defined characteristics independent of their statuses in these "lower-order" particularistic solidarities. Thus there have been rights to enter into contractual relationships, the consequences of which were defined as independent of the kinship or local community relations of the contracting parties. Or in a political context, certain obligations have been applied to citizens as such, or subcategories of them, again independently of their differentiation by these particularistic subsolidarities.

By specificity in this connection I mean the definition of legal rules in such a way that the rights and obligations thereby created could be abstracted from the status and expectations of certain particularistic solidary memberships, without destroying that membership. This is to

---

areas" there are strong presumptions that there will be political primacy on the *agency* level in the process of development, and that this will be associated with predominance of "socialistic" ideologies. It is very unlikely that ideological appeals to establish the system of "free enterprise" will have much positive impact on such societies and they may well prove to be boomerangs. This situation is, on the other hand, a main basis of the force of the Communist appeal.

say that, with respect to certain specific subject matters, such as the fulfillment of the terms of a given contract, the membership status would,
as it were, be "bracketed," would neither create obligations for the contractual relation nor would the latter have any consequences for it. The
primary solidary structures would therefore be "insulated" from the cross-
cutting relationship. This insulation is a primary condition and aspect
of structural differentiation in the relationship system itself.

The most relevant areas of content of legal institutionalization for
present purposes are those which may be called economic and political,[8]
and I shall turn presently to a sketch of the principal subareas of each.
Before that, however, it should be noted that a very important feature
of the place of these Western legal systems in the societies in which they
have functioned is their relative independence of the political structure
and processes in the narrower, governmental sense of that concept. It is
in the nature of the place of law in societies that there should be, especially with reference to jurisdiction and sanctions, a close integration
between the legal system and government. Law must be the law of
"politically organized society" as Roscoe Pound put it. But this is not to
say that the law is, in the social organizations involved in it, particularly
the system of courts and the legal profession, simply an "agency" of
government. Its involvement in the social structure is far more complex
than that. Even in relatively centralized or "absolutist" situations there
has been some independence of the judiciary from both executive and
legislative organs of the state. A "government of laws and not of men"
in the American sense, a *Rechtsstaat* in the German, implies this. I suggest that the relative weakness or near-absence of an independent legal
system in this sense is a major condition making for predominance of
political agency in the process of industrial development, as in the Soviet
case and even more in Asian cases.

Though the institutional focus of the normative systems under consideration is in the legal system, it should be clear that there is a shading
from this level to various orders of "private" and informal modes of institutionalization. Certainly the large-scale "formal organizations" of modern
societies have systems of norms which are cognate with law in the politically organized sense; but they do not have the "force of law" in the
sense of interpretation through court procedures and enforcement through
governmental agencies. Of course even where there are no private formal
definitions or agencies, there may still be important sets of institutionalized norms, as in cases like "trade practice." My present concern is
not, however, with the relations between these levels, but rather with
the structure of the normative systems relevant to industrialization.

[8] In this connection, I may again note that I mean "political" in an analytical
sense, which includes collectivity organization at *all* levels of the society, not only
that of government.

Economic institutions. What I am calling the "economic complex" can be broken down into three subcomplexes — those of contract, property, and occupation.[9] Of these contract is the more general and central institutional focus, while property and occupation, through the contract of employment, may be treated as derivative from it. The broad connection between contract and both the market complex and the mobility of resources should be fairly obvious. One aspect is the freedom of various categories of individuals and collectivities to make *ad hoc* agreements to exchange goods and money, and to enter into mutual obligations involving future performances. But these freedoms could not be institutionalized within a stable system of social relationships unless there were adequate systems of general rules defining the content of permitted contractual relations, the limits of such permission, and a number of other matters. Without attempting to justify such a statement here, I would like to suggest that there are four essential fields in a contractual system which must be adequately defined and regulated if the system is to be stable.

The four fields are: (1) definitions of permitted and prohibited content of contractual agreement; (2) definitions of legitimate and illegitimate means of securing the assent of the other party to a contract; (3) definitions of the situations of risk and uncertainty which are considered and of the legal, or normative, consequences of various kinds of unforeseen changes in circumstance; and (4) definitions of the societal interest in contractual relations, including particularly interest in their consequences for third parties.

For defining the institutional prerequisites of industrialization, the crucial problem of contract concerns the freedom of consumers' markets and of the supplies of the factors of production, hence freedom of mobilization for combining these factors in accord with economic interests, individually or collectively defined. This in turn involves freedom from anchorage in other ties which would impede such structuring. Once industrialization is an important societal interest it can, therefore, provide the main orientation to the fourth category above. But a system of norms governing contractual relations must function as a system and must therefore adequately cover the other three fields enumerated above. We not only permit freedom in many contractual fields elsewhere barred to such treatment, but we also prohibit it in certain very important areas. The most important perhaps is where contracts would infringe on the freedom of the individual, by slavery or other forms of involuntary servitude. In the field of means, the crucial prohibitions concern coercion and fraud as means of gaining assent. In the field of risk and uncertainty, the most general principles concern relieving contracting parties from crippling

---

[9] The formal bases of the classification presented in this and the following section are briefly outlined in the Technical Note at the end of the chapter.

obligations, the seriously onerous character of which could not have been foreseen at the time the obligation was assumed.

With specific reference to property these general principles apply, but can be more fully specified. Where the objects of possession are physical objects, the key institutional complex is the institution of ownership which was clearly developed in Roman law. This has two main aspects. The first is the gathering together of *all* property rights in the same object into one bundle to be held by a single owner, whether the owner be individual or corporate. This clearly was not the case in medieval law where several holders could have property rights in the same piece of land, for example. The essential rights may be classified as those of use, of control (specifying who shall use and for what purposes), and of disposal. Some of these elements may of course be kept out of the contractual context altogether by ascriptive restrictions, as in the common case of inalienability of land. Indeed, in the medieval manor even use was to a considerable extent "traditionalized."

The second aspect concerns the differentiation of property rights from other rights in the same object. The most obvious case here is political jurisdiction and the most obvious example is land. Again in European medieval law it was impossible to have property rights in land without carrying with them elements of status in the political structure. For instance, the land-owner was at the same time the land-*lord* in the sense of holding jurisdiction over the land — the manorial court being one expression of this. Ownership thus involves the differentiation of the previous bundle which included both property and jurisdictional rights. Essentially the same thing can be said about involvements in obligations of collective solidarity — in many property systems it is impossible to differentiate property rights from obligations of solidary membership. On informal levels this would be largely true even today within the household.

A particularly important special case of property rights is of course the whole field of the institutionalization of money and instruments involved in contractual relations which involve monetary considerations. This is in detail a highly complex field. Suffice it to say that in modern Western societies property in monetary assets, including securities as claims to income and repayment, is, from one point of view, the center of the whole property system. From that point of view property is the right to acquire possession through monetary transactions and conversely the right to alienate for monetary consideration. These rights, that is to say, tend to "govern" the lower-order rights of control of physical objects and use of them. Money is thus an institutionalized standard for the evaluation of commodities, and of course services, in terms of their *economic* significance, and is itself an object of possession in which property rights are institutionalized — the latter is the economist's conception of money as medium of exchange.

The second main aspect of contractual rights and obligations concerns the use, control, and "disposal" of human services, individual and collective. The most important case is the contract of employment resulting, in the case of the individual, in an occupational role, where for the duration of the contract he assumes obligations of performance within the employing organization and in certain respects recognizes the legitimacy of the control exercised over his performance by the collectivity, through leadership, authority, and the like. I shall argue presently that this means that economic and "political" patterns of institutionalization interpenetrate at this point. The "formal organization," which is the most important type of collectivity employing persons in strictly occupational roles, is a system with political primacy on its own level though not necessarily in the society as a whole.

From the point of view of production the important point is the mobility of human services for economic production, and hence their freedom from ties and imperatives which would interfere seriously with economic production. There is a set of components of the occupational role which corresponds to use, control, and disposal in the case of property. First, there are rights to specify and supervise the tasks of occupational activity, independently of traditionalized specifications. Second, there are rights to control such activity in terms of the decisions as to who shall act in the interest of these task-goals, and what procedures they should use. Finally, there are rights to transfer services from one employing organization to another. The free artisan, for example, may enjoy the first level of occupational rights. The management of an employing organization, in allocating jobs within the organization and laying down rules for their performance, may be exercising the second level of rights, that of control. Full "alienation" of labor, the operation of a full-fledged labor market, involves the third level. The wider the scope of contractual freedoms on each of these levels in turn, the greater the mobility of labor as a factor in production.

The structural tendencies in the institutionalization of occupational roles have, in the Western world, paralleled those of the case of property. On the one hand, the tendency has been to tie all these components of the control of human services into one bundle. One aspect of this is the full-time job — one individual can, so far as this governs, have only one full job at one time. All his other role-commitments are defined as non-occupational or secondary, such as the familial, "political," and so on. Another, even more important, aspect is the tying of the three levels together, so that employment, once accepted, gives the employing organization rights of control and of "use" — that is, specification of particular tasks.

The parallel also holds in the other principal respect, namely that the occupational role comes to be sharply differentiated from other roles in which the same individual is involved. Perhaps the most important case is the differentiation between occupational and kinship status and expectations. There has been a strong tendency for industrialization to be associated with increasingly sharp differentiation in this case, but it has had to go through a number of stages and has taken long periods to approach completeness.

A particularly important example of incomplete differentiation, for the history of industrial development, has been the case of managerial position in the "family firm." Here three components, which ordinarily would be analytically distinguished, are fused in the same status-role unit. These are, first, what I should call an occupational role-element in a strict sense. This concerns managerial responsibilities within a formal organization devoted to some phase of economic production. The second component is that of kinship organization. The individual has a status in his kinship group which certainly involves expectations and responsibilities which on occasion may not coincide with the productive interests of the firm. The third element, in turn, is the property component. The manager, in his familial role usually, is also a proprietor of the organization. Legally his managerial control has generally rested mainly on the property element. There is no doubt that the family firm played a crucially important part in the early industrialization of the West; indeed, I think it can be argued that it was indispensable, largely because it was the only way in which, at one stage, responsibility for production independent of governmental authority could be institutionalized. Thus it could focus entrepreneurial responsibility beyond the interests or lifetime of a single individual; it could accumulate and safeguard capital; it could establish a solid reputation in the community. At the same time, beyond certain levels, it can become a serious obstacle to further development.[10] The more recent tendency has been clearly toward differentiating these components from each other. The typical occupational manager is no longer in his position by virtue of kinship ascription, and property ownership is not a significant factor in his leadership and authority within the firm.

Political institutions. Let us turn now to what I called above the political complex of institutionalization. This concerns the normative structure of those aspects of collectivities which bear most directly on the effectiveness of their operation for the achievement of goals of the collectivity. Defined in this way the category "political" applies at any

---

[10] Among the best available sources on both of these aspects of the family firm are David S. Landes, "French Business and the Businessman: A Social and Cultural Analysis," in *Modern France,* ed. Edward Mead Earle (Princeton, 1951); David S. Landes, "Religion and Enterprise: The Case of the French Textile Industry" (manuscript); and J. R. Pitts, "The Retardation of the French Economy" (Harvard University, unpublished dissertation, 1958).

level of the social structure. It is particularly relevant to those "formal organizations" which are organized about some particular category of goal-attainment, of which economic production is one particularly important case. Seen in these terms government is a special type of "politically" oriented collectivity, that which organizes the society as a whole in the interest of collective goals. But because of the imperative of consistency in a normative system, the same basic principles of institutionalization tend to apply both to government and to many "private" organizations within the society.

I would like to treat the "political complex" of institutions as involving, in a sense parallel to the economic, three subcategories. One of them, which I call "leadership," is, like contract, more general while the other two, which I shall call "authority" and "regulation," are, like property and occupation, more specific.

By the institutionalization of leadership I mean the pattern of normative order by which certain subgroups within a collectivity are, by virtue of the "positions" they occupy within it, permitted and expected to take initiative and make decisions bearing on the attainment of the goals of the collectivity which bind it as a whole. It is in leadership roles that the more active functions with reference to collective goal-attainment are institutionalized. This basis of differentiation is, in certain respects, cognate with the division of labor in the economic sense.[11]

Leadership can be broken down into a series of functional contexts which are cognate with those set forth in the case of contract. We may speak first of the institutionalization of the social interest in leadership. This is essentially what Max Weber meant by "legitimation" in his treatment of the concept which has been translated as "authority" (*Herrschaft*). Legitimation in this sense includes the question of incumbency, that is, who is permitted to exercise the functions of leadership, on the basis of what process of selection for this role. Among the alternatives are hereditary succession, appointment, election, and so on. Secondly, there is the problem of institutionalization of the goals in the interest of which leadership is legitimized. This, like the others, of course leads up to the value system as discussed in the previous section. Certain goals, like forcible seizure of governmental power, are often prohibited. Third is the question of the means allowed in the exercise of leadership. The general exclusion of coercion, except in cases of the negative sanctions imposed for resistance to ligitimate authority, and of fraud apply as in the case of contract. In industrial organizations, not only the law of the state but union contracts are important foci for the definition of these rules. Finally, the orientation to risk and uncertainty may be thought of in

---

[11] It should be remembered that in complex organizations there are many levels and types of leadership function — it is not a simple matter of bifurcation into leaders and followers.

terms of the problem of collective responsibility. This applies both to the leadership and to the follower elements of a collectivity. For the leader it may mean that they must pay certain penalties if something goes wrong even though it could not clearly be said to be "their fault," and conversely "get the credit" in cases of good fortune. For the rank and file it means above all that they are bound by the consequences of the action of leadership, even though these consequences could not have been foreseen or approved in advance.

Again, for problems of industrial organization the crucial point about leadership is its freedom to organize human services in the interest of production goals, without being impeded by the nonrelevant commitments and ties of the persons involved. It is quite clear that such organization, at a level which is capable of coping with complex technological tasks, cannot be attained by purely egalitarian and "democratic" processes; there must be institutionalized leadership, whether by private "entrepreneurs" or in various types of public agencies. This leadership pattern, then, can be spelled out in each of two directions, which I should like to call authority and regulation.

I would like to use the much-controverted term authority here for a special subcategory of leadership, one which in "political" usage corresponds to property in the economic complex. This is the case which focuses on the disposability of human services in the context of organization for a definite collective goal. The important point is the legitimation of the right to make decisions which are binding on the members of the collectivity. By regulation, on the other hand, I mean a set of controls over activity where the regulating agent, to be sure, exercises functions of leadership but specifies only limits of acceptable action on the part of the units under his control. One of the main contexts in which regulation instead of authority operates is that in which the content of roles or of suborganizations is technical in a sense which precludes detailed supervision by agencies which are not technically qualified.

Authority in this sense, like property and occupation, may be said to involve three elements of direct concern. These are not defined in terms of the contribution of the unit of organization and its control — above all the contributions of individuals in roles — but rather of control of the policies of the organization as a system. The highest of the three levels is the general power of making binding decisions which commit the organization to one among a range of alternative directions of action. This is cognate with the right of disposal in the case of property. The other two are different cases of authority to implement this general decision-making power. The first of these is the power to allocate responsibilities of subunits within the organization. This is the crucial point at which the institutionalization of authority and that of occupation converge. The other focus is that on allocation of facilities which, in modern societies, becomes primarily that of control of budgetary resources. As in the economic cases, these three constitute a hierarchy in the control sense. In general, he who holds the more general decision-making power controls the allocation of responsibilities within the organization, and he who controls these responsibilities controls the allocation of facilities to their functions. There may of course be various restrictions on such control, such as through seniority and tenure rules.

The tendency in the modern Western world has been more and more to tie these three components together in a single "package." This, I think, is the central point in what Weber called "rational-legal" authority.[12] It is the condition of maximum disposability of human resources in the productive, as in other, processes. It is the focal institution of the ideal type of "bureaucracy."

As in the other cases, however, this consolidation has occurred through a process of differentiation of the authority complex from other, in this sense, nonpolitical patterns with which it has previously been fused. One major type of this pattern is kinship, which still persists at the political top in monarchical regimes and was formerly much more widespread. In economic organization it has been the pattern, as noted above, of the family firm. Another type of differentiation which has had to take place is from elements of "political" interest at the governmental level which, though of great social import, have been distinct from and often in conflict with the interest in the effective attainment of the specific organizational goal. The whole field of the spoils system, the use of administrative appointments as rewards for deserving Democrats or Republicans, is a case of this type.

Regulation may also be broken down into a similar set of three components. The first is again cognate with the task level. The distinction from authority would here involve the range of discretion with reference to access, specific facilities required, and the like, or to the funds necessary to acquire them. A good example is the provision of facilities through monetary funds rather than through controlling access to specific physical objects. Hence from the point of view of leadership, or the regulating agency, it is budgetary control. The second component is at the role level and concerns function or responsibilities within the collectivity. But here, as contrasted with authority, the function is performed with reference to some kind of standard which is beyond the control of the regulating agency. One of the most important types of standard is technical, such as with reference to engineering, research, or medical procedures. But from the point of view of public regulation of independent business, the standard of profitability within the institutional framework is such an independent standard. Finally, the third level concerns the

[12] Max Weber, *The Theory of Social and Economic Organization* (Glencoe, 1957), ch. 3.

basis of commitment to the interests of the regulating collectivity, to the "public interest."

There has been, in Western institutional development, the same general tendency in this as in the other fields to merge these components, and therefore to make it possible to "tie in" complexes of activity which could not be controlled through direct authority with the interests of important collectivities and their goals. This has been particularly important in areas where higher-level technical processes were concerned. Under the guild organization of the medieval economy, the artisan's skills were very closely bound in with a special type of social organization so that they could not be used in the contexts which foreshadowed the Industrial Revolution. For this to happen a differentiation had to take place, making such services more widely disposable. But this in turn meant differentiation from the solidarity of the guild system. The most important examples of full differentiation in this sense are such organizations as university faculties, hospitals, and industrial-research laboratories, where individuals performing such services are on full "occupational" status and the organization exercises all three levels of regulation over him.

It is, however, important to realize clearly that it would probably not be possible to institutionalize such services on the basis of what I have called authority; it would interfere too much with the necessary order of independent responsibility. Such institutions as academic tenure seem to be related to this situation. They are ways of protecting high-level professional personnel against "arbitrary" interference by administrative authorities. Similarly, governmental civil-service tenure may be said to protect the civil service against the spoils system; there is a sense in which an administrative bureaucracy is a "technical" subsystem which can only be "regulated," not "administered," by the top political authority.

Failure to deal adequately with the field I am calling regulation and to distinguish it from authority constitutes, it seems to me, the most serious defect, in the present context, of Weber's famous analysis of bureaucracy.[13] With these qualifications however, there seems to be little doubt that bureaucracy, in the sense of "package" institutionalization in this area of leadership of specific-function organizations, is a central feature of institutional structures which are favorable to industrialization.

It should also be clear that full realization of an "ideal type" is considerably more difficult to attain in this area than in that of property — in the whole area, that is, which involves the overlapping patterns of occupation, authority, and regulation. This is essentially because in the case of property either the physical object or the monetary funds can be fully dissociated from permanent involvement in other organizational contexts. A machine can be controlled exclusively by the particular manu-

---

[13] This is particularly concerned with the increasing role, in formal organizations, of *professional* services in roles other than the exercise of "line" authority.

facturing unit. Human service, however, has a fundamentally different character. If it is to be specialized at all, the specialized service must be differentiated out of a matrix of interests and role-commitments, the other components of which are different from that involved in the specialized part. Only within very severe limits can a total human being be specialized to a particular function of the occupational order. There must, therefore, be a dynamic equilibrium between the occupationally involved elements of the personality and the rest of it, and the more specialized the function the greater the relative importance of these other parts.

It is for such reasons that authority over human beings in specialized roles never approaches the degree of absoluteness of control that is institutionalized as ownership in the case of property, and the more extreme types seem to be unstable. Trade unions go back to this problem to a large extent, as does the development of regulatory forms of leadership instead of authority forms.

The problem of "social control." Another area of institutionalization is that which the sociologist tends to call in a narrower and more technical sense "social control." What I have called the economic and the political complexes of institutionalization concerns the definition of patterns of legitimized behavior and the structuring of sanctions with reference to such behavior. They presuppose motivational commitment of the individual to conformity with such normative patterns, as far as such conformity is not a function of expediency or of rational responses to situational sanctions. There is another whole set of institutionalized mechanisms which operate in this "motivational" area, having to do with the control of tendencies toward deviant motivation. In a modern society like our own I would include an important part of the functioning of such professions as medicine and law, and others such as social work, in this context. Most important for the larger outlines of structural development, however, are probably certain aspects of religion and ideology. In some respects religion and ideology serve as mechanisms of value "indoctrination" and maintenance. But they also operate at lower levels in the normative structure of the society. In a good deal of the Protestant Western world the revival movements can be interpreted in this light, and it seems also that the aspect of ideological manipulation which is analyzed by Inkeles as "agitation" for the Soviet cause also belongs in this category.[14] I shall not attempt to go into these mechanisms here, but only to call attention to their existence and importance. Perhaps the most important single brief statement which can be made about their relevance to industrialism is that they must somehow reinforce motivation to participate in higher-order, more mobile types of organization than would be the case in a more highly "traditionalized" and particularistic society.

[14] Alex Inkeles, *Public Opinion in Soviet Russia* (Cambridge, Mass., 1951).

Hence the generality of ideological slogans may be of great importance because attachment to them serves to emancipate the individual from attachment to overly specific loyalties.

v

As my last main task I should like to take up briefly the relevance for industrialism of the factor of political organization at the societal level, as distinct from that of the producing organization. The first essential to point out is the importance on the societal level, in historical and comparative perspective, of the institutionalization of the general patterns I have just reviewed in the case of politics, and indeed of economics. It is quite clear that the political organization of European feudal society was intimately involved with its economic organization and that feudal "governments" could not have sponsored and carried through processes of industrialization without fundamental structural alteration not only in their own organizations, but also in the institutional patterning for the society with which they articulated. The same is equally true of the governmental structures of China and India of about 1700.

Government, this is to say, must either articulate adequately with an independently established (or at least independently functioning, whatever the role of government in its origins may have been) institutional structure or must itself be capable of a fundamental initiating role in the establishment of such a structure. This is not of course to say that in a narrower sense any particular form of government is required, above all not that it must be a "democratic" government. It means only that government must be sufficiently stable and also sufficiently differentiated from institutionalized structures in the society which are incompatible with industrialization, so that it does not interfere too drastically with factors favorable to industrialization independent of government, or that it is itself sufficiently independent to be able to exert a strong leverage on the society to create new structures which are more favorable than their predecessors.

Indeed, it seems to be clear that it is with respect to the role of government that the most important differentiation of types of the process of industrialization must be made. Furthermore, it seems to be true that the appearance of an industrial economy for the first time requires a predominance of "private" initiative and thus the institutionalization of an important set of restrictions on the intervention of government in the economy; whereas once an industrial system is in existence, the adoption of its patterns by other societies can proceed effectively through predominant governmental initiative. At the very least there are two further arguments to be made in this area: first that governmental initiative provides the most rapid way to achieve significant industrialization and, second, that in the total balance of the societies in question this is the most likely path which will be institutionally, rather than simply economically, feasible.[15]

In the Western case, which in the world perspective has been of the first type, perhaps the most crucial barrier to government intervention was a legal system, to which governments were committed, which institutionalized the rights of private initiative in this area. In addition, of course, once the process was under way, governments derived great advantages from it, in revenue, in a basis for power in foreign relations, and in other respects. But this does not mean that governmental initiative could have brought it about. A crucial factor here was the motivation of elements of the population which were involved in the types of value-commitment sketched in an earlier section of this chapter. These could operate, however, only where the proper constellation of factors of opportunity was present. I think the institutions focusing on the legal system were the most fundamental of these opportunity factors because they underlay the factors of the "extent of the market" and the availability of mobile resources.

In the cases of political predominance, starting with the Japanese,[16] including the Soviet, and going on to the more recent cases, especially in Asia, one might say that the opportunity factor was external to the society — in the existence elsewhere in the world of industrial systems and the networks of trade and communications associated with them. Here the analogue of the "individual" level of value-commitments, classically delineated by Weber, is the national commitment, first to enhancement of national power and prestige and, instrumental to this, but under modern conditions fundamental, the development of industrial productivity. Given, then, the combination of the model and the pressures of the external industrial systems, the necessary patterns can, under favorable conditions, be institutionalized from this focal point. These conditions include the seriousness of the national commitment, to which ideological mechanisms are obviously relevant, but also the possibility of creating the essential internal opportunity factors of the sort sketched in the preceding section.

This general pattern seems to have been repeated twice on a major scale. Great Britain took the leading role in the first major process of industrialization to appear in history, starting in the later eighteenth century. The reactions to the British development, particularly on the continent of Europe, but also to some degree in the United States, were in many respects parallel to the more recent cases of "political" predominance. All of them, except Holland, which was more commercial than industrial, were characterized by a much more active role of politi-

---

[15] I have presented a fuller argument for this view than is possible here in, "Some Reflections on the Institutional Framework of Economic Development," cited in note 7.
[16] On this aspect of Japanese industrialization, see Bellah.

cal agency, such as in railway building, than was the case in Britain. All of them were, in terms of the goal of industrialization itself, conspicuously oriented to the British example. Thus the first great phase was laissez-faire Britain vis-à-vis the rest of the West, which has been considerably less "individualistic," with the non-Western world little touched. The second great phase has become the "capitalistic" West vis-à-vis the more "collectivistic" underdeveloped areas of the world.[17]

On the most general level of the theory of social systems, the two types of pattern thus need not be considered fundamentally different. The same framework of analysis is applicable to both. This does not mean, however, that on more concrete levels the balance among the various factors which have been reviewed is likely to be the same, for there are still lower-level ranges of variation within each of the two major types.

For example, it seems clear that in the political cases, particularly the Soviet, there has been a far sharper emphasis on the authority component of the total institutional structure than in the Western cases. This could be tolerated, I am inclined to think, for three primary reasons. First, there seem to be features of the cultural tradition of Russia, ultimately rooted in Eastern Orthodox Christianity, which make the exercise of sharply defined authority more tolerable than in Western Europe and the United States. Second, nationalistic interest has been very closely identified with successful industrialization, and hence the whole complex of sentiments involved in nationalism has been mobilized behind it. Third, there has been the *élan* of a revolutionary movement, which was able to mobilize and fuse with the nationalistic components through basing the national position of Russia on its position of leadership in the world communist movement, and defining the rest of the world which did not go along as "reactionary." Without some such fusion of components it is difficult to see how it would have been possible for the Soviet system to get over the problem of the "take-off," as Rostow calls it.

There may, however, be serious factors of instability in the Soviet case which are not readily visible. One I would particularly like to call attention to is the problem of the balance between what I have called authority and regulation. It seems clear that the institutionalization of organizational leadership has, within the Soviet system, been heavily skewed in the direction of authority. In its relevance to industrial efficiency, as distinguished from the stability of the governmental system, the problem would seem to focus at two points. One of these is the question of whether and how far allocation of accounting responsibility to the firm has set up, as some of Berliner's material suggests,[18] a tendency for it to acquire

[17] For many insights, particularly on the relation between Britain and Continental Europe in these respects, but on a number of other points touched on in this paper, I am indebted to Professor David S. Landes, both through personal discussions and through certain of his unpublished papers.

[18] Joseph S. Berliner, *Factory and Manager in the USSR* (Cambridge, Mass., 1957).

such a large sphere of genuine managerial independence that the authority itself may in time be jeopardized. This is to say that an element of market freedom would have to be permitted and eventually legitimized. The second and perhaps (though I am not sure) more crucial focus is the problem of the status of highly trained technical personnel and organizational subunits. It seems correct to believe that attempting to keep them within a rigid system of control through line authority is likely to involve serious strains. These are in part mitigated by recruiting "engineers" for administrative positions so that the operating technical people do not feel they are being directed by "laymen." Also I suspect that there is a good deal of informal leeway granted in actual operations. But the question whether this leeway will not have to be institutionalized, with considerable repercussions on the general system of authority, remains. The necessity for extraneous controls through the party is apparently related to this in both cases, but these controls presumably generate their own tensions and tendencies to change. This whole area of supplementary controls and their relation to propaganda and ideology is in need of much further investigation.

One more remark about the Soviet case may be in order. Apparently through Tsarist despotism a situation was created wherein there were remarkably few "middle-level" structures in the society which were in a position to offer serious resistance to the Soviet dictatorship and structurally crystallize to form a focus for change. The church was already highly centralized and politicized and could almost directly be taken over. The middle classes were weak, and such as there were could either be liquidated or absorbed in the new occupational system. Hence the main problem with repect to the old Russia seemed to be the "socialization" of the population according to the values of high-productivity industrialism. Ideology and education plus a field of realistic opportunity of great magnitude seem to have been the main instruments of this process, and it appears to have been highly successful. It therefore seems reasonable to suggest that the main sources of instability and change in the Soviet system should be looked for not in the strains entailed by the problem of integration with pre-Soviet social structures, but in the internal dynamics of the Soviet type of industrial society, including of course not only the economy but perhaps above all the governmental system. This case stands, for instance, in marked contrast to Great Britain where the preindustrial class structure and church have remained strong and have considerably influenced the present outcome.

A word about Japan may also be in order. Abegglen has called attention to the persistence, in middle-sized Japanese industry, of "particularistic" bases of organization of the labor force, especially in kinship terms of a type which has often been thought to be incompatible with industrialization.[19] When such phenomena are found, I think they should be used as clues to look for other compensating factors. In the Japanese case one of the most important seems to be the high pressure toward achievement which has been developed within the kinship context. I should therefore expect the organization of services about kinship to be more nearly compatible with industrial conditions than would be the case for all but a few other kinship systems. Even here, however, I would expect the situation described by Abegglen to be seriously unstable and to show a marked tendency to change in the more expected direction with the further development of the industrial system. The case would be partly parallel with the strains involved in the rigidity of the Soviet authority system.

I have introduced these very cursory comments on the Soviet and Japanese cases not in any way to claim a general understanding of them, but to illustrate that the view of the factors of industrial society which I have presented is not meant to imply rigid uniformity at the empirical levels. Not only is there the distinction between the two main types, but there are very important variations within each of them. At the same time, it is not legitimate to conclude that there are no important common elements, that an industrial economy would be compatible with any set of values, any institutional structure, and any governmental system. As these things go in comparative sociology, the specifications for successful industrialism are relatively narrow and definite.

VI

This chapter has been concerned with the problem of what kind of society is compatible with an industrial level and type of economy. It first pointed out that, though the focus of the characteristics of industrialism is in the economy and not the political organization of the society, the question should not be begged of what role political, in the sense of governmental, agency might or might not play in the development and maintenance of such an economy. Indeed, two main types of industrial society were distinguished, the one in which the main focus of agency has been in "free enterprise" relatively independent of governmental control and the one in which governmental agency has had primacy.

I then attempted to outline the essential features of an industrial economy as such. With respect to the structure of the society in which such an economy existed, these features could be said to be dependent on their relative compatibility with three other "primary subsystems" of the society, which I called the cultural system, with special reference to societal values and their internalization in personalities, the institutional

[19] James C. Abegglen, "Continuity and Change in Japanese Industry," in his *The Japanese Factory: Aspects of Its Social Organization* (Glencoe, 1957).

system, referring to the institutionalized norms especially formulated in legal systems but also extending to private and informal levels, and the political system focusing at the societal level in the structure of government.

The most crucial noneconomic factors underlying the industrial type of economy may be classified as, first, the factor of "drive" or capacity, which I focused more than anywhere else in the cultural system of values, and, second, the factor of "opportunity" which I focused in the institutional system. Economic productivity for the society may be translated into the valuation of achievement for the individual. There must be widespread motivation to active achievement in instrumental, "worldly" activities, essentially the type of pattern which Weber classically delineated for ascetic Protestantism, though it is now clear that Protestantism is not the only cultural base on which such a value-orientation can develop.

The institutional prerequisites center on the problems of the mobility of commodities through markets and access to them, on the mobility of the factors of production, and on the institutionalization of effective organization for their utilization. Institutionally considered, all of these factors go back to *differentiation* relative to preindustrial institutional systems. I paid special attention here to what I called the economic complex of contract, property, and occupation, and what in the analytical sense is the political complex of leadership, authority, and regulation. In both cases, and their subtypes, the essential pattern is a dual one. On the one hand, components of the institutional category, which in other systems have been segregated from each other, have come to be put together in a "package." On the other hand, each of the components has been differentiated from previous fusions with functionally different components, such as kinship. The modern institution of ownership in the property field is the paradigmatic case, seen against the background of feudalism. These processes of institutional differentiation have proceeded to different levels in different societies, but the general directional trend in relation to the industrial economy is clear.

It was possible only very briefly to call attention to the possible importance of what sociologists call, in a narrowly technical sense, the "mechanisms of social control," particularly religion and ideology in certain aspects of their functions. It would be expected that cognate processes of differentiation have taken place in this field.[20]

Finally, the relevance to the industrial economy of the system of political organization at the societal, that is, governmental, level was very briefly dealt with. It is here that the basis of differentiation between the two main types of industrial society comes to focus. I argued that the

[20] I have attempted to deal partially with this problem in a paper on "Definitions of Health and Illness in the Light of American Values and Social Structure" in E. Gartly Jaco, ed., *Patients, Physicians and Illness* (Glencoe, 1958), 165–187.

differentiation has mainly, though of course by no means exclusively, to do with the timing of the process of industrialization. The development of industrial economies for the first time had to be independent of predominant governmental initiative. On the other hand, "catching up" occurs in a situation which puts a strong premium on governmental initiative, hence a collectivistic emphasis, especially where there is a strong sense of urgency involved. I also argued that not only is there this primary differentiation of types, but a good deal of variation within each, which can be described in terms of a balance between the various components which have been reviewed.

Within the limits of a single chapter the above analysis has had to select out a very limited sector of comparative considerations. It should, however, be regarded as an essay in comparative sociological analysis. Its validity therefore rests not only on its empirical correctness with reference to the facts of known industrial societies, but also on the way in which it fits into a broader scheme of comparative structural analysis, including many nonindustrial cases. Such a scheme, in my opinion, to be adequate must include an explicit and well-analyzed evolutionary dimension. It is quite clear that no "primitive" society (defined, for example, as nonliterate) could develop a full-fledged industrial economy. In the long run, our ability to handle this type of problem will depend on the level of comparative evolutionary theory of social structures that we are able to work out.

TECHNICAL NOTE

The classifications and the treatments of structural differentiation and integration employed in the above analysis all use concepts as well as illustrative references which have been widely current in the literature. My own most important single source, however, has been the system of ideal types presented by Max Weber in *The Theory of Social and Economic Organization.* Many of the specific forms taken by the definitions and hence the ways in which distinctions are drawn, and the framework of systematization into which the concepts fit, are part of a more general attempt on which I have been working, to categorize the analysis of social systems. For the benefit of the reader who is interested in this more technical level of theoretical work, I shall here attempt very briefly to indicate the main ways in which I conceive the elements used here to fit into that more general scheme.

I conceive the structure of all social systems, however complex, to be capable of analysis in terms of the relation of structural forms to a scheme of four functional "system-problems" or dimensions: pattern-maintenance, integration, goal-attainment, and adaptation. Macroscopic and complex systems are characterized by these system-problems and "governed" by the structures and mechanisms organized around them, and subsystems are ordered in cognate terms at various different levels of organization and cultural generality.

Seen in these terms, the economy is a subsystem of the society organized about adaptive function.[21] I have therefore organized my own discussion about the problem of the interdependence of the economy with the other three primary functional subsystems of the society, the pattern-maintenance system centering on values, the integrative system centering on institutional norms, and the goal-attainment system centering on political organization and functioning. Since the emphasis of this paper is structural, I have not entered into any technical analysis of process, an analysis which I tend to categorize in terms of input-output interchanges between subsystems.[22]

Furthermore, it did not seem possible, within the present space limits, to attempt to present formal classifications within the field either of the pattern-maintenance system or the goal-attainment system at the operative level which is comparable to an economist's treatment of the economy. Indeed, I have attempted to be formal in this sense only within the integrative system and even there only for essentially half of it. This is to say that I have not attempted to deal with the highest-level structure of institutional norms, as embodied particularly in legal systems, nor with the details of the structure of systems of social control in the technical sense used above.

What I have done is to confine this more formal treatment to the areas of economic and political institutionalization which are most directly relevant to the functioning of the economy, what I have called the economic and the political complexes, respectively. These two, in turn, I have dealt with on two different levels of classificatory breakdown. The first concerns the primary functions of integrative control with respect to the functional area in question, economic or political as the case may be, while the second concerns a cognate functional breakdown of each of the subfunctions distinguished in that way. It is these functional differentiations which provide the lines of distinction between the major structural types and between the components of the "packages" I have discussed.

The paradigm of classification is the same in all cases. Each functional category is "governed" at the highest level by a value-system, which is a *specification* at the relevant level of generalization and situational reference of the general societal value-system. In its relevance to a differentiated system of units, then, there is a set of norms less generalized than the values, which specify patterns of behavior expected of these units in differentiated situational contexts. These norms in turn are differentiated by reference, along with their own integrative imperatives and their reference to the values, to each of the two primary aspects of the external situa-

---

[21] See Parsons and Smelser.
[22] Parsons and Smelser, esp. ch. 2.

tion in which they must be implemented by a unit, the definition of goals it is expected to try to attain, and the definition of expected (permitted, prescribed, prohibited) means to these goals, namely adaptive orientations. The following table is a schematic representation of the classifications at the two levels.

1. Higher Level of Generality

Economic complex

Means:	Goal-specification:
Property	Occupation
Values:	Primary norms:
Economic rationality[a]	Contract

Political complex

Means:	Goal-specification:
Regulation	Authority
Values:	Primary norms:
Organizational effectiveness[a]	Leadership

[a] I did not deal with economic rationality or organizational effectiveness as values in the body of the Chapter (Parsons and Smelser, ch. 3).

2. Lower Level of Generality[a]

Economic complex

Property

Use	Control
Valuation of physical facilities[b]	Disposal

Occupation

Task assignment	Role assignment
Valuation of human services[b]	Control of membership in organization

Economic rationality[b]
(valuation of the factors of production)

Valuation of control of organization[b]	Valuation of control of capital[b]
Valuation of productivity[b]	Valuation of control of human productive capacities[b]

Contract

Definition of consequences of risk and uncertainty	Definition of legitimate content of agreement
Definition of societal interest in contract[b]	Definitions of legitimate means to assent

Political complex

Regulation   Authority

| Range or limits of discretion in definition of tastes and access to facilities | Definition of range and limits of technical role-function | Allocation budgetary resources | Allocation of organizational responsibility |
| Valuation of "technical contributions" | Commitment to the higher level collective interest e.g., "public interest" | Valuation of control of membership contributions[b] | General powers of making binding decisions |

Value of effectiveness[b]
(valuation of the factors of power)   Leadership

| Valuation of collective responsibility[b] | Valuation of control of facilities[b] | Definition of consequences of external wish and uncertainty | Definition of collective goals leadership can strive for |
| Valuation of effectiveness[b] | Valuation of decision-making authority[b] | Definition of societal interest in leadership[b] | Definition of legitimate means which leadership can use |

[a] For simplicity I have omitted the titular reference in each box for the classifications at this level — they remain the same as at the more general level.

[b] These categories were not made explicit in the text of this chapter.

PROBLEMS AND PATTERNS OF RUSSIAN ECONOMIC DEVELOPMENT

ALEXANDER GERSCHENKRON

I

The emancipation of the peasantry stands at the threshold of the period under review. The question of whether, on the eve of the reform, the system of serfdom was disintegrating for economic reasons or whether its vitality and viability were still essentially unimpaired has been the subject of much controversy. But even those who, like the present writer, tend toward the latter view must admit that the development of the nonagrarian sectors of the economy was virtually premised upon the abolition of serfdom.

To say this, however, does not at all imply that promotion of economic development was a paramount objective of the emancipation. As was true of most of the agrarian reforms in nineteenth-century Europe, the authors of the Russian reform either considered industrialization undesirable or, at best, were indifferent to it. The actual procedures chosen reflected these attitudes. In many ways they were bound to hamper rather than facilitate economic growth. The emancipation involved, first of all, a determination of the land area to be given over by the landowner to peasants for permanent use. There is no question that over wide parts of the country (and particularly in the black-earth belt) the peasants received a good deal less land than had been customarily assigned to them prior to the reform. Second, there was the question of the magnitude of the quitrents (*obrok*) to be paid by the peasants as compensation for land allotments. It is true that once those rents were set, subsequent acquisition of land by the peasants (the so-called redemption procedure, by which the right of use was changed to the right of ownership) was rendered very easy and as often as not did not entail any *additional* burdens upon the peasantry. But the original rents were set far above the contemporaneous market prices of the land. The example of the immediately preceding agrarian reform in Europe — that of Austria in 1848 — where peasants' obligations were mostly determined on the basis of "equity," or cadastral values (much *below* their market prices), was not followed in Russia.

It might be argued that the two features of the Russian reform just mentioned should have provided a favorable climate for subsequent industrialization; the inadequacy of the peasants' landholdings in conjunction with the considerable financial obligations imposed upon the peasants' households could have been expected to favor the flight from the country and thus to provide a large reservoir of labor supply to the nascent industry. Such might have been the consequences indeed, if the reform and the later legislative measures had not erected considerable barriers to land flight by strengthening the *obshchina,* the village commune, wherever it existed.

An English yeoman who found the cost of enclosing the land excessive could sell his farm and use the funds so obtained for business ventures outside agriculture or, at worst, for covering his transfer cost. A Russian peasant who wished to leave the village commune not only had to relinquish his rights in the land, but in addition had to pay, under the terms of the redemption procedures, what often were very sizable sums before he could receive his release. A member of the household, rather than the head thereof, wishing to leave the village permanently also had to secure the consent of the head of the household. Where the periodic repartitions of land by the village commune were conducted on the basis of manpower at the disposal of the household, permanent departure of a family member was bound to reduce the extent of land to be made available to the household at the next repartition. In conditions of relative scarcity of land, the willingness of the head of the household to permit such departures could not be, and in general never was, very great. Nothing was more revealing of the irrational way in which the village commune functioned than the fact that the individual household had to retain the abundant factor (labor) as a precondition for obtaining the scarce factor (land). On the other hand, the readiness of the member of the household to sever for good his connection with the land and become firmly committed to non-agricultural pursuits naturally was adversely affected by these arrangements.

It is often claimed that the Russian emancipation procedure followed the "Prussian model." It seems that Lenin was the first to give currency to the thought. The analogy is hardly felicitous. The outstanding feature of the Russian reform was that instead of a class of landless laborers, it had firmly established the landowning peasantry and had taken special precautions to keep the peasants attached to their land. To be sure, this was done *inter alia* in order to satisfy the gentry's need for cheap labor. But here again the similarity with the Prussian reform is rather superficial and deceptive. Unlike the Prussian Junkers, the Russian gentry seldom showed much interest in technological innovations on their estates. The traditions of serfdom may partly account for that. Under these circumstances, the cheap labor assured the estates by the Reform Act may have been a very undesirable gift, inasmuch as it discouraged rather than encouraged them to introduce those improvements in the mode of cultivation which tended to have labor-saving effects and to increase the capital intensity of agricultural output.

While permanent migration to the city was rendered difficult, temporary moves on the part of the members of peasant households were much less so. Yet even in such cases, the permissive rights vested in the heads of the village administration and the heads of the household created various opportunities for impounding some portion of the earnings made in the city. The right to demand and to enforce the return to the village of the departed member certainly left much room for pressures and extortions of all kinds. If it is considered that age-long tradition and inveterate inertia would have hindered migration to industry under any circumstances, the Russian government by assigning to the obshchina and the mir such a strong role in the emancipation procedure and in the life of the post emancipation village had created a considerable obstacle to the formation of a permanent industrial labor force in Russia.

If the double pressure to which the peasant economy was exposed — the inadequacy of land and the magnitude of the financial burdens — was prevented from causing a steady and considerable migration from the land, then that pressure itself was bound to assume the role of a retarding factor in the economic evolution of the country. The peasant economy was unable to increase its productivity because its income net of taxation and redemption payments did not permit sufficient investment; at times the low level of income even led to capital depletion. In addition, the prospect of repartitions militated against land improvements, even if and where they were financially possible; and the egalitarian nature of such repartitions prevented consolidation of landholdings assigned to individual households and precluded changes in cultivation methods and crop-rotation systems even where ignorance and inertia of the peasantry did not constitute an effective obstacle to such improvements.

In the long run, the scarcity of land available to the peasants in conjunction with the increase in population implied a steady deterioration in the economic position of the peasantry, despite purchases by village communes and individual peasants of gentry land and despite the formation, in the 1880's, of special institutions designed to finance such transactions.

It is true that the position of state peasants was more favorable than that of the former serfs in that their land allotments were somewhat larger and their financial burdens somewhat lighter, while the so-called imperial peasants were in between the two groups. Yet these differences, particularly in the longer run, were not sufficiently large to warrant a different appraisal of the state and imperial peasantry. They too experienced the restrictive effects of the village commune, and the economic development of their farms also was restrained by the action of the government whose deliberate policy it was to bring their burdens in line with those imposed upon the former serfs.

It should be added that it would be a mistake to interpret the secular rise in land prices which characterized the period between the emancipation and the First World War as providing relief to the peasantry in the sense of reducing the real burden of their obligations. Over large areas of Europe market values of peasant land tended to be a good deal above the capitalized yield values. But in Russia that tendency was particularly strong. Land values moved upward even when prices of agricultural products were falling. The land hunger of the peasantry, stimulated by population growth, largely accounted for this discrepancy. Thus, the rise in land values, far from relieving the peasant economy, was an expression of its precarious position.

There is little doubt that the inhibitions upon the growth of output of the peasants' economy and the consequent limitations upon the peasants' purchasing power for industrial products were a serious obstacle to the industrialization of the country. They made it improbable from the outset that peasant demand for industrial goods could exercise a strong pull on industrial growth. This was clearly seen by a large number of Populist writers. Their conclusion was that industrial development in Russia was unlikely to start and, if started, was bound to founder in the shallowness of the "internal market."

This prospect left the Populists undismayed because of their aversion to industrialization and their fears of its social consequences. Yet the predictions did not come true. By 1914, Russia had taken very long strides along the road of industrial development. What had vitiated the Populists' predictions was their failure to see the manifold flexibilities and adjustabilities which are inherent in processes of economic development. The growing purchasing power of the peasant economy can be indeed important as a motive force of industrialization. Yet it is but one among a number of possible alternatives.

Economic development in a backward country such as Russia can be viewed as a series of attempts to find — or to create — substitutes for those factors which in more advanced countries had substantially facilitated economic development, but were lacking in conditions of Russian backwardness. Such "substitutions" are the key to an understanding of the way in which the original disabilities were overcome and a process of sustained industrial growth was started in Russia. It is these acts of substitution that came to determine the specific pattern of industrial development.

But the process of industrialization is also a process of diminishing backwardness. In its course, factors that were lacking formerly tend to become evident and acquire increasing importance within the body economic. What was once in vain looked for to serve as a "prerequisite" or a "cause" of industrial development came into being as its effect. It is a fascinating pursuit in the history of modern industrializations to see to what extent the original "substitutes" were thereby rendered obsolete and disappeared after having fulfilled their function; and to what extent they were preserved and continued to dominate the pattern of industrial development in its subsequent stages, even though the special need for them no longer existed.

The present assignment requires this writer to supply, within the scope of a few pages, a background chapter on the last hundred years of Russian economic history — a period of unprecedented economic change. Obviously, no more can be done than to select for discussion some significant aspects of that change. Perhaps the processes touched upon in the preceding paragraph may serve this purpose.

Over long stretches of the period under review, in manifold ways, in ever-changing forms, and at different levels, innovation and anachronism seem to coalesce and to separate, to follow and to displace each other. The remainder of this chapter will be devoted to an attempt to see the peculiarities of Russian industrialization in terms of these relationships.

II

The great spurt of Russian industrialization in the prerevolutionary period largely coincided with the decade of the 1890's. Thus, almost thirty years had passed over the land before the great effort could come about. This is not surprising. The peasant reform would have had to be very different if a direct and immediate impact upon industrial growth could have been expected from it. Moreover, even if the reform had been deliberately designed to favor industrialization rather than to obstruct it, a certain preparatory period of slow growth was almost inevitable. The judicial and administrative reforms which came in the wake of the emancipation were essential in creating a framework for modern business activity. But other changes, at least equally significant, were much slower in coming. Certainly a radical improvement in communications was crucial. One does not have to conjure up the dramatic and pathetic vision of a huge boiler being dragged by teams of oxen through the deep mud of the Ukrainian steppes on its way to the construction site of the first blast furnace in the *Donbas* in order to understand that some railroad building had to antedate the period of rapid industrialization. Railroads were indispensable to sustain a level of exports consonant with the needs of an industrializing economy. Railroad materials had to be imported from abroad, which in turn meant pursuit of a liberal foreign-trade policy with but a modicum of encouragement to domestic industry. Besides, a period of rapid growth does not materialize overnight simply because an institutional barrier to industrialization has disappeared. Such a period requires a simultaneous development of complementary efforts in many directions. The component elements of growth in the individual industrial branches must be adjusted to each other, and only when a number of such "development blocks," to use Erik Dahmén's felicitous phrase, has been created is the stage set for the initiation of the great spurt.

There is little doubt that the decades following the emancipation can be conceived as such a period of preparation. And yet it is only in retrospect that they can be so viewed. The deficiency of the internal market, so untiringly stressed by the Populist writers, might have postponed the period of rapid growth until a far and indefinite future. The strategic factor in the great industrial upsurge of the 1890's must be seen in the changed policy of the government. The fear of industrialization, so much in evidence in the 1860's, was gone. Industrial development became an accepted and in fact the central goal. Once this happened, the problem of the peasant demand lost its previous significance, and its relation to industrialization was thoroughly reversed. It was as though a rotating stage had moved, revealing an entirely new scenery. The growth of peasant demand for industrial goods no longer was a prerequisite of successful industrialization. On the contrary, its curtailment became the objective. To reduce peasant consumption meant increasing the share of national output available for investment. It meant increased exports, stability of the currency, chances for larger and cheaper loans from abroad, and the availability of foreign exchange needed to service foreign loans.

The Russian state under Vyshnegradsky and Witte put the peasantry under very considerable fiscal pressure. It left the agricultural economy of the country to its own devices, satisfied that conversion of pastures into grain lands and some modest rise in productivity on those estates which were cultivated as such rather than leased to the peasants were sufficient to support the process of industrialization. Population of course was growing rapidly. In the closing years of the 1890's Russian agriculture produced less breadgrains per capita of the population than had been the case three decades earlier. If the increased exports are taken into consideration, the domestic availabilities were still smaller. A central principle of governmental policy was to impound a larger share of the peasants' output rather than to take active steps to raise that output.

Thus, the government's budgetary policy was effectively *substituted* for the deficiency of an internal market. The continuation of railroad construction on a large scale throughout the 1890's provided the government with convenient machinery for the maintenance of demand for industrial products. At the same time, in multifarious ways the government either supplied investment funds to industry directly or encouraged and facilitated investment in industry. Government action took the place of what in other countries was achieved by the pull of a growing free market, or by forced savings generated either by credit creation or by the impact upon current income of previously accumulated claims.

Those, however, were not the only processes of substitution that were taking place during the period of the great spurt of Russian industrialization. The Russian government, far from favoring all branches of industrial endeavor indiscriminately, concentrated its primary attention on the output of iron and steel and the machinery industries. The strategic interest in railroads and general political considerations certainly prompted the government in that direction. But as may be deduced from comparisons with other countries, this cannot be more than a part of the story. In a sense, this concentration upon certain branches of industry also was an emanation of substitutive processes.

Russia on the eve of its great industrial spurt suffered from many disabilities. Its entrepreneurs were far too few; their time horizon often limited, their commercial customs backward, and their standards of honesty none too high. The influx of labor to industry was inadequate because of the institutional framework that had been imposed upon agriculture. Such labor as was available was uneducated, restless and fitful in its habits, often trying to submerge the sense of frustration and loneliness in alcoholic excesses with consequent absenteeism, low productivity, and rebellion against the rules of the factory discipline. One of the few advantages that Russia, as many other backward countries in similar conditions, possessed was the possibility of borrowing technology from more advanced and more experienced industrial countries. In this field alone, Russia could equal, if not excel, them. It could concentrate on modern technology so that its factory equipment, though much smaller in the aggregate, could be much more up-to-date in its average composition. But the introduction on a large scale of technology from advanced countries, in its very nature, also meant a substitution of capital for labor. Far from being irrational in conditions of a backward country, it was the modern Western technology which enabled the Russian entrepreneurs to overcome the disability of an inadequate labor supply and very frequently also the inferior quality of that labor.

This is not to say that lack of suitable industrial labor in itself was not a hindrance to Russian industrialization. Introduction of a labor-saving process may mean lower cost per unit of the product; and still the entrepreneur may find the resulting saving insufficient to justify the effort of reorganization and modernization of the plant. His decision may be positive only if he feels that cost reductions will lead to a great expansion of output, thus increasing the total profits very considerably. But a sizable expansion of output, even though the innovation is labor saving, will require a large increase in the labor force; accordingly, the decision may still fall against the innovation, unless the labor needed may be expected to come forth without too great a rise in wage rates. The point, therefore, is not that the difficulties which Russia experienced with the formation of an industrial proletariat were not a bothersome obstacle. The point rather is that the assurance of government demand for a considerable portion of the growing output in conjunction with the introduction of modern technology created a situation in which the quantitative and the qualitative inadequacy of the labor supply could be neutralized to an extent that still permitted a relatively high rate of industrial growth.

A historian of the period cannot fail to be impressed with two aspects of this process of assimilation of foreign technology. It may be taken for granted that throughout the nineteenth century technology tended to become more and more labor saving. This was true of the individual industrial branches, and even more so of industrial economies as a whole, because of the increasing share of those industries where technological progress led to particularly rapid increases in the capital-labor ratios. It is true of course that, broadly speaking, the Russian entrepreneurs had to accept Western technology such as it was. But if they had wanted to keep down the capital-labor ratios, they might well have tried to obtain second-hand equipment built in earlier phases of Western industrialization. The least they could do was to try to import technology from those countries where technological progress had been less rapid. In fact, the opposite was true. In the period of the great spurt of the nineties, it was no longer the English technology, but the more progressive German technology that came to dominate Russian imports; and increasingly, the eyes of engineers and factory managers turned toward the United States whence even more capital-intensive equipment was brought into the country. Thus alternatives were available, and there is no reason to assume that the choices made were not the rational ones.

On the other hand, it would be wrong to see the process of technological acquisition as one of mere imitation. True, in the last decade of the nineteenth century, the Russians had as yet very little opportunity for producing equipment which combined certain features of, say, American and German machinery (as began to happen several decades later). But they exercised discretion in the processes that were modernized and those that were left unchanged, often within the same plant. While the Russian blast furnaces were rapidly becoming bigger and technically more advanced, the processes of introducing the charge into the furnaces remained untouched by this development, and workers equipped with wheelbarrows still carried out the job. Where industrial work was still similar to that used in agriculture and capable of being performed by an unskilled and fluctuating labor force, it was allowed to continue to do so.

Finally, there is the problem of bigness. Bigness, in a broad sense, is of course inherent in the concept of a great spurt. But the industrialization in Russia, as in so many other backward countries in the nineteenth century, was also characterized by bigness both of individual plant and individual enterprise. There were many reasons for this. For one, the technology of the nineteenth century typically favored the large plants, and to accept the most advanced technology also meant accepting larger and larger plants. The state promoting industrial establishments, for good and not so good reasons, showed remarkably little interest in small businesses. Large enterprises were a much more lucrative source of graft; and the corruption of the bureaucracy tended to reinforce a tendency that was already present for weighty economic reasons. Similarly, the Russian government did little to check the strong cartelization movement within Russian industry which acquired momentum after the great spurt of the nineties. But what is of interest here is that the bigness of plant and enterprise, too, must be viewed as a specific substitution process. The lack of managerial and entrepreneurial personnel was compensated for by a scale of plants which made it possible to spread the thin layer of available talent over a large part of the industrial economy.

But what were the results and the aftermath of these developments? In purely quantitative terms, in terms of growth of industrial output, the spurt was truly a great one. The average annual rate of industrial growth during the nineties was around 8 per cent, and it was even better than that in the last years of the decade. None of the major countries in Western Europe had experienced a comparably high rate of change. The very rapidity of the transformation, however, was making for maladjustments of various kinds. The discrepancy between the industrial segment of the economy which was forging ahead and the relatively stagnant agricultural segment perhaps was the most crucial among those lags and tensions. But others were by no means unimportant.

The specific processes of substitution, which have been referred to above, tended to reinforce the heterogeneous character of the resulting economic structure. Contrasts between the new and the old appeared within the industrial group itself and within the individual plants and enterprises. Technology as a strategic factor in the industrial spurt implied modernization of some industrial branches and not of others. Within an industrial plant age-old processes based on tools used in the construction of the Pyramids were carried on side by side with methods representing the last word of the inventive genius of the nineteenth century. This inevitably was reflected in human contrasts within the labor force.

But the contrasts obviously transcended labor; they extended into the managerial group. The technical director, as the chief engineer frequently was called in a Russian factory, may have been indistinguishable from his Western counterpart. The commercial manager or the entrepreneur as likely as not was a much more complex phenomenon. He was able to understand and willing to exploit the economic advantages of the new technology, but at the same time he carried on attitudes and displayed forms of behavior which differed little, if at all, from those of preindustrial entrepreneurs in Russia. This was true of his relations to consumers, suppliers, credit institutions, and competitors. In addition, his relations with the governmental bureaucracy called for special, often very devious, actions. He had to be a different man in his way of dealing with a German firm which supplied his business firm with machinery and know-how, and in dealing with an official in the Ministry of Finance whence he obtained both subsidies and orders for deliveries. The great spurt in conditions of Russian backwardness could not fail to give rise to manifold stresses, tensions, and incongruities. Sociological research which would view those tensions against the economic background of the mechanics of backwardness should discover a rich field for empirical findings and analytical comprehension.

All these disparities, created almost inevitably in the course of the great spurt, can be seen as problems for the succeeding phase of Russian industrial development that followed. However, overriding all of them in importance was the problem which the emancipation of the peasantry did not solve and the gravity of which was greatly enhanced precisely by the policy of rapid industrialization. Industrialization required political stability, but industrialization, the cost of which was largely defrayed by the peasantry, was in itself a threat to political stability and hence to the continuation of the policy of industrialization. The immediate effect of the basic substitution of the government's budgetary policies for the deficiency of the internal market was growth of industrial output. In the longer run, the effects were more complex.

III

What happened in Russia in the nineties of the last century was the great upsurge of modern industrialization. Nevertheless, certain aspects of it were not modern at all. Several times before in the course of Russian history, economic development seemed to follow a curious pattern: the military interests of the state induced the government to bring about a rapid spurt of economic growth. In the course of the process, heavy burdens were imposed upon the peasant population of the country, the enserfment of the Russian peasantry having been inextricably connected with the policies of economic development. So great were the burdens, and so heavy the pressure, that after a number of years the spurt tended to peter out, leaving an exhausted population to recover slowly from the stress and the strain that had been imposed upon it.

There is little doubt that military considerations had a good deal to do with the Russian government's conversion to a policy of rapid industrialization. True, no immediate military discomfiture preceded the initiation of the new policy. But the war of 1877 against the Turks was won on the battlefields in the Danube Valley and the Balkan Mountains, only to be lost in Berlin against the British and probably the Germans as well. In the course of the Berlin congress, particularly during its dramatic moments, the Russian government had much opportunity and reason to reflect that it was not much better prepared for any military conflict with a Western power than it had been a quarter of a century earlier on the eve of the Crimean War. In the short run, Russian reaction consisted in shifting the direction of its expansionist policy away from Europe to Central Asia and the Far East. Taking a somewhat longer view and further prompted by the formation of military alliances in Central Europe, the government turned toward the goal of a drastic increase in the economic potential of the country.

In the 1890's, a renewed enserfment of the peasantry was, of course, not in the realm of practical politics. Nor was there any need for such a measure. The reforms of rural administration which had been introduced with the advent of reaction under Alexander III gave the central bureaucracy sufficient tax-exacting power over the peasantry; at least for some time it was possible to keep the peasantry in the state of docile compliance. The joint responsibility of the village commune for tax payments was helpful, though far from indispensable. The considerable shift to indirect taxation further increased the government's ability to pay for the industrialization in conditions of a relative price and currency stability. The fiscal policy of the government was able to perform the function which at an earlier age had been performed by the institution of serfdom.

The great spurt of the 1890's came to an end in 1900. The depression of that year was variously interpreted as an overproduction crisis, a financial crash, or a response to economic setbacks abroad, particularly in Central Europe. It is fairly clear, however, that below the surface phenomena lay the exhaustion of the tax-paying powers of the rural population. The patience of the peasantry was at its end. The following years were characterized by growing unrest in the villages until the folly of the war with Japan fanned the isolated fires into the flame of a widespread peasant rebellion in the course of the 1905 Revolution. All this was very much like the consummation of the traditional pattern of Russian economic development: a quick upsurge compressed within a relatively short period ending in years of stagnation. And yet there was a great deal more to the industrial spurt of the 1890's than simply a repetition of previous sequences of economic development. It would seem more plausible to view those similarities as the last emanations, in prerevolutionary Russia, of the traditional pattern. For the differences were fully as important as the similarities. Also in this broad sense, the new and the old appeared curiously commingled. Along with the resurrection of a specifically Russian past, there was also the assimilation of Russian economic development into a graduated but still general pattern of European industrialization.

Two, and perhaps three, factors stand out in distinguishing the upswing of the 1890's from similar episodes in the more remote past. One of them has just been mentioned. During the decade of the 1890's, the Russian government abstained from introducing for the sake of the industrialization any far-reaching institutional change which, while aiding the process in the short run, would have become a serious obstacle to its continuation in the long run. Neither the institution of the *zemskii nachal'nik* nor the additional steps taken in the 1890's to preserve and protect the village commune could of course compare in any way with the enserfment of the peasantry. That a government firmly committed to the policy of industrialization went out of its way to safeguard the obshchina seemed paradoxical. But apart from the fiscal value of the arrangement, it was felt that its existence contributed to political stability within the country. Neither reason was persuasive. Satisfactory substitutes for joint responsibility for tax payments could easily have been found; and the events of the subsequent years showed clearly that the village commune nursed rebellious rather than conservative sentiments. The abolition of the commune still remained a problem of industrial policies in Russia, but it was one which antedated the period of rapid industrialization.

The other factor was positive. A modern industrialization based on the creation of fixed capital of considerable durability was not followed by periods of protracted stagnations as easily as had been the earlier, much more labor-intensive spurts of economic development ("stagnation" of course is to be understood simply in terms of a very low or even negative rate of growth). The recuperative power of a capital-intensive economy was greatly superior to that of its historical predecessors. And, finally, a modern industrialization is characterized also by a more substantial investment in human capital. In particular, it tends to bring about, over a relatively short period, a considerable change in entrepreneurial and managerial attitudes as well as, though to a lesser extent, in those of skilled labor. All this means that the effects of the great spurt reached out strongly into the future; that the process of industrialization could be resumed at diminished *faux frais* and in a form more efficient and less dependent upon the support of the state.

Such were the characteristic features of Russian industrial growth in the years between the 1905 Revolution and the outbreak of World War I. This, too, was a period of rather rapid growth (some 6 per cent per year), even though the rate of change remained below that of the 1890's. During those years industrialization could no longer be the primary concern of the government. War and revolution had greatly strained budgetary capabilities. The redemption payments (as well as the institution of joint responsibility) had disappeared under the impact of the revolution. Kokovtsev, first as Minister of Finance and later as head of the Cabinet, pursued a cautious policy of thrift. Railroad building continued, but on a much reduced scale. The execution of such armament plans as were conceived was being postponed from year to year. In the eighteenth century, the death of Peter the Great and the withdrawal of the state from active economic policy spelled the doom of the contemporaneous economic development. But in Russia of the twentieth century, Count Witte's fall and the abandonment of his policies did not prevent a renewed outburst of industrial activity.

Nothing underscores more clearly the changed attitude of the government than the fact that its most important action in the field of economic policy was Stolypin's legislation against the obshchina. In a radical reversal of the agrarian policies pursued only a few years earlier, Stolypin's reforms of 1906 and 1910 made it possible for the peasants to sever their connection with the obshchina through a simple and advantageous procedure, to acquire personal ownership of the land, and in the process often to swap the numerous strips of their former allotment for a single consolidated holding.

There is no question that many aspects of the reform were harsh and unfair to the less prosperous members of the village communes. There is also every evidence that the government's *volte-face* was caused by political considerations, that is to say, by the impressive lesson learned from peasant uprisings during the preceding revolution. The consequences of the reform for the process of industrial development were accidental from the government's point of view, despite some liberal phraseology ("liberal" in the European sense of the term) used in defending the reforms.

Nevertheless, the potential positive effects of the reform on industrial development were indisputable. The authors of the reform, despite considerable opposition within the government, refused to accept the concept of family or household ownership; the ownership of peasants leaving the village commune was vested in the head of the household. For the first time, the road was open for an unimpaired movement to the city of peasant family members; for the first time large groups of Russians peasants could, like their counterparts in the West, sell the land and use the proceeds for establishing themselves outside agriculture. The war of 1914 necessarily cut short the implementation of the reform, but its initial effect was considerable. Both those peasants who had felt that leaving the commune would enable them to increase the productivity of their farms and those peasants who had been anxious to leave the village hastened to avail themselves of the separation procedure. It was a considerable step on the road of Russia's westernization.

And this is the aspect of the reform that is of primary importance from the point of view of the present discussion. The economic stagnation that followed the reign of Peter the Great was burdened by the legacy of serfdom. The very modernization of the state machinery under Peter meant that the government was much better equipped to enforce the serfdom condition upon the peasantry and to deal effectively with fugitives from serf status. At the same time, the territorial expansion of Russia kept reducing and making more remote the frontier regions which formerly had been the sanctuary of so many peasants in their flight from oppression. It was under these conditions that the edict granting the nobility and the gentry freedom from service obligations marked the acme of the state's retirement from active guidance of the country's economic life. That act finally severed the original connection between serfdom and economic development and sealed the perpetuation of serfdom as a main obstacle to economic progress. With regard to both its historical locus and its "liberalizing" character, the Imperial Edict of Peter III (1762) bears a certain resemblance to Stolypin's reform. And yet, despite these similarities, it is the difference between the two measures which may be taken as a guage of the contrast in historical situations. The great spurt under Peter the Great had not led to sustained growth. The traditional pattern of Russian economic development was allowed to work itself out fully. By contrast, the withdrawal of the state after the upswing of the 1890's was marked by a measure which was designed to further rather than thwart industrial progress.

The westernization of Russian industrialization between 1906 and 1914 expressed itself in a large variety of ways. To use the previously adopted terminology, one could say that the pattern of substitutions was changing rapidly. To some extent banks stepped into the vacuum left by the state. In this way, credit-creation policies and some entrepreneurial guidance by the banks continued to substitute for the scarcity of both capital and entrepreneurship in Russia. But this mode of substitution tended to approximate the pattern of Russian development to that prevailing in Central Europe. The credit policies of the banks were still a substitute for an autonomous internal market, but there is little doubt that one of the consequences of the industrial creations of the nineties was the gradual emergence of such a market.

It may be quite tempting to view again the change between the period under review and that of the 1890's in terms of Erik Dahmén's dichotomy between development blocks in the state of full completion and development blocks in the beginning stage. The years 1906–1914 were characterized by the relative scarcities of coal, oil, and metals, in conjunction with the rapid forging ahead of metal-processing industries. There is a persistent and very much exaggerated tendency in present Russian historiography to present those scarcities as consequences of monopolistic policies in the basic-materials industries. It is probably more reasonable, still following Dahmén, to say that during the years preceding the First World War the structure of Russian industry was distinguished by specific disproportionalities and that once again, though on a much higher level, industry may have been passing through a period of dynamic preparation for another great spurt. Such a spurt, of course, never materialized. The point, however, is that considering the years 1906–1914 as a period of formation of new development blocks may help to explain why the rate of growth during those years was not higher than it was. It cannot explain the high growth that was actually attained in a situation where the outside aid to industry had manifestly declined to a fraction of its previous volume. It is more helpful, therefore, to regard this period as governed by the effects of diminished backwardness, and in this sense to view the whole stretch between the end of the 1880's and the outbreak of the war as consisting of two disparate and yet connected parts: the great spurt of the 1890's had prepared for the subsequent continuation of growth under changed conditions.

Many of the tensions and frictions that could be so strikingly observed during the 1890's reappeared in the second period, if at all, in a considerably modified and tempered form. There is no question that great progress had taken place with regard to entrepreneurial attitudes. Without such progress and, in particular, without the general rise in trustworthiness of Russian businessmen, the banks could never have come to play a powerful role as suppliers of long-term credit to industrial firms. The general modernization of entrepreneurial attitudes no doubt made the complex of actions and relations of the individual entrepreneurs less heterogeneous. The decline in the importance of the government as an economic agent pointed in the same direction.

The years that had passed since the second half of the 1880's considerably increased the stock of permanent industrial labor in the country. At the same time, after 1905, more tangible improvements both in real wages and in working conditions became noticeable. The reduction in the importance of foreign engineers and foremen in factories and mines also tended to diminish friction. At the same time, the great pressure upon the peasantry had subsided. In contrast to the last decades of the nineteenth century, the quantity of breadgrain available for domestic consumption rose faster than did the population. The industrialization between 1906 and 1914 no longer offers a picture of a race against time and of progressive exhaustion, physically and mentally, of the population's power to suffer and to endure.

Those elements of relaxation and "normalization" in the industrial process should not, however, disguise the fact that in other respects the great spurt of the 1890's, the industrial upsurge under conditions of extreme backwardness, still dominated the course of the development in the later period. The composition of the growing industry continued to favor the same branches as before. As in the earlier period, the stress on bigness was characteristic of both the productive and the organizational structure. The movement toward cartelization, which was mentioned before, must be regarded as a part of this continued emphasis on bigness. As was true in countries west of Russia, the policies of the banks tended to accelerate the process. In this sense they were the true heirs to the policies previously pursued by the bureaucracy. And like the latter, they tended to exaggerate and accelerate the process both for good and bad reasons. Interest in small enterprises would have strained the organizational and supervisory powers of the banks as it had proved unmanageable for the bureaucracy. On the other hand, just as many a civil servant had found opportunities for personal enrichment in his official connection with large enterprises, similarly increases in capital, mergers, and mediation of monopolistic agreements, also when not required by the process of growth, proved a considerable source of profit for the banks. Still, when everything is said and done, it was of utmost importance that the stress on large-scale business, the very essence of industrialization in conditions of backwardness and the basis for its successful implementation, could be preserved after the withdrawal of the state.

Russia before the First World War was still a relatively backward country by any quantitative criterion. The large weight of the agrarian sector of the economy and the low level of the national per capita output placed her far below and behind neighboring Germany. Nevertheless, as far as the general pattern of its industrialization in the second period was concerned, Russia seemed to duplicate what had happened in Germany in the last decades of the nineteenth century. One might surmise that in the absence of the war Russia would have continued on the road of progressive westernization.

It is not entirely pointless to speculate on what might have happened in the course of such a development. Diminution of backwardness is a complex process. As has already been noted, certain paraphernalia of backwardness are shed fairly soon after the beginning of the process. Other elements are more resistant to change. Thus, the great school of industrialization tends to educate the entrepreneurs before it educates the workers; and it takes still longer before the influence of the industrial sector of the economy penetrates into the countryside and begins to affect the attitudes of the peasantry. In the latter respect, prerevolutionary Russia saw no more than the first modest traces of such an influence. Yet the likelihood that the transformation in agriculture would have gone on at an accelerated speed is very great.

In addition to the age-long attitudes which are more or less rapidly modified under the impact of economic development, there are specific institutional and economic factors which are created in the very process of industrialization, and which often appear strange and incomprehensible from the point of view of an advanced country. But they are the stuff that industrialization in backward areas is made of. Some of them disappear after they have fulfilled their mission, teleologically speaking. Thus did the Russian government leave the economic scene after the upswing of the 1890's. It is again extremely likely that the banks would not have been able to keep their ascendancy over Russian industry for a very long time to come. Diminishing scarcity of capital, further improvements in the quality of entrepreneurship, and the sheer growth of industrial enterprises in all probability would have in due time enhanced the position of industrial firms to a point where they no longer needed the banks' guidance. That is what happened in Germany after 1900, and the natural course of events might well have moved Russian industry in the same direction. Even so, if the German example had predictive value, the banks would not have necessarily been transformed into the English type of commercial bank. They would have retained their interest in long-term investments, and in this sense the Russian economy would have remained characterized by a peculiarity created in the earlier stages of its development. Even more important, the stress on bigness, the specific composition of industrial output, and the significance of cartels and trusts within the industrial structure are likely to have increased rather than diminished over the years. One of the curious aspects of the European development was that the process of assimilation of backward countries to advanced countries was by no means a one-sided affair. To some extent, as the degree of backwardness was reduced, the backward country tended to become more like the advanced country. Yet precisely because in the process of its industrialization the backward country had been forced to make use of very modern technological and economic instruments, in the long run it was the advanced country that in some respects assimilated its economy to that of the backward country. A comparison of the structure of, say, the German and the English economy in 1900 and some decades later would serve to illustrate this point.

Russian industrial development around the turn of the century was frequently decried as "artificial." Count Witte used to reject the accusation with considerable vehemence as meaningless and irrelevant (probably with justice). For what matters is both the degree and the direction of "artificiality" or "spontaneity" in the process seen over an appropriately long time. Taking into consideration the economic conditions that prevailed in Russia prior to its great spurt of industrialization, it is difficult to deny that the Russian development fitted well into the general pattern of European industrialization, conceived, as it properly should be, in terms of a graduated rather than a uniform pattern.

The only purpose in speculating about the probable course of Russian economic development as it might have been, if not interrupted by war and revolution, is to try to cast more light on the general industrial trends that dominated the last period of industrialization in prerevolutionary Russia. Still the question remains whether war and revolution cannot be interpreted as the result of the preceding industrial development. Some Soviet historians certainly incline in that direction. If the Russian bourgeoisie could be saddled with the main responsibility for the outbreak of the war and if, in addition, it could be shown that in bringing about the war it had acted in response to the pressure of its economic interests — if, in short, the process of Russian industrialization carried in itself the seeds of the coming military conflict — then to abstract the war from the process in order to elucidate the course and prospects of Russian industrialization would mean to abstract the process as well. Some Russian manufacturers indeed may have welcomed the wartime orders for their products. Yet the precise mechanism through which such interests of the bourgeoisie were in fact translated into the decisions reached by the emperor and his government has remained altogether obscure.

The view just described seems to magnify the political significance of the Russian bourgeoisie out of all proportion and to substitute suppositions of various degrees of plausibility for historical evidence. It might be more persuasive to argue that the government saw a relatively short and victorious war as a chance to solidify the regime and to avert the danger of revolution. And the question then would be to what extent the preceding industrial development may be said to have been leading to another revolutionary cataclysm.

It is true, of course, that the social and political structure of the empire was shot through with manifold serious weaknesses. Opposition to the regime was nearly universal among the intelligentsia and certainly widespread among the industrial and mercantile groups. Since 1912, the year of the famous massacre in the Lena gold fields, the strike movement of the workers was again gaining momentum. And at the bottom of the social edifice there was the old resentment of the peasants who had never accepted the rightfulness of the gentry's ownership rights over the land. The peasantry's land hunger was a steady source of ferment. The sentiment in the villages was no doubt further exacerbated by the blows struck against the village commune and the threat of its dissolution. A new outbreak of revolutionary violence at some point was far from being altogether improbable.

And yet, as one compares the situation in the years before 1914 with that of the nineties, striking differences are obvious. In the earlier period, the very process of industrialization with its powerful confiscatory pressures upon the peasantry kept adding, year in and year out, to the feelings of resentment and discontent until the outbreak of large-scale disorders became almost inevitable. The industrial prosperity of the following period had no comparable effects, however. Modest as the improvements in the situation of peasants were, they were undeniable and widely diffused. Those improvements followed rather than preceded a revolution and accordingly tended to contribute to a relaxation of tension. Stolypin's reforms certainly were an irritant, but after the initial upsurge their implementation was bound to proceed in a much more gradual fashion.

Similarly, the economic position of labor was clearly improving. In the resurgence of the strike movement economic problems seemed to predominate. It is true, of course, that in the specific conditions of the period any wage conflict tended to assume a political character because of the ready interventions of police and military forces on behalf of management. But this did not mean that the climate of opinion and emotion within the labor movement was becoming more revolutionary; as shown by the history of European countries (such as Austria or Belgium), sharp political struggles marked the period of formation of labor movements that in actual fact, though not always in the language used, were committed to reformism. There is little doubt that the Russian labor movement of those years was slowly turning toward revision and trade-unionist lines. As was true in the West, the struggles for general and equal franchise to the Duma and for a cabinet responsible to the Duma, which probably would have occurred sooner or later, may well have further accentuated this development. To repeat, I do not mean to deny that there was much political instability in the country. There clearly was. What matters here is that from the point of view of the industrial development of the country, war, revolution, or the threat thereof may reasonably be seen as extraneous phenomena. In this sense, it seems plausible to say that Russia on the eve of the war was well on the way toward a westernization or, perhaps more precisely, a Germanization of its industrial growth. The "old" in the Russian economic system was definitely giving way to the "new." It was left to the regime that finally emerged from the 1917 Revolution, generated in the misery of the war and the shame of defeats, to create a different set of novelties and to mix them with old ingredients of Russian economic history in the strange and powerful infusion of Soviet industrialism.

IV

The 1917 Revolution redeemed the ancient hopes of the Russian peasantry by letting them seize the lands of the gentry. In addition, after the end of the Civil War, when the NEP compromise was put into operation, the peasants found themselves greatly relieved of obligations toward the state as compared with the prewar years. At length, the "internal market" of the Populists seemed to have become a reality.

If the revolution had effected nothing else but a change in the position of the peasantry, one might perhaps have envisaged a slow but steady growth in agricultural output and a rate of growth in industry perhaps slightly exceeding that of agriculture, if for no other reason because of a sustained shift of many industrial activities from the farms to urban industries. The increased strength of peasant demand was bound to effect a change in the composition of Russian industry in the direction of greater stress upon "light" industries. Presumably, the rate of investment would have been lowered and the over-all rate of growth of industrial output slowed down thereby. It was apparently in these terms that Stalin, during the twenties, envisaged the course of the country's industrial development.

Yet, in addition to the new role of the peasantry, the revolution also established a dictatorial government controlling the large-scale industry. Instead of asserting itself through a market mechanism, the peasant demand, if it was effectively to change the structure of relative prices and the composition of industry, had to be reflected in government decisions. These decisions, however, might or might not be the appropriate ones. During the NEP period, the problem expressed itself largely in the so-called scissor crisis: in the fact that the government-dominated industry had insisted upon terms of trade that were unfavorable to agriculture. Nor was any shift toward greater stress on consumer-goods industries visible. If anything, toward the end of the NEP the share of heavy industries in total output was somewhat larger than before the war.

It is true that through most of the NEP period the high rate of industrial growth overshadowed the difficulties and prevented them from becoming overpowering. As long as the problem was to rebuild the prewar industry, largely using prewar equipment and prewar labor and technicians, the incremental capital-output ratios were very low and the rapid increases in the supply of consumer goods kept discontent at bay. The situation was bound to change as the prewar capacity of Russian factories was being reached and further increases in output began to require much more sizable investment funds.

This, no doubt, was a crucial and critical moment in the economic history of Soviet Russia. The adjustment to a lower rate of industrial growth would have been difficult under any circumstances. In the specific Soviet conditions of the later twenties it was aggravated by political factors. To prevent too deep and too sudden a fall in the rate of industrial growth, either voluntary or politically enforced savings were necessary. But the savings of the peasant economy were small, since, despite all improvements, the absolute levels of peasant incomes still were very low. To increase the rate of taxation carried the threat of peasant resistance; and a rise in industrial prices charged to the peasants after the experience of the scissor crisis, when such prices had to be *lowered* in relation to farm prices, was hardly within the range of practical politics. The legacy of the NEP policies, with their low taxes, downward pressure upon the industrial terms of trade, and the failure to provide in time for a shift in the composition of industrial output in favor of consumer goods, expressed itself in a situation of inflationary pressures where too large a volume of purchasing power of the peasantry pressed upon too small a volume of available consumer goods.

The "internal market" supported by the peasantry had been regarded for decades as the natural and spontaneous form of industrialization. After what has been said above, it may be doubtful whether in conditions of still considerable backwardness the peasant demand alone would have sustained any reasonable rate of increase in industrial output. Too low a rate of increase in demand may have proved insufficient to solve the problem of indivisibilities and complementarities inherent in the process of development. Without a strong flow of external economies (in the broad sense of the word), the nascent industrial enterprises might have found themselves burdened with costs of production that were too high for successful operation. Paradoxical as it may sound, industry might have been better able to satisfy a strong rather than a weak increase in demand.

The immediate problem, however, was different. The change in the economic position of the peasantry greatly increased the flexibility of Russian agriculture. Under certain circumstances, higher outputs per farming household will lead to an increase in the peasants' demand for industrial goods — whether adequate or not from the industry's point of view. Under different and less favorable circumstances, the peasant economy can reduce the extent of its connections with outside markets by diverting cereals to production of converted products for its own consumption; and by assigning a larger portion of the land to fibrous crops for home spinning and weaving. For the Russian peasantry with its weak marketing tradition the escape into greater self-sufficiency suggested itself as an easy and natural response to the economic conditions which prevailed in the second half of the 1920's. As the marketings of grain began to fall off, the inevitable adjustment to a lower rate of industrial growth seemed to turn into the threat of a negative rate of growth, of de-urbanization and agrarianization of the country.

The economic crisis that thus marked the end of the NEP period was at the same time a political crisis of first magnitude. Inability to maintain the food supplies to the cities and the growing resistance of the millions of peasants, strong in their intangible diffusion, seemed to spell the doom of the Soviet dictatorship. To be sure, a change in the political system of country would not have in itself solved the economic problem. The inflationary pressures still would have called for a solution. It is possible that a government truly representing the peasants might have been able to raise taxes and by so doing to establish the equilibrium between rural purchasing power and the volume of industrial consumer goods available, and at the same time to reverse the declining trend in agricultural marketings. Such a government might have sought and found foreign credits and used the proceeds for importation of consumer goods from abroad — thereby making the increases in taxation less unpalatable. The immediate problem might have been solved in this fashion. The question of industrial growth would have been another matter. Barring further fundamental changes in the economic structure of the country, the conditions for resumption of industrial growth would seem to have been rather unfavorable under such circumstances.

In retrospect, the threat to the continuation in power of the Soviet regime appears blurred by the indubitable successes achieved subsequently. But it was real indeed. It was under the pressure of that threat that Stalin underwent a radical change of mind and embarked upon the gamble of the First Five Year Plan. Viewed as a short-run measure, the purpose of the First Five Year Plan was to break the disequilibrium through increase in consumer-goods output based on increase in plant capacity. It was a daring scheme if one considers that its coming to fruition presupposed a further though temporary deterioration in the situation as a result of deflecting a larger share of national income into investment and away from consumption. Again, in the best Russian tradition, it was to be a race against time. If the Soviet government could keep peasant resistance within bounds for the relatively short period of a few years, it might be able to offer sufficient quantities of consumer goods to the peasants at terms of trade not too unfavorable to them, and thus it could eliminate the dangers and place the relations between the villages and the city on a sounder basis.

Not unlike the imperial government after the revolution of 1905, the Soviet government was keenly aware of the peasants' hostility to it. In a very similar fashion it was anxious to find or to create at least some points of support in the villages which might facilitate its task during the difficult years to come. Stolypin had gambled on the "strong and the sober," expecting the prosperous peasant outside the village commune to neutralize in some measure the antagonism of the majority. After certain adjustments, the collective farms were originally supposed to perform the same function. They were conceived as limited injections of communal vaccine into the individualistic climate of the villages. As long as the number of collective farms was kept small, it would be possible to provide them with sufficient state aid, so that membership in the collective farms would carry real advantages.

The plans, however, did not succeed; alternatively, they succeeded only too well. The resistance of the peasantry proved much greater than had been expected. The peasantry which had emerged victorious from the revolution and the civil war was very different from the docile masses of the imperial period. The bitter struggles that followed developed a logic of their own. In the course of the "revolution from above," as Stalin termed it and which more justly might be called a "counterrevolution from above," the original plans of the Soviet government were quickly rendered obsolete. The dogged defense by the peasants of the revolutionary land seizures evoked an all-out offensive by the government. The peasants went down in defeat and a complete, or nearly complete, collectivization was the result.

The collectivization supplied an unexpected solution to the besetting problem of disequilibrium, the actual starting point of the great change in Soviet economic policies. But it also affected profoundly the character of the government's plans with regard to industrialization. Once the peasantry had been successfully forced into the machinery of collective farms, once it became possible to extract a large share of agricultural output in the form of "compulsory deliveries" without bothering much about the *quid pro quo* in the form of industrial consumer goods, the difficulties of the late twenties were overcome. The hands of the government were untied. There was no longer any reason to regard the First Five Year Plan as a self-contained brief period of rapid industrialization, and the purpose of the industrialization no longer was to relieve the shortage of consumer goods. A program of perpetual industrialization through a series of five-year plans was now on the agenda. What was originally conceived as a brief spell became the initial stage to a new great spurt of industrialization, the greatest and the longest in the history of the country's industrial development.

Any historical contemplation of Soviet industrial history must begin with a description of the proximate chain of causations which connects the period of the NEP with that of super-industrialization under the five-year plans. Such a description brings out and explains the precise timing of the change that took place. The discussion must be in terms of the answers found by the Soviet government to the pressures and exigencies of a given situation. Yet to place the whole weight of emphasis upon those aspects of the evolution may not be sufficient. Other forces, perhaps less clearly visible may have been at work determining the course of development and its outcome. Much of what happened at the turn of the third and fourth decades of the century was the product of that specific historical moment; however great the change, and however drastic the momentary discontinuity in the process, the deep historical roots and its broad historical continuity must not elude the historian.

If Peter the Great had been called back to life and asked to take a good look at Russia, say, in the second half of the thirties, he might have had some initial difficulties because of changes in language and technology; he might have found the purge trials unnecessarily cumbersome and verbose; and he might have upbraided Stalin for the unmanly refusal to participate physically in the act of conveying the modern *Strel'tsy* from life to death. Yet it should not have taken him long to understand the essentials of the situation. For the resemblance between Soviet and Petrine Russia was striking indeed.

Nothing has been said so far about the role of foreign policy in molding Soviet economic decisions. Yet it must not be forgotten that the smashing defeat of the country by Germany stood at the very cradle of the Soviet regime. Foreign intervention in the Civil War, however halfhearted, certainly left memories that were long in fading. The 1920's witnessed a gradual improvement in Soviet diplomatic and commercial relations with foreign countries. But tensions were ever-recurring, and in 1927 there was much talk of military dangers in the course of the diplomatic conflict with England. Germany, despite the Russian aid to the *Reichswehr,* was still the military vacuum of Europe. After 1930, with the beginning disintegration of the Weimar Republic both Russian fears and Russian ambitions were increasingly concentrated on Germany; until after Hitler's advent to power the ambitions were frustrated and the threat of a military attack began to loom larger and larger each year. There is very little doubt that, as so often before, Russian industrialization in the Soviet period was a function of the country's foreign and military policies. If this is so, however, one might argue that there was more instability in the second half of the NEP period than that stemming from inflationary pressures alone. If, as has been indicated above, the continuation of NEP policies even after a successful removal of monetary disequilibriums was unlikely to lead to a period of rapid industrialization, pressures for a revision of those policies might well have materialized in any case.

A resurrected Peter the Great would have found sufficient operational resemblance between Charles XII and Adolf Hitler, however much he might have preferred his civilized contemporary to the twentieth-century barbarian. Nor would the great transformation in rural Russia cause him much trouble. He would have quickly recognized the functional resemblance between collectivization and the serfdom of his days, and he would have praised collectivization as the much more efficient and effective system to achieve the same goals — to feed gratis the nonagricultural segments of the economy and at the same time provide a flow of labor for the public works of the government, which the Soviet regime accomplished by the institution of special contracts between the factories and the collective farms. He would no doubt have acquiesced in the tremendous human cost of the collectivization struggles, once it had been explained to him that the quantitative difference between the Soviet period and his own time in this respect was largely the result of the colossal growth in population in the two intervening centuries. And while regretting the loss of animal draft power in Russian agriculture, he may have even understood that the reduction in cattle herds in the course of the "great slaughter" actually facilitated the task of industrialization inasmuch as the amount of calories per unit of land available for the feeding of the population was greatly increased as a result. Neither the formidable stress on technology in the earlier portions of the period of industrialization nor the resolute concentration upon heavy industries would have evoked the visitor's astonishment. True, at times Peter the Great was given to flights of fancy and attempted to launch in Russia production of Venetian mirrors and French Gobelins, but the great line of his policy, so different from that of French mercantilism, was essentially devoted to the increase of the country's military potential.

Thus a pattern of economic development which before the First World War seemed to have been relegated to the role of a historical museum piece was re-enacted in Soviet Russia. The anachronistic — or rather parachronistic — character of the Soviet experiment in rapid industrialization did not, however, prevent it from attaining a very high measure of success. On the contrary, the combination of ancient measures of oppression with modern technology and organization proved immensely effective. All the advantages of industrialization in conditions of backwardness were utilized to the hilt: adoption of the fruits of Western technological progress and concentration on those branches of industrial activity where foreign technology had the most to offer; huge size of plant and the simultaneity of industrialization along a broad front assuring large flows of external economics.

To be sure, the tendency to exaggerate and to overdo was ever-present. In many cases, smaller plant size would have been more rational. In addition, the very breadth of the effort kept creating and recreating bottlenecks; and the excessive bureaucratization of the economy absorbed an undue share of the available manpower. Yet when everything is said and done, the result in terms of growth of industrial output were unprecedented in the history of modern industrialization in Russia. True, the Soviet official index exaggerated the speed of growth. The rates of 20 and more per cent a year that were claimed never materialized in reality. It is, however, possible now on the basis of the computations performed by American economists and statisticians to conclude that the average annual rate of industrial growth in Russia throughout the first ten years after the initiation of the First Five Year Plan was somewhere between 12 and 14 per cent; the rate fell in the years immediately preceding the outbreak of the Second World War, but rose again after 1945. Its high level was maintained far beyond the period of reconstruction from war damages. In the first half of the fifties, industrial output still kept increasing at some 13 per cent a year. And it was only in the second half of the decade that the rate of growth began to decline, though very gradually. One has only to compare these rates with the high rate attained during Witte's great spurt of the nineties (8 per cent) in order to gauge the magnitude of the Soviet industrialization effort.

The success of the Soviet experiment is frequently described as a proof of the efficiency of a "socialist" system. That is how the leaders of Soviet Russia like to refer to their achievements. On the other hand, there is a good deal of unwillingness to accept the fact of rapid growth of Soviet industry because of the prevailing assumption of the fundamental inefficiency of socialism. Much of it is a question of semantics. It is at the least doubtful, for instance, whether Stalin's Russia could be described as a socialist country in terms of Anatole France's definition of socialism: *Le socialisme c'est la bonté et la justice.* A historian has little reason to get enmeshed in these discussions since he may find himself discussing the problem as to whether or not Peter the Great was a socialist. Nor is this the place to explain why in the opinion of the present writer Marxian ideology, or any socialist ideology for that matter, has had a very remote, if any, relation to the great industrial transformation engineered by the Soviet government.

What matters much more is the specific nature of the Soviet spurt and the economic mechanism which sustained it. The essential juxtaposition is between an approximate sixfold increase in the volume of industrial output, on the one hand, and, on the other, the level of real wages which in the fifties was still substantially below that of 1928, with the peasants' real income probably registering an even greater decline in comparison to 1928. By holding down forcibly the consumption of the population and by letting the area of consumer-goods output take the brunt of errors and miscalculations that occurred in the process of planning, the Soviet government succeeded in channeling capital and human resources into capital formation, thus assuring the rapid growth of the only segment of the economy in which it was interested. The Soviet leaders have kept asserting, and the Soviet economists have kept repeating after them, that according to Marx the rate of growth of producer-goods output must necessarily be higher than that of consumer-goods output. The reference to Marx is hardly meaningful within the context of the Soviet economy, which has no specific marketing problems with regard to consumer goods. Nevertheless, the assertion is quite correct as a description of the actual policy pursued by the Soviet government, pursued not by force of economic necessity but by virtue of *political choice*. It means implicitly that as the volume of output grows, so does the rate of investment in expanding output; in other words, a larger and larger portion of national output is allocated to the production of nonconsumable goods. It is these relationships that contain the essence of Soviet industrial development. This has been the strategic lever that permitted the Soviet government to make use of every advantage of backwardness to a degree unknown to all its predecessors.

v

As suggested above, the effects of industrialization begun in conditions of backwardness may continue for a long time to come. But the specific advantages of backwardness by their very nature must disappear in the course of a successful industrialization. Even if no restrictions on trade were imposed by the West, Russia today would stand to gain much less from imports than was the case a quarter of a century ago. What is true of foreign technology is also true of many other factors of growth. The exhaustion or at least the diminution of readily available labor surpluses in rural areas and the depletion of the reserves in high-grade minerals, conveniently located, point in the same direction. There is no question that after the war Russia experienced the drag of all these vanishing advantages or growing disabilities. If she was still able to maintain the rate of industrial growth at a level fairly close to that of the thirties, the reason must be sought partly in the government's ability to keep consumption down so that the growing disadvantages were successfully offset by increasing supply of capital; and partly in the great effort to increase the quality of the labor force by an ambitious program of training and education.

It is too early to judge whether the recent declines in the rate of growth will be transitory or whether they will have marked the end of the great spurt of economic development. It cannot be my purpose to indulge in prophecies. Rather, the contingency that the great spurt of industrial growth in Russia may be nearing its end may be used here to cast some additional light upon the recent economic history of the country. In discussing the origins of Soviet industrialization, some emphasis was laid upon military dangers with which the Soviet government had to reckon. It is, however, a frequent though natural pitfall in historical writings to assume that a genetic approach provides full explanation of a given phenomenon. If the policy of super-industrialization in Soviet Russia had been dictated exclusively by the needs of defense against foreign aggression, one might have expected a radical change in Soviet economic policy to follow the end of the war. This, however, did not happen. The stress on heavy industry and high-speed industrialization continued unabated.

Many reasons can be advanced to explain the fact. Perhaps not the least important among them lies in the peculiarities of the country's political system. It is a truism that a policy of high and rising investment rates could not be pursued in Russia unless by a ruthless and all-powerful dictatorship. But the obverse may also be true: the dictatorial system could not exist without an economic policy which provides it with a social function and a justification for its existence. If this is true, the prolongation if not the perpetuation of the economic spurt would be inseparably connected with the fate of the dictatorial regime. This is the point at which comparisons with the era of Peter the Great break down. The dynastic ruler of those days could stop and relax with impunity, but a modern dictatorial system is propelled by a specific dynamism which it can abandon only at the penalty of grave perils.

After the death of Stalin the problem of succession has proved a very difficult one. Concessions to the peasantry, Malenkov's attempt to shift Russian industry toward increased production of consumer goods, Malenkov's fall, Khrushchev's decentralization of the industrial organization and renewed promises of greater supplies of consumer goods, to say nothing of the two recent purges following each other in quick succession — all these seem to reveal a deep crisis in the Soviet dictatorship. Khrushchev's original effort to dissociate himself from his predecessor has unleashed a series of effects the consequences of which apparently have just begun to unfold. An entirely open situation has been created in which everything seems possible except perhaps one thing: continuation for any length of time of the present confusion. The road may lead back to a revival of Stalinist policies, including an undoing of the inchoate measures of relaxation taken in recent years. It may lead to a period of progressive resistance to the regime, culminating in a definite abandonment of the policy of high-speed industrialization, thus concluding the Soviet industrial upsurge in a way not unlike that at the end of the nineties. If, however, the former alternative were to prevail, it is a moot question as to what extent the rate of industrial growth could be maintained at levels comparable to those of the thirties and early fifties. The continuation of a steady increase in the rate of investment would be the most important single factor the Soviet government could rely upon to counteract the growing effect of the many retarding factors, including, it might be added, the increasing difficulty of agricultural output in keeping pace with the increase in population. This means that, in matters of economic policies, Stalinist policies would have to be pursued with a vengeance and consumption standards would have to be held down severely. Yet even in such a case one might assume that eventually the retarding factors would assert themselves and that a gradual fall of the rate of growth to much lower levels would be very difficult to resist.

VI

At the time of the emancipation, Russia was an agrarian country with a sprinkling of inefficient industry. Russia of today is a big industrial power. In terms of aggregate levels of industrial output it has overtaken and surpassed the advanced countries of Western Europe. A profound transformation has occurred with regard to technology, organizational methods, and labor skills. The last century of Russian economic history has resulted in a far-reaching westernization of the country's economy. And yet the old curse, so clearly perceived by Plekhanov, remains on Russia's economic development: the processes of Russian westernization are un-Western. It still seems to be true, as it was several centuries ago, that for every step which Russia takes along the road of westernization in one respect, it must pay, and pay dearly, by taking steps which, in other respects, lead it away from the West.

The process of industrialization in a backward country inevitably involves a certain period during which consumption is being reduced in favor of capital formation. After the initial phase is over, consumption begins to rise, reaches again the level at which it was curtailed previously, and then continues to increase more or less *pari passu* with the increase in national income. The extent to which this generalized sequence is reproduced in reality varies from case to case. The depth of the decline in consumers' real incomes, the length of the time that elapsed before consumption could return to its "ante-spurt" level, the speed at which further increases in consumption were diffused throughout the various groups of the community, all depended on many factors: the country's degree of backwardness, the course of the international cycle at the time of the great spurt, the role of foreign trade and capital imports in the process, the strength of the labor movement, the institutional framework in agriculture, and so on. By and large, however, the sequence is a simplified but correct description of the story of the nineteenth-century industrialization in a number of major European countries.

As has been stressed in the foregoing pages, Russian economic history tells a different story or, more precisely, it tells only the first half of that story. Except for a brief and uncertain glimmer of coming improvements in the years preceding the outbreak of the war in 1914 — and except for the period of return to prewar levels (or somewhat better than that) from the ravages of the Civil War — the Russian population has failed to derive any perceptible advantages from the long period of industrialization.

The reason for this lies in the existence of the dictatorship which no doubt has contributed to the course of industrialization more than any other single factor and which at the same time has prevented the consummation of the process on patterns observed in the West. The westernization achieved under the aegis of an Oriental despot has had to remain unfinished.

Again, it is possible and indeed likely that in the future the Soviet dictatorship may have to acquiesce in a gradual fall of the rate of industrial growth to levels considerably below those attained in the past. This could result from a growing scarcity of several ingredients of which industrial growth is made. But this decline in the rate of growth need not be caused or accompanied by larger shares of consumption in national income. There is no *economic* reason why the Soviet system could not go on, more or less indefinitely, channeling most of the annual accretions to national output into investment and keeping the levels of per capita consumption fairly stable. In other words, there is no economic force compelling the Soviet government to complete the process of industrialization.

And that is as far as an economic historian can go. It is with a certain sense of frustration therefore that he turns away from his contemplation of a century of Russia's economic history. It always was a "political" economic history and it is that now to an extent never witnessed before, at least in its modern periods.

The keys to an understanding of the nature of past economic change, let alone to its probable future course, lie outside the narrow purview of economic factors and relations. They must be sought in a sociology-of-power exercise by dictatorial governments, in a sociology of popular discontent. So far, students of Russian economic development have been compelled to work with rough and ready generalizations. It has not been difficult for them to see, with Bertrand Russell, power as the fundamental concept in social science. They know that much in Soviet industrialization makes sense in terms of a "power for power's sake" assumption. They realize that the Soviet identification with socialist ideology, though the latter has been thoroughly revised and denaturalized, has wrested from the Russian people the weapon of socialist protest which, along with other factors, has contributed so much to the humanization and consummation of industrial processes in Western Europe. They are aware that the policy of perpetual foreign tensions has been an effective tool in the hands of the dictators for eliciting a modicum of allegiance from an unwilling and sullen population. Yet more is needed than impressionistic insights and *ad hoc* hypotheses. An economist concerned with the process of Russian economic growth has every reason to hope that this volume will make a serious contribution to a searching and systematic exploration of these problems.

POPULATION CHANGES

WARREN W. EASON

From a demographic point of view, the population of Imperial Russia and the Soviet Union has shown both stable and changing characteristics since 1861. In total number of persons, the country has continued to rank as one of the largest in the world, second only to China and India. At the same time it has been one of the least densely populated, having a land area more than twice that of any other country. In terms of population increase, it has ranked fairly consistently among the most rapidly growing countries, although its relative position has declined significantly in the past few years. And it has retained the characteristics of a relatively "young" population, while developing a sharply widened deficit in the number of males relative to females, both conditions reflecting the impact of successive national crises beginning with World War I.

From an economic and social point of view, the effects of major reorientations of national objectives dominate indexes relating to the population. Some indexes have been changed which remained relatively stable for years: for example, the percentage of the population living in urban areas, which rose noticeably only after 1928. In other indexes, the direction of growth has been accelerated or reversed: for example, the percentage of the population in the socioeconomic class receiving income as individual employers was reduced essentially to zero, and the percentage in the class based on wages and salaries experienced accelerated growth. And wholly new indexes have been introduced: for example, collective farming, which rose to include a majority of the population during the 1930's.

These and other demographic and socioeconomic characteristics of population change since 1861 will be examined in this chapter by presenting the quantitative indexes themselves, and by relating them to the broad pattern of developments in the economy and society.

I

As a point of departure for discussing population changes since 1861, data on the total population are reproduced in Table 1. Most years are represented, with the principal exception of 1942–1944 and 1946–1949,

Table 1. The Total Population: Imperial Russia and the USSR
Census Data and Soviet Estimates, 1861–1959, and Series Estimated
on the Basis of Reported Vital Statistics and Other Data, 1926–1960[a]

(In thousands)

| Date | Census data and Soviet estimates | | Date | Census data and Soviet estimates | | Estimated series | |
	Pre-Soviet territory	Soviet territory		Prewar sources	Postwar sources	Based on reported vital statistics	Based on adjusted vital statistics
1861[b]	73,648	61,327	1926 census	147,028	147,028	147,028	147,028
1865	75,126	62,550	1927	147,128	—	147,100	147,100
1870	84,521	65,208	1928	150,450	—	150,500	149,900
1875	90,219	69,899	1929	154,288	155,000	154,100	153,100
1880	97,705	78,592	1930	157,700	—	157,200	155,600
1885	108,787	84,955	1931	160,600	—	160,100]	158,100
1890	117,788	92,822	1932	163,692	160,700	163,200]	160,700
1895	123,920	100,276	1933	165,748	164,000	165,300	(160,600)
1897 census	125,640	103,933	1934	168,000	—	—	(160,600)
1900	131,710	109,593	1935	—	—	159,300	160,500
1905	140,180	120,083	1936	—	—	161,300	162,200
1910	153,768	130,354	1937	—	166,100	163,500	164,100
1913	161,723	137,403	1938	169,000	169,100	166,900	167,300]
1914	165,138	139,913	1939	—	—	170,400]	170,400
1915	(168,435)	142,588	1939 census	170,467	170,557	170,557]	170,557
1916	(169,759)	142,260					
1917	(169,230)	142,472	1940	193,000	190,700[c]	196,300	
			1941	—	—	198,700	
1918		140,903					
1919		139,701	1945		171,700	171,000	
1920		137,093					
1921		134,276	1950		181,300	178,700	
1922		133,890					
1923		133,467	1955		197,400	194,500	
1924		135,021	1956 April 1		200,201	—	
1925		140,619	1959 census		208,826	208,826	
1926		143,796	1960		—	212,500[d]	

[a] Sources and methods are set forth in W. W. Eason, "Soviet Manpower: The Population and Labor Force of the U.S.S.R." (unpublished dissertation, Columbia University).

[b] All dates are January 1, except as indicated.

[c] TsSU, *Narodnoe khoziaistvo SSSR v 1958 godu: statisticheskii ezhegodnik* (Moscow, 1959), 9. Earlier postwar sources report 191,700,000 for 1940. Both figures are net of the natural increase of the population after the 1939 census, but inclusive of the estimated population of the annexed areas.

[d] Estimated from the census total, by assuming the same natural increase of the population during 1959 as reported for 1958 (18.1 per thousand population).

for which there are no Soviet estimates and which are particularly difficult to estimate on the basis of available information. The data are from the following types of sources: (1) the censuses of 1897, 1926, 1939, and 1959; (2) Soviet estimates for most years, based on both census and non-census materials; and (3) estimates for certain years after 1926, constructed with the aid of Soviet materials. With respect to the Soviet period, the data prior to 1940 refer to the territory up to the time of the 1939 census, and for 1940 and thereafter to the territory as of the date in question.[1]

[1] Specifically, this means that the non-Soviet estimates for 1940–1941 include all territories annexed during 1940, and for 1945 and thereafter exclude territories ceded to Poland in 1945 and include territories annexed during 1944 and 1945. The Soviet estimate of 191,700,000 for 1940 is net of the territories subsequently ceded to Poland and of the natural increase of the population after the 1939 census.

These data show that in almost one hundred years since 1861 the population of Imperial Russia and the Soviet Union, on Soviet territory, has increased from 61 million to about 210 million, or by more than three times. Allowing roughly for the territorial changes of the 1940–1945 period,[2] this represents an average increase of slightly more than 1 per cent per year. In the sixty-year period prior to 1861 (on Imperial Russian territory), moreover, essentially the same average rate of growth of 1 per cent per year was maintained.[3]

A long-run average growth rate of 1 per cent per year since 1801 may be compared to a world average rate of 0.45 per cent per year between 1750 and 1850, and 0.8 per cent per year between 1850 and 1950.[4] Since Imperial Russia and the Soviet Union probably have not suffered less in terms of wartime population losses than other countries, and since population emigration has exceeded immigration, the comparison suggests that the peacetime natural rate of population increase over the last century and a half has been considerably above the world average.

This conclusion is borne out by an examination of the vital statistics on births and deaths since 1801, reproduced in Table 2, where annual rates of increase on the average of about 1.5 per cent are suggested.[5] Correction for underregistration of births and deaths, especially in the early Soviet and pre-Soviet years, would probably lower the net population increases as reproduced in Table 2, but the corrected figures should still be above the world average.

For the pre-Soviet period, the decline in the crude death rate between 1861 and 1914 (from 38.7 to 25.3 per thousand) and the decline in the crude birth rate (from 51.9 to 41.0) combine to register a slight increase in the rate of population growth (from 1.32 to 1.57 per cent), but this cannot be interpreted as significant, due to shortcomings in the statistics.[6] The crude birth and death rates for the earlier years are of a

---

[2] This is to say, an allowance for approximately 22 million persons in the annexed territories at the time of annexations, plus births minus deaths in the intervening years, and net of emigration.

[3] Calculated from Soviet estimates of the total population of Imperial Russia in 1801 (37,540,000) and 1861 (73,648,000), in E. Z. Volkhov, *Dinamika narodonaseleniia SSSR za vosem'desiat let* (Moscow-Leningrad, 1930), 8.

[4] Calculated from data on the world population for 1750, 1850, and 1950, in United Nations Population Division, "The Past and Future Population of the World and Its Continents," *Proceedings of the World Population Conference, 1954,* III (New York, 1955), 266.

[5] This is not to say that the rate of population increase exceeded the rates in each and every other country throughout the period. As noted by F. Lorimer, *The Population of the Soviet Union: History and Prospects* (Geneva, 1946), 12, "The average rate of natural increase in Russia may . . . have been somewhat higher than in western Europe during most of the eighteenth and nineteenth centuries; it certainly never approached that of the white population of the United States in the early nineteenth century. . . ."

[6] These shortcomings, in the form of incomplete reporting by administrative units and underregistration of the births and deaths themselves, lead the Soviets to present

Table 2. Reported Birth and Death Rates Per Thousand Population
and Percentage Rates of Natural Increase, Imperial Russia
(European Part) and the USSR, 1801–1958[a]

Year	Birth rates	Death rates	Annual increase (per cent of total population)	Year	Birth rates	Death rates	Annual increase (per cent of total population) — Consistent with birth and death rates	Annual average between census totals	Adjusted for consistency with inter-censal annual average
1801–1810	43.7	27.1	1.66	1926[b]	43.6	20.0	2.36		
1811–1820	40.0	26.5	1.35	1927	42.7	21.0	2.17		1.90
1821–1830	42.7	27.5	1.52	1928	42.2	18.2	2.40		2.14
1831–1840	45.6	33.6	1.20	1929	39.8	20.3	1.95		1.64
1841–1850	49.7	39.4	1.03	1930	39.2	20.4	1.88		1.59
1851–1860	52.4	39.4	1.30	1931	38.2	19.1	1.91		1.65
1861–1870	51.9	38.7	1.32	1932	—	—	1.25		(−.03)
1871–1880	49.1	35.5	1.36	1933	—	—	—	1.24	(−.03)
1881–1890	48.7	34.2	1.45	1934	—	—	—		(−.03)
1891–1895	49.0	36.2	1.28	1935	28.6	16.3	1.23		1.05
1896–1900	49.4	32.4	1.70	1936	32.3	18.8	1.35		1.17
1901–1905	47.7	31.0	1.67	1937	38.7	17.9	2.08		1.92
1906–1910	45.2	29.0	1.62	1938	38.3	17.8	2.05		1.90
1911–1913	43.3	26.9	1.64	1940	31.3	18.1	1.32		
1913[b]	43.4	27.9	1.55	1950	26.7	9.7	1.70		
1914	41.0	25.3	1.57	1951	27.0	9.7	1.73		
				1952	26.5	9.4	1.71		
1920	29.1	38.1	−0.90	1953	25.1	9.1	1.60		
1921	34.1	29.1	0.50	1954	26.6	8.9	1.77		
1922	32.1	33.8	−0.17	1955	25.7	8.2	1.75		
1923	40.5	21.5	1.90	1956	25.2	7.6	1.76		
1924	43.1	22.0	2.11	1957	25.4	7.8	1.76		
1925	44.7	23.2	2.15	1958	25.3	7.2	1.81		

[a] Sources and methods for data before 1940 are set forth in Eason. Data beginning with 1940 are from *Narodnoe khoziaistvo SSSR v 1958 godu*, 31.

[b] Prewar birth and death rates for certain years appearing in postwar sources differ slightly from those listed above (prewar sources): birth rates: 1913, 47.0; 1926, 44.0. Death rates: 1913, 30.2; 1926, 20.3.

magnitude typical of many "underdeveloped" countries.[7] The decline in the crude rates starting around the turn of the century is sufficiently great to suggest a corresponding lowering of age-specific rates. However, this cannot be stated with certainty, first, because there are no accurate measures of change in the distribution of the population by age and sex after 1897, a factor which by itself could alter crude birth and death rates; and second, because the lowering of the crude birth rates themselves tends to lower the crude death rates (age-specific rates remaining unchanged).

In any event, the birth rate was low and the death rate high during the years following World War I and the Civil War, a period surveyed

the summary materials for these years in five-year averages. At the same time, it is clear from the data on the total population in Table 1 that sharp changes in the rate of growth follow from annual vital statistics as reported. According to Volkhov, 22, these can be related to epidemics, wars and famines.

[7] *Proceedings of the World Population Conference, 1954*, I (New York, 1955), 351–562, 775–1040.

in some detail by Lorimer.[8] The effect of these years, as shown below, is still apparent in the distribution of the population by age and sex.

Moving on to the Soviet period, it appears that, following the recovery after the wars, the crude birth rate returned to approximately the same level reported in 1913–1914 (41–43 per thousand), while the crude death rate dropped from 25–28 per thousand in 1913–1914 to about 20 per thousand in the late 1920's. The result is that the population of the Soviet Union during the year in which the First Five Year Plan began (1928) was increasing at an annual rate of 2.4 per cent, or more rapidly than at any other time for which statistics are available. Correction for under-registration of births and deaths might reduce this figure to something less than 2 per cent, as shown in the last column of Table 2, but a similar correction of the data for earlier years would probably leave the comparison over time essentially unchanged.

The possibility that the decline in the crude death rate between the turn of the century and the eve of the five-year plans represents a genuine improvement in conditions affecting mortality is supported by Soviet estimates of average life expectancy at birth for both sexes of the population, which rose from 32 years in 1896–1897 to 44 years in 1926–1927.[9] It is also reflected in Lorimer's estimate of the net reproduction rate for the European part of the USSR, showing an increase from 1.60 in 1897 to 1.72 in 1926.[10] This is despite a decline in the crude birth rate and a slight shift in the age distribution of the population toward the reproductive ages, which, other things being equal, would have raised the birth rate in 1926 as compared to 1897. In other words, more children born alive had the expectation of living through the adult ages in 1926 than in 1897.

The period of the five-year plans and the establishment of "socialism" is sharply differentiated from earlier Soviet and pre-Soviet years so far as the peacetime pattern of population growth is concerned. Almost immediately after the start of the plans, the rate of increase of the Soviet population declined sharply, recovering to the preplan rate only by 1937 (according to the reported vital statistics in Table 2). As a result, over the twelve years between the censuses of 1926 and 1939 — including 1927 and 1928, the First and Second Five Year Plans and part of the Third — the average annual geometric rate of population increase derived from the census totals was 1.24 per cent, or almost half the reported rate for 1928.

This intercensal average rate of increase is equal to or less than the

    [8] Lorimer, ch. 3.
    [9] TsSU, *Narodnoe khoziaistvo SSSR v 1956 godu* (Moscow, 1957), 270. The estimates actually stand for 50 guberniia of European Russia, in 1896–1897, and the European part of the USSR, in 1926–1927. Corresponding data for the entire country would probably show a lower life expectancy for each date, but the comprehensive data should still reveal an increase between the two dates.
    [10] Lorimer, 131.

rates based on vital statistics and reported for all years except 1933 and 1934. Since emigration and immigration were negligible, the discrepancy stems from the relatively greater underregistration of deaths than births in the vital statistics,[11] and from the probability that population growth was seriously affected by events during 1931–1934. An attempt is made in the last column of Table 2 to correct for underregistration in the intercensal years for which data are reported and to derive a "residual" average annual rate of increase for the period 1932–1934 by requiring that the average of the annual rates of increase for the twelve-year period be equal to the average annual intercensal rate of 1.24 per cent.[12]

By 1940 the rate of increase of the Soviet population registered another decline, to the same level as in 1926, largely through a fall in the birth rate.[13]

No comprehensive vital statistics on births and deaths have been reported for the nine-year period which includes World War II and its aftermath (1941–1949). Aside from reference to the "children born during the war years, when the birth rate fell significantly," made in the publication of postwar data on school attendance,[14] and the wartime population losses implied by the preliminary total of 208,800,000 from the census of January 15, 1959, compared to a 1940 population (on comparable territory) of almost 200 million, one must infer the pattern of population growth during these years from the data of other years. The result, as shown in the estimates of Table 1, is an absolute decline in the population between 1940 and 1945 on the order of 25 million. Assuming that the population would have increased by about 20 million by 1950 had there been no war, and allowing for a loss of about 2 million persons through emigration and net territorial adjustments, the implication is a total of what might be called "war losses during the war and postwar years," including excess deaths (military and civilian) and reduction in births, on the order of 45 million.[15]

[11] Lorimer, 117–119.

[12] The steps, in somewhat more detail, are: (1) to adopt Lorimer's hypothetical correction for underregistration in the beginning of the period (1926–1927); (2) to assume that by 1939 underregistration was either negligible or, at least, affected birth and death rates equally; (3) to interpolate this correction linearly between 1927 and 1938, inclusive, yielding corrected rates for each year within the periods 1927–1931 and 1935–1938; and (4) to set the corrected rates for these years and an unknown average rate for the years 1932–1934, averaged, equal to the intercensal average. of 1.24 per cent. The result is an absolute decline of .03 per cent per year during the period 1932–1934.

[13] We must assume from the introductory notes in the source in which the rate for 1940 appears, that the annexed areas are included, but we cannot be sure of adjustments for comparability with postwar territorial boundaries. For example, the officially estimated total population for 1940 is exclusive of both the area ceded to Poland in 1945 and the areas annexed by the Soviet Union in 1944 and 1945 (see Table 1).

[14] TsSU, *Kul'turnoe stroitel'stvo SSSR: statisticheskii sbornik* (Moscow, 1956), 76–77.

[15] W. W. Eason, "The Soviet Population Today," *Foreign Affairs*, XXXVII (July 1959), 598–606.

It would seem that by 1950, if not earlier, the pattern of Soviet population growth had recovered from the direct effects of the war, by virtue of the fact that between 1950 and 1958 the rate of increase of the population was relatively stable, near 1.7 per cent per year (see Table 2). This is a lower rate than in 1928 (2.40, corrected to 2.14) and 1938 (1.90), but higher than the prewar intercensal average (1.24) and higher than in 1940 (1.32).

However, if the distribution of the population by age and sex in 1954–1955 were the same as in 1926, the crude birth rate would be about 21.8 per thousand and the crude death rate about 9.6 (instead of 26.0 and 8.6, respectively), for an average rate of increase of 1.22 per cent per year.[16] In other words, with subsequent changes in the age and sex composition of the population eliminated, the Soviet population may be said to be increasing in recent years at approximately the same rate as during the prewar intercensal period as a whole, or at about two thirds of the preplan rate. Depending on the correction assumed for under-registration in the Imperial Russian statistics, this standardized rate of 1.22 per cent for 1954–1955 may not differ significantly from the "true" rate at the end of the nineteenth century. Some of the implications of these developments since 1928 may be seen through a comparison of trends in birth and death rates.

Birth rates. The population of the Soviet Union entered the period of rapid industrialization and national economic planning with a tradition of high birth rates in comparison with other countries of the world, the rates for virtually all peacetime years in the preceding century exceeding 40 per thousand. Throughout the period since 1928, in contrast, the birth rate has apparently always been lower than 40 per thousand. By 1931 the rate had dropped to 38.2 and by 1935 to 28.6, or 32 per cent below the rate for 1928 (42.2), and it may have been even lower during 1932–1934. After 1935, the birth rate increased rapidly, reaching 38.7 in 1937 and 38.3 in 1938. The difference between the crude rate in 1938 and that in 1928 is of a magnitude which could be explained solely by the shift of the population from rural to urban areas, on the assumption that rural and urban birth rates with respect to women of child-bearing ages were the same in 1938 as in 1926.[17]

Some rather obvious developments seem to have contributed to the dip

---

[16] Actual birth and death rates for 1954–1955 are calculated as the average of those actually reported for 1954 and 1955. Hypothetical birth rates are derived from the ratio of reported births to the estimated female population age 15–49, applied to the population having the same distribution by age and sex as in 1926. Hypothetical death rates are derived by applying UN model-life table mortality rates corresponding to a life expectancy of 64 years to the population at the time of the 1926 census.

[17] Age-specific rates for the female population of rural and urban areas for 1926 are from TsSU, *Estestvennoe dvizhenie naseleniia soiuza SSR v 1926 g.* (Moscow, 1929), 13–14.

in the birth rate during the early 1930's, namely, the rapid rate of rural-urban migration, especially during 1931, the disruption in the country-side over collectivization, and the food shortages of 1932–1933.

Whatever the causes of this movement in the birth rate during the 1930's, however, the rate returned to approximately preplan levels by the end of the decade. On the other hand, the fact that the birth rate for each of the past eight years has been as low as about 25 per thousand suggests a more fundamental development. Furthermore, as shown above, the magnitude of the change since before the plans, as reflected in the reported rates, somewhat understates the real decline, due to changes in the distribution of the population by age and sex.

A portion of the decline may appropriately be assigned to continued rural-urban migration, assuming stable rural-urban fertility differentials. But the change is much too great to be explained by this factor alone; it clearly suggests that the average Soviet woman, in the cities and probably also in the countryside, is having fewer children than formerly. As re-flected in average size of families, this is a condition which is generally confirmed by recent visitors to the Soviet Union.

Specific factors to explain this change may include the widening in the deficit of males relative to females (age 15–49), from 3 million in 1939 to possibly 14 million in 1955, although, as Sauvy has illustrated,[18] something like this could account for only a portion of the decline. Other factors bearing on attitudes toward size of family may include the larger share of work falling on women and the worsened housing conditions. These questions fall directly within the interests of other chapters in this volume.

Death rates. Following what is apparently a gradual improvement in conditions affecting mortality between the last half of the nineteenth century and the eve of the five-year plans, the crude death rate for the 1930's appears relatively stable. During the period of 1932–1934, however, although no data are reported, the rate must have been very high, as suggested by the recalculation of annual rates of increase between the censuses, shown above.

A reported crude death rate of 7.2 per thousand for 1958 places the Soviet Union ahead of virtually every other country. This represents in good part a genuine improvement in conditions affecting mortality, as may be seen in data on life expectancy at birth: 32 years in 1896–1897, 44 years in 1926–1927, 48 years in 1938–1940 and 67 years in 1955–1956.[19]

[18] A. Sauvy, "Population et doctrine de population en Union soviétique," *Population,* VII, no. 1 (January–March 1952), 145–147. Furthermore, the male deficit in 1926 (3,372,000), which occurred as a result of World War I and the Civil War (in 1897 there was almost no deficit), did not prevent the birth rate from reaching 43.7 per thousand population seven years after the war.

[19] Figure for 1938–1940 is estimate by Lorimer, 125; others are Soviet estimates, in *Narodnoe khoziaistvo,* 270.

At the same time, the rate is as low as it is, compared to some of the other countries, partly because of the age and sex distribution of the population (see note 15).

The most important component of the decline in the crude death rate and the increase in life expectancy would seem to be the reported fall in infant mortality from 184 deaths under one year of age per thousand births in 1940 to 60 in 1955 and 41 in 1958.[20] It may be shown that this effect accounts for at least one half of the drop in the crude death rate from 18.3 in 1940 to less than 8 in recent years.[21]

Aside from these several effects, the remainder of the decline in the crude death rate represents increased chances of survival for persons in the population other than infants.

II

The distribution of the population by age for both sexes, for males and females separately, and for the number of males per 100 females, by age groups, are reproduced in percentages in Table 3. In addition to the basic age distribution, the data are also grouped according to child-bearing ages (15–49) and working ages (16–59).

For 1897, 1926, and 1939, the distributions are derived from respective census data, while the 1931 distribution is a Soviet estimate as reported. For 1955, it was necessary (1) to estimate the population age 0–14 from annual data on school attendance, and (2) to age the population from 1940 to 1955 so as to obtain the number of those age 15 and over, by age groups, by means of a "projection," modified by the adaptation of survival ratios from United Nations model life tables corresponding to the reported Soviet life expectancy at birth of 64 years in 1954–1955, and adjusted for consistency with the total population and the number of males and females reported in the preliminary results of the 1959 census.[22]

The pattern of change in the distribution of the population by age and sex is related to the pattern of change in birth and death rates, as summarized above, and to the incidence of several national crises, beginning with World War I. Declining birth rates in and of themselves tend to reduce the percentage of the population in the younger age groups and raise correspondingly the share in the older age groups. Declining infant mortality by itself tends to operate in the other direction — in other words, to have the same effect as a rise in the birth rate. General improvements in the conditions affecting mortality other than infant

---

[20] *Narodnoe khoziaistvo SSSR v 1958 godu,* 31.

[21] This may be done by applying to the estimated population by age and sex in 1954–1955 age-specific mortality rates from UN model-life tables, adjusted so as to reflect, successively, the infant mortality rates for 1940 and 1955.

[22] The method is summarized in detail in Eason.

Table 3. Percentage of Age Distribution and Number of Males
Per 100 Females, Total Population, Imperial Russia
and the USSR, 1897, 1926, 1931, 1939, and 1955[a]

Age	1897	1926	1931	1939	1955	1897	1926	1931	1939	1955
			Male					Female		
0–9	27.4	26.6	28.2	24.2	21.5	27.2	24.6	26.1	22.0	16.7
10–14	11.3	12.2	9.6	12.8	8.3	11.0	11.1	9.0	11.9	6.7
15–19	9.7	11.4	11.1	9.9	12.0	10.8	11.7	10.2	9.3	10.7
20–39	28.9	28.8	30.5	33.6	31.0	28.7	30.1	32.0	32.5	32.7
40–59	16.0	14.8	14.8	14.1	21.0	15.9	15.3	15.5	16.6	23.6
60 and over	6.7	6.2	5.8	5.4	6.2	7.0	7.2	7.2	7.7	9.6
Total	100.0	100.0	100.0	100.0	100.0	100.0	100.0	100.0	100.0	100.0
0–14	38.7	38.7	37.8	37.0	29.8	38.2	35.7	35.1	33.9	23.4
15–49	48.0	49.1	50.4	52.0	56.2	48.1	50.5	51.2	51.3	57.1
50 and over	13.3	12.2	11.8	11.0	14.0	13.7	13.8	13.7	14.8	19.5
0–15	40.8	41.2	39.6	39.2	32.8	40.3	38.2	36.8	35.8	23.2
16–59	52.5	52.6	54.6	55.4	61.0	52.7	54.6	56.0	56.5	67.2
60 and over	6.7	6.7	5.8	5.4	6.2	7.0	7.2	7.2	7.7	9.6
			Both sexes				Males per 100 females			
0–9	27.3	25.5	27.1	23.0	18.8	100	101	101	101	102
10–14	11.1	11.6	9.3	12.3	7.4	101	102	100	99	98
15–19	10.0	11.6	10.7	9.7	11.4	95	92	102	98	101
20–39	28.8	29.5	31.3	33.0	31.9	100	90	89	95	75
40–59	15.9	15.1	15.1	15.4	23.4	99	91	90	78	70
60 and over	6.9	6.7	6.5	6.6	8.1	96	81	76	64	52
Total	100.0	100.0	100.0	100.0	100.0	99	94	94	92	79
0–14	38.4	37.2	36.4	35.4	26.2	100	101	101	101	101
15–49	48.1	49.8	50.8	51.6	56.6	99	91	92	93	78
50 and over	13.5	13.0	12.8	13.0	17.2	97	83	81	68	56
0–15	38.4	37.2	36.4	35.4	28.9	100	101	101	101	101
16–59	52.5	53.6	55.3	56.0	63.0	99	90	91	90	75
60 and over	6.9	6.7	6.5	6.6	8.1	96	81	76	64	52

[a] Sources and methods are set forth in Eason. Data for 1955 also include modifications based on the preliminary results of the 1959 census. Since the census data contain the number of males and females, but no distribution by age, the estimates by age for 1955 in this table must be regarded as highly tentative.

mortality tend to have a relatively small influence on the distribution of the (corresponding) population.

Between 1897 and 1939 the proportion of the population age 0–14 declined, the proportion age 15–39 rose, and the proportion age 40 and over remained essentially constant. This should reflect the effects of (1) a relatively greater decline in the birth rate than in infant mortality, during ordinary peacetime years, and (2) the lower birth rate and higher infant mortality during World War I and the Civil War as well as during the early 1930's.

The trends in the age distribution between 1897 and 1939 are accentuated between 1939 and 1955, due primarily to World War II and the lower postwar birth rate.

Higher mortality during two world wars and during the early 1930's appears to have fallen more heavily on males than females. In 1897 the number of males was roughly equal to the number of females, except in the age-group 15–19 (which could have resulted from bias in reporting ages) and 60 and over. By 1926, a marked deficit of males appears in all adult age-groups, and in the population as a whole there are 94 males per 100 females. These deficits widen by 1939 and again sharply according to preliminary results of the 1959 census, reflected in the estimates for 1955. The ratio of 79 males per 100 females age 16–59 in 1955 represents an absolute difference of about 18 million.

III

Largely through the stimulus of economic development, the urban population of Imperial Russia grew from about 7 million in 1861 to more than 20 million in 1914, or by three times (see Table 4). However, because of the rapid rate of growth of the total population, the urban population as a percentage of the total increased by only three points, from 11.6 to 14.6 per cent.

The data referring to the Soviet period in Table 4 comprise Soviet estimates with respect to the territory of the USSR, but they are based on pre-Soviet definitions of urban and rural areas. For this reason they may be misleading for comparison with the data of other countries or those of the Soviet period.

The pre-Soviet definition of an urban area is limited to places officially designated as cities, or possessing municipal self-government. According to the 1897 census,[23] which reported 13.4 per cent of the total population in urban areas (12.4 per cent of the population located on USSR territory, as in Table 4), there were, in addition, 6,376 "rural" settlements with anywhere from 2,000 to 41,000 population, many of which would be counted as "urban" according to the census methods of Europe or the United States and, most important, according to definitions established during the 1920's by the Soviets themselves and used in deriving the data for these years (Table 4). These "rural" areas (with respect to Imperial Russian territory) included a total population of 23.2 million, which, if added to the 16.8 million persons in the 932 official urban areas, would yield an "urban" population of 40 million, or 32 per cent of the total, instead of 13.4 per cent. Certainly some of these "rural" settle-

[23] TsSK, *Pervaia vseobshchaia perepis' naseleniia 1897 goda,* summary volume I (St. Petersburg, 1905), iv-v.

Table 4. Reported and Estimated Data on the Total, Urban and Rural
Population, Imperial Russia and the USSR, 1850–1956[a]

| Year | Population in thousands | | | Percentage distribution | |
	Total	Urban	Rural	Urban	Rural
1850	57,076	3,118	53,958	5.5	94.5
1860	61,720	6,993	54,727	11.3	88.7
1870	65,208	8,040	57,168	12.3	87.7
1880	78,592	10,159	68,433	12.9	87.1
1890	92,822	11,816	81,006	12.7	87.3
1897	103,906	12,870	91,036	12.4	87.6
1900	109,593	14,058	95,535	12.8	87.2
1910	130,354	18,586	111,768	14.3	85.7
1914	139,912	20,445	119,467	14.6	85.4
1920 Jan. 28	130,863	20,787	110,076	15.9	84.1
1923 Mar. 15	133,504	21,563	111,941	16.2	83.8
1926 Dec. 17	147,028	26,314	120,714	17.9	82.1
1928	(149,900)[b]	27,600	(122,300)	18.4	81.6
1929	(153,100)	29,200	(123,900)	19.1	80.9
1930	(155,600)	30,900	(124,700)	19.9	80.1
1931	(158,100)	32,000	(126,100)	20.2	79.8
1932	(160,700)	36,300	(124,400)	22.6	77.4
1933	(160,600)	39,700	(120,900)	24.7	75.3
1934	(160,600)	41,100	(119,500)	25.6	74.4
1935	(160,500)	—	—	—	—
1936	(162,000)	47,000	(115,200)	29.0	71.0
1937	(164,100)	—	—	—	—
1938	(167,300)	—	—	—	—
1939 Jan. 17	170,557	56,125	114,432	32.9	67.1
1940 Yr. av.	(197,500)	62,400	135,100	31.6	68.4
1959 Jan. 15	208,800	99,800	109,000	48.0	52.0

[a] Sources and methods are set forth in Eason, except for 1955, which is from *Narodnoe khoziaistvo SSSR v 1958 godu*, 9. Territory is USSR: 1850–1939, pre-1939; 1940–1959, post-1939. Dates are January 1 unless otherwise indicated.

[b] Total population figures in parentheses are estimated from Table 1.

ments were too sparsely settled to be considered urban under any reasonable definition, but many would qualify by later Soviet and present Western standards.

That the urban population of Imperial Russia in 1897 was actually more than 13.4 per cent of the total population — if not as high as 32 per cent — is also suggested by the fact that the percentage of the population dependent on nonagricultural occupations (25.4 per cent) was much higher than the percentage living in urban areas. Although some of the nonagricultural population undoubtedly resided outside of urban areas, however broad the latter concept, it seems unlikely by comparison with the data of the 1926 census that as much as one half of the nonagricultural population so resided. In 1926, 17.9 per cent of the total population resided in urban areas (Soviet definition) and 23.6 per cent were dependent on nonagricultural occupations. The same proportionate relationship to the nonagricultural population in 1897 would have meant an urban population of 20.8 per cent, instead of 13.4 per cent.

Although the percentage of the population living in urban areas in the half century before the revolution, using the Soviet definition, would probably be higher than that indicated by the 1897 census,[24] it is difficult to say what the corrected figure should be — perhaps 20 per cent or more.

It is also difficult to say whether a correction would yield *trends* from 1861 to 1914 significantly different from those set forth above, namely, an urban population which was more or less a constant percentage of the rapidly growing total population. The critical factor, for which we have insufficient evidence, is the change in the population density of the aforementioned settlements located in "rural" areas.

Nevertheless, even without a correction to ensure comparability with Soviet concepts, a decline in the urban population (on comparable overall territory), both absolutely and as a percentage of the total, is registered between 1914 and 1920. The period of World War I, the revolution, and the Civil War drove many urban dwellers back to the countryside (and others out of the country). As shown in Table 4, the urban population on USSR territory declined from 24.7 million in 1914 to 20.8 million in 1920, or by 15 per cent, and the total population also declined. The net result was a decline in the urban as a percentage of the total population, from 17.9 to 15.9 per cent.

If the pre-Soviet data were reconstructed using the Soviet definition of urban areas, the indicated decline would be greater — from 20–25 per cent of the total to 15.9 per cent. In other words, probably one third or more of the urban population as of 1914 had left the urban areas for one reason or another by the beginning of the New Economic Policy.

In the following years, the urban population again increased, both absolutely and percentagewise, to the extent that in 1928, on the eve of the five-year plans, 18.4 per cent of the total population were in urban areas. Applying the Soviet definition uniformly, this represents a smaller proportion of the total than in 1897 or, for that matter, than in any year since the 1850's. However, whether one is entitled to infer from these gross measures that the Soviet population in 1928 was less "urbanized" than previously requires some qualitative index of the extent to which urban residents had severed ties with the countryside — that is, of the extent to which they had made the transition from a rural to an urban way of life.

In any event, with the beginning of the five-year plans, the urbanization of the country was greatly accelerated. During the twelve years be-

[24] See Volkhov, 27.

tween the censuses of 1926 and 1939, the urban population rose from 17.9 to 32.9 per cent of the total. The annexation of territory in 1940 reduced this percentage only slightly.

Between the estimate for 1940 and the preliminary results of the 1959 census, the urban population (on roughly comparable territory) increased from 62.4 to 99.8 million persons, or by about 60 per cent, and from 31.6 to 48.0 per cent of the total. A further absolute decline in the rural population is implied by these figures, from 135 million in 1940 to 109 million in 1956.

Although the increase in the urban population since 1928 has been generally substantial, the annual increases in the early 1930's were quite irregular, as may be seen from the following data comparing net rural-urban migration with the increase in the urban population through 1935.

	Net rural-urban migration	Increase in urban population
1929	1,392,000	1,700,000
1930	2,633,000	1,100,000
1931	4,100,000	4,340,000
1932	2,719,000	3,399,999
1933	772,000	1,439,000
1934	2,452,000	3,704,000
1935	2,527,000	—

Except for 1930, the increase in the urban population each year is somewhat greater than the net rural-urban migration, a difference attributable to the natural increase of the urban population. The greatest increase in the urban population took place in 1931 and 1932, reflecting the flight from the countryside following mass collectivization.

Considering the twelve-year intercensal period as a whole, the urban population increased by 29.8 million, of which approximately 23 million may be accounted for by net migration to areas which by 1939 had been classified as urban, and the remainder by natural population increase. The total of net migration, in turn, is the sum of 18.5 million persons migrating (net) to areas which were urban at the beginning of the period (according to the lists of the 1926 census), and 4.5 million migrating to areas whose status was changed from rural to urban by the time of the 1939 census. The total 1939 population of these areas of changed status was 5.8 million.[25]

The sources of increase in the urban population in recent years appear to be similar to those for the period 1926–1939 as a whole. Of the 17 million increase in the urban population during five years including the last year of the Fourth Five Year Plan and the first four years of the Fifth Five Year Plan (1950–1955), more than 9 million was derived from

[25] N. Vosnesensky, "K itogami . . . ," *Pravda* June 2, 1939. The estimate of 4.5 million migrants to these areas is Lorimer's, 149.

rural-urban migration.[26] This is more than 53 per cent of the increase due
to migration, compared to 63 per cent between 1926 and 1939.[27] If the
fraction of the increase due to the reclassification of areas from rural
to urban was the same as in the intercensal period, or about 20 per cent,[28]
these data imply, as a remainder, a somewhat higher rate of natural increase of the urban population in the last five years than in the intercensal
period. This is not necessarily inconsistent with lower crude birth rates
for the total population in recent years, because the fall in the birth
rate during the early 1930's was probably more than proportionately an
urban phenomenon.[29]

With almost one half of the population now living in urban areas, the
Soviet Union stands among the more urbanized countries of the world,
although below such countries as the following.[30]

	Urban population as percentage of total
United States	59
Argentina	61
Denmark	61
Western Germany	60
United Kingdom	80
Australia	69
New Zealand	61

IV

Soviet discussions of economic and social change refer frequently to
changes in the distribution of the population by "social groups" or "social
classes," by which is meant, principally, changes according to type of
income earned. The categories of the distribution themselves have
changed considerably in the last thirty years, but the following appear
in one form or other in the available data: wage and salary workers,
collective farmers, cooperative handicraftsmen, private farmers, private
(noncooperative) handicraftsmen, "bourgeoisie," the military, and persons receiving their source of livelihood from one of the state or social
institutions.

"Classes" in the contemporary Soviet connotation really consist of sub-
strata in a population which is considered homogeneous in the sense that
virtually everyone receives income from "labor." State forms of labor,
based on income from wages and salaries, continue to be distinguished

[26] *Pravda*, February 3, 1955. The specific time reference in the source is "over
the past five years."

[27] From the data above: migration of 18.5 million as a percentage of the total
increase in the urban population of 29.8 million.

[28] From the data above: 5.8 million as a percentage of 29.8 million.

[29] Lorimer, 126–130 and ch. 2.

[30] *Demographic Yearbook 1948* (New York, 1949), 214–219. The figures must be
used with caution because of differences in definition.

from cooperative forms, based on income from labor shares; and the worker is distinguished from the peasant. But the category of the "bourgeoisie" has been eliminated, and it is being urged that distinctions between workers and peasants and between mental and physical labor also be eliminated.

Changes in the "class" composition of the population, so defined, are cited by the Soviets as the bellwether of social change under their system; and numerous quantitative measures (published and unpublished) have been designed by them to reflect these changes. There is no space within the limits of this discussion to compare the various measures and to summarize the steps which must be followed to obtain a reasonably consistent and complete series over time. All published measures reflect the principal change brought about by the revolution itself, namely, the sharp reduction in the class comprising "landlords" and "capitalists"; in addition, socialist and cooperative forms have been introduced.

The major difficulty in working with the available materials is that the more recent the publication, the less the detail presented. In other words, not only has the importance of various categories changed since the 1920's, but the number of categories has been drastically reduced. This has continued to the point where the recent measure of the "class composition of the population of the USSR" [31] includes only two classes: (1) wage and salary workers, (2) collective farm peasantry and cooperative handicraftsmen. All private forms of economic activity have been merged into a third class, which includes only 0.5 per cent of the population in 1955. A residual "other" class, which used to account for a significant fraction of the population in prewar measures (and which, according to our estimates, still does), has been eliminated entirely, in effect, by reassigning the members to one of the two major groups.

By means of an extremely laborious series of calculations and comparisons, which are not at all apparent on the surface of the data for selected years summarized in Table 5, an attempt has been made to reconstruct consistent estimates of the "class" composition of the Soviet population, using the main categories of the early and middle 1930's. These relatively detailed categories themselves do remain in the basic construction (by the Soviets) of recently published Soviet estimates, but in publication (in percentage terms) they have been grouped into the two large categories mentioned above.

The only note on method which might be appropriate concerns the category, "discrepancies in derivation." This arises from attempts to maintain consistency of concepts over time. It includes, in effect, many of the errors in estimation and many of the shortcomings of the original data which could not be removed otherwise, and it also includes any "nonreporting" of categories in years after 1928. Problems of estimation

[31] *Narodnoe khoziaistvo,* 19.

Table 5. The Population by Socioeconomic Groups,
USSR, 1928, 1932, 1938, and 1955[a]

Socioeconomic groups	1913	1928	1932	1938	1955
Population, including dependents, in thousands					
Wage and salary workers	23,300	26,100	44,600	55,500	86,900
Coop. handicraftsmen	0	2,000	4,200	4,900	4,000
Noncoop. handicraftsmen	(10,000)	4,100	1,900	1,500	1,400
Collective farmers	0	2,400	66,300	82,800	75,000
Private farmers	97,800	108,800	33,400	4,000	300
"Bourgeoisie"	5,000	3,700	371	—	—
Employed labor force categories	136,100	147,200	150,700	148,700	167,600
Unemployed and transients	?	1,900	1,100	—	—
Discrepancies in deviation	0	0	4,400	12,900	13,600
Civilian labor force categories	136,100	149,100	156,200	161,600	181,200
Military	1,100	700	700	1,900	5,000
Total labor force categories	137,200	149,800	156,900	163,500	186,200
Others, economically active	2,100	2,500	4,100	5,400	10,000
Total population	139,300	152,300	161,000	168,900	196,200
Nonagricultural population[b]	31,029	38,100	48,100	57,400	80,500
Agricultural population[b]	108,271	114,200	108,000	91,300	87,100
Percentage distribution					
Wage and salary workers	16.7	17.1	27.7	32.9	44.3
Coop. handicraftsmen	0	1.3	2.6	2.9	2.0
Noncoop. handicraftsmen	7.2	2.2	1.2	.9	.7
Collective farmers	0	1.6	41.2	49.0	38.2
Private farmers	70.2	71.5	20.7	2.4	.3
"Bourgeoisie"	3.6	2.4	.2	—	—
Employed labor force categories	97.7	96.6	93.6	88.1	85.5
Unemployed and transients	?	1.2	.7	—	—
Discrepancies in derivation	0	0	2.7	7.6	6.9
Civilian labor force categories	97.7	97.8	97.0	95.7	92.3
Military	.8	.5	.5	1.1	2.5
Total labor force categories	98.5	98.3	97.5	96.8	94.9
Others, economically active	1.5	1.7	2.5	3.2	5.1
Total population	100.0	100.0	100.0	100.0	100.0
Nonagricultural population	22.3	25.0	30.8	38.6	48.0
Agricultural population	77.7	75.0	69.2	61.4	52.0

[a] Sources and methods are set forth in Eason.
[b] Includes reported civilian categories only.

and therefore margins of error vary enough from one year to the next so that probably one should not attach great confidence to the magnitude of this category for any given year, at least to the nearest hundred thousand, or to relatively small changes over time. The introduction of this category also requires that trends in the other categories be interpreted with caution.

Of most general interest from the data of Table 5 is the indicated distribution of the population according to dependence on agricultural and nonagricultural occupations (reported civilian categories only). The period of rapid industrialization brought about both an absolute and relative decline in the agricultural population, from 114 million and 75 per cent of the total in 1928 to an estimated 87 million and 52 per cent of the total in 1955. (The data for 1955 are on the larger, postwar territory.) This suggests an understandable relationship to the distribution between rural and urban areas, although the relationship cannot be indicated with precision because of the "discrepancies in derivation."

At the same time, it is interesting, in view of the key role of state enterprises in the economy (including state farms and machine-tractor stations, in agriculture), and in view of the central position of the "proletariat," that less than half (44.3 per cent) of the population can be considered dependent on wages and salaries. Recent Soviet estimates place the percentage at 58.3 for 1955, but this includes such categories as the military, students receiving stipends from the state, and various otherwise nonreported categories, assigned to the category of wage and salary worker if individuals' former position or family status warranted. Similarly, the Soviets reckon 36.2 per cent of the population in the category of wage and salary workers in 1937, compared to 32.9 per cent for 1938 in Table 5.

The category of cooperative handicraftsmen increased rapidly after 1928, largely at the expense of the private or noncooperative handicrafts category, but the number as a percentage of the total has remained at about 2–3 per cent since the middle 1930's. The category of noncooperative handicrafts, along with that of private farming, has declined almost to insignificance (0.5 per cent). However, this is not necessarily an indication of the role of private economic activity measured on a part-time basis. For example, the full-time equivalent (annual average) number of persons occupied as "members of families of wage and salary workers occupied in subsidiary agriculture" in 1955 was reported at 3.7 per cent of the full-time equivalent civilian labor force.[32]

The degree to which Soviet agriculture had become collectivized by the late 1930's is shown in the total of 83 million persons in 1938, comprising virtually one half of the total population. The highest percentage,

[32] *Narodnoe khoziaistvo*, 204.

as far as can be estimated, was in 1936, with 54 per cent of the total in collective farming. The implications of the subsequent decline in absolute numbers of the collective-farm population are amplified by the fact that the figure for 1955 refers to the larger territory.

PART TWO

LAW, POLITICS, AND SOCIAL CHANGE

THE PATTERNS OF AUTOCRACY

ZBIGNIEW K. BRZEZINSKI

Executive power combines policy making with direction of policy execution. It is this combination which endows the executive organ in the governmental structure with its crucial functional importance and which vests it, or rather the persons who symbolize or control it, with the mystique that normally surrounds a head of state or a monarch. In the minds of most people, a president, a king, or even a premier, and today in one third of the globe a first secretary of *the* party, plays the role of leader, much in the tradition of the family head, the village elder, or the tribal chief. It is on the chief executives that society has depended through the ages for a sense of direction, and they have stood at the apex of the social and political hierarchy whenever men have come together because of necessity. Executive power may in fact be the oldest and the most necessary social institution. It has taken many forms, has established various channels for its achievement ranging from birth to purposely perpetrated death, and has been endowed, at various places, times, and in response to varying requirements, with different ranges of authority. Nonetheless, for our purposes it might be useful to distinguish in broad terms between the two types of executive power usually found since the rise of the modern state: the constitutional and the autocratic.

The first, of somewhat more recent vintage and normally a product of a more sophisticated stage of social, cultural, and political development, generally involves an executive organ operating within confines delimited by an institutional structure in which the executive power is both shared with other governmental organs and restricted even within its own sphere by a series of formal and informal restraints. The most classical sharing of power is, of course, that involving the separation of power into the executive, legislative, and judicial parts, each relatively free from the domination of the other. There are legal restraints on the arbitrary exercise of power as well as those inherent in the pluralistic character of modern society which produces its own shifting patterns of social alliances, pressure groups, and veto groups. In such a context the executive power, while not deprived of its functional significance, is prevented from becoming the dominant and relatively unrestrained source of political leadership.

The autocratic executive, by way of contrast, is relatively unhindered in the exercise of its power and does not share it with other organs, such as the judiciary or the legislature, since they are either absent or subordinated to the executive. Formal restraints, such as legal injunctions, are also either absent or circumvented, while informal restraints — for instance, those involving the church as a major institution — are somewhat more elastic in the assertion of their claims against the executive. The autocratic executive is, in brief, the central, dominant, and leading governmental organ.

It should further be noted that the autocratic form of executive power is in many ways the older and more basic of the two types. The constitutional form, much more complex, has arisen only under certain favorable conditions of social stability and economic well-being, and under the guidance of an enlightened elite. These conditions have not been as frequent as it might be desired. A mere glance at the political history of mankind reveals that in most places, at most times, most people have lived under some sort of autocratic, that is to say, nonresponsible and nonrepresentative, form of government. This observation, possibly trite, is nonetheless pertinent to the problem of continuity and discontinuity in the Russian executive in the years since 1861. Throughout the century, with one brief interlude measured not in years but in mere months, the Russian executive has been an essentially autocratic one.[1] As we shall see, however, within this dominent autocratic pattern varying degrees of intensity and directions of change have been discernible.

I

The autocratic character of the Russian executive during almost this entire period, with the consequently important element of continuity, can be brought out in sharper focus if we attempt to examine more closely some of the salient features of the Tsarist and Soviet executives to see how they show a definite perpetuation in autocratic pattern. What have been some of the important political characteristics of the Russian executive during the last one hundred years?

To a political observer the concentration of power in the executive organ to the detriment of the judicial or legislative bodies might well be the crucial criterion. The supreme authority of the emperor as the autocrat was acknowledged by basic law and cemented by tradition. The supreme power, vested in the emperor, was exercised on his behalf and at his will by ministers selected, appointed, and dismissed by him. The ministers were sometimes headed by an informal chairman of the ministerial council who, at least nominally, was the emperor's closest adviser.

---

[1] More will be said later about the implications and nature of the Duma period just prior to World War I. It is not possible, in this brief space, to present both a detailed institutional account of the roles played by the Tsarist and Soviet executives and a meaningful analysis of their continuities and discontinuities. I will concentrate on the latter and merely point to certain relevant institutional aspects.

However, unlike Western practice, it was always the emperor, and not the chairman (a post not regularized until the twentieth century), who personally selected and nominated the members of the ministerial committee. Thus even the element of indirect restraint on the emperor, inherent in the cabinet system with the ministers' developing a measure of institutional authority of their own, was in this case absent. As a result, cabinet ministers did not feel compelled to coordinate their operations with the chairman of their council and rarely did they meet in a body. The normal practice was for the emperor to closet himself with especially trusted ministers and to decide in this small group what the policy on an issue ought to be. In the case of the more important policy posts, such as foreign affairs or defense, the ministers dealt directly with the emperor even as late as the twentieth century when the practice of appointing a premier became institutionalized.[2] V. N. Kokovtsov recalls with a touch of bitterness how the minister of internal affairs neglected to keep him abreast of developments or how the minister of war used to obtain funds for the ministry without even consulting with the prime minister.[3] Of course, a particularly strong-willed chairman such as Stolypin could resist these tendencies; nonetheless, it was not the general pattern. As a result of this poor bureaucratic coordination on the top governmental levels, matters of high policy involving the executive power were resolved through the direct intervention of the emperor, to whom the central governmental organs — the Ministerial Committee, the Council of the Empire, the Senate, and the Holy Synod — were directly subordinated.[4]

[2] In the late nineteenth century the Committee of Ministers was composed of the following: War and Navy, Finance, Interior, Communications, State Domains, Education, Justice, Foreign Affairs, Control. The Ministry of the Interior was probably the most important ministry for domestic matters, directing not only the state bureaucracy but, in a sense, setting the broad patterns of domestic policy. It frequently competed for power and prestige with the Finance Ministry which shaped fiscal policy. Budgetary provisions for the respective ministries suggest their relative weights (except for the Foreign Ministry, the importance of which was less dependent on the vastness of its bureaucratic apparatus). Thus, for instance, in 1887, the expenditures of the Ministry of War and Navy were 251 million rubles; Finance, 109; Interior, 73; Communications, 26; State Domains, 23; Education, 21; Justice, 20; Foreign Affairs, 5; Control, 3. See C. Skalkovsky, *Les Ministres des Finances de la Russie* (Paris, 1891), 292. In the case of the War Ministry, many of the expenditures were for the purpose of constructing strategically important railroads which were otherwise non-profitable.

[3] *Iz moevo proshlago* (Paris, 1933), II, 153; *Out of My Past* (London, 1935).

[4] The Council of the Empire, composed in the mid-eighties of 64 members, was a consultative body for legislative matters. The members, appointed by the tsar, were usually members of the imperial family, former and present ministers, and distinguished servants of the tsar. The Senate, likewise composed of appointed dignitaries, was to be the highest judicial body, a court of cassation, and the supreme body for adjudicating administrative conflicts. One of its seven departments also handled governmental auditing. The Holy Synod, headed by a lay Procurator General and composed of the metropolitans and bishops, dealt with religious matters as well as problems of general state morality, and such.

A further aspect enhancing the personal power of the emperor was the monarch's practice of relying on a coterie of personal favorites, who often filled chief governmental posts. These appointments did not necessarily involve men distinguished by specialized knowledge of a particular aspect of government but rather persons considered as personally loyal to the emperor and to the general orientation that he held at the moment — be it a liberalizing or a conservative one. As a result, the emperor became the focal point for competing groups: those in favor of reforms and those against change felt that their objectives could be achieved only if the emperor could be won over and make his appointments accordingly. Growing political conflict thus enhanced the political influence of the emperor since reform, of whatever kind, could be achieved only with him and through him.

An additional factor in the autocratic pattern was the device of parallel informal and formal channels of executive power. Apart from his chosen ministers — whom after a while the emperor would begin to suspect of harboring views alien to him, and which in fact the ministers frequently acquired by being brought into contact with the realities of Russia once they were appointed to cope with them — the emperor would consult special advisers not burdened with executive posts. These would most frequently be drawn from among his personal courtiers, many of whom held high military ranks and were his devoted and disciplined servants, jealously protecting his power but often suffering from lack of native intelligence.[5] The most notable exceptions in this period from the pattern of courtier-advisers were Pobedonostsev and Rasputin; the latter, however, was influential through the empress.[6] Pobedonostsev's relationship with Alexander III is particularly illustrative of the role played by *eminences grises* in autocratic regimes. His influence had far wider ranges than justified by his post of Procurator General of the Holy Synod. He was Alexander's adviser on important matters of policy and a vigorous defender of the emperor's power against real and imagined encroachments on the part of those allegedly favoring constitutionalism. He effectively torpedoed Loris-Melikov's cautious reforms and successfully urged the emperor to replace Loris-Melikov with a more rigidly minded minister. Pobedonostsev's correspondence with the emperor skillfully exploiting the prejudices of this intellectually limited monarch, who was fearful of further reforms and mindful of the assassination of his father, and his personal intrigues, his little coups, his distrust of intellectuals, and his general philosophical position[7] — immediately bring to mind an analogy with Stalin. Pobedonostsev was in one person Stalin's

---

[5] For excellent descriptions of some of the leading figures in the court life of late nineteenth-century Russia, see the diaries of such dignitaries as A. A. Polovtsev, E. A. Peretz, K. Golovin, or P. A. Valuiev.

[6] See, for instance, the texts of the tsarina's letters to the tsar while he was at the front, in F. R. Golder, *Documents of Russian History* (New York, 1927).

[7] *Mémoires politiques, correspondance, etc.* (Paris, 1927).

Poskrebyshev and Zhdanov, but without the latter's political role and position as erstwhile heir apparent.[8] He provided the monarch with informal sources of information and served as his ideologue: chief defender and rationalizer of the status quo.[9]

Soviet political practices have not, on the whole, deviated significantly from the pattern sketched above. Throughout most of the political history of the Soviet Union one-man rule has been the norm, and recent events do not augur an imminent departure from long-established practice. Indeed, it has been argued cogently that a system such as the Soviet cannot operate without producing overwhelming internal pressures toward the elevation of some individual to the top of the political structure. Soviet political leaders, furthermore, have not come from the ranks of the administrators but from the party which endows them with a certain aura of "scientific" insight into history, analogous to the personal charisma of the anointed emperor. The party secretaries, while not ignoring the significant role played by the bureaucrats, have maintained the tradition of keeping the administrators tied to administrative procedures and have retained policy making as their own domain, to be shared with those of their own choosing. It was only following Stalin's assumption of the premiership that the party administration came to be closely linked at the top, but even throughout the Stalinist period, marked by a growing ascendancy of the administrative structure, little doubt remained as to which post was politically the more important. Khrushchev's career is mute testimony to this point. While coordination of decision making has probably improved since the Tsarist days, there is no doubt that problems of policy are still resolved by informal cabals of "politicians" and not by administrators: Stalin with Poskrebyshev and Malenkov for administrative-personnel matters, Zhdanov for ideological issues, and his more trusted Politburo members (depending on the dictator's whims) for broader consultation; Khrushchev with his reliable *apparatchiki* as the source of necessary support and counsel, and sometimes as the manpower for important administrative appointments.[10] Given the voluminous literature on Soviet politics, these brief observations might suffice to suggest

[8] Note Khrushchev's sarcastic remark in his secret speech, referring to Poskrebyshev as Stalin's "loyal shield-bearer."

[9] It is interesting to reflect that Pobedonostsev's insistence on a rigid system based on law strongly suggests that his ideal would have been the Platonic society — with its reliance on state religion, family training, indoctrination of the intellectual, all within a firm legal framework. These were precisely the things that Pobedonostsev was advocating and, in some measure, implementing. However, judging by his criticisms of the idea of a search for Truth, one might speculate that the *Laws*, rather than the *Republic*, would have been more to his liking. For some discussions of his views, see A. A. Kornilov, *Kurs istorii Rossii XIX veka* (Moscow, 1918), III, 269, and R. F. Byrnes, "Pobedonostsev on the Instruments of Russian Government," in *Continuity and Change in Russian and Soviet Thought,* E. J. Simmons, ed. (Cambridge, Mass., 1955).

[10] A recent example was the appointment of the relatively unknown party functionary, I. I. Kuzmin, to head the Gosplan.

some strong parallels with the previously outlined pattern of Tsarist executive power.

Another important area of political relationships pertinent to this investigation involves the related questions of political centralization and political coercion. While the latter, as we all know, does not necessarily follow from the former (as with France), there is a strong tendency in regimes which are not constitutionally based for the two to merge. That was the case under the tsars, and that is the case today in Soviet Russia. In Tsarist Russia centralization and coercion took the form of strict subordination of local authority (such as the *Gubernator,* the *Gradonachal'nik* or, since 1889, the *Zemskii nachal'nik,* as well as the *Stanovoi,* the *Ispravnik,* and the *Uriadnik*) to the Minister of the Interior[11] and the employment of centrally controlled police power for political ends. Of course, a particularly dynamic governor could achieve a certain amount of autonomy, especially in an outlying region, but usually by virtue of his ability to anticipate the *desiderata* of St. Petersburg and to execute them even more efficiently than anticipated.[12] In this sense, there is a strong resemblance to the able and energetic Stalinist satraps in the republics: people like Bagirov, for instance, who held his post for some fifteen years without interruption. Centralization, however, normally breeds overbureaucratization, and the Russian local officials were frequently swamped with dreary paper work and red tape — again much like their Soviet counterparts.[13] A measure of internal decay is a corollary of autocratic bureaucracies.

[11] A good source is I. Blinov, *Gubernatory: istoriko-iuridicheskii ocherk* (St. Petersburg, 1905).

[12] The check supposedly provided by the local procurator, subordinated to the Ministry of Justice, unfortunately often proved illusory since the governor normally wielded more influence back in St. Petersburg. Cf. N. Flerovsky, *Tri politicheskiia sistemy* (no place, 1897) 54–55. Another check involved the periodic inspections by delegated senators. In a sense, they performed the functions of control somewhat like the party control commissions or RKI. But again, personal factors were of critical importance.

[13] Marc Raeff, in his "The Russian Autocracy and Its Officials," *Russian Thought and Politics,* McLean, Malia, and Fischer, eds. (Cambridge, Mass., 1957), 80, mentions the example of a somewhat earlier provincial governor whose routine included signing 270 papers daily, or about 100,000 a year. Recent Soviet discussions of bureaucratic difficulties suggest a striking continuity in this reliance on written and signed instructions: one regional agricultural administration reported that during 1953 it received from the Ministry of Agriculture no less than 7,569 letters; in 1954, 8,459, and on the average about 30 instructions per day (*Partiinaia zhizn,* no. 3 [1956], 60–61). Tsarist literature, and more recently even some Soviet, gives us brilliant descriptions of crushed bureaucrats, fearful of inspections, giving their all to the daily dose of instructions, requests, statistics, and so on. See also *Krokodil* for cartoon treatment, and Khrushchev's 1957 speeches on decentralization. For an interesting and informative account of bureaucratic vicissitudes under the Tsarist regime, see the recollections of Flerovsky, esp. 19–136. In them he describes his initial career as a civil servant of the Ministry of Justice in St. Petersburg, the internal intrigues and nepotism, the lack of expertise of some of the higher functionaries, and the rather widespread disregard for established laws and rights on the part of higher and also lower officials.

Political coercion was also a major preoccupation of the Russian executive organ, a preoccupation lasting to this day. The police was under the administrative supervision of the Ministry of the Interior, and the chief of the police was appointed by the minister, was personally responsible to him, and retired whenever the minister retired. Following the reorganizations of 1880 and 1882 the Assistant Minister of the Interior became the commander of the Special Gendarme Corps, a security formation. The Okhrana, part of the police department of the Ministry of the Interior, provided the intelligence and counterrevolutionary operations. This was the political branch.[14] With rising ferment there was a growing tendency to exempt political cases from judicial "interference" by placing them under the jurisdiction of military courts. Between 1891 and 1901 all political cases were handled by military tribunals, and the extraordinary procedures provided in the decree of August 14, 1881, "Measures for the Preservation of State Order and Tranquility," were renewed every three years until the fall of tsardom.[15] Death sentences, which (as in Soviet Russia until very recently) were applied only in political cases, for acts undermining the executive power, were imposed with sufficient frequency to underscore the autocratic character of the regime.[16]

A common characteristic of autocratic regimes is the effort on the part of the executive branch to subvert judicial independence for the sake of political ends. In Tsarist Russia this took the form of direct and indirect pressure on judges trying political cases,[17] removal of such cases from

[14] According to the 1897 census, the Gendarme Corps numbered 800 officers and 50,000 men, the police force 104,500 men, and an unknown number of Okhrana functionaries and collaborators. This should be compared to the 435,000 public officials in the same period. G. Alexinsky, *Modern Russia* (London, 1913), 178, 182, 186.

[15] S. Kucherov, *Courts, Lawyers, and Trials under the Last Three Tsars* (New York, 1953), 201–203.

[16] The Russian criminal code was quite liberal in defining antistate activities, and even more generous in assigning the death penalty for them. The death penalty was provided for any actions or conspiracies which would endanger the "life, liberty or health" of the tsar, or would "limit" the powers of the throne (arts. 99, 101). The death penalty furthermore was provided for anyone plotting to change the Russian government, or to change it in any part of Russia, or for anyone plotting to separate any part of Russia from the Russian state (art. 100). The death penalty was again provided for anyone who made an attempt on the life of a member of the imperial household (art. 105). Furthermore, "armed resistance to authority or attacks on army or police officials and on all official functionaries in the execution of their assigned duties" would be punished by the death penalty" if these crimes are accompanied by murder, or attempted murder, infliction of wounds, grievous assault, or arson." See M. I. Gernet, *Smertnaia kazn'* (Moscow, 1913), 54. Other offenses, punishable by death, are also enumerated. For various statistics on the frequency of the death penalty, see Kucherov, Alexinsky, Gernet, and S. Usherovich, *Smertnie kazni v tsarskoi Rossii* (Kharkov, 1933). These sources also include accounts of mistreatment and flogging of political prisoners.

[17] The judges were subordinated administratively to the Minister of Justice. Flerovsky, a civil servant in the ministry, cites cases of the overbearing treatment of the judges by the minister, 65.

the jurisdiction of established tribunals (as indicated above), promulga-
tion of emergency punitive measures (as in 1905), and administrative
dispensation of justice. In the words of the last chief of the Okhrana:
"There was only one form of extra-judicial punishment, and that was
administrative banishment; sentences of up to five years could be pronounced." [18] He adds further that this was "frequently but leniently applied." The absence of a strong legal tradition in Russia facilitated these
deviations from the rule of law which, when firmly rooted, inherently
serves as a check on executive power.[19]

The Soviet parallels are self-evident. Political centralization in the
USSR is achieved, despite constitutional provisions, by the subordination
of republican (and lower) organs to the central political administration
in Moscow. Beyond that, the party acts as the chief coordinating instrument and has lately acquired an even more important coordinating capacity as a result of the economic reorganization. Soviet archives, such
as the Smolensk *Obkom* and *Oblispolkom*,[20] leave little doubt that, underneath fictitious lip service to federalism and the importance of local initiative, central executive control is indisputable and has been so during the
entire Soviet period despite some modest efforts during the NEP to give
meaning to republican autonomy. Organized violence, to protect the
Soviet form of government and hence to destroy all real and potential
opponents, has been associated from the very beginning with central
executive power and has not been impeded by excessive judicial sensitivity on the part of the Soviet leaders. Vyshinsky's statement that "the
contents and form of judicial activities cannot avoid being subordinated
to political class aims and strivings" [21] still holds today, even though its
author may have been at least partially repudiated. Death penalties for
political crimes have been applied more generously than under the tsars,
and administrative organs have freely imposed severe penalties on those

---

[18] A. T. Vassilyev, *The Ochrana*, (Philadelphia, 1930), 39. See also N. N. Beliavsky,
Politseiskoe pravo (Petrograd, 1915), and A. I. Elistratov, *Uchebnik russkago
administrativnago prava* (Moscow, 1910). Vassilyev, quoted above, was not entirely
correct, for under emergency circumstances captured revolutionaries were frequently
executed on orders of the provincial governors who based themselves on articles 17
and 18 of the Special Law for the Preservation of Order.

[19] P. L. Lavrov observed in 1870: "Law in Russian eyes never stood on the level
of 'written reason,' never became sacred just because it was law. Law was regulation
convenient to the momentary whim of the government." "Philosophy of the History
of Slavs," quoted in J. Kucharzewski, *Od Bialego Caratu do Czerwonego* (Warsaw,
1931), V, 53. See P. Milyoukov, *Russia and Its Crisis* (Chicago, 1905), esp. 165–185,
for a general analysis of the weakness of the legal tradition. The failure of the Senate,
which was meant to be the watchdog of laws, is illustrative. Filled with retired administrators and even former police functionaries, it never fulfilled its role and became a mouthpiece for the executive. See Flerovsky, 62, for some specific instances.

[20] Merle Fainsod, *Smolensk under Soviet Rule* (Cambridge, Mass., 1958).

[21] A. Vyshinsky, *Teoriia sudebnykh dokuzatel'stv po sovetskomu pravu* (Moscow,
1941), 31.

accused of political offenses. Centralization and coercion continue to be important attributes of the executive in Russia.

One final similarity between the executive organs of Russia before and after the 1917 Revolution lies in an area which need not be a characteristic of autocratic regimes but which has been important to the maintenance in power of these Russian regimes. That is the relation of the executive to the military. In many autocratic regimes, political power becomes so dependent on the military establishment that power ultimately passes to the military, or the military, as a group, are continually involved in attempts to "salvage" the national interest. Not so in Tsarist Russia (except for the short and untypical period after 1916) nor in Soviet Russia. Apparently the Russian military leadership has developed, somewhat like the Russian Orthodox Church leaders, a sense of political noninvolvement which makes it difficult for any would-be Bonapartist leader to use the army as a cohesive unit for political purposes. In the case of the tsar there were the elements of personal loyalty and wise personnel policy: for instance, many high officers occupied influential and lucrative administrative posts. In the USSR there may be ideological loyalty, and there is certainly a complex network of police and party controls and purges. Whatever the technique or causes, the political effect is similar.[22]

In view of the preceding it might be said that a crucial element of continuity in the Russian executive since 1861 has been the almost uninterrupted maintenance of an autocratic pattern of executive power, with the resultant minimization of restraints on the arbitrary exercise of that power. In this sense Soviet Russia merely continues on a trail blazed by centuries of earlier Russian political tradition. But this merely establishes the broad outlines of continuity and hardly exhausts our problem. Are historical parallels enough to posit historical continuity?

II

Within the framework of an essentially autocratic pattern there are significant differences between the Tsarist and Soviet executives, both in degree and kind, which demand investigation and theoretical evaluation. To that task I shall now turn. In so doing, it might be opportune at this stage to examine again the nature of restraints on political power and see to what extent these in fact had been subverted by the Tsarist and

---

[22] Of course, there have been plots among younger officers, impatient with the Tsarist policy of status quo, such as the *Voennaia Organizatsiia Partii Narodnoi Volii.* The officers, however, were all of junior rank, and this made it quite impossible to use the army as a unit of political purposes. These traditional considerations, apart from the more immediately significant factor of highly institutionalized controls and intense indoctrination, might have also been taken into account by those who for the last few years made a profession out of predicting an imminent take-over of political power in the USSR by the military.

Soviet executives. A useful device might be to distinguish between: (1) the direct restraints, expressed through *pacta conventa* such as the English Magna Carta or the Polish *Nihil novi* . . . , the Bill of Rights, constitutional guarantees, a rule of law, or even the broad consensus of tradition which rules out certain types of conduct, such as the use of violence; (2) the indirect restraints which stem from the pluralistic character of all large-scale societies and which necessitate adjustment and compromise as the basis for political power — the churches, the economic interests, professional, cultural, or regional pressure groups, which all impede the exercise of unrestrained power; and (3) the natural restraints, such as national character and tradition, climatic and geographical considerations, kinship structure and particularly the primary social unit, the family.[23]

Having made these distinctions we cannot fail to note that the Tsarist executive, in the final analysis, effectively subverted only the first kind of restraints, sometimes came into conflict with the second, and never challenged the third. Its relationship with the church or the zemstvos was one of control, especially in the case of the former; with the growing industrial and middle class, broadly speaking, one of adjustment. Insofar as the family is concerned, it never went beyond the point reached by most modern states — insistence on education and a degree of patriotic conformity. The Soviets continued this subversion of the direct restraints, but went beyond that in destroying the second kind and effectively challenging, if not entirely overcoming, the third. We thus have a broad area in which important differences appear in significant focus and demand closer scrutiny.

The question arises: if both executives can be considered autocratic, why is there such variation in the relation between political power and political restraint? The answer is to be found in the nature of the basic attitude of these executives toward the existing society. A traditional regime, with its paternalistic sense of authority, recognizes a transcendent system of values which inherently limits its otherwise institutionally wide scope of action. The Tsarist executive was motivated precisely by such curious mixture of autocratic paternalism and strong belief in the immaturity of the people. This made it frequently resort to violence but yet never allowed it to seek the logical conclusion of that violence — complete extermination of enemies — because of the conscious and unconscious assumptions inherent in the paternalistic attitude. Conflicts that did arise, such as the challenge to the economic interests of the gentry due to

[23] One might also consider a supernatural restraint in the sense of a transcendent moral order to which many governments pay lip service. In fact, however, its *political* significance is probably covered fully by the three outlined above, and particularly by the first two. For a full discussion of the role of these restraints and their implication, see the author's "Totalitarianism and Rationality," *American Political Science Review,* L (September 1956), 751–763.

state-encouraged industrialization or subsequently through the Stolypin reform, were still the function of an attempted response to changes in society and not a matter of preconceived policy of subordinating or destroying rural interest groups for the sake of eliminating restraints on the power of the regime. The powers-to-be in the Tsarist executive, ranging from Pobedonostsev or Rasputin to Loris-Melikov or Stolypin and including the tsars, all shared in the desire to defend the broad outlines of the status quo, although obviously differing on such specific measures as need for reform or desirability of reaction. But commitment to the status quo inherently involves a limitation on power by that status quo and a measure of acceptance of the values inherent in the status quo. If one takes society and the political system as they are, then one's power is fitted into the existing framework of that society, even if such things as law and constitution (direct restraints) are not too vital. The other types of restraints compensate somewhat for this absence of the direct restraints.

The Soviet attitude, motivated by an ideology which puts a premium on *conscious* political action on the basis of a relatively defined and dogmatic action program (qualities lacking in the more general and traditional viewpoints of the Tsarist reforms), aims at the transformation of existing society and hence initially rejects it as it exists. This act of rejection liberates the Soviet leadership from limits inherent in the status quo, and the conviction of the Soviet leaders that they possess an insight into the inevitabilities of history justifies all their acts. The reliance on a revolutionary movement, for which there is no parallel in Tsarist Russia, gives the leadership an independent tool for the destruction of restraints on its power, even if some bureaucrats (because of their professional interest in a measure of stability) are wary of excessive change. As a result, the power of the executive becomes pervasive, penetrating the entire society and maintaining its grip even as the impetus of the initial blows fades, as the new society begins to take shape and as its rulers develop a vested interest in the new status quo. By then the society has become both molded and penetrated by political organs which parallel the purely administrative structure and which give the top executive a significantly greater scope of action. It could even be argued that at this stage the distinction between the political system and society, which could be made in the case of Tsarist Russia, becomes meaningless. At the same time, because of the dynamic and ideological quality of the struggle undertaken, the executive is much more conscious of the need to keep its movement vital, especially since the elimination of pluralistic groups tends to give the movement a monopoly on power without the invigorating effect of continuing competition. Purges thus become the inherent device for coping with this situation and maintaining the revolutionary dynamic.

The process of pulverizing society destroys effectively all political op-

position and leads to the mobilization of all social energy for the achievement of the politically defined goals. The result is a far greater pattern
of compliance to political power than under the Tsarist executive. While
many examples could be cited involving such fields as the arts, sciences,
or the press (despite censorship, the Tsarist press was an example of diversity when compared to the Soviet[24]), let us look again at the handling
of political cases and the general problem of political opposition to the
regime in power. We have noted the summary treatment of political opponents by Tsarist military tribunals and the relative absence of inhibition
with respect to the execution of such opponents. At the same time, we
must note spectacular cases of judicial independence even in the more
violent days of Russian political history. In the trial of Vera Zasulich, the
presiding judge, at the risk of prejudicing his future career, effectively
resisted political pressure from the executive; the defense made impassioned appeals on behalf of the defendant, and the jury, acting with an
overriding sense of justice, acquitted her to the accompaniment of thun-
derous applause. What a contrast with the behavior of the auditorium and
the judges in the Hall of Crystals exactly sixty years later! At the nonjury
trial of the emperor's assassins (the government had become more cautious), the chief defendant Zheliabov unflinchingly defended his position and forcefully demanded that a jury trial be held — a behavior not
noted in Soviet political cases. Until the collapse of the empire, many defense lawyers courageously and devotedly defended, in many cases successfully, political prisoners accused of subversion or revolutionary activity. Soviet judicial history since Stalin is not marked by such episodes.

The executive power in Russia under the tsars was committed to a
defense of a political status quo in which the autocratic power was traditional while the society itself was changing with increasing tempo under the impact of slowly expanding literacy, economic reforms often initiated by the regime itself, growing urban centers, and spreading consciousness of the need for change. This meant that the regime's security
was more and more frequently challenged by revolutionary groups desiring drastic reforms. The executive could not take measures violent enough
to uproot and wipe out all opposition without shattering much of the
status quo. Absence of technology, while important, was not crucial; certainly revolutionary regimes in the past (Cromwell or Napoleon) have
been able, because of their revolutionary liberation from existing societal
limitations, to cope effectively with domestic opposition. As a result, much
of the political history of the last few decades of the empire could be

---

[24] For comparative treatments of the censorship systems, see M. Karpovich,
"Historical Background of Soviet Thought Control," in W. Gurian, ed., *The Soviet
Union: A Symposium* (Notre Dame, 1951); Merle Fainsod, "Censorship in the
USSR: A Documented Record," *Problems of Communism* V (March-April 1956),
12–19; and Alex Inkeles, *Public Opinion in Soviet Russia* (rev. ed.; Cambridge, Mass.,
1958).

written in terms of political plots, conspiracies, assassinations of countless important officials (not to mention the emperor), and intensive revolutionary propaganda.[25] While it would be erroneous to exaggerate their political significance, they did help to set the political atmosphere of the time. Pobedonostsev's letter of advice to Alexander III, shortly after Alexander's accession to the throne, catches the atmosphere of internal fear, bred by conspiracy, terror, and ineffectual counterterror. He writes:

(1) When you are retiring, Your Majesty, do shut the doors behind you not only in the bedroom but in all adjoining rooms, the hall included. A trusted person should carefully check the locks and make certain that inside door bars be slid shut. (2) Definitely check every evening before retiring whether bell wires are intact. They can be easily cut. (3) Check every evening underneath the furniture to see whether everything is all right. (4) One of the aides-de-camp ought to sleep near Your Majesty in the same apartments. (5) Are all persons around Your Majesty trustworthy? [26]

And the revolutionaries whom Pobedonostsev so feared, even though frequently tracked down, arrested, and executed, combined their revolutionary zeal with a mixture of romanticism and fanaticism which somehow would seem out of place among the current Soviet generation of *tekhnikum* students.[27]

The Soviet executive has until now avoided such a situation by stamping out the opposition while engaged in the process of constructing a new society. This revolutionary procedure freed it from traditional limits on power. By the time a new generation grew up, matured, and prepared to take stock (a development delayed by the world war and the cold war until the mid-fifties), a situation had been created in which opponents of the policies of the present Soviet executive face what might be called

[25] For detailed treatment of the conspiratorial activity, see A. P. Men'shchikov, *Okhrana i revoliutsiia* (Moscow, 1925–1932), and A. Kornilov, *Obshchestvennoe dvizhenie pri Aleksandre II* (Paris, 1905). Count Pahlen reported to Alexander II that the chief reason for the success of revolutionary propaganda was the sympathy that existed for it among large parts of the population (Kornilov, 160).

[26] *Pis'ma Pobedonostseva k Aleksandra III* (Moscow, 1925–1926), I, 318–319.

[27] Compare I. Berlin's "The Silence in Russian Culture," *Foreign Affairs* (October 1957), with the following account of a meeting of young Russian revolutionaries on New Year's Eve of 1880, when arrests were already auguring a not too happy future for them: "The preparation of the punch left a particularly plastic image in my memory. On a round table in the middle of the room a vase was placed, filled with pieces of sugar, lemon, roots, sprinkled with arac and wine. It was a magic sight when the arac was fired and the candles extinguished. The flickering flame, mounting and waning, lighted the severe faces of the men surrounding it; Kolodkevich and Zheliabov stood closest. Morozov took out his stiletto, then another, then another, placed them, crossed, on the vase and, without preparation, with a sudden impetus, the powerful, solemn melody of the known *haidamak* song was heard: 'Hai, ne dyvuites, dobryie ludi, shcho na Ukrainie povstaniie.' The sounds of the song spread and mounted, they were joined by fresh voices, and the shimmering flame flickered, bursting out with a red glow, as if steeling the weapons for struggle and death. . . ." Olga Lubatovich, *Byloe* (June 1906), 123–124, quoted in Kucharzewski, V, 304–305.

"the dilemma of the one alternative." Even if rejecting the system in a personal sense, any critic is forced to admit that by now no meaningful alternatives to it exist. That seems to have been the position of many Soviet students whom I met in the USSR in the fall of 1956.

The point of these remarks, following the admission of a broad pattern of continuity in the autocratic character of the Russian executive, is to suggest that a sharp distinction in the roles played by the Tsarist and the Soviet executives nevertheless must be noted. The distinction is inherent in the apparent difference between an autocratic regime based on certain traditional values and generally committed to the status quo, and an autocratic regime which is revolutionary in its policy and is committed ideologically to a radical destruction of the past and long-range programs of utopian reconstruction. Regimes such as the latter have been called totalitarian, and it is this totalitarian development *within* the broad autocratic pattern which presents us with a sharp discontinuity in the role and character of the Russian executive since 1861.

III

A further question now arises. After all, if we were to compare the British government of today with the British government of 1861 we would note certain very important differences within the constitutional pattern which could lead us to the conclusion that a sharp discontinuity is involved. The change from a parliamentary form of government to one which is fundamentally a centralized party form of government might be considered a sharp discontinuity, despite its occurrence within the constitutional pattern. Continuity and change, however, are in constant interaction, and the British form of government as it exists today evolved out of yesterday's. The change took place gradually even though the product at the end is quite different from what it was at the beginning. The question which we must now raise is whether the totalitarian pattern of the present Russian executive was implicit in the gradual changes occurring in the autocratic Tsarist executive. If that is the case, then the totalitarian role of the Soviet executive, though different in many respects from the Tsarist, is yet the natural child of trends implicit in the past.

To examine this position we must take a broad look at the confusing and multidirectional courses pursued by the antecedent regime in Russia and attempt to extract from them some indication of a general trend, meaningful to our quest for patterns of fundamental continuity or proofs of an essential discontinuity. That the record of the Tsarist executive was mixed insofar as liberalizing and reactionary policies are concerned is clear from a cursory glance at Russian political history. Yet it also becomes evident that the second half of the nineteenth century and the beginning of the twentieth were periods of great changes — and ones that we might call spontaneous — in the social and economic life of Russia.

Heavy industry, railroads, and coal and iron complexes were beginning, and the cities reflected the growing opulence and power of a new class of bankers, merchants, and industrialists. These changes, even if under the cloak of a political power dusty with antiquated traditions of autocracy, were beginning to make themselves felt. Violent radical conspiracies were their extreme expression. But much more important than these was the conscious striving of many for reform, for a constitution, for a liberal monarchy.[28] This consciousness penetrated even the cold walls of the Winter Palace, and the emperors gradually found themselves surrounded by whispered, and sometimes loud, warnings that something must be done.

To reform from within an old autocracy is not an easy task. Many vested interests are always against any change other than the natural, imperceptible one. This proved to be so in Russia. Yet the executive power, which, given the system, was the only effective source of reform, did initiate a number of significant changes. These reforms involved not only important areas of the social and economic life of the community, such as the liberation of the peasants or the later Stolypin agricultural reforms, but also political changes which had direct bearing on the power of the executive. The law reform and the organization of jury trial (1864), while still subject to severe limitations in statute and practice,[29] meant that the judicial branch was gradually becoming institutionalized. The law on assemblies, passed in the same year, similarly implied a modest development in the direction of regularized patterns of self-government, albeit on a very limited scale. The press reforms of 1865, the growing vocal activity of the zemstvos, and Loris-Melikov's projects were all efforts to bring the autocracy in line with the requirements of the changing society, to bridge the gap between political institutions designed to fight off the Tatar yoke, and to build a society which was now beginning to feel more strongly the impact of growing pains in an age of economic and social revolution. The dilemma of power in such a context — to liberalize or to contain — meant frequent oscillations and reversals. And yet, even though the executive would shrink back into the apparently only safe refuge of reaction (as in 1882), parts of the society would continue their pressures for change and the executive would finally respond. But the ambivalence would persist: the Duma period, the desire for a buffer between society and the executive (as explicitly stated by Witte), the electoral reforms, would be followed by a relapse, by electoral amendments designed to limit representation by a re-emphasis of Tsarist autocracy, by a reassertion

[28] For an interesting recent analysis, see George Fischer's *Russian Liberalism* (Cambridge, Mass., 1957).

[29] See Kucherov or Alexinsky. The latter comments: "To be elected a juror, a man must be a landowner. The composition of the jury was subject to the control of the bureaucracy. . . . Preliminary examinations fell almost exclusively to the charge of the police" (193ff).

of violence, all often welcomed by those who feared change.[30] Nonetheless, a residue of change would remain and would serve as a springboard for further intensification in the pressures for reform. The development of the prime ministership[31] and the embryonic growth of a multiparty system were part of institutional changes which even subsequent relapse into reaction could not undo in their entirety. That the change was slow, too slow, seems to have been the final verdict of history, and the regime did not surmount the accumulated pressures when they came to be combined with external blows. However, these considerations still lead one to suggest that the role played by the Soviet executive, given its policies and power, involves a reversal in an admittedly timid and regrettably blurred trend.

In the process of carrying out the Communist revolution, the successor government expanded its powers to a degree unprecedented in modern political history: it reversed the trends toward an independent judiciary, toward a freer peasantry, toward a modest system of political representation based on a pluralistic society. Much of the violence used to build the new Communist society was a product of the need to overcome the inertia which is the usual social response to rapid, purposeful, and ideologically motivated change pushed forward by an organized minority. Much of it was a product of brutal zeal and a lust for power. But one must remember also that the terror used by the empire against the revolutionaries in itself contributed to the sharpening of their dogmatic convictions and strengthened their belief in the necessity of violence for the sake of "morally" good ends. This psychological legacy of the empire makes the rulers of the past share responsibility with the rulers of the present for the continued reliance on violence despite the deep existential and normative differences between the Soviet and Tsarist executives.

Recently there have been some indications that with a decline in the momentum of internal transformation voices might be raised inside Russia to dispute the unlimited claim of the executive to rule over the destinies of the Russian people. But the occasional voices of nonconformity are still timid when compared to the literary outcries of the disaffected intellectuals or the heroic declarations of the revolutionary brethren of less than a century ago. The Tsarist executive was very gradually, indeed haltingly, moving in the direction of closing the gap between the political regime and society at large by adjusting to the requirements of the society. It moved too slowly. The Soviet leadership changed society in the image of

---

[30] See S. L. Levitsky, "Legislative Initiative in the Russian Duma," *American Slavic and East European Review*, XV (October 1956), 315–24; also S. A. Piontkovskii, *Ocherki istorii SSSR XIX i XX veka* (Moscow, 1935), for a discussion of the electoral system.

[31] The October 1905 reform formally set up a Council of Ministers with a prime minister, both modeled on the Western pattern.

its own doctrines so that no such gap should exist. The 1957 reforms in the Soviet administrative structure, allegedly granting more, say, to component federal and economic units, could have been significant in altering the role of the executive and its relation to society. But unlike the empire, there is always the parallel and pervading structure of the party, and all indications point to the fact that the party is as powerful as ever. This party, having surmounted domestic obstacles and being rather optimistic about current world trends, is not likely to atrophy in the foreseeable future. True, success in itself breeds conservatism and vested interest in the status quo. These in turn gradually imply restrains on power, especially as an industrializing society becomes more complex and literate. But neither industrialism nor education are incompatible with totalitarian autocracy. The former itself breeds pressures for central control and direction;[32] the latter, popular slogans to the contrary, is *divisible* and subject to manipulative controls which stress only those aspects compatible with totalitarian demands and de-emphasize those which are not. Scientific training unaccompanied by the humanities does not inevitably come into conflict with a totalitarian regime which puts a premium on scientific achievement and gives it every opportunity for development. Modern scientific education, furthermore, by being dependent on specialization, instead of fostering a true spirit of inquiry can also be used to promote the acceptance of certain purposes and to instill a peculiar perspective which increases the power of the regime by making it accepted. A commitment to science or to industrial technology and management, especially if accompanied by a high system of rewards, can be used as effective blinders to social dilemmas and political questions.

Beyond this, given both the situation in the USSR and in the Communist camp in general, a myriad of decisions which are political in essence will have to be made and will require an elite with political skill and a sense of purpose. With the screening process for promoting such an elite developed over the long period dominated by Stalinism, we can expect that for many years to come only dedicated "politicians," or those who successfully pretend that they are, will rise in the hierarchy and ultimately shape decisions. Even if partially due to mere inertia, motivation for such decisions is thus likely to continue stressing common ideologically defined purposes. Considering their revolutionary character and fundamental commitment to struggle, such purposes are bound to cultivate a profound hostility toward even incipient manifestations of social pluralism. And without it, effective restraints on political power cannot develop. For this reason it would seem idle to speculate at this moment on the durability of the Soviet executive's unlimited power. A political scientist, when glancing into history, must not forget that there are too many cross-

[32] For a fuller discussion, see the author's "Totalitarianism and Rationality."

roads in the paths pursued by politicians to permit the use of the past as a compass to the future.

THE PARTIES AND THE STATE:
THE EVOLUTION OF POLITICAL ATTITUDES

LEOPOLD H. HAIMSON

I

The common observation that the concept of political parties developed in the West in the context of representative institutions — and of the struggle for control of these institutions — and that in Russia, on the contrary, it was shaped in the absence of such institutions is substantially correct, of course. It really raises more questions than it answers, however; for underlying the problem of the emergence of both political parties and representative institutions is the broader question of the evolution of relations between state and society as expressed in the changing attitudes that social groups entertain toward one another and toward political authority.

What broad continuities appear to distinguish these underlying political and social tendencies in Russia before 1855, before the reign of Alexander II and the Great Reforms? However broad and controversial the problem, it seems to me that, aside from the Marxist school, most Russian historians, from Solov'ev to Miliukov and Presniakov, have tended to agree on three general propositions concerning it.

The first is that through most of its history — in the sixteenth- and seventeenth-century Russian state and society of service groups, as in the late eighteenth- and early nineteenth-century gentry-dominated state and society of estates — state power played a central role in the organization, indeed in the very definition, of large social groups, in the delineation of the rights and duties, privileges and "burdens," that constituted the basis of individual and group position in Russian society. The second generally held proposition is that through these centuries the relations among large social groups were marked by very sharp cleavages, by almost insuperable differences and conflicts of outlook, interests, and experience, reflected in and strengthened by the caste character of the administrative organs that governed their lives. Finally, most Russian historians would generally agree that, as a result of these two factors, individuals and social groups throughout this period did not generally seek to extend their privileges or to ease their burdens by collaborating with each other in order to impose their joint will on the existing political order. Instead they turned directly and individually to the state power as the only real and legitimate source of rights and duties in the Russian land, to favor or assist them against all other groups in society.[1]

For groups that felt themselves to be oppressed by the existing political authority there appeared to exist, by the middle of the seventeenth century, only two real alternatives to this political orientation. The first was to seek a change in the person of the supreme arbiter, a change of tsar or dynasty which, while leaving the existing framework of political and social organization completely intact, might bring about a redirection of the favors and benefits extended by the throne. The other was a *bunt*, an "elemental" revolt against the whole political and social order — elemental in that it involved a wholesale rejection of the existing framework of national life, without any conception of an alternative political and social order.

To state that these broad continuities may legitimately be found in the history of Russian political attitudes from the seventeenth to the early nineteenth centuries is not to deny that relations among individual social groups, or between them and the state power, changed in many significant respects during this long historical period. To mention only the aspect of these changes that is closest to our interests here: these three centuries saw an evolution in attitudes toward state power by a shift from the highly personal image of the tsar — as an arbiter between relatively fragmented and still relatively balanced service classes — which prevailed in the seventeenth century. The attitude shifted to the Petrine and post-Petrine conception of the state power as a dynamic, revolutionary, westernizing agency in social life; and finally to the disillusioned image held by advanced opinion in the mid-nineteenth century of a conservative, obscurantist autocracy, the willing prisoner and ally of gentry caste interests.

Yet, despite the obvious significance of these and other political and social changes, the broad continuities that we have detected in Russian attitudes toward state and society seem to persist throughout the seventeenth and eighteenth centuries, and to make their imprint on the early nineteenth-century political scene. Even the oppressive years of the reign of Nicholas I, and the general sense of political and social bankruptcy that they were ultimately to arouse in society, would not destroy the antagonism among the estates and the consequent centrality of state power. Indeed, it is during Nicholas's reign that we observe the articulation of the three strands of opinion which would challenge the validity of modern

---

[1] For reasoned, if not wholly persuasive, Marxist critiques of this dominant view in Russian historical writing, see: M. S. Aleksandrov, *Gosudarstvo, biurokratiia, i absoliutizm v istorii Rossii* (St. Petersburg, 1910); M. N. Pokrovsky, *Russkaia istoriia s drevneishikh vremen* (4 vols.; Moscow, 1922–1923); M. N. Pokrovsky, ed., *Russkaia istoricheskaia literatura v klassovom osveshchenii* (Moscow, 1927); and N. L. Rubinshtein, *Russkaia istoriografiia* (Moscow, 1941).

representative institutions (and of a party system operating within their framework) in the early decades of post-Reform Russia.

We may observe at this time, in the thought and activities of Kiselev and his disciples in the state bureaucracy as well as in the more abstract formulations of the "state" school of history and jurisprudence, the emergence of a revitalized conception of the autocratic power as the dominant force in Russia's development — the only one capable of upholding the national interest against the selfish claims of factions and of leading the way to the realization of social justice.

It is also during this period, in the late 1830's and 1840's, to be exact, that we witness the spread of utopian socialist views among the intelligentsia, views that would impel its members to reject the "futile" struggle for constitutional limitations and representative institutions, in the name of utopias in which not only social and economic differences but also the very existence of the state on which they rested would be eliminated.

And, finally, in the writings of the small Slavophile circle we observe, beneath the elaborate edifice of historical and philosophical fantasy, the more sensible, or at least the more influential, notion that the proper task for men of good will was not to struggle for control of a political structure which already exercised too pervasive an influence in Russian life, but rather to strive for the development of cultural and social forms free from the evil embrace of the political process.

All sharing the sense of the inextricable interdependence of the dominant forms of political authority and socioeconomic organization, these three strands of Russian opinion, though sharply divided during the post-Reform period on many issues of political and social life, persistently were to manifest a common and fatal reluctance to invest their energies in the "narrow" and "futile" work of political reform.

II

There is a general note of awe in the reports of contemporary observers in the first years of Alexander II's reign about the metamorphosis that Russian society had suddenly undergone. "I can no longer recognize the old caravanserai of soldiery, the baton, and obscurantism," the historian Kavelin wrote in 1857, the year of the Nazimov decrees and of the opening of problems of reform to public discussion. "Everyone is talking, everyone is studying, including people who never before read anything in their lives."

Underlying the general aura of excitement, there appeared to exist at this moment a remarkable consensus in Russian society that the "old order" was doomed and that Russia was in need of "comprehensive" reforms, including the abolition of serfdom. There was even a general recognition that the elimination of serfdom would necessarily require a whole series of peripheral changes — changes in the administrative framework, in the judiciary, in military organization, in the whole structure of state and society.[2]

On these points the most diverse strands of opinion appeared in agreement. Under the shock of Russia's humiliating defeat in the Crimean War, the web of common interests and common fears that had kept state and privileged society so long paralyzed had finally come undone. Consequently, to the clamor of advanced opinion — to the shouts of Westerners, Slavophiles, and budding young Realists — were now joined the more sedate, and influential, voices of articulate spokesmen for gentry interests, and those of champions of the "state principle," in and out of the bureaucracy. But what was to replace the old congealed autocracy and society of estates? On this question, following the original call for "reforms," "modernization," and "rule of law," fissures were soon to appear in public opinion.

The conflict first broke out over the issue of "public participation" in the work of reform. To most of the deputies of the first and second calling, just as to later elected spokesmen of the gentry, the rule of law — the elimination of arbitrariness in Russian life — meant first and foremost that the range of bureaucratic control and interference should at all costs be restricted, and that the great work of reform should be taken out of the stranglehold of secretive bureaucratic agencies and largely placed in the hands of elected representatives of the public. This claim of the "gentry liberals" for public participation in the reform movement, a claim which was extended by some gentry spokesmen to a demand for a permanent national representation, appeared to most of the officials entrusted with the reforms (as indeed to other spokesmen for the "state principle") as suspect and premature, at the very least.

Some of the champions of state interest were opposed to the idea in principle. They too favored a "rule of law," indeed civic equality before the law, but under the cloak of these legal principles they visualized the emergence of a rejuvenated, yet unhindered, autocracy — freed from the pressure of gentry interests and from the limitations of gentry *votchina* rights — governing a now united nation on the basis of uniform legal procedures with the assistance of a modernized, disciplined, noncaste bureaucracy. This was essentially the viewpoint of Pobedonostsev, a firm opponent of serfdom, an enthusiastic advocate of the legal reforms (in

---

[2] For a brilliant tableau of the movement of opinion during the reign of Alexander II, see A. A. Kornilov, *Obshchestvennoe dvizhenie pri Aleksandre II* (Moscow, 1909). For briefer sketches, see A. A. Kornilov, "Istoricheskii ocherk epokhi 60-kh godov," in D. N. Ovsianiko-Kulikovsky, ed., *Istoriia russkoi literatury XIX veka* (5 vols.; Moscow, 1908–1911), III, 9–41; and L. Martov, "Obshchestvennyia i umstvennyia techeniia 70-kh godov," *ibid.*, IV, 1–52.

the early sixties), but then, as in later life, a resolute defender of the integrity of autocratic power.[3]

However, opposition to gentry liberalism among the *gosudarstvenniki* (as the advocates of the state principle were called) was not confined to such firm champions of autocratic and bureaucratic rule. The defeat of the constitutional movement was ensured at this time by the fact that many of the more progressive figures who were responsible for the "democratic" features of the reforms discerned in the pressure for public participation and representation the reflection of antipopular, antinational, gentry caste interests. It was due to the chasm that they detected between the interests of the gentry and those of the peasant masses that an enlightened bureaucrat such as Nicholas Miliutin, a progressive public figure such as Kavelin, and even Slavophile sympathizers such as Iuri Samarin or Cherkassky so firmly opposed in 1858–1859 any large-scale participation by the elected deputies of the provincial nobility in emancipation legislation. Considering an unimpeded state power the only current representative of the national interest, these leaders of the reforms repeatedly expressed their concern lest the various deputies of the gentry reconcile their views and join in "party" pressures, which would inevitably be directed against the best interests of the people and of the state. When public clamor rose once again for the establishment of national representation in 1864–1865, Kavelin, Miliutin, and Samarin once more opposed the demands of the constitutional movement on the ground that any national legislature would necessarily be dominated at this time by gentry interests and by a gentry party.[4]

To add to the weakness of the movement for representative government, the *gosudarstvenniki* were joined in their opposition to national representation by the spokesmen of two other strands of Russian contemporary opinion: the Slavophile elements in the older generation of the liberal gentry and intelligentsia, and the radical spokesmen of the younger generation of Realists, Nihilists, and Populists.

The Slavophiles' abstract formulations of their hostility to Western constitutionalism and "legalism" need not detain us here. But it is important to note that underlying their arguments there was a general diagnosis of Russian conditions which, then as later, influenced much wider circles of Russian opinion, if only because it unquestionably incorporated some accurate perceptions of existing realities. Just as the *gosudarstvenniki* did, the Slavophiles recognized the centrality of the state power in Russia's historical development and in contemporary Russian life. However, it

---

[3] For a lucid summary of Pobedonostsev's conception of the state, see Robert F. Byrnes, "Pobedonostsev on the Instruments of Russian Government," in Ernest J. Simmons, ed., *Continuity and Change in Russian and Soviet Thought* (Cambridge, Mass., 1955), 114–128.

[4] See B. E. Nolde, *Iurii Samarin i ego vremia* (Paris, 1926), 119–121, 188–189; and B. B. Veselovsky, *Istoriia zemstva za sorok let* (St. Petersburg, 1911), III, 14–22.

was precisely to this preponderant role of the state that they attributed all the social, economic, and spiritual evils in Russian society: the chasms separating the various estates, particularly "society" and the "people," the tendency of Russian social groups to look to the state for the definition of their rights and duties, and indeed for the delineation of the very course of their lives. The way out of these fundamental distortions in Russian life, the Slavophiles argued, was clearly not greater public participation in the political process, which in a different form would merely involve a perpetuation of the fundamental evil — the one-sided, altogether excessive orientation of individuals and groups toward the center, toward the state power. The only real remedy was to encourage the autonomous development of social, economic, and moral life, the emergence of organs of "self-administration," and class collaboration *outside* the prehensile arms of state institutions. Hence the Slavophiles were animated by a bitter hostility to the very idea of the party system. They viewed political parties as organizations of factional interests, feverishly seeking by servile maneuvers or by intimidation the favors which the state itself was not legitimately entitled to bestow upon them.[5]

The Slavophiles' ideal of a relationship of noninterference between the state and the land was reflected at this time, however diluted or distorted, in the political attitudes of broader strata of Russian opinion. Indeed it was subtly expressed in the image of government entertained by some of the firmest Russian constitutionalists, who considered the appurtenances of constitutional government that they advocated (such as a national legislature or an independent judiciary) not as functions or organs of the state, not as aspects of public involvement or participation in state affairs, but rather as agencies of society rooted outside the state framework and intended to contain or limit its influence. It is perhaps not surprising that such a viewpoint should have been entertained by the numerous advocates of decentralization among the Russian constitutionalists, but we find it upheld at this time by as firm a centralist and advocate of the "state principle" as B. N. Chicherin.[6]

More significant for the subsequent history of political attitudes and parties in Russia, however, was the reflection of the Slavophile diagnosis of the existing relationship between state and society in the outlook of the post-Reform radicals, the Realists and Populists of the 1860's and 1870's. Two broad continuities characterize the political and social attitudes of the various strands of the radical movement in this period.

The first is a sense of almost total estrangement from the values, mores, and institutional forms discerned in the prevailing political and

---

[5] For a summary of Slavophile views about the zemstvo institutions, see Veselovsky, III, 19–32.

[6] For Chicherin's contemporary views on the proper functioning of the state, see B. N. Chicherin, *O narodnom predstavitel'stve* (Moscow, 1866); and *Vospominaniia Borisa Nikolaevicha Chicherina. Moskva sorokovykh godov* (Moscow, 1929), 283ff.

social order. We find this common note of alienation in the writings of almost all the Realists and Populists of the 1860's and 1870's. We detect it in Pisarev's praise of the "thinking individual" who "recognizes no regulation, no moral law, no principle over and outside himself," as well as in his famous plea to his followers to "hit out boldly left and right," since whatever did not stand up to their blows was clearly "trash" and "not worth preserving." [7] We discern it in a quite different and more conventional Populist form in the pleas of Lavrov and Mikhailovsky to the student youth of the early 1870's to give up their "tainted" privileged stations, "born out of the sufferings of millions," and to pay their *dolg*, their duty and debt, to the oppressed masses of the people. We find it in the savage stories and essays of Saltykov Shchedrin, with their descriptions of the hopeless struggle between the *malchiki*, the young utopian advocates of a better world, and the *Tashkentsy*, the selfish, cruel, and corrupt representatives of property and privilege in the existing order. And finally, of course, we observe it in the insistence of the *buntarei* of the 1870's that the intelligentsia give up its distinctive social identity and fuse with the elemental masses of the people — to blow the whole existing order to bits and replace it with a new world of liberty, equality, and justice.

The second broad continuity is an acute sense of the interdependence, and ultimate concordance, of the various institutions and dominant groups of the existing political and social order. It is among the radicals of the 1860's and 1870's that we find the most absolute formulation of the belief in the close interrelationship between the political and socioeconomic structures that we have already found in other strands of Russian contemporary opinion. To the Russian radicals of the period any effort aimed at partial political, social, or economic reform within the existing framework seemed bound to fail — precisely because all the traditional aspects of the existing order, and all the modernizing forces then active beneath its surface, appeared mutually supportive, or at least by radical standards equally antagonistic to the intelligentsia's ideals of social harmony and individual moral and intellectual liberation. And for this reason, with the possible exception of the handful of Pisarev's followers in the middle 1860's, all strata of radical opinion were convinced that any useful political or social action would have to be based on forces estranged from both the traditional caste system and the emerging "capitalist elements" in national life.

In their search for supporters, the radicals of the 1860's and 1870's were consequently impelled to concentrate their attention on those groups that seemed to them estranged, or at least potentially estranged, from the ruling political and social order. Three such groups were singled out in

[7] See especially "Bazarov," in *Sochineniia D. N. Pisareva* (St. Petersburg, 1894), II, 377–378.

the radicals' programs and appeals: the youth, particularly the student youth, the intelligentsia, and the communal peasantry. These three groups were the common targets, or at least the common objects of attention, of most of the radical appeals of the 1860's and 1870's. But the nature of the respective roles assigned to each of them within the framework of a people's party differed, in substance or in detail, from one party program to another. If we put these party and factional programs of the 1860's and 1870's side by side, from M. I. Mikhailov's "To the Younger Generation" of 1861 and Zaichnevsky's "Young Russia" of 1862, to the programs of the far more substantial "Land and Freedom" (1876–77) and "People's Will" (1879) parties,[8] we can find, under the many differences in shadings, two major variants.

The first of these is the relative importance attached by the authors of these programs to the "political" as against the "economic" struggle. The most significant point to note about the difference between these two orientations is that, during those two decades, they did not involve broad differences in programmatic conceptions or objectives: the advocates of both the "political" and the "economic" struggle still tended to view the existing political structure and the dominant socioeconomic forces, old and new, as inextricably intermeshed. Both were aiming, in theory at least, at the complete destruction of the whole framework of national life; both proclaimed as their ultimate objectives — as the only legitimate objective of a people's party — the establishment of an anarchic federation of free, "self-administering" communes and *artels*.

Actually the conflict between *politiki* and *ekonomiki* was a purely technical one: it revolved solely on the question of how the mutually supportive political and socioeconomic structures could successfully be overthrown. To most advocates of the "political" struggle it appeared that the path to success lay in the organization of a revolutionary element in society — all those who appeared ready to join the proletariat in the struggle for political freedom — as the actual or potential dictatorship that would "eliminate" or neutralize the sources of support for the existing order. Then, and only then, could the way be cleared for the calling of a Constituent Assembly or People's Duma to carry out the establishment of the new social and economic utopia.[9]

The advocates of the "economic" struggle, on the other hand, believed that even if such a revolutionary *coup de main* were actually carried off, it would merely pave the way for the replacement of one arbitrary government by another, equally contrary to the people's interest. A "political"

---

[8] For the texts of these programs, see V. L. Burtsev, *Za sto let, 1800–1896* (2 vols.; London, 1897), I, 25–152.

[9] See, for example, "Molodaia Rossiia" (1862), *Nabat*, no. 1 (1875), and "Narodnaia volia" (Program of Executive Committee, 1879), in Burtsev, I, 44, 134–135, 150–152.

movement was necessarily condemned to futility for lack of any adequate social base. All of the ruling estates and emerging new privileged classes in contemporary society were the more or less willing allies of the existing order. The only possible path to the desired transformation was the organization of a wide popular movement, based on the cultivation of the people's own demands and needs.[10]

A second major variant in the radical programs of the 1860's and 1870's was the relative emphasis placed on the "readiness" of the peasant masses for revolution, and therefore on the intelligentsia's role in the preparation and execution of a revolutionary overturn. Naturally it was the advocates of the "political" struggle who, as a group, tended to stress the role of the intelligentsia conspirators instead of the people's. But even within their camp there were notable differences of emphasis — from the ruthless, elitist tone of self-affirmation characteristic of "Young Russia," and to a slighter degree of Tkachev's *Nabat*, to the more sober notes struck by the People's Will group. Similarly, we find among the advocates of the "economic" struggle varying degrees of idealization of the existing foundations of popular life and of the readiness of the people to revolt — from the Lavrovists' stress on the need for intensive socialist propaganda by the intelligentsia, to the Bakuninists' insistence that all the people needed was stimulation and the harnessing of their rage.

In the last analysis, from the range of attitudes represented one may draw two alternative images of the role and organization of a people's party, which the various radical programs approached with differing degrees of fidelity. At one end of the continuum was the image of a centralized, largely conspiratorial, intelligentsia-dominated party, aiming to destroy the whole existing social and political order by striking at its apex, the central state authority; a party intent on the establishment in the people's interest of a provisional revolutionary dictatorship as the most reliable instrument for the elimination of all forms of political, social, and economic oppression. At the other end of the continuum was the image of an infinitely broader and looser revolutionary movement, aiming to destroy the political and socioeconomic structure at its base, by mobilizing against it the instincts and aspirations of all those inchoate elements of Russian society which were "humiliated and insulated." But note that in both variants one can discern the outline of only one party — of one people's party acting as the spokesman or catalyst for all the groups estranged from the existing framework of national life.

In the preceding pages I have attempted to describe the confluence of anticonstitutionalist tendencies in Russian opinion which sapped the vitality of the liberal movement and influenced attitudes toward the party

[10] See, for example, "Nasha programma," *Vpered*, no. 1 (1873), *Zemlia i volia*, no. 1 (1878), and "Pismo k byvshim tovarishcham," *Chernyi peredel*, no. 1 (1880), in Burtsev, I, 106–112, 136–138, and 203–208.

system during the two decades following the beginning of the Great Reforms. Underlying these various tendencies — the different programmatic stands of conservative and "democratic" *gosudarstvenniki*, Slavophile anti-*gosudarstvenniki*, and "political" as well as "economic" radicals — one finds certain common, or at least related, assessments of Russia's contemporary position, which reflected current Russian realities as well as the political and social traditions of the past: the sense of the centrality of the role of the state power in the general framework of social organization; or, conversely, the sense of the inextricable reflection by the state power of the existing organization of classes and estates; the sense of the chasms separating individual classes and estates, and of the lack of free, politically unmediated, interaction or collaboration between them.

Not only did these pervasive social sentiments cause the constitutionalist movement to lose potential recruits to both conservative and radical opinion, but they also influenced attitudes within its own thin ranks. Among the older, and more moderate, of its members, this heritage from the past would periodically tend to confirm the views and, at crucial moments (1864–1865, 1881–1882), strengthen the influence of those who considered any large-scale political movement, any wholesale pressure for a national representation, premature — it would lead under existing conditions to complete anarchy, or to the hegemony of a selfish, gentry-dominated representation. Among the more idealistic and radical members of the constitutionalist movement, the same heritage would often be reflected in the feeling that to struggle for political reforms, to press for their *own* participation in the political process, was not enough — that nothing would do but a radical transformation of social and political forms by a truly national representative assembly with broad constituent powers.[11]

In a study of Russian liberalism, written in 1889, the publicist Dragomanov discerned in the weakness of the Russian liberal movement up to that moment, and particularly in the zemstvo liberals, an underlying "lack of determination."[12] This failure of nerve Dragomanov attributed in part to the difficult conditions of illegality under which any struggle for political freedom had to proceed in contemporary Russia. But underlying this timidity, I think, there was a more basic deficiency, characteristic of moderate and radical constitutionalists alike: this is the ultimate absence, in their confrontation of the redoubtable and omnipresent state power, of the sense — so pervasive among English county gentlemen in the eighteenth-century House of Commons and among the deputies of the

[11] For surveys of the trends of opinion within the liberal movement during this period, see I. P. Belokonsky, *Zemskoe dvizhenie* (2nd ed., Moscow, 1914), chs. 1–2; and Veselovsky, III, chs. 1–12.

[12] M. P. Dragomanov, *Liberalizm i zemstvo v Rossii, 1858–1883* (Geneva, 1889), 43.

French Third Estate in 1789 — that they constituted in their own right the adequate representatives of country and nation. That the Russian constitutionalists still lacked such a sense of legitimacy in the 1860's and 1870's was in large measure due to certain persistent facts of Russian contemporary experience: the role of the state power in upholding the framework of national life was still too great; the mutual antagonisms of the various estates were still too sharp; the new noncaste organs of self-administration to which the Great Reforms had given birth were still too recent and imperfect to enable any organized social group to feel confidently that it could oppose the pretensions of the central political authority in the name of an already existent, let alone united, nation.

III

In the history of Russian political attitudes, the decade of the 1890's may be viewed as the opening of a new chapter, marked by a range of dramatic developments: the attraction in the early and middle 1890's of varied strands of intelligentsia opinion to Marxism; the appearance, with the strikes of 1895–1896, of the industrial proletariat as a dynamic and potentially revolutionary force on the Russian scene; the emergence at the turn of the century of the ideological and organizational nuclei of potent liberal and neo-Populist movements. This confluence of events would lead by 1905 to the confrontation of the Russian autocracy with a seemingly irresistible coalition of opposition and revolutionary forces. But when viewed in the broad perspective of the evolution of Russian attitudes toward political action and political parties, the overriding significance of the decade is that it marks the time when significant strands of Russian opinion became persuaded of the need, and possibility, of mobilizing a broad political movement to gain political freedom and establish representative government in Russia.

To be sure, there had appeared some veiled and timid previsions of this point of view in earlier decades, particularly at the end of the 1870's and the beginning of the 1880's, but it was only in the 1890's that the spokesmen for significant strata of Russian opinion began to argue openly and unashamedly that political freedom was in and of itself a worthy and significant objective — for the attainment of which a wide combination of social forces, cutting across ideological and class lines, could legitimately and profitably be mobilized. Perhaps the best indication of the depth of this change in the public temper is that the new orientation toward "politics" made simultaneous inroads into the otherwise sharply divided Marxist and Populist camps.

It was the change within the Populist fold that appeared at the time more worthy of notice, if only because the adoption of the new point of view meant to its Populist converts nothing less than a dramatic renunciation of the basic assumptions of the past, of the deeply inrooted

Populist prejudice against constitutionalism and liberalism, of the long-held axiom that the only objective worthy of a people's movement was a "basic" social and economic overturn. Yet these were the traditions that many of the most orthodox spokesmen of the *Narodnichestvo* — Stepniak, Mikhailovsky, Annensky, Korolenko — now repudiated in the most unequivocal terms.

"There are moments in the life of a state when one question assumes the leading place, relegating all other interests, however basic, to the background. Russia is confronting such a question at the present time, the question of political freedom." Thus stated the manifesto of the People's Rights Party (*Narodnago prava*), drafted by some of the editors of the Populist journal *Russkoe bogatstvo* in 1894. The only way to achieve this objective was to oppose to the government "the organized force of public opinion." This would be the main task of the projected party, the manifesto concluded: "to unite all the opposition forces in the country" in order to win for one and all "the rights of man and citizen." [13]

Two years earlier, Stepniak-Kravchinsky, hitherto one of the most dogmatic exponents of the "economic" struggle, had argued more heretically that the only practical path to political freedom was the establishment of a constitutional monarchy. Socialists would have to shed earlier prejudices and say right out that their immediate objective was the conquest of a constitution for Russia. Even more, they would need to give up their "utopian belief" that in the struggle against autocracy "an independent, let alone a leading, role" could be assumed by either the working class or the peasant masses. Political freedom would have to be won by the joint efforts of the only two significant progressive forces on the contemporary scene: the socialist intelligentsia and the educated liberal elements of "society." [14]

To be sure, neither Stepniak nor the editors of *Russkoe bogatstvo* were intent on cutting off completely their ideological ties to the Populist tradition. They did not demand that the Russian radicals give up their ultimate socialist objectives for the sake of the political struggle. Indeed, they argued that the attainment of political freedom was a "prerequisite" for the solution of broader social problems. But even in these arguments they displayed little willingness to appease old Populist prejudices: "We vigorously protest against the habit prevalent among many of us to subordinate the objective of political freedom exclusively to the resolution of the social question," Stepniak belligerently asserted in 1892. "We cannot view freedom solely as an instrument for this or that, as if the

[13] The full text of this manifesto may be found in Burtsev, I, 260–262. See also "Nasushchnyi vopros" (1894), a fuller statement of the party's credo drawn up by Bogdanovich; and the background article by Aptekman, "Partii 'Narodnago Prava' po lichnym vospominaniiam," in *Byloe* (St. Petersburg, July 1907).

[14] "Chego nam nuzhno" and "Nachalo Kontsa" (1892), in Burtsev, I, 251–256.

feelings and needs of a free people were foreign to us, as if, for the sake of our obligations to the People, we did not understand our obligations to ourselves, to human dignity." [15]

For the Russian Marxists, such an awareness of the need for a nation-wide movement to win political freedom did not, of course, represent quite so radical a break with ideological tradition. After all, Plekhanov and Akselrod had been stressing the point ever since the organization, in 1883, of *Osvobozhdenie truda*.[16] Yet it is nonetheless symptomatic of the new mood of Russian radical circles in the early 1890's that, despite the in-toxication with the discovery of "irresistible economic laws" and the con-sequent quietism which then temporarily possessed most of the younger generation of Russian Marxists, the one practical plank, the one call to action, to which many of them responded was Plekhanov's and Akselrod's statement of the political tasks of Social Democracy.[17] This was the call to lead the movement for the overthrow of absolutism, duly enlisting in the process the support of the "less politically mature" bourgeois-liberal elements in society; to mobilize the Russian workers to fight for the "bour-geois revolution" that would win them their civic and political rights.

We should note that both the Marxist and the new Populist programs of the early 1890's provided for a staggering of tasks which Russian radi-cals had once viewed as inextricably joined: both now drew a line (at least in timing) between the gaining of political freedom and the eventual social overturn. In the Marxist program this staggering of objectives was articulated in the conception of a two-stage revolutionary process, whose first stage (the bourgeois revolution) was be separated from the glorious socialist revolution by a proper, largely historically determined, interval. In the Populists' case, this differentiation was reflected in the more impre-cise vision of a political revolution which would enable Russian public opinion to effect, in due course, broad social and economic reforms.

What basic changes in the radicals' image of the existing political and social order did this new orientation toward political action ultimately reflect? The first was the disappearance of the sense of the inextricable interconnection between political and social-economic organization that had characterized the radicals' view of the framework of national life. Beyond the long arm of the state power, both Populists and Marxists were now able to discern the independent shape of an already existent — or fast emerging — society, animated at least for the moment by a certain com-munity of values or interests transcending the barriers of caste and class differences. The second and related change in this image of national life

---

[15] Burtsev, I, 255.

[16] See, for example, G. V. Plekhanov, *Sotsializm i politicheskaia borba* (Geneva, 1883), and his *Nashi raznoglasiia* (Geneva, 1885).

[17] Cf. the organization in the winter of 1893 of the *Peterburgskaia Gruppa Osvobozhdenii truda*. For fuller discussion, see Leopold H. Haimson, *The Russian Marxists and the Origins of Bolshevism* (Cambridge, Mass., 1955), chs. 3–4.

was that in the chief constituent groups of the new society the Populists and Marxists now detected the emergence of a "public opinion" in *radical conflict* with the values and policies of state power, and in accord with the immediate interests, if not the ultimate objectives, of the socialist cause.

Both of these dimensions had been absent from the radicals' world view in the 1860's and 1870's. Both were prerequisites for the appearance of a favorable attitude toward the struggle for representative institutions. For a struggle confined to winning political freedom to appear practical, indeed conceivable, to the Russian radicals, it was necessary for them to perceive in national life a body of public opinion seeking political self-expression, and therefore to discern a society, a nation, distinct from the state. For such a struggle to appear useful in their eyes, it was equally necessary for them to see this public opinion as favoring objectives similar to their own.

The sources of this new image of society and public opinion must be traced ultimately to the Great Reforms which had created the legal setting for greater social mobility and closer contacts among classes in national life. But it was really only in the 1890's that the Russian radicals began to perceive at all clearly the shape of this new society and to discern in it a growing opposition to the state. The Populists and Marxists derived their discovery of the tension, the "dialectical conflict," between state and society from a common source: the process of rapid industrialization that Russia had begun to undergo in the late 1880's under the direction and sponsorship of the state. Both camps now diagnosed this process as a growth of capitalism at the expense of Russia's "natural" or "popular" economy, and they derived their belief in the inescapable conflict between state power and society from their sense of the contradictions attendant to this growth. Yet, in the last analysis, the two groups viewed this development of "capitalism" in sharply contrasting lights and held quite different pictures of the chief protagonists in the conflicts to which it was giving rise.

It naturally appeared to the Marxists that the growth of capitalism, in Russia as everywhere else, was merely a reflection of the unfolding of irresistible, "objective," economic laws. Whatever its social cost, whatever sufferings it was now producing, this process was to be welcomed by all enlightened elements in society, partly because it was giving birth to a conscious proletariat, the future agent of the socialist transformation, and partly because — in the more immediate perspective — it was giving rise to a modern, "bourgeois," westernized class society, whose interests strongly demanded the conquest of the civic and political rights that would so greatly benefit the development of the proletariat's consciousness.

Possessed, as most of them were, by this vision of a budding capitalistic society struggling for political self-expression against an out-dated "feudal" state order, the Russian Marxists naturally looked to its two "objective" class representatives — the proletariat and the bourgeoisie — to provide the chief impetus in the struggle for political freedom. It was the industrial proletariat that now showed "the most certain signs of political awakening." The bourgeoisie was still "politically inert" — but there was no doubt that this "other new class," even if more backward, would "be forced under the threat of ruin to become conscious of its own interests." [18] In the meantime, the Marxists were prepared to identify all "liberal" elements in society — all those who appeared ready to join the proletariat in the struggle for political freedom — as the actual or political spokesmen for a would-be politically mature, class-conscious bourgeoisie.

The Populist constitutionalists readily succumbed to precisely an opposite temptation. Ever since the 1880's they had viewed "capitalistic development" in Russia as merely the reflection of arbitrary, "unnatural" governmental policies which were driving the people's communal and artel existence, and indeed the nation's economy as a whole, to bankruptcy.[19] It was their conviction that the governmental policies were, or would be, widely opposed, not only by the peasantry and the intelligentsia but also by enlightened members of "privileged society," which drew the Populists of the 1890's to the idea of political freedom, to the vision of an aroused and mobilized public opinion replacing the existing regime by one more sympathetic to popular interests. Hence, the Populists were now tempted to consider all their actual or potential allies in "society" as spokesmen for antibourgeois, anticapitalistic tendencies, struggling against a procapitalistic state.[20]

By the turn of the century, the Populists had good reason to feel that the anticapitalistic, antibourgeois, antibureaucratic tendencies that they had discerned in contemporary society were now beginning to coalesce into a "public opinion" opposed to the policies of the state. Their chief cause for continued anxiety was that most "academic" and gentry liberals were still persuading themselves, as the 1890's drew to a close, that legality, self-administration, and concern for the popular welfare could be introduced into — or at least temporarily reconciled with — the political structure of autocracy. Some of the gentry liberals, such as D. N. Shipov

[18] G. V. Plekhanov, *O zadachakh sotsialistov v borbe s golodom v Rossii* (1893), in *Sochineniia* (Moscow, 1923–1927), III, 405. See also P. B. Akselrod, "K voprosu o sovremennykh zadachakh i taktike russkikh sotsial demokratov," and "Istoricheskoe polozhenie i vzaimnoe otnoshenie liberal'noi i sotsialisticheskoi demokratii" (Geneva, 1898).

[19] See, for example, V. V. (V. P. Vorontsov), *Sud'by kapitalizma v Rossii* (St. Petersburg, 1882), and Nikolai-on (N. F. Danielson), *Ocherki nashego poreformennago obshchesvennago khoziaistva* (St. Petersburg, 1893).

[20] See, for example, Nikolai-on, "Apologii vlasti deneg," *Russkoe bogatstvo*, I (1895), and V. V., "Proizvoditel'nye klassy i intelligentsia v Rossii," *Novoe slovo*, (March 1896).

and N. Khomiakov, the future leaders of the liberal right, still held on to the hopeful Slavophile vision of a benevolent, antibureaucratic tsar, peacefully consulting with the enlightened representatives of the Russian land.[21] Others of a more Western outlook, such as B. N. Maklakov, still looked forward to a gradual introduction, from the bottom up, of legal and eventually of constitutional principles into the machinery of government.[22] But only a handful of liberal spokesmen appeared prepared for an open militant struggle to secure these civic and political rights from the clutching hands of autocracy.

IV

If the Populists still suffered from a relatively thin diet as the 1890's drew to a close, they were to be surfeited at the opening of the new century by an embarrassment of riches. Not only did the years leading up to 1905 see the appearance of the coalition between liberals and democratic intelligentsia for which the Populist constitutionalists had been calling since the early 1890's, but they also witnessed the emergence of an impressive neo-Populist movement, built along somewhat more traditional lines. In the ideological and organizational definition of both these movements, the Populist constitutionalists were to play a major, if not central, role.

In remarkable contrast to the travails of the past, the creation of the "all-nation" coalition against absolutism proceeded during these triumphant years with remarkable rapidity, comprehensiveness, and ease — and in a relative spirit of sweet reasonableness without parallel in the earlier or later history of Russian political attitudes. By the beginning of 1905, an imposing front was to be systematically mobilized against the autocracy, ranging all the way from the zemstvo congresses (or at least their dominant wing, the zemstvo constitutionalists) at the right, the professional unions, organized under the aegis of the Union of Unions at the center, to the Social Democrats and Socialist Revolutionaries at the left. All these more or less independent political groups were determined, ostensibly at least, to maintain their distinct programs and tactics; yet most of their leaders and followers asserted themselves to be equally intent on "striking together" against absolutism for the attainment of common, immediate political objectives.

I have deliberately omitted from this already impressive list the most influential, most remarkable, and most symptomatic political organization of the period, the Union of Liberation (*Soiuz osvobozhdeniia*). I have done so simply because the Union of Liberation did not at any time represent a particular political grouping or tendency in any conventional

---

[21] See D. N. Shipov, *Vospominaniia i dumy o perezhitom* (Moscow, 1918), 145ff.

[22] See V. A. Maklakov, *Vlast' i obshchestvennost' na zakate staroi Rossii* (Paris, 1936), and *Iz vospominaniia* (New York, 1954); also Michael Karpovich, "Two Types of Russian Liberalism: Maklakov and Miliukov," in Simmons, 129–143.

sense. What we actually find represented in the councils of the movement is nothing less than an array of ideological tendencies and attitudes, embracing almost the whole spectrum of contemporary revolutionary and opposition attitudes: the moderate gentry constitutionalism of Nikolai Lvov and Kokoshkin, the more fiery and uncompromising liberalism of Petrunkevich and Miliukov, the modern "scientific" liberalism of Struve, the reformist Western Social Democratic outlook of Prokopovich, as well as the Populist ethos of Peshekhonov and Annensky. Indeed, these capsule descriptions are but bare, unsatisfactory approximations, for what was truly characteristic of the individual components of the movement, as well as of the whole complex, was an amorphousness and fluidity, reflecting a common desire to absorb, or at least to comprehend, the whole swirling flow of oppositional and revolutionary opinion.

But the truly remarkable feature of the Osvobozhdentsy is that they saw it as their role not merely to unite or reconcile the variety of tendencies that they represented under a common platform or organization, but rather to take a hand in the actual creation, ideological delineation, and "independent" organization of a whole spectrum of political groupings and tendencies. In this fashion, between 1903 and 1905, the Osvobozhdentsy played a more or less central and public role in the organization of the Group of Zemstvo Constitutionalists — and through it, in the political mobilization of the whole zemstvo movement (on the basis of a carefully delimited, "political," constitutional platform) and in the political organization of the city intelligentsia into professional unions (in this case, in support of an appropriately more radical program of political and social reforms). Through the personal agency of Peshekhonov and Annensky, they even took a hand in the ideological and organizational development of the radical Socialist Revolutionary Party and, most astonishing of all (if true), in the formulation — in properly "folksy" style — of the platform of Father Gapon's Assembly of Russian Workers.[23]

What was the Osvobozhdentsy's purpose in performing this juggling act, and what was the basis of their success? Only in the most limited sense was it intended to impose on the various groups a single, definite political purpose and direction. Zemstvo groups, intelligentsia liberals and radicals, rebellious workers and peasants, all were to be persuaded of the need to win political freedom. But aside from this, there was not the slightest attempt to prevent, indeed there was many an effort to encourage, these various groupings to develop distinct and even conflicting political physiognomies — if only in the interest of a truly broad and successful mobilization of a national movement.

What did the Osvobozhdentsy expect from the society that they were helping to bring to life? What was the theoretical basis for their confidence

---

[23] For a convenient summary of the activities of the Osvobozhdenie, see George Fischer, *Russian Liberalism* (Cambridge, Mass., 1958), chs. 5, 6.

that the different pieces, which they had helped shape, would somehow fall together in a reasonably coherent pattern? To be sure, a similar confidence is already to be found in the theoretical formulations of intelligentsia leaders during the 1890's. We find it in the orthodox Marxists' conception of the bourgeois revolution that was to be followed, after a proper interval, by the glorious socialist overturn, as well as in the Populist constitutionalists' more flexible vision of a political revolution that would give Russian citizens their civic and political rights — and create the political setting for eventual social reforms. But in both of these earlier conceptions, the hope to enlist "all-nation" support for the struggle against autocracy had rested entirely on the assumption that this struggle was to be confined to the conquest of political freedom. Under the exhilarating stimulus that the Osvobozhdentsy and their SR allies drew from the rising momentum and articulateness of the opposition movement, the distinction that the radicals of the 1880's had drawn between impending "political" changes and the eventual social transformation was to be largely swept away, or at least significantly blurred.

The "Westerner" elements among the Osvobozhdentsy — for the most part, the men of Struve's stripe who had matriculated earlier in the school of legal Marxism — were perhaps the least affected by the intoxicating mood of the moment, if only because their own long-range objectives for Russian society were no longer particularly radical. Yet even they now looked forward with remarkable sanguineness to the emergence at one stroke of a modern social and political order, to the appearance full-blown on Russian soil of the most advanced and progressive form of Western society. If they were so little concerned about the need to impose certain common, moderate, political objectives on the various elements of the opposition to absolutism, if they were in fact prepared to assist these groups, however disparate or radical they might currently appear, to organize independently, it was because they saw the end result of their efforts as largely predetermined. The new enlightened social and political order that was about to be born would necessarily bring in short order the domestication of all radical elements, the transformation of Russian revolutionary extremists into social reformers of the Western type. If this was now happening in Germany, Struve could well argue, why should it not also happen in Russia? [24]

As for the representatives of the school of Populist constitutionalism now active in the councils of the Osvobozhdentsy and their friends among the Socialist Revolutionaries, they looked forward to an equally hopeful, but quite different, perspective. It now seemed to them increasingly apparent that no insurmountable "objective" ideological differences really separated the vast majority of the opposition movement: the SD's, the

[24] See "Germanskie vybory," *Osvozhdenie,* no. 25 (June 1903).

SR's, and the advanced (that is, "real") liberals. All of these groups were, potentially at least, equally radical; all of them were "instinctively" opposed to both "feudalism" and "capitalism."

As early as 1898, Peshekhonov had insisted on the identity of the economic interests of industrial workers and toiling peasants and, almost from the very first, he and his disciple, Victor Chernov, expressed and elaborated this view in the pages of the official SR organ, *Revoliutsionnaia rossiia*. Of course, they conceded, capitalism was now spreading in the countryside and giving birth to a new kulak class — but all this meant politically was that the toiling peasants' traditional instincts for economic equality and cooperation would now be largely directed against capitalistic, rather than feudal, exploitation.[25] As we turn over the pages of *Revoliutsionnaia rossiia*, between 1902 and 1905, we observe the neo-Populist image of the nation-wide front against capitalism being extended (with increasing confidence) to include most of the members of the liberal opposition. From the original conception of a careful, rather distant, and wholly provisional collaboration, lasting only up to the moment when the autocracy would be overthrown,[26] the emphasis of the journal gradually but unmistakably shifts to an optimistic vision of the core of the liberal movement as the expression not of gentry, let alone bourgeois, interests but rather of the social conscience, however confused, of a nonclass, noncaste intelligentsia.[27] From 1903 to the outbreak of the 1905 Revolution, the neo-Populist leaders would feel increasingly certain, if only on the basis of their own experience with the Osvobozhdenie movement, that most of the liberal leaders were "antibourgeois" and "antigentry" in their instincts, if only "vulgarly so," and that they were not "hostile to socialism, but simply believe in it badly." [28]

These particular distortions in the neo-Populists' vision of the character and composition of the coalition against absolutism impelled them, far more seriously than their Westerner collaborators among the Osvobozhdentsy, to stretch the limits that had originally been assigned to the struggle for political freedom. The "democratic" revolution that they saw in the offing was no longer to be confined to mere "superficial" political reforms; it was to encompass radical social and economic changes (such as the socialization of the land) which would pave the way for the socialist transformation. Nor was this revolution any longer to depend in any sig-

---

[25] See especially "Krest'ianskoe dvizhenie," *Revoliutsionnaia rossiia*, no. 8 (June 1902), and "Programnye voprosy," I and III, in *Rev. ros.*, nos. 11, 13 (September, November 1902).

[26] See "Novoe vystuplenie russkikh liberalov," *Rev. ros.*, no. 9 (July 1902), and "Oppozitsiia ego Velichestva i g. von-Plehve," *Rev. ros.*, no. 13 (November 1902).

[27] See N. Novobrantsev (A. V. Peshekhonov), "Osnovnye voprosy rev. programmy," *Rev. ros.*, nos. 32, 33 (September, October 1903).

[28] See "Sostav liberal'noi partii," *Rev. ros.* (October 1903), and "Sotsialisty-revoliutsionery i nesotsialisticheskaia demokratiia," *Rev. ros.*, no. 56 (December 1904).

nificant degree on the support of an established group in privileged society; the broad social and economic changes that it would effect would be imposed by a "firm democratic regime" against the resistance of both gentry and bourgeoisie.[29]

These were the two ideologically different, yet equally optimistic and almost equally elastic, conceptions that animated the neo-Populist, neo-Marxist, and ex-Marxist figures who, in the years immediately preceding 1905, largely led and manipulated the growing forces in the opposition to absolutism. Both conceptions presented a challenge to the Menshevik and Bolshevik leaders of Russian Social Democracy who, however divided on other issues, were still in ostensible agreement on the need for "Social Democratic hegemony" in the "bourgeois" revolution.

To the Mensheviks, particularly to Plekhanov and Akselrod, it was the Westerner, liberal vision that seemed by far the less objectionable of the two, since it corresponded fairly closely to their own minimum program for the first, the "bourgeois," revolution. By contrast, the SR platform — with its "hopeless confusion" between the tasks of the impending bourgeois revolution and the objectives of the eventual socialist overturn — appeared to them calculated to produce dangerous divisions within the ranks of the opposition to the regime.[30]

But Lenin and his Bolsheviks would have been hard put to decide which of the two views was the more harmful. To be sure, it was the SR's who, in their long-range program and especially in their definition of immediate objectives (in their program minimum), were coming closer — disturbingly close — to the conception of the "democratic revolution" for which Lenin himself was groping. Like the SR's, Lenin now looked forward to a democratic revolution that would encompass broad social and economic changes to facilitate the transition to socialism. Like the SR's, he foresaw that these reforms would be resisted not only by the gentry but also by the bourgeoisie — which would try for compromises and some sort of reconciliation with the autocracy. And like the SR's, he foresaw that this resistance would have to be overcome by a "firm democratic regime," truly reflective of the interests of the toiling masses.[31]

We should note that both conceptions were directed equally against the "feudal" gentry and the "capitalist" bourgeoisie — in fact, if not in theory, against all dominant groups and existing social forms in Russian life. Both views contained (though for quite different reasons, as we shall see) the implicit assumption of the legitimacy of only one party as the suitable voice for the toiling masses. But there the similarity ended. Although the SR's envisaged the overturn as the culmination of a natural,

[29] See Novobrantsev, and "Proekt programmy partii S-Rev," *Rev. ros.*, no. 46 (May 1904).
[30] A more comprehensive discussion may be found in Haimson, ch. 8.
[31] Haimson, ch. 8.

and hence irresistible, process — faithfully expressing the clear aspirations of a crushing majority of the Russian people — Lenin visualized it merely as one of two, almost equally possible, historical alternatives. The bourgeoisie might well patch up its differences with the autocracy and succeed in denying the fuzzy, instinctive desires of the popular masses, since its influence was infinitely more pervasive — and the masses infinitely less prepared to resist it — than the SR's chose to assume.

There is no need to summarize here the two revolutionary perspectives that Lenin was now to develop, and which he would later summarize in his "Two Tactics," but we should recognize the rationale that this theory offered for the legitimacy of a single-party center: the relative isolation of "conscious" revolutionary elements in existing society and the enormity of the tasks confronting them. They had to extricate the "spontaneous" peasant masses, and even the working-class movement, from the shackles of feudalism and from the more insidious and potent influence of the capitalist bourgeoisie; to place these masses under conscious socialist leadership and control; to expose ruthlessly the perfidious bourgeois influence, the "dressed-up liberals," hidden even in the most revolutionary parties.[32] The SR's, on the contrary, drew their instinctive sense of the legitimacy of a single party, at least at this moment, from the optimistic, exuberant image of a broad popular movement of peasants, workers, and intelligentsia, all equally intent on the overthrow of autocracy and the eventual establishment of socialism.[33]

On the eve of 1905, the programs of the Bolsheviks and the SR's were the most extreme manifestations of the general tendency in the opposition movement to stretch the careful, deliberate schedule that the Marxists and Populists of the 1890's had drawn of their political and social tasks. This blurring of vision was in most cases to be quickly dispelled by political realities. Yet it should be amply clear that it was precisely that confusion of political and social tasks, precisely this melange of visions and objectives, which — compounded by the blindness and ineptness of the autocracy — permitted the triumphant build-up of the opposition and revolutionary forces. It was this very confusion that facilitated the mobilization of the remarkably checkered coalition of antiautocratic, antibureaucratic, antifeudal, and anticapitalistic forces which, by October 1905, the autocracy was unable to curb. And, by the same token, it was this confusion that reflected most clearly the internal weaknesses to which this majestic movement would eventually succumb.

In 1889, the liberal publicist Dragomanov had argued hopefully that a nation-wide movement for political freedom could not be thwarted by a lack of brute strength, by a monoply of armed force in the hands of its opponents. "If a political regime is deprived of a surrounding atmosphere

[32] Haimson, ch. 8.
[33] See "Otvet Zare," *Rev. ros.*, no. 4 (February 1902).

of support, or at least of neutrality," he wrote, "it will fall — just as the French monarchy did in 1789, and Prussian absolutism, in 1848. These events transpired, not because the governments [in question] lacked physical strength, but because the moral atmosphere surrounding them prevented its use. . . . The Bonapartists found the strength to shoot up Paris, and the Hapsburgs, Vienna; the Hohenzollerns returned their army to Berlin [only] after divisions in public opinion were exposed." [34] The course of the 1905 Revolution was to confirm Dragomanov's diagnosis.

V

The "all-nation" movement against autocracy, which the leaders of the Osvobozhdenie had so deliberately and energetically mobilized, reached its majestic peak with the general strike of October 13–17, 1905. Confronted by the almost unanimous opposition of society, into which even the faithful business and industrial bourgeoisie had been swept in the summer and fall of 1905, the demoralized autocracy was forced to follow the course predicted by Dragomanov sixteen years earlier. Despite its continued monopoly of the instruments of violence — with all its talk of an armed uprising, the Bolshevik-dominated Central Committee of the RSDRP had at this moment fifty-odd Browning revolvers[35] — it was compelled to promise, in the October Manifesto, the civic and political rights demanded by Russian society.

The October Manifesto marked the high point of the nation-wide opposition movement. It also marked the beginning of its downfall. From this moment on, momentarily deceptive indications to the contrary — such as the working-class strikes of November and December 1905, the Moscow uprising, and the originally enthusiastic popular reception of the First Duma — the power and cohesion of the revolutionary forces slowly but surely began to decline, to the rising chorus of the mutual recriminations of the various opposition and revolutionary parties.

During the ensuing twenty months of political struggle, culminating in the dismal finale of the Stolypin *coup d'état* of June 3, 1907, each of the opposition parties would be guilty of more or less serious tactical errors. And since the errors of each party were based in part on a failure to predict accurately the course followed by its political rivals and allies, each felt justified in blaming the fiasco on other parties' inability, or unwillingness, to follow their "proper" political course. To weigh the relative merits of this long series of mutual recriminations would be futile: each of them, at least in part, was but a rationalization for failure; yet in the limited sense that each party's prospects had been adversely affected by

[34] Dragomanov, 51.
[35] V. S. Voitinsky, *Gody pobed i porazhenii* (2 vols.; Berlin, St. Petersburg, Moscow, 1923–1924), I, 162. Voitinsky's memoirs constitute perhaps the most dispassionate and revealing single account of 1905.

the political course of the other parties in the political spectrum, each was partially justified. More important for our purpose is to try to understand the precise character of the trials that the broad conceptions of political dynamics now underwent in the turmoil of the revolutionary storm.

The first of these conceptions, we must recall, one already elaborated by the orthodox Marxists in the 1890's, was that the coming revolution would be in the last analysis a bourgeois revolution which would bring to Russia the advanced Western, democratic political institutions corresponding to the interests and aspirations of the industrial proletariat and of the "capitalistic" bourgeoisie, the two class representatives of the new society. The Osvobozhdentsy liberals and the orthodox Marxists — the future Kadet leaders and the future Mensheviks — had been equally insistent that the coming revolution should not go beyond the objective limits assigned to it by history, by the current level of Russia's socioeconomic development, and by the aspirations or level of consciousness reached by the majority of Russian society. Both had foreseen, and would continue to foresee, that if the revolutionary movement swept beyond its historical limits, if it should seek through unwise political action to overturn its "objective" base, it would be condemned to defeat by an inexorable "Thermidorian" reaction. It is probably fair to say that, both before and after 1905, the Kadet and Menshevik leaders were as conscious of this danger as any revolutionary leaders in history. Yet despite this, their vision of the revolution and the political diagnoses that they drew from it were soon to be shattered on the reefs of political reality.

Why was the Kadet-Menshevik picture of the revolution so confounded by the course of events after October 1905? In the following period the two parties unveiled some serious tactical differences, and each consequently accused the other of having "deviated" from the original true vision. These differences gave rise to periodic practical conflicts between the two groups which in some degree hindered the effectiveness of their alliance. But it is the degree to which the leaders of both parties succeeded, through the vicissitudes of these revolutionary years, in remaining true to their common vision and to each other that is truly remarkable. And it is in the very character of this common vision that the ultimate sources of their defeat must be sought.

In the years leading up to 1905 the Mensheviks and the Kadets had predicted repeatedly, and quite accurately as it turned out, that — to misuse a Marxist adage of the 1890's — either the bourgeois revolution would be achieved with the aid of the bourgeoisie or it would not be achieved at all. The ultimate cause of their defeat was that, unknown to them, the 1905 Revolution was not a bourgeois revolution. To be precise, it was a bourgeois revolution during the short period from the summer of 1905 to the October Manifesto when certain elements of big business and the industrial bourgeoisie actually joined in the nation-wide movement against the autocracy. But then there had come the momentous, unsettling events of October, November, and December 1905 — the issuance of the October Manifesto itself with its sweeping promise of political reform, the November economic strikes of the Petersburg workers, the bloody Moscow uprising — and as precipitously as they had been swept into the opposition movement, the business and industrial elements had withdrawn to join with frightened "gentry liberals" and representatives of the bureaucracy in the formation of new parties. In the programs of these new parties, such as the Commercial-Industrial Party and the larger Union of the 17th of October (the two would merge after the dissolution of the First Duma), the Mensheviks and their Kadet allies might have discerned the emergence of a far more up-to-date, more explicitly bourgeois ideology than the constituent elements of these parties had ever before manifested. In the face of the revolutionary threat of the expropriation of their landed estates, the gentry supporters of the Octobrists now abandoned all traces of their earlier paternalistic attitudes toward the village commune and firmly supported Stolypin's program of agricultural reorganization as the proper basis for the development of a spirit of "individual enterprise" and "respect for property" among the peasant masses. As for the businessmen and industrialists who had now allied themselves with the gentry, many of them now displayed a new appreciation for the importance of legality in the functioning of the Russian state. And most significant of all, those new "moderate" parties of the right supported, in the name of these very principles of "order," "legality," and "respect for property," the government's suppression of revolutionary disorders and its eventual dissolution of the first two Dumas.[36]

The significance of the appearance of the Octobrists was not only that it indicated where the sympathies of the bourgeoisie really lay, but also that it provided the demoralized government with a new basis of support in "society," freeing it from the paralysis of the October days. From this point on, the government felt able to strike back at the opposition and revolutionary forces.

Since both Kadets and Mensheviks had been so emphatic about the danger of transcending the objective limits of political action, and since the Mensheviks in particular had been so insistent on the need for bourgeois participation in the bourgeois revolution, why did neither group call a halt to the "assault on autocracy" in the light of these symptomatic signs after the issuance of the October Manifesto, or at least after the opening of the First Duma? Why did they not accept the new legal and political framework that had been established, as one truly corresponding to the existing equilibrium of forces, and rest their hopes for Russia's

---

[36] See the remarkably dispassionate account in F. Dan and N. Cherevanin, "Soiuz 17 Oktiabria," in Y. O. Martov, D. Maslov, A. Potresov, eds., *Obshchestvennoe dvizhenie v Rossii v nachale XX — go veka* (3 vols.; St. Petersburg, 1909–1914), III.

political future in the further natural development of social, economic, and cultural forms? This was the kind of self-restraint for which Struve now desperately called, but the Kadet and Menshevik leaders failed to display it, due (so Struve insisted) to their traditional intelligentsia revolutionary psychology.[37]

I think that we can ascertain two main assumptions underlying the two groups' head-on pursuit of the "bourgeois revolution" well after the bourgeoisie had actually deserted from their camp. The first of these, to which the Kadets held with particular devotion, was that the development of the modern, advanced, industrialized society that they saw irresistibly emerging in Russia would necessarily entail the progressive realization in political and social life of the principles of freedom and social justice. One may find touching expressions of this faith in the writings of most Russian liberals of the period — from the naive and inflated sociological demonstrations of Maxim Kovalevsky to the far more sophisticated historical analysis of Paul Miliukov.[38] It was this instinctive belief in the golden laws of progress which made the Kadets so confident of the objective basis in Russian life for the realization of their "advanced" social and political objectives (all immediate evidence to the contrary), and which blinded them to the possibility that an excessive radical course might involve permanent political setbacks.

The second of these deluding assumptions, which was especially important for the Mensheviks, was that the Kadets represented a "bourgeois" party. Even though the Kadets occasionally attracted bourgeois voters, this was an erroneous, or at best a meaningless, assumption: for the Kadets were, first and foremost, a party of the intelligentsia, a quite distinctive social and political category even if it happened to be missing in the Marxist scheme of things. The assumption that the Kadets were a bourgeois party helped the Menshevik leaders to rationalize, indeed impelled them to believe in, the "objective" validity of the political course that after October they were all too inclined to pursue. For as long as the Kadets stood with them in the opposition, as long as this "bourgeois" party had not fully assumed the reigns of political power, they felt justified in believing that the historically prescribed course of the bourgeois revolution had not yet been completed — and that they had, therefore, every right to push on.

Underlying the readiness of these two groups to hold on to these assumptions in the face of adverse political circumstances, there was undoubtedly the large dose of the traditional intelligentsia prejudice to

[37] See especially, "Iz razmyshlenii o russkoi revoliutsii," in P. B. Struve, *Patriotica* (St. Petersburg, 1911), 20–43.

[38] See, for example, Kovalevsky's "Vzaimootnoshenie svobody i obshchestvennoi solidarnosti," in K. Arsenev, ed., *Intelligentsiia v Rossii* (Moscow, 1910); and Miliukov's *Russia and Its Crisis* (Chicago, 1906).

which Struve had pointed: a persistent — if now less overt — sense of estrangement from the whole fabric of the existing order; a consequent impatience for broad social, as well as political, reforms; a readiness to use the instrumentalities of the state power to enforce changes rather than waiting for "objective processes" to bring them about.

But to what extent could the Kadet and Menshevik leaders have changed the course of the opposition and revolutionary movement had they more sternly contained these "fatal inclinations" of their intelligentsia natures? Very little, I think, for the simple reason that once again 1905 was not an orderly "bourgeois" revolution, but rather a spontaneous upsurge of heterogeneous elements seeking to overturn the whole existing order. The seemingly irresistible character of the revolutionary wave in the initial stages of the revolution was due to the fact that it mobilized not only the long-standing protests against the crumbling traditional order but also the resentments against the pains and dislocation of the early stages of the "capitalistic," and specifically industrial, development that the autocracy had attempted to push at so rapid and forceful a tempo. Thus, to use the language of the intelligentsia left, 1905 was the compressed expression of outbursts of revolt against "capitalism" as well as "feudalism," against "bourgeois" as well as "gentry" rule.

VI

During the politically torpid and often demoralizing years that immediately followed the *coup d'état* of June 1907, a number of prominent intelligentsia figures issued a series of powerful appeals for a fundamental reassessment of the intelligentsia's traditional attitudes and values. They urged the intelligentsia — now that a modern society perfectly capable of deciding its own fate had come to political life — to give up their "outdated" wholesale involvement in politics and instead to follow the rules, to enjoy the fruits of a normal civilized existence.[39]

Of these appeals, perhaps the sharpest and the most pointed were those issued by that remarkable figure, Peter Struve. In his contribution to the *Vekhi* symposium (1909),[40] and in his articles in *Russkai mysl',*[41] Struve urged the intelligentsia to alter their ways in two important and largely complementary respects. First he called on them to give up their obsession with revolutionary politics, their tendency to evaluate all prob-

[39] See contributions by N. A. Berdiaev, S. N. Bulgakov, M. O. Gershenzon, A. S. Ozgoev, B. A. Kistiakovsky, and P. B. Struve, in M. O. Gershenzon, ed., *Vekhi* (Moscow, 1909). Also N. A. Berdiaev, *Dukhovnyi krizis intelligentsii* (Moscow, 1910); B. A. Kistiakovsky, *Stranitsy proshlago. K istorii konstitutsionnago dvizheniia v Rossii* (Moscow, 1912); A. S. Izgoev, *Russkoe obshchestvo i revoliutsiia* (Moscow, 1910); and P. B. Struve, *Patriotica* (St. Petersburg, 1911).

[40] Entitled "Intelligentsiia i revoliutsiia."

[41] See particularly "Velikaia Rossiia," *Rus. mysl',* I (1908), and "Otryvki o gosudarstve," *Rus. mysl',* V (1908), in *Patriotica,* 73–108.

lems — all areas of life — on the basis of rigid, usually completely mis-
placed, ideological criteria. He urged them to lead stable and fruitful
lives, to invest their energies, in an orderly way, in suitable social and
cultural activities, and to enjoy these activities for their own sake. His
second major point was that the intelligentsia should develop at long
last what he termed a sense of *gosudarstvennost'*. By this word, Struve
now meant to denote a sense of the continuity of institutions, a respect
for, or at least a certain restraint in the face of, historical traditions, a
sense of law — in substance, an understanding of the slow, halting, and
painful character of the process that had been involved in the growth of
Russian civilization and of the social and the political forms in which
it was now enclosed. Only such an understanding, Struve firmly believed,
only an awareness of the "elemental" conditions of cruelty and savagery
from which existing institutions had ultimately emerged and to which
their destruction might bring a return, could impose on desires for radical
political changes the restraining influence of a sense of reality.

In this appeal for a more acute and realistic sense of the public interest, and in his more specific political pleas of the period, Struve was attempting to convince his readers that only by agreeing to operate under
the existing social and political order — by dedicating themselves within
its framework to professional pursuits, helpful to the development of
Russian society and culture — could they expect to exercise a genuinely
creative and transforming influence on the evolution of the state order
itself.

But most of Struve's critics chose to interpret his appeal as a complete
repudiation of the intelligentsia's glorious revolutionary tradition, a slur
on its saintly succession of heroes and martyrs. Those who felt compelled
to answer the substance of his arguments concentrated on one major
debating point: the alleged contradiction between Struve's plea for the
repudiation of the intelligentsia's tradition of *sotsialnost'* (the almost
compulsive absorption that it had displayed throughout its history in
political and social problems) and his appeal, on the other hand, for a
new sense of *gosudarstvennost'*, for a new statesmanlike concern for the
national interest.[42] In Struve's eyes such a sense of political responsibility
required above all a display of political moderation and realism. But to
his traditionally minded intelligentsia critics a call to "public duty" could
only mean one thing: a demand for an even more intensive effort to mold
Russia's fate "directly" by destroying, reforming, or assuming control of
the state power — the organizational center of the whole complex of
Russia's economic, social, and cultural institutions. Hence they discovered
in Struve's pleas a contradiction which was not really there, a misunder-

---

[42] See N. Avksentev and others, *Vekhi kak znamenie nashego vremeni* (Moscow,
1910), especially the contributions by L. Shishko and N. Gardenin (V. M. Chernov).

standing which mirrored only too clearly the persistent hold of their own "intelligentsia" prejudices.

Actually, in the years following the dissolution of the Second Duma, the leadership of the Kadet Party, and indeed much of the intelligentsia at large, heeded Struve's conception of duty in practice if not in theory. Many in the intelligentsia, deserting their traditional allegiance to the revolutionary cause, were now absorbed into the normal, humdrum, and useful professional existence that they had formerly despised and had undergone as a result an inevitable mellowing of outlook. The Kadet deputies in the Third Duma, their numbers now drastically reduced by changes in the electoral law, as well as by the unquestionable, if temporary, swing of public opinion to the right, began to follow cautious, businesslike, "constructive" parliamentary tactics, of which even a Maklakov could feel proud.

This Kadet sagacity — compounded by the Octobrists' subservience to the arbitrary and often illegal turns in government policy — was to be rewarded in the elections to the Fourth Duma by a sharp rise in the Kadet vote, particularly in the pre-eminently bourgeois First and Second Curiae of the cities.[43] And most helpful of all, the sessions of the Fourth Duma saw the emergence of a growing collaboration between Kadets and now dissillusioned Octobrists which promised the eventual ascendancy of a moderate, yet liberal, center. This almost came about, but only during the First World War with the organization in the summer of 1915 of the Progressive Bloc.

Did the gravitation of so many in the intelligentsia toward the new semiparliamentary institutions, the already established organs of self-government, and the normal cares of professional roles that occurred in the wake of 1905 indicate that Russia had now entered an era of growing social and political stability? Most historians of the period would say that it did and would argue that only the added strains and dislocations of the First World War kept the bright promise of the years leading up to 1914 from being fulfilled.

Indeed, there were many further signs of progress in Russian national life during those years: evidence of a new flowering in the cultural life of the intelligentsia, now largely freed from the obsession of radical politics; indications that, beginning in 1909, Russia's industrial growth had not merely resumed much of its earlier pace but had become more self-sustaining and independent of the artificial stimulus of state subsidies; evidence that the communal institutions which had so greatly hindered the development of Russian agriculture were rapidly disintegrating, and that a new class of ambitious, property-minded peasant proprietors had

[43] See A. Martynov, "Istoriia konstitutsionno-demokraticheskoi partii," and Cherevanin in *Obshchestvennoe dvizhenie*, III.

emerged in the Russian countryside. Yet, by the light of historical hind-
sight at least, one might have discerned certain disquieting features in
this bucolic scene, or raised a number of disturbing questions.

One might even have questioned the optimistic inferences that were
now being drawn from the evident disintegration of the sectarian dogmas
and ethos that had hitherto kept so many in the intelligentsia together,
and apart from existing society. To be sure, for a large and vocal element
in the intelligentsia, this disintegration of traditional values and loyalties
opened the way for a genuine reabsorption into the framework of national life. But to what degree did this breakdown of traditional bonds also
contribute to the embitterment, the "hardening," of those irreconcilable
factions of the intelligentsia "left" which, in 1917, would help sweep away
both the existing order and the traces of old intelligentsia culture? And
perhaps most important of all, how many of those in the intelligentsia
who joined in the flight from radical politics, and indeed from any political involvement, after 1905 found themselves unable in succeeding
years to gain new values to replace those that they had lost? How many
were there who shared, however inarticulately, Alexander Blok's sense
of the continued thinness of Russia's civilized layers and his readiness to
capitulate, as one of the privileged few, before a new revolutionary
holocaust? [44]

Blok's pessimism about the thinness of contemporary Russian culture
brings to mind perhaps the most important and the most difficult issue
to be raised about the developments of this period. To what extent did
the contemporary mood of the Russian masses correspond to the sentiments of those in the intelligentsia who were now reabsorbed into existing society? The industrial workers and, to a lesser degree, the peasantry
had risen in 1905 in a largely instinctive burst of revolt against the conditions of their existence. Were their varied, amorphous resentments against
the crumbling traditional order and the painful dislocations attendent
to the rise of a modern world now being assuaged, or were they slowly
building up toward a new — more general and more violent — outburst?
If the latter was the case, the new mood of political moderation and, in
some cases, political indifference which was now being displayed by
many intelligentsia circles could well have meant that the few connecting
links between these intelligentsia groups (and the society that they had
rejoined) and the masses were now gradually being cut, leaving the latter
completely exposed to the embittered pleas of the intelligentsia extreme
left.

Even the greatest governmental achievement of the period, the measures that Stolypin so forcefully initiated for the dissolution of communal
agriculture, opened some disturbing immediate perspectives in this connec-

---

[44] See A. Blok, *Intelligentsiia i revoliutsiia* (St. Petersburg, 1918), a collection of
articles written between 1905 and 1917.

tion. For these policies meant the introduction of new dislocations in village life, largely imposed in practice if not in theory by governmental fiat. How would the masses of the peasantry respond to these dislocations? Would their grievances mount up against the more prosperous individual farmers and, combined with their never wholly suppressed desire to obtain the remaining gentry lands, give rise to new and more potent revolutionary outbreaks? To be sure, the peasants were quiet in the years leading up to 1914, but how might they respond to new revolutionary disorders in the cities, particularly among the industrial workers? The question is not entirely academic since we do witness a new upsurge of opposition sentiments in 1913–1914 and, particularly, a dramatic rise in the curve of industrial strikes which, even according to official governmental statistics, were now assuming an increasingly "political" character.[45]

VII

A student of 1917 finds it hard to escape the impression that Lenin and his followers won their victory largely by default — largely as a result of the failure of the other parties of the left to grasp the opportunities that had once been theirs. The burden of responsibility for the defeat that the concept of multiparty representative government now underwent lay most heavily on the leaders of the Menshevik and Socialist Revolutionary parties; for, unlike the Kadets, these parties were not lacking in popular support at the moment when the breakdown of the old regime called them to the center of the political stage.

Yet the failure of the leaders of the moderate left in 1917 is by no means easy to specify. Indeed, the first impression that one might draw from a comparison between the political attitudes that they now expressed and the sentiments which had been voiced by the earlier generation of Russian radicals would be the realization of how close they had finally come to the spirit of representative government. In practice, if not in theory, the Mensheviks and SR's of 1917 were no longer animated by the sense of radical estrangement from society which had traditionally impelled Russian radical circles to dismiss any but the most drastic changes

[45] The statistical data published by the Ministry of Trade and Industry list 466 strikes involving 105,110 workers in 1911, 2,032 strikes involving 725,491 workers in 1912, 2,404 strikes involving 887,096 workers in 1913, and 3,466 strikes involving roughly 1,300,000 workers during the first seven months of 1914 (the highest figure since 1906). Of these totals the following percentages are listed as "political": 5.1 per cent of the strikes, 8 per cent of the strikers in 1911, 64 per cent of the strikes and 75 per cent of the strikers in 1912, 54 per cent of the strikes and 56 per cent of the strikers in 1913, and 70 per cent of the strikes (2,565) and 75 per cent of the strikers (1,059,111) in 1914. These figures only cover strikes in factories under governmental inspection. See Ministerstvo torgovli i promyshlennosti, *Svod i otchetov fabrichnykh inspektorov* for the years 1911, 1912, 1913, and 1914 (St. Petersburg, 1912, 1913, 1914, 1915).

in existing political and social institutions. Unlike the Radicals of the
1860's and the Bolsheviks of 1917, they were possessed by no burning
desire to seize the levers of political power to destroy the old, or to install
a new, framework of national life. Indeed, they were now, all too eagerly,
prepared to recognize the legitimacy of the current demands and interests of other groups in Russian society, and the claims to political authority of the parties through which these groups purportedly spoke.
On almost every major issue that arose in 1917 — the question of peace or
war, the settlement of the land question, the timing of the election to the
Constituent Assembly — the majority leaders of the Mensheviks and
the SR's compromised with the wishes of the rightist parties, at the price
of denying the clear aspirations of their own popular following.[46]

Paradoxically, in the visage of political moderation that the Mensheviks and the SR's maintained through 1917, in the exaggerated degree to
which they consistently made concessions to parties which, by a more
natural logic, they might have viewed as their rivals for power, we might
find the reflection of the traditional intelligentsia prejudices still present
in attitudes toward representative government.

To understand the Mensheviks' and the SR's reluctance to assume
the responsibilities of power at this time, one must recall the terms under
which the Russian radicals had been converted to the view that something useful could be achieved by winning a decisive voice in the political
process for the constituent groups of Russian society. In the radicals'
theoretical tenets at least, the conversion to the cause of political freedom
had not been based on any wholehearted reconciliation to the legitimacy
of the existing framework of national life. Rather, it had been justified by
the historical forecast that once the existing social order was liberated
from the shackles of autocracy, it would more quickly destroy itself and
give birth to the socialist utopia.

To be sure, the adoption of a more dynamic view of the interplay
between politics and social life had given rise among the Russian radicals
to more positive attitudes toward the role of representative institutions.
It had awakened in many of them a new sense of the legitimacy, or at
least of the inevitability, of the presence of the variety of social and political tendencies that were now emerging in Russian life. Yet this recognition of the legitimacy of a multiparty system had been, and continued to
be, phrased by most of the Russian radicals in wholly provisional terms.
Until 1917 it remained an almost axiomatic article of their faith that
"basic class conflicts," and therefore the legitimate existence of basic po-

[46] The literature on 1917 is, of course, enormous. The accounts that I have found
most useful are P. N. Miliukov, *Istoriia vtoroi russkoi revoliutsii* (Sofia, 1921–1924),
I, pts. 1–3; and *Vospominaniia* (New York, 1955), II; Oliver H. Radkey, *The
Agrarian Foes of Bolshevism* (New York, 1958), a splendid study of the SR's in
1917; and N. Sukhanov (N. N. Gimmer) *Zapiski o revoliutsii* (7 vols.; Berlin, St.
Petersburg, Moscow, 1922–1923).

litical differences, would come to an end with the establishment of socialism.

It was in part this dogma — that the legitimacy of a genuine multiparty system was not rooted in any natural order of things and was justified only for a limited historical period — which crippled the effectiveness of the right-wing Mensheviks, and even of the moderate SR's, in 1917. From this dogma the Mensheviks concluded, and taught their followers (including many of their SR allies), that they should not assume any of the prerogatives of power until "objective conditions" had finally put an end to the legitimacy of "bourgeois" rule. From this they also drew the inference that their assumption of power would coincide with the end of the legitimate tenure of bourgeois interests and bourgeois parties in Russian life. In the last analysis, it was these two beliefs which, more decisively than the political immaturity of the masses or the wiles of the Bolsheviks or even the war, trapped the parties of the moderate left and brought on the decisive defeat of representative government in 1917.

The realities of political life now confronted the moderate socialist parties with an insoluble dilemma. To refuse to assume any of the responsibilities of power would have meant, so they thought, to surrender the country to anarchy, to an eventual counterrevolution of the right or, as events actually demonstrated, to their eager Bolshevik rivals on the left. To assume all the prerogatives of power, on the other hand, would have amounted to a declaration that the legitimate presence in Russian society of bourgeois interests and bourgeois parties had once and forever come to an end.

It may well be that at this moment of truth the Mensheviks and the majority of the SR's hesitated to assume power because they had finally come to realize the inherent falseness of the view that freedom could be maintained without a permanent recognition of the legitimate presence in political life of basic differences of values and interests. In practice, however, they strove to straddle the issue. Confronted by the evident inability of the bourgeois parties to mobilize adequate social support, they entered a coalition government to prolong the life of the democratic political order that had come into being. But, obsessed as they were by the illegitimacy of assuming political authority in such a pluralistic political context, they failed to assume the prerogatives of power, and thus failed in their duty to represent with sufficient vigor the aspirations of their own following, the majority of the Russian people.

After all, what did the mass followers of the parties of the left desire in 1917? Clearly they wanted peace and land, at virtually any price. But even more, from the opening days of the revolution, most of the workers, in Petrograd at least, appeared to feel that they were arrayed against "bourgeois society" and a "bourgeois state," as well as against the crumbling autocracy. From the first they recognized only the authority of their "own" leading organ, the Petrograd Soviet, and pressed their reluctant "representatives" in the Soviet to check the menace of "bourgeois reaction" — to take more and more of the "power" into their own hands.[47]

Such a sense of isolation from "society" had already arisen among the Petrograd workers in the closing days of 1905. But in this earlier episode, this feeling had come to them as an unwelcome discovery, as the bitter fruit of their defeats after the exhilarating days of the October general strike. Twelve years later, it assumed from the very start the character of a more belligerent, more articulate, and more generalized opposition to the whole existing political, social, and economic order.

It was the sense of the chasm that had now opened between "society," including the liberal intelligentsia, and the masses which impelled Miliukov, in the first days of 1917, to plead — in the tones of a Struve or a Maklakov — for the rights of the youthful Alexis to succeed to the throne. Much to the surprise of some of his colleagues, the leader of the Kadets now argued that it was imperative to maintain some continuity in the state power, if the country was not to descend into anarchy.[48] It was this same sense that the Provisional Government and his own party were operating in an almost complete vacuum that also impelled Miliukov to insist from the very beginning on the formal support of the Petrograd Soviet and of the moderate socialist parties.[49] The most prominent figure of the liberal intelligentsia had now been transformed in the eyes of the Petrograd workers into one of the "Messieurs, the bourgeois Ministers," and he knew it.

By July 1917 the unrest among the Petrograd workers (skillfully exploited by the Bolsheviks, to be sure) would explode into a rebellious insistence that *their* socialist representatives, *their* Soviet, take all the "power" away from the "bourgeoisie." "Take the power, you son of a bitch, since it is being offered to you," an irate worker told the frightened Chernov (then already Minister of Agriculture) during the July demonstrations.[50] In the face of such popular feelings, the more moderate socialist leaders had already felt compelled, some months earlier, to take some of the power for fear that otherwise they would shortly have to take it all.

Such problems did not embarrass a man like Lenin. He, alone among the socialist leaders, was from the first moment of his return to Russia not only prepared but eager to take all of the power — even at the price of exploiting the blind, "spontaneous" instincts of the masses. Indeed it may be argued that, in part, Lenin's image of the revolution and the

---

[47] There is substantial agreement on this general point between Miliukov and Sukhanov, two observers of quite different political views, but equal political acumen. See Miliukov, Istoriia, I, pt. 1, chs. 2–4, and Sukhanov, I, chs. 1–6.

[48] See Miliukov, Istoriia, I, pt. 1, 53–56, and Vospominaniia, II, 316–318.

[49] Miliukov, Istoriia, I, pt. 1, 46–49.

[50] Miliukov, Istoriia, I, pt. 1, 244.

revolutionary instincts of the workers had now temporarily merged. The mood of the workers in 1917 was clearly to destroy the whole existing political and social structure — the "capitalistic" as well as the autocratic state, "bourgeois" as well as "gentry" rule. And this was precisely what Lenin was now urging them to do. The task of the socialist proletariat, he argued in *State and Revolution,* was not merely to conquer the existing state structure, but to destroy it. The working class had to "shatter," "break up," "blow up," the whole existing "state machine" until "not a single stone" would be left standing.[51] This vision — along with Lenin's demagogic appeals — put him temporarily in accord with the mood of the popular masses.

To be sure, we find even in *State and Revolution* a more ambivalent view of the state than most of Lenin's rank-and-file followers were able to discern. Almost every page in this curious document reflects, under the thin coating of Marxist phraseology, an emphasis on the centrality of the role of state power in organizing, controlling, propping up (for the time being at least) the whole structure of Russian social and economic life. In terms reminiscent of the revolutionary appeals of the 1860's, *State and Revolution* repeatedly stresses the proposition that it is only after the proletarian dictatorship is consolidated that it will begin to wither away.[52]

This belief in the centrality of the role of state power was perhaps the key element in Lenin's image of the revolution. If from the very first he was so eager to wrest the "power" away from the bourgeoisie — and from any parties willing to compromise with it — it was not because he was less aware than any other socialist leader that, by all the conventional Marxist yardsticks, Russia was "still a peasant country, one of the most backward in Europe."[53] Rather it was because he assigned less significance than they to "objective" social and economic criteria, and more to the role of political power, in the overthrow of bourgeois society and in the building of socialism. Similarly, if, before and after the Bolshevik seizure of power, Lenin was so unwilling to abide by democratic electoral procedures, if he was so reluctant to let the Bolsheviks share the power with other parties, it was not simply because he was more driven than other socialist leaders by personal ambition. It was also because he was ani-

[51] See *State and Revolution,* Vanguard Press edition (New York, 1929), 135, 138, 144, 146–147, 218–219.

[52] Lenin repeatedly denounces the view of the Marxist "opportunists" that capitalism can be eliminated without the complete overthrow of the bourgeois state, without the most ruthless elimination of its political and administrative institutions and relations (pages 125–126, 128–129, 210–211, 213, 220). But he is equally impelled to point out to his opponents on the left, the Anarchists, that during the transition to Communism, the power of the state will be an indispensable lever for the class transformation — for the suppression of the evil minority by the majority (pages 166–170, 216–217, 220–221).

[53] "Farewell Letter to the Swiss Workers" (April 8, 1917), in *Sochineniia* (3rd ed., Moscow, 1935–1937), XXIX, 343.

mated by a far more "generous" view of the uses to which he and his party could put the political authority imbedded in the state.[54]

Political action always represented for Lenin a crucial, and quite independent, dimension in human affairs. Throughout his career he was never willing to concede that his party should constitute merely the passive expression of the level of consciousness and organization attained by the working class which it purported to represent. Almost as consistently he tended to discern in the political authority of the state not simply the reflection of an independently developing society but perhaps the chief mold in which the attitudes and institutions of this society were shaped. And, largely for this reason, the Western view of political representation, as an instrument of control over the state by social groups in some way independent of its influence, always remained in his eyes a meaningless or at best a highly deceptive conception.

After the dissolution of the Constituent Assembly and the elimination of the representatives of all other socialist parties from any significant share in the "Soviet power," Lenin wrote, in answer to his critics:

Now it is this dialectic which the traitors, numbskulls, and pedants of the Second International could never grasp: the proletariat cannot conquer without winning a majority of the population over to its side. But to limit this winning over of the population, or to make it conditional, on "acquiring" a majority of votes in an election, *while the bourgeoisie is in power,* is an impracticable imbecility or simply cheating the workers. In order to win a majority of the population over to its side, the proletariat must first overthrow the bourgeoisie, and seize the state power into its own hands; secondly, having smashed to bits the old state apparatus, it must introduce the Soviet power, by which action it immediately undermines the dominion, authority, and influence of the bourgeoisie, and the petty-bourgeois compromisers among the majority of the nonproletarian laboring masses, through the revolutionary fulfillment of their economic needs at the expense of the exploiters.[55]

In this statement, written well before the authoritarian tendencies in Soviet life had reached their full bloom, one can already see the degree to which the Bolsheviks would feel free — by the "natural" and "logical" order of things — to use the power of their party and state to shape the conditions of "representation" in the society over which they ruled.

To be sure, the picture of the proletarian dictatorship during the "transition to socialism" that Lenin drew in 1917 was almost anarchistic in its simplicity and mildness: no independent administrative class would be needed to govern it, no special police would be needed to guard it, since it would constitute, in the most literal sense, the rule of the majority of the people.[56] In this measured, almost miserly, image of authority no

[54] See Leonard Schapiro, *The Origin of Communist Autocracy* (Cambridge, Mass., 1955), part 1, for a splendid account of the evolution of Lenin's attitude toward the seizure of power and collaboration with other socialist parties in 1917.

[55] In *Sochineniia* (3rd ed.), XXIV, 641.

[56] See *State and Revolution,* 149–151, 155–156, 165, 195, 205–206.

specific role was even assigned to the party, the molder and guardian of the workers' consciousness which had been given such sweeping powers in the struggle to overthrow the old order.

It is at least possible that in the days before October Lenin actually visualized the role of his party — following the destruction of the autocratic and bourgeois state — as one of relatively gentle leadership and guidance rather than heavy-handed control. But the modest image of the future role of the party that he may have held at the time hinged on a false assumption which, along with so many other aspects of his outlook, he had inherited from the radicals of the 1860's: a belief that the more radical the destruction of the existing state order and of the whole complex of social and economic relations that it supported, the easier it would be eventually to establish a stateless, truly free, and harmonious society. Little, probably, did Lenin realize that, before destroying all other, independent, social and administrative forms, in a society born in a vacuum, resting solely on the ruins of the past, individuals would necessarily be compelled to look, more than ever before, for the definition of their rights and duties, for the pattern of their lives, for their very identity — not to themselves or to each other — to his new party and state.

THE COURTS AND THE LEGAL SYSTEM

JOHN N. HAZARD

I

The Soviet court had achieved a complete break with the past by early 1919 in the eyes of the Commissar of Justice, D. I. Kursky. In jubilation he wrote:

Neither Roman law nor subsequent bourgeois law gave such authority to a judge. Perhaps we can find some analogy in more ancient primitive law. But one has only to consider the whole complexity of contemporary social relationships and to contrast these with the primitive usage which was developed into a norm by the elders, by the immeasurable difference between the sources of primitive law and of the new law created by the proletarian revolution.[1]

The commissar was saying that the Russian revolution had ended continuity between the Imperial and Soviet legal systems, not only in law but in the culture pattern of Russian society. Yet within the brief span

[1] See *Proletarskaia revoliutsiia i pravo*, no. 12–14 (1919), 24.

of three years he was back on the platform before his fellows of the
Commissariat of Justice explaining an apparent reversal of policy.[2] A civil
code was to be enacted which he admitted created a close resemblance
to the legal pattern existing prior to the revolution and to the pattern of
law found in other states influenced by Roman law. In short, continuity
of civil law was being restored in the cultural sense, and the blame was
being laid at the door of the English bourgeoisie. It was this hated class
through its prime minister, Lloyd George, that was said to be forcing
the new Soviet Russian state to adopt a system of law which was sufficiently predictable and familiar to attract English capital to a nearly
destitute Russia.

It is tempting to draw the conclusion from developments in the Soviet legal system as it was prepared for the needs of the New Economic
Policy that continuity with all that had happened since 1864 was being
re-established in the legal sphere after nearly five years of experimentation with novel institutions and novel law and procedure.[3] There is much
evidence to support such a conclusion. Yet the Bolsheviks continued to
claim that their legal system, even in its NEP form, could not be considered related to that of the past. Soviet legal philosophers attempted
to explain the difference in terms of new wine in old bottles, or as Eugene
B. Pashukanis preferred to say, as new content in old bourgeois forms.[4]
Pashukanis was subsequently denounced for even this limited acceptance
of the influence of the past, and those who came after him belittle the
affinity of Soviet and pre-Soviet codes by saying that there was continuity
only of terminology, while both form and content had been changed with
the advent of the new Soviet type of socialist economy.[5]

Two distinguished non-Communist legal scholars in France have also
held that continuity with the past was broken by the Bolshevik revolution.
Baron Nolde has written that "the Soviet legal system, though it has borrowed important rules from the German and Swiss Codes, is nevertheless
an original and autonomous system. One might say that it is more economic than legal." [6] René David has said that of the five principal legal
systems of the world, one is the "system of the Soviet world, profoundly
different from the former [the Christian] by reason of the socialist structure of the societies to which it is applied, with all the consequences

[2] See D. I. Kursky, *Izbrannye stati i rechi* (Moscow, 1948), 70–73.

[3] "Continuity" is used herein to refer to continuation of forms and functions, and
not to the continuing applicability after the Russian revolution of Imperial statutes
and codes.

[4] See E. B. Pashukanis, "The Soviet State and the Revolution in Law," Lenin
et al., *Soviet Legal Philosophy*, trans. Hugh W. Babb (Cambridge, Mass., 1951),
268–280.

[5] See P. Yudin, "Socialism and Law," *Soviet Legal Philosophy*, 294.

[6] See Pierre Arminjon, Boris Nolde, and Martin Wolff, *Traité de droit comparé*
(Paris, 1950), I, 51.

which such a socialist structure, which is essentially an economic order, inevitably impose on the political, social and moral order." [7]

The fact that distinguished non-Soviet jurists deny as loudly as Soviet legal theorists that the Soviet system reflects historical continuity provides strong evidence that continuity has been broken, but there are eminent voices raised against this evidence. Oxford's Professor of Comparative Law, F. H. Lawson, has written:

How far is it [the Soviet] an original system? The question is complicated by the presence of an ideology which has not prevailed in the West, though it is not Russian but western in origin. However Russian the Soviet leaders may be they are in the Russian sense of the term westerners and not easterners of the Panslavic school drawing inspiration from the glorious Russian past. Yet some western observers are inclined to mark off Soviet law from western law precisely because of this prevailing Marxist ideology, which they say transforms the whole system. I doubt the accuracy of this diagnosis.[8]

The effort to determine whether continuity exists is made even more difficult by another complicating factor, namely that of semantics. The present writer has been criticized violently on occasion for using terminology of non-Soviet legal systems in describing Soviet legal institutions. He has been told that he should not use the words "court" or "judge" or "code of law" to describe Soviet tribunals or the rules they claim to be applying.[9] Such criticism requires the invention of new terminology to meet the special conditions of Soviet society, and, indeed, there is reason in support of such a demand because terminology automatically creates the impression of continuity when none may exist.

The basic difficulty in reserving established terminology for the Anglo-American system, and perhaps that of Western Europe and its heirs in Latin America, is that there exists wide variation throughout the world in the form of tribunal that settles disputes and in the principles used in their settlement, whether one looks at the ancient past or even at systems in various parts of the modern world such as pre-1911 China. Were the view to be adopted that established terminology must be reserved for a specific type of court and law, it would be necessary to develop a vocabulary of considerable size to describe the varying institutions that settle disputes and keep order in varying types of society so that those who read and run might not draw inaccurate conclusions.

[7] See René David, *Traité élémentaire de droit civil comparé* (Paris, 1950), 224.

[8] See F. H. Lawson, book review, *University of Chicago Law Review*, XXI (1953–1954), 780–781. The same view is held by Harold J. Berman: "Yet Soviet law is not a product of Marxian socialism alone. . . . Soviet law is also a product of Russian history. It is Russian law — just as our law is not 'capitalist' law or 'democratic' law but American law." See his *Justice in Russia: An Interpretation of Soviet Law* (Cambridge, Mass., 1950), 3.

[9] See Michael J. Kerley, *Washington State Bar News*, VI, no. 7 (February 1952), department of criticism page.

To the present writer, at least, the world seems to have given a negative answer to a demand for the creation of a new vocabulary, for in
every land and at every time legal institutions have generally been described in universal terms. Not many scholars have insisted that the
positivist is not a philosopher of law merely because he denies that
the principles enacted by a legislature as rules of conduct for a society
rest upon any immutable base such as that claimed by the natural-law
philosophers. If the positivists generally have a place in the pantheon of
the law, then the Soviet jurists cannot be excluded, for as John C. H. Wu
has written in the *Catholic Encyclopedia,* the doctrines espoused by
Andrei Vyshinsky when he was the foremost definition maker in the
USSR are but "positivism pushed to its logical end." [10]

Use of terms common to different societies in describing institutions
and rules designed to settle disputes must somehow be divorced from
any implication of continuity in Russian and Soviet society if we are to
avoid a debate over semantics. This will not be easy to achieve, for weight
is given to the continuity argument when words in continuous use for
centuries are employed to describe modern Soviet institutions; yet the
effort must be made to think of the words as "colorless," or the inquiry
into continuity will be defeated before it begins.

II

The contrast between old and new was drawn by the Bolsheviks
promptly after the Russian revolution. The institutions created by Alexander II in the judicial reform of 1864 [11] were nominally abolished by the
first Soviet decree on the courts.[12] It closed the doors of the three levels
of general courts created by the 1864 reform as well as the commercial
courts which had been functioning in Petrograd, Moscow, Odessa, and
Warsaw. The general courts had been created in 1864 to provide a forum
for the trial of all but relatively minor offenses and for the settling of
civil disputes except those of small value, the value varying with the type
of claim involved. While abolishing the general courts, the 1917 decree
was less disruptive of the former courts closely associated with the people
in whose name the revolution had been fought, namely the *volost* courts
and the Justice of the Peace courts.

The volost courts had been created by the Emancipation Act of 1861 [13]
to provide a state-sponsored tribunal for the peasantry to replace the
village courts previously functioning among the serfs. The jurisdiction of

[10] See the article "Law" in *The Catholic Encyclopedia,* Sixth Section, Supplement
II (1955), 13, column 1.

[11] For an analysis of the reform of 1864, see Samuel Kucherov, *Courts, Lawyers
and Trials under the Last Three Tsars* (New York, 1953).

[12] Decree No. 1 on the Courts, November 27, 1917 (1917) 1 *Sob. Uzak. RSFSR,*
No. 4, item 50.

[13] See *Polnoe sobranie zakonov,* no. 36657.

these volost courts as they continued to exist up to the time of the revolution had been limited to petty civil claims and criminal prosecutions
among the peasants. Control over them was exercised by the Ministry of
the Interior.

The Justice of the Peace courts had passed through periods of vicissi-
tude, but they had survived to 1917 in many urban communities of the
empire.[14] They had jurisdiction over civil claims up to five hundred rubles
in value, in contrast to the jurisdiction of the volost courts of one hundred
rubles, and in some cases they could hear claims of higher value, as with
real property actions. At the time of the revolution, their criminal jurisdiction was also limited, largely to crimes for which penalties might be
fines up to three hundred rubles in value or imprisonment for periods not
exceeding eighteen months.

The Soviet system inherited, as a result of the imperial legislation, a
structural pattern which included three court systems, and this fact was
reflected in the earliest Soviet decrees. The first Soviet decree abolished
only the general court system and declared that subsequently a decree
would define the courts that would replace it. The activity of the Justice
of the Peace courts was only suspended, to be undertaken by a substitute
institution composed of a single full-time judge and two lay judges to be
chosen in turn for each session of the court from a panel prepared for the
purpose. The work of the volost courts was absorbed in this new institution. Jurisdiction of the new court was limited as the Justice of the Peace
jurisdiction had been, the maximum in civil cases now being three thousand rubles, and in criminal cases crimes for which a penalty of up to
two years' imprisonment was provided by law. Appeals were to be forbidden unless the judgment exceeded one hundred rubles or there had been
a sentence in excess of seven days' detention. To hear such appeals there
was to be a review of the record without rehearing of witnesses by all of
the full-time judges of the county assembled as a "congress" from time to
time.

Outside of the new court system there was to be established a separate
set of tribunals to deal with cases of alleged counterrevolution. To the
Soviet officials of the time this tribunal seems to have been conceived as
being not a deliberative body bearing any relationship to the courts of the
past, but an instrument of the revolution, which meant in their minds an
institution which acted quickly and without any attempt to assure complete accuracy in determination of guilt if this seemed necessary to save
the regime of the Bolsheviks.

By February 1918, the specialists in the Commissariat of Justice had
prepared a second decree on the courts,[15] by which they created a system

---

[14] See Paul Vinogradov, *Self-Government in Russia* (London, 1915), 101.

[15] Decree No. 2 on the Courts, February 1918 [undated] (1918) 1 *Sob. Uzak.
RSFSR*, No. 26, item 347.

of courts, called District People's Courts, to try cases exceeding the jurisdiction of the local people's courts created by the first decree, and to hear cases held over from the old regime. There was to be more emphasis upon professionalism in the district courts, as evidenced by their structure. Civil claims were to be heard before a bench of three professional judges, supplemented by four lay judges, while criminal cases were to be heard by a bench of twelve lay judges and two alternate lay judges, chaired by one of the members of the staff of professional judges assigned to the court. The decree made no mention of any requirement of legal training for the professional judges, although it permitted judges of the old courts to be selected for the new positions, and, in fact, most of the early judges in these district courts were legally trained. To provide control over these courts a review of the record was to be permitted by a panel of judges elected for the purpose from among their own number by all district court judges in each province. Remand for new trial was permitted if the errors were found to be substantial, and also if the decision was found to be clearly unjust in substance. A "supreme court control" was ordered established in the capital to assure uniformity of practice in the district courts. Neither it, nor the intermediate review meetings of district court judges, was ever established, and the district courts themselves were reduced in jurisdiction by the third decree on the courts of July 20, 1918 [16] and absorbed completely in the local people's courts by the People's Court Act of November 30, 1918,[17] although the courts did not cease functioning until January 15, 1919.

Those who look for continuity see in the district courts the heirs of the general courts of the empire, and in the new people's courts the heirs of the Justice of the Peace and volost courts. Here was, indeed, a double system of courts structured in such a way as to place before one court the lesser cases measured in terms of money claimed or crime committed and the more complex cases, measured in the same terms, before a court of superior training and experience, and having as an integral part of its structure what amounted to a jury. To be sure, the jury now bore a new title, but it was similar in structure to a jury in that it was composed of laymen called to serve for the single case on which it sat. Further, the professional judges in the new district court usually had legal education as had been the case in the Imperial general courts, while the judges in the people's court had no such education but only such experience as they acquired in practice, like most of the Justices of the Peace in the empire whom they had replaced.

[16] Decree No. 3 on the Courts, July 20, 1918 (1918) 1 *Sob. Uzak. RSFSR*, No. 52, item 589.

[17] People's Court Act of 1918, November 30, 1918 (1918) 1 *Sob. Uzak. RSFSR*, No. 85, item 889.

Weight is lent to the theory of continuity by the evolution of the people's court after absorption of the district court in 1919. In this evolution specialization emerged. By a circular dated August 27, 1920 [18] and signed by Commissar Kursky, the councils of people's judges which had become the reviewing authority for the people's courts by the People's Court Act of 1918 were authorized to establish "special sessions" to have jurisdiction over cases referred by the provincial military tribunals and the security police (the Cheka), and also over the most important cases falling within the general jurisdiction of the people's courts. Here was a return to the concept of hierarchy within the court system based upon the complexity and seriousness of a case. Since the revolutionary tribunals and the Cheka continued the function of finding and eliminating political enemies, whether presumed or real, the hierarchy concept seems to have been based on the recognition that the courts created by the People's Court Act of 1918 were inadequate to the task of the complicated nonpolitical case.

The policy makers appear to have been forced against their will, after abolition of the district courts created by their Decree No. 2, to return in mid-1920 to a hierarchical court system. They thought this a retreat and continued to talk about a "single people's court," but in fact they had left behind the simplicity of structure for which they had struggled in earlier years. The actual establishment of the "special session" waited for another instruction of the Commissariat of Justice, dated September 16, 1920,[19] but the vital decision had been taken in August 1920.

Control by a supreme court was a concept to be approached carefully in Bolshevik thinking, but such control was foretold by a three-line note to the People's Court Act of 1920. By this note it was provided that the Commissariat of Justice would have the supreme control over criminal sentences and civil decisions of the people's courts and of the councils of people's judges in each province. The act gave no particulars of the new institution, but it was followed by a decree of March 10, 1921,[20] establishing details of what was called two years later by a Soviet historian "the prelude to the organization of a supreme cassational court."

By the events of 1920 and 1921 the stage was set for the judicial reform accompanying the introduction of the New Economic Policy. The draftsmen of the NEP reforms chose to pretend that they were creating a simple system, but in fact they created a three-stepped system, headed by a Supreme Court, no longer a department of the Commissariat of

[18] This circular seems not to have been placed in any published collection but was distributed in printed form directly to the courts and has been preserved as such with other circulars of the period.

[19] (1920) 1 *Sob. Uzak. RSFSR*, No. 100, item 541.

[20] (1921) 1 *Sob. Uzak. RSFSR*, No. 15, item 97.

Justice but an independent agency of government. The Judiciary Act of 1922[21] reintroduced a structure bearing an external resemblance, at least, to the three-level system of general courts in the empire. To be sure, the jury, as it had been operated under the empire, had disappeared in the 1922 act, but the courts of original jurisdiction were to have two lay judges on the bench. One could argue with the philosophers that quality changes with quantity to find that the element of popular control created by a jury had vanished because the number had been reduced from twelve to two. But if one takes such a position, it amounts to formalization of what is necessary to introduce popular influences into judicial decision making, and the Supreme Court has intimated in the United States that there is nothing mystical in the number twelve.[22]

Commissar Kursky might also have argued, in customary Marxist fashion, that the new court system was further different in quality from that of the empire. The old judges held over from the Imperial regime had gone. The judges were now men and women presumably imbued with the principles espoused by the Bolsheviks, if not themselves members of the Communist Party, and they were applying a law enacted by the new regime and not held over from the Imperial era.

This latter point is of major importance in any search for continuity and change, for it may well be that not institutions but what they do is the factor of major importance in any such determination. Before advancing to a consideration of substantive law, there must, however, be an examination of two factors of paramount importance in any study of courts: the prosecution and the bar.

III

The policy makers of 1917 seem to have felt that they required continuity of the institution called "court" to cope with disputes in society, but they were completely certain that they were through with a professional prosecution and bar. Neither institution was to survive the revolution, for it was presumed that in the new society with its anticipated high level of social consciousness, the community or at least an injured individual or his relatives would rise up to bring a social offender to court, and the accused or his relatives would appear in protection of the innocent if such protection had any foundation in fact. The judge was to be like a primitive chieftain, authorized to explore the dispute in detail, calling such witnesses as he wished, taking such views as he thought necessary, and interrogating the parties in his effort to make up his mind as to what had happened and what should be done.

[21] Judiciary Act of 1922, October 30, 1922 (1922) 1 *Sob. Uzak. RSFSR*, No. 69, item 902.

[22] See *Maxwell v. Dow*. 176 U.S. 581 (1899) in which the court held that since trial by jury had never been a necessary requisite of due process of law, a state statute permitting trial for a capital offense by a jury of eight was not unconstitutional.

Decree No. 1 [23] abolished the professional bar of the empire and thus broke institutional continuity with the past. It also abolished the system of prosecutors. Any blameless citizen of either sex having civil rights was to be permitted to appear as accuser or defender before the court from the moment of the beginning of the investigation. Yet the first decree did not prohibit payment of lawyer's fees, and some lawyers continued to practice and to appear under the permission granted to blameless citizens, but usually only when an appeal was taken to the congress of people's judges. The second decree on the courts,[24] recognizing as it did the need to carry on with cases inherited from the past and to try complicated new matters, permitted lawyers to appear on a professional basis. The decree also permitted courts to call to their aid professional accusers, although these were not yet organized as state prosecutors. Both defenders and prosecutors were to be enrolled in a "college" which was a panel from which courts might call persons to prosecute and individuals might see counsel. There was no prohibition against selecting persons from outside the college if no fee was paid, but to the extent that any professionalism was to enter into the relationship, the college could not be avoided.

The professional bar which was brought into existence for the district courts did not serve in the people's courts. Soon judges at the local level began to complain about their tasks, for they found the presentation of facts on behalf of the accused inadequate even when every effort was made to give the accused the opportunity to defend himself directly or through relatives. In June 1918, a general meeting of the Moscow professional local court judges adopted a resolution in favor of establishing a college of legal defenders to assist them with their work.[25] The first rules of procedure created for the people's local courts in the summer of 1918 [26] provided for practice by members of a college of defenders, although no such colleges had been created officially. Even with the new authorization, judges were permitted to exclude lawyers if a civil case seemed uncomplicated or concerned with divorce.

The People's Court Act of 1918 [27] created a "college of defenders, accusers, and representatives of the parties in civil suits." It made of the bar a salaried civil service available to the court. Here was something unimagined during the Imperial regime, but its novelty did not keep it alive even in a society favoring novel institutions. The Commissar of Justice returned to expose the abuses which had arisen under the civil-service system and demanded separation of the institution of accusers

[23] Cited above, note 12.
[24] Cited above, note 15.
[25] See *Proletarskaia revoliutsiia*, no. 12, (1918), 30.
[26] (1918) 1 *Sob. Uzak. RSFSR*, No. 53, item 597.
[27] Cited above, note 17.

from that of defenders and the discarding of the salary concept for counsel.[28]

Legal aid as a labor duty of those with legal education was made the next experiment by the People's Court Act of 1920.[29] A registry carried the names of those with competence, and a person desiring a lawyer requested a man from the registry, paying no fee. The lawyers, whether serving in a civil or criminal suit, were to receive their regular wages at their regular place of work. This was their service, like that of jury duty in common-law countries. Relatives might still appear in defense of a party, as well as representatives of labor unions, but this was but retention of a symbol of the thinking of the early days. It suggested that the Communist leaders were unwilling to accept the fact that their system of legal institutions was becoming complicated and was moving away from the influence and control of the people on farms and in the factories.

The legal-duty idea broke down, as can be imagined, under the impact of the restoration of a measure of private enterprise with the NEP. Everyone expected the courts to be flooded with lawsuits, and the whole question of legal representation required rethinking. A congress of employees of the Commissariat agreed in January 1922 that a professional bar had to be established in a college of defenders tied to the courts.[30] Members were to be admitted to the bar only on examination. It was to elect its own officers and discipline itself. A system of legal fees was reinstituted, although subject to a tariff for workers and clerks and to be waived for those unable to pay. On May 26, 1922, the decree incorporating the new concept became law.[31]

The institution of the professional prosecutor was undergoing a parallel metamorphosis. The People's Court Act of 1920 placed the accusatorial function in a newly created institution to be organized in each province by the provincial executive committee's department of justice. Candidates nominated by the executive committee would be appointed by the provincial soviet. When a judge required help, he would file a request and the assignment would be made.

The introduction of the New Economic Policy hastened the disintegration of the system as it had come into being, for it seemed obvious that with the restoration of some measure of capitalism, there would be restored the economic basis for class enemies. After vigorous debate which was resolved only with the intervention of the Politburo of the Communist Party, the office of prosecutor was created in the Commissariat of Justice, with the commissar himself as chief of the office.[32] The office was

---

[28] The commissar's view is given in Ia. L. Berman, *Ocherki po istorii sudoustroistva RSFSR* (1924), 37ff.

[29] People's Court Act of 1920 (1920) 1 *Sob. Uzak. RSFSR*, No. 83, item 407.

[30] See Berman, 55.

[31] (1922) 1 *Sob. Uzak. RSFSR*, No. 36, item 425.

[32] (1922) 1 *Sob. Uzak. RSFSR*, No. 36, item 424.

highly centralized so that even the provincial prosecutors were to be named by the prosecutor of the republic and to be transferred and removed solely by him, and the provincial administrations were to have no say whatever in the oppointment or activity of the prosecutors assigned to them. Not until June 20, 1933, was there a major change in the office, for at that time republic autonomy in the field of prosecution ended.[33] There was created a prosecutor's office in the USSR with general direction over the activities of the prosecutor's offices in the several republics. The basis was laid for the highly centralized system of prosecution which was incorporated in the Constitution of 1936 [34] and is retained to the present day.

The 1922 reforms may be said to have created a multistepped system of courts, a professional prosecutor, and a professional defender. To be sure, they were not entirely like institutions charged with similar functions in other lands, but they had lost with the 1922 reforms their most extreme features of difference. The courts were no longer the primitive tribunals hailed by the Commissar of Justice in early 1919, nor were the prosecutors and defenders citizens who came forward on a nonprofessional basis to accuse and to defend. Later, in 1930, the bar was completely collectivized without special legislation in that private practice was discouraged by discriminatory taxation, and practice became centered in associations subject to the control of the college, which in turn was subject to the control of the Commissariat of Justice. This supervision went beyond the usual control over the bar exercised by the courts in the United States, and to some analysts of the Soviet bar it made impossible the independence of the bar which they felt to have been an outstanding feature of the bar of the Russian Empire. It has been said that "The organization of Soviet lawyers is not a bar in the western sense of the word — the kind of bar which functioned in prerevolutionary Russia." [35] This is so, but it can probably be found to have sufficiently similar functions to those of the bar elsewhere to merit the appellation. Its shortcoming has been in the way in which it has feared to perform its duties courageously in political cases. In this aspect continuity has been broken with the past.

IV

If one turns from institutions to the law applied by them, one finds a similar progression of events, from simplicity to complexity. It was the dream of the Bolsheviks to institute a system of law which would facilitate the emergence of economic and social relations on which a new type of society might be built. Yet the new leaders were sufficiently realistic to

[33] Law of June 20, 1933 (1933) 1 *Sob. Zak. SSSR*, No. 40, item 239.
[34] Art. 115.
[35] See Samuel Kucherov, "The Legal Profession in Pre- and Postrevolutionary Russia," *American Journal of Comparative Law*, V (1956), 443–470.

appreciate that this could not be done quickly, the more so since they had given no thought before the revolution to the multitudinous details of which the law is made. They were prepared only on some major points, dictated by Marxist principles, headed by the concept that private ownership of producer goods must be abolished and ownership of these goods placed in the state. Their first act was to abolish private ownership by great landlords of their land,[36] and as soon as the influence of the Socialist Revolutionaries could be overcome, they acted to abolish all private ownership of land.[37]

The details of law and procedure had to wait until the new rulers had time to invent them. In consequence the first decree on the courts[38] instructed the new people's judges to use as a guide the laws of the ousted government to the extent that they had not been revoked by the revolution and were not contrary to the revolutionary consciousness of the judges. The second decree[39] creating the district courts authorized them to be guided by the civil and criminal laws existing up to that time, to the extent that they had not been revoked and did not conflict with socialist justice. While the formula had been changed slightly, it suggested that judges would take what they could from the laws of the past in deciding a case, tempering the provisions by the judge's own concept of the type of justice compatible with Soviet Russia's new variety of socialism. Not until the People's Court Act of 1918 [40] was reference to the laws of prerevolutionary governments forbidden. The judges were now to apply decrees of the new government and in the many circumstances not covered by decree to be guided by their socialist concept of justice. At this point, formal continuity of law was indubitably ended.[41]

The formal break with the substantive law of the past had been made complete, for judges after 1920 were expected to apply common sense, revolutionary expediency, and whatever residual concept of law they might have. An examination of practice by the Commissar of Justice disclosed so wide a variation of views as to appropriate law that codification was ultimately undertaken in the interest of establishing uniformity.

The Commissar of Justice was himself less of a prisoner of the concepts of the past than some of his judges. He found it desirable to correct their decisions in a 1919 article[42] by selecting those which seemed wise. In most of the cases the problem was whether the Imperial law should be

---

[36] Decree on the Land, October 28, 1917 (1917) 1 *Sob. Uzak. RSFSR*, No. 1, item 3.

[37] Decree of February 19, 1918 (1918) 1 *Sob. Uzak. RSFSR*, No. 25, item 346.

[38] Cited above, note 12.

[39] Cited above, note 15.

[40] Cited above, note 17.

[41] To this effect see Vladimir Gsovski, *Soviet Civil Law* (Ann Arbor, 1948), I, 273, and also Kazimierz Grzybowski, "Continuity of Law in Eastern Europe," *American Journal of Comparative Law*, VI (1957), 44–48.

[42] See *Proletarskaia revoliutsiia i pravo*, no. 11 (1919), 29.

applied, not because of any legal value but because of the wisdom of its solutions even for the new state. He praised a decision which had found a crime in the paying of a minor to have sexual relations, even though in the court's view such an act was not criminal under Imperial law. He praised the leniency of a court hearing a charge of murder when it was indicated that the killing had occurred without prior planning and as a result of intoxication, and because there must have been some group psychological influence at work. He thought an acquittal of a charge of attempted robbery justified when it was found that the defendant, motivated by his sympathies for idealistic anarchy, had entered a house armed with a revolver and a bomb to take over an apartment from the owner. The man was punished lightly only for unauthorized requisition. Civil cases were also held up as models.

A suit against a railway company for injury caused to a passenger was decided in favor of the passenger in spite of the fact that experts needed to be examined to determine whether the plaintiff could work. The court refused to call additional experts on the ground that they could imagine no employment for an amputee subject to hysteria, and that people of the world knew better than experts what was necessary to hold a job. A claim for maintenance of a child born out of wedlock was granted, but a plea for costs was rejected because the court found that the defendant had two families and that to require him to pay costs would be "like putting a noose around his neck." A suit for maintenance of a spouse was rejected because the marriage seemed to have been contracted fictitiously to permit the woman to escape from the difficult situation in which someone had placed her, and the woman was still able to work. Commissar Kursky liked these decisions because they were "shot through with the spirit of unhindered imagination."

All of this was to change with the coming of the NEP and the enactment of codes of law. If we turn to the new criminal code, we find it epitomized by Professor N. S. Timasheff who has said, "But not all is unique in that [Soviet] law; there are also many elements in which Soviet law differs only slightly from pre-Revolutionary Russian law." [43] For Timasheff, Soviet law is unique insofar as it expresses the ideocratic nature of Soviet society, but he maintains that there are especially abundant similarities in the sphere of criminal law. He declares that all of the legally trained draftsmen of the 1922 Soviet criminal code were conscious of the 1903 Imperial Russian criminal code, and that an inspection of the 1922 code makes it clear that structurally there is nothing revolutionary in it over the 1903 predecessor. The major contrast is in the Soviet code's authorization to courts to apply criminal law by "analogy," which the 1903 code specifically forbade. Yet the 1845 criminal code of

[43] N. S. Timasheff, "The Impact of the Penal Law of Imperial Russia on Soviet Penal Law," *American Slavic and East European Review,* XII (1953), 441.

the empire had permitted such application, and Timasheff concludes, "There can be no doubt that the provisions of the Soviet codes reproduce, with verbal change only, the provisions of the code of 1845." [44]

In the important "analogy" provision, the Soviet criminal code has broken the continuity with what had immediately preceded it, but a legal historian might say that it was the interlude from 1903 to 1917 which itself had broken the continuity of more than half a century, and that the Soviet code had but restored the continuity.

The Soviet criminal code's provisions on the general properties of criminal actions are found by Timasheff to be generally similar to those of the 1903 code. Thus, the provisions relating to responsibility of the criminal because of psychological disturbance, self-defense, and various types of intent are found to bear similarity. The distinction between attempt and preparation is that of the 1903 code, although in the revision of 1926 a departure from 1903 and 1922 was introduced, in that preparation was assimilated with criminal attempt and both were made punishable as the consummated crime.

Some elements of the new Soviet code represent a complete break with the past in Timasheff's view. He notes the "expanded jurisdiction" by which he presumably means the reaching out by the Soviet code to make it a crime against the Soviet state to participate abroad in activity harmful to the workingman's cause. He also notes the penalties prescribed by the code and the rules for their application, by which he apparently means the penalty of required work at the criminal's job with reduction of pay and loss of seniority, but without guard. He also draws a clear distinction between the provisions of the Soviet criminal code on so-called counterrevolution and the Imperial law, saying that the whole chapter on counterrevolutionary crime is an improvisation.

Timasheff finds similarity, however, in the Soviet approach to murder, placing at another's disposal means to commit suicide, or instigating a minor or an irresponsible person to commit suicide, bodily injury and violation of bodily integrity, incarceration by use of violence, kidnapping, suppression or substitution of a child, and sexual offenses. Even property crimes were defined in terms substantially similar to those of Imperial law, sometimes that of the code of 1845. Also crimes by officials, which are sometimes considered as having been developed in unique fashion under Soviet pressures, are shown to bear close resemblance to those of the Imperial code, although by 1926 the second Soviet criminal code had adopted some new limitations. As to the 1926 code generally, Timasheff concludes that it is merely a restatement of that of 1922 and, since it is still in force, the impact of prerevolutionary law on Soviet law is

[44] Timasheff, 449.

still there, and he adds "the Revolution has been not so complete as one might expect *a priori*." [45]

Civil law has fared somewhat similarly. Vladimir Gsovski, who has made the most thorough comparison of old and new, is much struck by the contrast in spirit or purpose of the Soviet code from what went before, but his monumental work is studded with comparisons which show that the draftsmen of 1922 were much influenced by the civil law of the empire. In the sphere of property law, he finds that "a non-Soviet jurist would look in vain for a new concept of ownership in the Soviet civil code." [46] The new feature of Soviet law in the property field lies outside the code in the provisions prohibiting the ownership of certain types of property, these being the types which can be used to gain income through the employment of the labor of others. For the items that may be owned by the individual, the law is as old as Rome itself. Milovan Djilas seems prepared to argue in his *The New Class* that even in the public-property sphere familiar concepts of property law have reappeared in the USSR. He declares, "As defined by Roman law, property constitutes the use, enjoyment and disposition of material goods. The Communist political bureaucracy uses, enjoys, and disposes of nationalized property." [47] With this analysis he concludes that there has been developed a new class with its feet resting on property ownership, in that the incidents of the new class's control over nationalized property are the same as the incidents of ownership known to Roman law and, therefore, to civil-law systems everywhere, including Imperial Russia.

To any sweeping conclusion that no new dimension has been added to property law by the Soviet codes, one must counter with the law of housing tenancy[48] and use of land.[49] Transformation of the tenant's rights from contract, on which they rested prior to the revolution, to status, on which they now rest, has everywhere been regarded as one of the major developments in law not only in the USSR but elsewhere since the social developments following upon the heels of the industrial revolution. In the land-law sector, the complete prohibition of alienation of use of agricultural land and the restriction on alienation of small private-house lots since permission of the local governmental authorities is required are noted changes in the postrevolutionary law of the USSR; yet they rest on laws outside the code, and for other property relationships the code offers no such innovations.

In contracts law Gsovski finds that Soviet law "has evolved from the

[45] Timasheff, 462.

[46] See Gsovski, I, 558.

[47] See Milovan Djilas, *The New Class* (New York, 1957), 44.

[48] See John N. Hazard, *Soviet Housing Law* (New Haven, 1939).

[49] See John N. Hazard, *Law and Social Change in the U.S.S.R.* (London, 1953), ch. 6.

efforts of Soviet legislators and jurists to use within the framework of socialist economy the concept of contract as developed in the civil law countries." [50] He finds that the Soviet draftsmen followed certain theoretical constructions of European law, as developed by Russian prerevolutionary writers of renown. He finds it necessary in discussing the law of sales to discuss Imperial law because this influenced the Soviet concept.[51]

Perhaps in tort the Soviet draftsmen provided a distinct break with the past in that they introduced the concept of liability without fault, while prerevolutionary law required the presence of fault to establish liability.[52] Here was indeed a change from the past at what is the very heart of the law of obligations. Yet the rest of the outside world has moved in the same direction since the Russian revolution and without regard to it, and prerevolutionary Russia was not impervious to the influence of social pressures in the law.[53] It is hard to decide whether continuity has been broken, for with the advance of the industrial process and the accidents which have accompanied it, there have been developed in Western countries beyond reach of the Russian revolution not only workman's compensation schemes, but also jury verdicts which have created what one Western scholar has been bold to call "negligence without fault." [54] Is one to say that this is not part of a continuum, but rather a "breakthrough" like those which occur in the progress of scientific research?

Perhaps continuity has been broken in that of recent years, in contrast to the development in Western nations, the Soviet courts have swung away from the provisions of the Soviet civil code making fault unnecessary to re-establish the principle that there must be willfulness or negligence in all but the extrahazardous case to permit a finding of liability, and in so doing they have reversed the continuing development common to Western countries and come nearer to the prerevolutionary attitude. Still, they have made what looks like a reversal with the realization that minimum damages will be forthcoming to an injured employee through operation of the scheme of socialized medicine and the social-insurance law administered by the labor unions and the ministries of social insurance throughout the Soviet republics. Thus there is a considerable part of the law which has progressed in step with legal systems of the West.

Inheritance law among the peasants has remained as it was before the revolution, as has been explained above. Although inheritance law among

---

[50] See Gsovski, I, 415.
[51] Gsovski, I, 455.
[52] Gsovski, I, 496.
[53] Gsovski, I, 486, 494.
[54] Albert A. Ehrenzweig, *Negligence Without Fault* (Berkeley, 1951).

the urban population was specifically abolished in a 1918 decree[55] in favor of a temporary substitute for the social-insurance plan which was expected to be introduced soon thereafter, the concept of inheritance for the urban population was restored with the 1922 code[56] and has been expanded in subsequent years. This expansion seems to have been made necessary as property incentives have been increased to encourage production for the five-year plans, and today the inheritance rules, including as they do the right to bequeath property by will, have much in common with civil-law countries everywhere.[57] Perhaps the major difference lies in limitation upon the circle of heirs to whom a testator may bequeath his estate, but even this circle has been expanded to include nephews and nieces, and the limitation serves primarily to exclude the creation or support of private charities which are notable beneficiaries of estates in the United States, although not such common beneficiaries in civil-law countries. Even the restrictions on bequests which appear in the code are illusory as to property of the type which a testator might wish to leave to persons outside the circle, for they do not apply to savings-bank deposits and government bonds, which may be left to anyone by simple notification to the bank or custodian.

The labor-law field was of great concern to the revolutionaries, for they were determined to escape from what they believed to be a major evil of capitalism, namely the hiring of labor power by contract without regard for considerations other than profit. Gsovski has found a break from the continuity of the past in this field in that a laborer is in many categories not a free agent to make an employment contract where he wishes, for students who graduate from higher schools and industrial-technical schools are obliged to work at the place of assignment.[58] Further, during the war and for ten years thereafter, freedom of choice of employment was restricted generally, for legislation required all workmen to remain at their jobs unless released by management.[59]

The legal forms of labor law have been maintained in spite of these changes in principle. The code of 1922 required that there be a personal contract in each employment situation. Yet management was limited by the code in the circumstances in which it could dismiss, and its right to set hours and wages in bargaining with the individual and eventually his labor union was circumscribed until in 1938 all wages and hours were set by the state.[60]

Some of these limitations on freedom of labor contract have come as natural developments in civil-service relations in many countries, and it

[55] April 27, 1918 (1918) 1 *Sob. Uzak. RSFSR*, No. 34, item 456.
[56] Art. 416.
[57] See Gsovski, I, 657.
[58] Gsovski, I, 800.
[59] Decree of June 26, 1940, *Ved. verkh. sov. SSSR*, No. 20 (1940).
[60] June 4, 1938 (1938) *Sob. post. SSSR*, No. 27, item 178.

would be hard to say that they were not a natural outgrowth of the state's assumption of economic functions. Other limitations, however, are far from the concept of freedom of bargaining associated with industrial development under Imperial law and may be regarded as a break in continuity.

v

The place of the courts in the governing process draws the major attention of those interested in public law. Yet the evidence on which a judgment must be based as to whether there is continuity between the Russian Empire and the USSR is controversial. A contrast between the empire and the Soviet system can be offered by comparison of Samuel Kucherov's "Was independence of judicial power achieved by the Reform? This question may be answered affirmatively but with some reservations" [61] with Andrei Vyshinsky's "From top to bottom the Soviet social order is penetrated by the single general spirit of the oneness of the authority of the toilers. The program of the All-Union Communist Party (of Bolsheviks) rejects the bourgeois principle of separation of power." [62]

While it is on record that Article 1 of the Basic Principles of the 1864 Statutes of Judicial Institutions declared that "The judicial power is separated from the executive, administrative, and legislative powers" [63] and that the Senate upheld the separation of judicial power,[64] there was reluctance on the part of the emperor to accept what he had caused to be proclaimed. Kucherov points to the exceptions to the principle in the continuation after the 1864 reform of the ecclesiastical and military courts and above all of the volost courts, which were responsible directly to the Ministry of Interior.[65] It was these courts which had attracted the attention of the French scholar, Leroy-Beaulieu, because of the fact that more than three quarters of the emperor's subjects were under its jurisdiction.[66] To be sure their jurisdiction was limited, but the fact that for most peasants they represented the sole court with which they would have contact made them a vital part of the judiciary, and clearly they had no pretense of independence.

The empire found it necessary for security reasons to permit the Minister of the Interior to create within the ministry Special Boards with the power to establish open or concealed supervision over untrustworthy

---

[61] See Kucherov, *Courts, Lawyers and Trials,* 35.
[62] Seen Andrei Y. Vyshinsky, *The Law of the Soviet State,* trans. Hugh W. Babb, (New York, 1948), 318.
[63] See Kucherov, *Courts, Lawyers and Trials,* 33.
[64] Kucherov, 34.
[65] Kucherov, 35.
[66] See Anatole Leroy-Beaulieu, *The Empire of the Tsars and the Russians,* trans. Zenaide A. Ragozin (3 vols., New York, 1893–1902), II, 270.

subjects and to exile the most dangerous to remote places for terms up to five years.[67] It was this system of administrative exile which attracted the attention of the first George Kennan and which has figured so prominently in histories of the exile of such prominent persons as Lenin, Stalin, and numerous other leaders of the Bolshevik revolution.

It is hard for one trained in the thinking of American public lawyers to conceive the totality of this situation as representing independence of the judicial arm, unless one is willing to narrow the definition of judiciary to the point that it excludes the courts having to do with the daily lives of most of the people and the police tribunals whose action was notorious at the place where the independence of any judiciary is put to the test — in the sphere of political dissent.

The Soviet concept of the place of the judiciary is admittedly vastly different even on the surface. The constitution has subordinated the judiciary completely to the Supreme Soviet, although there has been an attempt to separate the judiciary from the administration by declaring the judiciary independent and subject solely to the law.[68] Still, the supremacy of the legislative authority over the judiciary is openly proclaimed in contrast to the situation in the empire, and this appears to break continuity.

Consideration of the exceptional role of the Soviet police with the authorization it has had up until 1953 to judge citizens in its own tribunals and to exile them to hard-labor camps for periods up to five years, subject only to audit by the Prosecutor General as a representative of the Supreme Soviet,[69] suggests still further that the Soviet era has departed extensively from the spirit of the West. Yet it is tempting to conclude that this development had its seeds in the imperial system, at least to the extent that those Soviet citizens who might have been revolted by the excesses of the Soviet police may have been led to accept them during the formative stages because it seemed that the Soviet police was only turning the tables on those who had exercised similar measures against the opposition a few short years before. In this manner, it may be said that there was continuity in the willingness of the mass of the people to tolerate terror because the humanizing concept of a really independent judiciary with a monopoly of the power of imprisonment did not run deep in the Russian people.

One cannot overlook in any analysis such as this the role of the Communist Party. It is outside the constitutional structure in a position which on paper suggests that it is like parties in other countries, yet all the world knows the place it has come to fill. While administrative officials are

---

[67] *Ustav o pred. i pres. prest.*, Section 1, notes 1 and 2. For details, see A. I. Elistratov, *Administrativnoe pravo* (Moscow, 1911), 91ff.

[68] Constitution of the USSR of 1936, Art. 112.

[69] Decree of July 10, 1934 (1934) 1 *Sob. Zak. SSSR*, No. 36, item 283 and decree of November 5, 1935 (1935) 1 *Sob. Zak. SSSR*, No. 11, item 84.

denied by Soviet law any right to interfere in the decision-making process of Soviet courts, the party is under no such prohibition. On the contrary, under party rules the members who find themselves in any Soviet organization are duty bound to observe party discipline and to caucus on policy questions so as to devise the party position and to see that it is adopted by the nonparty members present. Westerners have already learned from a former Soviet lawyer how the party has intervened to influence the court in some cases which it has considered of great political importance.[70]

If one considers the relation of the Communist Party to the entire Soviet judicial system, one can find in this fact the major break in continuity, for no such monopoly party existed in the empire. Even prior to 1906 when the emperor himself was a monopoly source of policy decision, he had no disciplined and ubiquitous corps of administrators comparable to the members of the Communist Party. Certainly after 1906 the emperor found himself hampered in the decision-making role by parties in the new Duma, and his efforts to monopolize the situation by proroguing the Duma and ruling by decree met more opposition than is possible today under Communist Party domination. Perhaps, therefore, the major break in continuity with the past as it relates to the courts and the legal system is to be found in the emergence of the monopoly of the Communist Party and not in the structure of legal institutions or the rules which they apply.

THE POLITICAL POLICE: THE DREAM OF A BEAUTIFUL AUTOCRACY

SIDNEY MONAS

I

On June 25, 1826, Nicholas I founded the Third Section of His Majesty's Imperial Chancery; this was a political police unprecedented in Russia. A certain legal and extralegal tradition for the special treatment of state crimes did exist. These, known as cases of "word and deed" (against the person or dignity of the sovereign), had been investigated and prosecuted not through normal administrative channels but by specially commissioned agents in the private chancery.[1] Such political-police nuclei were distinguished by two traits: their lack of continuity and their perpetual reappearance. The Third Section, however, survived

---

[70] See Boris A. Konstantinovsky, *Soviet Law in Action* (Cambridge, Mass., 1953).
[1] M. Semevsky, *Slovo i delo* (St. Petersburg, 1885).

Nicholas and was abolished in 1880 only to have its apparatus transferred intact to the Ministry of the Interior, where it was reinforced by a closer connection with the everyday police and where it remained, through some changes, until February 1917.

The uprising of December 14, 1825, cast a long shadow over Nicholas's reign. The Decembrists, whatever differences existed among them, agreed that the unlimited power of the Romanov dynasty, unchecked by law or popular institutions, could not utilize for Russia the energies of nationalism and democracy which had been unleashed in Europe by the French Revolution. It could only perpetuate the backwardness, inefficiency, corruption, ignorance, and injustice that separated Russia from the more advanced countries of the West. Constitutions, parliaments, courts, opinion spontaneously and freely expressed, all appalled Nicholas; he was not averse to change and reform but it must come, in the Romanov tradition, from above. In a world in which the traditions of the *ancien regime* and the power of absolute monarchy were dissolving, Nicholas found his ideal of "unconditional legitimacy" on the parade-ground; there was something reassuring about watching stiffly uniformed soldiers respond instantly to orders, one movement flowing from another, executing delicate maneuvers precisely as issued from above.[2] To the testimony and depositions of the arrested Decembrists, Nicholas responded with a direct, personal ferocity. At the same time, he systematically studied their account of the conditions which had provoked them and their suggestions for reform. Problems and state tasks which they envisaged resolving through constitutional arrangements, Nicholas turned over to the political police.[3]

The decree establishing the Third Section is extremely vague. It prescribes a general surveillance over all areas of life: not only the power of arrest and investigation in crimes against the state, but also the prevention of such crimes. The Third Section was to serve as a public-opinion poll, a house of representatives, a school, a court, a jail, and a family-counseling service.[4] The official histories note that when General Benckendorff, as the appointed head of the Third Section, asked Nicholas for his orders, the emperor handed him a white handkerchief: "Here are your orders," he said. "Take this and wipe away the tears of my people."[5]

The Third Section consisted of two parts: the Corps of Gendarmes and

---

[2] N. Polievktov, *Nikolai I* (Petrograd, 1918), 35.

[3] *Vosstanie dekabristov: materialy* (Moscow-Leningrad, 1925), I, introduction; A. S. Borovkov, "Avtobiograficheskie zapiski," *Russkaia starina*, XCVI (1898); B. E. Syroechkovsky, ed., *Mezhdutsarstvie 1825 goda i vosstanie dekabristov* (Moscow-Leningrad, 1926), 32–34; *Vtoroe polnoe sobranie zakonov rossiiskoi imperii* (St. Petersburg, 1833), I, no. 449, 666 (hereafter cited as II *P.S.Z.*).

[4] N. Shil'der, *Nikolai I* (St. Petersburg, 1903), I, 780–781; A. Lomachevsky, "Zapiski zhandarma," *Vestnik Evropy*, no. 3. (1872), 245.

[5] Shil'der, I, 467.

a network of secret agents, directed from the chancery, which in turn was staffed by gendarme officers. Administrative channels were at first irregular and informal, reflecting the emergency conditions of their creation and their intended impermanence. Gendarme officers were recruited from among the more promising young Guards Officers, offered the inducement of larger salaries, a handsomer uniform, more awards and decorations, and a greater opportunity for promotion. The secret agents were recruited from among former police detectives, young men seriously compromised by their associations with the Decembrists, people compromised by debt or a criminal past, servants and adventurers. There were not many; probably no more than a hundred during the entire reign of Nicholas.[6]

Benckendorff's first aim was to make the political police respectable. He considered his own moral qualifications impeccable and, to be sure, he was a polite, honest, mildly disposed, rather lethargic courtier. A Baltic German of no particular distinction, he had a great yearning to shine at aristocratic balls and deeply regretted that society ladies sometimes considered him a "gendarme" and a "spy."[7] He had a record of obeying orders as a courier and adjutant, without improvisation. Nicholas appointed him Chief of Imperial Headquarters to keep him in his closest entourage. He showered him with every sign of favor and prestige. Benckendorff in turn inculcated a code of chivalry and high good manners among his officers, constantly exhorted them to relieve the suffering and oppressed, rescue "widows and orphans" in distress, and to take full advantage of the opportunity their service offered them to do good. They must make themselves prominent, liked, and respected, so that people would not hesitate to come to them with denunciations of political intrigue. When the Third Section set up an independent headquarters in 1838, it became the custom for all important personages arriving or leaving the capital to call and pay their respects. Poor people came with complaints, appeals, petitions; offended conservatives or careerist spies came to make political denunciations; suspects under surveillance came to "check in." All were treated with ineffable politesse.[8]

Nevertheless, men trained in the officers' corps and imbued with the military code of honor felt qualms about dealing with informers. One director of chancery is said to have paid his secret agents in sums from which the number thirty had been subtracted — "to remind them of the thirty pieces of silver."[9]

During the early years of its existence, a certain inner dynamism moved the Third Section. It expanded into the provinces, and its person-

[6] See the staff and budget allotments published as supplements to II *P.S.Z.*
[7] "Iz zapisok grafa A. K. Benkendorfa," *Istoricheskii vestnik*, XCI (1903); "Petersburgskoe obshchestvo pri vosshestvii na prestol Imperatora Nikolaia I," *Russkaia starina*, XXXII (1881), 175.
[8] A. Gertsen, *Polnoe sobranie sochinenii* (Petrograd, 1919), XIII, 45–54.
[9] P. Karatygin, "Benkendorf i Dubelt," *Istoricheskii vestnik*, XXX (1887), 172.

nel increased fivefold.[10] Surveillance over other state institutions turned rapidly into interference and expedition. The corruption of provincial governors was exposed; cases were hurried through, or removed from, the courts. A militant optimism glows through all the early reports to the emperor.[11]

In the surveys of public opinion submitted by the Third Section to the emperor, a careful analysis is made of the state of mind of various segments of the population. Stray rumors, "what people say" at street corners and at banquets, are also thrown in, but the reports are more methodical than one might expect. The Third Section notes that serfs are becoming increasingly conscious of their bondage and that the religious sects act as "Jacobin Clubs" among them. Much is expected of the new regime, and the appearance of gendarmes in "deaf corners" is said to be greatly appreciated by the provincial population. Even forces of nature reinforce the police, and the outbreak of *cholera morbus* in 1830 has the beneficial effect of "taking people's minds off politics." When the Fifth Section of the Chancery, under Count Kiselev, becomes the Ministry of Court Properties, the Third Section assumes a more conservative tone with regard to the peasantry — it is dangerous to arouse too many expectations.[12] Among the high aristocracy, the Third Section notes a dangerous nationalism, independent of the official nationalism of the regime, but here again the political police have the matter in hand and the tide is turning. Above all, the surveys concentrate on a somewhat heterogeneous "middle class" referred to as "the soul of the Empire," or simply "the public." [13] This consists mostly of the educated middle-gentry, the class which Pushkin referred to in his journal as the Russian *tiers état*, and it was from this milieu that the Decembrists had come.[14]

The Third Section points out the importance of university circles and the growing power of the press. University students are few in number, not more than three thousand, and the circulation of the periodical press never exceeds twenty thousand during Nicholas' reign, but the political police is very much aware of the immanent importance of both.[15] Here, the reports say, the ideas of the Decembrists, and the constitutional ideas of Europe, still have certain sway. Here aspirations for a national literature and a new national consciousness are beginning to take shape. Michael von Vock, the first director of the Third Section's chancery,

[10] "Tret'e otdelenie sobstvennogo ego imperatorskogo velichestva kantseliarii o sebe samom," *Vestnik Evropy* (March 1917).

[11] "Graf A. K. Benkendorf o Rossii v 1827–1832 gg," *Krasnyi arkhiv,* XXXVII– XXXVIII, XLVI (1929–1931)

[12] N. M. Druzhinin, *Gosudarstvennye krest'iane i reforma Kiseleva,* I (Moscow-Leningrad, 1946).

[13] "Benkendorf o Rossii," *Krasnyi arkhiv,* XXXVIII (1929), 145.

[14] A. S. Pushkin, *Dnevnik* (Moscow-Petrograd, 1923), ed. V. F. Sanodnik et al., 40.

[15] A. S. Nifontov, *1848 god v Rossii* (Moscow, 1931), 202.

recommends that the regime take full advantage of this ripening force, place itself in the forefront by subsidizing and encouraging writers, periodicals, and the "well-intended" in general. Just a twist, an organizing impulse from above, and a great new power will be in the emperor's hands.[16] Censorship should be relaxed (its administration, in any case, belongs to the Ministry of Education), and those who show a spirit of opposition, instead of merely being reduced to silence, should be submitted to the political police.[17] This genuine totalitarian impulse from the Third Section — implicitly recommending, on the one hand, an enthusiasm campaign and, on the other, police terror — found no reinforcement, however, either from above or from below.

Nicholas treated the most talented officer of his police with stony condescension. When von Vock died, the emperor remarked: "I have lost Vock. I am sorry I was not able to like him." [18] Enthusiasm campaigns were not to his taste: "Neither to praise nor to blame" fell to the subject's lot, merely "to obey." [19] Not even the only private newspaper in Russia subsidized by the Third Section was removed from the normal censorship, and Nicholas, by and large, remained true to his principle that "It is beneath the dignity of the monarchical power to enter into the political arena with common journalists." [20]

If the Third Section proved unable to launch a police press, its responsibility for public opinion gave it full opportunity to harass the censorship. Censors, caught in a difficult position between the writers and professors among whom they lived, and the police who watched over them, were frequently rebuked, fined, confined for days in the guardhouse, dismissed from their posts, and occasionally even apotheosized by university students as martyr-heroes.[21] Only three periodicals, however, were actually closed down on the Third Section's recommendation during Nicholas' reign, and these were insignificant. As soon as a journal numbered more than a thousand subscribers, the political police became reluctant to suppress it, even though, like "The Contemporary" in the 1840's, a radical, even a socialist, influence was suspected.[22] A banned journal sent rumors flying and disturbed the placidity of public opinion, which the Third Section had been founded to maintain.[23]

Among student groups the Third Section sent its paid informers, often of the servant class, occasionally a compromised student. Amateur denun-

[16] "Benkendorf o Rossii," *Krasnyi arkhiv*, XXXVII, 162; "Peterburgskoe obshchestvo," *Russkaia starina*, XXXII, 548.

[17] "Peterburgskoe obshchestvo," *Russkaia starina*, XXXII, 538; "K istorii russkoi literatury," *Russkaia starina*, CIII (1900), 579–591.

[18] Pushkin, *Polnoe sobranie sochinenii* (Moscow-Leningrad, 1949), XII, 201.

[19] Nifontov, 200.

[20] Shil'der, II, 713–714.

[21] A. Nikitenko, *Dnevnik* (Moscow-Leningrad, 1955), I (1826–1857).

[22] M. Lemke, *Nikolaevskie zhandarmy i literatura* (St. Petersburg, 1908), 175.

[23] M. Sukhomlinov, *Izsledovanii i stat'i* (St. Petersburg, 1889), II, 429.

ciation (*donos*) was encouraged and prodigiously harvested. So many more denunciations reached the Third Section than its limited staff could investigate that a decree of 1842 made false accusation punishable to the same extent as the crime reported.[24] Gendarme officers, who came from the same class by and large as the students, often treated the arrested more solicitously than the spies who reported them. Interrogations usually began in an atmosphere of patriarchal benevolence: "I knew your father. What would he say if he could see you here. . . ." A written questionnaire of the suspect's education and opinions was submitted: why were such-and-such books found on your shelves? What, in your opinion, is the best form of government? [25] Administrative exile to some provincial city where the political "criminal" often worked in an office of the bureaucracy, confinement to his home under parental supervision, or simply a school-teacherlike reprimand, were the most usual forms of punishment. Petty interference in their lives, the disruption of their careers, and the violation of their privacy were, however, bitterly resented by the students. Nor was the hypocrisy of police benevolence popular among them.[26]

In the years following 1848, two circumstances combined to spur the Third Section into renewed activity. First, the European revolutions of 1848 found sympathetic echoes among the Russian "public," whose zealous adherence to the autocracy the Third Section had once been so confident of securing. An independent public opinion, even a national literature, proclaimed by Belinsky and entirely independent of official nationalism, had in fact arisen.[27] Secondly, a competitor for police honors appeared on the scene. The Ministry of the Interior had always controlled the everyday police, which had secret agents of its own. When the ambitious Perovsky became minister in 1844, he turned a jealous eye toward the special position, the special quota of state honors and awards, accorded to the Third Section. In 1849, one of his agents uncovered, or rather manufactured, the Petrashevsky conspiracy, the second great political case to occur during the reign of Nicholas. While the ministry did

[24] I. M. Trotsky, *Zhizn' Shervud-Vernogo* (Moscow, 1931), 141–150.
[25] Gertsen, XII, 212; D. D. Akhsharumov, *Iz moikh vospominanii* (Moscow-Leningrad, 1930).
[26] I. M. Trotsky, *Tret'e otdelenie pri Nikolae I* (Moscow, 1930), 1.
[27] "It is only in the realm of literature," Belinsky wrote in 1846, "that we cease to be Ivan the Terrible and Peter. Only here do we talk freely as men about human problems. Our literature has already . . . created a kind of public opinion." In short, only literature was free, and it was from literature that social critics like Chernyshevsky received their education in freedom. This education was unfortunately incomplete, and following a spurious logic they concluded that literature henceforth was morally obliged to pursue the particular conception of freedom they arrived at, morally obliged to destroy the old order. When the heirs of Chernyshevsky finally seized power they transformed literature's "moral obligations" into a seven-days-a-week *barshchina*, enforced by a far deadlier police than that of the old order. Cf. H. E. Bowman, "Art and Reality in Russian 'Realist' Criticism," *Journal of Aesthetics and Art Criticism*, XII (1953–1954), 386–392.

its best to magnify, the Third Section bent every effort to minimize its significance. Perovsky triumphed, however, and fifty men were sent to hard labor in Siberia.[28] The Third Section was forced into a flurry of activity. Surveillance was increased. Bookstores were raided. Gendarmes clattered more prominently than ever down the main boulevards. But in all its reports and recommendations, the Third Section urged that Russia remain "somnolent and at peace" and advised against banning periodicals, against commitment of Russian troops in Hungary, against continuation of the Crimean War, against anything that might serve to increase the distance between the regime and the "public." [29]

Meanwhile, a young student of plebeian origin who was to play a crucial role in the formation of the consciousness of the 1860's noted in his diary:

The secret police have taken [the Petrashevtsy] — this is a fearfully base and stupid story: these animals, these swine . . . they should be hanged! How easy it is to go down in history — I myself, for example, never doubted that I would join their society, and eventually I would have joined.[30]

This was Nicholas Chernyshevsky. The political police had undoubtedly made its impression.

II

In 1876, when Alexander II was considering the abolition of the Third Section, he had one of its high officials prepare for him a history of that institution. In this official history, the repressive aspects of the political police are barely referred to. It dwells instead on information-gathering and welfare functions: the relief of the poor from cumbersome litigation in the jammed courts, plans for railroads, foreign-intelligence information, inspection of factory conditions, recommendations for the abolition of serfdom and for greater religious tolerance — all calculated to impress on the emperor the indispensability of the Third Section to "reform from above." [31] The political police appeared to Alexander, as it had to his father, to be the necessary tool of a beautiful autocracy. By a number of interrelated reforms, Alexander limited the application of police action. At the same time, with the first indications of a revolutionary movement, he returned to the police many of its old powers, more exclusively concentrated on the segments of revolutionary youth. When Alexander did abolish the Third Section, it was only to unite its apparatus more effectively with that of the everyday police in the hands of Loris-Melikov and his commission. A deadly dialectic of police and revolutionaries ensued,

---

[28] M. Gernet, *Istoriia tsar'skoi tiurmy* (Moscow-Leningrad, 1946), II, 204.
[29] "Tret'e otdelenie i Krymskaia Voina," *Krasny arkhiv* (1923), no. 3, 294; Nifontov, 119–178.
[30] N. G. Chernyshevsky, *Polnoe sobranie sochinenii* (Moscow, 1939), I, 274.
[31] "Tret'e otdelenie," *Vestnik Evropy* (March 1917).

culminating in October 1917. Far from connecting the sovereign with the public, as Nicholas I had envisioned, the political police guaranteed his isolation and ineffectiveness.

The heads of the Third Section were still military men. Some, like P. A. Shuvalov, had considerable influence on Alexander II, but Shuvalov was the exception rather than the rule. The police were more specialized. The upper hierarchy became even more acutely aware of its needs as an institution, of tasks that could not be performed adequately, and of mouths that needed to be fed. The Third Section at the very beginning of its existence had informed Nicholas that liberation of the peasantry was inevitable, but P. A. Dolgorukov, who, as head of the Third Section, sat on Alexander's liberation committee, opposed the reform — insisting he would not be able to answer for the public peace if the measure went through.[32] Technical accomplishments became a more important criterion in the choice of high police personnel than their record of filial devotion or their manners. At the same time, a sense of technological inadequacy made police leadership doggedly conservative.

Police manners deteriorated rapidly. The students remained as before the main object of police surveillance, but there were many more of them, and they were no longer exclusively of the gentry class. The students became more violent, and so did the police.

The countryside, furthermore, was tense. The Corps of Gendarmes had frequently to act in quelling peasant disturbances. The Third Section, anticipating a juncture between the disturbed student element and the peasantry, feared the consequences. When the "going-to-the-people" movement of 1874 began, Shuvalov suggested that the root of the problem was not in getting at the students, but at the peasantry. In a curious way, he anticipated Stolypin's attack on the village community, not, like Stolypin, seeing it as an obstacle to economic development, but rather, like Herzen, viewing it as a breeding ground for socialism.[33] Long before this, however, as early as 1860, the Third Section had been concerned with the possible spread of oppositionist sentiment from the students to wider segments of the population. As part of a campaign to spread literacy, Alexander had permitted a number of reading rooms and Sunday courses in instruction for workers (still, in large part, semipeasants) to be opened in the cities, staffed largely by volunteers from among the students. Dolgorukov warned of danger. With the outbreak of mysterious fires in St. Petersburg and student disturbances in 1862, the reading rooms and the Sunday courses were abolished.[34]

In 1866, the demented former student Karakozov attempted to assassinate the emperor. The Third Section, after Dolgorukov had been forced

[32] N. Dzhanshiev, *Epokha velikikh reform* (St. Petersburg, 1899), 18.
[33] S. S. Tatishchev, *Imperator Aleksandr II* (St. Petersburg, 1903), II, 76.
[34] Tatishchev, II, 221, 536–537.

to resign for his ineptitude in protecting the emperor, discovered that
Karakozov had belonged to the Ishutin circle at Moscow University, the
members of which "aimed to move closer to the people." [35]

The special investigating committee into the Karakozov affair, under
M. N. Muraviev (the subduer of Poland), including representation from
the Third Section, discovered "the ruinous corruption of a whole generation of Russian student youth by the plague of socialism." [36] In 1868, the
first revolutionary pamphlet aimed directly at the peasantry appeared
from a clandestine student press in Moscow.[37]

Meanwhile, the Third Section had divested itself of the censorship.
On April 6, 1865, preliminary censorship was abolished entirely, and a
system of warnings and fines, administered by the Ministry of the Interior,
was introduced instead.[38] The improvement cannot be overestimated.
Nevertheless, it should be pointed out that, on the one hand, the press had
grown sufficiently so that preliminary censorship was no longer feasible
(if it ever had been) and, on the other, that the Third Section, supplemented by the rigid Buturlin Committee, had a certain formative influence on the press committee of the ministry. Government officials approached the problem of a free press with a nervousness the Third Section
had tutored and shaped: they maintained a tendency to look on the press,
as Nikitenko put it, "with police eyes," and with the excuse of any
emergency, real or imagined, to behave in the manner of "a high court
dealing with ideas as with thieves and murderers." [39] During the first two
years of "freedom of the press," four periodicals were suspended.[40]

The Third Section concentrated its attention on the illegal press, imported and domestic. Herzen, in England, corresponded with young men
in Moscow and St. Petersburg. They sent him news, and he sent them
material from the Free Russian Press. They soon began duplicating
Herzen's material at home, aided by the common practice of hectograph-
ing their professors' lectures. In Moscow, a student, Zaichnevsky, set up
the first underground Russian printing press in 1861. Even after his arrest
by the Third Section, his pamphlet, "Young Russia," the first propaganda
leaflet calling for open revolt and complete overthrow of the regime, appeared and was distributed. In 1862, in response to a government order
abolishing student organizations and cutting down on scholarship aid to
needy students, riots broke out in St. Petersburg and Moscow universities.
Street demonstrations occurred. Herzen remained fully informed of the
course of events, denouncing gendarme action against the students. Revo-

---

[35] *Istoriia Moskvy* (Moscow, 1954), IV, 332.
[36] Tatishchev, II, 539.
[37] *Istoriia Moskvy*, IV, 336.
[38] *Ministerstvo vnutrennikh del: istoricheskii ocherk* (St. Petersburg, 1901), 150.
[39] Quoted in Dzhanshiev, 324.
[40] Dzhanshiev, 359.

lutionary pamphlets were sent through the mail, and some even appeared on the steps of the Winter Palace.[41]

On November 20, 1864, Alexander introduced widespread legal reforms, trial by jury, irremovable judges, independent courts, and a free and independent bar. That he intended the reform to go as far as it did is questionable. In the case of a judge who had rendered a decision against the emperor's will, Alexander ordered him removed; when the Minister of Justice informed him that he had, after all, issued a law making judges irremovable, Alexander looked startled: "Did I really sign that?" he asked.[42] In any case, the courts remained the most radical and, in a sense, the most successful of all Alexander's reforms. It was there that political lawyers, in the full glare of publicity (jury trials were fully open to the public; other courts were more restrictive, but accounts of the trials often appeared in the press) put the beautiful autocracy itself — and its executive instrument, the police — on trial.

The Third Section retained formidable powers, which were, however, frequently and publicly called into question. The political police could still, by a petition to the Minister of Justice or the emperor himself, dispose of cases in administrative order rather than have them come before the courts. Under such circumstances, a maximum sentence of five years could be pronounced by a special board including the political police. But this procedure was open to intense criticism, not merely from the public, but from legally trained and legally minded high officials in the government as well.[43] The conditions of administrative exile, to placate public opinion, had to be considerably easier than the conditions of prison or hard labor.[44] The frequency with which the administration order was resorted to increased with increasing disturbances — there were 260 persons in administrative exile in 1875, 7,000 in 1880, and 45,000 were sent out annually in the years 1905–1907 — but this in itself created a serious limitation. The provincial authorities, even in eastern Siberia, were by no means equipped to look after so many. In comparatively easy circumstances, revolutionaries could carry on their work in exile, spreading opposition to the interior, and then return with five years of experience and education behind them.[45]

The usual alternative, in political cases, to the administrative order was a trial before the Senate, or before a *sudebnaia palata*, a court con-

---

[41] Tatishchev, 536–537.

[42] S. Kucherov, *Courts, Lawyers and Trials under the Last Three Tsars* (New York, 1953), 35.

[43] Kucherov; see also the several volumes of reminiscences by the distinguished jurist, A. F. Koni.

[44] A. T. Vasilyev, *The Ochrana* (Philadelphia-London, 1930), 39.

[45] Tatishchev, 547, 586; A. A. Lopukhin, *Otryvki iz vospominanii* (Moscow-Petrograd, 1923), 93.

sisting of a professional judge and four "class representatives" appointed by the zemstvo (a representative institution with limited powers of local government). If a case were disposed of in this way, the Third Section labored under serious limitations. Within two weeks of arrest, the political police had to turn over the accused to the prosecutor's office, with right of counsel, for inquiry and interrogation. It had no right to appeal to the court; on the other hand, it had occasionally to suffer serious criticism by the courts of dubious methods and improprieties. A much higher premium came to be placed on the accumulation of evidence before arrest, thereby stimulating police use of secret agents and external surveillance. The advantage to the Third Section, and to the regime, in securing the sentence of a court was the identification it provided of "society" (represented by a free court) with the regime in opposing the revolutionaries. If the sentence proved "unfavorable," however, the regime suffered.[46]

Occasionally, the Ministry of Justice, consulting with the Third Section, decided to dispose of a case in open court, before a jury, with the greatest possible publicity. Theoretically, this implied a nonpolitical trial, an "ordinary" criminal case. In cases of terrorist action, where guilt seemed fairly evident, the Third Section and the ministry hoped to identify the terrorist-revolutionaries with common criminals in the public eye. The first such case was that of Nechaev's murder of Ivanov in 1868. Nechaev himself had escaped abroad, but the Third Section had rounded up all those who had in any way been implicated in his secret society. Almost a hundred young men and women, mostly students, were brought before a jury.[47]

The Third Section, aware of the stakes involved, requested investigative powers that had been denied it by law. In May 1871, two months before the trial began, Alexander restored inquisitorial privileges to the political police, on condition that they be exercised in the presence of a representative from the prosecutor's office. Nevertheless, the trial was not a success. Fifty-six of the eighty-seven persons brought to court were acquitted. The fact that the Third Section rearrested them, committing them to administrative exile, did not, as had originally been hoped, increase the popularity of the regime.[48]

In 1874, the junction of the Petersburg "reds" with the discontented peasantry seemed indeed to be taking place, as several hundred students left their universities to spread among "the people." Shuvalov, meanwhile, had been appointed ambassador to Great Britain, and General Mezentsov, a hard-bitten, merciless garrison commander, took over the Third Section. With the arrest of the Populists and the famous "Trial of the 193," Mezent-

[46] Kucherov.

[47] V. Bazilevsky, *Gosudarstvennye prestupleniia v Rossii v XIX veke* (St. Petersburg, 1906–1908), I, 159–227.

[48] Tatishchev, II, 542–543.

sov was convinced that the revolutionary movement had been crushed. Encouraged by the response of the peasantry to police appeals, the Third Section began to treat political prisoners with a severity that departed from tradition. From 1875 to 1881, forty-three political prisoners died while under arrest, twelve committed suicide, thirty-eight went mad.[49] In the Trial of the 193, Mezentsov used all his influence to prevent an acquittal. When the court recommended clemency, Mezentsov preferred sending the condemned to Siberia in administrative exile.[50]

In 1878, Vera Zasulich shot and wounded General Trepov as a reprisal for the illegal flogging of a prisoner, the student Bogoliubov. She freely admitted the deed, affirming it as an act of justice. Mezentsov and the Minister of Justice decided to try the case before a jury, and she was acquitted. Zasulich's testimony and the eloquent pleading of her attorneys aroused such sympathy that she became a kind of exemplary heroine, setting a precedent for the behavior of revolutionaries in court. Trepov, by implication, was condemned. The day after the acquittal, the Third Section attempted to dispose of her administratively, but she had been whisked abroad by friends. Shortly thereafter, Mezentsov himself fell victim to a reprisal attack. Walking in broad daylight down a prominent St. Petersburg boulevard, he was approached by a young student who quietly slipped a knife into his stomach and left him dying. From this time on, the head of the political police was a marked man. Henceforth, moreover, the lawyers "put into the limelight the question of the lack of rights of political prisoners," explaining the entire revolutionary movement in terms of the measures taken by the police against political offenders.[51]

Lack of discrimination with regard to the enemies of the regime was a built-in tradition of the political police. Although the welfare ideology of Nicholas' time had slipped away, the dream of the beautiful autocracy still tolerated no distinction among opponents. Those who participated in street demonstrations were arrested along with bomb-throwing terrorists. After 1878, the practice of appointing temporary governor-generals, the use of military courts issuing only the death sentence, and the rapid growth of the Third Section's personnel served only to heighten the intensity of revolutionary activity, and to provide it with a certain base in public sympathy, or at least public apathy.[52]

With Loris-Melikov's "dictatorship of the heart," the Third Section was abolished, and an attempt made to unify police administration, first in the supreme executive commission, then in the Ministry of the Interior. Loris-Melikov himself, however, urged the inadequacy of a merely ad-

---

[49] Tatishchev, II, 549.

[50] A. Iakimov, "Bol'shoi protsess ili protsess 193-kh," *Katorga i ssylka,* no. 8 (1927).

[51] Kucherov, 224.

[52] E. Naryshkin-Kurakin, *Under Three Tsars* (New York, 1931), 55–57; Tatishchev, II, 553–561.

ministrative solution to the problem of revolutionary terror. "To go further on this path is quite impossible," he told the emperor. "This task cannot be accomplished by punitive and police measures alone." [53] He pleaded the necessity of distinguishing real revolutionaries from the more innocent, of guaranteeing a return to a more fully legal order as soon as the emergency subsided, of calling a consultative assembly to clarify local and class needs, and of restoring "dignity and self-respect to the schools." [54] On the same day that Alexander signed the document calling for a consultative assembly, he was assassinated by remnants of the scattered organization of the People's Will. The positive aspects of Loris-Melikov's program were drowned in Alexander III's autocratic indignation. His reorganization of the police remained, however, placing an unprecedented concentration of power in the hands of the Minister of the Interior.

III

The preponderance of the Ministry of the Interior was to prove fatal to Witte's plans for the industrialization of Russia, but it did not guarantee an effectively functioning political police. [55] The minister controlled all the police organs, political and ordinary, but the farther from St. Petersburg, the more their activities diverged; he was chief of the Corps of Gendarmes, but as a civilian he frequently encountered the stubborn resistance of military tradition. [56]

The chief of the department of police in St. Petersburg was no longer a military man, but usually a lawyer, trained in the prosecutor's office. He controlled both the everyday police and the *okhrana*, or security section. Immediately subordinate to the minister, he was, so to speak, his man and resigned when a minister resigned. In the last fifteen years of the Imperial regime, in part because of the high toll of assassination and intrigue over Ministers of the Interior, there were twelve chiefs of police. [57]

The special importance attached to the okhrana also facilitated a certain maneuvering in the higher circles of the government. Zubatov, for example, smarting under Plehve's criticism of his workers' organizations, intrigued with other ministers against both the Minister of the Interior and the chief of police. With the re-emergence of a terrorist group, far more powerful and systematically organized than the old People's Will, and with the penetration of that group by secret agents, the power of the

---

[53] Tatishchev, II, 588.

[54] Tatishchev, II, 594.

[55] *Ministerstvo*, 211–217; A. A. Lopikhin, *Nastoiashchee i budushchee russkoi politsii* (Moscow, 1907), especially 31–33; S. Witte, *Vospominaniia. Tsarstvovanie Nikolaia II* (2 vols.; Berlin, 1922).

[56] A. I. Spiridovich, *Pri tsarskom rezhime* (Moscow, 1926), 9; Lopukhin, 17.

[57] P. P. Zavarzin, *Rabota tainoi politsii* (Paris, 1924), 8.

okhrana section over even the highest figures of state assumed, potentially at least, sinister proportions.

With the industrial expansion of Russia in the 1890's a new segment of the population, the proletariat, engaged the special interests of the police. Rapid industrialization was vital to Russia and, to encourage it, the regime fostered the growth of various kinds of syndicates among industrial enterprises, while at the same time forbidding any kind of organization among the workers. This made mockery of the pretense of a free labor contract. The system of factory inspection, administered by the Ministry of Finance, theoretically arbitrated disputes over the labor contract and investigated workers' grievances. In practice, however, the workers stood little chance of making their grievances felt through this channel. Illegal strikes were their only recourse, and these outbursts of violence became, as the policemaster of Moscow put it, "the primary school for the political education of the workers." The regime feared this political education above all, and often attempts on the part of employers to compromise with or surrender to the demands of their employees were actually forbidden by the Ministry of the Interior, acting on advice from the police.[58]

As late as 1895, the Ministry of Finance denied the existence of a Russian proletariat, but its administration of the factory inspection reflected a great fear of the factory. Inspectors' reports were carefully labeled "secret." Inspectors were enjoined to keep a sharp eye out for breaches of order, and especially to report any contacts between the intelligentsia and the workers. Many factory inspectors, and Witte himself when he was Minister of Finance, protested against this use of the factory inspection for police purposes, but pressure from the Ministry of the Interior remained inexorable.

In 1901, Sviatopulk-Mirsky, then chief of Gendarmes, reported that bad conditions in the factories created a receptive soil for propaganda by the radical intelligentsia:

In the last three or four years it has made out of the good-natured Russian bloke a unique type of semiliterate *intelligent* who considers it his duty to negate religion and the family, who holds law in contempt, and who is not only disobedient to authority, but contemptuous of it.[59]

Not only factory inspectors, but even some police officials, pointed out that the best way to frustrate revolutionary propaganda was to remove its basis. The right of workers to their own organizations, however, was not recognized until 1912. Until the police unions of Zubatov and Rachkovsky were to introduce a new note, the main aim of the Ministry of

[58] I. Kh. Ozerov, *Politika po rabochemu voprosu v Rossii za poslednie gody* (Moscow, 1906), 24–29, 56, 112–131.
[59] Ozerov, 131.

the Interior was to convert the factory into a barracks. Police were maintained in the factory (often at the expense of the owner), and Cossacks were quartered nearby. Police spies, sometimes unknown to each other — one set reporting to the gendarmes, another to the local police — were sent among the workers. The factory inspectors, some through police pressure, some through their own inclinations, were almost turned into another police force. Employers were restrained from making concessions to their workers without the approval of the factory inspection. Strikes, when they occurred, were violent and were violently suppressed.

During the depression years 1899–1903, strikes and street disorders were common occurrences. Police behavior in their suppression caused Lenin to gloat:

It is physically impossible to make thousands and tens of thousands of people responsible for refusing to work, for strikes, for meetings. It is politically impossible to initiate court proceedings for every such case. . . . "Justice" takes off its mask of impartiality and loftiness takes to flight, leaving the field of action to the police, gendarmery and Cossacks.[60]

The police were educating the population in a sense quite different from that intended by Benckendorff.

With the founding of the Social Democratic Party in 1898 and the Socialist Revolutionary Party in 1902, the police found itself faced with a revolutionary movement of unprecedented scope and organization and increasing strength. The SR's soon grew into a vast, amorphous mass party with membership in all classes of society. Its "battle organization" formed, on the other hand, a tightly knit, conspiratorial group, which took a high toll of state dignitaries. It had bases abroad and unknown sympathizers throughout Russia.[61] The okhrana attempted — and quite successfully — to filter secret agents into the highest reaches of the battle organization but, anxious to discover all the ramifications of the group, sometimes abided terroristic acts in order not to show its hand too soon. The Bolshevik faction of the SD's, on the other hand, did not advocate terroristic acts. In dealing with the Bolsheviks, the okhrana resorted most frequently to administrative exile, even proffering the option of exile abroad — a process which helped rather than hindered the formation of a highly trained revolutionary "elite." [62]

A small group of double agents came into being, which gave the political police in the last fifteen years of its existence a special air of intrigue and treacherous manipulation. They were people who lived in two worlds, each of which made absolute demands of service and loyalty. Some were

---

[60] V. I. Lenin, *Sochineniia* (2nd. ed., Moscow, 1926–1932), IV, 116, quoted in Kucherov, 201–202.

[61] A. I. Spiridovich, *Partiia S. R. i ee predshestvenniki* (Petrograd, 1918); *Histoire du terrorisme russe, 1886–1917* (Paris, 1930).

[62] Vasilyev; Zavarzin, 13; Spiridovich, *Pri tsarskom rezhime*, 16.

mere adventurers, like Azev, who tried to manipulate both worlds. Some were demoralized revolutionaries, like Malinovsky. Some, like the aristocratic young lady, Zinaida Zhuchenko, conceived a kind of idealistic mission against the terrorism of the revolution.[63]

The man who developed the network of secret agents to a degree of refinement was Zubatov, the chief of the Moscow okhrana. He separated the personnel under him into two distinct groups: those whose training (military or legal) had imbued them with a sense of honor, fitness, and "correct procedure," and those who labored under no such scruples. In organizing the "unscrupulous" part, he displayed a special flare.

For "external surveillance" (those — cab drivers or "casual" pedestrians — who secretly observed the movements of suspects, but from the outside) he recruited discharged noncommissioned officers. He was careful to select men without strong family or personal ties, over whom the revolutionaries could find no obvious hold, and whose social isolation created a frame of mind suitable for the service. For his secret agents, Zubatov recruited revolutionaries — his interrogations of political prisoners always inserted an offer of service to the police, and over prisoners with a criminal past he applied pressure of various kinds, including the threat of exposure. Money, of course, helped; the okhrana operated on a limited budget, but Zubatov was not averse to the spread of rumors concerning the gold of the police. He encouraged his officers to recruit on their own, but found that he had to overcome a strong revulsion on their part against men willing to betray their comrades. He tried to explain to them in language they would understand. "You, sirs, should look on an agent as a loved woman with whom you have an illicit alliance. Preserve her as the apple of your eye. One incautious step and you compromise her." [64]

It was Zubatov who, in his curious *fin-de-siècle* way, reawakened echoes of the Third Section's "educational" and "welfare" mission. He viewed the recruitment of secret agents not merely as a weapon against the revolution, but as a means of bringing revolutionaries back into respectable society. When an inevitable psychological crisis destroyed an agent's usefulness, he urged police officers to "draw him cautiously out of the revolutionary circle, set him up in some legal business, give him a pension, do everything you can to show your gratitude to him. . . . You will lose an agent, but acquire a worthy member of society." [65]

Later, as head of the special section in St. Petersburg, Zubatov systematized the filing system, adopting a more scientific recording of anthropometric detail. Using Zabatov's files, and engaging in further research, the police officer Spiridovich later wrote scholarly histories of

[63] Zavarzin, 23.
[64] Spiridovich, *Pri tsarskom rezhime*, 14.
[65] Spiridovich, 15.

both the SD and SR parties for the emperor. The history of public opinion in Russia, which the Third Section had undertaken in the nineteenth century, was in the twentieth reduced to that.[66]

The innovation for which Zubatov is best known also evokes echoes of the day when the political police was supposed to be "the moral physician of the people": his organization of labor unions sponsored by the police. Unfortunately for him, these organizations merely served to demonstrate the weakness of the police and relative strength of the revolutionaries. In Odessa, in 1903, revolutionary elements took over Zubatov's union and called it out to join a general strike. Zubatov was dismissed under a cloud and sent into a brief period of administrative exile.[67]

One of the most bizarre and futile attempts on the part of the police to revert to its old "opinion-forming" and "opinion-correcting" role was its campaign of anti-Semitic propaganda. This was an attempt to gain support for the autocracy by identifying the revolutionaries with Jews, a semiofficial policy, never openly acknowledged by either the police or the regime; and the police were by no means the only agency engaged in this venture. But as early as the 1880's, okhrana sections had included a "specialist in Jewish affairs," and no Jew was ever allowed to become an officer of the okhrana. In 1901, Rachkovsky set up a special secret press in the office of the Petersburg okhrana for the printing of anti-Semitic propaganda. The liberal chief of police Lopukhin first called the existence of this press to public attention, and Witte warned that official anti-Semitism would compromise Russia's financial position abroad.[68]

During the period of the 1905 Revolution and after, police agents and underground revolutionaries inhabited a common shadow world of perpetual distrust and suspicion. Almost anyone might be a police agent. Almost any police agent might be a revolutionary spy. When Lopukhin inadvertently admitted to V. Burtsev, a moderate SR, the identity of Azev (at that time head of the battle organization) as a police spy, Lopukhin was tried and exiled, in a broadly publicized case.[69]

If the police occasionally applied pressure on arrested revolutionaries to become agents, revolutionaries used the same device against revealed agents to turn them into revolutionaries. Thus, Stolypin and General Karpov, governor-general of Kiev, were both assassinated by former agents Bogrov and Petrov, respectively. The most useful agent in the employ of the okhrana was Roman Malinovsky, leader of the Bolshevik faction in

[66] Vasilyev, 90–91; L. Trotsky, *The History of the Russian Revolution* (New York, 1936), 52–77.

[67] Ozerov, 195–259.

[68] Lopukhin, 82.

[69] *Delo A. A. Lopukhina* (St. Petersburg, 1910); the world of double agents emerges dramatically from the Provisional Government's investigation into okhrana activities, *Padenie tsarskogo rezhima, po materialam chrezvychainoi kommissii Vremennago Pravitelstva* (7 vols.; Leningrad, 1924–1927), esp. vol. 3.

the Duma, member of a revolutionary counterespionage committee, and Lenin's protegé. He was exposed as a police spy in the Duma in 1914, but escaping abroad threw himself under Lenin's protection. A revolutionary court acquitted him — it was too difficult to believe in those days (in marked contrast to the Stalin and post-Stalin periods) that a distinguished revolutionary could be a police spy. In 1917, when the Provisional Government, investigating the okhrana archives, discovered indubitable proof of Malinovsky's work for the police, Lenin defended him in a curious way. He argued that it made no difference whether he was a police spy or not. Surrounded by alert Bolsheviks, Malinovsky could not help being of more use to the revolution than to the police.[70]

The Provisional Government, in spite of Burtsev's recommendations to the contrary, disdained the use of *any* political police. The Bolsheviks, unfortunately, had no such scruples.

IV

The Cheka, or Extraordinary Commission to Combat Counterrevolutionary Crimes and Sabotage, was "created," as Stalin quaintly put it, "on the second day of the revolution" (on the first day God created the earth) with Feliks Dzerzhinsky as its chairman.[71] Until 1921–1922, it existed as the instrument of revolutionary terror, operating not merely to deal with emergencies, but to anticipate them. Its founding decree makes that of the Third Section a model of conciseness by comparison; but even there, rights of judgment and execution are denied the Cheka — a limitation that had no effect in practice. As the advance guard of the revolution, the Cheka not only investigated, tried, and shot those who resisted, not only searched out and disposed of "class enemies," potential enemies, and hostages, but gathered in crops, requisitioned supplies, ran the railroads, guarded the border, inspected factories, and taught school. Its standard of procedure was not legality, but "revolutionary conscience." [72] Criticized from the beginning, both from outside and from within the Bolshevik Party, on two grounds — violation of the rights of individuals and interference with the function of more normalized institutions — the Cheka incorporated its already established empire into the constitutional structure of the Soviet Union.[73] This was done by a process by which the everyday police became the "militia" and the death sentence "the highest measure of punishment" — with little relevance to actual practice.

The imperial political police, in spite of occasional totalitarian impulses, had been fundamentally dedicated to preserving a dream of

---

[70] B. Wolfe, *Three Who Made a Revolution* (New York, 1948), 554.
[71] Stalin, *Sochineniia*, X, 234.
[72] S. Wolin and R. M. Slusser, *The Soviet Secret Police* (New York, 1957), 6–7, 78; M. Latsis, *Chrezvychainye komissii po bor'be s kontr-revoliutsiei* (Moscow, 1921).
[73] Wolin and Slusser, 11.

autocracy, which looked to the past and tried to come to frightened terms with the present. Soviet political police operated in terms of an apocalyptic vision of "new man," conceived by men living underground, members of a secret revolutionary party, for whom membership in the party had become a more important condition for existence than the living and continuing "spontaneous" world. To understand the Soviet police, we must first look at the party.

Although Bolsheviks had criticized the use of individual terror as a tactical device, they never objected to it in principle; indeed, Lenin had affirmed its necessity as an instrument of the dictatorship of the proletariat. "We do not enter the kingdom of socialism with white gloves on a polished floor," as Trotsky put it.[74] The preservation of the revolution justified hostages, arrests by category, and "preventive" punishment. In this, the Left SR's agreed with the Bolsheviks, and participated with them in the early days of the Cheka. This was part of a revolutionary tradition dating back to the Jacobins; the French revolutionary terror, however, had shown a direct correspondence in incidence and ferocity to the threat of immediate foreign invasion and domestic counterrevolution.[75] In contrast, the application of terror by the Soviet political police during the emergency period of War Communism was relatively mild, and assumed monstrous and unique proportions only during 1937–1938, although the practice of terror (not usually in the form of summary execution, it is true, but exile and preventive arrest) began to show a marked increase from the time of the stabilization of the Soviet state.[76]

The Bolsheviks differed from the other revolutionary parties not because their conceptualization of this category was broad, but because of what we might call their exclusiveness and their inner party discipline. The maintaining of this discipline, wrought largely by Lenin to preserve the integrity of his group against suppression and infiltration by the police, on the one hand, and against the formless and form-threatening "spontaneity" of the workers' movement, on the other, became a problem once success swelled the ranks of the party and once the special difficulties of running a state complicated leadership. Lenin's cry of "Schism! Schism!" to all disagreement and dissent within the party before the revolution found institutional form later in the party purge commissions. Purge meant expulsion from the party and was used by the leadership to eliminate opponents and dissenters within; terror meant execution, exile, imprisonment, and was used by the leadership to eliminate opponents and dissenters, actual or potential, outside the party. Party commissions con-

---

[74] E. H. Carr, *The Bolshevik Revolution* (New York, 1951), I, 157.

[75] D. Greer, *The Incidence of the Terror During the French Revolution: A Statistical Interpretation* (Cambridge, Mass., 1935).

[76] Carr, I, 176; H. Arendt, *The Origins of Modern Totalitarianism* (New York, 1950), 379; Z. Brzezinski, *The Permanent Purge* (Cambridge, Mass., 1956).

ducted the purge, and the political police conducted the terror; both were in the hands of the executive committee of the party, dominated by the Politburo. Stalin's domination of the Politburo was marked by his use of the political police to purge the party and his use of party controls to purge the police.

Feliks Dzerzhinsky, the chairman of the Cheka, had previously served on Bolshevik counterespionage committees, had been a member of the military-revolutionary committee of the Petrograd Soviet, and had assumed responsibility for the security of Bolshevik headquarters at Smolny during the first days of the revolution. He had a thorough knowledge of the old political police, having spent more than a fourth of his life in jail or exile. So many years in prison do not, as Albert Camus has written with regard to the Marquis de Sade, "produce a very conciliatory form of intelligence. . . . If the mind is strong enough to construct in a prison cell a moral philosophy that is not one of submission, it will generally be one of domination." [77] Beyond that, he was a singularly selfless, thorough idealist, a kind of saint of the revolution, who took on his own head the responsibilities of the terror. Reading his scattered speeches, articles, letters, and his prison diary, one is struck by the sentimentality of his language, his sense of isolation from the world, and his view of the party as a kind of religious order.[78] "Love," he wrote to his sister in 1919:

Today as many years before I feel it in my soul and hear its hymn. This hymn calls me to struggle, to unbending will, to tireless work. . . . I am a perennial wanderer. . . . In the process of change and creation of new life . . . I see the future.[79]

As a child he wanted to become a priest. "A small but spiritually strong handful of people," he later wrote in his prison diary, "will rally the masses round them." His jailers made a horrible impression on him. "I felt myself," he wrote after an interview with a prison official, "defiled with filth." [80] He could not abide the world of imperial prisons and would not tolerate any compromise between that world and his vision of the future which a "spiritually strong handful" would create. Later he had no tolerance of those who, like Tomsky or Bukharin, threatened to compromise that future on the grounds of the immediate needs of the masses. Although himself a Pole, he had no sympathy with local independence and was even (along with Stalin) accused by Lenin of Great Russian chauvinism.[81] His devotion to the leadership of the party was fervent and personal, attaching itself first to Lenin, then Stalin.

[77] *The Rebel* (New York, 1956), 36.
[78] F. Dzerzhinsky, *Dnevnik i pis'ma* (Moscow, 1956); *Izbrannye rechi i stat'i* (Moscow-Leningrad, 1947).
[79] Wolin and Slusser, 374–375.
[80] Wolin and Slusser, 69.
[81] R. Pipes, *The Formation of the Soviet Union* (Cambridge, Mass., 1954), 273–277.

The cult of Dzerzhinsky blossomed forth after his death and has not ceased to this day. Stalin wrote a glowing memorial tribute. Children's books appeared, featuring Dzerzhinsky as the kindly little father of the Cheka.[82] In the party he had never risen above the rank of candidate member of the Politburo; he was an instrument rather than a will. But he had created an elite political police for party service which, if the party is considered as the advance guard of the proletariat, might be called the advance guard of the advance guard.[83] "Chekist" became a Communist term of approval. During Dzerzhinsky's lifetime to be a Chekist meant to do unpleasant, often self-searing, work in the interests of the party, to sacrifice oneself for the party. The term Chekist, to this day, connotes the party's special approval for services rendered.

During the period of the New Economic Policy, the political police played a special role in preventing the generally relaxed and permissive conditions from producing any kind of organized opposition to the party leadership, either within or outside the party. It was only during the collectivization and industrialization drives, however, that the Soviet political police demonstrated the special zeal of men, whether idealists or opportunists, who were isolated by character, and further isolated from broad human sympathies by the special conditions of service in the political police. Legal restraints meant little; control by the prosecutor's office meant far less than in imperial days, for the prosecutor's office now merely represented another branch of the same party, and one inherently less capable of rendering spectacular service to the party leadership. The "liquidation of the kulaks" reinforced and augmented the already vast administrative machinery of the police. Industrialization brought it into the factory. Penetrating everywhere, the political police became the institutional prototype of the totalitarian state as a whole: characterized by aggressiveness, insecurity, and a sense of isolation, the men of the police did their best to engender these qualities in the population at large. No other institution could have lent itself so effectively to the collectivization and industrialization drives in the circumstances under which they occurred.

With the social and economic stratification of Soviet life in the 1930's, the political police ceased to be an ascetic order for the highly paid elite. The higher and more privileged the position, the less secure the tenure. Insecurity balanced privilege, and the police maintained its basic characteristics in a moving equilibrium as it grew in scope and terror.

The purges culminating in the *Ezhovshchina* are still obscure in their motivation. Stalin's fear of assassination, his avidity for total control within the party, the threat of war, the possible consolidation of amorphous

---

[82] Iu. German, *Rasskazy o Felikse Dzerzhinskom* (Moscow-Leningrad, 1947).
[83] Wolin and Slusser, 81; F. Beck and W. Godin, *Russian Purge and the Extraction of Confession* (New York, 1951), *passim*.

resistance inside the country with opposition outside, all played their part. Once the political police was set in motion, however, in an operation according to plan, in which "overfulfillment of norms" received due reward along with the encouragement of political denunciation among the population at large, whereby denouncing others became the only frail hope of saving oneself, terror threatened to engulf the entire nation.[84] Stalin, by exerting all his ingenuity, managed to avail himself of the police capacity for self-liquidation and thereby brought the process to a timely halt.[85] Accidents and personal excesses were deplored.[86] Thus began the Beria chapter of police history.

Like his predecessors, Lavrenti Beria was of non-Russian ethnic background. Unlike them, his entire career had been under Stalin's immediate supervision, first as a Chekist, then as a party leader in Georgia. With the personal tie to the leader definitely cemented, and under the excellent growing conditions of war and postwar reclamation, the political police expanded in size and function beyond all previous bounds. Building canals and roads, extracting raw materials, displacing entire populations, controlling a vast espionage and counterespionage network, supervising the church and the army, developing athletes for Olympic competition and atomic energy for the cold war, the police became an empire — not merely an instrument of the party, but an instrument over the party, with the ageing figure of Stalin alone guaranteeing its subordination.

Stalin's anxiety over the popularity of war heroes and the possibility of a political basis in that popularity contributed to the enhancement of the power and prestige of the political police. He accorded a unique position in the party hierarchy and an unprecedented number of awards and official distinctions to Beria. Service under Beria became a stepping stone to leadership in the provincial party apparatus, especially in Georgia. Army ranks and decorations were instituted among the armed forces of the political police. As an empire, however, the political police was faced with the problems of stabilization and loyalty. After Stalin's death, Beria began to make a bid for public support: first, by exposing the fabrication of the "doctors' plot," then by displaying the benevolence of police institutions — revising the Criminal Code and granting an amnesty. At the same time, he tightened still further his personal control over police administration.[87]

That Beria failed to seize power, in spite of his empire, marks the inherent limitations of the political police. The empire itself had been the necessary physical counterpart of Stalin's ideological authority. Without

---

[84] Beck and Godin; I. Deutscher, *Stalin* (New York, 1949), 372ff.

[85] Brzezinski, 65–131.

[86] Stalin, *Sochineniia*, VII, 380ff; A. Weissberg, *The Accused* (New York, 1951), 421; and, for irony, N. Khrushchev, secret speech, in *The Anti-Stalin Campaign and International Communism* (New York, 1956).

[87] Wolin and Slusser, 27–28, 322–337, 382–384.

its apparatus of totally organized, totally organizable men, Stalin could never have held total sway over an increasingly complex society. A world war had been waged successfully on an unprecedented scale, and in this war inevitably a secondary leadership arose, closer to the public at large than was entirely compatible with Stalinist totalitarianism (one should not, of course, exaggerate this closeness — these men were still Communists) and which had acquired some degree of confidence in its own ability and its own worth. Without Stalin's ideological authority, the political police had to face more than the direct hostility of the public: the newly confident leadership of the army, the bureaucracy, the party, which might (being Communist) acquiesce in the necessity of unlimited police power against the inertia and the political "shortcomings" of the population at large, but not in its supremacy over them. In any appeal to a larger public, the apparatus of the political police would not only be at an obvious disadvantage but unfitted by its very nature. In order to capture Stalin's position, Beria had first to dissociate himself from his own apparatus, to find some base of support outside the police empire. For this he had not the time. In the face of a threat from Beria, the leadership of the party and that of the army managed to submerge their differences for a decisive action.

One should not underestimate the impact of the war on the new Soviet leadership: literally new, since so much of the old had been undone by the purges. For the first time an enormous enterprise had been carried through — had to be carried through — without the illusion of Stalin's omnipresent hand, no matter with what increased intensity propaganda and the police tried to maintain that illusion. Big as the police were blown, enormous as the Generalissimo was made to appear, the real experience of the war was larger still. Indeed, as Khrushchev repeatedly and indignantly emphasized much later in his famous speech, Stalin and the police were felt as an unwarranted and insulting intrusion. Out of the confidence acquired by successful prosecution of the war, something like a sense of community emerged in the party leadership and persisted in spite of Stalin's postwar efforts to destroy it.

Parallel with this sense of community in the leadership of the Soviet Union, the war created a larger sense of community as well. Relatively vague and ill-defined, it consisted nevertheless of a feeling shared by a large number of people that the validity of the common war experience was something quite different from the official pronouncements of validity. The new leadership was aware of this public feeling and was convinced that the party could not maintain its rule without taking it into account. Opinions as to how it should be taken into account apparently differed. From the repeated charges that have been brought to bear against Malenkov since his dismissal — charges of "inexperience" and "timidity" — it may be inferred (as Boris Nikolaevsky has recently suggested [88]) that his attempts to reach an agreement with the West ("atomic war would mean the end of civilization," he insisted) and his program for consumer-goods production were considered by Khrushchev and others as a policy too far in the direction of complete capitulation. Khrushchev, on the other hand, seems to rely squarely on the party leadership itself — a leadership now based, however, on a closer proximity to the public and, if still aggressive, at least more responsive to the larger sense of community I have suggested than was true under Stalin. This has been reflected in recent changes with regard to the political police.

Khrushchev's exposure of Stalin and Beria was accompanied by the administrative division of political-police functions. No public mention of the security organs was henceforth made without some included reference to the observance of "socialist legality." [89] Many political prisoners were released and, at the Twenty-first Party Congress, the recently appointed head of the state security organs, A. N. Shelepin, proudly announced that, "Today there is no one incarcerated in our prisons out of political motives." [90] The concept of terror, of course, has been reaffirmed — but only in proportion to the danger threatening the Soviet state. Khrushchev indignantly denounced the Stalinist thesis that the enemies of the Soviet state become increasingly dangerous the closer it approaches communism. No doubt this seemed to Khrushchev and his supporters a shocking mistrust of the very accomplishments on which their confidence was based. But celebrating the fortieth anniversary of the Cheka, Ivan Serov (then chief of the security organs) affirmed the terror at the same time that he derided Stalinist abuses: "Now that Soviet science and technology have been shown to be in advance of the United States'," he warned, "espionage against the USSR has a special significance." [91] Serov concluded by urging mass cooperation with the police in denouncing violations of security. In this way, the tense international situation served both as an excuse for the continued existence of an imposing political police and as a brake against the more extreme forms its activity had assumed in the past.

General Serov who succeeded Beria (or more accurately Abakumov) as chief of the security organs was a hard-bitten police professional who had begun his career under Stalin, and whose name was linked with such somber enterprises as the massive evacuation and exile of citizens of the Baltic countries and the total dispersion of the Kalmyk, Chechen, and Ingush Autonomous Republics. There is no indication that he did not

[88] B. Nikolaevsky, "Vneshniaia politika Khrushcheva," *Sotsialisticheskii vestnik* (April 1959), 56.

[89] I. Serov, "Sorok let na strazhe bezopasnosti sovetskogo gosudarstva," *Pravda* (December 21, 1957), 6; Khrushchev, secret speech.

[90] A. Shelepin, "Rech' tovarishcha A. N. Shelepina," *Pravda* (February 5, 1959), 8.

[91] Serov, *Pravda*.

perform his new role faithfully and well. It was he, following Khrushchev, who carried through the purge of Beria appointees in the political police; it was he who attempted to reassure the public about the maintenance of "socialist legality"; and it was he who called for the formation of vigilance committees against foreign espionage and mass cooperation with the organs of the police. Mikoyan, at a news conference in Los Angeles on January 12, 1959, insisted that Serov had not been "dismissed," but merely reassigned "somewhere in the army." With the initial task of an "old-fashioned" type of purge of the police apparatus accomplished, Serov simply did not fit the current requirements for a chief of political police.

These requirements are admirably met by Aleksandr N. Shelepin, who was appointed to replace Serov on Christmas day, 1958. A young man, barely turned forty, very much a part of the war generation, Shelepin's rise to prominence coincided entirely with the prominence of Khrushchev. Unlike Serov, he was a public figure, if a relatively minor one and if only for a short time. He was not associated with any of the police abuses of the past. His career in fact had been in the organs of propaganda, persuasion, and indoctrination, not in those of repression. As head of the Komsomol, he had indeed cried out against the corrupting influence of the West, and had conducted the anti-*stiliagi* campaign, but had at the same time discouraged the eruption of this campaign into the "old-fashioned" kind of crude violence.[92] As a member of the Central Committee of the party, he had been associated with the organs of propaganda, and this association he apparently retains as head of the political police. His speech before the Twenty-first Party Congress is most instructive in this regard.

He begins with an affirmation somewhat stronger than the usual ritual incantations: "The twentieth century will be known as the century of communism!" He sketches the glories of the proposed seven-year plan, and only then begins to expatiate on the role of the security organs. These, "now that the last traces of Beria's activities have been liquidated and revolutionary legality restored," are directed primarily against agents from abroad. But this *agentura* is a very formidable business. The American C.I.A. employs more than 20,000 spies and spends more than a billion and a half dollars annually on espionage work, he says. Its staff is "twelve times" what it was during the immediate postwar years. In order to meet this threat, he urges closer "ties with the people," vigilance committees, correctional work on wavering members undertaken by the Komsomol, the trade unions, and the various collectives. He insists that the sphere of activity of the state security organs must be limited, that their "punitive function has been curtailed and will be still further curtailed." He adds, however, that "this does not mean that there are fewer cases before us or that the enemy's activities have diminished." What Shelepin is indeed

---

[92] Cf. "Kto iz nikh stiliaga?" *Komsomolskaia pravda* (August 11, 1956), 2.

urging is that Soviet institutions convincingly persuade every man to become his own Minister of the Interior.[93]

All this had already been adumbrated, less elaborately and less eloquently, by Serov, who had also attempted to by-pass the Stalin era in order to find a more viable police tradition in the period of Lenin and Dzerzhinsky. "Dzerzhinsky," Shelepin insists, "knew how to tell the difference between a real enemy of the Soviet state and a citizen who accidentally fell under the influence of the enemy." There are, however, even more ominous, if still muted, references in Shelepin's speech. For one thing, "revisionists" are coupled with "imperialists" as threats to the fulfillment of the seven-year plan, and it is not entirely clear whether it is only the vigilance committees that are being alerted to their activities or the state security organs as well. For another, the "antiparty group" — explicitly, Malenkov, Molotov, Kaganovich, and Shepilov — are accused of "a real plot against the party," and it is similarly unclear as to whether Shelepin's boast of "no political prisoners" will remain of long standing. Shelepin's attempt to associate himself with Khrushchev first, and with the "Leninist Central Committee" secondarily as a symbolic support for Khrushchev's policies, goes considerably further than Serov's; Shelepin is clearly Khrushchev's man. As long as the determination of party leadership is based on a more or less open struggle among the top members of the party hierarchy, it seems inevitable that such a struggle for control of the party necessarily involves a struggle for control of the police, and that the terroristic potentialities of the political police may well be released in the process.

Meanwhile, criticism of the political police and the terror, with their mindless violation of privacy and personal integrity, their human waste, and their stifling of initiative, has found a voice — stronger at first than it is now, to be sure — in literature. Again, the impact of the war, and the disillusioning repression that followed it, should not be underestimated. Dudintsev's *Not by Bread Alone* was not explicitly a political novel, but it was not merely, as some would have it, a plea for "the career open to talent." It was, on the contrary, a strong assertion of the validity of personal inspiration independent of politically imposed criteria, the validity of personal experience and private knowledge. In this light, in any case, the students excitedly discussed it; in this light, it had meaning for them. In Galina Nikolaeva's *Battle Along the Way*, a series of police arrests and personal "disappearances" is described in detail. These arrests are, in the novel, explicitly attributed to Beria, and there is no overt condemnation of the system that made such arrests possible. Nevertheless, the experience of arrest is concretely and dramatically presented — down to the neighbor who draws her blind to avoid noticing — and this has a

[93] Shelepin, *Pravda*.

kind of meaning that the ritual denunciations of Beria that appear almost daily in the press cannot have. Both Dudintsev and Nikolaeva were attacked in print, the former much more systematically. Both replied, eventually going through the form of a capitulation. Nikolaeva, a party stalwart, did not, indeed, retreat very far. Dudintsev, on the other hand, after months of obscurity, published a short story that seems to belie his capitulation. Neither was arrested. The latest move against Dudintsev has in fact been the publication of a novel, *The Brothers Ershov* by Kochetov, which purports to refute him. It is a very dull novel, however, and in spite of all encomiums lavished on it by Shelepin's propaganda apparatus seems to have caused but little stir.

Of an entirely different dimension, but by no means unrelated to the literary thaw, has been the Pasternak scandal. Pasternak was not a novice like Dudintsev, nor a party writer like Nikolaeva. He represented a connection with the prerevolutionary past; he was the last living monument of the old Russian literature and was looked on as such by a small but significant group of younger intellectuals, writers, and would-be writers. *Doctor Zhivago*, which has not been published in the Soviet Union but which enjoys an underground circulation in the manner of Pushkin's "liberal" poems or Lermontov's poem about the death of Pushkin, both thematically and in effect proclaims the existence of a community not based on party standards but on the values of art and literature as these are recreated in the work of an individual man. Tolstoy once implied that what occurred in the Rostov home (and others like it) had more importance for the ultimate course of history than the plans and proclamations of Napoleon and Alexander I; Pasternak similarly insisted that the work of a single gifted man, no matter how shut off from what seem to be the major events of his time, by drawing others into a spontaneous community springing directly from the same human needs and aspirations that Russian writers once saw as centered in the family, may prove to be of greater significance than all the party proclamations and police decrees. Those who might be inclined to take this significance lightly are referred back to the first flowering of Russian literature — which occurred at a time when, as Nikitenko put it, there were "more censors than books" and the gendarmerie was "the moral physician of the people" — and its consequences. Russian literature, however faintly, still preserves, against the Stalins and the Khrushchevs, some of the best ideals of the old Russian intelligentsia, which destroyed one political police and may yet topple another.

THE STATE AND THE LOCAL COMMUNITY

ALEXANDER VUCINICH

Russia's "epoch of great reforms" during the sixties of the last century produced the village community, the township, and the zemstvo. These three units were local political communities: all had at their command the necessary administrative agencies to perform specified functions of local import. The municipality as a political-administrative unit antedates the reforms of the 1860's; credit for its establishment goes to Peter the Great and Catherine II. However, a new Statute on Cities, passed on June 16, 1870, liberalized the election of city councilors and expanded the administrative competence of local municipal authorities.

To understand fully the place of these four local communities in Russia's political system it is necessary to study the internal organization of their elected and administrative agencies, to indicate the institutional mechanisms which linked them with the central state authorities, and to point out the basic trends in their relation to the state.

I

When on November 20, 1857, the government announced its intention to abolish serfdom, one of the most vital and complex problems it faced was the blueprinting of new rural communities and their relations with the central authorities. Both these demanding tasks were thrown into the lap of an administrative section of the commission entrusted with drafting the General Statute on Peasants. The members of this section were in agreement from the outset that the basic tasks confronting them were the creation of uniform types of local communities, the definition of the political and administrative attributes of these communities, and the specification of their ties with the central state machinery.

In searching for a precise definition of the primary rural community the members of the administrative section endorsed unanimously the proposal of the Ministry of the Internal Affairs that (1) the new village units be so organized as to ensure "the replacement of the former irresponsible police authority and the irresponsible landlord courts by an appropriate police and judiciary-police organization of the peasants," and (2) necessary institutional devices be introduced to safeguard "the general peace and order." [1] A synchronization of these two tasks was the

---

[1] A. A. Kornilov, *Ocherki po istorii obshchestvennago dvizheniia i krest'ianskago dela v Rossii* (St. Petersburg, 1905), 320.

key problem with which the administrative section was faced. The first task was tantamount to laying the foundations for an autonomous status of the rural community vis-à-vis the central political authorities. The second task was of opposite cast: it was directed, above everything else, toward the preservation of the autocratic regime. The prodigious assignment which the members of the section faced was how to grant a modicum of self-government to rural communities without abrogating any attributes of monarchical absolutism.

No wonder then that from the outset they subscribed to the idea of two types of rural political communities: one to handle the purely local "cultural" and "economic" problems, and therefore not to be formally linked with the government, and the second to function as a police and administrative unit connected by formal ties with the central government. The proposed dichotomy was based on the premise that one type of community should be dedicated to local interests and the second to the interests of the state. This dichotomy became the cornerstone of the General Statute. At the beginning most members of the administrative section shared the opinion that the land commune (*pozemel'naia obshchina*) and the village community (*sel'skoe obshchestvo*) should be the units of the proposed dichotomy.[2] However, the final draft of the General Statute recognized the village community and the township (*volost*) as the two primary rural communities.

The village community appeared in two general forms. In the areas in which communal agriculture (through the existence of the obshchina) was predominant a village community was more often than not coterminous with the traditional commune. Thus the peasants who previously were subordinated to a single landlord were likely to form a peasant community. This phenomenon was a result of the philosophy of gradualism which dominated the thinking of the drafters of the General Statute. The second type of village community consisted of rural households which were not previously organized on a communal basis although they were an integral part of the system of serfdom. Each type of community was bolted together by the institution of "collective responsibility" (*krugovaia poruka*): the entire community was held legally responsible for the failure of a single person to meet his obligations to various state authorities. In communities based on the obshchina principle, the rule of collective responsibility was extended to include the obligations to former landlords. The peasants, individually or collectively, had no legal right to leave their community before they completed their land payments.

The General Statute granted the peasant a series of rights. For the

[2] For a detailed description of the various types of obshchina and their relation to the village community, see Geroid Tanquary Robinson, *Rural Russia Under the Old Regime* (New York, 1949), 67–78.

first time he could enter into all sorts of contractual relations and run his family affairs independently of the landlord, who was also divested of his traditional responsibility for the collection of peasant taxes and for the meeting of military obligations by the rural populace. However, the landlord had retained a number of traditional prerogatives and, as a substitute for his "lost" land, he acquired certain new power attributes. He continued to play the role of guardian in all court proceedings whether or not the peasants desired his services. New police functions of village authorities were placed under his direct control.

The new village community did not signify a full termination of serfdom. The peasants' annual payments (*obrok*) and services (*barshchina*) to their former landlords were preserved as a form of payments for land. The "installment" system of redemption payments made it practical for the government to retain the *krugovaia poruka*. On the other hand, the landlords' loss of such important responsibilities as the supervision over the tax payments and military obligations by the peasants created an administrative vacuum in the countryside. The newly founded administrative agencies of the village community and the township became the legal heirs to the "state functions" previously performed by the landlord. The big question was how to define the authority of the new communities, the more so because at the time the emphasis on self-government had gained wide currency among many intellectuals and progressive landlords. The problem of local autonomy versus centralized autocracy became a burning issue in Russia's internal politics during the remainder of the monarchic era.

All household heads of a village community made up the village assembly (*sel'skii skhod*), which in turn selected the elder, the tax collector, and a number of other officials. The elder and the officials were responsible for the assessment and collection of various taxes, maintenance of rural roads and bridges, assistance to families impoverished by fire and natural accidents, and several obligations of purely local significance.

The township consisted of two or more village communities including a total of from three hundred to two thousand male members, and with a maximum distance of eight miles between individual villages. The General Statute defined the township as the lowest administrative unit of peasant self-government, in contrast to the village community which was defined as an "economic" unit. The organizational blueprint of the township included three institutions: the township assembly (*skhod*), the township headman with the administrative officials, and the township peasant court. The township assembly consisted of all elected village and township officials and of additional peasants elected by each village community at a ratio of one delegate per ten households. The law vested the assembly with limited authority in the fields of local "economic" interests, public order, and local schools. Since an appallingly high number of deputies were illiterate and totally unversed in administrative intricacies, these institutions made no appreciable contribution to the cause of rural self-government. Experience had shown that there were no substantial township properties, capital investments, or public undertakings to give the township assembly a vital place in the life of the rural population. Moreover, from the very beginning most tax, land, and public-work obligations were handled by village assemblies.

The township headman and other administrative officials were obliged to acquaint the mostly illiterate local population with the substance of relevant laws and government decisions. It was their duty also to search for and detain law violators and in general to maintain peace and order in their respective areas. The township court, the third institutional component of township government, consisted of from four to twelve members elected by the township assembly. It settled small debt conflicts among local peasants and punished individuals guilty of minor misdemeanors.

The administrative mechanisms of the village community and the township had no precedents in Russia: they were the first institutions which recognized the peasant as a political quantity. The situation in municipalities was quite different. Local government of a special type had existed in towns and cities since the early eighteenth century. Peter the Great instituted various *Landrats,* urban guilds, magistrates, and elective commissions in an effort to make up for the obvious inability of centralized bureaucracy to cope effectively with the growing demands of both the state and the local community.[3] These agencies were granted no effective local autonomy and had no deep roots in the community. They became mere bureaucratic appendages and an added burden to the citizens. A student of the growth of the idea of self-government in Russia concludes correctly that Peter's administrative reforms had contributed considerably more to the consolidation and expansion of the bureaucratic system than to the cause of local self-government.[4] As the economic and political life of the country grew more complex, the contrast between local and state demands became increasingly more pronounced. In 1785, Catherine II issued the Statute on Cities which ruled that the members of "all" estates (with the exception of peasants, of course) take part in electing the deputies of city councils (*duma*). The latter were empowered to manage independently a sizable array of local cultural and economic activities. Dzhanshiev, an eminent student of Russia's social reforms, stated that none of the nineteenth-century city statutes was "more pro-

---

[3] A. A. Kizevetter, *Mestnoe samoupravlenie v Rossii* (Moscow, 1910), 99–112. See also: B. B. Veselovsky, "Detsentralizatsiia upravleniia i zadachi zemstva," in B. B. Veselovsky and Z. G. Frenkel, eds., *1864–1914, Iubileinyi zemskii sbornik* (St. Petersburg, 1914), 35–36.
[4] A. A. Kizevetter, 112.

gressive" than the one promulgated by Catherine II.[5] Although the city duma became a permanent body, it did not achieve the autonomous status specified by the 1785 statute. Within a very short time the duma authorities became fully subordinated to the government-appointed chief of local administration.

After prolonged preparations, the second Statute on Cities was made public on June 16, 1870. All city property-tax payers participated in the election of the city duma councilors, who in turn elected an administrative board and a mayor. Such local "economic" matters as construction and maintenance of public market places, sanitation service, certain types of educational facilities, charity, and fire protection were under the jurisdiction of this body. During the 1870's the city duma was introduced throughout Russia and in certain parts of Central Asia.

The most original and tangible contribution of the reform-oriented government of the late 1850's and the 1860's to the political autonomy of the local community was made through the Statute on Zemstvos of January 1, 1864. The zemstvo institutions were among the principal forces in the reform period which transformed Russia's social life along "completely new lines of citizenship."[6] The zemstvos were organized on district (*uezd*) and provincial (*guberniia*) levels, and their authorities consisted of zemstvo assemblies and zemstvo administrations. The district assemblies had from ten to ninety-six deputies (*glasnykh*), who were elected by three electoral groups (*curiae*) defined in terms of property holdings: the landholders, city property holders, and village communities. The district zemstvo assemblies elected the provincial deputies at a ratio of one delegate per six district delegates. The district assemblies also elected the members of the district zemstvo administration for a three-year term to perform specified administrative functions. The zemstvo institutions were entrusted with such purely local "economic and cultural" functions as the management of the rural means of communication, mutual insurance, charity, and food stores. They also fought cattle plagues and natural causes of harvest failures, and were in charge of local commerce and industry, public health, elementary education, and jails.[7] In order to finance their undertakings and to pay the salaries of their employees, the zemstvos were authorized to collect property taxes. The zemstvo agencies were introduced gradually; it took ten years after the passage of the 1864 statute before they were established in thirty-three provinces of European Russia. In Siberia, the Baltic areas, most of Central Asia and the Caucasus, they were never introduced lest any autonomy of

[5] N. Dzhanshiev, *Epokha velikikh reform* (Moscow, 1900), 508, 520.
[6] Veselovsky and Frenkel, vii.
[7] For a detailed description of zemstvo achievements during the period from 1864 to 1914, see Prince G. E. Lvov and T. I. Polner, *Nashe zemstvo i 50 let' ego raboty* (Moscow, 1914).

local communities might spur the growth of nationalism among non-Russian peoples.

II

The political-administrative agencies of the village community, the township, the new city duma, and the zemstvo were the results not only of the rising pressure for local self-government generated by the country's intellectuals of various ideological orientations, but also of a need to find working substitutes for the defunct local administrative machinery of the serfdom era which placed in the hands of landed aristocracy extensive police, judiciary, and other functions. They were also results of the determination of the top-level state authorities to "solve" the problem of local self-government without surrendering any essential attributes of monarchic absolutism.

The idea of local self-government was one of the most popular ideas of the reform epoch. It was only the tradition-imbued, high government bureaucrat who was quick to discern its utter incompatibility with the monarchical order and to condemn it outright. The champions of local self-government represented a strange conglomeration of intellectual circles; each bestowed all its blessing on local political autonomy and yet each defined it in its own terms. Out of the ocean of general intellectual confusion there emerged three dominant theories of self-government which may be labeled the communal theory, the social theory, and the state theory. The proponents of the communal theory — among whom the most vociferous were various antiwesternization factions — were content with the idea that the existence and perpetuation of land communes as corporate bodies were synonymous with sound local self-government. Many proponents of this theory identified the commune both as an indigenous Russian institution and as a primordial — that is, pre-feudal — organization. They provided no serious challenge to the champions of the autocratic regime; yet while the Slavophiles sought the perpetuation of the commune as a bulwark in the struggle against westernization, the spokesmen of autocracy sought its survival to avoid undue complexities in the policy of gradual dissolution of serfdom.

The social theory of local self-government was championed by a majority of intellectual groups and by a solid core of state councilors. This theory was based on the cardinal assumption that society, with its own demands and functions, was independent of the state and that, therefore, the peculiarly "social" functions should be carried out by special "social" agencies which must be outside the bureaucratic pyramid of the government and must enjoy appreciable autonomy in the performance of their functions.[8] This theory was obviously based on a false

[8] N. N. Avinov, "Glavnyia cherty v istorii zakonodatel'stva o zemskikh uchrezhdeniiakh," in Veselovsky and Frenkel, 3.

dichotomy of society and the state, and its official supporters were committed to overlook the creation of any formal ties connecting the local political communities with the trunk of the central government. The society-state dichotomy came to be a part of the futile effort to blend two ideologically disparate parts of the Russian body politic: the romanticized democratism of the local rural community and self-sanctified autocratism.

The state theory of local self-government revolved around the assumption that there were no specifically local affairs, that so-called local affairs were state affairs which were placed by the "will of the state" into the hands of the organs of local self-government. The state authority, according to the champions of this theory, was one and indivisible and had two arms: the units of the bureaucratic pyramid and the institutions of local self-government. During the late 1850's and early 1860's the state theory was still in an embryonic form; it did not receive full theoretical treatment before the last two decades of the century.[9]

The four local communities as finally blueprinted by their respective statutes were predominantly the results of the ideas and designs set forth by the proponents of the social theory. The representative and administrative bodies of these communities became known as "social institutions." Their drafters did realize, however, that an unqualified application of pure social theory would lead to a polarization of the two types of authority between which no formal links would exist. Therefore, the lawmakers were compelled to define for all four communities not only their self-governing mechanisms and jurisdiction, but also what amounted to government control over the local elected bodies. The legal acts which paved the way for the establishment of the four communities were based on the premise that the difference between "state" functions and "social" functions was the difference between important and unimportant functions as these were defined by the state. In practice, the autocratic government did not surrender any of its functions; it merely authorized the local "self-governing" authorities to perform the tasks with which the state was not traditionally concerned. Of course, as some of the social functions grew in complexity and importance the central government was ready to redefine them as state functions and place them under its jurisdiction.

It is obvious that from the outset the local communities were politically subordinated to the state authorities in two ways: their authority was limited to the powers delegated to them by nonelective central authorities, and they were subjected to strict control by government bureaucracy. The elected authorities of the village community and the township were obliged by law to carry out all tasks assigned to them by numerous government officials, including the ubiquitous police and court

---

[9] For a brief review of the leading exponents of this theory, see P. P. Gronsky, "Teorii samoupravleniia v russkoi nauke," in Veselovsky and Frenkel, 76–85.

investigators. The village and township authorities were also dominated by a special government official, the arbitrator, who was appointed by the governors upon recommendation by the local gentry. His original function was to prepare so-called basic documents, which specified size and location of land acquired by the peasants and their financial and other obligations to the former owners. From the beginning, however, the arbitrator commanded enough authority to annul any decisions by local authorities which he considered illegal, to discharge or even arrest elected officials, and to give formal approval or disapproval of local deputies. In 1874 the arbitrator was replaced by the district office for peasants' affairs, which consisted of permanent members and was dominated by the district police chief whose orders were law to all township and village authorities. In 1889 the land captain became the new master of the countryside; he possessed unqualified power to overrule all orders and judicial decisions made by rural authorities. While the arbitrator was an amateur with vaguely defined power attributes, the land captain was a high-ranking bureaucrat with expert proficiency in wielding a far-reaching authority.

Municipal self-government was subject to similar limitations. The mayors of larger cities needed official approval by the Minister of the Interior and those of smaller municipalities by the provincial governor before they could officially begin their public service. Zemstvo self-government — widely extolled as the highest form of local political autonomy achieved under the Tsarist regime — was also subject to control by the bureaucratic apparatus, although this control was not explicitly stated in the Statute of 1864. The latter document, however, did rule (through Article 108) that the zemstvo institutions should direct their activities in accordance with the regulations provided for by special laws. These laws regulated the stupendous "obligations" of rural communities to the state, the methods of rural communication, public-construction projects, distribution of provisions, mutual insurance, charity, and the assessment and collection of taxes.[10] The zemstvo authorities were hamstrung by outside regulations establishing most of the substance and procedure of their "self-government." It is also noteworthy that most of these regulations came into existence before the establishment of the zemstvo and even before the enactment of the General Statute. Thus zemstvo agencies were expected to conduct their affairs in accordance with legal measures which came into force in prereform days and were totally alien to the idea of local self-government.[11]

There is another element that occupied an important part in the network of relationships which linked the local community with the state and which throws significant light on the political-administrative status of the local community in the Russian polity. In addition to the assign-

[10] Avinov, 28.
[11] Avinov, 28.

ments of local importance, labeled as "social" rather than "political" assignments, the local communities performed many functions of "state significance" which were subsumed under the general category of "obligations to the state." The state functions bestowed no rights or prerogatives on the local communities and their representative bodies; they simply imposed burdensome duties on them. At the end of the 1870's, for example, the municipal government of Moscow disbursed 37 per cent of its budget for the needs of the army, police, gendarmerie, and similar institutions which were subordinated to the central government and over which the city fathers had no jurisdiction.

The case of the zemstvos is particularly instructive in this regard. In 1899 the government issued a voluminous charter which stipulated the "obligations" of rural communities to the state. In the regions where zemstvos were in existence they were the chief carriers of these burdens. In 1906 and 1907 additional burdens were added as the old ones tended to perpetuate themselves. The zemstvo obligations to the state were divided into cash obligations and goods-and-services obligations. The former were earmarked for the maintenance and construction of roads; the needs of civil administration (such as post offices); direct donations to the state treasury; local economy, welfare, and improvements; and military needs. Later the zemstvos were obliged to finance the building of detention stations for convicts transported from one place to another, and in the western regions to pay the salaries of local priests. The goods-and-services obligations were equally extensive.[12] Zemstvo administrations were required to organize the local populace for mandatory work on roads; to supply horses for local policing and mail-distributing purposes and for the transportation of official persons; and to provide living quarters for certain police and other officials.

Another important feature of the newly established local communities influencing their relationship with the central agencies of the state was the peculiar class composition of their elected and administrative bodies. In the elections of the deputies of the various assemblies the social category of "estate" (*soslovie*) was the key element. The estates were neither social classes nor castes. They were social strata that were more dynamic — and more susceptible to vertical mobility — than castes; yet they were more rigid and subject to appreciably less mobility than social classes. Estates were defined by law and legal customs and were characteristic of the social system of the empire. The fathers of the great reforms of the 1860's recognized that the abolition of serfdom and the attendant creation of new local communities as political-administrative entities necessitated a modification of differential legal and political rights and duties based on the estate principle. The problem of estate stratification was of prime significance in the preparation of laws for the regulation

[12] A. P. Feodorov, ed., *Ustav o zemskikh povinnostiakh* (St. Petersburg, 1908).

of procedures for the election of deputies to the assemblies of local communities.

At a time when the idea of equal citizenship was alien, in Russia hardly more than in most of Europe, the proposals for electoral procedures could follow one of three paths: they could be based on an estate, an all-estate, or a nonestate principle. These principles were widely discussed, officially and academically, although quite often without clear differentiation. The estate principle stood for the participation of a single estate in the election of the delegates of local assemblies. The all-estate principle denoted the participation of all estates *qua* estates in elections, that is, each estate participated as a separate and distinguished entity. The nonestate principle stood for the substitution of a class principle for an estate principle in the designation of groups which voted as separate units. This principle replaced the hereditary status by the type, size, and value of property holdings as the official criterion for the division of population into voting groups.

Of the four communities under discussion, the village community and the township elected their representatives on an estate principle; they were defined as purely peasant bodies and only the peasants were allowed to participate in the elections. The official reasoning behind the estate nature of the assemblies of these two communities was quite obvious: through the estate unity of peasantry the government expected to prolong the existence of the obshchina as the most potent guaranty for the fulfillment of the financial and other obligations of the peasants to their former landlords. Through the estate unity of the township the government expected to enhance both its control over the rural community and the fulfillment of peasant obligations to the state.

The deputies of city councils and zemstvo assemblies were elected on the basis of the nonestate or property-class principle. In cities the voters were divided into three groups, each entitled to one third of the total number of deputies. The first group consisted of the comparatively small segment of large property owners who paid in aggregate one third of the city taxes. At the bottom was the bulk of city populace who jointly paid as much tax as the few members of the top group.[13] Similar procedures were applied in the elections of zemstvo delegates. The members of district zemstvo assemblies were elected by persons who acquired the right to vote by virtue of owning a legally defined minimum ("census") of property. The voters were grouped into three electoral aggregates (*curiae*): the owners of agricultural land, the owners of real estate in

[13] The 1892 Statute on Cities replaced the three-class division of the electorate by territorial election units (districts) which contributed neither to a more equal representation of various segments of the population nor to a reduced "dependence of municipal self-government on the administrative organs of the state." Kizevetter, 153.

urban communities, and the members of village communities.[14] The first two groups elected their delegates by direct vote, while the members of village communities elected a group of "electors" (at a ratio of one elector per three hundred households), who in turn selected the requisite number of zemstvo delegates. The intent of the lawmaker to abate the deeply rooted estate bias in the election of district zemstvo delegates did not materialize. Although the electoral curia of landowners included not only the former landlords who retained substantial property but also small peasants, the latter, with few exceptions, played no independent role within their voting group. In cases where they did win decisive victories, it was not difficult to discover formal "irregularities" and proclaim the elections invalid, or to secure the victory for the gentry through administrative influences on the muzhiks.[15]

That the zemstvo assemblies were not based on a principle of proportional representation of the social groups of individual districts was obvious. Moreover, the two strongest groups — the landed gentry and the peasants — formed a strange constellation of forces separated by the inequality inherent in the estate system. An authoritative source puts it this way: "The difference between nonaristocratic and aristocratic estates was preserved in full force. In zemstvo assemblies there met two groups of people with totally different political and civil rights. Totally different also were the economic positions of these groups. The foundations of serfdom, despite some external changes, continued to live after 1861 in a new style." [16]

The zemstvo as a resounding myth differed qualitatively from the zemstvo as a cold reality. As a myth it epitomized the highest achievement of "the epoch of great reforms" for it stood for two novel principles of progressivism: local self-government and nonstate representation. In reality its self-government had but little substance, and its representative character hardly took a step away from the system of feudal estates. It was largely as a myth — at least in the beginning — that the zemstvo acquired its strange conglomeration of ideologically disparate supporters. In the words of Prince D. Shakhovskoi: "Hundreds of persons with sharply developed individualities took part in zemstvo work, and here we met the adherents of the total spectrum of political allegiances, from extreme Westerners to typical Slavophiles, from resolute radicals to stub-

[14] For various reasons the townfolk showed little interest in zemstvo elections. B. Veselovsky, *K voprosu o klassovykh interesakh v zemstve* (St. Petersburg, 1905), 35–36.

[15] D. Shakhovskoi, "Politischeskie techeniia v russkom zemstve," in Veselovsky and Frenkel, 444. For the distribution of zemstvo deputies in terms of their estate identifications, see *Kalendar spravochnik zemskago deiatelia, 1912 g.* (St. Petersburg, 1912), 96.

[16] Shakhovskoi, 444.

born upholders of the existing order, and from consistent democrats to lukewarm defenders of the estate principle." [17]

III

To ask what happened to the zemstvo institutions during the remaining years of the empire amounts substantially to asking what happened to the relationship between the Russian state and the Russian local community in general. The growth of zemstvo institutions was paradoxical. On the one hand, a long series of government orders, laws, and statutes combined to curb any appreciable development of local self-government and even abrogated most of the original guarantees of administrative autonomy. On the other hand, the zemstvo acquired a remarkable degree of stubbornness and vitality and became a rallying point for movements directed against rigid centralism, and dedicated to a general amelioration of social and economic conditions.

While the 1864 statute entrusted the zemstvo institutions with a considerable area of activity, it also curbed their authority by vesting the provincial governors with what amounted to a veto power over the decisions of zemstvo officials. The weakest original feature of zemstvo self-government, however, came from its institutional inability to command adequate executive staff and to have its lower echelons operating on the township level. The zemstvo institutions were granted a considerable area of activity but little genuine authority. For the execution of many of their decisions they were dependent on the assistance, and whims, of local government authorities. The government's attitude toward the zemstvos was generally negative; the government officials viewed zemstvo agencies "not as organic elements of the system of our local administration," but as "an incidental appendage which was tolerated but not desired, and without which local administration could exist and function." [18]

During the first two decades of the existence of the zemstvos, the central government was concerned primarily with the enactment of measures limiting the work of zemstvo institutions. On November 21, 1866, the government imposed drastic limitations on the right of zemstvo assemblies to tax commercial and industrial enterprises. On May 4, 1867, an official act ruled that it was illegal for zemstvos of different provinces to maintain any kind of formal relations among themselves. On June 13, 1867, the government granted more power to chairmen of zemstvo administrations (usually persons favored by provincial governors) at the expense of zemstvo assemblies. At the same time it was decided that all zemstvo publications were to be subject to censorship by provincial authorities. The act of September 19, 1869, ruled that zemstvos must pay postage for all their correspondence because "neither by their composition nor by their

---

[17] Shakhovskoi, 449–450.
[18] Avinov, 17.

basic principles are zemstvos government agencies, and therefore they
have no other legal rights than private persons and societies. . . ." [19]
The Statute on Schools of May 25, 1874, imposed wide limitations on the
domain of participation of zemstvos in the supervision of teaching and
the right of zemstvos to select the members of district school boards. The
government decision of August 19, 1879, authorized the provincial governors to supervise the transfer and appointment of zemstvo employees.

The crowning assault on self-government came with the enactment
of the 1890 Statute on Zemstvos. Unlike the document of 1864, this statute
made no reference to self-government as an attribute of the zemstvo
organization. It ruled that without the governor's approval no person
could be either a deputy of the zemstvo assembly or a member of the
administrative board. The governor was also vested with authority to
annul the decisions of zemstvo assemblies not only in cases where they
were incompatible with existing laws but also where they were regarded
as "unsuitable." The nature of zemstvo representation was also changed;
the new statute replaced the class principle by the all-estate principle in
the selection of deputies. The three electoral groups now included the
landed gentry, the townfolk, and the peasants. The 1864 statute ensured
the landed gentry of a relative majority in zemstvo assemblies; the 1890
document gave them an absolute majority. In a very few zemstvos —
known as peasants' zemstvos — did the peasants command a majority of
votes.[20]

It should be emphasized that by this time the estates had begun to
break up into subgroups with distinct styles of life and unequal wealth.
The gentry consisted of a small group of land magnates and a large group
of small-town aristocrats who were increasingly forced to seek employment in various professions. These two groups did not have common
estate interests of any substance. The estate of townfolk consisted of an
even more diversified group including merchants, city owners of real
estate, industrialists, and larger or smaller nonaristocratic landholders.
The peasantry, despite its superficial homogeneity, had already begun to
show signs of economic inequality: the terms "working peasants" and
"agricultural proletariat" came into existence.[21] For these reasons the all-
estate principle of the new statute did not produce the officially expected
alignment of social forces. The aristocracy had produced a segment of
progressives who were dedicated to the zemstvos and their principles of
self-government. In general, the electoral procedures stipulated by the
1890 statute did not seriously impair the zemstvo gains during the preceding decades. The tradition created by the zemstvos and the new social

[19] Veselovsky, "Detsentralizatsiia upravleniia i zadachi zemstva," in Veselovsky and
Frenkel, 43.
[20] Boris Veselovsky, *Istoriia zemstva* (St. Petersburg, 1911), IV, 195–201.
[21] Vladimir Trutovsky, *Sovremennoe zemstvo* (St. Petersburg, 1915), 33.

and economic conditions worked against a successful application of all-estate representations. Indeed, after 1890 the zemstvos generated a more uncompromising struggle against the political role of estates as social entities.[22]

Despite the obvious antizemstvo orientation of the central government, the zemstvo institutions became a social force of great and diverse significance. Their work in education, sanitation, construction of roads, veterinary service, mutual insurance, and public charity assumed unprecedented proportions. Much of this work was carried by the so-called third element, the army of zemstvo employees. In 1912 it was estimated that there were 85,000 members of the "third element" in forty provinces which had zemstvo organizations. For each elected zemstvo official there were fifty appointed employees.[23] These people were officials of a new kind. The government employee represented the state, was subordinated only to higher echelons in the bureaucratic pyramid, and *ruled* even though he may have been at the bottom of the administrative machinery. The zemstvo employee had no authority and was dependent upon the local electorate. He became an antidote to government bureaucracy and was to a remarkable degree responsible for the fact that the term "bureaucracy" acquired a generally negative meaning. A famous encyclopedic dictionary, published in St. Petersburg in 1895, summed up the prevalent views on government bureaucracy by identifying it as a term denoting a method of administration peculiar to political communities in which "the central government authorities have concentrated all power in their hands," and in which there exists a "privileged segment" of officials who display "caste exclusiveness" and are "poor members of communities" because of their full identification not with the society which they serve but with the authorities who employ them.[24]

Through the third element the zemstvos brought large numbers of progressively oriented professionals in close contact with the rural community. The congresses of individual professional groups were the most effective means for formulating remedial actions to meet the pressing demands of the population in education, social security, medicine, and agriculture, and for providing an opportunity for zemstvo experts to discuss their professional problems. The third element was also instrumental in spearheading the crystallization of a political movement anchored to the zemstvo institutions. This movement sought a reorganization of the state administration, from top to bottom, along the lines of local autonomy

[22] Veselovsky, III, 681.

[23] In 1912 there were in thirty-four provinces approximately 3,000 physicians, over 1,000 veterinarians, 1,100 agricultural experts, 1,000 insurance agents, 1,400 medical technicians and midwives, 300 statisticians, 500 engineers and technicians, and 45,000 teachers. Trutovsky, 47–48.

[24] A. Ia., "Biurokratiia," in F. A. Brokgauz and I. A. Efron, eds., *Entsiklopedicheskii slovar'* (St. Petersburg, 1895), V, 293.

and representative government, and was of some consequence in the events of 1905. It also revealed the basic inherent weakness of the zemstvos. When the zemstvo followers were faced with the constitutional issues that dominated the events of 1905, the overrepresentation of the landed gentry was instrumental in breaking the unity of zemstvo delegates and bringing to an abrupt end the zemstvo political movement. In the three successive Dumas the zemstvo-affiliated deputies became identified in increasing numbers with the conservative forces. B. B. Veselovsky, the most eminent chronicler of the history of zemstvos, made the following self-explanatory table of the distribution by per cent of zemstvo affiliates in the first three Dumas.[25]

	First Duma	Second Duma	Third Duma
Left	5.2	7.5	0
Center (Const. Dem.)	78.0	54.7	12.7
Rightists and Octobrists	16.8	37.8	87.3

Thrown back upon their purely local work, the zemstvo institutions found themselves surrounded by new problems. The hegemony of bureaucracy became more consistent and stubborn. The zemstvo authorities were ordered to submit their annual budgetary estimates to the government for scrutiny and approval. The government began to make financial donations to zemstvo administrations earmarked for various educational and other purposes. This practice intensified government interference with zemstvo activities and proved that government donations were directly related to zemstvo self-government: the larger the financial donation of the government, the more drastic were the limitations on the meager attributes of self-government. Small groups of Duma deputies introduced several bills aimed at giving the zemstvo more local authority and clearer jurisdiction. But these bills died before they left the chambers of the appropriate committees. The creation of the All-Russian Union of Zemstvos for the Relief of Sick and Wounded Soldiers in 1914 was a patriotic gesture unaccompanied by any legislative measures aimed at the solution of the burning problem of zemstvo self-government.

The zemstvos were a historical force which marshaled and inspired the liberal-minded groups of various ideological bents and which, on a small scale, made the democratic process a known quantity in Russia's political life. The legions of politically conscious individuals learned by experience that unalloyed zemstvo self-government was "the best school for the development of independent activity without which no people, past or present, could achieve lasting prosperity." [26] The zemstvos provided avenues

[25] Veselovsky, IV, 80, 83. In the First Duma the zemstvo adherents made up 33 per cent, in the Second Duma 18.4 per cent, and in the Third Duma 50.2 per cent of all deputies from the regions which had zemstvo organizations.

[26] S. I. Shidlovsky, Zemstvo (St. Petersburg, 1904), 8.

for thousands of young people to participate in a political process which stood apart from the domains of autocratic competence. Their weaknesses did not come from a shortage of dedicated men but from institutional limitations imposed by monarchical absolutism. These weaknesses were:

1. The peasants, the bulk of the population, were underrepresented in zemstvo assemblies which bore the mark of indisputable domination by the landed gentry. The demands to reduce the property "census" in the determination of voting rights fell on deaf ears.

2. The zemstvos had no local branches, remained substantially isolated from small local communities, and were in no position to exercise effective control over their numerous undertakings.[27] The repeated demands for so-called small zemstvo units, or township zemstvos, were consistently ignored by the government.

3. Because they possessed no instruments of coercion, the zemstvo assemblies were compelled to depend to a large extent on local government officials and their discretionary rights for the execution of their decisions.

4. With few exceptions, the government prevented the zemstvo institutions from organizing larger alliances which would lend more weight to zemstvo demands and would give these institutions a more influential place in the Russian polity.

5. The government refused to establish zemstvos in those non-Russian areas where it feared that these institutions would give an impetus to nationalist aspiration, or would work against the interests of Russian settlers.

6. From the very beginning the government considered the zemstvo institutions inimical to the established political order and was concerned primarily with curbing the domain of their activities and their influence on the local populace.

IV

In May of 1917 the Provisional Government passed a law establishing the township zemstvo. The intent of the law was to provide the zemstvos with small administrative units which could maintain direct contact with the local populace; to give new life to the township which had become an antiquated political-administrative unit;[28] and to democratize the elective procedures. The law stipulated that all local inhabitants be granted the right to vote for township zemstvo deputies and that the suffrage be equal (no property "census"), direct (no elections of "electors"), and secret.[29]

[27] K. Golovin, *K voprosu o volostnom zemstve* (St. Petersburg, 1912), 1–2.

[28] The estate character of the volost meant in practice that although all rural inhabitants were equally entitled to the benefits from this unit, only the peasants paid the taxes for its maintenance. Moreover, the township headman was gradually transformed into an agent of the government rather than a spokesman of peasants.

[29] P. P. Gronsky, *Novaia volost* (Petrograd, 1917), 4ff.

To give more substance to local self-government the law also ruled that all nonelective township offices — such as those of the police officials and land captains — be abolished and that their functions be transferred to local elective units. The implementation of the new law appeared during the last weeks of the existence of the Provisional Government and even continued during the initial weeks of the Soviet regime. However, the October Revolution prevented it from becoming a reality.

History has shown that this law was more a corrective of the drastic limitations which the empire had imposed on local self-government than a herald of things to come. It embodied the demands and aspirations of the liberal-minded groups which were inspired and to a large extent politically educated by zemstvo institutions. It was predicated upon the condition that the state surrender some of its important traditional prerogatives to the representative bodies of the local community. It was exactly for these reasons that the Soviet authorities allowed the zemstvo institutions to be squeezed out of existence during the turbulent weeks following the October Revolution. Lenin scorned the zemstvos of the Tsarist regime as "the fifth wheel of the Russian state administration";[30] and he was quick to see that the democratic township zemstvo, established by the Provisional Government, was incompatible with the centralized system of Soviet government. Ironically, in their antizemstvo moves the Bolsheviks benefited from the unfavorable attitude in many localities toward the new elective local assemblies which, as O. H. Radkey points out, "were handicapped by being called 'zemstvos' and 'dumas,' which made it seem as though they continued to be weighted, as under the tsars, in favor of propertied classes." [31]

v

The empire created a political tradition which revolved around the dichotomy of state and society; the two were considered separate and unequal entities. The basic premise of the Soviet regime's political philosophy has been the identity of state and society. Both regimes apotheosized the state: the empire identified it with the most vital aspects of social welfare, and the Soviet regime equated it with the totality of social life.

The monarchical dichotomy of state and society justified the creation of two sets of separate agencies: the bureaucratic hierarchy of the state and the elected "social" assemblies of local communities. The Soviet concept of the unity of state and society led to the institutional blending of bureaucratic and elective bodies. The local soviets are elected assemblies and nonelective officials put together. To district soviet combines in prin-

[30] V. I. Lenin, *Sochineniia* (4th ed., Moscow, 1946), V, 32.
[31] Oliver H. Radkey, *The Agrarian Foes of Bolshevism* (New York, 1958), 431–432.

ciple two institutions of the empire: the local echelons of government bureaucracy and zemstvo assemblies.

The local soviets form one of the most complex and confusing parts of the Soviet political system. There is a qualitative difference between the constitutional and official Communist definitions of the local soviets. The 1936 Constitution states that the soviets are the only legitimate source of power in the USSR, whereas, according to the official Communist interpretation, they are a "form of political organization of the masses," which unites "all the working people and thus facilitates the political guidance by the Party." According to the Constitution, the soviets are a *power locus*; according to the authoritative Communist interpretation, they are a *power instrument* or a "transmission belt" through which the party policies are carried out. We must therefore recognize the essential fact that the local soviets perform important political functions both as the loci of fictitious power and as power instruments.

The tasks of local soviets as loci of fictitious power are to neutralize the pronounced discrepancies between the revolutionary-democratic traditions of the original Russian Communist Party and the practical aspects of present-day centralization of authority; to serve as vehicles through which official policies are equated with "the general will"; and to provide an outlet for, and to harness for officially approved social ends, the tendencies in group behavior developed under the empire.

As power instruments or "transmission belts" the local soviets perform their functions through three distinct institutional mechanisms: the assemblies of elected deputies, the appointed officials, and the *aktivs*. The elected assemblymen, representing the local populace, make decisions on local matters. Each decision must have a political preamble indicating the party edict or pronouncement in the spirit of which it has been formulated and must pass the scrutiny of the "guiding core" of the party operating within the local soviet and of the executive committee of higher soviets. The appointed officials are of two types: those who carry out the decisions of assemblies and those through whom the decisions of higher government authorities are channeled to local communities. The latter officials are "controlled" by local soviets, but actually they are subordinated to the corresponding officials at the higher bureaucratic echelons. The *aktivs* are groups of volunteers which perform various auxiliary functions and through which larger segments of the local population are mobilized to perform many socially useful functions in a manner approved by the government. These *aktivs* are a vital vehicle through which the identification of society with the state is given concrete expression. The street committees, which operate as "social" units within the framework of local soviets, are only one example of such *aktivs*. These committees perform "political and educational" work among the nonworking inhabitants (housewives, elderly people), give assistance to the Red Cross

and various other voluntary associations, help government credit officials
in screening applicants for loans, assist various children's institutions (day-
care centers, nursery schools), track down petty violators of peace and
order, work toward curbing juvenile delinquency, and undertake a multitude of other assignments.[32]

Under the empire *samodeiatel'nost* (independent action) was considered the dynamic aspect of *samoupravlenie* (self-government). The
scorn for local independent action paralleled the official curbs imposed
on local self-government. Yet the proof is abundant that zestvo institutions
achieved appreciable results despite, rather than because of, the government authorities. Undoubtedly, a kernal of self-government was present.

In the Soviet system the term *samodeiatel'nost* has become very popular; yet it is never identified, and has no connection, with *samoupravlenie*.
It simply stands for the existence of voluntary groups clustered around
legitimate institutions and entrusted with the performance of minor functions in the immediate sphere of everyday life. In the Soviet Union there
are no areas of independent associative life. In the Tsarist system there
were such areas, but they were results of a traditional lack of official concern with certain domains of social activities. The Soviet system is totalitarian in the full sense of the word; the Tsarist system was totalitarian in
its basic orientation but not in its institutional make-up.

THE STATE AND THE ECONOMY

THEODORE H. VON LAUE

I

The changing relations between state and economy in the development of Russian society since 1861 is a highly complex and voluminous
subject. It might therefore be more suitable in this context to select only
those aspects which may help to put the entire topic in the proper light
and deepen our understanding of "the Russian condition."

These crucial aspects — they will emerge more clearly later — center
around a persistent problem: how could the Russian state sustain the role
of a great power with the imperfect and limited resources of an underdeveloped country? This essay will deal, at least tangentially, with the
Russian state as a member of the European, and from the 1890's on, of
the emerging global state system; it will do so not only in the objective

[32] V. V. Kopeichikov, *Pravovye akty mestnykh organov gosudarstvennoi vlasti i
upravleniia* (Moscow, 1956), 51.

terms of international relations but also according to the subjective estimate of the Russian public and the government as to what political role
Russia should play. As for the objective facts, one reminder may suffice:
in the twentieth century the Russian state has twice passed through
crises far more extreme than those faced by any other of the present great
powers of the West. And as for the evolution of Russian state ambition,
there is room only for a very brief but necessary characterization. For a
minimum goal it aimed at, it is fair to say, the protection of the boundaries
of Russia, the preservation of her native institutions: in short, at sovereignty in the traditional sense. For a maximum goal — coming to the
fore at a time when the other great powers either voiced or actively pursued universal aims — it expressed a desire for the expansion, even global
expansion, of the Russian way of life, or her system of government.

The fact that Russian state ambition has been a product of Western
influence and not of native origin has never received the attention which
it deserves. Even the theory of Russia as the Third Rome has its Western
antecedents. One need only look at the origins of Spanish or French
nationalism in the fifteenth and sixteenth centuries, or of English Protestant imperialism in the seventeenth. Western nationalism became secularized earlier than its Russian counterpart. Yet concerning global universality, what could be more ambitious than the Girondist sense of
mission in 1792, German philosophy in the age of Schiller and Fichte,
Palmerston's arrogance, or, say, Cecil Rhodes' boast that if he could reach
the planets he would annex them too?

Imperial and Soviet state ambition can be interpreted properly only
in the European context. Seen in this perspective it will appear that it
was by no means extreme, and that it followed, like an echo, the Western
trends. For instance, when Lenin said in 1915 that, if he came to power,
he would stir up the European proletariat against their governments and
the colonial peoples against the imperialists, he merely put into revolutionary and Russian phraseology a sentiment voiced by German national
liberals. They proclaimed at the same time that it was Germany's task not
only to win a place in the sun for herself but also for the Egyptians,
Persians, Moslems, Boers, Chinese, and others. In other words, Germany
too had a world mission, the liberation of human civilization from the
yoke of English influence. In the last analysis, of course, both German and
Russian imperialists expressed sentiments taught them by the British
imperialist example.

If there was an ingredient peculiar to Russian state ambition, it was
not the reckless sweep of her global pretensions, but the hypersensitivity
concerning all threats to her power, a sensitivity conditioned over the
centuries very largely by the tremendous disparity between the material
and cultural resources of Russia, on the one hand, and those of her political rivals, on the other. The great powers of the West were, and to

this day are, able to support their ambitions from the wealth and achievement created more or less spontaneously by their citizens. Russia, by contrast, was a backward country with an underdeveloped economy for the better part of the period under consideration. How, then, could she sustain her political aims with her greatly limited economic resources? How could she do so in a century in which the material progress of Western civilization was breathtakingly rapid, the gap between the advanced and the backward countries widening, and the price of sovereignty constantly and steeply rising? What, in short, were the unique experiences over the past hundred years of an underdeveloped country which also claimed to be a great power (or a great power which also happened to be an underdeveloped country)? The following sketch, starting with specific problems of economic policy and advancing to a general thesis, will offer an answer to this question.

II

Modern Russian economic policy began, vaguely, when Alexander II and his advisers recognized that the defeat of Russia at Sevastopol called for a far-reaching recasting of Russian society and economy after the Western pattern; from the outset Russian economic policy thus stood under the *Primat der Aussenpolitik*. The emancipation of the serfs was the most spectacular and obvious corollary, yet by no means the first one. The adoption of an extensive program of railroad construction and of a unified budget under the Minister of Finance, the lowering of tariffs in order to permit a freer influx of Western European goods, the effort to restore the convertibility of the ruble — all preceded emancipation. These innovations were intended to help Russia achieve the advantages of private enterprise which had given her enemies their superiority. Yet it was paradoxical that, in its efforts to increase the economic resources of Russia, the government should adopt a policy of nonintervention in the economic affairs of the country and abdicate — for the time being — its control over Russia's economic development.

Thus for the next decades the roots of modern Russian economic policy cannot be found at the top level, in the decisions of the emperors, but within the more limited responsibilities of the finance ministers. How could the Minister of Finance find enough funds for all the expenditures it took to become a great power? He had to finance the Russian army and navy, which claimed rarely less than one quarter and more often around one third of the budget; and the court, church, civil administration, education, and public works as well. While he never managed to satisfy the military, he had to be even more thrifty in regard to cultural and economic needs. As for revenue, the taxes were harsh and increasing. In the forty years before 1900 indirect taxes were raised four and a half times, direct taxes doubled (while the population increased by only

78 per cent and the price level remained fairly constant).[1] Each retiring Minister of Finance warned his successor about the exhaustion of "the paying powers of the population." Inevitably, the deficits in the budgets rose rapidly.[2] Obviously the Russian government could not make ends meet, even though it taxed its population to the utmost, curtailed its expenditures drastically, and under its policy of free trade shifted the burden of Russian economic development largely to its subjects. But how could they fully assume this responsibility when the government took from them almost every kopek which they might have invested in economic expansion?

In one respect, indeed, the government had to come quickly to the rescue: the financing of railroad expansion. Immediately after the Crimean War, the government had launched an extensive construction program. Russia needed railroads for defense and, still more, for economic development. While the construction and management were left to private initiative, the expense had to be borne by the state, which guaranteed the railway loans. Yet even so, what with the poverty of the treasury, there were definite limits to the speed of railroad construction and thus to the economic and cultural development of the country as a whole.

Deficits and the overriding need for railroad expansion drove the Minister of Finance to heavy borrowing at home and abroad and raised the state debt to new heights. By the end of the century it amounted to about three and one half billion rubles, of which one billion was held abroad, the largest foreign debt of any great power.[3] The management of such a large foreign debt imposed upon the Minister of Finance — and the government as a whole — a tremendous responsibility. The financial sacrifices needed for the prompt service of this debt and for the maintenance of Russian credit abroad were very considerable. For the sake of its foreign credit, the government also was forced to maintain an unusually optimistic if not false interpretation of Russian economic conditions — which was bound to antagonize the public. And inevitably Russian, unlike American, foreign credit became a tool of power politics and a limitation upon Russian sovereignty in general. No other great power found its foreign policy so hampered by its dependence upon foreign credit, and its foreign credit subject to such political pressures.[4]

[1] Cited by A. P. Pogrebinsky, *Ocherki istorii finansov dorevoliutsionnoi Rossii (XIX–XX vv.)* (Moscow, 1954), 98.

[2] Between 1862 and 1870, for instance, the deficits amounted to about 300 million rubles (Pogrebinsky, 88); between 1866 and 1888 the budget was officially balanced only three times (87). Even thereafter deficits prevailed, but were concealed more skillfully.

[3] Cited by P. P. Liashchenko, *Istoriia narodnogo khoziaistva SSSR* (2 vols.; 3rd ed., Moscow-Leningrad, 1952), II, 189.

[4] One of the better-known examples was Bismarck's action in 1887 which drove the Russian securities from the Berlin stockmarket; another was the French demand in 1901 that Russia build the Sedlets-Bologoe railway line in return for the granting of a loan.

The urgent need for foreign capital also foisted a number of other obligations upon the Minister of Finance, some of considerable technical complexity. In order to facilitate the influx of foreign loans into Russia and to promote international trade in general, he had to provide a stable currency — a freely convertible currency based on gold. The experiment of free conversion was made twice after the Crimean War, with disastrous results. No subsequent Minister of Finance until Witte dared to undertake it again, although all worked hard to prepare for it. Their problem, not unlike that of modern British Chancellors of the Exchequer, was how to accumulate a sufficient gold reserve in the face of an uncertain balance of trade and a passive balance of payments. Remedies were difficult. The modernization of Russia required heavy imports for the sake of her economic and industrial development and her cultural progress in general. In order to offset these heavy imports, the Ministry of Finance did its utmost to facilitate Russian agricultural exports — the railway network was designed primarily for this purpose. In the late 1880's, a period of falling world prices, it even began forcing the peasants to throw their grains on the market when they were cheapest, thus deliberately depressing the level of domestic consumption and indirectly also drying up its future sources of revenue and again slowing down the modernization of the countryside. These measures slowly took effect. While in half of the years between 1860 and 1880 the balance of trade was negative, it improved thereafter and provided a constant surplus almost to the end of the century.[5]

Yet the surplus was not sufficiently large to create an active balance of payments; the invisible imports were too large. Among them loomed very prominently — and gallingly — the expenses of Russian travelers in Europe. One Minister of Finance even proposed a prohibitive tax on passports for foreign travel in order to reduce the loss of valuable foreign currency.[6] At any rate, with a constantly adverse balance of payments convertibility was hopeless. But without convertibility the supply of foreign capital remained limited and thus also the rate of economic growth. At the most, the Minister of Finance could hope to build up a sufficient gold reserve through a constant recourse to state-guaranteed or state-owned foreign loans paid in gold, which however only increased the foreign indebtedness of the government and all the evils thereof. Wherever, in short, the Russian Minister of Finance turned for an escape from the basic poverty of Russia, he ran into a network of interrelated and highly technical dilemmas, each reinforcing the other.

[5] Figures from P. A. Khromov, *Ekonomicheskoe razvitie Rossii v XIX–XX vekakh* (Moscow-Leningrad, 1950), 469, table 14.

[6] Vyshnegradsky, who otherwise had no prejudice against travel in Europe. The State Council, however, turned down his request. I mention this fact especially in order to underscore a point made about a "materialist interpretation" of the Iron Curtain by Ragnar Nurkse in *Problems of Capital Formation in Underdeveloped Countries* (Oxford, 1955), 76.

How did the successive Russian Ministers of Finance try to break out of the vicious circle of poverty breeding further poverty? Reutern, who had reorganized Russian finance after the Crimean War, succeeded fairly well in making ends meet at the three buckles of state finance: the budget, the balance of trade, and the balance of payments. He taxed heavily, limited government expenditures as much as possible, and covered the deficit in the budget and the balance of payments by foreign loans. Then came the Turkish War and its staggering costs, which undid all of his work. The next Minister of Finance to cope with the fiscal riddles was Bunge. Except for some tariff increases, he concerned himself less with the buckles — they were all left gaping — than with the fabric of the Russian economy. He tried to improve public welfare by winding up the transition period of emancipation, abolishing the capitation tax, establishing a Peasant Land Bank and a Nobles' Land Bank, and assisting Russian industry by a series of excellent labor laws. But when the international crisis over Bulgaria demanded extraordinary expenditures, his deficits were held against him and he gave way to a new man, Vyshnegradsky. Vyshnegradsky devoted his attention again to the official buckling points. He created surpluses both by skillful accounting methods and by curtailing government expenditures, even those for railroad construction; he forced the agricultural exports to the utmost so as to cover both visible and invisible imports. Equally drastically, he curtailed imports by a monster tariff, the tariff of 1891. Fortune played into his hands the sympathies of the French money market, which strengthened Russia's foreign credit. Yet after five seemingly highly successful years, the old misery suddenly reappeared with a vengeance. While the buckles held, the very fabric of the Russian economy went to pieces in the great famine of 1891. The state had taken everything from the peasants, who had no surplus whatever to guard against crop failures. And to add insult to injury: German and Austrian diplomats sneered that Russia was too poor to be a great power; a civilized state did not suffer from disastrous famines.[7]

Russian economic policy thus experienced a profound setback at the very moment when the government, for reasons of state, was contemplating further heavy expenditures in connection with the building of the great Siberian trunk line. The decision to build the Siberian line was the result of the rise of Japanese power in the Far East, the increasing Western penetration of China, and rising imperialism in general. In view of such competition, Russia — given her political ambition — had to build a modern link between the European and Far Eastern boundaries, and had to start building it at a time of economic catastrophe.

[7] See W. L. Langer, *The Franco-Russian Alliance, 1890–1894* (Cambridge, Mass., 1929), 228.

III

Thus the famine of 1891 also became a turning point in modern Russian history in the relations between state and economy. In the thirty years since the emancipation, the economic condition of the Russian government and of Russian society had not improved. On the contrary, the countryside showed many signs of deterioration. The government, even while avoiding international complications, was unable to carry out needed state projects like the Siberian railroad. While the high tariff restricted the influx of Western goods, it also slowed down the modernization of Russia — although it gave some encouragement to Russian industry. To make matters worse, the public grew increasingly hostile to the government over its unsuccessful financial policy and the persistent poverty of Russia. The Russian Ministers of Finance were fully familiar with the special urgency of the accursed Russian question: what was to be done? It was at this point that for the first time in modern Russian history a comprehensive economic policy emerged, linking state and economy under a common necessity. It was the work of Sergei Witte.

In Witte's view — to give a brief summary of the "Witte system" and advance the analysis one step further — economic policy was more than ever an instrument of power politics. "Russia," he said, "needs perhaps more than any other country a proper economic foundation for her national policy and her culture," so that she will be "a great power not only politically and agriculturally, but also economically." [8] And in an age of rapid industrial progress in the West, economic development meant to him above all the most rapid industrialization.

International competition does not wait. If we do not take energetic and decisive measures so that in the course of the next decades our industry will be able to satisfy the needs of Russia and other Asian countries which are — or should be — under our influence, then the rapidly growing foreign industries . . . will establish themselves in our fatherland. . . . Our economic backwardness may lead to political and cultural backwardness as well.[9]

Thus from the start Witte had a clear recognition of the backwardness of Russia. Repeatedly he spoke of her colonial economy in contrast to that of the Western "metropoles." Occasionally he even dropped hints about "the peculiar conditions of Russia" in general which slowed down her economic development. In education, for instance, he observed that Russia was not only behind Europe but behind some Asian countries as well.[10]

At the same time he adjusted Russian state ambition to the rising

[8] "Dokladnaia zapiska Vitte Nikolaiu II," *Istorik marksist*, no. 2/3 (1935), 130.
[9] "Dokladnaia zapiska. . . ."
[10] In Witte's letter to Nicholas II on agrarian reform. See Sergei Witte, *Vospominaniia. Tsarstvovanie Nikolaia II* (2 vols.; Berlin, 1923), I, 467–473.

tide of imperialism. "Russia is an empire," he always emphasized with a keen sensitivity for the ambitions of the other great powers. She had a great cultural and political task in Asia and Europe. Now she must catch up to what had been missed in the course of two centuries, since Peter the Great. This required great sacrifices, but "a great power cannot wait." [11] All of Witte's work thus was permeated by a sense of extreme urgency and haste. As he once remarked with reference to Nicholas II's indifference: "Was Russian power to increase as it had after 1861, or was it to decline again? . . . He who does not go forward will, for that very reason, fall back compared with the countries that move forward." [12] Hence there arose for the first time the question of the forced tempo of economic development, of "artificial" measures disrupting the organic pattern of a native economy.

Witte thus jettisoned the premises of liberal economics. It was up to the state, he wrote in his first budget report, to order the country's economic life:

As a result of the special historical conditions of its political structure and development, fiscal policy in our fatherland cannot be contained in the strictly limited framework of the financial needs of the government as they are traditionally understood. In the understanding of the Russian people the conviction prevails that it is within the power of government authority to be concerned with everything touching the welfare and the needs of the people. In all cases of public misery, whenever it assumes considerable proportions, the people turn to the authority of the Tsar with their hopes and their trusts. Considering the weak development of the habits of self-help among the population, the whole burden of the struggle with public misfortune falls inevitably upon the government. [13]

But, furthermore, the government's policy must be comprehensive: "Every measure of the government in regard to trade and industry affects almost the entire economic organism and influences the course of its further development." Hence, Witte continued, Russia required "that this policy be carried out according to a definite plan, with strict system and continuity." [14]

Witte's plan, or "the protective system" as he called it in connection with the tariff of 1891, called for stepped-up government expenditures for the development of Russia's riches. [15] And under his guidance between

[11] Witte, *Vorlesungen über Volks- und Staatswirtschaft* (2 vols.; Stuttgart, 1913), I, 140.

[12] Witte, *Vospominaniia*, I, 467–473.

[13] In Witte's budget report for 1893.

[14] Cited in Theodore H. Von Laue, "A Secret Memorandum of Sergei Witte on the Industrialization of Imperial Russia," *Journal of Modern History*, XXVI (March 1954), 65.

[15] Witte always spoke of "the protective system," although strictly speaking the motives for the tariff of 1891 were fiscal, that is, designed to prevent imports for the sake of an active balance of payments. The terminology of protectionism, however, was a useful propaganda tool for industrialization.

1894 and 1902 more than two thirds of the government's ordinary and extraordinary expenditures were poured into the economic development of the country, the highest proportion of any period between 1861 and 1917.[16] The largest single item, of course, was spent for railroad construction. Witte's emphasis upon railroad construction served a double purpose. It not only improved communications but, even more important, also stimulated industrial expansion. The Witte system was based on a rudimentary theory of economic development. Through extensive railroad construction the heavy industries and their subsidiaries could be developed, giving Russia a heavy industry of her own. The expansion of the heavy industries in turn would stimulate the growth of the light industries, and eventually agriculture would improve through the increased demand for food and the cheaper supply of better equipment and chemicals. In the end, the government would be amply repaid for its outlay through the increased prosperity of the country and the rising tax yield.

For the time being, unfortunately, the sacrifices of the population were even greater than ever. As Witte admitted himself, in strictest secrecy, the population was paying for industrialization out of current necessity.[17] And what was not paid from tax revenue and the limited domestic capital was financed by foreign loans. Under Witte the foreign indebtedness of Russia mounted drastically, particularly after he introduced the gold standard, and thus prepared the way for the influx of foreign capital under nongovernmental auspices as well. But, as Witte argued, except for foreign capital the population would have to make still further sacrifices.[18] As one of his apologists added: it was difficult enough for Russia not to fall further behind, even with the utmost efforts. The only way to make some progress was through the resort to foreign capital.[19]

[16] My figures are based on the budgets published in Khromov, 514ff. For this rough estimate I have added the expenses listed in the Ordinary Budgets for the service on the government debt, for the Ministries of Finance, Communications, State Domains and Agriculture, State Control, and the Administration of the State Stud-farms, and in the Extraordinary Budgets the funds for the expansion of railroads and ports and for the conversion of loans. This estimate for the economic expenditures of the government is probably slightly high: part of the debt service covered loans which had a military rather than an economic significance.

Total ordinary and extraordinary expenditures (in 1,000 rubles):

1861–1870	1894–1902	1908–1914
4,594,000	15,137,000	22,128,000

Total economic expenditures (as itemized above):

2,091,000	10,611,000	12,223,000

[17] Cited in Von Laue, 64–74.

[18] Von Laue, 64–74.

[19] B. F. Brandt, *Innostrannye kapitaly. Ikh vliianie na ekonomicheskoe razvitie strany* (2 vols.; St. Petersburg, 1898–1899), I, 87.

There is no need to discuss the results of such "artificial" stimulation; they are stated in Alexander Gerschenkron's chapter. Suffice it here to cite the fact that of all types of industrial enterprises existing in 1900, 40 per cent were founded after 1891; and that the smallest ones employing less than fifty workers multiplied most rapidly.[20] The boom reached quite deeply into Russian society. Concerning fiscal necessities, Witte succeeded not only in making ends meet in the budget but also in the balance of payments, so that he accumulated a gold reserve sufficient for convertibility. Thus he made possible a stable currency and all the advantages for Russian credit and foreign trade which followed from it. Yet in the last analysis he balanced accounts only by borrowing heavily at home and abroad. He also charged the current expenditures for the economic development of Russia up to the future, and the question remained whether the development of Russian productivity would ever overtake Russian foreign indebtedness. But how could her productivity win this race, his critics demanded, considering the misery of the mass of the Russian population to which attention was again called by the onset of the depression in 1899? Someday soon, the pessimists declared, Russia would have to face the results of having lived beyond her means for so many years.

The depression of 1899 laid bare again the weaknesses of the Witte system: when the foreign loans stopped, as they did in 1899 and through no fault of the government, the boom also collapsed. Obviously Russia was not master of her own economic development. Furthermore, the latent discontent with the government's economic policy, muffled by the industrial boom of the nineties, broke out in a rising crescendo that led to Witte's fall and culminated in the revolution of 1905. But what else could the government have done? There was no escape from the dilemma: the Russian people would remain poor and backward whether the government pursued a policy of laissez faire or whether it made a special effort through a planned protective system. And they were to remain poor and backward while the peoples of Western Europe and the United States became noticeably more prosperous. Was the Russian public to stand for this seemingly perpetual backwardness?

Witte was quite aware that his economic measures were insufficient for the industrial progress of Russia; they were constantly obstructed by a hostile social and political framework. Thus he was increasingly driven to recast Russian society in the image of the capitalist society of the West. His "system" was, one might say, a huge wager on the Russian capitalists. For its success, however, Witte needed a legal and institutional setting in which the Russian capitalists could eventually take over the development of Russia's resources. He wanted to enhance, not limit,

[20] A. V. Pogozhev, *Uchet chislennosti i sostava rabochykh v Rossii* (St. Petersburg, 1906), 80–81.

private initiative. But, like Colbert and Peter the Great, he discovered that he and his businessmen did not necessarily agree. He found the Russian *kupechestvo* sluggish and inflexible, reluctant to take advantage of the opportunities which he held out. They in turn complained about the heavy hand of the government. Thus there was a flaw at the very center of his system.

Of greater consequence, however, was the collective order of peasant life. Witte realized that capitalism in industry, in order to stimulate the Russian economy, must be backed by capitalism in agriculture. Thus after 1897 he became a determined foe of the extended peasant family, the peasant commune, strip farming, and the legal separation of the peasantry from the rest of Russian society. He was also a keen protagonist of elementary and, still more, advanced education. Perhaps education was undermining the loyalty of the people, so he told Tsar Nicholas, but even if it did, it was necessary so that Russia could move forward.[21]

There was no stopping point in this line of reasoning. The logic of economic development pushed the Minister of Finance ever farther afield. From his concern over economic institutions he progressed to criticism of the social structure of Russia, and thence to a questioning of the bureaucracy, of foreign policy, and even of the nature of autocracy. In 1898 Witte demanded the overhaul of Russian local administration in order to produce a streamlined, modernized civil service.[22] In 1900, finding himself opposed on all sides by government officials who did not share his ideal of an industrialized Russia, he demanded that all economic policy be concentrated in his hands. The emperor, he pleaded, should make it clear that he considered industrialization of primary importance for the spiritual and political welfare of the country and should enforce compliance for the views of the Ministry of Finance in all branches of the government.[23] Constantly he meddled, in the name of economic necessity, in Russian foreign policy. Industrialization, he knew, demanded peace, stopping the arms race, and avoiding any costly ventures in foreign policy. And even in the Far East, where he became committed to an expansionist policy for the sake of the prosperity of his Siberian railroad, he was constantly restrained by his fear for the financial stability of the government.[24]

But the most significant conclusion which Witte drew from his economic policy was concerned with the nature of autocracy. Russia, he realized, required an autocratic regime, but an autocracy with its ears

---

[21] Witte, *Vospominaniia*, I, 467–473.

[22] My source for this is Witte's pamphlet *Samoderzhavie i zemstvo* (Stuttgart, 1903), and his correspondence with Pobedonostsev of that time, published in *Krasnyi arkhiv*, XXX (1928), 89–116.

[23] In "Dokladnaia zapiska," cited above.

[24] B. A. Romanov's *Rossiia v Manchzhurii* (Leningrad, 1928) gives a very misleading account of Witte's Far Eastern policy.

to the ground and working patiently and with modern efficiency for the welfare of all its subjects. He demanded greater unity of purpose at the center of the government, concentration upon the task of catching up, and a streamlined bureaucracy reaching from the capital to the smallest village and motivated by one will. Extensive public relations creating a close relationship between the ruler and ruled were also essential. He himself set forth in his annual budget reports the reasons for his economic measures and the overriding need for industrialization, and he was in constant consultation with the economic groups whose fortunes were affected by his policies. He was the first to celebrate industrial victories by parading favorable statistics. The government as a whole, he said, must discuss and consult with its subjects, and convince them that all its acts were necessary for their welfare. Only thus, he warned amidst incredible incomprehension, could a revolution be avoided.[25]

The foregoing discussion, I trust, has shown how the political ambition of the Russian state and economic necessity combined to prompt a revision of the very basis of the Russian state and society. Starting from the need for industrialization, Witte was driven step by step to advocate a profound reform of current autocratic practice. What he envisaged was a government capable of carrying out a revolution from above, a revolution which would recast not only the Russian economy but also her society and administration after the contemporary pattern of Western urban-industrial life. Yet at the same time he was a prophet crying in the wilderness.

How alien his "system" was to public opinion may be seen from the fact that his most famous accomplishment, the introduction of the gold standard, was carried out by an unusually sharp assertion of autocratic prerogative against the determined opposition not only of the public, but also of the bulk of the imperial bureaucracy as voiced by the State Council.[26] The gold standard, like all his other measures, and above all his entire philosophy of rapid industrialization, would have been instantly repudiated by an overwhelming majority, if it had ever been submitted to a popular vote. At the turn of the century Witte had enlisted against himself the zemstvos, many committees of trade and industry, the overwhelming majority of the intelligentsia, the peasants, the revolutionaries, the bulk of the imperial bureaucracy, and the emperor himself.

The public distaste for Witte's policy was understandable, for its appalling cost in terms of popular welfare were well understood at the time. Few Russians shared Witte's faith in modern industry; the scientist

---

[25] If the government was bad, wrote Witte to Pobedonostsev in 1899, a revolution was fully justified. *Krasnyi arkhiv*, XXX (1928), 104.

[26] In the State Council, Nicholas II was likened to the mad Paul for issuing the decisive ukaz on the gold standard. See A. A. Polovstov's diary, *Krasnyi arkhiv*, XLVI (1931), 116.

Mendeleev was his only ally among the public. Russian society was still deeply rooted in an agrarian orientation. It despised not only factories and cities, but also the cold rationality, punctuality, and uniformity of modern industry, its adaptability and pride in specialization. On the other hand, there is no evidence that the bulk of the population did not favor the basic political ambitions of the government; on the contrary, too often they wanted more than what the government considered feasible. Incredible as it may seem in retrospect, the public craved the benefits of the European, urban-industrial way of life without being willing to change its own essentially preindustrial habits.

At this point another unjustly neglected phase of the relations between state and economy in a backward country with the ambitions of a great power must be briefly discussed: the element of constant subversion of all governmental authority as a result of the constant comparison with the advanced countries of the West. In Witte's Russia one could always hear the reproach that the other countries, France, Germany, England, the United States, could manage to be powerful and civilized without excessive sacrifices on the part of their populations. Why not Russia? Just as the Russian public was eager to buy foreign goods in unlimited quantities without any recognition of the limits set by their poverty, they also wanted to be powerful without making any undue exertions. In their ignorance of the dilemmas of backwardness they simply would not accept the fact of Russian poverty, which in itself was an indication of their ambition. The difficulties of government under these circumstances, even of one more efficient than that of Nicholas II, can be imagined. The government, after all, was obviously assuming full charge of economic development. Yet everybody saw how little it could accomplish. Therefore, so the conclusion ran, it was no good. As Stalin put it many years later: you are backward, therefore you are wrong.[27]

There were lesser, yet equally insoluble, problems posed by the Witte system. How would Russian society agree to the government's wager on the Russian capitalists? From Witte's point of view, of all social groups in Russia only the *kupechestvo*, the energetic elements in the *meshchanstvo*, and the kulaks could be expected to make intelligent choices for the productive investment of scarce capital. But would these groups ever be able to win the confidence of the other groups of Russian society as they rose to prominence? All evidence points to the contrary: no segments of Russian society were more despised or hated than these "bourgeois" groups. And how was the government to overcome the elemental antagonism of the emerging industrial working class or of the

[27] Stalin's speech to the business executives of February 4, 1931. *Sochineniia*, XIII, 39. For a theory of "the revolution from without," see my "Die Revolution von Aussen als erste Phase der russischen Revolution 1917," *Jahrbücher für Geschichte Osteuropas*, IV (1956), 138–158.

peasants whom rural starvation and unemployment drew into the factories? Witte was more aware of this second problem than of the first. Yet he never gave it his full attention.

Finally, there was the problem of foreign intervention in Russian affairs resulting from the foreign indebtedness of Russia. As mentioned above, Russian foreign loans had assumed from an early moment an unusually political character. It could hardly have been otherwise considering the power competition in the European system. The Russian government thus always faced the danger that its financial dependence would be exploited as a check on its sovereignty. It could not pursue a foreign policy liable to antagonize its creditors or an internal one that undermined their confidence in the financial stability of the country. Thus it had far less freedom of maneuver than its rivals among the great powers. Whatever it undertook, it had to consider the reactions of the European investing public. The suppression of political disorders or anti-Semitic measures, for instance, tended to reduce Russian creditworthiness and thus, in fact, exerted a restraint. Between 1887 and 1917 Russian policy was tied to French policy, inasmuch as French investments in Russia were controlled, to a large extent, by the French government. The degree of foreign control through financial ties has often been exaggerated, yet there can be no question that it was a very real check bitterly resented not least by the emperor himself.[28] One can well understand the desire for true economic sovereignty stated so often before 1917 in Russian economic literature. Yet here lay another unpalatable paradox of the underdeveloped: they must become more dependent on foreign aid in order to become independent of it — unless, of course, they were willing to "go it alone."

Needless to say, in Witte's time the full consequences of Russian backwardness and conversely of her rapid need for industrialization were barely perceived; his work remained incomplete. After his fall as Minister of Finance no further effort was made by the emperor to carry out his vision. Tsarist economic policy never assumed the comprehensive character that Witte had planned to give it. Stolypin carried out only part of Witte's grand design, and that incompletely. This is not to deny that considerable industrial progress occurred before 1914, much again with the help of large state orders.[29] Yet the basic disparity between Russian industrial production and Russian political ambition remained. No matter how much the rate of growth in Russian industry exceeded that of the other great powers, imperial Russia did not command the industrial

[28] There is much good material in an article by Olga Crisp, "Some Problems of French Investment in Russian Joint Stock Companies, 1894–1914," *Slavonic and East European Review*, XXXV (December 1956), 223–240.

[29] Liashchenko, II, 406.

potential necessary for her station.[30] In 1913 — to cite but one example
— 37 per cent of Russia's annual consumption of technical equipment
was imported, and more than half of her industrial machinery.[31] When the
war came she did not possess industrial equipment sufficient to hold her
own and accordingly she suffered brutally.

IV

How then — to advance the analysis to a final thesis — did the Soviet
regime cope with the dilemmas of backwardness? It would appear at the
outset that the new masters of Russia found themselves in the years after
1917, and particularly with the advent of Stalin, in an even worse plight
than their predecessors, at least with respect to the discrepancy between
their political ambitions and their economic resources. On the one hand,
they were confidently expecting victory not only in a world revolution
but also in the field of industrial production. Even in their minimum aims
they were more demanding, adding economic self-sufficiency to political
sovereignty. On the other hand, they suffered from incredible devastation,
loss of territory, and the elimination of the skills and know-how of the
former ruling groups at a time when the power competition for global
prestige and power was becoming sharper.

While the discrepancy between political ambition and economic resources seemed greater under the Soviets for at least thirty of their present
forty-three years than earlier, the new rulers of Russia had certain
advantages over their predecessors. They went a step beyond the vision
of the Witte system. They represented — to submit only a brief summary
— a unified government led by a party with monolithic discipline and
motivated by an ideology in which industrialization and the economic
rationalism of the Western urban-industrial system were paramount ideals.
Russia could hardly have acquired a more economics-minded group of
rulers. The Bolsheviks furthermore were painfully aware of the backwardness of their country and were determined, even more than Witte,
to remedy it by extreme means. They were willing to concentrate almost
all of their resources on economic expansion. Moreover, they dealt with
a self-contained socialist economic system in which class antagonism had
been largely suppressed and the old dependence on foreign capital ended.
Having abolished private income, except in agriculture, they could control
the manpower of their country with unprecedented force. Under socialist
theory, particularly the Bolshevik version, they also suffered from none
of the liberals' hesitations over the extension of state power, which had
hampered Witte. Finally, they were experts in the art of mass manipula-

[30] For comparative statistics on industrial growth before 1914, see the League of
Nations volume, *Industrialization and Foreign Trade* (New York, 1945).
[31] Liaschchenko, II, 760.

tion and propaganda, capable of utilizing the latent energies of their subjects to a degree undreamt of in the time of the empire.

Most important, perhaps, as masters of an avowed dictatorship, they had no qualms about invading the deeper levels of resistance to the prescribed urban-industrial mode of life. In their efforts to produce a "new Soviet man" they applied for the first time the full logic of the Witte system: if the economic policy of the government was industrialization, the government must try to remake all of Russian society according to the needs of industrialization. It must not only adapt agriculture to the rationality of the factory, but also reshape the social structure, the predilections of the population, and their subconscious minds. The extremes of social engineering in the Soviet Union have always shocked the Western observer. But given their determination to close the gap of backwardness, the Bolsheviks had no choice. Spontaneity in Russian life, in the arts, literature, philosophy, in economic action or individual conduct, meant free play for all the preindustrial instincts, habits, and values.[32] Hence it could not be permitted.

There is no need here to discuss the elaborate technique evolved in this practice of social control. Suffice it to say that all the Soviet measures against the spontaneous creativity of the people are inherent in the basic necessity governing the relations between state and economy in Russia. Nor need it be related how the Soviet government coped with the inevitable opposition aroused not only by the extreme material sacrifices of the five-year plans but also by the state's constant invasion of the privacy of its subjects. One vitally essential feature must nevertheless be mentioned: the prevention of invidious comparisons with Western conditions and of the hankering for expensive imports. It was done both by the positive method of assuring the Russian people, if necessary by outright lies, that they lived in a socialist society and therefore in the best of all possible worlds, and by the negative method of the Iron Curtain which kept out not only the foreign goods but foreign models in every field of life. In this manner the Soviet regime limited drastically the constant subversion from without. In short, it tried to create artificially the optimism and secure self-esteem of the Western peoples which had contributed so much to the development of their modern institutions, economic and otherwise.

If, then, the Soviets have succeeded in narrowing the gap between

[32] For support of my contentions I should like to refer to other contributions to this volume — for instance that of Talcott Parsons, which deals with the values and institutions underlying a modern industrial society. He does not make reference, however, to the deep-seated habit of conformism, the "aggressive desire to do the right thing," which characterizes, for instance, American urban-industrial society and which has contributed so much to its smooth functioning. Other chapters in this volume discuss the absence in Russia of the values, institutions, and habits — in short, of the social discipline — required for a functioning urban-industrial society.

their political ambition and their economic resources, they have done so less through economic means, such as the refined techniques of over-all planning and the adaptation of modern standards of industrial efficiency, than through social, psychological, and political means, through a total attack on the traditional fabric of Russian life. And while they have had the advantage of Western experience in the fields of technology, science, and even industrial management, they have had to proceed on their own in the larger framework of institutions, emotions, and attitudes in which these accomplishments could be put to maximum use.

How much the Soviets have succeeded in creating a "new man" suitable for the urban-industrial way of life may well be questioned. Their drastic efforts have more often than not provoked their own deep-seated resistances. At any rate, it was inevitable that they should prefer the experiment to defeatist inaction. And choosing action they had to aim at a total remolding of their society. The Western European pattern is a total one, encompassing all aspects of life, and for quick imitation requires a comprehensive recasting of any society differing from it. The economic and cultural discrepancy between the advanced and the underdeveloped country thus inescapably tends to force a totalitarian grasp upon any effective reform in the latter, at least where speed is considered essential.

In looking over Russian development in the past hundred years, one sees an ever closer identity between state and economy and an ever deeper invasion of the spontaneous creativity of the Russian people by both. The state has been shifting its attention increasingly from the economic aspects of backwardness to its noneconomic aspects, to the organization of government and society, and even to the subconscious motivation of human behavior, all in an overriding effort to narrow the gap between its resources and its ambitions in the global state system. If this premise is correct, the transformation of Russian society since 1861, particularly after 1917, has been prompted very largely by the desire of Russia's leaders to overcome the handicaps and inferiority of backwardness.

In conclusion, throughout the course of recent Russian history one observes an understandable unwillingness to surrender Russia's great-power status, on the one hand, and an equal readiness, on the other, to try all means, whether legitimate or illegitimate according to Western political theory and practice, to overcome the humiliation of backwardness. The incredible cost of this ambition, above all in terms of human life and well-being, of freedom and spontaneity, only points up the fiercest of all the dilemmas of backwardness: the gap between humaneness and state necessity. That gap is wide enough even in the experience of the great powers of the West; it is insurmountable in the case of a backward country that also wants to be a global power.

SUMMARY AND REVIEW

MERLE FAINSOD

Any analysis of the relations of political, legal, and economic institutions to the transformations in Russian society since 1861 must inevitably take into account a bewildering array of interacting forces and influences. The pressure for modernization is an insistent theme — perhaps the most insistent. The resistance to modernization is equally apparent in a prolonged and stubborn adherence to preindustrial traditions and in the dramatic rear-guard action of the Slavophiles and their successors against the Westernizers. The transcendent role of state power is everywhere manifest, weakening in the last years of the empire and powerfully reasserting itself in the Soviet period, sometimes seeking to bar social change, at other times manipulating, guiding, and even accelerating it in the regime's interest. Law reveals itself as both obstacle and opportunity, sometimes working to freeze existing social relations, at other times attempting to adapt and reform them, and after 1917 operating as a potent instrument to recast the social structure on a new revolutionary and industrial model. Economic policy emerges as a handmaiden of state policy, only incidentally concerned with meeting the welfare needs of the population and focused on overcoming the consequences of retarded economic development. The state looms large, overshadowing the individuals who are its subjects. While there is still a place for society apart from the state under the empire, with the fulfillment of the totalitarian impulse in Bolshevism the penetration of society by the state became almost complete. It is within this frame that the essays devoted to law, politics, and social change will be reviewed.

Zbigniew Brzezinski's paper is essentially a comparative analysis of the structure of authority in the Tsarist and Soviet system. Although he does bring out parallels and continuities within a basic autocratic pattern, he is more concerned to emphasize the significant differences between the two systems. Tsarist power is seen as merely one variant of pretotalitarian authoritarianism, committed to preserving the main outlines of the status quo and operating within a framework of societal and traditional restraints. Soviet power, on the other hand, is viewed as an expression of totalitarian dynamism, dedicated to the total control and reshaping of society in a new revolutionary image.

Brzezinski sees a crucial difference between the two systems in the treatment accorded to elements in opposition. The tsars vacillated between repression and concession, but even in their most brutally repressive moods they lacked the cold-blooded efficiency of the totalitarian regime, and the concessions they were prepared to make fell far short of propitiating the forces which were arrayed against them. Pointing to the work of the tsar-reformers, Brzezinski suggests that they tried by occasional reforms from above to narrow the gap between the regime and society, but because they conceded too little, their history is a record of failure. In contrast, he suggests, the Soviet leadership has sought to reinforce the durability of its unlimited power by ruthlessly stamping out all opposition and by so transforming and dominating society that no gap can exist between the society and its leadership. As Brzezinski puts it, a situation has been created in which there is no meaningful alternative to rule by the Communist Party leadership; opponents of the regime face "the dilemma of the one alternative." Thus, if this thesis be valid, the Soviet regime has transcended the dilemma of the empire in which the choice was between allowing opposition pressures from below to build up into a revolutionary explosion or, alternatively, introducing reforms from above and accepting self-denying ordinances which developed into institutionalized restraints on autocratic power.

While speculation on the durability of Soviet totalitarianism is not the most profitable of all occupations, it may not be amiss to point out that the Soviet leadership is faced with its own revolution of rising social expectations. How it responds to them over the long term may well determine its own capacity for survival. We know too little of the dynamics of totalitarian systems to be certain that the unlimited authority which the Soviet leadership presently exercises may not be subject to ultimate erosion or displacement by forces which are not now visible on the horizon. History has a way of confounding those who claim to have mastered its secrets.

In turning to Leopold Haimson's essay, one is confronted again with the strength of the autocratic tradition in Russian public life. Unlike Brzezinski, Haimson does not deal with its current manifestations; he is chiefly concerned with seeking out its roots and the attitudes which nurtured it. If I may perhaps oversimplify Haimson's major thesis, it seems to me that it adds up to this: the weight of Russia's political and social experience created a powerful barricade to a parliamentary path of development, and the organization of Russian society was essentially uncongenial to the development of a pluralistic party system in the Western sense of the term. In elaborating this thesis Haimson emphasizes the central role played by state power in defining the forms of social organization, the chasm separating classes and estates, and the historic tendency of social groups to turn directly and individually to the state as the only legitimate source of authority through which grievances could be redressed.

As Haimson demonstrates, there was little disposition, even among reformers in the pre-emancipation era, to look to the Western parliamentary model as one to be followed. Reformers in the state bureaucracy might have favored the elimination of serfdom and the modernization of administration, but they continued to affirm the view that the autocratic power was the dominant force in Russia's development and that it remained the custodian of national interests against the selfish claims of estates and factions. For the Slavophile reformers the task was not to impose constitutional limitations on the autocratic power, or to establish a party system which would involve them in the political process, but rather to achieve the recognition of an area of autonomy for society free from political direction and control. Among the radical intelligentsia, the dominating attraction was exercised by utopian socialist views, which involved a rejection of the very idea of the state along with constitutional limitations, representative institutions, and other partial political reforms.

These diverse strains of thought — all joined in hostility to Western parliamentarianism — were to exert a powerful influence in the post-emancipation period. The confluence of these anticonstitutionalist tendencies in Russian opinion undermined the position of those constitutional reformers who were groping their way toward a system of national representation. Indeed, even when the constitutional movement finally scored its partial triumph in the 1905 Revolution, the parties which moved to the center of the political stage remained in a sense estranged from the broad base of Russian society and operated in an environment in which the aspirations of the masses of peasants and workers could not readily be fulfilled through parliamentary channels. The revolutionary holocaust when it came in 1917 testified to the thinness of Russia's constitutional commitment; the historic achievement of Lenin and the Bolsheviks was to reassert the centrality of state power.

Although Haimson does not assert that this process was in any sense inevitable or that the outcome was foreordained, he does emphasize the predisposing factors in Russian public opinion and social development which facilitated a revolutionary resolution of Russia's crisis. While I share Haimson's view that the Russian constitutional movement was a fragile plant, it does seem to me important to stress perhaps more than he does that the forces which rallied around it were growing in the prerevolutionary decade, and that the chaos and disorganization of 1914–1917, the years of war and revolution, may have done more to undermine constitutionalism and made a greater contribution to Lenin's victory than Haimson's analysis allows. The triumph of the Bolsheviks makes appear inevitable what may not have been at all inevitable at the time. The victor's retrospective history may be as dangerously distorted as the defeated's "might-have-beens."

John Hazard's essay also puts primary emphasis on the claims which the past makes on the present. His careful, scholarly examination of what actually occurred in the legal sphere in the first years after the revolution leads him to conclude that the continuities between Tsarist and Soviet judicial practice quickly reasserted themselves. Essentially, he contends, the Bolsheviks, after proposing a radical break with the Tsarist past, ended up with a hierarchical court system not unlike that of their imperial predecessors, reverted to reliance on professional judges, professional prosecutors, and a professional bar, and adopted a substantive body of law which in many respects drew heavily on prerevolutionary precedents and practice. While Hazard is not unaware of the paramount role of the Communist Party in shaping the uses of legal doctrine, the full dimensions of the party's impact on the law tend to become submerged in his discussion. His contention that the Tsarist judiciary was not significantly more independent of political direction and control than the Soviet judiciary is open to question and misses the important distinction drawn by Brzezinski between Tsarist authoritarianism and Soviet totalitarianism. Nor does his discussion give adequate weight to the dynamic and transforming role of Soviet law as an instrument of the party dictatorship — the utilization of the law to provide an institutional discipline and legal sanction for a society which was being rapidly collectivized, industrialized, and, until Stalin's death at least, totalitarianized. The major concern of Hazard's paper is with formal continuities. As a result, the role of law as an instrument of social change emerges only dimly.

Sidney Monas' chapter contributes a vivid account of the role of the political police in imperial Russia and a more condensed treatment of police developments during the Soviet period. As becomes a historian, the method is primarily historical, and the thesis of the essay, if I may take the liberty of extrapolating one, is suggested by tantalizing leads which are thrown out in passing. Briefly put, the objective of Nicholas I in founding the Third Section was the consolidation of order; the duty of the subject was to obey the autocrat; and the task of the Third Section was to make certain that the subject fulfilled his duty, that Russia remained "somnolent and at peace." What Monas calls "The Dream of a Beautiful Autocracy" is essentially the vision of a people united in subservience to a stern but beneficent and paternal Autocrat.

During the nineteenth century this dream lost contact with social reality. With the increasing estrangement of important segments of society from the autocracy, the political police, although never completely casting off its early mask of benevolence and welfare, became an increasingly repressive organ — dedicating its energies to stamping out opposition wherever it appeared. Nevertheless, as Monas demonstrates, the Tsarist political police operated over a considerable period within a framework of legal restraints; these together with its relative inefficiency rendered it powerless to check the growth of the revolutionary forces which it sought to eradicate. The Tsarist political police not only failed to arrest social change; it prepared many segments of the public to support a revolutionary break with the old order and provided a model from which the Soviet political police borrowed many of its techniques.

But Monas also properly points out important differences between the Tsarist and Soviet political police. The object of the Tsarist police was to safeguard the status quo; the aim of the Soviet political police has been to facilitate a reshaping of Soviet society by eliminating all those who bar the way to its realization. The Tsarist political police contained potentially totalitarian impulses which were never altogether fulfilled. The Soviet political police became a totalitarian instrument penetrating every corner of Soviet society. The Tsarist political police numbered its victims in the thousands and tens of thousands; the Soviet political police stamped its mark on the millions. The Tsarist political police provided a school for revolutionaries; the Soviet political police left most of its victims cowed and subdued. Although Monas takes note of the moderation of the terror in the years since Stalin's death, he is not inclined to see its early disappearance and indeed concludes that the "struggle for the control of the party necessarily involves a struggle for control of the police, and that the terroristic potentialities of the political police may well be realized in the process."

While there are many suggestive leads in Monas' excellent essay, one of the most interesting problems which it poses involves the relation of the political police to social change. The Tsarist police sought to freeze the social forces that were in motion and was ultimately overwhelmed by them. The Soviet police in the initial phases of the revolution served as an instrument of forced change; it helped to destroy an old society and to create a new social order. Once the main contours of the new order crystallize and solidify, the task of the political police again becomes essentially conservative, defending the status quo and its array of beneficiaries. Does this mean that the Soviet police agencies will take on more and more of the characteristics of its Tsarist predecessors, battling against the immanent forces of changes at work on the Soviet scene, and destined ultimately, like its progenitors, to be estranged from society and to be replaced by new political formations? Or has the Soviet regime discovered a new magic formula for survival, the special secret of responding to and manipulating rising social aspirations while avoiding the alienation which dealt a deathblow to its predecessor?

Monas' emphasis on the differences between the Tsarist and Soviet regimes is further elaborated in Alexander Vucinich's admirably lucid analysis of the development of local governmental institutions in the Tsarist period and of their analogues, the local soviets, under the Bolsheviks. After demonstrating the grudging character of the zemstvo reforms, the deep suspicion with which they were regarded in high bureaucratic circles, and the mounting restrictions imposed on zemstvo initiative, he nevertheless concludes that they embodied and practiced a degree of self-government which the local soviets under the Bolsheviks were never able to attain. The dichotomy between state and society under the empire provided the zemstvos with a field of maneuver which, though circumscribed, was nevertheless real. In contrast, the Soviet regime's claim to determine the totality of social life narrowly restricts, where it does not obliterate, all areas of autonomous associative life. As Vucinich points out, the local soviets encourage mass participation in the performance of local governmental function, but the activity of the masses is guided and directed by party edicts and pronouncements, and the local soviets neither claim nor enjoy independence from central direction or control. The Communist leadership seeks to surround the soviets with an aura of democratic mythology while in fact denying them independent authority; the Tsarist regime uncompromisingly rejected the democratic myth, while in fact permitting the zemstvos a limited degree of self-government. In other words, the distinction is one between a totalitarian regime which has largely made good its pretensions and an authoritarian regime whose more narrowly conceived authority and more limited resources fell short of controlling the totality of social life.

With Theodore Von Laue's chapter we move into the area of economic policy, and again the stress is on continuity rather than change. In examining the evolving relations between the state and the economy since 1861, the question to which Von Laue addresses himself is this — how could the Russian state sustain the role of a great power with the imperfect and limited resources of an underdeveloped country? Von Laue sees the origins of modern Russian economic policy in the defeat suffered in the Crimean War, and the answer to his question in the assumption by the state of large responsibilities for industrial development which had to be financed by foreign loans and sacrifices in current consumption by the peasantry. The dream of Count Witte, the apostle of industrialization, was the transformation of Russian society in the image of the capitalist society of the West, the rationalization of the autocracy to create a modernized bureaucracy, the establishment of a social structure and educational system designed to stimulate innovation and economic progress, and the creation of a legal and economic climate in which private entrepreneurship would flourish. As Von Laue points out, Witte's work remained incomplete; despite a very impressive spurt of industrialization during the 1890's and a lesser, but not insignificant, effort in the period between the 1905 Revolution and the outbreak of the First World War, Russia's backwardness interposed formidable obstacles to modernization, and the sacrifices exacted by industrialization were to contribute to the tensions which the revolutionary movement was able to exploit.

Turning to the Bolsheviks, Von Laue visualizes them, in one sense at least, as the spiritual heirs of Witte, similarly dedicated to industrialization, but prepared to embrace far more brutal and thoroughgoing expedients to transform the traditional fabric of Russian life in order to attain industrial efficiency and accumulate an industrialization fund. In this perspective the Bolsheviks emerge as the industrializers par excellence, achieving the great-power status of which Tsarist Russia could only dream. Given the Bolshevik commitment to rapid industrialization, Von Laue sees reliance on totalitarian methods as virtually inevitable. Indeed, he tends to view totalitarianism as a necessary path for any underdeveloped country which is intent on rapid industrialization.

Even if one regards the last thesis as dubious, or at least debatable, one may grant with Von Laue that Stalin's decision to overcome Russian backwardness through a program of rapid industrialization and collectivization powerfully strengthened the totalitarian component in his system of rule. One may concede further that continued dedication to a policy of high-speed industrialization, if purchased at a price of severe pressure on living standards, carries its totalitarian consequences if the policy of superindustrialization is to be maintained. But what happens when economic backwardness is at last overcome, when the great-power status of Russia has achieved its technical coefficients, when the threats from the outside world begin to appear somewhat less menacing, and the rationale of totalitarianism loses its persuasiveness, at least to its subjects if not to the rulers themselves? If it be true, as Von Laue contends, that the last century of Russian history has seen a powerful extension of the state and an ever-deeper invasion of society, largely prompted "by the desire of Russia's leaders to overcome the handicaps and inferiority of backwardness," it is also well to remember that it has been accompanied by a strong undercurrent of discontent with the sacrifices which have had to be borne, and that suppressed aspirations have a way of eventually forcing a reckoning. Indeed, some of the major welfare concessions of the regime since Stalin's death may be interpreted in these terms, and we should not be surprised if they turn out to be merely a harbinger of wider claims which future Soviet regimes will dare ignore only at their peril.

PART THREE

SOCIAL STRATIFICATION

SOCIAL CLASSES AND POLITICAL STRUCTURE

ROBERT A. FELDMESSER

the equalization of the estates is a simultaneous
victory for the general interest of the state
as well as for personal freedom.[1]

I

An examination of the dynamics, or of the statics, of social classes in
Russia, or anywhere else, requires initially that we have an understanding
of exactly what is being examined. We may start from Hans Speier's
simple, almost self-evident, statement: the "specific characteristic" of social
classes, that which distinguishes them from other elements of social structure, is hierarchy.[2] Yet even if we accept this proposition, the identification of concrete social classes is still no easy matter. A particularly troublesome problem has been whether we are to look for "real" groups, "objective" in nature, with boundaries and composition clearly recognizable
by all concerned, their members as well as those who observe them; or
whether we are to study subjective perceptions, attitudes, the way the
individual members of society themselves feel. The key to this venerable
question seems to lie in the recently developed concept of reference groups.
We shall find, as might well have been expected, that the struggle has
been taking place over another false dichotomy.

The reference-group concept is the logical sequel to a number of
fundamental theorems of human behavior: that behavior is motivated;
that motivation is, in large part, the product and anticipation of rewarding
and punishing interaction with other humans; and that rewards and punishments are meted out in accordance with the degree to which behavior
conforms to the expectations of these other individuals.[3] These propositions, when combined, lead to another: that a given act or pattern of acts
is undertaken, consciously or unconsciously, in order to satisfy the perceived expectations of those people who are psychologically significant to
the actor in his given situation. The expectations are commonly designated
as "norms"; at a more organized and explicit level, they become an ide-

---

[1] V. O. Kliuchevsky, *Istoriia soslovii v Rossii* (3rd ed., Petrograd, 1918), 28.
[2] Hans Speier, *Social Order and the Risks of War* (New York, 1952), 20.
[3] The clearest relevant statement and illustration of these theorems is that by
George C. Homans, *The Human Group* (New York, 1950), to which the present
formulation is heavily obligated.

ology; at a more diffuse and implicit level, a value system. A reference group, then, is a set of individuals who share distinctive norms which are used by a given actor in the determination of his own behavior.[4]

Now, if our interest is in the study of human behavior, a group is "real" if it has an impact on behavior. It is real, in other words, to the extent that it serves the reference-group function. This implies two essential properties: (1) The group possesses its own at least partly unique system of norms which distinguishes it from some other group or groups. Otherwise, no definable, peculiar influence on behavior could be attributed to it. (2) It has power effective in enforcing these norms — resources for rewarding and punishing its members, for controlling the consequences of their behavior. What is specifically excluded is the application of the term "reference group" to an aggregate of individuals who merely find themselves in similar situations; what we are concerned with, rather, is the group-shared norms in terms of which they respond to their typical situations. And without power, a group would have no way of keeping its members "in line," conforming to one another's expectations, and no way of defending the integrity of its norm system against "outside" pressures. Indeed, it is difficult to see how a group's norms could be learned or become known at all except through the periodic application of power (sanctions). Of course, this power may be subtle or overt, and it certainly need not be exercised through any formal organization, though it may be; it may reside in nothing more than the power of parents to socialize their children.

A hierarchical stratum, therefore, is a social class — it is real, it has significant and distinctive effects on behavior — to the extent that it is used as a reference group. Any society provides a rich array of potential reference groups; what distinguishes social-class reference groups from others is that their members occupy contiguous positions in a hierarchical scale. Hence, whether a society has a social-class system or not is an empirical question, to be determined in each instance by inquiring into the frequency with which hierarchically arranged categories are in fact utilized as reference groups. The more frequently this is the case (bearing in mind both the number of individuals and the number of areas of behavior), the more nearly real are the social classes in the society, and the more important they are to an understanding of the behavior of its members; the less frequently it is the case, the less will information about social classes contribute to that understanding.

A number of revealing corollaries follow from this approach. First, it is not necessary, or always even wise, to ask people about social class in order to ascertain what influence it has on their lives, or whether the

---

[4] For a number of specific applications, as well as for further theoretical elucidation, see especially Robert K. Merton, *Social Theory and Social Structure* (revised and enlarged ed.; Glencoe, 1957), 225–386.

phenomenon exists at all. There is no substitute for observation of and generalization from behavior. What a person says about his social class, in response to direct questions about it, is important information — for verbal statements are behavior, too — but it cannot be regarded as a better index of fact than what he says about his family, another of his potential reference groups. "Class consciousness" — of which more will be said subsequently — is, in other words, a pre-Freudian term. Conversely, mere legal definitions do not of themselves create social classes, although the sanctions which accompany them may exert some influence. Second, it is not necessary to establish the fact of consensus as to the boundaries and composition of hierarchical groups before one can legitimately speak of social classes. They can be said to exist in a society if some sizable proportion of its members refer, in the determination of their behavior, to the norms characteristic of people located in some limited range of a socially recognized hierarchy. It is altogether reasonable to expect some variation (though surely it will not be entirely idiosyncratic) in the definition of this range, but such variation does not disprove the existence of social classes any more than — to make an analogy with another common type of reference group — the failure of the members of a society to agree on the precise year when old age begins entitles us to say that there is really no such thing as old age. The boundaries of reference groups are heuristically defined. "Objective" groups are those whose boundaries and composition are matters of intersubjective agreement;[5] but we cannot legitimately infer the absence of social classes from the absence of such agreement.

Third, and most significant for what follows, the extent to which hierarchically ordered positions or ranges of positions — one possible set of reference groups among the many which may hypothetically be made available — are normatively defined or actually used as sources of guides to behavior may vary from one individual to the next, from one situation to another, from one society to another, from one era to another within the same society.[6] The American ideals of equalitarianism and democratic behavior, for instance, do not deny the existence or the desirability of a hierarchy of economic wealth; they express opposition only to the transformation of ranges of this hierarchy into reference groups. One may be rich, but one should not "put on airs," behave differently from those with less money.

[5] "Inter-subjective norms are not agreed to by members of a society because they are objective, but, in effect, become objective because they are jointly accepted." Henry D. Aiken, *The Age of Ideology* (New York, 1957), 23.
[6] It may also vary within the ranges of the hierarchy itself. Social classes may include, among the norms to which they exact conformity, definitions of the situations in which they themselves are appropriate in the determination of behavior. This raises a host of intriguing problems and possibilities, which are, however, tangential to the purposes of this essay.

II

If social classes are to be understood and analyzed in the terms set forth above, Russian society on the eve of emancipation might be characterized boldly and simply: there were no social classes. Admittedly this is hyperbole, but it nevertheless expresses a basic truth. At most, we might speak of "conflicting" class patterns — but that would mean, essentially, the lack of a close correspondence between position in a hierarchical segment, on the one hand, and a wide range of distinctive norms, on the other, and thus, by the criteria which have been adopted, no true class system existed. There were value differences within the society, to be sure, and that there were differences of wealth and property needs no belaboring. But the crucial point is that these differences were far from being neatly aligned with one another.

The legally authorized, and thus most explicit, form of hierarchy was the system of estates and the associated Table of Ranks.[7] At the most general level, there were two estates: the nontaxable and the taxable (*podatnoe*). Along with the privilege of exemption from the poll tax went freedom from compulsory military service and from corporal punishment. Within these two broad categories there were a number of subdivisions. The hereditary nobility (*potomstvennoe dvorianstvo*) stood at the top of the privileged estate, marked off particularly by the further privilege of owning serfs. Below them came the personal nobility (*lichnoe dvorianstvo*), who were granted a title for life but whose children were not nobles but honored citizens (*pochetnye grazhdane*), this latter status then being transmitted by inheritance. They were thus distinguished from the next group, the merchantry (*kupechestvo*), who enjoyed their privileges only so long as they continued to pay for them in legally specified amounts.[8] Personally honored citizens were granted the privileges of the merchant group for life but could not pass them on to their children. The taxable estates were composed of town inhabitants, among whom were the *meshchanstvo,* small shopkeepers or artisans, in effect the lowest stratum of merchants though without the privileges of the merchants; and of the mass of rural inhabitants, the peasantry (*krest'ianstvo*). The clergy stood outside these categories, being subject to ecclesiastical rather than civil authority. In addition, there were a number of groups, such as

[7] The picture which follows was pieced together principally from the following sources: Kliuchevsky; G. B. Sliozberg, *Dorevoliutsionnyi stroi Rossii* (Paris, 1933), 97–107; and Anatole Leroy-Beaulieu, *The Empire of the Tsars and the Russians,* trans. from the 3rd French edition by Zenaide A. Rogozin (New York and London, 1893), I, 314–375. See also Max Beloff, "Russia," in A. Goodwin, ed., *The European Nobility in the Eighteenth Century* (London, 1953), 172–189.

[8] Actually, only the two highest "guilds" (*tsekhi*) among the merchants belonged to the privileged estate. Guild membership was determined by ownership of a specified minimum of capital and payment of a corresponding license fee. For further detail, see Leroy-Beaulieu, I, 338.

Cossacks and Jews, for whom special provisions were made which did not place them in any of the estate categories.

These estates were only rough equivalents of the similar institutions of Western Europe. They differed in two ways. First, membership in them was somewhat less permanent, even in those which were nominally hereditary. Birth into the nobility or the hereditarily honored citizenry was a valid claim to the privileges of membership only so long as the tsar chose to recognize it. Imperial condemnation was sufficient for exclusion.[9] Conversely, the tsar could confer membership in the privileged estates on whomever he would, and not infrequently court favorites were so honored on little more than the imperial whimsy. Moreover, although the requirement of the Petrine era that high rank and the privilege attendant upon it be *conditional* on continued service in the state bureaucracy had disappeared a century before emancipation, it remained true that distinguished service could be so rewarded, and often was.[10] Attainment of a certain rank brought ennoblement with it automatically, without regard to origin. Although over the years this minimum qualifying rank was successively raised, the lowest rank always remained open to holders of a university degree and, from there, promotion brought the same result. Anyone who wished to engage in trade and paid the requisite fee could have his name inscribed on the merchants' rolls, and even peasants, as well as artisans and noblemen, found themselves able to do so.[11] Membership in the estates of Western Europe certainly was not immutable, but the difference was more than one of slight degree. Russia, unlike the Western nations, was marked by a "lack of respect paid . . . to noble birth as such." [12]

Both cause and consequence of this difference was another: none of these strata had the facilities with which to create an effective reference group based on its own collectively defined norms. Most of the estates and subestates had forms of corporate organization, but these bodies were purely local and their powers chiefly administrative, such as the keeping of membership registers. They had no political favors to dispense, no offices or votes to control. The tsar felt no obligation to heed their wishes, and on many occasions simply ignored their appeals or advice. No group, in short, had "any rights that the governing power need consider." [13]

[9] Leroy-Beaulieu, I, 392.

[10] For a number of examples, see Marc Raeff, "The Russian Autocracy and Its Officials," in Hugh McLean, Martin E. Malia, and George Fischer, eds., *Russian Thought and Politics* (The Hague, 1957), 81–86.

[11] Leroy-Beaulieu, I, 338; P. A. Berlin, *Russkaia burzhuaziia v staroe i novoe vremia* (Moscow, 1922), 40ff, 87–89.

[12] Beloff, 181. There was, however, a small number of "distinguished families" (known collectively as *znat'*) who held a position of high social prestige over several generations which was not dependent on the tsars' beneficence; interestingly enough, this position did not rest on membership in any particular estate, and was no more often adorned than unadorned by noble title.

[13] Leroy-Beaulieu, I, 313.

Legally, the reward of membership (and the punishment of exclusion) was not at the autonomous disposal of any estate, and though the nobility might have sought to exercise a *de facto* control over its own composition, either through social exclusiveness or by refusing to inscribe new names in the registers, it actually did so only rarely.

Underlying both these differences was the fact that the Russian estates, unlike those of Western Europe, were not so much the accommodative outcome of a struggle between a powerful autocrat and a powerful nobility (and, later, a powerful bourgeoisie) as they were, both in law and in accepted tradition, the tsar's instrument for preserving his own power. The nobility had perhaps come close to asserting itself as a class with inalienable rights in the second half of the eighteenth century, but its efforts never quite reached full fruition. The tsar managed to make clear, by word and deed, that such grants of privilege as he conferred were for the sole purpose of enabling the nobility and other groups to become more effective administrators of his own policies — the collection of taxes on behalf of the imperial authority, the maintenance of internal order, and the production of goods which he felt were needed by the state. Whenever it appeared that these privileges might be used to frustrate the imperial desire, they were modified or withdrawn. The nobility itself, in effect, accepted the principle of its own subordination. Thus, for example, when it was allowed to appoint certain local officials from among its own ranks, the actions of these "class representatives" turned out to be indistinguishable from those of their centrally appointed counterparts. Or, again, even after the requirement of state service had been ended, high bureaucratic rank remained a major source of social prestige, and the scramble for the tsar's favor continued unabated. The attraction of life in the capital, especially of reception at the imperial court, served as an efficacious substitute for the formal imperative of the law.[14] It is true that the nobility, by brute force, did occasionally influence or change the dynastic succession. But, to paraphrase a later belittlement of a different political method, this power amounted to no more than the ability to determine which claimant to the throne would be the next oppressor.

Similarly, economic weapons of defense against the tsar were not at hand. The nobility is commonly identified with the landlords, but the tsar freely granted lands as well as titles to those who met his pleasure. Yet the absence, in both law and custom, of primogeniture or other forms of single inheritance meant that landed property was rapidly diffused after the initial grant. Moreover, the profligacy of the wealthy in Russia is legendary. Just prior to emancipation, well over half of the nobility's land, and almost two thirds of its serfs, were mortgaged to state credit institutions, and other portions to private persons and banks. Only some 10 to

---

[14] Beloff, 177, 180–184, 187–189.

12 per cent of the nobility owned serfs at all, and only about 1 per cent owned more than one hundred.[15] While many nobles were certainly well-to-do, numbers of merchants, and even a few peasants, were also able to amass substantial wealth and to obtain *de facto* control over serfs.[16] In such cases, however, their attention was often concentrated not on realizing the aspirations of their estate, but on winning their way into the nobility.

Indeed, it is difficult to discern any aspirations or other norms proper and peculiar to one or another estate. The nobility and the merchants, after all, had not been legally separated long or sharply enough for clearly disparate traditions to arise: it was only in 1762 that the hereditary nobles were given the exclusive rights of serf ownership and freedom from corporal punishment, and the merchants were granted the latter a brief twenty years later; other distinctions dated only from the Charter of the Nobility of 1785.[17] Many of the merchants, in turn, were only one generation removed, if that, from the peasantry. Internally, each estate was a motley collection of people with widely varying interests. There were undoubtedly some characteristics more or less widely shared among the nobility, for example, but these were chiefly cultural refinements, such as the use of the French or German language rather than Russian, which had "little impact on their behavior as administrators." [18] This was understandable enough, since there was little of importance that conformity to such affectations could bring which could not be had without it. Otherwise, attitudes and styles of life among the noblemen were as heterogenous as their economic statuses. If some had aristocratic pretensions, others leaned toward a leveling ideology; if some favored freeing the serfs, others opposed it.[19] The older aristocrats were often at odds with the newer; those residing in Moscow and Petersburg with those who lived in the provinces; those whose lands were in the fertile zones with those whose land was less productive; those who owned large quantities of land and serfs with those who owned less or none; those whose properties were managed by hired help or by serfs with those who managed or even tilled the soil themselves; those who had established industrial works with those who had not. It was due, in part, to these very divisions that the nobility had been unable to unite for an effective challenge to the power of the tsars. Yet, at the same time, the legal barriers that did separate the estates added to their common powerlessness, helped to block the emergence of

---

[15] Peter I. Lyashchenko, *History of the National Economy of Russia to the 1917 Revolution* (New York, 1949), 393; Leroy-Beaulieu, I, 322, 354, 393, 417.

[16] Berlin, 63–64, 90.

[17] Berlin, 18; Beloff, 188; Leroy-Beaulieu, I, 392. The last author points out (351) the absence of so much as a *de* or a *von* to distinguish aristocratic family names from "ordinary" ones.

[18] Raeff, 86.

[19] George Fischer, *Russian Liberalism* (Cambridge, Mass., 1958), 5.

genuine social-class reference groups which would ignore estate distinctions and coalesce around vital interests and shared ideologies. In the last analysis, each aristocratic, or would-be aristocratic, family felt that what mattered most for its social position was neither estate membership nor economic activity, but its personal standing in the eyes of the tsar.

It could be argued that the peasantry formed a massive exception to these generalizations. Here, if anywhere in pre-emancipation Russia, there was a group concentrated in one segment of the economic hierarchy which largely coincided with the boundaries of a legally designated estate, and whose members lived within a broadly similar normative framework governing not only their work habits but also their family life, their religious behavior, and their attitudes toward their own and others' positions in society, as well as their speech, dress, and manners. Strip farming, the mir, the difficulties in leaving the village, and an exceptionally strong patriarchal family provided the conditions under which the peasantry maintained a way of life more or less common to all. To introduce such qualifications as the differences (even if in some respects considerable) between household and field serfs, crown peasants and private, might perhaps be quibbling. What can be questioned, however, was the degree to which at least some of the more important attitudes were distinctive to this group. There were many people who were not peasants themselves but who regarded the peasant as the victimized hero of Russia, or who, at any rate, reacted to the peasant's situation in much the same way that he did — in other words, used the same values to judge it and, like him, found it unsatisfactory. The widespread agitation which led to emancipation, and in a sense the emancipation itself, attest to that fact.

III

The reforms of Alexander II and, to a lesser extent, of his successors went far toward dissolving the legal supports of the estate system, without actually abolishing it altogether. Chief among them, of course, was the Emancipation Act of 1861, which deprived the hereditary nobility, in principle, of the right to own serfs. Two years later, it was decreed that town inhabitants could not be subjected to corporal punishment except on the judgment of a court, and the application of corporal punishment to the peasant was placed in the hands of the mir; in 1904, this authority, too, was turned over to the courts.[20] Later edicts extended the obligation of military service to all estates (1874), a measure which had implications reaching far beyond mere legal equalization;[21] abolished the poll tax (1886);[22] and transferred the authority to issue internal passports from

[20] Sliozberg, 101–102; Michael T. Florinsky, *Russia* (New York, 1953), II, 895.
[21] Leroy-Beaulieu, I, 317.
[22] On the significance of this act, see George Vernadsky, *A History of Russia* (New Haven, 1951), 197.

the estate organizations to the police (1894–1906). The new courts were taking less notice of the appurtenances of estate and title than had hitherto been the case,[23] and both the courts and the zemstvos produced a new group of lawyers, doctors, teachers, and administrators to whom existing definitions of rank and legal status could not easily be applied. They were educated in the universities, whose importance was thereby increased, along with that of the classical gymnasiums; and a series of reforms slowly and fitfully, but unmistakably, broadened access to these institutions. It is significant that, even when reaction set in after the initial educational reforms, it did not take the form of providing separate schools for each estate, but of higher tuition fees, alterations in the educational ladder in the direction of separating vocational from classical schools, and regulation of the composition of the student body in terms of the occupations of their fathers — as, for example, in Delianov's famous "circular on cooks' children" of 1887.[24]

The quickening pace of economic change in the late nineteenth century had similarly corrosive effects. Managerial, engineering, and scientific occupations could not be dealt out by inheritance, or assimilated to the structure of *chiny* and estates, any more than could those which grew out of the new political institutions. The degree of economic overlap among the estates was intensified: first, by a decline in the amount of land owned by the nobility, in favor of the merchants and later increasingly of the peasants; and second, by the construction of railroads and factories, in which no estate held a monopoly.[25] A factory proletariat appeared, recruited from several estates without ever receiving an official designation of its own. The Stolypin reforms, by a combination of political and economic means, accelerated and extended the process of change, both thrusting the centrifugal forces of differentiation into the peasantry and somewhat obscuring the remaining distinctions between it and the rest of the population.[26]

While making their respective contributions to the destruction of the old estates, political reform and industrialization were at the same time preparing the ground for the growth of genuine social classes. The zemstvo was a potential forum for the articulation of differentiated class norms and seemingly promised a diffusion of political power which could be useful in enforcing those norms. Even if — or, perhaps, especially if — the zemstvo assemblies were dominated by large landowners, the diminution of purely autocratic power would nevertheless be significant. Meanwhile, through journalistic media and formal organizations, groups of

[23] Donald MacKenzie Wallace, *Russia* (London, 1905), II, 278–280.
[24] Nicholas Hans, *History of Russian Educational Policy, 1701–1917* (London, 1931).
[25] Geroid Tanquary Robinson, *Rural Russia Under the Old Regime* (New York, 1949), 132–135; Berlin, 114–115, 118–119, 120–121; Lyashchenko, 476ff.
[26] Robinson, 211, 222, 224, 238–240.

businessmen, professionals, and workers expressed vital interests, moved in the direction of shared economic and political values, and gathered the forces with which to promulgate them.[27] Thus there are grounds for believing that hierarchical groups and ideologies might eventually have become aligned in Russia, creating reference groups out of stratified categories. The amorphous political parties which began to appear in the early years of the twentieth century might well have acted as the catalysts in the transformation.

Nevertheless, during the decades in question, there were major obstacles to the emergence of social-class reference groups. For one thing, there were a few anachronistic attempts to preserve the estate character of Russian society. Thus, separate land banks were established for the nobility and the peasantry, with, of course, more favorable terms for the former;[28] a few schools were still reserved for children of the nobility; and, of greater moment, access into the nobility through the attainment of rank was for the first time entirely cut off.[29] Second, the tsars remained as adamant as ever in refusing to yield any element of power, whether to estates or to more "natural" groupings at any point in the socioeconomic scale. The powers of the zemstvos and the courts, never very great, were steadily restricted, nor did the Dumas fare any better. The appointment of personal favorites to ministerial positions — and the frequent disregard of ministerial advice — continued to be the practice.[30] The tsars' own definitions of the political and military interests of the state received precedence over the pleas of economic interest made by manufacturers and railway buildings, and strict prohibitions were placed upon the formation of workers' organizations, unless they were small, isolated, and under close government supervision.[31]

Finally, the nascent strata in the economic hierarchy were unwilling, perhaps unable, to make an unequivocal break with tradition and stake out positions based unambiguously on their mode of economic activity. A large proportion of the workers were more anxious to find a way to return to the peasant villages whence they had recently come, and where they still frequently lived and worked for substantial parts of the year,[32] than they were to organize for the sake of improving their lot as workers. Among the merchants, one could still find many who lived a peasant

[27] Berlin, 121, 124–128, 134–137; Leroy-Beaulieu, I, 465n; Fischer, 57–59; Mark G. Field, *Doctor and Patient in Soviet Russia* (Cambridge, Mass., 1957), 47–48.

[28] Margaret S. Miller, *The Economic Development of Russia, 1905–1914* (London, 1926), 97; Robinson, 131.

[29] Leroy-Beaulieu, I, 349, 395n.

[30] Florinsky, II, 899, 1093–1104; Wallace, II, 29, 242–246, 280–281, 447–458. A number of other chapters in this volume deal with these developments in greater detail; see especially Zbigniew Brzezinski, "The Patterns of Autocracy," and Alexander Vucinich, "The State and the Local Community."

[31] Miller, 184–185, 190–191, 234–237; Robinson, 248.

[32] Robinson, 296.

way of life and others who strived to imitate or outdo the nobility.[33] The newly developing kulaks were similarly divided. Industrial entrepreneurs operated under widely varying conditions, with decisively different relationships to both their capital and their labor force, and the presence among them of a large number of foreigners added further to their heterogeneity.[34] Conversely, where groups did appear with some kind of common attitude (even if only of a very general sort), they were not closely linked with a common economic position. The epitome of this situation were the *raznochintsy* — "men of various ranks" — and the intelligentsia. These might have been reference groups, but they could not accurately be called social classes because of their wide dispersion over the economic hierarchy.

Thus, upon the outbreak of World War I, Russian society contained, at most, only embryonic social classes. Given time, they might have been transmuted into true reference groups — as is suggested by the rising frequency, after the turn of the century, of strikes and peasant uprisings — but the time was not given, and the question must remain forever moot. One fact, though, is clear: Russia, as it has often been said, was the last place in which to expect a class-based revolution of the Marxist type. And, indeed, a Marxist revolution, in the conventional sense, never did occur there.

IV

Lenin was one of those rare historical figures who created a reference group rather than adopted one. He was singularly unwilling to adjust his behavior to the normative demands of others. For him, the realization of the Marxist goal of a socialist society came first, and the group with which he would cooperate was defined by prior acceptance of this goal and of the means which he felt were requisite for its achievement. Having embraced the overt aspects of Marxism, he did believe that the proletariat was the most likely source of collaborators, but he did not overlook the possibilities that equally valuable adherents could be found in other classes and that not every worker could be relied on to follow him.

This viewpoint was revealed most explicitly in the early rules of admission to the party which Lenin forged into a revolutionary instrument. Originally, no social-class distinctions were made at all; to become an accredited Bolshevik, one had to submit two personal recommendations, pledge loyalty to the party program and obedience to its decrees, and pay dues. Thus, workers were not admitted automatically on the strength of their social-class position alone, although this would seem to be the logical implication of the Marxist understanding of history. Later, admission was made easier for proletarians and peasants than for other categories,

---

[33] Leroy-Beaulieu, I, 341–342.
[34] Miller, 223.

but all candidates still had to submit personal recommendations and undergo a probationary period before admission, and no one was absolutely excluded from membership. The distinctions were a matter of degree: fewer recommendations and a shorter probation were demanded of candidates from proletarian origins. Significantly, the stiffest requirements were those made of former members of other parties — *whatever* their social-class origin.[35] In other words, an applicant's political inclinations were given first consideration, and his hierarchical economic position was secondary.

The precedence thus assigned to political compatibility over economic position has been described as "Marxism stood on its head." But if we trace the inversion to its source, we find that Leninism was but a logical outgrowth of Marxism, from which the structure of the contemporary Soviet state just as logically follows.

The central concepts in the Marxist theory of social change are class consciousness and the class struggle. Marx apparently believed that the technology of production, in any given era, gave rise to an economic organization which, in turn, produced groups of men with radically opposed interests. One of these groups, by virtue of its strategic position of control in the process of production and distribution of material goods, was able to dominate and exploit the others. Gradually, however, the opposition of interests generated a corresponding opposition of ideologies. Class consciousness and class solidarity emerged, and the upshot was a violent battle, out of which issued a new mode of organization, leading to yet another struggle. Capitalism was the penultimate stage in the cycle; its classes were the bourgeoisie and the proletariat, and the struggle between them would be the final one, ending in the proletarian revolution and the establishment of a form of organization, socialism, in which there would be no opposed interests, ideologies, or classes.

I have prefaced this oversimplified recapitulation of a familiar theory with a cautious "apparently," for, although it does represent the general understanding of his theory, Marx did not seem to be utterly certain at all times that every step in this process was inexorable.[36] In particular, he spoke of a time during which the members of a class were not yet fully conscious of their common interests and mistakenly adopted "alien" ideologies. This was one aspect of what he called "false consciousness"; usually he insisted that it would eventually be overcome, though he himself studied one situation in which it was not.[37] Until it was, the only proletarians, for example, who were truly class-conscious were those who

---

[35] Merle Fainsod, *How Russia is Ruled* (Cambridge, Mass., 1953), 211, 524.

[36] His indecisiveness is well demonstrated by Reinhard Bendix and Seymour Martin Lipset, "Karl Marx' Theory of Social Classes," in Reinhard Bendix and Seymour Martin Lipset, eds., *Class, Status and Power* (Glencoe, 1953), 26–35.

[37] Karl Marx, *The Eighteenth Brumaire of Louis Bonaparte,* especially ch. 7.

conformed to the ideology which he, Marx, regarded as "appropriate" to the worker's situation.

Therein lies the origin of the Leninist "reversal." For when would "eventually" come to pass? At any given time, workers with false consciousness might be found, and they could not yet be accepted as true proletarians, ready for revolution. On the other hand, as Marx stated in the *Communist Manifesto*, it can also be expected that "a small section of the ruling class" — "in particular, a portion of the bourgeois ideologists, who have raised themselves to the level of comprehending theoretically the historical movement as a whole" (that is, who accept the Marxist view) — will join the revolutionists. For Marx, too, then, the composition of the revolutionary group was determined by ideology and not by economic position. Put into practice, the doctrine implies that it is ideology which must be scrutinized by the revolution's organizers, not the credentials of "objective" position; and that someone, consequently, must decide exactly what attitude is "appropriate" in each historical moment (bearing in mind that the workers may be deluded). The Marxist proletariat turns out to be not a social class but an authoritarian political party, and Lenin can justly claim the mantle of Marxist succession.[38]

If a social class — reverting now to my own terms of analysis — is a hierarchical category used as a reference group, then class consciousness may be defined as the tendency of an individual to utilize his social class as his dominant, possibly his only, reference group. For the class-conscious person, the ways in which people in his own and adjacent hierarchical positions think and act have become overwhelmingly important.[39] Obviously, this is not an occurrence whose inevitability can be postulated *a priori*, since every person is socialized by — is subjected to the sanctions of — a multiplicity of reference groups. Hierarchically patterned interests and sanctions are potentially important, but they compete with the interests and sanctions of religious, national, and other groups for psychological attention. In different circumstances, different reference groups will come to the fore. Marx sensed this dimly, but then assumed away the problems it raised, rather than attacking them with a methodical inquiry into the forces affecting the formation of reference groups and the selection among them by individual actors. He simply took it for granted that each worker, finding himself in the "same" objective position, would sooner or later arrive at the same ideological conclusion; and that all workers would then naturally cooperate to give institutional form to their

[38] See the discussion in Robert A. Feldmesser, "Aspects of Social Mobility in the Soviet Union" (unpublished dissertation, Harvard University, 1955), 35–38; and Reinhard Bendix, *Work and Authority in Industry* (New York, 1956), 345.

[39] It may be noted, in passing, that, by this formulation, class consciousness and prejudice become two species of a single social-psychological genus, which has come to be known as the "authoritarian personality."

shared values.[40] But false consciousness, in this context, is nothing but the observation that individuals do not necessarily limit their reference groups to the social class to which they "objectively" belong, or to any other; it may be but one among many, and not necessarily the most important.

It is, of course, far from inconceivable that people occupying similar positions in a hierarchical order would come to adopt a common ideology and form a reference group on its basis. But whether, and under what conditions, this convergence of an ideology and an economic or other group occurs is an empirical question, which ought not be theoretically prejudged. The analysis to this point suggests that the Bolshevik revolution was not a class revolution, and the Bolshevik party not a class party. It follows that the Bolshevik state would not be a class state.

v

The question to be asked about the class structure of Soviet society, as of prerevolutionary Russia, is not whether "objective," hierarchically graded differences exist; such differences have by now been well documented,[41] and they cannot and need not be denied. It is a matter of what their consequences are for the behavior of Soviet man, and thus for our understanding of Soviet society. From this standpoint, the contemporary Soviet Union contains no social classes.[42] Loyalty to a political leader and his ideology is again the cause, not the consequence, of one's hierarchical position; and occupants of all hierarchical statuses respond to the same norms, not to differentiated and autonomously enforced ideologies. Once more, I am exaggerating, but with a purpose.

If that is a correct, albeit simplified, description of Soviet social structure — and the evidence for it will be presented shortly — it cannot be facilely assumed that we have an instance of simple historical reversion, repetition, or coincidence. For in other respects Soviet society is vastly different from its prerevolutionary predecessor. Most prominently, of course, it is now an advanced industrial nation. A number of observers of another such nation, the United States, have commented upon the fact that it is, in many ways, highly conformist or standardized — which is to say that the norms and behavior of its subgroups are surprisingly undifferentiated, despite the indubitable existence of considerable "objective"

[40] This blithe assumption confers a great polemical advantage on Marxism: it can never be proven wrong, since any existing false consciousness is by definition temporary. Cf. Merton, Social Theory and Social Structure, 479.

[41] Among many other treatments, see especially, Alex Inkeles, "Social Stratification and Mobility in the Soviet Union: 1940–1950," American Sociological Review, XV (August 1950), 465–479; Barrington Moore, Jr., Soviet Politics — The Dilemma of Power (Cambridge, Mass., 1950), 159–188, 221–349; and W. W. Kulski, The Soviet Regime (Syracuse, 1954), 405–508, 573–590.

[42] Limitations of space preclude discussion of the NEP period, during which Soviet society made its closest approach to a full-blown class system. For further treatment, see Feldmesser, 77–168.

differences among them. Many of the same forces which have tended to "homogenize" American society are operative in Soviet society as well: the narrowing of occupational specializations toward a middle range of skill; mass education and mass communications; the pressures toward centralization of effective power and the other obstacles to meaningful political and economic participation which are inherent in the aggregation of great numbers of people.[43] Hence, merely knowing that the Soviet Union is a large-scale, advanced industrial society would enable us to predict a certain degree of "classlessness" for it.

But we know more than that. Taxonomically speaking, we have only so far determined that the Soviet Union belongs in the family of societies called "advanced industrial." What, then, are the distinguishing features of its genus? What is it that prevents us from saying that the Soviet Union is just like any other advanced industrial society? The answer seems obvious: while the other members of the family have maintained their economic establishments within a pluralistic political framework, it is totalitarianism which singles out the genus *Sovieticus*. The governing principle of totalitarianism is that there are to be no autonomous subgroups; broadly speaking, all sanctions are at the disposal of a single ruling group, and they are to be so used that, except for differences which may be necessary in the exercise of technical functions, the norms guiding the behavior of all citizens shall be the same. This is the political objective emanating from the Marxist doctrine that there is a single group which knows what is historically right and necessary, and it boils down, ultimately, to a restatement of the Tsarist principle that only the autocrat can decide what is right for his people — although there is good reason to believe that the Soviet regime has succeeded in realizing it in greater degree. To the leveling forces of advanced industrialism have been added those of advanced totalitarianism.

The hypothetical implication of these propositions is that the hierarchical strata of Soviet society should be more nearly and more often alike in their attitudes than their counterparts in other industrial societies. Although the difficulties which stand in the way of making such a comparison are enormous, the evidence presently available seems to confirm the hypothesis. A comprehensive survey of the opinions of Soviet displaced persons reveals a remarkably low relationship between hierarchical position and many of the elements of ideology which we customarily associate with class-differentiated structures. Soviet intelligentsia, white-collar employees, workers, and peasants agree almost completely on the general mode of economic organization they prefer, and on the desirability of such specific institutions as state ownership of transportation and heavy industry and governmentally administered programs of medical

[43] Cf. the comments on modernization in the contribution to this volume by George Fischer, "The Intelligentsia and Russia."

care and education, guaranteed employment for all, and cradle-to-grave welfare; and they do not differ in the degree of their disapproval of the kolkhoz, the role of the secret police and the Communist Party in the

Comparisons of class differences in attitudes

Soviet Union			United States	
Per cent favoring state ownership of				
	Heavy industry[a]	Light industry[a]	Per cent favoring state ownership of "mines, factories, and industries"[b]	
Intelligentsia	85	23	10	Businessmen, professionals
Peasants	86	52	37	Ordinary workers
Ratio	1.0	2.3	3.7	
Per cent expressing "least hostility" toward regime[c]			Per cent "conservative" or "ultra-conservative"[d]	
Intelligentsia	71		76	Businessmen, professionals
Peasants	40		22	Ordinary workers
Ratio	1.8		3.5	
Per cent wanting to "change everything" if Bolshevik regime is overthrown[e]			Per cent "radical" or "ultra-radical"[f]	
Intelligentsia	20		8	Businessmen, professionals
Ordinary workers	34		46	Ordinary workers
Ratio	1.7		5.8	
Per cent saying Lenin did "much harm" to the Russian people[g]			Per cent expressing "general disapproval" of President Roosevelt in 1938[h]	
White-collar	78		61	"Prosperous"
Skilled workers	70		25	"Poor"
Ratio	1.1		2.7	

Note. For the sake of economy of presentation, only the groups with the highest and lowest percentages are shown. In the American data, the other groups showed a smooth progression from high to low in every case; in the Soviet data, the other groups either showed the same sort of progression or exhibited small and irregular variations. The ratios following each set of answers are of the higher figure to the lower, as a measure of the spread between the extremes.

[a] Alex Inkeles and Raymond A. Bauer, *The Soviet Citizen* (Cambridge, Mass., 1959), 234.

[b] Richard Centers, *The Psychology of Social Classes* (Princeton, 1949), 60. The figures shown are proportionately weighted averages of the figures given (1) for owners and managers of large and small businesses, and professional and semiprofessional persons, and (2) for semiskilled and unskilled manual workers.

[c] Lowest score on a 5-point scale. Per cent of total sample with this score: 56. Inkeles and Bauer, 260, 447.

[d] Lowest two scores on a 5-point scale. Per cent of total sample with these scores: 50. Centers, 57.

[e] Inkeles and Bauer, 235. Per cent of total sample giving this response: 26.

[f] Highest two scores on a 5-point scale. Per cent of total sample with these scores: 22. Centers, 57.

[g] Inkeles and Bauer, 252.

[h] Arthur W. Kornhauser, "Analysis of 'Class' Structure of Contemporary American Society: Psychological Bases of Class Divisions," in Bernard Berelson and Morris Janowitz, eds., *Reader in Public Opinion and Communication* (Glencoe, 1953), 73.

Soviet Union, and the results of Lenin's leadership.[44] Moreover, where there are differences among them, they are often more moderate than among corresponding groups in the United States. A few illustrations are given in the accompanying table. This evidence is all the more impressive on two counts: (1) Most of the displaced persons left the Soviet Union during World War II, before the full effects of totalitarianization could have been felt.[45] So far as age differences are an index, the trend in Soviet society is toward a convergence of attitudes among hierarchical groups.[46] (2) The emphasis by the analysts of the opinion survey is on the importance and magnitude of the hierarchical differences as a salient feature of Soviet society.

Such emphasis is not entirely unwarranted, and I ought not overdraw the picture. Some degree of hierarchical differentiation is inherent in the very nature of social structure,[47] and the extreme specialization of labor and the consequent need for authoritative coordination which characterize industrial societies (relative to *other kinds*) increase differentiation far beyond whatever minimum might be otherwise necessary. The resultant differences in individual life experiences are bound to have some effect on norms and values; there are many confirming instances of this influence in the data obtained from the displaced persons.[48] Even in Soviet society, there are informal means of compelling conformity to these differentiated norms: witness the numerous official complaints about *blat* and *semeistvennost'*. Perhaps a balanced statement would be that the Soviet Union, as a specimen of industrial society, may have more elements of class structure than other, nonindustrial societies, but fewer than other societies of its own type.

Yet to those who, like ourselves, already have firsthand familiarity with industrial society as a type, it seems more important to stress the

[44] Alex Inkeles and Raymond A. Bauer, *The Soviet Citizen: Daily Life in a Totalitarian Society* (Cambridge, Mass., 1959), 234, 236, 238, 243, 245, 252, 321. It is a bit of supreme irony that there is even little difference in the frequency of the various reasons which members of different strata offer for having left, or not returned to, the Soviet Union (272). It should be pointed out that, regardless of the extent to which the displaced persons are "representative" of the Soviet population as a whole, there is little doubt that they do more or less accurately reflect internal differentiation —or the lack of it—*within* that population; and that the varying content of what they agree on rules out the explanation that "unanimous" political opposition to the Soviet system has simply overwhelmed any class differences (21–64).

[45] See note 42 above.

[46] Inkeles and Bauer, 155–156, 220–230, 273–279. In some instances, an apparent increase in attitudinal differentiation over time was actually the product of converging values applied to divergent objective situations (95–97, 147–149).

[47] Talcott Parsons, "A Revised Analytical Approach to the Theory of Social Stratification," in Bendix and Lipset, 92–128.

[48] Inkeles and Bauer, *passim*. Some of these findings, however, amount to no more than saying that a man with high income perceives his standard of living to be better than does a man with low income, or that a person who has completed college "feels" that he has had better educational opportunities than one who has not.

distinctions rather than the similarities among the subtypes.[49] The hall-mark of the totalitarian variety is that no group, other than the political leaders themselves, can be permitted to acquire a material or social basis of support strong and stable enough to allow it to regulate the composi-tion and behavior of its own membership.[50] From this point of view, Soviet income and related differentials are the conditional rewards of the regime for services rendered. Hierarchical differentiation is itself only a convenient tool of the regime, which it uses to suit its political needs. It dilates or contracts the range of differentiations; it establishes and re-moves duties and privileges; it alters the position of particular indi-viduals. We can speak of "social classes" in the Soviet Union only in the same limited sense that we can speak of trade unions, professional or-ganizations, political parties, or regional or ethnic groups. Even the so-cializing functions of the family have been shaped to the regime's de-mands.[51] Knowing that a man belongs to one of these groups may tell us something about the objective conditions of his life, but relatively little about his state of mind.

Covertly, cliques or similar formations may resist this domination, but they are at best localized and precarious, tolerated in principle only so long as the regime finds it in its own interest to do so. With its ultimate control over virtually all the resources of the nation, the regime retains the capability of disrupting them at will, and frequently does so. The only qualification is that it must first discover them — to which end a well-organized system of cross-checks, "self-criticism," and mutual spy-ing is devoted.[52] Under such conditions, the members of the society do not crystallize into social classes; rather, they form a single, relatively undifferentiated mass.

[49] It is worth noting that although, as has been indicated, the main theme of the Inkeles and Bauer volume is that the Soviet Union is an industrial society ("the single most important conclusion to emerge from our study" — 383) and a class-differentiated one, there are some interesting indications of second thoughts. Com-pare, for example, chapter 13 ("Social Class Cleavage," 299–320) with an earlier analysis of the same data: Alex Inkeles, "Images of Class Relations among Former Soviet Citizens," *Social Problems*, III (January 1956), 181–196. The later version differs by the inclusion of a number of phrases and passages intended to minimize the significance of such class "conflict" as is shown and of comparative data which "might be interpreted as suggesting that if anything the extent of class antagonism in the United States is greater . . ." (318).

[50] Barrington Moore, Jr., *Terror and Progress, USSR* (Cambridge, Mass., 1954), 197–210.

[51] Kent Geiger, "Changing Political Attitudes in Totalitarian Society: A Case Study of the Role of the Family," *World Politics*, VIII (January 1956), 187–205. See also Inkeles and Bauer, 210–230.

[52] Here the superior effectiveness of Soviet organization over that of the Tsarist regime, which faced a similar problem, is clearly illustrated. Cf. Raeff, 88.

THE INTELLIGENTSIA AND RUSSIA

GEORGE FISCHER

Few aspects of Russia, or the life and role of intellectuals anywhere, have interested the West more than the intelligentsia. At present this interest is divided between the "old" intelligentsia of a century or more ago and the "new" intelligentsia of our own time. The differences between the two groups are great. I believe, nonetheless, that the disjunction between old and new intelligentsia has been neither abrupt nor complete. I also believe that to the extent that the disjunction actually exists it is largely a product of modernization: the transformation of a whole society in the course of seeking and attaining the "modern." [1]

I

The middle of the nineteenth century saw the emergence of the intelligentsia as a self-conscious and distinct group. This old intelligentsia consisted of two very different generations. These were (to follow the dichotomy of Turgenev's *Fathers and Sons*) the Fathers, or the "Generation of the Forties," and the Sons, the "Generation of the Sixties." Although the similarities between noblemen-Fathers and commoner-Sons are many, the differences make it desirable to consider them separately.[2]

In the 1830's, the decade during which the Fathers coalesced, Russia revealed limited but unmistakable tendencies toward modernization. They consisted of scattered instances of industrialization; significant innovations in agriculture and in state administration; the expansion of schools and universities; an increased output of books and periodicals. But these first stirrings of modernization occurred in a largely non-Western society composed mainly of peasants and highly privileged noblemen-landowners, and under the shadow of an ever-dominant traditionalistic and autocratic state. As had been the case since the modernizing efforts

[1] The revision of this essay has profited by visits to Moscow in 1958 and 1960, made possible by the Inter-University Committee on Travel Grants and the American Council of Learned Societies; and by a year's leave at the Center for Advanced Study in the Behavioral Sciences and my association there with Edward Shils, whose pioneering comparative essays on intellectuals are brought together in a forthcoming volume of the Free Press of Glencoe, Illinois.

[2] Since World War II, no Western monographs have dealt with the old intelligentsia in terms of institutions. Partly institutional studies of its ideas appear in Alexander von Schelting, *Russland und Europa im russischen Geschichtsdenken* (Bern, 1948), and J. M. Meijer, *Knowledge and Revolution: The Russian [Student] Colony in Zurich* (Assen, Netherlands, 1955).

of Peter the Great at the turn of the eighteenth century, most innovations aroused little sympathetic response from a society which on the whole remained static and primitive economically, culturally, and politically. It is within this context of incipient and faltering modernization that the intelligentsia's first generation must be viewed.

The criterion by which the intelligentsia was defined in the middle of the nineteenth century was a subjective one. It was their outlook or *Weltanschauung*. No matter how well educated, no matter how proficient in scholarship or science and intensely involved in the pursuit of knowledge or in the cultivation of the arts, one was not considered a member of the intelligentsia if he did not share its outlook. This outlook was one of anguished alienation from a society unwilling or unable to modernize. No accurate estimate appears to exist of the number of Russian intellectuals that belonged to this first generation of the intelligentsia. It seems reasonable to assume that the number was in the thousands — of the 1835 population of thirty-six million, hardly more than one or two hundredths of one per cent.

Since higher education was on the whole confined to the nobility, the intelligentsia of the generation of the Fathers also came largely from this class. The exceptions — Belinsky, Polevoy, Botkin — were few and for this reason all the more notable. It is not clear to what extent the various levels of the nobility were represented in the intelligentsia. But it appears that the Fathers came from the middle nobility rather than from the top or bottom layer of the highly privileged landowning elite of Russian society.

The Fathers inherited the tradition of a rich cultivation in Western European letters and science characteristic of Russia's earlier noblemen-intellectuals like Pushkin. Education still tended to be through private tutors, often Western Europeans. An elaborate liberal education, followed or accompanied by familiarity with "Europe," was the precondition of a certain style of life and intellectual pursuits not rare among landed aristocrats. The Greek and Roman classics, leading Western works of fiction of the eighteenth and early nineteenth centuries, and philosophy and history were read widely. So were Russia's "fat journals," as important in distant country estates as in the intellectual centers of Moscow and St. Petersburg. The nobility's leisurely existence, together with a sizable income, made possible periodic visits to the resorts and metropolitan centers of France, Germany, and Italy. That a large part of Russia's nobility did not share either the cultivation or the outlook of the Fathers only enhanced the feeling of alienation and the actual isolation of this early intelligentsia.

A problem appears here which in a transmuted form recurs in connection with later generations of the Russian intelligentsia: the actual relationship between intellectual activity and political freedom. The belief that political restraints must reduce the quantity or at least the quality of intellectual activity is a keystone of the modern Western outlook. Yet the culture of Russia's early intelligentsia points to an opposite conclusion. This intelligentsia was linked to the Golden Age of Russian culture, and both coincided with the politically most oppressive era of the country's recent history, that of Nicholas I. To be sure, the greatest figures of this Golden Age tended to stand outside the intelligentsia, while the intelligentsia itself sired much that appears adolescent, arid, and imitative. But it is the Fathers, the same intellectuals who identified most completely with the Superfluous Man prototype of Russian fiction, who looked back on the era as "a marvelous decade." And it is the zealously individualistic Herzen who stated that this era combined outer slavery with inner freedom.

Although ideas and aspirations were changing rapidly, the occupational pattern of the Fathers continued to be that of propertied intellectuals in a largely premodern society. Most of them concentrated on gentleman farming and amateur intellectual pursuits, usually after serving for a few years as officers or government officials. Unlike those in Germany or England, highly educated young men with wide intellectual interests and a modern outlook did not enter the church. A growing minority, however, entered the slowly expanding professions like administration, law, and university teaching. The newer field of journalism tended to attract and support plebeian members of the early intelligentsia who depended for their income on writing and often lacked the formal training and contacts required for the older professions.

Intellectual life in the generation of the Fathers was centered largely in the universities. It was at the universities that a few younger nobleman-intellectuals for the first time encountered and mingled intimately with commoners of similar occupational and intellectual aspirations. At the universities, so often the seedbed of ideas of modernity in less advanced countries, the new and socially "open" discussion circles became the birthplace of the intelligentsia. Long thereafter, the universities — principally the University of Moscow — served as its recruiting area and a link which in later years served to bind the intelligentsia into a single body. As in other premodern societies of the nineteenth and twentieth centuries, university students continued to furnish much of the leadership and elan of a modern intellectual life. To the Fathers this usually meant no more than private circles for ideological discussions. So small, close-knit, and isolated was this intelligentsia itself, and so unpropitious were political events in both Russia and Western Europe, that the world of the intelligentsia was highly circumscribed. It encompassed little except the universities, the aristocratic salons and country houses so important at that time, occasional public lectures, and a gradually growing number of literary and general periodicals.

Becoming a separate entity at a time when public affairs promised little to the ideals of intellectuals in Western Europe and very much less in Russia, the intelligentsia developed its values through romanticism, passionate philosophizing and a no less passionate melancholy. It is at this time, too, that members of the intelligentsia began ardently to champion action on behalf of the homeland or "the people." For this isolated and discomfited first generation alienation culminated not in action but in complete withdrawal. The withdrawal took the form of the often noted flight of the Fathers into abstract theory and extreme programs. Such an "escape from reality" recurs again and again among comparable modern-minded minorities.

One common by-product is xenotropia, an attraction toward things foreign. Foreign ideas, vogues, and precedents become the prime stimuli for emotions and actions. To non-Western intellectuals "foreign" usually meant the West. To most of them modernization was also equivalent to westernization or at least its utilitarian "practical" aspects. This is just as true of assertively nationalist intellectuals, like the Slavophils of Russia, as of their purportedly more cosmopolitan "westernizing" compatriots.

The initial status of the intelligentsia in Russian society was determined not by its own values, however, but by the overriding fact that it was a new and miniscule group. Neither the state nor the bulk of the population esteemed its outlook or showed appreciation of its functions within society. Yet the intelligentsia did acquire a notable influence over that majority of intellectuals who were in their attitudes less involved and less extreme in opposition to their society. This influence is directly traceable to the lagging modernization of the country.

As a result of the lag, few Russian intellectuals shared the decisive experience of most intellectuals in Britain, Germany, and France. In Russia, and generally outside the West, modern-minded intellectuals were rarely incorporated occupationally or spiritually into society, into its system of central, "established" institutions and values. Nor did they develop affinity with the society's ruling authorities — economic, political, and ecclesiastical. Instead, individuals and even whole groups within the educated minority came to sympathize somewhat with the alienated, critical outlook of the intelligentsia. In the generation of the Fathers, the center of gravity for Russian intellectuals thus became the oppositional intelligentsia — that is, those intellectuals who were least incorporated into their society.

So many things did the Sons have in common with the Fathers that the two are rightly grouped together as the "old" intelligentsia. The differences between them arose partly from the changing intellectual and political climate of Russia as well as Western Europe, and partly from the characteristic antagonism of a younger generation toward its elders.

At this time, too, Russia's modernization, albeit still partial and halting, was altering the composition and ideas of the intelligentsia.

The definition of "intelligentsia" remained unchanged in the 1860's and 1870's. An intellectual's outlook remained the sole criterion which determined his membership in the intelligentsia. As with the number of Fathers, we have no accurate estimate of the size of the second generation. By the 1860's the intelligentsia seems to have grown from thousands to tens of thousands. But with the population of Russia doubling within one mid-century generation, the proportion of the intelligentsia to the 1859 total of seventy-four million increased only slightly.

The most dramatic difference between Fathers and Sons was in their social origin. Not a few of the Sons, including their leaders, were as in the past of noble origin. Yet increasingly the Sons were commoners rather than noblemen. What lent drama to the change was that most of the commoners came not from the bourgeoisie of that time, the prosperous but deeply traditionalistic and anti-intellectual old merchant group, but from the *raznochintsy*. *Raznochintsy*, or "men of different ranks," were an amorphous semiofficial category between merchants and peasants. They included lower officials and lower clergy, and a smattering of provincial teachers and doctors. It is from this improvident but aspiring group that the intelligentsia's second generation received not only much of its numerical increment but also its distinctive tone. If Herzen, Belinsky, and Turgenev symbolized the Fathers, the Sons were characterized by the Bentham-like Chernyshevsky and the petty urban milieu of Dostoevsky's novels.

The lower social origin, as well as the economically less assured and less elaborate style of life of the commoner-intellectuals, led to a new cultural division within the intelligentsia. Observable in other modernizing societies as well, it is the division into an upper and a lower intelligentsia. Socially, educationally, and occupationally, the Fathers as a rule belonged to the upper intelligentsia. The lower intelligentsia, on the other hand, first emerged with the Sons who often were far less worldly, less cultivated, and professionally less well established. This new phenomenon of the only partially educated and culturally limited half-intellectual — so largely a product of modernization and its novel educational and occupational opportunities — was at the time portrayed acidly by Dostoevsky and more charitably by Turgenev. As their novels illustrate, the division between lower and upper intelligentsia was not long governed by social origin. Nor did the ideas of that period diverge simply in accordance with social origin. But in a stubbornly traditionalistic society, social origin did at the time seem crucial to all concerned.

There was another change in the intelligentsia's culture which arose in connection with modernization. The Sons no less than the Fathers tended to be general intellectuals par excellence — the opposite of specialized intellectuals whose training and interests encompassed one field only. They were broader, too, than the "middle-range" type of intellectuals. The scope of middle-range intellectuals is not quite so confined as that of specialized intellectuals, but beyond their own field involvement is apt to be passive rather than active. As general intellectuals, most Fathers and Sons treated as their domain all ideas and ideals, all of culture and society. At the same time, in contrast with the philosophical and political concerns represented in the Enlightenment and the revolutions in England, America, and France, mid-century Europe became immersed in the specifically technological, scientific, and economic aspects of modernization. One outgrowth of the shift, in Russia almost as much as in Western Europe, was the increased demand for more technical training and occupations. The Sons who received or sought this training partook of the important concomitant shift in styles of life — the shift from a leisurely aristocratic style of life to the professional and generally more utilitarian outlook so prevalent in modern societies.

"Nihilism" was a vital new element in the culture of the Sons. Its theme was the sterility of the life of the earlier intelligentsia, and praise of unyielding contempt for the traditional and the ceremonial. This theme, embodied in the figure of Bazarov in Turgenev's *Fathers and Sons* and the hero of Chernyshevsky's *What is to be Done?*, expressed the typically ascetic culture of gifted and ambitious young men whose plebeian origin excluded them from the refinements of an aristocratic or bourgeois life. In this and other ways, England's "angry young men" since World War II recall the culture of the Sons.

While together social origin and culture dramatized the differences between Fathers and Sons, it was probably in the realm of occupations that the greatest change occurred. As science, technology, and engineering became recognized as the means of transforming Russia into a modern society, more and more opportunities developed for new kinds of specialized training and professions. In Russia the total number of such opportunities was as yet frustratingly small. But by comparison with the preceding generation, the number was large enough to attract many young *raznochintsy* to whom the earlier general education and liberal professions had as a rule been inaccessible. That these technical professions were themselves new and modern and utilitarian added to their appeal. So did the possibility in the field of engineering of obtaining a state-supported education, which penurious students could then do nowhere else except in theological seminaries.

For the same reason the theological seminaries served as a major funnel for *raznochintsy* who, like Chernyshevsky, subsequently played an important role in the intelligentsia. As before, such less technically oriented intellectuals most often found positions in journalism and the universities. The lower intelligentsia also found employment as teachers and as clerks in government and business offices, particularly in the provinces. Yet even such often unsatisfying positions were far from numerous, while the outlook of the intelligentsia itself foreclosed major careers in the state or most of the older professions in some way affiliated to government. The nature and distribution of occupational opportunities was undergoing a significant change, but there was no numerical expansion sufficient to absorb the less opulent and more ambitious intellectuals now coming from the universities.

Organizationally, university students and private discussion groups arising around the universities retained their importance for the Sons, as did the universities themselves and the "fat journals." As yet no daily press or professional organizations of their own augmented this rather undifferentiated group. The one major change was the initiation by the Sons of political activity. To be sure, theory still prevailed over practice. Moreover, most political activity was confined to two sources — the circles in Western Europe of expatriated Russian noblemen-intellectuals and students, and Herzen's widely read émigré periodicals — both of which originated among the Fathers rather than the Sons. But it was the Sons who in the 1860's first started sporadic and mainly local clandestine organizing and distribution of leaflets. In the following decade, they extended their revolutionary political activity. Initially it took the form of the ambitiously conceived but ill-fated "going to the people" of the mid-1870's. This was followed by the establishment of Russia's first underground revolutionary organization which planned and in part carried out assassinations of high officials as well as mass agitation. To the end, however, the scope of this political activity was minute.

Like the definition of "intelligentsia" — the term itself originated in the 1860's in Russia — the outlook did not change decisively. Russian society was regarded with complete hostility, and its transformation to something more modern remained the passionate goal of the Sons. Within this over-all continuity, a notable shift did occur.

Greater economic deprivation and uncertainties, together with changes in Russian life and the Western models, made such a shift in specific ideas inescapable. Despising the romanticism, the metaphysical speculation, and the philosophical idealism of the preceding decades, the Sons enthusiastically accepted scientific, materialistic, and utilitarian creeds from the West. For the Sons as for the Fathers, aesthetic and literary criticism remained a preferred ideological battleground. But now social and economic problems replaced philosophical ones, and socialism shared the stage with science.

The austere devotion to science by the Sons enshrined their idealization of the rational, the new, and the modern, as opposed to what the Sons in their nihilist asceticism scorned as the sentimentality and aimlessness of the Fathers. The Sons felt that the problems of life could be resolved only through a tough-minded, matter-of-fact, and utterly impersonal scientific attitude. The social and political physiognomy of the future did not engage the attention of the Sons in any great detail — no more than it had held the interest of the Fathers. Most of the Sons were preoccupied with foreign countries, above all the West, but they hated capitalism, industrialism, and the bourgeois mores. Therefore the spreading faith in socialism took an agrarian and populist form. They idealized "the people" and proclaimed the socialist propensities of the peasantry. They asserted the sacred duty of intellectuals to serve them — and the necessary extinction of the existing society. In this respect the Sons differed from the Fathers, whose alienation never took on such a revolutionary visage.

In another respect, however, Fathers and Sons were wholly alike. Both found "reality" outside the structural framework and territorial boundaries of their own society. Some chose German metaphysics in its most abstract form, others combined scientism and populism, and still others turned to the religious and explicitly messianic variety of nationalism that culminated in Dostoevsky. Yet there was a common thread through these ever-shifting ideological tides. This was the belief that something outside the normal processes of society itself must act as the decisive force in Russia's destiny. The fact that Russia lagged so far behind the West in modernization, although it was a major society in close proximity to Europe with vast territories, great natural resources, and numerous past glories — this fact intensified the nationalism of the intelligentsia and made that nationalism all the more xenotropic. Thus many of the more sensitive members of Russian society were not only looking at Russia despairingly but were constantly angered and humiliated by looking at their homeland as they believed it must appear to critical Western eyes.

This anxiety about modernization explains the "agonized belief in a single, serene vision, in which all problems are resolved, all doubts stilled, peace and understanding finally achieved" which characterized not only Tolstoy but so much of the Russian intelligentsia up to the present. This almost obsessive "hedgehog" preoccupation was very much part of a craving for some total and finite formula about the country's obscure future. Most often such a future was not wholly different from the existing state but only "better" than it in some essential way — more spiritual, more ethical, more efficient, more grandiose or potent. Whatever the reaction, it revealed a common attitude toward Russia's future among most of the intelligentsia, an attitude of deeply felt pessimism.

The particular variety of these grand schemes did not affect the fundamental pessimism. Some of them idealized the present, others the past, most the future. Some identified the existing state as the means to salvation, some offered an alternative form of strong government, while others saw a still mightier central force in "a Russian Christ" or "the people." With a few notable exceptions, even the old intelligentsia's antipathy to authority was the very opposite of Western individualism. Not infrequently the West also denied the virtue of authority, but it did so in the name of an optimistic image of society and its future. In Russia, on the contrary, the anarchist denial of all authority was but an inverted form of pessimism. It came from the same underlying feeling of the intelligentsia that Russia was too unprepared, too amorphous, and too limp to live in any condition other than total centralization or total anarchy. Nor should this sense of hopelessness be attributed to some black humor of the Slavic soul. Often hyperbolic but not at all baseless, the pessimism about prospects of modernizing their country marked the values and actions not only of Fathers and Sons but of innumerable other intellectuals outside the centers of the West.

In relation to Russian society, the Sons had one influence that the Fathers did not. Their clandestine revolutionary organizations, small and limited though they were, touched off a variety of forces in other parts of society. Although we do not know enough about this, it is clear that the intellectuals, if only as a source of disturbance and annoyance, were increasingly on the minds of government officials. Intermittently this produced a militant, crisis-laden atmosphere, a state of anxiety and distrust which decreased rather than enhanced the intelligentsia's fruitful performance in Russian society.

In general, although the formative years of the Sons were spent in a politically less hostile climate than that of the Fathers, the Sons were just as alienated from the central institutions and values of their society. Even aside from isolated revolutionary ventures, the intelligentsia had grown too slightly, and modernization had advanced too little, to improve the attitude of society and state toward the intellectuals. While their potential technical usefulness to Russia increased as more of them studied engineering, agriculture, chemistry, and the like, this was not reflected in a parallel rise in their status or influence. As a result, the alienated intelligentsia retained moral ascendancy over the more incorporated intellectuals in government service and the professions. Leading intellectuals often opposed the intelligentsia sharply and disassociated themselves from it. This was true of Dostoevsky, Tolstoy, and Gogol, and of many publicists and scholars as well. Yet they also retained a bond with the intelligentsia and identified in part with its insecure position and its oppositional outlook.

II

By the turn of the twentieth century Russian society had changed considerably and so had the place of intellectuals within it. Russia for the first time was modernizing actively and extensively. This acceleration of the pace of modernization was dramatically marked in the 1860's by the economic and administrative transformations growing out of the Great Reforms. It had continued to gain momentum through railroad building, the intense industrialization of the 1890's, and an increasingly active public life even before the 1905 Revolution.

The role of the state was now a highly ambiguous one. It remained a traditional autocratic monarchy hesitant about the amount of modernization it desired or considered safe. On the other hand, where it did sponsor modernizing activities, it often lacked the determination as well as the means to hold in check the many changes — economic, political, cultural — which were repugnant to it but were inherent in modernization and were especially close to the hearts of intellectuals. This ambivalence led to very diverse official actions. Some government officials championed modernization and modern politics, others opposed them, and still others temporized.

The intelligentsia of the two decades surrounding the turn of the century may, by extrapolation from Turgenev's *Fathers and Sons,* be labeled "the Grandsons." Located halfway chronologically, its central characteristics also show it to be equidistant from old and new intelligentsia in most other ways. So great was the change in the role that intellectuals could play in society that the definition of "intelligentsia" itself shifted by the 1890's from the earlier subjective criterion of attitude to an objective one of occupation. The ideological conception of the intelligentsia as an oppositional stratum lingered on, but among the Grandsons there were many who did not fit into it. The term now referred to all persons, regardless of their outlook, who followed certain occupations. These were the modern professions which required a high degree of educational qualification or other extensive technical training. Still excluded were groups who at the time did not receive a modern formal higher education, notably executives of the government, business, and church. The incomplete figures of Russia's first national census of 1897 suggest that the intelligentsia had expanded drastically. Its size fell between one-half and three-quarters of a million — perhaps half of one per cent of a population of one hundred twenty-six million.[3]

A series of rigorous modernizing efforts accelerated the earlier influx from the lower middle classes into the intelligentsia. These efforts also resulted in a further sharp decline in the economic position of the nobility, thereby adding to the intelligentsia a considerable new element: the offspring of an indigent petty nobility. Another new element, of which we

[3] On the intelligentsia at the turn of the twentieth century, recent Western institutional studies are limited to Samuel Kucherov, *Courts, Lawyers and Trials under the Last Three Tsars* (New York, 1953), and George Fischer, *Russian Liberalism: From Gentry to Intelligentsia* (Cambridge, Mass., 1958).

know little, originated in the business world. These new recruits came from both the formerly distant old merchant group and the rapidly rising modern entrepreneurs. By the end of the nineteenth century, therefore, all but the lower classes — workers and peasants — were widely represented in the intelligentsia.

The culture of the Grandsons was shaped most directly by three factors: the tremendous quantitative increase of the intelligentsia, the continuing decline of the aristocratic style of life that had been prevalent among earlier Russian intellectuals, and the simultaneous ascendancy of modernization and modern professions. These developments considerably increased not only the size but the prominence of the lower intelligentsia, less reflective and more technical in its culture. They also furthered the emergence of a large middle intelligentsia with some intellectual interests but moderate educational qualifications. Like the comparable American "middlebrows" of today, this middle intelligentsia took over some of the traits and style of life of the milieu above them as well as that below. The plays and stories of Chekhov record this group most vividly.

An accretion likewise took place in the upper intelligentsia. It consisted of a significant number of eminent and politically moderate figures in the professions — especially professors, lawyers, and writers — who often acted as spokesmen for the Grandsons. Their professional predecessors had been refused inclusion in the old intelligentsia as a result of the generally accepted ideological definition. The cause of this particular change was the more general absorption of all intellectuals into the same modern professions and hence an important blurring of lines. This is applicable to all the formerly decisive divisions — between aristocratic and modern styles of life, between upper and lower intelligentsia, between isolation and incorporation into society. The culture of the Grandsons thus was representative of a significant trend toward a "philistine" outlook, and from the general to the specialized or middle-range intellectual, which not infrequently accompanies modern technical education and professions.

The further course of modernization increased the weight of these technical occupations and the training, outlook, and style of life engendered by them. More and more people entered those professions — formally trained, highly specialized, and profoundly rationalized — which are no less significant in modern society than the world of business. Although much of the state apparatus continued to be characterized by traditionalism and the limited development of rational-legal methods of administration, its newer and more advanced branches (notably the judiciary and certain economic bodies) needed and preferred personnel trained in the modern professions. So did the vast network of self-governing rural and municipal institutions (zemstvo and duma) spawned by the Great Reforms. Their new educational, communal, and administrative organizations employed many thousands of teachers, doctors, economists, agricultural experts, statisticians, and the like. Corresponding to the increase in the "third element," as this zemstvo corps of salaried professionals came to be called, there was a rapid increase in the number of university graduates, particularly in technical fields; of economic and engineering specialists for private industry and to a lesser extent agriculture; and of lawyers and journalists.

Nowhere is the difference between the free-lance or rentier members of the old intelligentsia and the institutionalized intermediate intelligentsia more noticeable than in the organizational realm. The employment of intellectuals now often meant their integration into the new kind of large-scale economic and administrative organizations that had not existed half a century earlier. The number, variety, and vigor of the intelligentsia's own organizations underwent a similar differentiation and growth. These included professional and semiprofessional associations like the Pirogov Society of Russian Doctors, the now very active Imperial Free Economic Society of St. Petersburg and Imperial Moscow Society of Agriculture, the Moscow Society of Jurisprudence, and the Writers' Union. In the Illiteracy Committees, the Literary Fund, and other national and local groups, professional men and their wives concerned themselves with various concrete aspects of public affairs and welfare such as mass education, the rights of minorities, famine relief, and legal aid. There was a striking expansion of publishing, which now consisted not only of the ever-popular journals but also of a flourishing daily press and innumerable book publishers who did not seem to lack purchasers or financial backing. Another new phenomenon was the continuous series of public conventions, meetings, banquets, and celebrations, which gave intellectuals unprecedented opportunities for promulgating their unity.

This pattern is in direct contrast to the very constricted and more or less private organizational life of the old intelligentsia. The contrast cannot be ascribed exclusively to the attitude of the state at the turn of the twentieth century. Although the state had not significantly changed its traditional autocratic make-up, it was nonetheless more tolerant toward many of the intelligentsia's organizational ventures. Yet factors that lie outside of politics are at least as important. With the intensification of the process of transforming Russia into a modern society, the intelligentsia became less political and less oppositional. More intellectuals acquiesced in a society which now offered them more satisfying occupations. There were of course important exceptions, and few Russian intellectuals ever forsook politics altogether. But the demanding virtues of professional life, and the numerous contacts made essential by it, produced a breadth and variety of activity that absorbed energies which had previously flowed into oppositional pursuits or emotions. It is significant that university students, who had formerly been involved in a whole range of intellectual activities, retained their importance only in radical politics. Now this domain alone tended to attract and hold none except university students and recent graduates. The organizational vitality of the newly emergent professional and technical intelligentsia, and the largely nonpolitical but nonetheless significant nature of its organizational life, bears out a fact already noted: not a few intellectuals can feel adequately rewarded professionally and fulfilled socially, and attain high standards of skill and competence, in societies which permit little or no political freedom.

The political activities of the Grandsons' generation of intellectuals were likewise much more numerous than fifty years before. And while assassinations, mass agitation, and other dramatic incidents continued to attract the most attention, the major forms of political activity had changed. One of these was closely related to the nonpolitical activities. The professional organizations, albeit inherently nonpolitical, were used systematically by the politically conscious members for political debates, articles, and petitions. The resulting mixture of politics and nonpolitical organizations is not unusual in modern life. But in Russia it made more lawyers and doctors, for example, politically sensitive. It also made for more government interference in the life of the professions. The second form of such activity was the crystallization and growth of three political parties dominated by the intelligentsia: the future Constitutional Democratic, the agrarian-populist Socialist Revolutionary, and the Marxist Social Democratic. Although they were illegal and functioned clandestinely from centers abroad, each of them developed an impressive apparatus, press, and scope. These parties are thus one more way in which the intelligentsia was undergoing the far-reaching differentiation that distinguishes modern from premodern societies.

The intermediate intelligentsia's values, like its other characteristics, were both varied and amorphous. Here differentiation is illustrated by a new ideological constellation which emerged in the 1890's. It did so in the course of a disaggregation and regrouping which left far behind the specific ideas of the mid-nineteenth century and often its general values as well. The improvement in the position of Russian liberalism was expressive of the change which was taking place in the intelligentsia. Liberalism had always espoused modernization, but by the beginning of the twentieth century it had become (in the West as well as Russia) a doctrine of gradual modernizing and of moderation in general. Such a doctrine, which had only a very limited appeal for the acutely alienated Fathers and Sons, was no more attractive to that small segment of the Grandsons which continued their tradition. That tradition of alienation, of rejection not merely of the existing society but of any hope of altering it without a revolution of some kind, still had a following. But with the acceleration of modernization, it receded markedly.

The decade of the 1890's, in particular, witnessed a whole series of liberal adaptations from the radical heritage of the intelligentsia, and at the same time a major change took place in Russian liberalism itself. To the liberal gentry's usually rural and moderate outlook which concerned itself largely with local issues, the younger constitutionalists from the professions opposed an eagerness to democratize Russian liberalism and to collaborate with nonextremist radicals. On the whole, however, Russian liberals remained ambivalent. They were torn between "small deeds" and "senseless dreams." Their values favored something less extreme than either but the situation in Russia did not. Like the liberals, a majority of Socialist Revolutionaries and Social Democrats inclined to facilitate or at least assume their country's steady if halting modernization. Thus they were able to reach some rapprochement with the younger liberals.

Aside from a cluster of Left Socialist Revolutionaries, only the small Bolshevik movement represented an extreme alienation in this generation. The Bolshevik movement was primarily of plebeian origin and, also continuing the pattern of the mid-century Sons, was closest to the lower intelligentsia. And the Bolsheviks manifested an ardent and total faith in the same values as the Sons. The earlier idealization of science became concretized in the Marxian system. And while the heirs of the future were now sought not in the peasantry but in factory workers and hope lay in industrialization rather than in agrarian socialism, the Bolsheviks shared the Sons' pessimism about the ability of Russia to modernize herself short of a cataclysmic transformation.

The Bolsheviks were likewise almost alone in combining the earlier preoccupation with public events and the earlier refusal to become involved in the round of civil life — a sort of political antipolitics. The non-Bolshevik currents, on the other hand, developed a more pluralistic, less exclusively political orientation; among them there began in different ways a shift to the individual, to private life, and to "noncivic" conceptions in philosophy, aesthetics, and literary criticism. Both the petty inanities and the exquisite sensibility to personal relationships that accompanied this shift in values are immortalized in the work of Chekhov. What seemed to prevail was a langorous rather than anguished melancholy, focused on private affairs and political quietism. Another form of withdrawal from the passionately political and oppositional was the complex individualistic philosophy of religious mystics like the ex-Marxist Berdiaev. The manifesto of this group, the later *Vekhi* collection of essays, consisted of a sharp frontal attack on the politically oriented segment of the intelligentsia (liberal no less than radical) for its extremism, its antinationalism, and agnosticism. From these roots flowered the Silver Age of Russian culture. This important movement of the early twentieth century was distinguished by aestheticism, cosmopolitanism, and Bohemianism, as well as a predilection for modernistic and experimental forms like symbolism. Its outlook, neoromantic and hence strongly antimodern and individualistic, was recently resurrected in the novel of Pasternak, himself a striking product of the Silver Age.

Even a compressed recapitulation of these novel currents in Russian life brings out a major pattern. Clearly the intermediate intelligentsia felt considerably less alienated than did its forerunners. Being radical, or being civic-minded at all, had become a matter of individual circumstances and inclinations. The once predominant influence of the radicals had greatly subsided. The Bolsheviks, the most direct heirs of the Sons, were then far from their later position. Radicalism was still attractive, however, because of the continued ambivalence of the intelligentsia toward the considerable but unsteady progress of the country and its own improved but nevertheless ambiguous position. Reflected in the wavering of the liberals and in the various nonpolitical currents as well, this ambivalence meant that the radicals could count on a considerable potential sympathy. Great though the change had been in the relation of the intellectuals to their society, it was ambivalence which had replaced the earlier alienation rather than a genuine and secure sense of affinity.

III

The new, the Soviet, intelligentsia of today differs much less from the intermediate intelligentsia of the Grandsons than from the old intelligentsia of the Fathers and Sons. And among the changes of the past half century, probably nothing has been more consequential than the unique variety of modernization evolved since 1917. The Soviet variety of modernization transformed the intelligentsia into a salaried and closely integrated component of the state. It greatly accentuated the general modern preponderance of the elaborately organized and differentiated technical professions over the "free" and humanistic professions. It contributed still more to a preponderance of specialized and middle-range intellectuals over general intellectuals.[4]

The new Soviet variety of modernization involved shifting from partial

[4] The intelligentsia of today is the subject of half a dozen recent Western institutional studies. Several types of monographs analyze the technical intelligentsia. Mark Field contributes to the sociology of professions in his *Doctor and Patient in Soviet Russia* (Cambridge, Mass., 1958). Professional training is treated in detail in Nicholas DeWitt, *Soviet Professional Manpower* (Washington, 1955), and Alexander G. Korol, *Soviet Education for Science and Technology* (New York, 1957). The one recent Western volume on the organizational pattern of the intelligentsia is Alexander Vucinich, *The Soviet Academy of Sciences* (Stanford, 1956). On the administrative intelligentsia, there are two studies embodying the sociology of the professions: David Granick, *Management of the Industrial Firm in the USSR* (New York, 1954), and Joseph S. Berliner, *Factory and Manager in the USSR* (Cambridge, Mass., 1957). Aside from applicable portions of Vucinich, *The Soviet Academy of Sciences*, no comparable studies have dealt with the literary intelligentsia.

and ambiguous change to an unprecedented exacerbation of certain trends
of modern development characteristic of all large-scale industrial societies. Soviet modernization is rooted in Russia's earlier modernization
and especially in the dialectical interplay between its progress and the
obstacles to progress. It has also been shaped by a special type of modernizing puritanism, an asceticism much like that of the Sons: a starkly
pessimistic conviction that their country is doomed to "backwardness" —
is condemned to remain behind the hailed and fascinating Western
model — unless it undertakes a total transformation of itself under completely dedicated, unified, disciplined (and modern) leadership. And
Soviet modernization could and did have recourse to institutions never
previously combined in comparable situations: an elite (the Communist
Party) severely organized and disciplined to accomplish the task; a
technology facilitating the grandiose modernizing program of the "new
class"; and a "maximalist" or *jusqu'auboutiste* doctrine that sanctifies such
revolution from above.

So great has been the impact of the Soviet state on the intelligentsia
that a preliminary comment is desirable at this point. The position of the
intelligentsia in Soviet society is profoundly affected by one circumstance:
the Bolsheviks from the outset suspected most intellectuals of softness,
self-absorption, purposeless curiosity, and incapacity for discipline. After
1917 this puritan and anti-intellectual suspicion fused with the determination of the state to confine all pursuits to what assisted the one central
task of modernization or at least did not retard it. This pattern would
appear to be confuted by the lavishness and enthusiasm with which the
state has often treated the intelligentsia, and its evident awareness most
of the time that excessive demands sap the intelligentsia's creativity and
morale.

Actually, these seemingly contradictory elements together led to the
"artificial dialectic": a continuous and more or less conscious alternation
of policy between severity and relaxation. When to the artificial dialectic
is added the loopholes for individual leeway that exist in any complex
society, the impact of the state on the intelligentsia shows itself to be
quite complicated. The intelligentsia is by no means completely centralized, or subjected to uninterrupted and total control at every step and
in every sphere. The situation is more intricate than a simplified conception of totalitarianism allows.

The current definition of "intelligentsia" adds to the liberal and technical professions of the Grandsons all administrative officials. Manual and
clerical workers alone are left outside the intelligentsia. This definition
is expressive of the conception of the intelligentsia which emerged in
Russia in the 1890's; it is a functional institutional conception and signifies
a more professional and less ideological image of intellectuals. To some
degree the new definition may be traced to the particular Soviet doctrinal

classification of the entire population into workers, peasants, and "employees" (clerical as well as professional). At least as much, however, the definition reflects trends in all advanced societies. One of these is the formal and specialized "professional" training increasingly required of executives and managers. A second trend is the lowering of barriers — educational, social, organizational — between these administrators and the earlier intellectual occupations.

The size of the new intelligentsia has been placed officially at fifteen and one half million and approaches 7 per cent of the 1956 population of two hundred million. Aside from the ever-growing need for specialists in all advanced societies, this striking increase is linked to the peculiar nature of Soviet modernization. So ambitious and all-encompassing is it that certain categories of specialists are in greater demand than would probably be the case in either a "normally" modernizing society or one no longer modernizing intensely, such as the United States. Likewise, the deliberate acceleration of Soviet modernization created a shortage of essential skilled workers and other subprofessional personnel. Such polarization perforce adds considerably to the size of the new intelligentsia. The prime example of both factors is the number of engineers required and trained in the USSR.

All this has meant the striking "plebeianization" of Russia's intelligentsia. The guess may be hazarded that today the members of the intelligentsia are largely of lower-class origin. The earlier prerevolutionary efforts at modernization added numerous intellectuals from the lower reaches of Russia's middle classes; now a later stage of the same process has opened the intelligentsia to offspring of worker and peasant families. While this phenomenon is not unique to the earlier Russian or the Soviet variety of modernization, it was greatly furthered by the characteristic revolutionary emphasis on "careers open to talent" and the removal of earlier elites. Also essential has been the doctrinal idealization of lower-class origin and the particular need for vast new armies of specialists, which the middle and upper classes alone could not satisfy.

The great increase in the lower-class component of the intelligentsia is neither complete nor sudden, however, since already by the beginning of the twentieth century the displacement of the erstwhile nobleman-intellectuals by commoners had gone very far. It is equally interesting, moreover, that there is still a considerable number of intellectuals of upper-class and middle-class origin who survived intervening upheavals and who have become an integral part of the new intelligentsia. Naturally, this has been more common in less political and less prominent domains, and may have involved disguising of actual social origin. For these reasons, the details of this element of continuity from intermediate to new intelligentsia remain at best obscure, although the fact is itself unquestionable. Indeed, it appears that offspring of the earlier intelligentsia have often fared better than their contemporaries of lower-class origin in one sphere at least: their more intellectual background and initial schooling enabled them to complete a higher education and consequently to secure positions which call for lengthy specialized training. For the "technical intelligentsia" such social origin could thus be decisive. It has also been appreciable in the "literary intelligentsia" — men of letters, artists, teachers in the humanities, journalists.

Very different has been the social origin of the newer "administrative intelligentsia." Since the administrator deals with people, the state has placed a premium on political reliability rather than on specialized skills, and on a "natural" talent for manipulation of human beings that does not require extensive schooling. This has meant easier entry from the lower classes without elaborate training and therewith a more complete break with the earlier culture of the intelligentsia. Hence it is within the new administrative intelligentsia that lower-class elements have gone furthest — not least in the governmental sphere. This profoundly significant pattern is illustrated by the present leaders of the Soviet Communist Party. Most of them are of lower-class origin, received only limited technical training and no liberal education, and became party functionaries after other administrative work.

The culture of the present-day intelligentsia is a complicated and revealing motley of qualities. On occasion it is vital, brilliant, original. But on the whole it appears markedly jejune and insulated from the outside world. This persists to date despite the rapidly growing complexity and prosperity of Soviet society; despite the increasing contact with other countries through governmental, scientific, cultural, and tourist exchanges; and despite the avid curiosity in the USSR about things foreign. A major explanation is the continuing governmental support of favored activities and proscription of activities deemed expendable or inimical. But here, too, the Soviet variety of modernization has played a very special role. For if "philistinism" accompanies the peak periods of modernization everywhere, the Soviet variety by its very intensity has accentuated and extended the negative manifestations. Outstanding among these are a general coarsening; bombast, artlessness, and insularity; lessened receptivity for things complex or unfamiliar; debilitating daily hardships and "materialistic" absorption in them.

More elusive is a second level on which the Soviet variety of modernization has deeply affected the intelligentsia's culture. It has sharpened rather than resolved an old inner conflict of the Russian intelligentsia which is shared by all non-Western societies and their intellectuals: their proper relationship to the long dominant and emulated West. While modernization narrows the gap between their own society and the West, it by no means eliminates the conflict. On the contrary, it may make the conflict still more acute. For as long as the West continues to be viewed as superior and hence as the model (and this is in many ways still the view held by the USSR and its intellectuals), a modernizing society remains in dire need of a more stable separate identity and self-esteem.

In the USSR the instability and the need are all the greater, for it has probably gone furthest in emulating the West while seeking to maintain a quite different social system and culture. This means overcoming, or at least reducing, the conflict between an unfading preoccupation with things foreign and a securely self-respecting modern nationhood. Without resolving this conflict no nation can be "modern," no nation can exact the remarkable active participation of the population in the national life which distinguishes modern societies from earlier complex societies — and which makes each modern society, including the USSR, in some ways unprecedentedly "popular" and unprecedentedly "civilized."

Although it is not confined to intellectuals, the conflict affects the intellectuals in particular. Not only does it determine the quality and stability of their own identity and self-esteem; it also affects the rest of the society because the intellectuals in various ways continue to articulate the values of the society. The whole history of the Russian intelligentsia indicates that much of it would welcome the speedy creation and imposition of a new, modern national identity. This need of modernizing societies to transcend their "groveling" before foreign models accounts in large measure for the systematic withdrawal of the contemporary intelligentsia from contact with Western and earlier Russian intellectuals, and its readiness to echo the state on the superiority and uniqueness of the USSR. Within this seemingly contradictory context — the context of striking progress and jejune qualities, insulation and xenotropia, the preoccupation with both daily material problems and a separate national identity — the intelligentsia of today consists of groups not unlike those of preceding generations of Russian intellectuals.

The group that is largest and culturally dominant is the lower intelligentsia. Alongside an earnest and energetic pursuit of knowledge, it partakes most completely of the noted negative cultural accompaniments of drastic modernization. A second group, the middle intelligentsia, is not as numerous or influential as were its Chekhovian forerunners half a century ago. The highly rewarded upper intelligentsia of today has produced universally acclaimed achievements in certain fields and the very opposite in others. The culture of this group appears closer to the lower or middle intelligentsia than to its own brilliantly cosmopolitan progenitors. Conversely, any cultural heirs of these progenitors tend to come from a quite different milieu and to be of a lower social origin and culture.

Like its culture, the occupational pattern of the contemporary intelligentsia continues the evolution before 1917. The technical professions, and especially the newer ones in engineering and related scientific and military fields, are steadily gaining in numbers and importance over the once prevalent liberal professions. It is more difficult to assess the nature and relative position of the third component, the administrative intelligentsia. Since the state is today performing functions far greater than in imperial Russia — especially in the economy, culture, and social welfare — comparisons are not easy. Moreover, we do not know whether the administrative intelligentsia is in fact proportionally larger than its likewise expanding equivalents in other advanced societies.

The degree to which Soviet intellectuals find fulfillment in work is noteworthy. They are responsive to the vast needs and opportunities connected with Soviet modernization. Also crucial is the survival of earlier professional traditions and standards, and the currently very high status and self-esteem of Soviet scientists and scholars due to remarkable achievements in some areas. It is all-important, moreover, that most Soviet undertakings are so vast, intensive, and often novel, and that the agencies of the state involved in either the same or related domains are so numerous. This gives members of the intelligentsia a considerable amount of discretion (either officially provided or imperceptibly appropriated) in determining or altering the pattern of their own work. The result is that outside of the domain of politics — and the infrequent occasions when official disapprobation affects an entire occupation — the intelligentsia is immersed in technical pursuits on which the life of individuals and groups can focus readily.

The social and organizational forms of the present-day intelligentsia are not entirely different from what they were fifty years ago. The principal disjunction grew out of the institutional incorporation of the intelligentsia as a salaried component of the state and the monolithic nature of political and public life. Continuity between intermediate and new intelligentsia lies in the proliferation of professional and semiprofessional organizations, and their renewed vigor at present through such imposing structures as the Academy of Sciences of the USSR. Nor do members of the new intelligentsia remain outside the public activities and organizations that the Grandsons patronized and that the state has since taken over. It is a major feature of Soviet life that intellectuals are encouraged and even pressed to take part in a wide variety of general activities. Among these are public lectures, electoral campaigns, legislatures and local councils, ceremonial and other festive occasions, and innumerable conferences and exchanges of delegations. It is not clear to what extent this type of public activity may be only symbolic. What does appear certain is that to considerable numbers of Soviet intellectuals it provides an important means of accommodation — be it affirmation or be it the often highly complex forms of accommodation that lie between affirmation and rejection.

The organizations employing members of the intelligentsia are usually as vast and complex in the USSR as in other advanced societies. A dimension peculiar to the USSR is the integration of all these organizations into a highly centralized whole. In some ways the extremely large scale of Soviet institutions routinizes and complicates the activities of the intelligentsia. Yet it is also a major source of the loopholes which permit flexibility — organizational no less than personal — in even the most paternalistic advanced society.

The outlook of the Soviet state seems to many in the West much too simplistic, rigid, and frequently anti-intellectual to be palatable for the intelligentsia. We do not actually know to what extent this is the case. It must be borne in mind that acceptance of the official outlook is highly compatible with the values of the intelligentsia throughout the past century — particularly the pessimism about the country's prospects of overcoming backwardness without a unitary and total solution, and the assumption that less arduous and extreme alternatives would be fruitless. At present the greater part of the intelligentsia shares these values, reinterpreted in ways which call not for the rejection of the Soviet state but for its affirmation. Such affirmation is implied in the nationalism that is so strongly espoused by the new intelligentsia. It takes the modernization-oriented form of ascribing the country's long-craved material progress and international standing to the state and its relentless modernizing.

To non-Western societies and their intellectuals, too, there is in politics an element of the sacred both in the religious and the colloquial sense of the word. Whether such intellectuals oppose or accept authority, they are seldom as receptive as the West to the modification and alteration of the "sacred." What those in authority do and their reasons for it are accordingly scrutinized and discussed far less matter-of-factly, systematically, and concretely. Within this very different context, members of the Soviet intelligentsia do harbor and at present express rather freely numerous specific critical sentiments, especially on internal affairs. No more than elsewhere are such criticisms incompatible with affirmation of the outlook of the society or state.

The very progress of modernization creates and exacerbates strains, ambiguities, and contradiction. With its singular and ubiquitous mixture of the modern, "transitional," and premodern, the USSR may well have even more such problems than other parts of the world. Yet by and large the Soviet intelligentsia has been persuaded by the state as well as by its own interpretation of the course of history that it is participating in an advance which is unique and immensely valuable, that it prefers Soviet socialism to Western capitalism, and that in any event no viable alternative exists in Russia now or is at all likely to emerge soon. Hence the relation of today's intelligentsia to the central values and institutions of the society, to The Establishment, is one of acceptance in many cases and of positive affirmation in others. A partial inner alienation may sometimes exist alongside these more affirmative attitudes. Alienation has been dethroned, however, from its position as the dominant trait of the old intelligentsia of a century ago. The singularly modernizing USSR has gone far in incorporating the new intelligentsia.

THE CIVIL SERVICE: ITS COMPOSITION AND STATUS

ALF EDEEN   .

I

A fundamental problem in evaluating the role of the civil service in Russia since 1861 is posed by the nature of the statistical materials. Not until the census of 1897 is there a reasonably firm statistical basis for estimating the size of the Russian civil service, and for the earlier years one must rely on scattered data in order to get an idea of the general trend. An illuminating example of the difficulties in this connection is that Kliuchevsky, in order to show the extent of the bureaucracy during the early part of the nineteenth century, was compelled to refer to indirect evidence. He found, for example, that 2.8 million cases were handled in the Department of Justice and its dependent organs in 1825, and that in 1842 there were 3.3 million uncompleted cases, involving 33 million sheets of paper, in the whole administration.[1] These impressive figures confirm the opinion of Hoetzsch who, referring to the conditions at the end of the same century, asserted that the huge government apparatus had brought about an administrative muddle, or as he put it, "oben zuviel regiert und unten zu wenig verwaltet."[2]

The general tendency of the development during the latter half of the nineteenth century may be seen from the budget figures for the administration, the judiciary system, the financial system, and the armed forces, which were the completely dominating expenses and which swallowed progressively larger sums.[3] Several factors contributed to the constantly rising curve for these national expenditures. In the initial stage of the so-called reform period in the beginning of the 1860's, great changes were made in the central and local administration, and the judicial system and later the armed forces were reorganized. Although it cannot be verified statistically, it seems reasonable to infer that these

[1] Vasilii O. Kliuchevsky, *Kurs russkoi istorii* (5 vols.; Moscow, 1937), V, 344.
[2] Otto Hoetzsch, *Russland* (Berlin, 1915), 270.
[3] See, for example, Pavel N. Miliukov, *Ocherki po istorii russkoi kultury* (3 vols.; St. Petersburg, 1904–09), I, 156ff, and Hugh Seton-Watson, *The Decline of Imperial Russia* (London, 1952), 122.

reforms tended to increase even further the already expanded number of civil and military administrative functionaries. In connection with the tightened police surveillance of the population at the turn of the century, the increased expenditures for the maintenance of the "secret" and "open" police had no small part in the over-all increase of costs. Miliukov cites as an example the fact that the budget for the Ministry of the Interior was almost doubled between 1899 and 1909.[4] Furthermore, the rapid development of industry and transport during the period in question meant increased demands not only on resources but on personnel as well. Thus, at the end of the 1880's the state owned 24 per cent of the railway mileage while the proportion by 1902 had increased to as much as 67 per cent. At the same time, the total mileage of railroads had more than doubled.[5] Finally, the "colonial" expansion in Siberia, Central Asia, and the Caucasus, and foreign engagements and wars placed demands for further augmentation of both civilian and military personnel. The size of the latter group, for instance, grew from about 800,000 soldiers during the Napoleonic Wars to 1.6 million during the Crimean War, and reached a figure of 4 million in 1905.[6] Parallel to this increase, of course, the number of army officers of different grades also increased, as the tabulation below indicates.[7]

Year	Generals and officers
1876	27,000
1880	32,000
1897	41,000

The 1897 census provides data concerning the occupational distribution of the population, which may serve as a basis for a comparison with the conditions after 1917.[8] For the earlier Soviet period there is a comparatively detailed statistical analysis of the composition of the administrative corps, made by Gosplan and bearing upon the situation in 1929.[9] After that time a period of complete silence follows with regard to this question; not until 1956 were the first cautious attempts made to lift the veil. But such a degree of secrecy still prevails that the total number of civil servants in the national economy is concealed under the collective heading "workers and other employees."

[4] Miliukov, I, 159.
[5] Seton-Watson, 115–116.
[6] Miliukov, I, 115.
[7] *Obshchestvennoe dvizhenie v Rossii v nachale XX-go veka* (4 vols.; St. Petersburg, 1908–1911), I, 433; and the 1897 census in *Obshchii svod po imperii rezultatov razrabotki dannykh pervoi vseobshchei peripisi naseleniia, proizvedennoi 28 ianvaria 1897 goda*, ed. N. S. Troinitsky (2 vols.; St. Petersburg, 1905), II, 256. The figures are rounded.
[8] *Obshchii svod*, II, 256ff.
[9] Ia. Bineman and S. Kheinman, *Kadry gosudarstvennogo i kooperativnogo apparata SSSR* (Moscow, 1930).

The difficulty in making comparisons between figures from such widely separated periods lies above all in the fact that different statistical methods were used and that the definitions are not identical. The following figures, which illustrate the growth of the bureaucracy, do not lay claim to any particular degree of accuracy but at least give an indication of the general trend.[10]

	1897	1926	1956
The entire intelligentsia	0.7	2.7	15.5
Intelligentsia exclusive of education and public health	0.4	1.9	10.3

These figures could be further refined. The figure for 1897, for example, includes an unknown number of *pomeshchiki* (estate owners).[11] The 1926 figure of 1.9 million might be further compared with Gosplan's information, for it appears that only about 700,000 persons can be designated as members of "the state apparatus" in the sense indicated.[12] This discrepancy is doubtless due to the fact that the term "intelligentsia" in Russian usage is a very vague and broad concept and seems at times to include almost all occupational groups not directly concerned with manual labor or with janitorial duties and odd jobs.

Rather exact figures can, however, be given for 1897 and 1929 concerning the personnel in the state administration proper and in the police and judiciary systems — exclusive of personnel in the armed forces. In 1897 this corps amounted to about 260,000, of which 105,000 were in the police system.[13] On the basis of information provided by Gosplan, one can deduce a figure (comparable on the whole) of 390,000 for 1929. Of these 390,000 persons, 142,000 were in the police system.[14] When comparing these figures, it is to be observed that the actual administrative territory in 1929 was considerably smaller than in 1897, so that the increase was proportionately a good deal greater than the figures would indicate. Unfortunately, exact and comparable figures for the present situation are lacking. The expansion of the bureaucracy in connection with industrialization is, however, indirectly apparent in official statistics concerning the development of the intelligentsia during the period between 1926 and 1956. Selected occupational groups, which are of special interest in this connection, are presented in the following table (in thousands).[15]

[10] The figures for 1956 are from *Dostizheniia sovetskoi vlasti za 40 let v tsifrakh* (Moscow, 1957), 255.

[11] *Dostizheniia*, 256.

[12] Bineman and Kheinman, 5.

[13] *Obshchii svod*, II, 256. The figure refers to central and local administration, excluding janitors and the like.

[14] Bineman and Kheinman, 5, 23.

[15] *Dostizheniia*, 255.

	1926	1956
Leaders in enterprise (industry, agriculture, building construction, etc.)	365	2,240
Technical engineering personnel (incl. foremen)	225	2,570
Agronomists, veterinarians, land-surveyors	45	376
"Plan economists" and bookkeepers	650	2,161
Others	575	2,609

It might be assumed that the category of "others" in this table includes functionaries in the state administration proper (probably functionaries in the party apparatus, too), in the police system, and in the officer corps. According to an official report, the personnel in the apparatus of the state and financial organs and in that of public organizations is supposed to amount to 1.4 million.[16] Since personnel in the "apparatus" of public organization is also included, the figure seems remarkably low in comparison with the 1929 figure of about 700,000. Thus, it must be that the term "apparatus" in the statistics for 1956 is considerably more limited than in those for 1929. There is no reason to suppose that the growth of the personnel here should differ essentially from other "apparatuses" (compare, for instance, the expansion of the central union republican and local during the 1930's and the continuous growth of the party apparatus). The fact that the number of "others" has quintupled between 1926 and 1956 should, at least in part, reflect this condition. An interesting and probably characteristic example of this trend is the growth of the finance apparatus. In 1922 the number of civil servants in finance amounted to 30,000; now there are 167,000 persons in the organization of the finance ministry — "excluding bookkeepers, cashiers, and comptrollers for savings accounts." [17]

Concerning the above-mentioned figure of 1.4 million, it is not certain that the general and officer corps have been counted. So far as is known, there are no current data concerning the size of this group. That this corps, which was reckoned at over 40,000 persons in 1897, must have increased is quite clear. The standing forces are now about the same numerical size as at the turn of the century; and the military-technical development and the changes in strategy and tactics necessitated by this development have caused a constant increase in the number of commanders, especially officers, in relation to the number of enlisted men.[18]

The administrative personnel in industry and commerce before 1912 — the predecessors of the "socialized" industrial and commercial management of today — comprised a group that is exceedingly difficult to estimate statistically. About 60,000 persons were accounted for in the 1897 census

[16] *Narodnoe khoziaistvo SSSR* (Moscow, 1956), 190.

[17] A. Kharionovsky, "Kadry finansovoi sistemy," *Finansy SSSR*, no. 10 (1957), 57, 63.

[18] *Obshchii svod*, II, 260.

under the rather clearly limited title "Administration of Commercial and Industrial Enterprises" (in the sector of private enterprise). This figure, however, can hardly cover the whole group which might be characterized as industrial and commercial employees; but there appears to be no practicable method for correcting the figure. Figures concerning the situation in 1912 and 1910 do exist, however, for the large cities of Moscow and St. Petersburg; and the number of employees is given as 92,000 and 41,000 respectively.[19] Figures available for 1929 record only 80,000, of whom 37,000 are in commerce and 42,000 in industry.[20] These figures must be seen against the fact that state commerce and industry were developed only to a small degree at that time. In 1956, not less than 133,000 civil servants (excluding salespeople)[21] were accounted for in commerce alone and over 2 million in industry, of whom about 750,000 were civil servants (others consist of technical engineering personnel).[22]

Even if the statistical material is scant and if the comparability can be questioned in several cases, it still appears obvious that the administrative corps has had, on the whole, an uninterrupted growth in numbers during the last hundred years. The particularly powerful acceleration during the Soviet period is partly connected, of course, with the institutional structure in the Soviet Union, which has, so to speak, in itself contributed to bureaucratization. But of the contributory factors, the decisive one has certainly been the continuous industrialization, begun during the second half of the nineteenth century and — after a momentary interruption during the First World War and the early years of the revolution — resumed once again with powerful force after the adoption of the First Five Year Plan.

II

With the Bolshevik seizure of power in 1917 a social order with roots in a backward agrarian society was destroyed. The leading social group in this old order was the nobility; and in a characterization of this social group the publicist Ogarev noted in 1860 that "the governing estate was made up of a caste of bureaucrats consisting of higher civil servants who owned serf-peasants and lower civil servants who were small landowners or completely without landed property."[23] This characterization seems to be correct insofar as the "ruling" nobility was divided into a class of

---

[19] A. G. Rashin, *Naselenie Rossii za 100 let* (Moscow, 1956), 333, in the table under the heading "Sluzhashchie torgovo-promyshlennykh predpriiatii," and 325, in the table under the heading "Sluzhashchie promyslovykh zaniatii."

[20] Bineman and Kheinman, the tables on 162 and 166, excluding custodians, workers, and the like.

[21] *Sovetskaia torgovlia* (Moscow, 1956), 115.

[22] *Narodnoe khoziaistvo SSSR*, 44.

[23] Mikhail S. Olminsky, *Gosudarstvo, biukrokratiia i absoliutizm i istorii Rossii* (Moscow, 1925), 107.

hereditary landowning nobility, whose members were mostly recruited to the higher civil-service stratum, and a nonhereditary titular or civil-service nobility, the main body of which — together with untitled civil servants (*chinovniki*) — appeared in the lower administration. On the other hand, it is not completely adequate in this case to speak of "caste," for the Russian nobility was not a caste in the recognized sense of the word. Persons from other social levels were continually being taken into the nobility, primarily through advancement in the civil and military administrations, but also through the bestowal of orders and even through purchase of titles. Entrance into the nobility occurred automatically in virtue of the Table of Ranks which Peter the Great introduced in 1722.[24] The purpose of this measure was to thwart the boyars, that is to say, the high nobility at that time, and to make room in the civil service for representatives of the low nobility (*dvorianstvo*), who were granted titles and prestige on the basis of the table. According to Kliuchevsky, the Table of Ranks meant that "an aristocratic hierarchy, founded on birth and family trees, was exchanged for a bureaucratic hierarchy, founded on merit and years of service."[25] This reform did not have such thoroughgoing effects, because once the *dvorianstvo* was established in its new position, the hereditary branch in this nobility grew, in its turn, into a new high nobility, which in the following centuries saw to it that "birth and family trees" did not lose their significance in recruitment to the state service.

The hereditary nobility (including family members) amounted to about 1.2 million persons in 1897; and the civil-service nobility and untitled civil servants (the latter, of course, could be regarded to a certain extent as being "potential nobility") amounted to about 0.6 million persons.[26] To judge from scattered statistical data, both groups had increased considerably since the middle of the century.[27] The social strata which could provide additions "from below" were the upper middle class in the cities, which included "honorary citizens" — hereditary and titular — and the merchant class (*kupechestvo*), especially merchants in the "First Guild." Together with the nobility and the untitled civil servants, they amounted to barely 3 million persons.[28] Thus, of the Russian population of 125.6 million, only 2 to 3 per cent at most had the opportunity to enter careers whch could lead to the higher positions in society.

What is interesting and remarkable about the Russian "ruling" nobility is the fact that it did not form itself into a homogeneous class or a "party" which could promote an independent policy contrary to the royal power.

[24] *Reformy Petra I: sbornik dokumentov,* ed. V. I. Lebedev (Moscow, 1937), 76.
[25] Kliuchevsky, IV, 86.
[26] *Obshchii svod,* I, 160.
[27] M. J. H. Schnitzler, *L'Empire des Tsars* (Paris, 1866), III, 287n1; and Anatole Leroy-Beaulieu, *The Empire of the Tsars and the Russians* (3 vols.; New York, 1893–1902), I, 350.
[28] *Obshchii svod,* I. 160; and Rashin, 322, who refers here to Lenin.

Leroy-Beaulieu characterizes the status of the Russian leading class in the following manner:

Superior as well as inferior classes existed only for the Throne and the State, not in or for themselves, and the sovereign was always free to raise or lower his subjects, in accordance with his needs or views, from one category to another.[29]

The exclusive position of the nobility in Russian society was not based on political power and control of the government machine, but was rather due to the fact that the nobility had a clear social, economic, and cultural advantage over other groups. This position was maintained by means of tax legislation directed against the peasantry. The tax legislation was combined with special privileges for the enjoyment of higher education as well as for entrance into and advancement in the central administration and other administrative areas. In 1885 — on the occasion of the centennial of Catherine II's charter of the nobility — an imperial "manifesto" was published in which it was stated as essential that "Russian Nobles should keep their leading position in the conduct of war, affairs of local administration and courts. . . ."[30]

The nobility could for a long time maintain its leading position within the administration for a very simple reason: the overwhelming majority of the population was completely disqualified in this connection since they were not even literate — in 1897, for example, 80 per cent of the population was illiterate.[31] The nobility and the civil servants — along with the clergy — had by far the highest percentage of literacy; but it may be inserted parenthetically that no less than about 25 per cent of the members of these culturally leading classes were illiterates.[32] For the nobility there were also special schools and educational institutions which were closed to other social groups — for instance, the lycées in Petersburg and Moscow and the page and cadet schools. Until 1880 the Alexander Lycée in Petersburg was so exclusive that only the sons of the hereditary nobility were admitted.[33] And this lycée — like the others — was intended "for education of youth destined for important areas in the state service."[34] On the military side, the cadet schools were mainly intended for the sons of officers. Concerning the recruitment of the officers corps — and of the clergy too, for that matter — something of a caste system had been developed, since the occupation passed from father to son and "outsiders" entered these careers only in exceptional cases.

---

[29] Leroy-Beaulieu, I, 313.
[30] Cited in Seton-Watson, 135.
[31] William H. E. Johnson, *Russia's Educational Heritage* (New Brunswick, 1950), table, 283.
[32] Johnson, table, 284.
[33] Leroy-Beaulieu, I, 395n.
[34] *Malaia sovetskaia entsiklopediia* (Moscow, 1930), IV, 688.

During the latter part of the nineteenth century and up to 1914, definite progress was made, particularly in the field of public education. In leading circles, however, there was a desire to prevent this progress from encouraging an undesirable social mobility. From the notorious instruction published by the Ministry of Education in 1887, the following deserves to be quoted:

Gymnasiums and progymnasiums are freed from receiving the children of coachmen, servants, cooks, laundresses, small tradesmen, and the like, whose children, with exceptions, perhaps of those who are gifted with extraordinary capacities, ought by no means to be transferred from the sphere to which they belong and thus brought, as many years' experience has shown, to slight their parents, to feel dissatisfied with their lot, and to conceive an aversion to the existing inequality of fortune which is in the nature of things unavoidable.[35]

The occupations listed above show that the authors were especially concerned about the diffusion of "unnecessary" knowledge among particular sectors of the urban population. Of interest also is the open recognition of the problem — just as urgent in our day — of how to maintain an authoritarian and hierarchical social order in a time of industrialization and urbanization with growing demands for increased formal education — a development which might lead to the undermining of the established order.

The question of the increased social differentiation in the towns — connected with industrialization — becomes particularly important with regard to the recruitment of the universities. The statistics concerning the social composition of the university students are incomplete, but one can discern certain rather clear trends.[36] As a consequence of the official school policy, the social selection was, on the whole, quite naturally completed at the time of entrance into universities. The dominating group consisted of sons of the nobility and the civil servants. For 1911 there is a distribution[37] which shows that the sons of civil servants and titular nobility represented 46 per cent of the university students. That only 9 per cent came from the hereditary nobility is, of course, connected with the fact that other exclusive educational institutions were at their disposal. The most striking trait, however, is the advancement of the other social groups during the latter part of the nineteenth century: the sons of peasants increased percentagewise very notably from a low initial figure, and the lower middle class in the towns appears as an important group. After having finished their studies, representatives of these groups took employment to a great extent as civil servants in local administrations in the provinces. This "rural intelligentsia" came into strong opposition to the authorities, reflecting a tendency which was also being expressed

[35] Cited in Johnson, 155.
[36] Johnson, table, 290.
[37] Cited in Hoetzsch, 311n.

among the craftsmen and the lower level of civil servants in the towns. The authors of the instruction from the Ministry of Education that was quoted above must have thought that their worst apprehensions had come true.

Birth, personal connections, and a certain educational level opened the door to a career in the state administration. After his entry into the service, the person in question was placed in a *chin* (rank) according to the Table of Ranks. The table included fourteen ranks for the courtiers, the military officers, and the civil servants; and its purpose was both to show the comparability *between* the different ranks of the three administrations and to denote the pattern of advancement *within* the respective administrations. During the time of Peter the Great, the new principles were applied rather arbitrarily, and capable men from the bottom of society could make overnight careers and consequently gain entry to the highest estate. With increasing bureaucratization, however, restrictions were gradually introduced for the particular purpose of preventing a leveling of the nobility. At the same time, however, these restrictions led to a stagnation within the administration. Thus, the attainment of the eighth rank from the bottom (major, collegial assessor) ensured the grant of hereditary nobility;[38] the "threshold" was moved successively higher and higher on the rank scale, and the right to be granted hereditary nobility automatically through service was finally discontinued under Alexander III.[39] There were still loopholes, however — for instance, bestowals of certain orders carried a right to such nobility with them. Of greater importance for the functioning of the state machinery, however, was the fact that the order of advancement became fixed: the civil servants had in principle to pass the different ranks successively — without "skipping" — and seniority was the universally decisive factor at the advancement from one rank to another.[40]

The marked differentiation in rank among the civil servants was combined with a similarly sharp differentiation in salary[41] — a few top salaries for the highest civil servants and extremely modest salaries for the great mass of lower officeholders. The widespread corruption for which the Russian administration was notorious was connected with this unsatisfactory remuneration system and the almost obligatory "prestige expenses," which were pressing for precisely these last-mentioned groups. State service was nonetheless extremely sought-after, primarily because of the social prestige which the possessor of rank enjoyed. The rank table comprised the standard by which a person's social position was measured. The impressive titles and uniforms, which grew all the more dazzling and

[38] Schnitzler, III, 284.
[39] Leroy-Beaulieu, I, 349.
[40] Schnitzler, 334.
[41] Hoetzsch, 270.

decorative with the rise in rank, invested the chinovniki with dignity and authority over the general public. This title-and-rank mania, however, was not a phenomenon prevalent only in the civil service. On the whole, when a person or a group — artists, scientists, teachers, and merchants — was to be especially distinguished before the public, grants of title and rank were resorted to as a panacea. Merchants in the First Guild, for example, had been granted the right to wear special uniforms (*gubernskii mundir*) and — after twenty years' membership in the guild — to receive the title "Counselor of Commerce and Manufacturing." [42]

III

When the Bolsheviks seized power in 1917, they were confronted with a Russian reality which hardly squared with the official ideology. This fact does not seem to have bothered the new leaders in their exercise of power, which was immediately concentrated on a consolidation of captured positions and on practical administrative work. The aim was to build up a completely new social order with no roots in the past, and the heritage from the overthrown Tsarist regime was formally severed by means of a series of governmental decrees. The administrative apparatus was rebuilt from the ground up and was provided with new labels. The chinovniki rule was formally "liquidated" by means of a decree as early as November 1917, entitled "On the Abolition of the Estates and of the Civil Ranks." [43] With the stroke of a pen, Peter's Table of Ranks, which for nearly two centuries had formed the cornerstone of the Russian administrative structure, disappeared. A revolutionary terminology was also introduced concerning the names of the civil servants' duties. "Minister" and "ambassador," for example, were replaced by "people's commissar" and "plenipotentiary representative," and in the armed forces the customary officers' ranks were replaced by the single term, *komandir* (commander). A new salary scale was put into effect in the state administration, and it was leavened by the universal leveling spirit.[44]

The decisive and eminently practical task with which the Bolshevik leaders were faced was to make the administrative machinery function and to man the various apparatuses. First of all, they had to organize the armed forces and next bring order into the civil administration. The dilemma was to meet, on the one hand, the political demand to recruit an administrative corps from social groups which were loyal and not infected with the chinovnik spirit and, on the other hand, to meet the technical-administrative demand for competence and expert knowledge. These two interests, however, were in conflict: the sources of the new

[42] Serafim V. Iushkov, *Istoriia gosudarstva i prava SSSR* (2 vols.; Moscow, 1950), I, 496.

[43] *Iuridicheskii slovar* (Moscow, 1956), II, 417.

[44] Abram Bergson, *The Structure of Soviet Wages* (Cambridge, Mass., 1946), 190.

regime's personnel — the workers and peasants — were to a considerable extent illiterate; and the competent cadres — that is to say, the civil servants from the old regime — had demonstrated their attitude toward the new regime through (among other things) repeated strikes which took place in 1917 and 1918 within the state administration.[45] The government was up against a grim fact and had no other choice than to gamble on the civil-service cadre that was at hand — despite its manifest enmity to the regime.[46] This circumstance, which has probably been of great significance for the formation and character of the Soviet administrative corps, has to a considerable extent been lost sight of. Nor have the Soviets, for their part, mentioned this fact until very recently. In 1957 it was pointed out in an authoritative journal: "During the course of nearly *two decades'* development of the Soviet state, persons who originated in the petty-bourgeois group, formerly the exploiting classes, comprised the dominant element in the composition of the civil-service corps." [47] A large group of these civil servants, of course, was comprised of people who, at least in earlier stages, "wintered the storm" in hopes of a change of regime.

This reliance on the "capitalistic" civil servants necessitated a rigorous political control over the civilian and military functionaries. It also promoted a further acceleration of the expansion of the educational system for the purpose of producing from the worker and peasant population an administrative corps which would be more acceptable from a political point of view. During the 1920's many improvisations in the area of education were temporarily adopted — for example, facilitation of entrance into the university and different kinds of preparatory short courses. At the same time, the functionaries were being exposed to a systematic social and, in certain respects, economic discrimination with regard to entrance into the party, admittance to educational institutions, the receiving of social benefits and rations, and the rate of taxation.[48] As a result of this deliberate policy on the part of the government, a large number of persons of worker and peasant origin were raised to leading posts in the state during this period. The worker and peasant element was large, of course, within the party, which served as the basis of recruitment for the new civil-service nobility; and it increased rapidly during the period in question. As has been mentioned, however, the dominant group within the state administration was of civil-servant origin, and it was only in the local units that the new recruitment had a more significant scope.[49] The educational level of these cadres — as in the party as a whole — was

---

[45] Bergson, 107.
[46] See the table in Bineman and Kheinman, 95.
[47] "Iz istorii partiinogo stroitel'stva," *Partiinaia zhizn'*, no. 20 (1957), 58; italics added.
[48] Bergson, 109ff.
[49] Bineman and Kheinman, table, 8.

naturally extremely low. Of special interest is the fact that the social composition of the military officers corps was most widely different from that of the higher civil administration. This difference reflects, of course, the efforts of the regime in this particular field: in 1927, 22 per cent of the officers were of worker origin — as against 12 per cent in 1921 — and 56 per cent of them were of peasant origin.[50] Analogous conditions existed in the police system.[51] Peasants accounted for 62 per cent and workers for 22 per cent of the policemen. Even among the higher functionaries within the police system there was a similarly safe majority of persons with the "right" background.

During the 1930's the internal situation was radically changed. In connection with the rapid industrialization, the consequent enormous increase of administrative authorities and personnel, and the expansion and building up of the educational system, the "radical" experimental spirit and amateurishness of the 1920's had to give way to the demand for internal unity, stability, and competence. This altered situation, partly brought about by a conscious policy on the part of the government, partly necessitated by the very pressure of events, produced particularly striking consequences in the social and economic status of the administrative civil servants.

The increase of the administrative apparatus resulted in a strong social mobility with new additions from the lower strata of society. The stream of workers' and peasants' sons into administrative work raised the question of the social status of the civil servants. Already in the beginning of the 1930's there appeared a clear tendency to do away with special rules which were directed against the functionaries; but they were still not welcomed into the party. The entrance requirements for this group were much stricter than those for workers and peasants.[52] In view of the fact that the new additions were introduced "from below" — a process which was accelerated during the macabre purges[53] — the result of the differential entrance requirements was that the more a person did to make himself useful to the state, the more difficult it became for him to become a member of society's elite organization. The situation became untenable and the differential entrance requirements were abolished at the party congress in 1939.[54] The measure was given particular emphasis through the fact that Stalin himself appeared with a speech in defense of the "new Soviet intelligentsia," [55] which was not, however, elevated to a

[50] Malaia sovetskaia entsiklopediia, IV, 69.
[51] Bineman and Kheinman, 56.
[52] D. Bakhshiev, Voprosy chlenstva v VKP(b) (Moscow, 1949), 84ff.
[53] See Stalin's pronouncement at the Eighteenth Party Congress that over 500,000 young Bolsheviks, party members, and those "near the party" had been advanced to leading posts in the administration and the party. Pravda (March 3, 1939).
[54] Bakhshiev, 100.
[55] J. V. Stalin. Voprosy leninizma (Moscow, 1947), 606ff.

"class" but was characterized as a "stratum" (*prosloika*). The pragmatic attitude toward the question of the civil-servant stratum was clearly expressed in a pronouncement of Malenkov at the party conference in 1941:

Despite the party's directives, the situation within many party and administrative organs hitherto has been that on choosing functionaries one has given more attention to finding out the family tree of the person in question, to finding out who his grandparents were, than to investigating his practical and political qualifications, capacity and talent.[56]

After the civil servants had been placed on a par with the other social groups, the doors were opened for their entrance into the party apparatus, where — particularly in the higher levels — the civil and military administrative corps is well represented.[57]

During the 1930's many rules and stipulations were once again introduced for the purpose of gaining control over and at the same time granting authority to the powerfully expanding and differentiated administrative apparatus.[58] The handbook issued in 1930 by the Worker and Peasant Inspection (RKI), "Nomenclature and Characterization of the Duties of the Civil Servants within the State Organs of the Soviet Union," included up to two hundred different duties and ranks for civil servants.[59] It might be mentioned that already at that time the traditional ranks of "attaché" up to "counselor" existed within the diplomatic service. In 1935, the title, "Marshal of the Soviet Union," was reintroduced. With the Second World War a sharp differentiation, along with a clear fixing of position and authority, followed within the armed forces. The titles of general and admiral were reintroduced in 1940 and the Guards' regiments reappeared in 1942. The traditional, international system of ranking was readopted for the rest of the officers corps in 1943.

At the same time, a completely new title, "chief marshal," was introduced in the air force and the artillery. The epaulettes were also restored to favor again, although according to the "Short Soviet Encyclopedia" of 1931, they had been abolished after the October Revolution "as being a symbol of class oppression in the army." [60] In 1943 and 1944, respectively, the Suvorov and Nakhimov schools were instituted after the pattern of the Tsarist cadet schools;[61] titles and ranks in the generals and officers corps of the interior and security organs were brought into agreement

[56] *Bolshevik*, no. 3–4 (1941), 31.

[57] Concerning the social composition of the higher organs of the central and local party organizations, see Alf Edeen, *Rysslands Nya Medelklass* (Stockholm, 1954), 23–34.

[58] Edeen, 55–63. Where nothing else is given these rules have been taken from *Sbornik zakonov SSSR i ukazov prezidiuma verkhovnogo soveta SSSR* for the period in question.

[59] *Nomenklatura i kharakteristiki dolzhnostei sluzhashchikh gosorganov SSSR* (Moscow, 1930).

[60] *Malaia sovetskaia entsiklopediia* (Moscow, 1931), VI, 624.

[61] *Entsiklopedicheskii slovar* (Moscow, 1954), II, 470; (Moscow, 1955), III, 341.

with those of the regular armed forces in 1945; and in the same year Stalin allowed himself to be designated "generalissimo," the title which had crowned Peter's famous Table of Ranks.

A parallel development also took place in the civil administration beginning in 1941, when the titles "ambassador" and "minister" were re-introduced into the Soviet diplomatic service — followed in 1943 by a regular rank-and-title ordinance, including stipulations for uniforms, for the entire service. Within the governmental machinery, the designation "people's commissar" was abolished in 1946 and was replaced with the respectable title of "minister." During the period between 1943 and 1949 rules concerning order of rank were announced successively. Along with these there were titles and descriptions of uniforms for civil servants in ten to fifteen different civil (especially in the economic) administrations. The purpose for this detailed categorization and uniforming of the civil-servant corps was — as emphasized by Soviet experts in administrative law — "to strengthen the service discipline and raise the titled civil servant's authority." [62]

These rules offer interesting insights into the functioning of the Soviet administration. Especially informative are the rules concerning the order of ranks within the prosecutor's office. [63] The civil servants are here divided into eleven "classes" with exact stipulations for advancement from a lower to a higher rank or class. The principle of seniority is carried out up to the fourth class. The normal progression can, however, be avoided in exceptional cases by the stipulation that the supreme prosecutor himself can permit a civil servant to "skip," according to the ordinance, "not more than two ranks above the rank a civil servant holds." In the original ruling there was also a "table of comparisons" that is extremely indicative. Here it was shown how the different ranks within the prosecutor's office were to be compared with the military ranks. The cycle in the Russian development was herewith completed; Peter's rejected Table of Ranks was in fact re-established with its ostentatious titles, rank distinctions, and uniforms, displaying the social status of the chinovnik before the general public. Only recently has the Soviet government attempted to eliminate the most grotesque manifestations of this mania for uniforms and ranks. [64]

The economic status of the administrative corps during the first Soviet period has already been mentioned. The doctrine of equality, which had been cherished from the beginning, was, however, written off rather quickly. Thus, already during the Civil War outstanding scientists, for

[62] S. S. Studenikin, V. A. Vlasov, and I. I. Evtikhiev, *Sovetskoe administrativnoe pravo* (Moscow, 1950), 137.
[63] Dated September 16, 1943, *Sbornik zakonov, 1938–1944* (Moscow, 1945), 336 ff.
[64] *Sbornik zakonov, 1938–1956*, 239, Ukase of July 12, 1954, "Concerning the Abolition of Personal Titles and Distinguishing Marks for Civil Servants within Civil Ministries and Authorities."

example, were allotted "academic rations" (*akademicheskie paiki*)[65] which were considerably larger than those of nonacademics. It appears from Bergson's work on the Russian wage structure that the average earnings for civil servants in industry were considerably above those of workers in 1928 and that the difference was even more marked in 1934, that is to say, after the first rush of industrialization.[66] Thus, already by 1928 the abandonment of wage leveling had brought about a wage gap between the civil servants and the workers. At the same time, however — up until the early 1930's — the functionaries were subjected to an economic discrimination in matters concerning social privileges (for example, social benefits, social insurance, and pensions), taxes, and rations. This policy was closely connected with the social discrimination against the functionaries that I mentioned earlier. After Stalin's speech before the business executives, which comprises one of the milestones in the advance of the managerial class during the Soviet era, this economic discrimination was abolished and was followed by a number of facilities and benefits — for example, special dining rooms and shops for, first of all, engineers and technical personnel. Later these privileges were gradually extended to other civil-servant groups.[67]

Russian data published more recently show that the economic position of the functionaries has not been altered in comparison to that of the workers. It also appears that the wage scale within the civil-service corps reflects the social differentiation in title and rank.[68] The Russian civil-service corps is already so differentiated socially and economically that what is now characterized as a stratum consists in reality of several distinguishable strata.

The higher-income level among the civil servants with "rank" involves a number of extra advantages owing to the particular structure of the Soviet economic system — for example, the absence of income-tax progression combined with heavy indirect taxation (turnover tax), social benefits and pensions (the size of which is determined by, among other things, income level), the right to extra living space, and the very favorable inheritance tax. In addition, there are "personal" salaries alongside the ordinary wage scale (these personal salaries are for specially qualified functionaries), and "personal" pensions for outstanding political, civil, and military functionaries.[69]

---

[65] M. Kim, *Kommunisticheskaia partiia — organisator kulturnoi revoliutsii v SSSR* (Moscow, 1955), 207.

[66] Bergson, 116–117.

[67] Bergson, 112ff.

[68] See, for instance, N. G. Aleksandrov, *Sovetskoe trudovoe pravo* (Moscow, 1949); Studenikin and others; E. L. Manevich, *Zarabotnaia plata i ego formy v promyshlennosti SSSR* (Moscow, 1951).

[69] These and other special privileges not mentioned in this essay have been assembled in Edeen, 64–66 and 80–82 together with references to the Soviet source material.

The enormous disparities in income and the extreme rewarding of certain categories with bonuses has now aroused irritation in the Soviet Union. The new leaders, who have been anxious to wipe out the most extreme manifestations of the Stalinist regime, have also reacted on this point. At the Twentieth Party Congress, Mikoyan — referring to the Russian economic and social background — stated that the enormous disparity in wages was "natural" for the purpose of turning out highly qualified cadres rapidly. He added that "the differentiation must be retained, but the gap will be narrowed." [70]

IV

The rise of a new Russian bureaucracy comprises one of the significant factors in an attempt to elucidate the question of continuity and change in Russian society after 1861. Certain main trends stand out distinctly from the material presented above. In some cases, the present state of affairs is strikingly similar to the old Tsarist order, which shows the force of tradition even in a society originating as a protest against that order. Again, in other cases, it is obvious that innovations have been introduced during the Soviet era.

The highly centralized government machinery and the state direction of the economy, which are often thought of as specific "communist" features, are completely in line with the Russian administrative tradition. The dominating position of state power in Russia is old, and the liberal Russian historian, Miliukov, has pointed out: "Since oldest times, the government has also regarded all areas suitable for industrial exploitation as its own property." [71] The chronic pressure on the economic resources in the interest of the state — especially in order to satisfy the growing demands of an enormous war machine — presupposed a widely ramified administrative apparatus, the higher functionaries of which had, of old, a favored and central position in Russian society. "Russia is ruled by 40,000 heads of bureaus (stolonachalniki)," [72] as Nicholas I expressed it. By that, of course, he meant the purely technical-administrative side of the question, not the political; for the bureaucrats at that time had just as little possibility of influencing great political decisions as do the present functionaries within the party and administration. The "inner circle" could in earlier times, as now, handle its cadres arbitrarily since the principle of the irremovability of the civil servant was and still is completely unknown. Even the top leadership is subject to frequent shifts, as "mysterious," inexplicable, and seemingly capricious as now, and the outsider is left to mere guesswork or to manipulating various kinds of

[70] XX s"ezd Kommunisticheskoi Partii Sovetskogo Soiuza; stenograficheskii otchet (2 vols.; Moscow, 1956), I, 307.
[71] Miliukov, I, 175.
[72] Malaia sovetskaia entsiklopediia (Moscow, 1929), II, 607.

more or less vague "theories." As under the tsars, the present-day Russian rulers rely heavily upon a strong, omnipresent, and harsh police power to enforce government policy and to control the conduct and loyalty of their subjects.

To the traditional features also belong the strong consciousness of rank and title in the administrative corps. It seems, however, as if an attempt is now being made to check this "tradition," which is particularly embarrassing against the ideological background. Yet the actual course of events has so far shown that this problem cannot be solved by decree. All of the evils and "beauty patches" inherent in the old chinovnik rule still exist, as is daily demonstrated in the Soviet press: abuse of power, bullying, red tape, paper drill, negligence, incompetence, and corruptibility. That these traditions have lived on so obstinately is not especially remarkable, considering the initial situation facing the Bolsheviks: the extremely low level of education among the population; the lack of qualified personnel; and the necessity of accepting in administrative work "alien" social groups from the old regime, whose representatives became — consciously or unconsciously — a connecting link in the seemingly broken chain of continuity and who left their mark on the present Soviet civil-service corps.

The decisive change introduced by the Soviet regime — the strong curtailment of the rights to private property — seems to be more relevant to questions which lie outside the subject treated here. However, the replacement of the right of private ownership of real estate and means of production with the right of use (which is usually attached to a post) has brought with it a specific disadvantage for the higher Soviet civil servant who has fallen into disfavor. He, in contrast to many of his Tsarist predecessors, does not have the possibility of quietly retiring, and enjoying the cozy daily life of the Russian provincial estate owner. Compared with the conditions in the 1930's, when the person in disgrace was simply liquidated, it is possible that the exiles of Molotov and Malenkov, for example, to "provincial" duties in the east imply something new, a return to methods which correspond somewhat to the prerevolutionary order.

It is, further, an innovation to have a system with a party apparatus that parallels the ordinary administrative apparatus — even in the remotest local unit — and has the task of minutely supervising and controlling it. This supervision is the more remarkable today, since the party functionaries often hold purely administrative posts and the the civil servants (including military officers), as a rule, are party members and often of high status. The higher up one goes in the hierarchy, the more difficult it becomes to decide whether a person shall be regarded as a party man or as a government official. This question is still more complex concerning the younger generation of party and state functionaries who have been trained at universities and other higher educational institutions. It seems as if these two administrations are on the way toward merging, and perhaps the development is moving toward some sort of gradual "withering away" of certain overlapping functions, even though it now appears still far off. The dualism or "control over the control" cannot, in any case, be regarded as rational or effective from a technical-administrative point of view. The present system can claim a "rationality" on political considerations alone.

The change which has had significant direct repercussions on the public administration is the improvement of the educational system and the extension of the recruitment to the state service. As has been pointed out above, the situation before the revolution was such that only a very small percentage of the population was recruited to the civil-servant corps. The social mobility and the rapid careers from the bottom of society during the Soviet regime — where the party in particular served as the basis for recruitment — have also been mentioned above. This mobility, however, is quite natural in a society subjected to rapid political, economic, and administrative change, especially in view of the institutional order in the Soviet Union. On the other hand, Russian society has now begun to settle or "ripen," and the earlier development should perhaps be regarded as a unique phenomenon, having to do with quite special conditions and causes. An interesting symptom is the fact that, already at the end of the 1930's, the functionaries and their descendants were clearly overrepresented at the universities in relation to their relative proportion of the total population.[73] Since this time, the complete lack of information concerning the social composition of the institutions of higher education must be regarded as an indication that the present composition is "unsuitable" and would not support the official thesis of equal possibilities for all. The existing social, psychological, geographical, and — to a lesser degree, however — economic "barriers" have so far been passed over in silence. Concerning the condition within the administrative apparatus, it is obvious that advancement now proceeds more slowly than earlier — in accordance with a fixed and well-established pattern which indicates that the changes in a person's social status will probably take place over short social distances. There are also many facts and circumstances which imply that there has been a stabilization in the sense that the basis of recruitment to the administrative corps will be narrowed in comparison to the situation a few decades ago.

On the other hand, it must be pointed out that the government is endeavoring to prevent stagnation. It is extremely doubtful, however, whether such measures can essentially change the present state of affairs. The real problem is the actual need for administrative personnel. If this need should decrease, as a consequence of an effective rationalization

[73] I. N. Medynsky, *Narodnoe obrazovanie v SSSR* (Moscow, 1952), 164.

within the administration, it is very likely, in view of the established social and economic order, that the descendants of the functionaries will be even more favored. Should the need increase, the probability is that the social mobility will not cease. It might not be too bold to maintain that, with regard to technical development, in the long run the need for functionaries tends to increase and thus secure the chances for social advancement — quite irrespective of the government's measures in this field. These additions "from below" will be absorbed in an administrative machinery which has increasingly acquired stability, authority, and competence over the last four decades. The social values and attitudes of this administrative corps are already fixed and, like the hierarchical structure of the "apparatuses," have their roots in a social order which the Bolsheviks thought they had definitely destroyed in 1917.

THE RUSSIAN PEASANT: FROM EMANCIPATION TO KOLKHOZ

LAZAR VOLIN

I

The very selection of the year 1861 as the starting point of the inquiry to which this volume is devoted is symptomatic of the importance attached to the peasantry in the Russian social fabric. This is, I am sure, not due to a mere physiocratic bias or predilection. For 1861 is associated with a great milestone in the historic fate of the Russian peasant — the Emancipation Act of February 19. It decreed the abolition of what the great Russian historian Kliuchevsky characterized as the worst form of serfdom in Europe.[1] By the same token, 1861 became a great national landmark, ushering in a new era justly remembered in Russian history as that of the Great Reforms of the early reign of Alexander II. Following in the wake of a severe jolt administered to the Russian autocracy by the humiliating defeat in the Crimean War of 1854–1855, these reforms re-

[1] V. O. Kliuchevsky, *Kurs russkoi istorii* (5 vols.; Moscow, 1910), I, 434. For a discussion of the Russian servile system, see also: G. T. Robinson, *Rural Russia under the Old Regime* (New York, 1932), chs. 3–4; Lazar Volin, "The Russian Peasant and Serfdom," *Agricultural History*, XVII (January 1943), 41–61, reprinted in Herman Ausubel, ed., *The Making of Modern Europe* (2 vols.; New York, 1951), II, 709–31. Of the voluminous Russian literature on the subject referred to in the above publications, there must be singled out the monumental *Velikaia reforma: Russkoe obshchestvo i krest'ianskii vopros v proshlom i nastoiashchem*, ed. A. K. Dzhivelegov and others (6 vols.; Moscow, 1911). The first four volumes are devoted to a description and analysis of various aspects of serfdom.

vitalized national life after the sterile reactionary regime of Nicholas I. Despite the abolition of serfdom, the dictum of Gustav Schmoller, that in Europe "from 1500 to 1850 the great social question of the day was the peasant question," [2] continued to be applicable until much later in Russia. For in one form or another, it has never disappeared as a central political-economic issue at every critical juncture in modern Russian history, even after the peasantry ceased to be the predominant element of population.

Half a century after the emancipation, the peasant question or, as it was then called, the land or agrarian question was again in the foreground during the 1905 Revolution, and it emerged as an explosive issue a decade later during the revolution of 1917. It was central in the transition from War Communism to the NEP in 1921 under Lenin and, of course, in the collectivization crisis of the early 1930's under Stalin. After Stalin's death this question came back to plague the heirs of the late dictator.

This cursory review should make it clear that the peasant question in Russia was not settled by the emancipation in the 1860's as it was in Western Europe by the French Revolution and the subsequent agrarian reforms, and the industrial revolution in the nineteenth century. On the contrary, the historic contest between the Russian peasant and the landlord, shielded by the Tsarist state, continued until a complete victory was apparently won by the peasant in 1917. However, this was a Pyrrhic victory followed by a new conflict, this time between the peasant and the Communist state, bent on collectivization of agriculture and a rapid but lopsided industrialization. Throughout this period, while the institutional agrarian structure underwent significant changes, the peasant continued to be the Cinderella of the body politic, except for some transitory and sectional improvements.

II

The period between 1861 and the revolution of 1917 poses a crucial question: why, having begun with a promising agrarian reform, did it end with a peasant revolt resembling in many respects Pushkin's celebrated "Russian mutiny — terrible and senseless"? Certainly Alexander II recognized the dilemma — agrarian reform or eventual revolution — when he warned the serf-owning landlords in the beginning of his reign that it is better to liberate serfs from above than to wait until they liberated themselves. He saw the handwriting on the wall and hoped to forestall a possible peasant uprising, a rumbling of which was to be heard in frequent local mutinies of serfs, keeping alive that nightmare of the serf-owner —

[2] *Volkswirtschaftslehre*, I, 520, quoted in J. H. Clapham, *The Economic Development of France and Germany, 1815–1914* (Cambridge, Eng., 1921), 1.

the *Pugachevshchina*.[3] When the government's intention to abolish serfdom became known about a hundred years ago, it was greeted with immense enthusiasm by the Russian intelligentsia of all shades of opinion:
from the Slavophiles at the right, to liberals like Kavelin and (at that
time) Katkov at the center, to Herzen at the left of center, and even
Chernyshevsky at the extreme left.

This enthusiasm, however, faded as the emancipation legislation,
which was to affect so profoundly the life of the liberated peasantry,
began to take shape.[4] Not only did radicals like Ogarev and Chernyshevsky damn the emancipation reform, but even Ivan Aksakov, the conservative Slavophile, was critical. For a strong impact was exerted on the
new legislation by the landowning nobility, which was strongly entrenched at the imperial court and in the governing bureaucracy. The
landowners were bent on making the liberation process economically as
painless as possible to themselves when they realized its inevitability.
The pressure of the landlord interests, though in some respects divergent
(as between different geographic regions), resulted in many a compromise unfavorable to the liberated peasants.[5]

To be sure, the peasant ceased to be legally what Herzen called
"baptized property." And, what is equally important in view of the
attachment of the Russian peasants to their land, they were not liberated
as landless proletarians. This was the fate of the peasants freed from
bondage much earlier in the Baltic provinces (1818), and the idea was
toyed with during the early preparatory stage of the emancipation reform
but later abandoned.

The peasants did not obtain all the land they hoped for in accordance
with the strongly implanted concept that land should belong to those who
toil on it. Actually, the landowning nobility retained about 45 per cent
of the best land.[6] In the allotment of the remainder to the more than 20

---

[3] A term for a peasant revolt derived from the name of Emelian Pugachev, the
leader of a formidable peasant rebellion in the 1770's during the reign of Catherine
the Great.

[4] For a detailed treatment of the emancipation legislation, see: Robinson, ch. 5;
George Pavlovsky, *Agricultural Russia on the Eve of the Revolution* (London, 1930);
P. I. Lyashchenko, *History of the National Economy of Russia to the 1917 Revolution*
(New York, 1949), ch. 21; *Velikaia reforma*, V, 4–5; A. A. Kornilov, *Krest'ianskaia
reforma* (Moscow, 1905), chas. 3–5.

[5] The divergence was principally between the landowners of the more fertile
regions of the black-soil area, where land itself was the most valuable element of
the estate economy, and the much less fertile nonblack-soil area, where the landowners to a large extent derived their income not from farming of their own, but
from quit-rents paid by the serfs, who gained their livelihood partly from agriculture
and partly from nonagricultural pursuits.

[6] Lyashchenko, 393. The reduction of the land area allotted to peasants after the
emancipation amounted to 9.9 per cent in 15 nonblack-soil provinces and 26.2 per cent
in 21 black-soil provinces, and 18.1 per cent for the combined 36 provinces. In some
provinces the reduction exceeded 30 to 40 per cent (Lyashchenko, 384). It should
be noted, however, that in addition to the more than 20 million private serfs there

million peasants, however, there were considerable regional variations, dictated by the divergent interests of the landowning gentry in different areas.

A large section of the liberated peasantry in the more fertile regions, where land was valuable, was allotted even a smaller area than it had tilled for its own needs under serfdom. The holdings allotted were also often of poor quality and location, and lacking such important components as meadows (hayland) and woodland, necessitating the leasing of these types of land from the former master. In these and other aspects of the land-allotment process was the genesis of the continued economic dependence of the liberated peasants on their former master which persisted long after the emancipation. Here was a source of irritation and conflict which poisoned the liberated peasant-landlord relations.

The situation was aggravated by the financial aspects of the emancipation reform. The peasants were saddled with a heavy redemption price for the allotted land that exceeded its market value before allotment. The fiscal burden of redemption payments and taxes, sometimes even exceeding the income from land, began early to figure as one of the chief causes of rural destitution in the findings of official investigating commissions and of private investigators and observers during the post-emancipation era. Moreover, fiscal considerations involved in the task of extracting the burdensome redemption payments and taxes were, to a large extent, responsible for the fact that the peasant was not made an independent land proprietor or full-fledged citizen and that his mobility was restricted.

Thus, over a large part of the country, ownership of peasant land was vested in the whole village community or mir and not held as private property in fee simple by the individual peasant farmer.[7] The mir apportioned the land on some egalitarian basis to the peasant family or household (*krest'ianskii dvor*), which was the actual farm unit. The latter could not even refuse to accept an allotment, however unprofitable. For taxes had to be paid under a system of unlimited responsibility of the whole membership — whether the land was tilled or not. Incidentally, the legal registrictions with which the allotted land was hedged and segregated from other privately owned land were further tightened by the law of December 14, 1893.

The mir also assumed much of the police authority over the peasants which was formely exercised by the landlords, including the power of deportation to Siberia. It shared with the heads of the households the

---

were also the so-called crown (state) peasants and those belonging to the imperial family, numbering altogether close to 20 million. These categories fared much better and suffered no reduction of their land area.

[7] For a discussion of the mir, see Lazar Volin, "The Peasant Household under the *Mir* and the *Kolkhoz* in Modern Russian history," in Caroline F. Ware, ed., *The Cultural Approach to History* (New York, 1940), 125–139.

important power to grant or withhold permission to obtain and renew the much-coveted passport, without which a peasant could not leave his native village for any length of time. It was, however, mainly the persistent and vexing tax arrears which lead to intervention of the mir in the affairs of the individual household. To ensure payment, a member of the defaulting household could be hired out or the head of the household could be removed and a different member appointed in his place.

Thus the mir, usually under the leadership of its more prosperous or more aggressive elements, lorded it over the average peasant. In turn, the mir and the volost (a unit of rural self-government which comprised several village communities) were dominated by government officials, whose legal power of interference was increased during the latter part of the nineteenth century. The elected peasant aldermen were "elective in name only and depend to such an extent on the local government bureaucracy that they cannot even think about defending the interests of their community. As a result the better element of the village as a rule shuns service and the positions are occupied by the scum of the peasant population." [8] Such was the testimony gathered from various sources by an investigation at the beginning of the century.

The peasants also had separate lower courts, where minor criminal and civil cases were tried in accordance with custom law. This "very often proved to be no law at all," [9] so ill-defined and unfairly and arbitrarily administered was it. The quality of the village judges was no better than that of other elective officials, who were tools of the *chinovniki* (government officials). Corporal punishment was retained in these peasant courts long after it was abolished in the penal system of the general courts, which had undergone a thorough and highly progressive reform in the 1860's.

Still another set of limitations to which the peasants, but not other classes of the population, were subjected stemmed from the customary joint family ownership of the property of a peasant household, which was retained after the emancipation. While it protected individual members against the improvidence of the head of the household, it also had disadvantages for the individual. For instance, all his earnings from whatsoever source were supposed to go into the common pool — a serious matter, considering the prevalence of migratory work in the overpopulated Russian village. Even peasants who had long lived and worked away from the village were often forced to continue their contributions to the household of which they legally remained members. The weapon here was the famous Russian passport, which hung like the sword of Damocles over the head of any peasant who wanted to live away from his native village.

Despite the various restrictions the traditional Great Russian large

[8] S. N. Prokopovich, *Mestnye liudi o nuzhdakh derevni* (St. Petersburg, 1904), 99.
[9] Paul Milyoukov, *Russia and Its Crisis* (Chicago, 1906), 343.

peasant family began to feel the disintegrating impact of individualism following the emancipation. This was manifested in numerous family divisions, notwithstanding certain economic advantages possessed by a large peasant family. In the 1880's the government became so alarmed over the adverse effects of family divisions that it tried to restrain them by law. Such restraint, however, was unavailing and served only to provide an additional source of vexation to the peasant.

This all adds up to a picture of the liberated Russian peasantry remaining "a peasant nation consistently segregated from the general life of the community (state)," instead of being drawn closer to the rest of the citizenry.[10] Such a view has not been seriously challenged. Writing fifty years later, as moderate a political thinker as V. A. Maklakov likened the postemancipation status of the Russian peasant to a "kind of caste" [11] — an oppressed caste, we may add — lorded over by the chinovniki and their stooges.

The segregation or insulation of the peasant class was enhanced by the growing cultural lag between the town and the country. Culturally, urban Russia made great strides during the second half of the nineteenth century with a significant democratization and broadening of the predominantly upper-class culture. But this progress hardly touched the Russian village, which continued to live in ignorance. Precious little was done by the Tsarist government even to stamp out wholesale illiteracy until the revolution of 1905. On the contrary, it did its best to hamper the educational and cultural activities undertaken by the local self-government (zemstvo), private organizations, and public-spirited individuals. The government attitude was summed up by a well-known authority, N. N. Kovalevsky, as follows:

The principal objective of the government was not to spread popular education as widely and as rapidly as possible, but to ward off some kind of a danger to the nation because the people will acquire too much knowledge unnecessarily through schools and books, and will broaden their intellectual horizon. There are still not a few persons who are convinced that popular ignorance is the best guarantee of social order.[12]

"The access of peasants to books was hindered to the utmost by the authorities; lectures and talks in the village, even when dealing with strictly specialized subjects, met actually almost insurmountable obstacles," wrote the eminent Russian economist and educator, A. A. Manuilov.[13]

It was the consensus of experts and observers of Russian rural condi-

---

[10] I. M. Strakhovsky, in *Krest'ianskii stroi* (St. Petersburg, 1905), I, 388.
[11] V. A. Maklakov, "The Agrarian Problem in Russia before the Revolution," *Russian Review*, IX (January 1950), 3–15.
[12] Prokopovich, 54.
[13] A. A. Manuilov, *Pozemel'nyi vopros v Rossii* (Moscow, 1905), 47.

tions at the turn of the century that the legal, social, and cultural isolation and ignorance of the liberated peasantry failed to develop its power of initiative, stifled the spirit of enterprise, and tended to reinforce the natural inertia. Thus it also contributed to the growing economic destitution caused by the inadequate land allotment in many areas and aggravated by a rapidly growing population and heavy fiscal burdens. This situation was complicated by a transition from a self-sufficient to a money economy and by inadequate outlets for the surplus manpower. These were lacking because of slow industrial development, failure to encourage agricultural resettlement, legal restrictions on mobility, and insufficient improvement and intensification of agricultural techniques. The latter process was, in turn, retarded by peasant poverty and the consequent shortage of capital, inadequate markets for farm products, lack of know-how, cultural backwardness of the farm population, and lack of agronomic assistance.

The idea that all was not well with emancipated rural Russia began to gain ground in the public mind soon after the emancipation reform. As a matter of fact, as we saw above, serious criticism of the reform began with its very proclamation. A decade later, in 1872, an official commission of inquiry into rural conditions was set up, the Valuev Commission, before which much pessimistic testimony was given. Twenty years later, following the catastrophic famine in 1891, an even gloomier view that the Russian village was in the throes of a serious crisis because of increasing impoverishment gained wide acceptance. The paradox of a chronic undernourishment of the farm population in a country which had become one of the leading exporters of grain and other foodstuffs was stressed by numerous observers and witnesses before the official investigating commissions, such as that established under the chairmanship of the Minister of Finance, Count Witte. The increase in the number of peasant households without work horses and the generally poor condition of peasant livestock lacking an adequate feed-supply base, the increasing parceling of peasant holdings, the piling up of tax arrears — these were some of the symptoms of the growing deterioration of peasant agriculture.

If the peasant could still, with some difficulty, keep his head above water in years of good or average harvests, he was faced with disaster when crops failed, as they often did, especially in the large semiarid belt of Russia. Famine conditions, epidemics, increased mortality, decrease in the number of livestock (including work horses which, by striking at the sole source of farm power, did more than anything else to undermine the very foundation of peasant farming) — this is the spectacle of the growing destitution of a famine-stricken Russian village. The adverse effects of such conditions were felt long after the worst of the famine had passed. What Kipling wrote of the Indian peasant in the 1890's could be applied to his Russian counterpart as well: "His life is a long-drawn question between a crop and a crop."

The chronic rural distress should not obscure the fact that there always had been a small group which was economically better off than the great mass of the peasants. Leadership in the village and also a tendency to exploit the poorer peasants through usurious loans, and such, was often characteristic of this group. Such economic stratification in the village was noted, for instance, as early as the 1870's by the astute observer, A. N. Engel'gardt, in his celebrated *Letters from the Village* which, incidentally, can still be read with much interest and were recently republished by the Soviets.[14] But growing economic stratification in the village was particularly stressed by Marxist socialist writers, who appeared on the scene in the 1880's. At that time a split took place in the Russian socialist movement between the new orthodox Marxist wing and the older populist (*narodnik*) or agrarian-minded current which based its socialist ideology on the peasant mir and not on the industrial proletariat. A vigorous controversy developed between the Marxists and the populists concerning the trend of economic development of Russia and, more specifically, the inevitability of its passing through a capitalist stage. The populists took a dim view of this. The Marxists, on the contrary, found supporting evidence for their traditional analysis of economic development (which postulates class stratification and polarization concomitant with the growth of capitalism) in the stratification process taking place in the Russian village. They claimed that the mir system with its egalitarian tendency of land tenure retarded but did not eliminate this process. However, in their preoccupation with economics, the Marxists neglected other influences in rural stratification, notably the demographic factor — that is, the composition and the size of the family. These, as Kaufman, Chaianov, and others showed, played an important role in the process of village stratification. Larger and stronger peasant holdings were usually associated with larger families, and vice versa.[15]

The public discussion of the agrarian question and the toil of scholars and official investigating commissions produced copious and highly valuable material on rural conditions in Russia for which a student of Russian agrarian history must be eternally grateful. But they did not result in any serious corrective measures until the revolution of 1905. To be sure, the peasant had the active sympathy of the progressive Russian intelligentsia which considered it a sacred duty to help the poverty-stricken masses. As ill-paid doctors, teachers, nurses, and zemstvo workers, the

[14] A. N. Engel'gardt, *Iz derevni. 12 pisem 1872–1877* (Moscow, 1937).
[15] The larger the family, the greater as a rule the number of workers as well as of the mouths to be fed. This meant that more land could be and needed to be taken on from the mir or leased from the neighboring estate or fellow peasants. If a large peasant family, however, was short of work horses or farm equipment, some of its workhands could seek employment in the city and, with the money thus earned, purchase the needed draft animals and implements. See A. A. Kaufman, *Voprosy ekonomiki i statistiki krest'ianskogo khoziaistva* (Moscow, 1918), 19–20; A. A. Chaianov, *Organizatsiia krest'ianskogo khoziaistva* (Moscow, 1925), chs. 1–2.

intellectuals threw themselves unsparingly into this work, undeterred by the discouraging opposition and persecution of the government. Famine relief especially brought out strenuous efforts by the intelligentsia on behalf of the stricken population. But all this devotion was a drop in the ocean of peasant need. However, it greatly helped to keep the issue in the public spotlight. And so did the sympathetic interest in the peasant by the Russian literature of the pre-Soviet era, imbued with a strong humanitarian tradition.

The more radical populist section of the intelligentsia also tried, against great odds, to arouse the peasantry by spreading socialist propaganda in the villages. It considered the Russian peasant partly prepared to embrace socialism because it detected a socialist germ in the institution of peasant communal land tenure, the mir, to which even Karl Marx gave qualified approval.[16] But this socialist propaganda, even if it had not been quickly suppressed by the government, proved an abysmal failure. The peasants were not interested in socialism.

"What will you do," one of the propagandists (Zheliabov) asked a peasant whom he thought entirely converted to the socialist doctrine, "if you should get some five hundred rubles?" "Well, I will open a saloon," said the peasant.[17]

And what about the peasant's attitude toward the crisis? What was his solution? It could be summed up in two words: "more land." He saw the root of all his difficulties in a shortage of land and his only salvation in extension of the cultivated area. It was easier, of course, to continue the same type of farming in a larger area than to reorganize the system of farming on the old holdings, especially when capital and knowledge were lacking. Moreover, some holdings were too small for any practicable improvement of farming. There were also historical and psychological reasons for the peasants' attitude. There was the traditional view that only the tillers of the soil were entitled to land; hence the disappointment of the peasants when they did not obtain all the estate land after emancipation. What rankled most, however, was the loss of the land which they tilled as serfs on their own — the so-called *otrezki* (literally, cut-off land). Lenin sensed this feeling when he sought, as a means of enlisting the peasantry, the inclusion of a demand for restoration of *otrezki* in the platform of the Social Democratic Party.

While the peasants acquiesced in the new land arrangements more peacefully than the government expected, despite a number of local mutinies,[18] they never fully accepted them as a just solution. The peasants

[16] See David Mitrany, *Marx against the Peasant: A Study in Social Dogmatism* (Chapel Hill, 1951), 31–35.

[17] Milyoukov, 408.

[18] Kornilov, 175. It was, however, by no means a submission without a protest, inasmuch as there were more than 1,100 cases of disorders and uprisings in different villages during the two years 1861–1863. V. Gorn, *Krest'ianskiia dvizheniia za poltora veka* (Moscow, 1909), 29.

continued to dream, after emancipation, of a new partition of land to be ordered by the kind tsar, once he was able to overcome the resistance of the nobles and his ministers. Naturally, as the crisis deepened, they looked with increasingly covetous eyes on the broad acres of the "nobles' nests" which adjoined their narrow strips. How he could lay his hands on this land, of which he considered himself unjustly deprived, became the central preoccupation of the Russian peasant.

There was another influence which tended to reinforce this peasant outlook with respect to estate land. This was again the mir. I shall not deal here with the intense controversy, historical, economic, and ideological, which this institution provoked and which did not cease until the revolution of 1917. I only want to call attention to the central feature of the repartitional mir system: the peasant family held its strips of land not permanently (except for the homestead and the attached kitchen garden), but only until the next repartition. Then the holding could change both in size and location. Such repartitions took place at regular or irregular intervals. If the land was given up for one reason or another by a member, it reverted to the mir, which had the right to redistribute it. But the member still retained his right to an allotment. In other words, the peasant had a right to a holding but not to a particular holding; and he could not sell it. The actual farming unit, however, was the individual peasant household and not the mir, just as the kolkhoz is at present.

The repartitions of land and physical changes in holdings kept alive in the peasant mind the idea of the egalitarian distribution of land in accordance with the dictates of rough primitive justice. And why should such egalitarianism stop at the boundary line that divided the allotted from the estate lands? The peasant mind, unaccustomed to legalistic niceties, saw no reason for such a segregation. With his peculiar concept of the right to land and the continuing practice of flexible landholding, the peasant considered the property right of the landlords less than sacrosanct.

III

Until 1905 the peasants, while constantly dreaming of a new partition to relieve their distress, were nevertheless resorting to legal means of allaying their land hunger. They purchased some estate lands and leased a much larger proportion, often on difficult terms. But as we saw, abundant explosive material was accumulating for a revolutionary conflagration in the village. The spark was provided by the outbreak of revolutionary disturbances in the cities in 1905, following the unpopular and unsuccessful war with Japan. Unrest, punctuated by numerous *jacqueries*, spread through the countryside. In the new Russian parliament, the Duma, in 1906 and 1907 the peasant deputies clamored for distribution of estate lands. And again, as during the emancipation reform half a century earlier, they were generally supported by all the progressive elements of Russian society. Even the moderate liberals, the Kadets, strongly advocated distribution of a major part of the estate lands with fair compensation of the landowners, in order to increase holdings of the poorer peasants. Many liberals acknowledged that such a land reform was no panacea for Russia's agrarian ills, which stemmed fundamentally from agricultural underproduction. But, with the peasant temper being what it was, this was a first inevitable step in the solution of a difficult problem. The government itself, when the revolutionary disturbances were at their height, toyed with the idea of a land reform, proposed by the Minister of Agriculture, N. N. Kutler. But as soon as it felt that it was riding out the revolutionary squall, the government, reflecting the aspirations of the majority of the landowning class, adamantly turned its back on all such schemes.

However, as an alternative to the radical and liberal proposals, P. A. Stolypin as prime minister (1906–1911) enacted his own kind of agrarian reform, epitomized by his famous slogan, a "wager on the strong." Its essence was to split the peasantry by the development of a class of independent, economically viable peasant proprietors who would be attached to the principle of private property, and therefore better coexist with the estate system and act as a bulwark against any future revolution in the village.

With this end in view, legislation was passed aiming at the breakdown of the mir and individualization of the peasant land tenure and other property relations.[19] At the same time, much greater attention was paid by the government to technical progress in agriculture in its various aspects; much more was done in the way of technical and credit assistance to peasant farmers and encouragement of agricultural resettlement in Asiatic Russia. The redemption payments also ceased in 1907, while the gradual abolition of mutual collective responsibility for taxes began even earlier. The peasant could now sell his allotted land with some limitations. Some other legal disabilities were removed, and the Russian peasant doubtless became a freer individual than he was prior to 1905.

Central in this program, however, was the turnabout of the government with respect to mir tenure, which it had zealously guarded during the preceding half century. The new policy was not supported by many conservatives, who feared the sharp break with the paternalistic tradition, and it had a highly unfavorable reception among the liberal and radical opposition, including even those who were critical of the mir.

[19] For a discussion of the Stolypin legislation, see: Robinson, ch. 2; Pavlovsky; A. D. Bilimovich, "The Land Settlement," ch. 2, in A. N. Antsiferov and others, *Russian Agriculture during the War* (New Haven, 1930); N. P. Oganovsky, *Ocherki ekonomicheskoi geografii SSSR* (2nd ed., Moscow, 1924), 119–121. K. P. Kocharovsky, "Vykhody iz obshchiny," *Zapiski Instituta Izucheniia Rossii* (Prague), II (1925), 43–101.

It was felt that the government's antimir policy was too precipitate, too arbitrary, and, above all, sharply slanted in favor of a minority of the peasantry as against the great majority. Paul Miliukov sums up the opposition attitude thus:

The Stolypin reform tried to divert peasants from the division of the land of the nobles by the division of their own land for the benefit of the most prosperous part of the peasantry.[20]

Lenin, by the way, did not share this sentiemnt, common to the liberal and radical opposition. He wrote in 1912:

Most reactionary are those Kadets from the [newspapers] *Rech'* and *Russkie vedomosti*, who reproach Stolypin for the breakup [of the mir] instead of demonstrating the necessity of a more consistent and decisive breakup.[21]

The peasant reaction to the legislation may be gauged from the fact that out of more than nine million peasant households with communal land tenure in European Russia, about three million shifted voluntarily or involuntarily to hereditary tenure during the decade before the revolution of 1917.[22] Thus, despite all blandishments and pressure, a majority of the peasants were still clinging to mir tenure on the eve of the revolution.

Whether this phase of Stolypin's policy contributed materially to agricultural progress, of which there was some after the revolution of 1905, is a debatable question. But this should not obscure the fact that other government measures, such as those leading to consolidation and segregation of fragmented peasant holdings, were clearly beneficial. Apart from any positive government action, however, the revolutionary storm and the freer climate after 1905, despite the reactionary character of the postrevolutionary political regime, doubtless had an energizing effect on the village. The vigorous growth during this period of the rural voluntary cooperative movement was a significant manifestation of the new spirit of grass-roots initiative.[23]

Even in the matter of land, though the revolutionary disturbances of 1905 were suppressed and peasant aspirations for a new partition thwarted, many landowners became insecure and anxious to liquidate their estate properties at a good price. Thus, the acquisition of estate land by peasants through purchasing from landlords, which began soon after the emancipation, gathered momentum after 1905. It was assisted by the much expanded financial aid of a special government institution — the Peasant Bank. To be sure, a smaller area was involved and a stiffer price was exacted than would have been the case under the proposed

[20] "Respublika ili monarkhiia," *Krest'ianskaia rossiia* (Prague, 1923), 54.
[21] V. I. Lenin, *Sochineniia* (2nd ed., Moscow, 1931), XVI, 14.
[22] Kocharovsky, 55. The number of households is based on the 1905 land census. See I. V. Chernyshev, *Sel'skoe khoziaistvo dovoennoi rossii i SSSR* (Moscow, Leningrad, 1926), 39.
[23] See E. M. Kayden and A. N. Antsiferov, *The Cooperative Movement in Russia during the War* (New Haven, 1929).

liberal land-reform schemes of 1906–1907. Furthermore, the land often
did not pass into the hands of those who needed it most. Be this as it
may, about 30 per cent of the estate area was purchased by peasants
between 1861 and the revolution of 1917. And on the eve of the revolution, small peasant farmers owned approximately two thirds of all land
in European Russia outside of the public domain, which consisted mostly
of nonagricultural land.[24]

Peasant agriculture also extended eastward as the growing railroad
network opened new agricultural areas for large-scale settlement beyond
the Volga and the Urals. This colonization process, resembling in some
respects the westward expansion of agriculture in the United States, was
aided by the peasant disappointment produced by the abortive 1905
Revolution as well as by the lifting of various legal obstacles to mobility
and by positive measures of government assistance. While speaking of
the railroads, their effect in a country of vast distances in reducing the
cultural and especially the economic self-sufficiency of the village and
bringing it within the orbit of the market and money economy cannot
be overestimated. Another important factor of change was the industrial
revolution, which began in earnest during the closing decade of the nineteenth century. It expanded the domestic market for farm products and
created new employment outlets for the underemployed rural manpower.
Also the growth of the industrial working class, subject to strong radical
propaganda by the intelligentsia, was bound to have political repercussions in the countryside, the more so since ties between the young Russian
city proletariat and the village were far from sundered.

It seems legitimate to speculate that if a prolonged and exhausting
war, culminating in a revolution and civil war, had not intervened in
1914–1918, agricultural improvement would have continued. If, in conjunction with such progress, the Stolypin policy of the "wager on the
strong" could have been further implemented for a period of several
decades, it is possible, though by no means certain, that the projected
bulwark against an agrarian revolution might have been created. Again,
it is probable that if a land reform could have been speedily enacted
after the overthrow of the monarchy in 1917 by the democratic Provisional Government — and the difficulties of such an undertaking cannot be exaggerated — a peasant revolution might have been obviated.
But all this was not to be.

IV

The contest of the peasant with the landlord and the Tsarist state
over land, which runs like a red thread through centuries of Russian

[24] N. P. Oganovsky, Sel'skoe khoziaistvo Rossii v XX veke: Sbornik statistiko-
ekonomicheskikh svedenii za 1901–1922 g.g. (Moscow, 1923), 60–61; A. N. Chelint-
sev, "Pomeshchich'e khoziaistvo v Rossie pered revolutsiei," Zapiski Instituta Izucheniia
Rossii, I (1925), 10.

history, ended with the long-anticipated and dreaded total partition of land (*chernyi peredel*). Not only was the whole estate system drawn into this vortex, but also the consolidated and segregated "Stolypin" peasant holdings. It was a total triumph for the small peasant farmer, culminating a process which began sixty years earlier with the emancipation.

Lenin and his followers, who did their best to inflame peasant passions before the seizure of power, gave official blessing to the partition in the famous Land Decree. Here was Lenin's unabashed flirtation with the populist peasantophile ideology, which he had previously so often roundly condemned. It did not last long, however. After a brief honeymoon, a new conflict developed between the peasant and the Communist party-state, imbued with all its traditional Marxist suspicion and disdain for small-peasant agriculture as a putative breeding ground of capitalism and an inefficient form of production. The latter notion stems from the classical Marxist dogma of the superiority of large-scale methods of production in agriculture as in industry. For Lenin this doctrine was reinforced by an unbounded enthusiasm for that American invention, the tractor, considered *ipso facto* a powerful vehicle of collectivism. According to him, if the peasants were given one hundred thousand tractors, which he acknowledged was a fantasy at the time, this would sway them in favor of Communism.[25] He did not live to see the horrors of collectivization.

Important as these ideological factors are, there is another perhaps overriding cause of the perennial peasant-Communist conflict. If the Tsarist state was bent on protecting the interests of the landowning class, with which the governing bureaucracy was strongly infused, the Communist regime has been preoccupied with the problem of extracting from the countryside foodstuffs for the growing industrial working class, on which it originally based itself. But the regime, bent on a rapid industrialization and primarily on developing heavy industry, did not want (and in the early years of its existence was unable) to compensate the peasant farmers properly. It preferred to exact, in a colonialist fashion, what Stalin in a frank moment called "something of a tribute"[26] — a tribute, of course, on the altar of collectivist industrialization. This squeeze, which evokes memories of the fiscal pressures of the postemancipation period, was manifested in price relationships between the monopolistic state industry and agriculture which were disadvantageous to the latter (the famous "scissors") in shortages and poor quality of manufactured goods, and in high taxes. Here is the principal basis of the peasant-Communist conflict, further accentuated, of course, by ideological factors.

Epitomized as a "struggle for bread," it was the key to War Com-

[25] Lenin, XXIV, 170.
[26] J. V. Stalin, *Sochineniia* (13 vols.; Moscow, 1946–1951), V, 12, 49–56.

munism (1918–1921) with its forced requisitions of farm products. It was likewise central in Lenin's decision to take a breathing spell through the NEP. Again, the struggle for grain, intensified by the growing requirements of Stalin's all-out industrialization, was at the root of the jettisoning of the NEP and of the horrible rural collectivization and man-made famine in the countryside of the early 1930's.

The rather short-lived NEP, viewed in retrospect, was probably one of the happiest periods in the Russian peasant's existence; he was more of his own master than at any time before or since. It is true that he had no voice in the government and that the land was legally nationalized. The peasant nevertheless was actually in full control of his small holding. Though excessive parceling of landholdings was not conducive to efficient farming, the peasant managed to make a living. Such grievances as he had over taxes and prices and shortage of capital pale into insignificance compared to what was to follow.

I shall not dwell here on the ordeal of collectivization during the early 1930's, which even Stalin found worse than that of the war, according to his confession to Churchill. A highly revealing document which recently came to light confirms once more the reports of the horrors perpetrated during the collectivization campaign. It is a secret Stalin-Molotov letter of May 8, 1933, addressed to all party and government agencies, including the secret police:

The Central Committee and the Sovnarkom are informed that disorderly mass arrests in the countryside are still a part of the practice of our officials. Such arrests are made by chairmen of kolkhoz administrations, by chairmen of village soviets and secretaries of party cells, by *raion* and *krai* officials; arrests are made by all who desire to, and who, strictly speaking, have no right to make arrests. It is not surprising that in such a saturnalia of arrests, organs which do have the right to arrest, including the organs of the OGPU, perpetrate arrests without basis, acting according to the rule: "First arrest, and then investigate." [27]

Consolidation of the fragmented peasant holdings, an operation which Stolypin and his Minister of Agriculture, Krivoshein, began in the name of individualism and which the revolution destroyed, was accomplished on a sweeping scale by Stalin in the name of collectivism; but it was at terrible cost, human and economic.

In the kolkhoz, the peasant found himself during the Stalin era a residual claimant to an uncertain and meager income after the state took its large share and provision was made for capital and current collective expenses. The method of payment, based on the so-called "workdays," was exceedingly complicated. By a steep differentiation of the remuneration system, based on skill and technology, a new economic stratification (tractor and combine operators) was created in the modern Russian village.

The Soviet rhetoric about kolkhoz democracy and self-government

[27] Merle Fainsod, *Smolensk under Soviet Rule* (Cambridge, Mass., 1958), 185.

proved to be merely fiction. Just as the prerevolutionary "elected" village officers were tools of the Tsarist officials, so are the kolkhoz "elected" officers usually stooges of the Communist officials by whom they are normally appointed and replaced at will. At least a member of the mir had a great deal to say about the repartition of land which was usually accomplished in a democratic fashion. And he was, of course, his own master on his little strips within the limits imposed by the usually common crop-rotation cycle. The kolkhoznik is fully subordinated in his work relations to the kolkhoz management over which he normally has no control. Thus, he differs from the ordinary Soviet factory or state-farm hired worker merely in that he does not receive a regular wage and must share with his fellow kolkhozniki the considerable risks of agricultural production.

Only on his little kitchen-garden plot is the peasant a complete master. Incidentally, a kitchen garden is allotted to the household as a whole and not to individuals, though the former may be penalized for the sins of its members. Since kolkhozniki, in addition to their kitchen gardens, privately own a considerable proportion of the livestock population, there is a significant dichotomy in the collective-farm structure. Thus the peasant is a kind of Janus, facing both toward the kolkhoz and toward his small private farming, which is especially dear to his heart. Since the private farming competes with the collective-farm economy for the labor and loyalty of kolkhozniki, the Kremlin has been looking with a jaundiced eye upon this dichotomy and pursuing an ambivalent policy with respect to the "acre and a cow" farming of kolkhozniki, now restricting and now relaxing. But the importance of this sector in the national food supply — though it is declining — and in maintaining peasant morale explains the reluctance of the Kremlin to dispense altogether with this thorn in its side.

Regimentation of the peasantry not only has not relaxed since the war but actually has heightened. The screw has been tightened, especially since the kolkhozy began to be merged into giant supercollectives during the last years of Stalin's life, with the consequently increased gap between the management, often consisting of outsiders, and the rank-and-file membership. This campaign, spearheaded by Khrushchev and continued after Stalin's death, resulted in a decrease in the number of kolkhozy from more than 250,000 in the beginning of 1950 to 89,000 at the beginning of 1955.[28] Since then, a section of the peasantry became even more firmly tied to the collectivist chariot, when a number of kolkhozy were converted into or merged with large state farms (*sovkhozy*). In these units the peasant becomes formally a wage-earning worker just as if he were employed in a factory, but he usually retains the little kitchen garden.

[28] *Narodnoe khoziaistvo SSSR v 1956 godu: Statisticheskii ezhegodnik* (Moscow, 1957), 139.

The seriousness of this move, which has not been accompanied by the usual Soviet fanfare and publicity, may be gauged from the fact that during the first six months of 1957 the number of kolkhozy decreased from 84,800 to 78,900, while the number of state farms correspondingly increased from 5,099 to 5,773.[29]

To a considerable extent, the conversion of collectives was concentrated in certain areas. The most important was that beyond the Volga and the Urals, in the so-called "new lands" zone, where large tracts of virgin land were brought under cultivation during the years from 1954 to 1956. This has been the *locus classicus* of Soviet large-scale mechanized farming. Since new capital investment was required to expand, conversion of collectives, together with machine-tractor stations (MTS) servicing them, to sovkhozy was a logical step. The situation was similar in the irrigated cotton-growing regions of the Uzbek Republic in Central Asia, where, likewise, new investment by the state to extend or reconstruct the irrigation network was needed. Still another area of conversion was the zone of German occupation during the war, where collective farming disintegrated and, though restored after the end of hostilities, remained weak.

But, even after making allowance for such specific regional and economic factors, the scale and the tempo of conversion posed the question whether this trend was likely to continue. Were we, in other words, witnessing the last stage in the proletarian transformation of the Russian peasantry, which so long and so tenaciously held on to the land and, even under serfdom, coined the slogan, "We are yours, but the land is ours"? This seemed to be the portent at the beginning of 1958, and it was bolstered by two additional lines of reasoning. First, the ideological line which postulates the superiority of the sovkhoz over the kolkhoz as a form of socialist organization — or, to use Soviet terminology, socialist property — and, implicity if not explicitly, points toward the former as the ultimate goal of collectivization. The second line is the fact that conversion also eliminates the dualism in management between the kolkhoz and the MTS with its attendant inefficiency. For in such an operation, both the kolkhoz and the MTS are absorbed in a sovkhoz.

However, a speech by Khrushchev in Minsk on January 22, 1958, reported in *Pravda* and *Izvestiia* on January 25, 1958, changed the whole complexion of things. For it heralded the beginning of another process, the absorption by the kolkhozy of the important functions of the MTS through purchase of their machinery and the reorganization of the MTS into mere repair-and-service centers. By the autumn of 1958, nearly 70 per cent of collectives purchased machinery from the MTS. If mass conversion of collectives into sovkhozy were contemplated in the immediate future, then why proceed in the opposite direction of strengthening the kolkhozy by allowing them to swallow the state property of the MTS, a

[29] *Forty Years of Soviet Power* (Moscow, 1958).

course, incidentally, which was tabooed by Stalin? As a matter of fact, Khrushchev and other Soviet spokesmen went to great lengths during the discussion of the new reform to boost the kolkhoz as a form of "socialist property" and to affirm the continued parallelism in the Soviet agrarian scheme of both the kolkhoz and the sovkhoz. Thus, the continued coexistence of the two types of socialized farming may be accepted as the prevailing official policy as of the end of 1958.[30]

The purchase of machinery from the MTS, involving the elimination of what Khrushchev called "two bosses on the land," doubtless enhanced the status of kolkhoz management. As to the rank-and-file peasantry, the impact differs between the skilled workers, like tractor drivers and combine operators, who were permanently employed by the MTS, and the ordinary kolkhozniki. The former were not only better paid but also had a more stable income through a guaranteed minimum wage. Now they were again joining the ranks of kolkhozniki as was largely the case prior to 1953–1954, when they were transferred to the permanent staffs of the MTS. Official pronouncements call for the retention of the prevailing minimium-wage system for the "cadres of mechanizers" transferred to the kolkhozy, but the extent to which this will be implemented raises some misgivings. The unskilled kolkhozniki, of course, would not suffer from any downgrading of the earnings of the skilled and might even benefit from such leveling. In the long run, both the skilled and unskilled kolkhozniki may gain from increased efficiency, a probable result of doing away with the dualism in farm management. But this gain will also depend on the extent to which the kolkhozy will be permitted to retain the fruits of increased efficiency. The present official emphasis on prospective lowering of state prices for farm products, unaccompanied by a sharp reduction of the high-priced manufactured goods, does not augur well.

How will kolkhozniki fare in the immediate future? Here it is essential to note the beginning of an improvement in the economic position of kolkhoz peasantry since the lean days of the Stalin era, when the reliance was placed principally on the proverbial stick rather than the carrot. This period was characterized by a large volume of compulsory deliveries of farm products to the state, and by very low prices paid for such deliveries. The reform of the procurement system and a substantial increase of prices of farm products in 1953–1954 by the post-Stalin regime made it possible to increase cash payments by kolkhozy to their members from 12.4 billion rubles in 1952 or a very low figure of 62.3 rubles per kolkhoz household, to 42.2 billion or 2,142 rubles per household in 1956. During the same period the total cash income of the kolkhozy increased from 42.8 billion rubles to 94.5 billion. Whereas in 1952, 29 per cent of the total cash income was distributed among kolkhozniki, in 1956 the propor-

[30] This is not to say that this policy may not suddenly veer in the opposite direction. There are many precedents for a zigzag course.

tion rose to 45 per cent of a total income that was double in size.[31] To be sure, there are some offsetting factors — mainly the declining receipts of kolkhozniki from sales on the kolkhoz (free) market. It can be also argued that the cash payments to the kolkhozniki could have been larger if kolkhoz investments were smaller and less wasteful; if, for example, the "cow palaces," the far too solidly constructed barns observed in the Soviet countryside, were not built.

Yet it cannot be gainsaid that the cash payments to kolkhozniki advanced substantially during 1954–1957 from their previous low level. While information on the still very important payments in kind is fragmentary, they probably also manifested an upward trend with increased production. The crucial question, then, is whether this trend may not be arrested because of the official pressure for heavy expenditures to purchase machinery from the MTS. Only time can supply an answer, but the danger certainly must be recognized.

v

It is time now to ask the key question: what does the review of a century of Russian peasant history reveal regarding basic continuity and change? First, as pointed out at the outset, the very persistence of the peasant problem throughout the century, despite the shrinkage of the agrarian sector in the national economy, exhibits a thread of continuity. But there have been significant changes. Until collectivization became an accomplished fact, the central issue for the Russian peasant was to expand and safeguard his possession of the land and be free to dispose of its product. This may still be the ideal of the Soviet peasantry. Attachment to such an ideal may explain in large measure the peasant's clinging to his little private plot. I say "may" because we have no objective information about the peasant's aspirations and moods as we had during the war, the peasants tried to jettison the kolkhoz in the occupied zone.

Be that as it may, there is enough evidence available from Soviet sources regarding the peasant's economic behavior and reactions to leave little doubt of his acute awareness of his economic interest and determination to act upon it within the framework and limitations imposed by the collectivist society. This explains the stress laid by the post-Stalin agrarian policy on economic incentives as a means of enlisting the peasant's cooperation in production.[32]

There are, of course, other significant changes, such as the predominant

---

[31] Cash payments to kolkhozniki reported by Khrushchev, *Pravda* and *Izvestiia*, January 25, 1958; number of peasant households and cash income of kolhozy, *Narodnoe khoziaistvo SSSR v 1956 godu*, 140.

[32] See Lazar Volin, "The Malenkov-Khrushchev New Economic Policy," *Journal of Political Economy*, LXII (June 1954), 187–209; and "Soviet Agricultural Policy After Stalin: Results and Prospects," *Journal of Farm Economics*, XXXVIII (May 1956), 274–286.

literacy of the peasant population, compared with the wholesale illiteracy at the beginning of the century. With this may be associated the impact of the new farm technology as a broadening influence on the peasant outlook and as an aid in the ascent up the economic ladder through the acquisition of new skills.

But perhaps the outstanding break in the historic continuity has been the reversal by collectivization of the trend toward independent peasant farming — the increasing proletarization of the peasant. Perhaps the peasant's status in Soviet society is epitomized by the old kolkhoznik's remark to a Soviet bureaucrat in Nikolai Zhadanov's fine short story, "A Trip to the Homeland," in the second volume of *Literary Moscow:* "You then are the bosses, we — the producers." And yet the kolkhozniki fare better than the Chinese peasants, whose thousands of years of family farming seem to have have been completely broken by the new serfdom of the communes.

THE RUSSIAN URBAN WORKER: FROM SERF TO PROLETARIAN

JERZY G. GLIKSMAN

The emancipation of the serfs in 1861 and the upheaval in industry and agriculture of 1928–1932 are undoubtedly the crucial milestones on the road to the formation of the Russian working class as we know it today. Emerging from serfs and peasantry, this class acquired the features of a modern urban proletariat in the continuous process of industrialization of the country.

I

Serf labor played a prominent role both in the first industrial enterprises of Muscovy and during the period of growth in Russian industry initiated by the reforms of Peter. It has been established, however, that for some years before emancipation there was a strong tendency to replace serf labor by more productive hired labor. Employers who were able to hire free workers competed successfully with those who did not; the proportion of hired labor was increasing rapidly and even began to predominate in many manufacturing industries. A law of June 18, 1840, allowing the liberation of serf factory workmen under certain conditions, facilitated this process.[1]

[1] M. Tugan-Baranovsky, *Russkaia fabrika v proshlom i nastoiashchem* (St. Petersburg, 1898), I, 151ff.

By 1860 industrial serf labor was still predominant in mining and metallurgy, but serfs formed only about one third of the total industrial labor force of approximately 800,000.[2] During these years before emancipation, however, the industrial labor force was neither quantitatively nor qualitatively adequate for the needs of an expanding industry. Recruitment of free workers was one of the main difficulties confronting the industrial entrepreneur. Emancipation improved the situation radically by creating an initial manpower reservoir of at least four million rural people, whom the reform left either landless or with extremely small allotments. The peasant manpower reservoir remained unexhausted for many decades.

Because of the high rate of natural increase among the rural population, and the continuing economic hardships incidental to emancipation, the number of village inhabitants seeking employment in the growing industries of the cities increased rapidly if intermittently. The emigration of the peasants was hampered, however, by certain rules which made it difficult for members of the *obshchina* (rural commune) to leave the village for any extended period. In the early postreform years, 1861–1870, the number of so-called long-term passports issued to peasants leaving for extended work in urban industries averaged 59,200 per year. It increased to 184,500 per year in the wake of the industrial expansion that occurred during the period from 1891 to 1900.[3] Under the impetus of this active migratory movement, the numerical growth of the industrial workers in Russia was rapid. During the quarter century following emancipation, the number of workers employed in large industrial enterprises, such as factories, mines, and railroads, increased from 706,000 to 1,432,000.[4] On the eve of World War I, the total number of industrial workers in Russia had reached the three and a half million mark.[5]

II

Inevitably the peasant origin of the bulk of Russia's urban workers stamped them with certain rural characteristics. Not only did they master industrial skills more slowly than Western workers, who came largely from generations of artisans and craftsmen, but their enduring links with

[2] A. G. Rashin, *Formirovanie promyshlennogo proletariata v Rossii* (Moscow, 1940), 91–92.

[3] P. I. Liashchenko, *Istoriia narodnogo khoziaistva SSSR* (2 vols., 3rd ed., Moscow, 1952), II, 28. It is unclear in Liashchenko's context whether the figure of 1,845,000 which he gives for the 1891–1900 period is an average annual figure, like the one for the years 1861–1870, or an aggregate for the ten-year period. In view of the magnitude of the figure, however, only the latter seems plausible.

[4] Computed by Lenin in his study "Razvitie kapitalizma v Rossii" (1899), *Sochineniia* (4th ed., Moscow, 1946), III, 436.

[5] *Dostizheniia sovetskoi vlasti za sorok let v tsifrakh: statisticheskii sbornik* (Moscow, 1957), 50.

the countryside also delayed their transformation into a modern industrial labor class.[6]

To begin with, there existed certain legal links tying the Russian worker to the village of his origin. Even after many years of continuous employment in industry, sometimes reaching down to the second or third generation, the emigrants from the countryside would remain legally within the *soslovie* (estate) of peasantry. By the turn of the century, about nine tenths of all Russian urban workers were so classified.[7] However, this was merely a passport classification and was of little practical consequence. More important, for the majority of the new workers, were the effects of the other legal link with the country, that of belonging to the obshchina. Up to the Stolypin reform, the former peasant, although now settled in the city, remained legally a member of the obshchina. Membership in the commune included the formal right to participate in the redistribution of land. In most cases, however, it was a *privilegium odiosum* to the new worker, for in practice it carried with it, up to 1903, liability to taxes levied by the obshchina and the duty to fulfill periodically the formalities connected with obtaining the obshchina's consent for the renewal of the worker's passport.[8] The legal association with the obshchina undoubtedly retarded for a long period the psychological divorce of the newly urbanized worker from his native village.

Much more important than these legal relationships were the strong economic and personal ties that bound the new urban workers to rural life. The patterns of urban-rural relations were quite diversified. Some of the workers had land in the villages, with relatives tilling it. They had come to the cities reluctantly, under the pressure of poverty, to supplement their agricultural earnings. Schulze-Gävernitz, in his description of Russian industrial life of the period, stresses the hatred felt by these persons toward factory work. Mainly heads of families, they would return periodically to their homes, often for prolonged intervals, to help with the field work. While in the city they would regularly remit a portion of their earnings to their families. By generalizing from the attitude of this group, Russian economists and sociologists of populist tendencies used to deny the very existence in Russia of a working class as an identifiable social group.

Besides those urbans workers who retained a strong attachment to their villages, there were others whose bonds with their previous rural life were rapidly fading away. These were mostly people without land or house in the place of their birth. They were most often young unmarried

[6] The term "class" as used in this chapter combines objective and subjective criteria and denotes a social group having a common occupational function, a consciousness of belonging, a distinctive social status, and the possession of certain basic common values.

[7] Liashchenko, 165.

[8] Tugan-Baranovsky, 416–417.

people or people whose family ties in the village were disintegrating under economic pressures. They were ready to become permanent industrial workers and to plan a future in the city.

Between these two extremes lay people with various degrees of rural attachment that determined whether and how their economic, social, and psychological assimilation to industrial life would occur.

There were also economic factors in the urban environment which delayed the formation of permanent cadres of industrial workers. Because of bad housing conditions a great many urban workers could not create for themselves a normal family life. According to the 1897 census, about 60 per cent of the workers in European Russia lived alone, and the average worker's family consisted of only 1.98 persons although an average family in the population as a whole consisted of 5.63 persons.[9] Life in wretched, employer-owned barracks, perhaps in one corner of a crowded room, was all that most Russian workers of the period could expect. This was hardly conducive to the national increase of their kind.[10]

The low level of wages was an even more important obstacle to the growth of an urban proletariat. A series of workers' budget surveys, conducted in various industrial cities during 1908–1910, revealed the close connection between the level of wages and the family situation of the worker. These surveys showed that only workers who earned at least 400 rubles a year, that is, skilled or semiskilled workers, maintained a normal family life, while the majority, who earned on the average less than 300 rubles, usually could not afford to support a wife.[11] A budget survey of 1908 in St. Petersburg, where the level of wages was above the national average, found that among a select group of workers (earning an average yearly wage of 472 rubles) nine tenths of those who earned less than 400 rubles lived alone, and only those with wages above 600 rubles tended to have families with children. The higher the father's earnings, the greater the number of children.[12]

Despite the unfavorable conditions for a natural increase among the industrial workers, some progress was made, and at the turn of the century between one third and two thirds of the industrial workers were what we may call "hereditary proletarians," that is, persons whose fathers had

[9] S. N. Prokopovich, "Krest'ianstvo i poreformennaia fabrika," *Velikaia reforma*, (6 vols.; Moscow, 1911), VI, 269. One must note, however, that according to the rules of the census the workers with families in the villages were registered as single.

[10] K. A. Pazhitnov, *Polozhenie rabochago klassa v Rossii* (n. p., 1906), 47–55, 125–139.

[11] According to S. G. Strumilin, the average yearly wage of an adult worker in Russia in the years 1908–1910 was about 290 rubles; see "Oplata promyshlennykh rabochikh v Rossii za 1900–1916 gody," *Problemy ekonomiki truda* (Moscow, 1957), 463.

[12] Prokopovich, in *Velikaia reforma*, 274; S. N. Prokopovich, *Narodnoe khoziaistvo SSSR* (New York, 1952), 65–72.

been factory workers.[13] Moreover, it should be noted that a favorable change was probably introduced into the family situation of the workers by the fact that the proportion of women among wage-earners was increasing: by 1913 women already formed almost one third of all factory workers.[14]

In the formation of a class of urban laborers a significant role was played by the trend toward a concentration of Russian industry. First, the bulk of industry was located in a few geographical regions. Second, employment was concentrated to a high degree in large-scale enterprises. This peculiarity of the Russian economy was partly due to the substantial foreign investment in Russian industrial development. Even in the eighteenth century many Russian factories employed 1,000 or more workers, a few individual mining enterprises in the Urals counting up to 3,000 workers on their payrolls.[15] The concentration of employment in large economic units was still further intensified after emancipation. While in 1866 enterprises with 1,000 and more workers employed 27 per cent of all workers in large-scale industry (enterprises employing over 100 workers), in 1890 this proportion reached 46 per cent.[16] By 1913 about 44 per cent of *all* factory workers were employed in enterprises with 1,000 or more workers,[17] a greater proportion than in England, Germany, or the United States.

The concentration of workers in large-scale enterprises, it is generally agreed, created among them a consciousness of fellowship in the factory community which replaced the old loyalties to the village. Moreover, it facilitated the propagandistic and organizational activities of various socialist and trade-unionist groups, all striving to bring about a crystallization of the class consciousness of the workers by appealing to their material interests.

The concentration of production in large units was often accompanied by increased mechanization, thus creating a growing need for a better-trained labor force. Russian industry, however, could draw but a negligible number of recruits from the small group of urban artisans. Even the peasant *kustari* (cottage-industry workers), who were compelled to give up work in their homes under the pressure of competition from factory-produced goods, formed a relatively small element in the factory labor force compared with the great mass of plain land-tilling peasants who entered it. Under such conditions the emergence of skilled cadres of industrial workers was considerably retarded. The former peasants, however, were gradually acquiring factory experience and learning new

[13] Rashin, 390–403.
[14] Strumilin, 462.
[15] Rashin, 20, 43–49.
[16] Lenin's computation, 447.
[17] *Dostizheniia,* 49.

trades in response to the demand for skilled factory labor. Their accomplishments strengthened their ties with industry.

Workers employed in mechanized production severed their relations with the land more easily as a rule, than manual workers. This was demonstrated in the 1880's by an industrial survey of a large part of Moscow province, which established that a high percentage of the manual workers returned to the country in the summer for field work, while those working with machines seldom did so. For instance, 82 per cent of the hand-loom cotton weavers used to return to their villages, but none of those weaving cloth on power looms.[18] In summary, as Russian industry matured the former peasants in the city acquired new skills, obtained employment in the mechanized branches of industry, and were generally inclined to become permanent industrial workers.

III

Contrary forces pulled at the emerging Russian urban labor class, some of them tending to integrate the former peasants into the industrial environment, others to draw them back into their former mode of life. This dual influence was partly responsible for generating the great debate of the 1880's and 1890's concerning the economic future and the prospects for a social revolution in Russia. The populists, with their extreme anti-industrial bias, were obviously waging a losing battle with reality by insisting that all urban workers were peasants temporarily seeking a marginal part of their incomes from industrial work. On the other hand, some of the Marxists overstated the separation of the industrial workers, "the carriers of the revolution," from their former rural milieu.[19]

In spite of what has been said, we lack the statistical data for a thorough understanding of the changes in the Russian urban labor force during the prerevolutionary period. Several contemparary Russian economists and sociologists were inclined to estimate the rural ties of the workers by the percentage of them who owned land and returned more or less regularly to their native villages for field work. Because of the intense contemporary interest in the growth of the urban labor force, several surveys were conducted at the end of the nineteenth century and the beginning of the twentieth.[20] The data obtained, though sometimes quite interesting within their limited scope, were rather fragmentary and showed wide fluctuations from region to region and from industry to

[18] E. M. Dement'ev, *Fabrika: chto ona daet naseleniiu i chto ona u nego beret* (Moscow, 1897), 4–11, 26, 36, quoted in Tugan-Baranovsky, 413–414.

[19] The "carriers of the revolution" theory *à rebours* also prevailed in some government circles concerned with the security of the regime. Donald Mackenzie Wallace reports that Witte, because of his proindustrialization policies, was accused by these circles of being "a revolutionist, with secret, malevolent intentions." *Russia* (London, 1912), 670.

[20] Several of these surveys are analyzed in Rashin, 403–417.

industry. The results often depended on the year, or even the season of the year, when the investigation took place. On the whole, the results of the several surveys were not comparable, nor were they a sufficient basis for any general quantitative conclusions.

Even the most comprehensive of these investigations was far from satisfactory. The labor census taken in the fall of 1918, which included about one million workers in various branches of industry in thirty-one provinces of Russia (the Ukraine, the Urals, and Siberia were not covered), revealed that immediately before the revolution one third of the workers investigated owned land and about one fifth also tilled it with the help of their family members.[21] But this census was taken at an atypical moment, when workers with rural connections had recently returned *en masse* to their native villages. For this reason the figures of the 1918 census cannot be regarded as an accurate reflection of the situation on the eve of the revolution.

The extent and intensity of the workers' rural ties are clearly not the only criteria that should be considered in assessing their maturity as a separate social class. No less relevant are subjective factors, such as the workers' attitudes and their sense of belonging to a group having common interests — that is, their class consciousness. It should be recalled in this connection that in the early 1880's Leroy-Beaulieu still saw in Russia only the "raw material" for a class-conscious and "ambitious" proletariat. To be sure, the crystallization of the political and social consciousness of the workers progressed noticeably with the development of capitalism. It found its expression in the intermittent but violent strike waves of the last decades of the nineteenth century, which culminated in the revolutionary events of 1905 and, finally, in the heavy involvement of the workers in the 1917 upheavals.

All the available evidence, a small part of which has just been reviewed, points to the conclusion that economic and social development in the half-century preceding the 1917 revolution generated permanent cadres of industrial workers who tended to form a separate social unit with the characteristics of a modern urban working class. On the other hand, on the eve of the revolution the urban labor force was extremely small in relation to the total population (estimated at about 140 million in 1913) and far from homogeneous in character. In fact, its most distinctive feature was its mixed composition, which varied with the passage of time and the increasing assimilation of the workers to industrial life. In brief, this group had a dual character, half-peasant and half-proletarian.

The revolution of 1917 affected the social status of the workers in many respects but did not initially change the dual character of the industrial labor force. In the period of War Communism this duality revealed itself

[21] Rashin, 412–414.

conspicuously when great masses of unemployed workers took advantage of their rural connections to flee from the famine-ridden cities and to participate in the redistribution of land. Soon thereafter the NEP reversed the trend and the number of industrial workers increased but in 1928 the industrial labor force, estimated at 3.1 million, remained smaller than it had been in 1913.[22]

The industrialization drive which began in 1928 immediately created the need for a great expansion of the labor force. The peasantry continued to be, as in the prerevolutionary years, the main source of the urban labor supply. The villages continued to harbor large numbers of underemployed persons. The distribution of the great estates among the peasants did little to alleviate rural overpopulation, while the subsequent collectivization of peasant holdings was bound to increase it. At first, collectivization tended somewhat to hinder migration to the cities, and thus, *mutatis mutandis,* the events of the immediate postemancipation years repeated themselves. The catastrophic famine in the villages, however, and the harsh measures against those who opposed collectivization brought about a mass exodus from the villages.[23]

During the First Five Year Plan the number of industrial workers almost doubled.[24] We have no vital statistics on the three million new industrial workers, so we do not know their origins. We do know, however, that the labor force as a whole increased by about twelve and a half million during the 1928–1932 period, and that more than two thirds came from the countryside.[25] It may reasonably be assumed that the proportion of former peasants among the newly recruited industrial workers was even higher.

The dynamics of labor growth during the First Five Year Plan was, by all odds, unique in the light of later Soviet history. Under the subsequent five-year plans developments took a somewhat different turn.

The rate of growth of the labor force, still immense in comparison with other industrial countries, slowed down steadily. During the Second Five Year Plan the number of industrial workers grew by less than one third.[26] It then took two decades, 1937–1956, for their number to grow by

---

[22] *Dostizheniia,* 50.

[23] For a detailed description of the developments in the early period of collectivization, see S. M. Schwarz, *Labor in the Soviet Union* (Syracuse, 1952), 7–20.

[24] *Narodnoe khoziaistvo SSSR v 1956 godu: statisticheskii ezhegodnik* (Moscow, 1957), 50.

[25] *Itogi vypolneniia pervogo piatiletnego plana razvitiia narodnogo khoziaistva SSSR* (Moscow, 1933), 174.

[26] Gregory Grossman accounts for the relatively low increase in the number of industrial workers during this period by the fact that the huge flow of labor into industry during the First Five Year Plan was not really absorbed until the following plan; see "Some Current Trends in Soviet Capital Formation," *Capital Formation and Economic Growth* (Princeton, 1956), 174n.

about 85 per cent.[27] In absolute terms, the influx of peasants into the cities was still quite sizable, and there were even occasional increases in the number of new arrivals with a rural background, as for instance during the immediate postwar period. In the years 1950–1954 some nine million people moved from the countryside to work in the cities.[28] But on the whole the proportion of rural people entering urban occupations has been declining significantly since the 1930's.

More and more of the industrial recruits have been persons of urban origin not previously engaged in production. New workers have been drawn from pauperized former members of the middle classes, unemployed youth, and particularly women, including housewives. The proportion of women among wage-earners and salaried workers in industry rose from 28 per cent in 1929 to 45 per cent in 1956.[29] Of course, once the workers enjoyed conditions favorable to a natural increase in their numbers, this became a regular source of labor supply. A sizable proportion of the new workers are now the children of workers.

As far as the future is concerned, Soviet planners recognize that the once vast rural reservoir of manpower has greatly diminished. The serious effort to improve agricultural output, under way since September 1953, has greatly curtailed rural recruitment for industry. Indeed, the drive to develop virgin lands has compelled the regime to transfer to agriculture a considerable number of city dwellers, mostly young people. No increase in the availability of labor from the villages can be expected in the future unless the government effects a reorganization of agriculture even more profound than the recent plan for dissolving the machine-tractor stations. But such measures are long-range and unpredictable.

IV

The Soviet worker's economic environment has exerted a far-reaching influence on his social status. The marked expansion of the Soviet economy was accompanied by a greatly increased trend toward the concentration and mechanization of industry. In 1955, about 62 per cent of the workers in large-scale manufacturing industry were employed in enterprises with 1,000 or more workers.[30] The degree of mechanization can be deduced from official data. These tell us that, between 1928 and 1956, the consump-

[27] The number of industrial workers was 6 million in 1932, 7.9 million in 1937, and 14.7 million in 1956. These figures do not include certain marginal categories of industrial workers, nor do they include those employed in some minor subsidiary enterprises. For the sake of data comparability, the half million members of the cooperatives taken over by the state in 1956 were excluded from the 1956 figure of the total number of industrial workers. *Narodnoe khoziaistvo*, 50.

[28] Khrushchev's speech at the January 1955 session of the Central Committee of the CPSU, *Trud*, February 3, 1955.

[29] *Narodnoe khoziaistvo*, 206.

[30] *Narodnoe khoziaistvo*, 48.

tion of electric power per industrial worker increased almost tenfold [31] and that, between 1940 and 1957, the size of the machine-tool inventory increased by a factor of 2.6, and the number of presses and forges in use by a factor of 3.2.[32]

After the beginning of the industrialization drive, a tremendous effort was made by the Soviet authorities to provide vocational training for millions of new workers who, as a rule, lacked any previous mechanical aptitudes or experience. Harsh disciplinary and coercive measures were applied to restrain labor mobility, absenteeism, and tardiness, and to teach new workers the value of time, orderly habits, and precision in work. In the process, old peasant patterns of life and behavior were uprooted.

The attractions and opportunities of farm life had weakened considerably. Under the system of collectivized agriculture, the peasants moving into the cities usually had neither desire nor opportunity to return to the countryside. This had a crucial effect on their attitude toward their new life. Most of them were young people "who did not care to farm any more, who were ready to become city folks."[33] Thus a voluntary return to agriculture by any substantial group of the Soviet workers became rather unlikely.

Advancement to administrative, supervisory, technical, and managerial positions became a common phenomenon among the more experienced workers during the first two decades after the revolution. In the process there emerged a new privileged, bureaucratic, and professional class with a proletarian background. As one would expect, this class quickly developed a desire to preserve its status from one generation to the next. While the principle of equality of opportunity, a sacrosanct part of the revolutionary tradition, still applies in practice to a certain extent, and while the workers' chances for advancement have not disappeared, there are considerably fewer opportunities for "promotion from the ranks" than there were in the twenties and thirties.[34] The factors restricting mobility between classes have been strengthened, and the early fluidity of Soviet society has given place to a far more stable pattern not altogether unlike that prevailing in Western industrial societies.

While the Soviet leadership clearly encourages the workers to improve their skills by education, it has to counteract the apparently widespread inclination to use education as a springboard to nonmanual occupations. Differences in educational and economic standards divide the workers into several strata, but the great mass of the urban workers now form a distinct social entity, with more or less clear boundaries.

[31] *Dostizheniia*, 53.
[32] *Narodnoe khoziaistvo*, 58.
[33] Schwarz, 19–20.
[34] For a discussion of the problem of social mobility in Soviet society in the Stalin period, see Alex Inkeles, "Social Stratification and Mobility in the Soviet Union: 1940–1950," *American Sociological Review*, XV (August 1950), 465–479.

V

Is this Soviet working class, we may ask, comparable in social status to its counterpart in the advanced Western industrial societies? More specifically, can it be called an urban *proletariat,* the term applied in Soviet literature to the working masses of the *capitalist* world? This is more than a question of semantics; it goes to the core of social stratification in the USSR.

The economic function of the workers is almost identical in both systems. Workers in the Soviet Union and in the West do the same kind of work in a very similar factory environment, whose character is determined on both sides largely by the technology of mass production. Both groups of workers have to sell their labor in order to live. The workers in the advanced Western countries have, however, a much greater bargaining power than the Soviet workers. The existence of free trade unions and the possibility of exerting political pressure strengthens the workers' position. Under the Soviet system the workers are not only deprived of these advantages, but are in addition subject to strong political, administrative, and propaganda pressures designed to make them accept the state's terms regarding wages and working conditions. In practice, however, the burden of these pressures is somewhat alleviated by the existence of full employment in the Soviet economy.

The worker in the advanced capitalist countries has an incomparably higher over-all standard of life and is subject to much easier rules of labor disicipline than the Soviet worker. In certain branches of welfare, particularly in facilities for medical assistance and education, the situation of some workers in the West compares unfavorably with that in the USSR. In both types of society, however, the average wage of the workers is usually below that of people doing nonmanual work; in both, physical labor is classed below brain work in prestige and importance. The constant efforts of the Soviet authorities to build up the prestige of manual labor have not altered the situation to any great degree.

Clearly there are basic parallels in economic function, working conditions, and social status between the workers in the Soviet Union and in the West. Soviet ideologists, however, admit no such similarities; they claim that the workers' position in a socialist society is necessarily different in essence from that of the worker under capitalism. This distinction underlies the standard, Marxist-derived, Soviet definition of the term "proletariat." It is only "by force of habit," as Stalin put it, that the word is used for the Soviet working class. Properly speaking, runs the official line, a proletariat is an exploited group that can exist only under a system of private ownership of the means of production and a market economy. In relation to the facts of Soviet life, of course, this line of reasoning is spurious. The Soviet definition of the proletariat as a group that has no real influence either on the disposition of the means of production or on the distribution of "surplus value" [35] very well describes the case of the Soviet workers.

As Bertrand de Jouvenel has pointed out in a recent assessment of Marx's theory of class struggle, the old fight between classes for the possession of "surplus value" ("the workers wishing to obtain the whole of it and to apply it to consumption, the capitalists wanting to retain as much of it as possible, and to apply it to investment") has found its parallel in the Soviet Union, where the government plays the part of the capitalist.[36] There can be little doubt that the conflict of interests between the employer and the individual worker, which Soviet writers regard as typical of the capitalist West, is to be found to a marked degree in the Soviet Union. Moreover, the Soviet system renders the worker much weaker in the economic struggle than his Western counterpart. The workers of the USSR, indeed, proved too weak to prevent the recurrence of some of those methods of primitive accumulation which are said to have marked the early stages of capitalism. Low real wages and inadequate housing accompanied industrial expansion in the USSR as they did earlier in the West. The Soviet leadership, while maintaining complete control over the distribution of the "surplus value," has applied various techniques to maximize it. These techniques have included the application of a heavy-handed system of incentives, rising work norms, "socialist emulation," and the whole range of speed-up devices underlying the three successive, officially sponsored movements called *udarnichestvo, stakhanovism,* and *novatorstvo.*

The reforms of the post-Stalin period have not altered any of the fundamental features of Soviet labor policy. True, some rather important improvements in the condition of the workers have been introduced. The most repressive features of the labor laws, particularly court penalties for violation of labor discipline, were abolished in 1956. In the same year, and in the early months of 1957, the abysmally low pensions for the aged and the disabled were increased, maternity leaves were lengthened, and the procedure for examining labor disputes was revised so as to enhance the role of the trade unions. The working week was shortened from 48 to 46 hours, and for some categories of workers to 40–42 hours. Last but not least, the meager wages of the lowest-paid workers were increased.

[35] V. S. Nemchinov, "Velikaia oktiabr'skaia revoliutsiia i izmenenie klassovoi struktury sovetskogo obshchestva," in Akademiia Obshchestvennykh Nauk pri Tsk KPSS, *Vsemirnoistoricheskoe znachenie velikoi oktiabr'skoi sotsialisticheskoi revoliutsii* (Moscow, 1957), 54ff. To be sure, the use of all subjective criteria for class definition is ruled out by Nemchinov as "unscientific," as is any distinction between classes based on differences in living conditions, size of income, or even ownership of property, as long as this property does not include means of production. Even the Western sociological term "class stratification" is rejected.

[36] Bertrand de Jouvenel, "On the Character of the Soviet Economy," *Bulletin of the Atomic Scientists* (November 1957), 329.

At present, too, the whole Soviet wage structure is being subjected to a systematic overhauling and modernization, with what results we do not yet know.

These long overdue reforms, it is generally agreed, have their roots not merely in the change of leadership and the general political thaw, but even more in the very nature of the new socioeconomic order that has begun to emerge in Russia after more than a quarter century of rapid industrialization. Under the new technological conditions of modern industry, with an urbanized labor force on the scene, the problem is no longer chiefly one of maintaining discipline, but rather one of evoking the initiative of the worker and of securing his goodwill. Moreover, the impending shortage of labor, which may affect significantly the rate of growth of the economy and the national income in the years to come,[37] is a crucial factor impelling the Soviet leadership to make concessions to the workers.

Reliable Western reports of labor restiveness and even occasional strikes in the USSR indicate that neither the new Soviet labor policy nor the recent material benefits accruing to the workers has eliminated their discontent. On the contrary, these changes have encouraged demands for more liberalization. The current flow of Soviet press reports suggests a widespread feeling among the workers that their demands for better housing and more consumer goods are not being met on an adequate scale.

Further, more substantial concessions to the workers and the mass of consumers will be less likely in proportion to the Soviet effort to force a more rapid development of heavy industry and military preparedness. This situation raises the question whether the Soviet regime will be able to continue its present course of internal relaxation without relinquishing at least some of its principal political, military, and economic goals, and whether, if faced with this choice, the regime will feel compelled to turn to more coercive methods.

THE MILITARY AS A SOCIAL FORCE

RAYMOND L. GARTHOFF

The pattern of change and continuity in Russian society over the past century has been the product of two complexes of determining factors: those common to the Tsarist and Soviet eras, and others specifi-

---

[37] M. Breev, "Nekotorye zakonomernosti raspredeleniia trudovykh resursov v SSSR," *Sotsialisticheskii trud,* no. 6 (June 1957), 38.

cally distinguished by the impact of the Russian revolution. It seems warranted and useful, even in its oversimplification, to identify the former on the whole with basically economic factors — above all, industrialization, with the many attendant social effects of urbanization. Similarly, the latter are most directly the political factors, though of course the origins of the revolution reflected the weakening of the social underpinnings of the political structure, and the consequences of the revolution were manifested in all aspects of life and society. In other words, the degree and direction of change in Russian society would have proceeded very much along certain of the lines which it has followed whether or not the revolution had occurred, while certain other lines have been given peculiar direction or impetus in consequence of the historical turns of Russian political developments. The evolution of the military as a social group and political force in Russian society markedly reflects these elements of historical continuity and disruption.

The present marks an uneasy comparison with the late nineteenth century — now, as then, a technological revolution is affecting military affairs and, in turn, the composition of the military. Now, as then, a new type of professional officer is coming into being. In a sense, a new military class is being born. But the differences are also quite significant. Then the military professionalization meant a contribution to the breakdown of a traditional, established social (and political) order; now the similar trend is as part of a broad build-up of a new class society. Now, as then, the military is largely apolitical — but for different reasons, against a different political trend in other classes of society, and with possibly different consequences. We shall return to these questions later.

I

The half century preceding the First World War was marked by important changes in the composition both of the Russian officer corps and of the enlisted ranks. The Crimean War, and later the Russian-Turkish and Russian-Japanese wars, pointed up a number of severe shortcomings in the personnel of the Russian army, as well as in the system of supply and level of weaponry.

From 1861 to 1881, War Minister Dmitri Miliutin (brother of the great reformer Nicholas Miliutin) instituted a series of important reforms of the army which had great significance for its subsequent social evolution.[1] The term of service of the enlisted man was in 1861 reduced from 25 to 16 years. Later, in 1874, there followed an unbonding of these virtual serf-soldiers, and compulsory universal military service was introduced. The

---

[1] The most complete account of these reforms, though not objective in its interpretation, is P. A. Zaionchkovsky, *Voennye reformy 1860–1870 godov v Rossii* (Moscow, 1952), which includes a useful bibliographical essay. For a good brief account in English, see Alexander Kornilov, *Modern Russian History* (New York, 1924), 157–162.

term of active duty was again reduced, to a period varying from six months (for those with university education) to six years for those without complete primary education. In the 1860's and 1870's the soldier's training was also broadened to include achievement of literacy by those many who had not had sufficient schooling. Generous exemptions were granted (essentially on economic grounds) for "only sons" and other breadwinners. Finally, conditions of service and discipline became less harsh, and corporal punishment was abolished. By means of these measures equality of all classes before the law was established, and higher military standards were achieved as well.

Equally great changes were made in the selection and preparation of officers. From the 1860's on, an officer had to have experience as regimental commander before becoming eligible for general's rank. In the mid-1860's Miliutin converted most of the military schools into gymnasia, and established certain higher *junker* schools for technical specialties.

In the 1880's, after Miliutin's departure, the caste distinction of the officer corps was revived with encouragement by the government. Officers were exempted from the laws prohibiting duels. The military gymnasia were changed into "cadet corps" schools. In the 1885 manifesto on the creation of the Bank of the Nobility the wish was expressed that "the Russian nobles preserve a dominant place in the military leadership."[2] Nonetheless, the basic line of development of the new officers' corps was not affected. From 1861 to 1914 the continuing trend of the officer corps was evolution from partial and sometimes part-time service of a segment of the nobility toward a professionally and technically qualified group drawn from all classes. This trend was in part a reflection of the general social change produced by the growing industrialization, urbanization, educational progress, and other factors. But in part it was also a response to the definite needs of a modern army. As war and armaments became more technologically advanced, it was necessary to have officers with corresponding technical qualifications. In the war years 1812–1813 some 14 per cent of the military budget was spent on military ordnance and technology; in 1904–1905 this share had risen to 25 per cent; and in 1914–1915 it had jumped to 60 per cent. (In absolute terms the jump was also notable; from 80 million gold rubles in 1812–1813 to 12 billion in 1914–1915.[3]) Measures taken to overcome the technical backwardness that had been revealed in the wars naturally affected some branches more than others — the navy, engineers, and artillery more than the infantry and cavalry. But it pervaded all to some degree. The rise of technically qualified officers, regardless of their birth, was opposed by many traditionalist line officers, but it necessarily continued. In some cases, notably in respect to the navy, the line-officer corps preserved an aristocratic

---

[2] Cited in Kornilov, 162.
[3] Col. A. Lagovsky, *Strategiia i ekonomika* (Moscow, 1957), 9.

character by reluctantly admitting the growth of a separate corps of naval engineers and technical officers, the vast majority of whom were not from the nobility. The latter, products of special naval engineering and shipbuilding schools, with high standards, were for a long time denied naval ranks (they became colonels, and even generals, of the navy rather than captains and admirals), and when finally given epaulettes, the shoulder boards were narrower. Incidentally, these two features of distinctive discriminatory ranks and insignia remain today in the Soviet navy, though they have long ago been discarded by other modern navies that once used them.

What about the nontechnical officer corps? The Guards, navy officers of the line, and much of the cavalry held with determination to their aristocratic character and composition despite many difficulties. Indeed, mere noble birth was often insufficient, and the necessary standard of living required much more expenditure than provided by the salary. The Guards officers were drawn from certain select preparatory cadet corps schools which, by tradition, were restricted to the nobility and associated with specific Guards regiments. Even there, only about 60 per cent were from the hereditary nobility, another 28 per cent being sons of "personal nobles" (usually officers).[4] Only in 1913 were all schools actually opened to all qualified applicants. But in the army as a whole, in contrast to the Guards, considerable changes were occurring. Let us look at the pattern of composition of one of the average military schools in Moscow. In the late 1860's, 81 per cent were from the hereditary nobility and 9 per cent sons of personal nobles; in the late 1870's, some 45 per cent were from the nobility, 33 per cent were sons of personal nobles, 13 per cent were of bourgeois origin, and 11 per cent from the clergy. By the late 1880's, only 12 per cent were nobles, 57 per cent were personal nobles, 16 per cent bourgeoisie, and 5 per cent were from the peasantry. Finally, by the beginning of the First World War, 9 per cent were nobles, only 28 per cent personal nobles, 28 per cent were bourgeoisie, and 19 per cent peasants.[5] In fact, by 1912 even in the Academy of the General Staff only 48 per cent were hereditary nobles.[6] Such an outstanding general as Alekseev, last commander in chief under the tsar, was not from the nobility. General Denikin, later Alekseev's successor as commander in chief of the White army, was the grandson of a serf. Both were graduates of ordinary *junker* military schools open to all. The officer corps of the Russian army, of course, remained composed of "nobles" due to the provision of Russian law and society whereby a man of nonnoble birth auto-

---

[4] Nikolaus Basseches, *The Unknown Army* (New York, 1943), 59.

[5] Colonel Sventsitsky, cited by D. D. Fedotoff White, *The Growth of the Red Army* (Princeton, 1944), 43–44.

[6] General A. I. Denikin, *Staraia armiia* (Paris, 1929), 59.

matically acquired "personal" nobility upon reaching officer status. Upon reaching the rank of colonel, he would acquire hereditary nobility.

We are accustomed to thinking of the nineteenth and twentieth centuries as the era of the decline of old pre-Napoleonic professional armies, and the rise of mass citizen armies. But this is only one aspect of a complex phenomenon. While in one sense the illiterate Russian soldier of 1860 who was handed over by his master for twenty-five years' service was unquestionably "professional," the soldier of a few decades later was more in tune with the professional requirements of contemporary warfare. In the officer corps this was even more true. It was not so many decades earlier that military service had been a part-time duty levied on all nobles in Russia. In the early and middle nineteenth century, many of the aristocracy served only a few years of active duty and then retired to full-time social life. The average length of duty of officers rose from ten years under Nicholas I to eighteen years by the first decade of the 1900's.

The professionalization of the officer corps occurring in the period 1861 to 1914, would have eventually evolved into a new vertical stratum of society. But the initial effect, in this period, was the disintegration of the once homogeneous aristocratic military caste into a heterogeneous compound. Moreover, the emerging group tended to become increasingly isolated from the horizontally demarcated strata of civil society.

An additional factor in the situation was the nationality question. During much of the nineteenth century there existed a "seesaw" controversy over discipline and military doctrine which, both directly and indirectly (symbolically), involved the ethnic Great Russians set against the Baltic-German nobility. I earlier cited the statement in the 1885 manifesto favoring the preservation of "a dominant place in the military leadership" by "the Russian nobles." Again, the regular army had come to include a large number of officers and generals from the various nationalities of Russia (including the Baltic Germans), while the Guards schools and officers were at the turn of the century about 90 per cent staffed by Russian officers (the balance being largely from certain favored minorities such as the Baltic Germans and the Georgian princely families).[7]

The political complexion of the officer corps became quite pale. The vast majority of the officers prior to the revolution were staunchly conservative, and of course loyal, but essentially apolitical. The echoes of the Decembrists were very faint by the latter part of the nineteenth century, for no longer were the intelligentsia and officer class intimate — another effect of the growing isolation of the military class from the rest of society. True, the social mores and traditions of service to the emperor were reinforced by conceptions of military discipline which

[7] Basseches, 59.

inhibited active political interest. Moreover, the training of the officer was, while by no means inferior, simply not a liberal education. While the social composition of the officer corps became more varied, the regular officers continued to be drawn very largely from the military-school systems, which remained isolated from the ardently political and frequently radical universities. The apolitical stance of the officer corps was reflected in the fact that there were no attempts at a royalist counter-revolution after the proclamation of the Provisional Government. The Kornilov affair, the sole superficial exception, was more inspired by the combination of a misunderstanding and a fear of the rising Bolshevik extension; it did not represent the spearhead of a monarchist movement. Former imperial army and Guards officers have quite frankly acknowl-edged their prevailing political ignorance prior to the revolution, the product of a simple lack of interest in political affairs.

In the crisis of 1905 many officers proved politically unsure, and in the face of widespread passive opposition in the army to dispelling the rebels, the Guards proved the most reliable support of the regime. In view of this evident political immaturity of the officers, courses on po-litical science and current political events were instituted in the military schools in 1907.[8] Three years later, however, these courses were aban-doned, as they proved more provocative than palliative.

During the First World War, the officer corps underwent further rapid change. The heavy losses of the first year, especially among the Guards, seriously diluted both the officer corps and the regular troops. The 50,000 regular officers, to whom 35,000 reservists were added upon mobilization in 1914, together totalled less than the number of officer casualties in 1914–1916 alone.[9] While the casualties included many of the new wartime officers, the depletion of the regular prewar cadre officer corps was tremendous. Thus it was necessary to commission several hun-dred thousand new officers during the course of the war, usually men with very little military training except perhaps for noncommissioned service.[10]

By 1917 the officer corps was of a very different nature than it had been in 1914. The new officers were drawn from the largely peasant noncommissioned officer staff, and from the young intelligentsia; both groups, for varying reasons, had been patriotically imbued in the early years of the war, but by 1917 and 1918 they were little inclined to con-tinue the war. The "Guards Regiments" which decisively defected to the

---

[8] For some background to this measure, see Denikin, 147–148.

[9] General N. Golovin, *Voennyia usiliia Rossii v mirovoi voine* (2 vols.; Paris, 1939), I, 160, provides the figures for casualties — totalling 92,500 by the end of 1916 (including 15,000 held prisoner by the enemy). The estimates of officer active duty and reservist strengths in 1914 are based on the careful study of Colonel N. Piatnitsky, *Krasnaia armiia SSSR* (2 vols.; Paris, 1932), II, 14.

[10] Piatnitsky, 14.

revolution in 1917 were not the real Guards regiments, the remnants of which were at the front; they were the regimental training battalions which by 1917 had little opportunity for selectivity of personnel or training to accord with traditional standards.

The Imperial Russian officer corps had undergone substantial changes of social composition and attitude during the fifty years preceding the First World War. Like Russian society as a whole, it was adjusting to the changed economic conditions of the country and of the world. The political evolution, however, while moving reluctantly in the same direction, had failed to keep pace with the times.

II

The Bolshevik revolution marked a violent rupture in the trend of development of the officer corps — though it was not by any means a totally new departure, nor an entirely new group of men. During the Civil War between 50,000 and 100,000 officers of the old army were taken into the new Red army (while some 200,000 entered the White armies).[11] Perhaps as important, a little over 10,000 civil servants of the Ministry of War were absorbed, as well as the major part of the general staff and military academies of the old army.[12] By August 1920, over 48,000 former officers of the Imperial army had been taken into the Red army[13] — though, of course, very many of these were wartime promoted officers. In 1921 a large number of these old officers were dropped.[14] But more important than the numbers was the influence played by many of these former officers, which was very considerable indeed. A number of former career general-staff colonels and lieutenant colonels, in particular, exerted considerable influence — men such as S. S. Kamenev, Vatsetis, Shaposhnikov, Kork, Uborevich, Primakov, Lebedev, and many others. But while these professional officers — some representatives of the new prewar technical experts, others of the career military drawn from the nobility — played a very important role, they were not as politically influential as the new breed of military chiefs who arose from the Bolshevik Party (Frunze, Podvoisky, Voroshilov) and from the very process of the revolution itself (Budenny, Blücher, and others). These revolutionaries and guerrillas were often more hostile to the specialists on military science and on modern weapons than had been the old line

[11] The official Soviet figures show that a total of 314,180 former officers, noncommissioned officers, and rated medical personnel from the prerevolutionary army had entered the Red army by August 1920: in *Grazhdanskaia voina*, ed. A. S. Bubnov et al. (3 vols.; Moscow, 1928), II, 95. The estimate for the White armies is from Erich Wollenberg, *The Red Army* (London, 1938), 73.

[12] *Grazhdanskaia voina*, II, 95. The exact figure is 10,339.

[13] *Grazhdanskaia voina*, II, 95. This figure (48,409) is line commissioned officers only.

[14] *Grazhdanskaia voina*, II, 97–98. During 1921, 37,954 officers were dismissed, including 14,390 who had been officers in the *White* armies at one time.

officers thirty years earlier. Thus for a decade or so following the Civil War a conflict raged between the "proletarians" and the "military specialists."

Beginning in about 1931, the professionalization of the army was renewed in earnest. The old officers had continued to dominate military thinking, though by this time they were but a small minority of total officer strength.[15] A survey of military writers, in 1929, showed that over 80 per cent were former Imperial army officers, including over one third who were former colonels or generals. And of the 100 authors of the 1929 *Field Regulations,* 79 had been officers in the old army.[16] The key turning point was the advent in 1931 of Mikhail Tukhachevsky — nobleman, ex-lieutenant of the Guards, future marshal of the Red army — to *de facto* control of the army. The Red army moved toward modernization, and the officer corps toward a distinctive place in Soviet society.

From the time of the revolution on, the Bolshevik Party felt hard pressed to ensure the control and assimilation of the new officers. While as late as 1924 only 32 per cent of the officers were affiliated with the Communist Party, by 1928 an estimated 65 per cent were members.[17] But in 1928 only 32 per cent of the influential category of military writers were party members.[18] Moreover, although party membership increased, the data on social (class) origins show how dependent the Red army remained on "alien" elements. In 1923 the officer corps was composed of 13.6 per cent workers, 52.7 per cent peasants, and 33.7 per cent "others." By 1927 the comparable figures were 22.4 per cent workers, 56 per cent peasants, and only 21.6 per cent others. But let us look at the breakdown by categories of officers. As late as 1926, "higher officers" (generals) were 7.3 per cent workers, 31.2 per cent peasants, and 61.5 per cent "others." Similarly, "senior officers" were 44.7 per cent from the other classes, and even "middle-rank officers" were 20.6 per cent in this category.[19] Likewise, in the Zhukovsky Air Academy in 1922 only 40 per cent were "workers and peasants" and 35 per cent party members, but in 1927 while over 77 per cent were party members, still only 50 per cent were workers and peasants.[20]

---

[15] Piatnitsky, 116, states that the percentage of former Imperial officers declined from 76 per cent in 1918 to 10 per cent in 1930. N. Efimov in *Grazhdanskaia voina,* II, 106, notes that in 1923 30 per cent of the officers had prerevolutionary military education, and in 1926 this was 15 per cent.

[16] S. Nikitin-Zubrovsky, in *Voina i revoliutsiia* (Moscow), no. 9 (September 1929), 111–114.

[17] N. Efimov, in *Grazhdanskaia voina,* II, 108, cites the official 1924 figure; Wollenberg, 72–73, gives the later one.

[18] Nikitin-Zubrovsky, 101.

[19] All data above are taken from the official reports cited in *Grazhdanskaia voina,* II, 105–109.

[20] These figures were compiled by the author from official data given in the Soviet air force journal, *Vestnik vozdushnogo flota,* during the 1920's.

The Soviet regime did not rely upon increased party membership among the officers to provide party control. "Military commissars" were introduced in 1918 to control directly the military specialists, as all former imperial army officers were termed. The institution of political officers has of course remained ever since, and as Marshal Zhukov and the world were recently reminded, the party intends it to continue to remain very much alive.

As has been noted, the period of stabilization of the evolution of the new officer corps was especially marked during Marshal Tukhachevsky's ascendancy, from 1931 to 1937. Again, as in the latter part of the nineteenth century, the driving motive was the establishment of a professional group comprising specialists in the military art and in military technology. But this phenomenon also generated certain social aspects not congruent with the official ideology. The new officer class wanted a return of traditional and hierarchical personal ranks, insignia, privileges, and the opportunity to give these same advantages to their sons. Beginning with the mid-1930's a number of these demands were met. In 1935 ranks were restored, and while general officer grades were not given (until 1940), the creation of the rank of marshal was an "imperial" addition that had not been found even in the prerevolutionary army. New salary scales not only favored the military greatly, but also reflected the growing gap between officers and enlisted men and between junior and senior officers. A whole network of literally hundreds of special stores were established for the military officers and their families. Theaters and clubs for officers and their families only were established. In 1937, in exchange for the execution of Marshal Tukhachevsky and his associates, the Red army officer corps was presented with an ultramodern rest sanatorium, at Sochi.

The emerging new class of officers began to receive lessons in French, in polo, in dancing, and in the social graces. Many of the newly "cultured" Civil War heroes divorced their too-proletarian wives and married new young ladies with more appropriate social savoir-faire. It again became necessary, as before the revolution, for junior officers to have the approval of their commanding officers before they could marry. Count Ignat'ev, the imperial army attaché in Paris before the revolution, returned to the Soviet Union in the 1930's and became a consultant on precisely such matters of cultural form. Thus in respect to custom and deportment, as well as military art and tactics, "specialists" from the old regime were found indispensable.

As this process of evolution of a new military tradition and class was developing, the political development of Stalin's dictatorship burst into the great purge. The *chistka* wiped almost clean the slate of senior officers in the Red army — it is sufficient to recall that three of the five marshals, 13 of the 15 army commanders, 57 of the 85 corps commanders, and 110 of the 195 division commanders were purged.[21] Up to one half of the whole officer corps were adversely affected. Nonetheless, even this severe jolt to the new military class in the long run contributed to the emergence of a more homogeneous group. Those most hard hit by the purge were precisely the two old groups, the Old Bolsheviks who took to military affairs in the Civil War and subsequently remained, and the former Imperial officers. In this sense, then, the purge actually furthered the natural process of the rise of the new officers. Indeed, the rapidity of the rise of some individuals was astonishing: for example, Rychagov, a senior lieutenant in 1937, had become a lieutenant general three years later, and briefly (at age 35) commander in chief of the air forces in 1941.

The proportion of party members continued to grow, though irregularly, as the purges hit party members heavily and led to an increase in numbers of nonparty officers both in 1934 and in 1937–1938. Similarly, in the armed forces as a whole, party membership in 1939 was where it had been in 1931, about 50 per cent, some ten percentage points below its high of nearly 60 per cent in 1933.[22]

During this period prior to the war, the army finally became entirely a regular army, and the last of the territorial troops were integrated by 1939.[23] Large numbers of the new officers had become competent specialists in the mechanized and technical arms — the air forces, armored forces, and others. A professional military leadership was developing to meet the prevailing state of military technology.

Like the purge, the Second World War decimated the ranks of the prewar professional officer class but also contributed to raising its standing. Under the impact of the preliminary campaign in Poland and Finland, generals' ranks were restored, and new firm discipline was established in 1940. Saluting was now required, including even of noncommissioned officers by privates. The political officer, the military commissar, had been again raised to a coequal position in 1937, but after 1940 (except for a year in 1941–1942) he was again reduced to a position of nominal subordination to the commanding officer. In 1942 the *pogony*, the once-hated golden epaulettes, returned to adorn the new military elite. Guards units were formed, with extra pay and privileges. Finally, the officers were granted the opportunity to cultivate a "hereditary" line, by sending their sons to new exclusive cadet schools, established in 1943. These schools, like the new orders for valor and achievement, were named for distinguished Imperial military heroes — the Suvorov and Nakhimov

---

[21] See R. L. Garthoff, *Soviet Military Doctrine* (Glencoe, 1953), 220.

[22] Piatnitsky, I, 21, gives the 1931 and 1933 figures (and other data showing the rise during the 1920's and early 1930's). The 1939 figure was given by Marshal K. E. Voroshilov at the Eighteenth Party Congress, *Rech' na XVIII s"ezde VKP(b)* (Moscow, 1939), 12. Other official figures for the years 1933, 1934, 1935, are given by Voroshilov, in *Stat'i i rechi* (Moscow, 1936), 574, 611, *et passim*.

[23] Voroshilov, *Rech' na XVIII s"ezde VKP(b)*, 32.

(naval) schools. Young boys are accepted at the age of eight or nine, so that they literally grow up in an atmosphere of military caste.

The Soviet officer today is the only military representative of a modern world power to sport epaulettes and velvet lapels, leather boots, and a dress dirk at his side. Marshals (in several grades), generals, field-grade officers, and then junior officers are rigidly separated categories with segregated messes and recreational facilities. A field-grade officer and a company-grade officer are not social equals. Needless to say, relations to enlisted men, save in giving duty orders, would ordinarily exist only in availing oneself of the services of the aides or orderlies assigned to field-grade, as well as to general, officers.

A strong sense of social solidarity has come to pervade the military. In present-day Russia more than in any other major power, garrison life has continued to exist. This and other features of Soviet life have accentuated the solidarity which fellow officers feel in any army. Class inbreeding is even literally true; and while the example may not be typical, it is relevant to note that one of Marshal Zhukov's two daughters is married to the officer son of Marshal Vasilevsky and one to the nephew of Marshal Voroshilov. It is clear from accounts of Soviet career officers that the regular professional officers and their families tend very much to be drawn to one another. Ever since the early 1930's, the line is even usually drawn short of association with the political officers — and almost always avoids the secret-police counterintelligence officers in the armed forces.

Travel to the Soviet Union has created new opportunities to observe and talk with Soviet officers. From such contacts, it is abundantly clear that they, and their wives, are quite content with their security and high standard of living relative to the rest of the population. Young officers — and enlisted men — show none of the skeptical criticism of the regime which is remarkably widespread and sometimes entices away the students. The pride of young air-force lieutenants in their sharp uniforms, the superior air of smartly elegant colonels (keeping together) at Sochi, the deference shown a general entering a Moscow hotel — all are, while not unique phenomena, little signs of the pronounced class structure in the Soviet army.[24]

How does the emergence of a privileged military caste affect the social structure at large? As we have noted, the military tend more to associate only with their fellow officers than do the other privileged groups — artists, writers, scientists, and managers. But while there may be more interclass contact among some other groups, the current trend of all Soviet society is toward a pyramid of increased class stratification.

[24] These illustrations and comments are based primarily on the author's experience in meeting and talking with Soviet officers while traveling in the USSR in the summer of 1957.

Hence the evolution of a separate military caste within the privileged
social layer does not contradict the broader trend.

The recent growth of a military caste is thus quite different in its
import from the growth of a new military class in the late nineteenth
century, for then it was at the cost of contributing to the disintegration
of long-established rigidly stratified classes based on birth. On the other
hand, the new tendency does widen the gulf between officers and enlisted
men, and provokes a certain degree of resentment in the latter.

So we see that the period since about 1931 has marked the growth
of a new traditionalism and military class, in many ways reminiscent of
the traditional military class as it was developing from 1861 to 1914.
Some individuals have even spanned the whole period. The last of the
former imperial line officers to leave an active field command was Admiral
Panteleev, who retired from command of the Pacific Fleet only a few
years ago. But while in many ways present social status has much in
common with the older period, due both to circumstances and to conscious efforts to revive past tradition, the political effect of this sociological phenomenon is quite different.

III

As the military developed into a social class with distinctive features,
it could not fail to become to some degree a political entity, due to the
enforced politicization of all Soviet society. As an institution the military
could not fail to be affected by the shifting political weight of other
institutions. And particularly in the brief post-Stalin period, important
changes in the political balance of Soviet institutions have greatly altered
and increased the potential political role of the military.

The death of Stalin was a key event. All other Soviet institutions automatically became more important as the institution of the all-powerful
autocrat disappeared. In the ensuing political readjustment, first the
secret police and later the governmental and managerial bureaucracies
have all been weakened. While, to be sure, it is the Communist party
machine which has gained most in political power, the military has also
almost by default been raised in stature. Particularly as a consequence of
the unavoidable involvement of the military in issues weighted with strategic decisions, but also contested between factions of party rivals, the
senior military chiefs came to play a significant political role. There is
no evidence that the military was driven by political ambition. Nonetheless, the nature of the issues forced its political involvement. Finally,
Marshal Zhukov was removed after he had become a political figure and
sought to pursue certain policies. The fact that at least some of these
policies directly related to the role of the professional military class did
not signify that his fall from power removed the military from its institutional involvement or basically reduced its status, though it did mark an

abrupt decline in active representation of the military in national policy making.[25]

While the military has shown no inclination toward political opposition, it has also displayed no great positive political interest of any kind. The constant harping of the party on increased political indoctrination, and the intensity of the reaction to party presidium member Zhukov's desire to ensure that such nonsense did not interfere with raising the professional qualifications of the military, bear eloquent recent witness to the awareness by the Soviet leaders of the essentially apolitical posture of the military as a whole. To be sure, 86 per cent of the officers are affiliated with the party, but the Soviet leaders well realize that party membership ordinarily reflects a formality more than zeal.

Today, as in the latter half of the nineteenth century, a new technological revolution deeply affects the military. In the mid-twentieth-century technological reorientation of the army, just as in the last century, new specialists are needed — men conversant in the military application of such fields as nuclear energy, rocket power, and space flight.[26] The social disruption of the introduction of such men is much less severe now than eighty years ago, due both to the different pattern of society and to the tendency to train career military men in these specialties. Indeed there is a strong tendency to advance these very scientific and technological fields substantially through the medium of research in military institutions. But the cultivation of an apolitical attitude is furthered by this trend. Many of the new military scientific-technical men do not even deign to join the Communist Party. While presumably all unit commanders and staff officers of the rank of major and above must be party members, a number of technical specialists became generals without even joining the party. Despite the intensive political indoctrination in the armed forces and the advantage to career, the percentage of officers who are party members (86 per cent) failed to rise between 1952 and 1958.[27]

This trend toward renewed professional concentration on military-technical development accompanies a rejuvenated approach to questions of military science and the military art, attuning them to the opportunities and constraints of the new geopolitical and weapons world. The

[25] The changing role of the military in Soviet politics from 1953 to 1958 is discussed more fully in R. L. Garthoff, *Soviet Strategy in the Nuclear Age* (New York, 1958), 18–39.

[26] This stress upon the need for increased technological preparedness in military men is well reflected in Major General G. I. Pokrovsky's *Science and Technology in Contemporary War*, translation, ed. R. L. Garthoff (New York, 1959).

[27] Marshal A. Vasil'evsky stated in 1952 that 86.4 per cent of officers were members of the Communist Party and Komsomol (*Pravda*, October 10, 1952). Marshal R. Malinovsky said in early 1958, that "over 86 per cent" of officers are members of the party and Komsomol (*Pravda*, February 23, 1958), thus confirming that the figure was still between 86 and 87 per cent.

renaissance in both fields is very largely a product of the post-Stalin era, and both were advanced particularly by Marshal Zhukov during his tenure.[28] But as with the parallel trend under Marshal Tukhachevsky two decades earlier, the facts of life are causing a continuation of professionalization regardless of the political fate of the most prominent innovators.

What does this mean for the future? In another decade or two a new generation of officers will have risen, men who have a new outlook. Gone will be the durable marshals who, like Konev and Timoshenko, earned their spurs in the Civil War. New generals will have assumed the reins to whom the horse-drawn *tachanka* sporting a heavy machine gun will be as foreign as the bow and arrow. Their outlook will almost surely be less, rather than more, political — unless, of course, in the meantime the political structure has been rent asunder.

Thus the military has acquired outstanding social status, material rewards, and prestige. It has neither sought nor been given commensurate political power, and the Zhukov affair has doubtless served to inhibit the military from seeking a more active political role.

IV

In conclusion it seems useful to review two key aspects of change and continuity in the role of the military as a social force during the last century. These two particular aspects are highlighted in view of their fundamental significance: (1) social status and stratification, the privileged place of the military in society and the social structure; and (2) political prestige and power, the apparent and actual extent to which the military share in national decision making.

The social status of a given group is not always a reflection of its operating role in society, due largely to the familiar phenomenon of cultural lag in evolution. But such status is usually related to either past or present functional importance — or, at the least, to the image of functional importance. Russian society in the latter part of the nineteenth century was in process of gradual but reluctant adaptation to new conditions of life. The Russian nobility, unlike, for example, the English aristocracy at an earlier parallel stage of development, did not adjust to the new economic system by merging with the class of mercantile and industrial entrepreneurs. In the army, in the Petrine period, feudal primacy of rank and command based solely on aristocratic hierarchy was ended. The reforms of Miliutin in the 1860's and 1870's laid the basis for the increasing merger of those (including technical specialists) who came from various classes with the military career segment of the nobility. So

[28] The questions of military doctrinal and strategic evolution in the period from 1953 to 1958 are examined in detail in Garthoff, *Soviet Strategy in the Nuclear Age*, 61–91.

the military aristocracy, unlike the Russian autocracy and nobility as a whole, did come to terms with the changing needs of the times. By 1914 the evolutionary emergence of a new military class was well advanced; though friction was not absent, it was overcome. The general result was the raising of the new military class, with its heterogeneous origin, virtually into the social plane of the hereditary nobility.

This viable solution of the problem of adjustment of the new military class in the social structure was accompanied by a corresponding political accommodation — though under the prevailing conditions this meant very little in concrete terms. Nonetheless it represented a fact of major significance. There were no shortcomings in the relationship of the military class, as such, to the regime. The basic shortcomings were in the relationship of the regime to society as a whole. When the autocracy evaporated, the military served the new Provisional Government without question. In fact, a surprising proportion later served the radical Bolshevik regime voluntarily. This was in part a consequence of the fundamentally apolitical attitude which reigned over the broad expanse within the vague and shifting limits of patriotism which could stretch from Russian tsar to Russian commissar. In fact, it proved a stretch sometimes easier to bridge than that between strong liberal opposition to the old regime and acceptance of the new Bolshevik autocracy of the self-styled vanguard of the proletariat. And in its positive aspect, this superprofessionalism of the military indeed had a certain influence on the new regime. This was foreseen by the Old Bolshevik Mekhonoshin, who reportedly told Lenin, after fulfilling the latter's behest to evaluate the inherited bureaucracy of the Ministry of War, "This machine cannot be remodeled. It is more likely to change us than be changed by us." [29]

The new workers' and peasants' Red army was no more a continuation of the old imperial army than the new regime was of the old one. The early social egalitarianism of the society was mirrored in the army. But the army has also been fully apace of the subsequent rebirth of the new, and in some respects even more highly stratified social structure, which has evolved in the Soviet state. The present social standing, material reward, hierarchical system, and public prestige of the military in the Soviet Union is unsurpassed among contemporary world powers, and in relation to the modern imperial Russian past.

The political role of any social class is an integral and important part of its being, but there is neither a logically inherent nor a historically established necessity that the social function of any class and its importance to society as a whole should determine its political power. Armies and police forces, as the armed guardians of society, have a unique potential for influencing political decision. But their actual political power depends

[29] Cited by Wollenberg, 74; and by Colonel J. D. Hittle, *The Military Staff* (Harrisburg, 1949), 242.

on the structure and stability of society as a whole and on the accepted locus of decision making.

The Soviet army, like the Russian army of forty-one and more years ago, is today essentially apolitical. Nonetheless, its potential political role, in the light of changes in the internal Soviet political balance over the five years since Stalin's demise, is peculiarly great. The sensitivity of the ruling party machine to this high potential was evident in the preemptive ouster of Marshal Zhukov, the first spokesman for the military to have been admitted (if but briefly) to policy-making councils.

The privileged military caste in mid-twentieth-century Russia is one component in an increasingly stratified society. Whether it and all the other new privileged classes will indefinitely be content to permit a single artificial and parasitic class, the career Communist Party machine, to hold a monopoly of political power remains a question for the historian of the future.

SUMMARY AND REVIEW: SOCIAL STRATIFICATION IN THE MODERNIZATION OF RUSSIA

ALEX INKELES

I

Near the core of every revolution lies a problem in social stratification. Indeed, we may define a revolution as a sudden intensification of an established trend, or a sudden break in the continuity of development, in a society's stratification system. Admittedly this definition is not adequate to account for the multiform processes which revolutions generally encompass. I do not argue that revolutions are always, or even regularly, "caused" by strains in the stratification systems of society, although quite a good case could be made for that position.[1] But it may certainly be argued that changes in the stratification system are a universal accompaniment of political and economic revolutions, and that the unfolding of such revolution is always in significant degree reflected in the shifting patterns of stratification. This is no less true of slower processes of social change than those following from political revolutions. It applies equally to more general or diffuse processes of change, such as those summed up

[1] On the French Revolution, for example, see Elinor G. Barber, *The Bourgeoisie of 18th Century France* (Princeton, 1955).

in the idea of "the industrial revolution," and to more specific and geographically limited processes such as the modernization of Russia.

Stratification results from the fact that societies distribute or allocate "scarce goods" more or less unequally. By scarce goods we mean all objects or states which are recognized as of value in any society but are in limited supply. The tangible free goods most commonly cited are air and less often water, as against land or money, which are generally scarce. Among the intangibles, all sorts of honors, prestige, and respect are to some degree scarce, as against a state of grace or faith which probably qualifies as free goods. Max Weber distinguished three main realms or "orders" in social life, each with its distinctive allocated object and each yielding its own pattern of differentiation. The political order refers to the pattern for allocating power, the economic order to the allocation of goods and services, and the status order to the allocation of honor, prestige, or "standing" in the community. To these we should, perhaps, add several others, assigning a more independent role to realms which Weber subsumed under the term status, including a whole complex of factors he summed up as "style of life." In modern times we need to give more independent standing to what might be called the realm of "experience" — wherein are allocated access to aesthetic experience and opportunities for the development and expression of individual talents and needs. Another is the realm of knowledge, wherein are allocated the skills, information, and wisdom which are the collective heritage of the society.

Each of these realms or social orders is characterized by a pattern or organization, a set of rules, which determines the allocation of the realm's distinctive scarce good. These rules determine who gets what, when, and how. To the extent that a good is differentially distributed and the differentiation is relatively enduring, we have the fundamental condition underlying the phenomenon of social stratification. All those who have more or less equal chances for a share of the particular good are designated a stratum. Such strata may be sharply separated from each other and even prescribed by law. Such were the Tsarist estates, including the hereditary and personal nobility, honored citizens, large and small merchants, and peasants. Each held precisely defined rights and privileges, such as the right to own serfs or the exemption from corporal punishment. Strata are, however, equally likely to be separated only by imprecise and perhaps even arbitrary dividing lines. This is eminently true in the case of income, where the categories used are generally quite conventional, and modest shifts in the "cut-off" points are of little significance.

Sociologists working on stratification have generally concerned themselves with a limited range of problems. One set may be summarized as the mapping problems. Here the main interest has been in describing the distinctive patterns of differentiation in one or more of the social orders and identifying the individuals who compose the different strata. Studies of the strata in particular orders, such as the income classes of the economic order, are supplemented by other studies of more general interest which map the larger and more complex system of stratification for the society as a whole. Such studies attempt to determine the extent to which high or low position in the realm of power, income, or status bears a systematic relationship to the individual's position in the other stratification hierarchies. Mapping studies have been most commonly undertaken in the United States, where sociologists have pioneered great refinements in the instruments for measuring stratification. Much of their energy has gone into research and debate over whether the strata should be defined on the basis of "objective" indexes, such as income, or "subjective" indexes, such as the class or social group of which a person feels himself a part or to which he aspires. An echo of this controversy is to be found in Robert Feldmesser's contribution to this volume, since he argues that groups are real only insofar as they serve as "reference groups" for people. On those grounds he regards the Soviet Union as having only one class, "composed of that small clique occupying the top positions of control."

A second set of studies deals with the determinants of stratification, especially the mutual influences between the different stratification orders. In such studies the status dimension has most commonly been at the center of attention, the main interest being in discovering how changes in an individual's or group's income or power influence their "standing" or prestige in the community. Numerous illustrations of such concern are to be found in the contributions to this volume. To choose but one example, Raymond Garthoff calls our attention to the fact that in the Tsarist army an effort was made to preserve the fiction that the officer corps was a "noble" group, by granting personal nobility to all of commoner birth who entered its ranks and hereditary nobility to all who attained the rank of colonel.

A third set of problems are those dealing with the general laws for the development and change of stratification systems, especially as they relate to the society as a whole. In the classical works of sociology it was mainly this aspect of the study of stratification which attracted attention. Gumplowicz, Ratzenhofer, Oppenheimer, Marx, Pareto, Weber, all were interested in stratification mainly in its relation to the larger social order, and each sought to work out general laws governing the interchange between the stratification system and the larger society. A typical example would be Weber's hypothesis that in times of stability the status system generally lies at the heart of a society's pattern of stratification, but in times of rapid change the economic or class pattern of stratification comes to predominate as the basis of classification.

Interest in the development of such general laws has unfortunately greatly weakened in contemporary sociology. This is perhaps reflected in the essays in this section, none of which, with the possible exception of George Fischer's, is cast in a comparative framework or treats its topic systematically as illustrating a general law of social development. In fulfilling the chairman's role of providing a framework for the individual contributions in Part Three, "Social Stratification," I propose to supplement their rich empirical efforts by suggesting such a generalization or hypothesis and partially testing it against the facts in the Russian case. To simplify matters, I will restrict myself largely to the information given in this section. This should certainly constitute a stringent test of the propositions I advance, since there was no central directive dictating the emphasis in these essays, and no central tendency was "built in" in advance through selecting persons sharing a common disciplinary frame of reference — the contributors being a lawyer, a historian, a political scientist, a civil servant, and a sociologist.

I offer two propositions on the effects of the process of modernization on stratification systems. The first holds that the modernization of a traditional social system leads to a decrease in the degree of differentiation in each of the stratification subsystems or orders. That is, a process of relative homogenization takes place, reducing the gap or range separating the top and the bottom of the scale in income, status, power, experience (self-expression), and knowledge (skill). More important, in each hierarchy modernization brings about a marked increase in the proportion of the total population that falls in the same or adjacent strata near the middle of the distribution.[2] The prototypical elongated income pyramid, for example, becomes truncated; both the broad base and the sharp tip are eliminated, and in its place there is a trapezoid or perhaps even a diamond shape. The distance from the top to the bottom of the scale is reduced, and more people will be found sharing relatively the same position within a narrow range of the total scale. Movement from one to another position on the scale, furthermore, will not be sharply proscribed. Fluidity will characterize the system as a whole, especially with regard to individuals occupying adjacent or close positions in any given status hierarchy.

The second proposition holds that under conditions of modernization there is a tendency to equilibration within the stratification system as a whole, a tendency that is, for standing on any one of the stratification scales to be the same or similar to the individual's or group's relative

[2] It is important to stress the location of the "bulge" because in a traditional peasant-based society there is extraordinary homogeneity, or concentration of the majority of the population in a single stratum. Thus in Russia some 80 per cent were peasants experiencing fairly homogeneous conditions. But this bulge was at the bottom of the distribution and in terms of "range" very far removed indeed from the top of the hierarchy.

standing on the other scales. The traditional society abhors discrepancies in standing, but generates them in abundance because of the rigidity of the several stratification orders. By contrast, the modern society is relatively indifferent to such discrepancies, but its greater flexibility in fact tends to minimize their number.

These rather sweeping assertions cannot be fully or even adequately documented in a chapter as limited as this in size and topic. Some few illustrations may, however, serve to suggest the direction in which a fuller account would go. This brief excursion should also help to highlight some of the reservations and restrictions which must be applied to the propositions sketched above.

II

Modernization may be defined as the process whereby a nation effects the transition from one state of socioeconomic and political organization to another, specifically from a traditional social pattern to a mature industrial society. We may somewhat arbitrarily define a society as "mature industrial" if 50 per cent of the total labor force is engaged in construction, industrial production, or services such as medicine, education, transportation, and others not requiring mere manual labor or totally unskilled work. It is implied that the production units will be of large scale, that the ratio of tools used and power consumed per worker will be high, that a substantial proportion of the labor force will have a minimum of formal education and occupational training, and that labor will be allocated on a basis approximating the conditions of a free labor market. Urban conglomerates will predominate over rural residence, extensive rapid transit will be available, as well as a network of mass communication media.

A traditional society, the point of departure, is defined as one in which two thirds or more of the labor force is engaged in agriculture, primary extraction, nonmanual labor, or unskilled — mainly domestic — service occupations. It assumes the predominance of rural residence, a weakly developed transportation network, and markedly limited access to mass communications. The village community and the extended kinship system are strong. Values tend to be centered around traditionally validated belief, and the dominant tone of life, even in its mundane aspects, is religious rather than secular. Individual autonomy is limited, and the values are prescriptive — that is, they narrowly define appropriate goals, motivations, and means for their attainment.

There can be little doubt that during the period of modernization from 1861 on there was in each of the stratification orders in Russia a definite reduction in the distance separating the extremes, and in each realm of stratification there were unmistakable tendencies for the proportion sharing more or less common life chances to increase. In the status realm we can point to no dramatic decree disbanding the formal system of status ranks as a whole, but the emancipation of the serfs, with which we date the beginning of modernization, certainly must be taken as a markedly significant improvement in the general status of the peasant. Other evidence of the homogenization of status is called to our attention by Robert Feldmesser, who cites certain interesting facts concerning the regulations governing corporal punishment. Since physical punishment, especially whipping, is in significant degree administered to demean a person, we may take it as a rough measure of an individual's status or social worth that he is exempted from it. We note with special interest, therefore, that in 1762 only nobles were exempt from corporal punishment, but twenty years later the merchants won this exemption, followed by all town inhabitants in 1863, and finally the peasants in 1904. This is clear evidence of the diffusion of a status privilege initially available to only the highest strata of the society. It is important to note, in this connection, that to our knowledge the application of the terror under the Soviet regime granted no particular favor according to the rank of its victims, either in interrogation practice or in assignment to camps.

The story of the revolutionary attack on the formal status system of the old order is well known, but perhaps not always correctly understood. The elimination of all titles, special forms of address, and legal privileges of the Tsarist nobility and other ranks was certainly in part motivated by equalitarian ideology. But the prime concern of the Soviet leaders was the destruction of the old status order which they saw as an important element of the larger Tsarist social system. Far from instituting strict equality, the new system asserted a new official status hierarchy, at the top of which stood the party, then manual workers, somewhat further down landless peasants, substantially below these clerical personnel and the "working" intelligentsia, and next middle peasants. Far below these came the somewhat more affluent peasants, or kulaks as they were later called, and last and virtually beyond the pale were all who had any standing in Tsarist society, including not only nobility, former officers, and civil servants of rank, but merchants, rentiers, and priests. Soviet Russia in the immediate postrevolutionary years was, therefore, a sharply stratified society. The strata were legally defined and frequently enjoyed markedly different privileges, as in the allotment of housing and ration cards. Their obligations also varied, as reflected in the fact that members of the former exploiting classes were to be called on first for such duties as street cleaning.[3]

In comparing later Soviet developments with the earlier period it is often stressed that the Soviets were unwilling or unable to maintain the marked equality of the early years. I submit that this emphasis is mis-

---

[3] For a review of these measures see Robert A. Feldmesser, "Aspects of Social Mobility in the Soviet Union" (unpublished dissertation, Harvard University, 1955).

placed. It is equally, indeed more, relevant to argue the lesson of Soviet experience to have been that in a modern industrial society Soviet leaders were unable to maintain the early *ine*quality and were in time forced to move in the direction of relative equalization of the formal status of all members of the society. In the Soviet Union today there are no formal legal distinctions of status. All citizens are at least formally equal before the law and the authorities.[4] This is not to deny that there is a definite status structure in Soviet society. But this system is informal and imprecise. It bears strong resemblance to the status system of the United States, which is generally acknowledged to have gone much further in equalizing or homogenizing status than have the industrial countries of Europe and Asia.

The greater homogenization in the access to experience and to knowledge is too evident to need to be argued at length. Traditional Tsarist society had a relatively closed stratification system. As modernization began, the needs of the state and of the expanding industry which it encouraged intensified the need for technically trained competent specialists of all kinds. The noble estates were neither large enough nor in many cases interested enough to fill the gap. Increasingly the society became open to talent, and increasingly the talent was drawn from a broader social base. All of our contributors stress this point. Raymond Garthoff gives us a particularly clear example in his discussion of the army, concluding: "From 1861 to 1914 the continuing trend of the officer corps was evolution from partial and sometimes part-time service of a segment of the nobility toward a professionally and technically qualified group *drawn from all classes*" (italics added).

Much the same pattern is revealed for the civil servant by Alf Edeen, the intellectual by George Fischer, and the scientist by Nicholas DeWitt (in Part Four). Underlying this spread of opportunity for personal development and advancement was the increasing accessibility of schools. From 1865 to 1914 the number of students per 10,000 of inhabitants increased by five times, from 105 to 545. In the case of higher schools the increase was even more marked, the ratio of university students to population for 1914 being seven times that for 1865. Not only were more being educated, but more came from humble origins. Thus in the universities in 1880 the children of workers and craftsmen were only 12.4 per cent and of peasants only 3.3 per cent of the enrollment, but by 1914 they accounted for 24.3 and 14.5 per cent, thus more than doubling

---

[4] There are perhaps a few exceptions, but not of great note. For example, on the window of the ticket booth of a Soviet airport, I noticed a list giving the order of priority in which Soviet citizens could purchase air tickets, beginning with members of the Central Committee of the Communist Party. But this seemed less a status privilege and more a necessary arrangement to meet priority needs of the state in regulating access to scarce airplane seats.

their proportionate representation.[5] The Soviet period may have deepened and intensified these tendencies, but the trend toward broadening opportunities to secure education and to develop one's talents was clearly evident as an accompaniment of the modernization process well before the revolution.

With regard to the distribution of income, the case is more complicated. Insofar as traditional society has mainly a two-class system, and the overwhelming majority are village peasants, the proportion of the population that is homogeneous in income is likely to be very large indeed. Furthermore, in the initial stages of modernization the development of large fortunes in trade, finance, and industry probably served in Russia to increase the spread from high to low earners, and to increase the diversity of income patterns. However, it has been stressed that only the long-range trend of modernization leads to homogenization of income. In this instance we would argue that the relevant period is the stage of late rather than early industrialization, which in the case of Russia means the Soviet period.

We must, of course, grant that the initial revolutionary equalitarianism was short-lived and that since the thirties the Soviet regime has stressed differential earnings as incentives to higher production. In addition, it has favored some segments of the population, such as artists and scientists, with unusually large earnings. Yet there seems little doubt that the long-range trend, while not moving toward equalization, does reflect a drift toward relative homogenization. The earnings of the factory director and collective-farm manager are today much closer to those of the worker and peasant than was the case with former owners and managers of plants and estates as compared to the workers and peasants of their day. With other formerly underprivileged groups, such as the common folk of Central Asia, the change has, of course, been much more dramatic. In recent times, furthermore, the regime has made moves to reduce the exaggeratedly high earnings of the most favored elite and has taken vigorous measures to raise the minimum wage. The substantial inequity between urban and rural earnings may be expected to be largely eliminated in time as the collective farms are converted to state farms where regular wages are paid. The fact that all work for the state leads to uniform and public pay scales, which become a standard and shape expectations, increases the probability of homogenization in earnings. And this, of course, serves in turn to ensure relative homogenization in style of life, housing, dress, and other consumption patterns.

Coming to the realm of power, our case may seem to break down. The essence of the Soviet system is that it justifies and practices an extraordinary degree of centralization of power. Because it is a totalitarian society the centralized political power takes on awesome dimensions,

[5] W. H. E. Johnson, *Russia's Educational Heritage* (Pittsburgh, 1950).

since it can reach into the smallest niche of personal life. To argue that the tsars were also great autocrats does not lessen the power of the General Secretary of the Communist Party. Nor does it do full justice to the fact that under the tsars groups such as the nobility, the industrialists, the merchants, and others could sometimes organize and exercise some degree of autonomous influence. But to restrict the contrast to the Soviet and Tsarist periods is to neglect the over-all trend, the long-range course of development in which Soviet history to date may be simply a short-term reversal.

Certainly the growth of political parties, the meetings of the Duma, and finally the calling of the Constitutional Assembly all reflected the tendency for the early period of modernization to yield more widespread sharing of political influence. Although the extreme centralization of power in the Soviet era apparently reversed the trend, this by no means does justice to all the facts. The Soviet leaders have gone much further than the Tsarist regime in creating at least the formal apparatus associated with shared power, through the elaborate institutions of local government, the vast display elections, and the encouragement of "self-criticism from below." Although the vital decisions remain the monopoly of the party leaders, the growing importance of technical problems in the governing of the state has forced an informal sharing of power with the many important scientists, engineers, managers, and other crucial technically skilled personnel. Certainly the recent reorganization of administration on a more decentralized basis represents a diffusion of decision-making power, however much the central elite may take precautions not to lose the decisive initiative and control. The full extent of such sharing has by no means been reached.

Even if we were to allow the monopoly of power in Soviet society to be an exception to the general principle of increasing homogenization of life chances in all spheres, this need not seriously impugn the value of the model. The model is, of course, an "ideal type" — a construct which reality can be expected only to approximate. The fact that Soviet experience shows little tendency toward homogenization in the access to power may be the distinctive characteristic which distinguishes the Soviet variant from the general model. It may also point to major areas of strain in Soviet society, since in this respect the Soviet Union is "out of line" with the requirements of the model. We might, therefore, predict that in the future one of the central problems of the system will be to deal with the strain between the leaders' desire to hold on to their monopoly in the face of growing desires and rational pressures from below for a greater share of power. If the model has commanding force we must anticipate that in the future there will be further shifts in the power structure of Soviet society, tending toward more equal sharing of power. On the other hand, it may be that the model should be revised and the prediction of increasing homogenization be restricted to realms other than that of power.

III

Up to this point I have not dealt with the second proposition, which predicts that under conditions of modernization there will be a tendency toward equilibration, toward consistency in the standing of individuals and groups in the different social orders which produce hierarchical strata. The space available precludes an extended exposition of this point, but the main lines of the argument may be briefly sketched.

In a traditional society there is relatively sharp separation between many of the different stratification realms because of religious and quasi-religious restrictions on certain types of activity. Thus, the noble may be free to engage in religious roles or war, but not in commerce or trade. As a result, the different status realms tend to be quite segregated. A Russian merchant might become quite wealthy yet he would have but little status. Indeed he might be legally a peasant and, if he fell into difficulty, might be treated not according to his occupation or wealth but according to his legal status. A monk might come to have great power over the royal family, but he might have little status and less money. In modern society two important departures from this situation may be noted. First, there is greater flexibility. The absence of traditional value proscriptions, religious injunctions, and legal regulations governing the estates contributes in obvious ways to allow adjustments of the sort which ultimately facilitate bringing one's position in the different hierarchies more or less into line. Second, there is a shift away from the relative diversity of the bases of stratification which characterizes traditional society; instead the modern industrial society gives overwhelming primacy to one structure, the occupational. In modern society the individual's position in the occupational system tends to pull with it, to shape or determine, a large number of his other characteristics.

In his contribution to this volume Talcott Parsons repeats a commonly made assertion that one of the distinctive characteristics of the modern industrial setting is that the occupational role is so sharply segregated from the other roles which the individual plays. While this may be technically correct, it is somewhat misleading. What is meant, of course, is that in the industrial society a man no longer carries on his work in the family setting, working within the village in which he lives, where he goes to church, and so on. But this formulation suggests to many the idea that in modern society there is less of a "bundle" or "package," less of a cluster of social characteristics which regularly go together. As Parsons would agree, I am sure, this is manifestly *not* the case. In Russia after the emancipation, by contrast, to know that a man was a noble was not at all to know whether he was wealthy or poor, powerful or weak and dependent, learned or ignorant. Such qualities varied much more independently of status than comparable qualities vary independently of occupation in modern industrial society. Knowing only a man's occupation in the modern society, we can predict with reasonable success a host of other characteristics, including the man's standing in the community, his income, education, aesthetic preferences, and housing.

I cannot here cite relevant evidence in any detail. But our report of the findings of the Harvard Project on the Soviet Social System[6] presents detailed evidence of the extent to which a man's position in the occupational structure in Soviet society falls into line with other important characteristics of his situation. The stratification profile presented by each major social group reveals marked consistency in the relative standing of the group in each of the several subsystems, spheres, or social orders which together make up the larger stratification system. High, middle, or low standing on one dimension is associated with high, middle, or low standing on the other scales measuring the share of scarce goods received by those in various groups. A few illustrative figures involving two groups near the poles of the hierarchy should suffice.

In income those in the professional-administrative category fell overwhelmingly in the highest bracket, 63 per cent earning 6,600 rubles per year or over (in 1940). Only 3 per cent fell in the lowest category earning 3,000 or less. But 60 per cent of the unskilled workers fell in that category, 87 per cent in the two lowest categories combined (earning 4,199 rubles or less). Those who had the well-paid jobs stood at the top of the educational hierarchy as well. In the more recent generation of Soviet citizens we found that at least 75 per cent of the college graduates entered the ranks of the professional and top administrative groups; of the remainder all but 4 per cent were at least semiprofessional. At the other end of the scale, those with four years of schooling or less were ordinary workers or peasants by occupation in 85 per cent of the cases, and only 3 per cent were at the white-collar level. The educational measure is particularly useful in highlighting the tendency of modern society to bring the different stratification measures into line. Among those who share humble origin, born into worker or peasant families, it is almost invariably true that those who secure more education also rise in the occupational scale. Thus, of those from such backgrounds who secured schooling for only four years or less, 88 per cent remained peasants or workers. But of those who managed to get beyond secondary school, 79 per cent secured white-collar or professional-administrative jobs.

Another realm of stratification in which the tendency toward equivalence of position in different hierarchies may be noted is that of access to

[6] Alex Inkeles and Raymond A. Bauer, *The Soviet Citizen: Daily Life in a Totalitarian Society* (Cambridge, Mass., 1959).

information. On every measure of involvement in the communications network, of the fullness of a man's contact with sources of ideas and information, the professional-administrative group was at the top of the hierarchy, the ordinary worker at the other pole. Of those in the intelligentsia 82 per cent were frequent readers of newspapers and magazines, and 62 per cent frequent radio listeners. The workers fell near the bottom of the scale, with only about 20 per cent being frequently exposed to such channels of official communication.

Finally, we may note that even in the realm of "psychic income," where we measure the gratification and satisfactions of daily living, the same pattern prevails. The professional-administrative group is consistently at the top of the hierarchy with regard to prestige and personal satisfaction; the working class consistently falls near the lower end. When our sample judged the regard or esteem in which selected occupations were held by the population, the highest scores were earned by the professional-administrative occupations. And when we asked the incumbents of various positions how they liked the jobs they held, the professional-administrative group was at the top, with 77 per cent satisfied, whereas the unskilled workers fell near the bottom of the distribution with only 23 per cent reporting satisfaction.

These are but a few of many illustrations which could be introduced to show that there is a striking consistency in the relative standing of each major occupational group on the several different hierarchies of stratification in the USSR. The Soviet Union is of course not unique in this respect. A similar situation prevails in the United States and in other large-scale industrial societies: a general tendency to minimize the discrepancies in the standing of any group as one goes from one to another realm of the stratification system. To put it in more positive terms, modern society tends to encourage comparability, congruence, or equivalence in the position of any group in each and all of the relevant distinctive hierarchies making up the stratification system as a whole.

IV

Several readers of an earlier draft of this chapter have pointed out that this hypothesis would apply better to the contrast between modern society and those which are *transitional* rather than traditional. The point is well taken. Surely in terms of the proportion or frequency of discrepant stratification "profiles," a traditional society would not rank high. The overwhelming majority of the population in a traditional society are peasants, whose position in all the stratification orders will be consistently low, and in that sense not discrepant. By contrast, in a transitional society, one moving away from the traditional order toward modern industrial forms, there will be a high absolute number and proportion of people with stratification "profiles" revealing many elements of discontinuity or discrepancy in position from hierarchy to hierarchy. Of course, we tend often to exaggerate the monolithic quality of traditional societies. Leaving this aside, however, I would still assert that, from a structural point of view, the distinction between traditional and modern society is most revealing.

The traditional society, like any other, cannot be permanently frozen. It changes, is forced to adjust and adapt to new situations and needs. New groups performing new functions arise, and old groups lose their function or the means for maintaining their old style of life. But the structural rigidity of the traditional society prevents the new groups from acquiring a status, or style of life, or education in keeping with their newly acquired income or power, as it forbids the denial of prestige, respect, or office to those high born who may have lost the means of economically validating their position. Thus we face the paradox that although it has a simple structure with only a few recognized stratification positions, abhors discrepancies in rank, and strains toward consistency, the traditional society will become in time, through the course of slow change, riddled by discrepancies which it lacks the means to resolve. By contrast, modern society, although regularly generating a multiplicity of new positions through the extensive differentiation of labor, and constantly experiencing changes in this realm, nevertheless has the necessary mechanism for allowing adjustment in position. Given a little time, therefore, most people will find their appropriate "level," adjusting power, income, and knowledge until these are all fairly well in line. Thus they bring to the stratification system as a whole the minimal number of sharp discrepancies or discontinuities in position in the different hierarchies.[7]

The accuracy and usefulness of the propositions stated here will become apparent only after they have been subjected to systematic testing not only on Russian materials but on those of other societies. Undoubtedly many refinements will have to be made and reservations introduced to account for distinctive local conditions. Indeed, the data may fail to support the propositions or require revisions so profound as to constitute a virtual refutation of them. But my purpose in this chapter has not been to settle a point, but to open a discussion.

[7] I am indebted to Irving Rosow for highlighting this paradox for me.

PART FOUR

EDUCATION, SCHOLARSHIP, AND RELIGION

EDUCATION: ORGANIZATION AND VALUES SINCE 1917

GEORGE Z. F. BEREDAY

I

One of the distinguishing features of American education is the fact that it is locally controlled and thus tied directly to the life of the community that supports it. The relationship of the school to the people is a two-way relationship. Through the school board, the Parent-Teacher Association, pressure groups, newspapers, and the more general web of informal relationships, the public directly influences the nature of school instruction. At the same time through a myriad of ways, of which the molding of the opinions of children is the most obvious, the school in turn has its impact upon the social life around it. The school and the community are in a fluid, flexible partnership. Their fate is one of a never-ending and direct mutual adjustment.

By contrast, the Soviet school has to function in a more complicated fashion. Officially it is the agent and exponent of the policies of the government. It represents the established ideology. It hands down official directives and training. Though the actual features of organization provide for separation of responsibility between the several ministries of education and culture and for decentralization at the union and republic level, the practical supervision of the party has never put into question the dependence of the schools on central direction.[1] They are, in an oft-repeated phrase, a political weapon. They are emissaries of the authority from above. They do not ask — they tell what is to be done.

But that is only one half of the story. Even in a police state no people can be wholly passive; no people can be forced or cajoled into a position of mere recipients of orders. The Russian people, long known for their acquiescence to authority, have now been wrenched through education and advancing industry from the age-old torpor. Even under central direction the ruled masses are bound to write into education aims and meanings of their own. Faced with authoritarian bureaucrats and teachers dispensing the will of the state, they are apt to invent ingenious measures to circumvent it and to adapt to their practical needs the official directives handed down to them. Still more significantly, they may prevent enforce-

---

[1] See G. Z. F. Bereday, "Changes in Soviet Educational Administration," *School and Society, LXXXVI* (January 18, 1958), 37–39.

ment of policies through passive resistance. To many of the pressures
they respond with counterpressures.

In Soviet education both the government and the people use the
schools for purposes of their own. When these purposes coincide, harmonious cooperation does occur. But when they diverge, the schools
become a scene of demonstrable tensions. The relationship is thus not two-
way as in the United States, but three-way. The schools are caught in the
middle between the state and the public and their respective interests.
Like the American schools, they carry out their task amidst frequent conflicts of interests. But unlike our schools, they serve as buffers between the
contending partners, not as partners in the enterprise.

This has significance for the functioning of Soviet education. From the
beginning, educational values, and the organization of schools which
manifest them, have been affected by two vectoral forces. In broadest
generalization, the aim of the Soviet government was to educate for un-
selfishness. It is as a corollary of this over-all objective that the schools
were made to serve the secondary aims with which we are familiar: the
teaching of urgently needed industrial skills and political indoctrination,
both as a shortcut to economic progress and ultimately as a road to the
Soviet form of socialism. But while the government pursued these aims,
the Soviet people developed at the same time a somewhat different though
familiar orientation. Perhaps taking too seriously the promises of their
leaders, they seem to have been seized with the ambition to attain a
better life for themselves and their dependents. Certainly cultural hunger
and ceaseless activity to win economic betterment appear to be a dominant
motivating force behind the mass demands for more education.

These two basic aims imposed upon the schools by the state and the
people are not only irreconcilable in theory; they are often hard to fit
together in practice. One will easily grant that as a theoretical premise the
official doctrine of education for selfless service is ethically sound. It is, in
fact, merely a restatement of the Taoist, Buddhist, and early Christian
doctrine. If every member of society could concentrate on being useful
to others, all would vastly benefit from the multiplicity of efforts thus
accruing to them. In this sense the regime's call is not only compatible but
has been responsible for galvanizing the masses into action.

In practice, however, once the awakening took place, Soviet authorities
found it hard to convince the people, bent on speedy satisfaction of increasing personal wants, that an indefinite postponement of this satisfaction would bring it more securely within their reach. Classical economics
has always taught that an economic system based on self-interest depends
on the willingness of investors to prefer future "deferred" consumption
over the satisfaction of present wants. An altruistic system seems to have
difficulty with this rule. The more persuasive the official slogan about the
better collective future, the more determined do individuals seem in de-

manding an immediate fulfillment in the present. Thus the cleavage between the short-range and long-range goals in education is a perennial problem everywhere, and certainly in the Soviet Union. At all times the schools stress to their pupils the imperative necessity of serving the state. At all times people respond by trying to serve principally themselves. There exists, and has existed throughout Soviet history, a potential source of conflict between the teacher as symbol of the state and the taught as symbol of the individual. But inevitably there has also taken place a degree of accommodation between the two. The system must develop along lines of compromise acceptable to both parties.

Through trial and error and through the now proverbial zigzags, no less applicable to education than to other spheres of Soviet life, the official policy has represented a series of surrenders to popular will and a subsequent series of balancing attempts to reassert the threatened Communist doctrine. Faced with the daily lessons of what makes people "tick," the regime was forced to modify its uncompromising altruistic stand in favor of incentives designed to supply more realistic motivation. Instead of materialistic samaritanism there had to be some concession to renascent religious feeling and only periodic revival of atheistic campaigns to keep matters in equilibrium. Instead of world communism there had to be patriotism and Russian nationalism punctuated by a revival of international campaigns and the stepping up of interest in ethnic minorities. Instead of progressivism in education there had to be the vacillation between a strictly formal college-oriented curriculum and readjustments in favor of politechnization.

On the other hand, the Soviet people also had to accommodate themselves to the Communist ideological scheme. Sometimes, though probably less often and less blatantly than is assumed in the West, this has taken the form of a mere careerist lip service. More often a genuine search for ideals was born of that mysticism which has been somewhat exaggeratedly proclaimed the Russian birthmark, ever since the romantic writers discovered that the peasant had a soul. This search was channeled into varying degrees of dedication to the Communist experiment. It does not take much imagination to understand how to a peasant-born student, and a significant proportion of students in each generation come from the countryside, the opening vista of a personal career becomes identified with the excitement of building a new and wonderful collectivist state.

It is submitted as a central thesis of this chapter that these collisions and accommodations between the postulates of official theory and the requirements of unofficial practice supply a meaningful clue to the understanding of the process of continuity and change in Soviet education. What follows will simply illustrate the various permutations resulting from the meeting of these two formative influences.

II

The general humanitarian concern of the Marxist doctrine for the education of the underpriviliged, ingeniously coupled with the industrial ambitions of Soviet policy makers, have combined to render the expansion of educational opportunities one of the major and most cherished aims of the Communist program. From the start it has been pressed for relentlessly and boasted about incessantly. The Soviet Union became, like the United States, committed to the belief that, to evoke and maximize the dynamic potential of the country, no less than full-scale education for all was needed. The cultural and industrial opportunities thus created had, as could have been predicted, a spiral effect. Growing opportunities for education stimulated the economy which in turn demanded more skills and provided fresh incentives. It is certain that the regime could not have survived the decimation of its educated class by the revolution and later by the purges had not the machinery of education been geared to speedy provision of replacements. It is equally certain that the Soviet economy could not have made its spectacular advances had not the need for enlarged cadres been anticipated by educating surpluses of specialists.

This policy of expansion has been pushed ahead on several fronts. Strenuous efforts were made first of all to abolish adult illiteracy. An ambitious program of supplying first primary and then secondary education to the whole population of the relevant age group was also undertaken. Finally, the build-up of the system of higher education has recently received first priority. To these we must add the activities under the jurisdiction of the Ministry of Culture. The provision of libraries, the advances of the theater arts and the film industry, the development of sports, the activism of youth organizations — these are among the most successful and most obvious of all Soviet achievements. It has been said with some reason that the cathedral or parish church dominates the view in a European town. In an American town the high school first attracts the eye. It is the Pioneers' palace (clubhouse for children aged nine to fifteen) that is assigned the choicest location and building in the Soviet scene.

The liquidation of illiteracy was a humanitarian, economic, and even political necessity. It is for the last-mentioned reason that it received the earliest attention: "A person who could not read was beyond the easy reach of communist propaganda." As described by George Counts, party organizations, schools, and voluntary civic action were immediately mobilized to deal with the problem.[2] It was, of course, understood that a literate public need not be a receptive public. Educated people might be ill fitted to the concept of a monolithic police state. But here modern techniques of thought control and mass persuasion were expected to provide the necessary safeguards. In addition, the growing school system was

[2] G. S. Counts, *The Challenge of Soviet Education* (New York, 1957), 180.

expected to provide for the young what Alex Inkeles refers to as a "predisposition to believe." [3] Having effectively created the means of total control of communications, the Soviet rulers could proceed without further restraint with the business of reclaiming the vast masses of people from the cultural neglect of the earlier era. In actual fact, as has been pointed out often, in doing so they merely duplicated the plans of reform that were developed in prerevolutionary days.

The major impact of the illiteracy campaign came in the first two decades of the regime. Lenin's first decree "On the Liquidation of Illiteracy" in 1919 marks its beginning and the Soviet pronouncements of the mid-1930's mark its official termination. From that time on the regime has considered its task wholly accomplished. Since World War II Soviet statistical sources have not cited statistics on illiteracy on the grounds that the Soviet Union is now "a country of complete literacy." [4] An official bibliography published in 1956 lists, among forty-two sources on liquidation of illiteracy, none published after 1935.[5]

But even this basic educational ambition is subject to some limiting qualifications. In view of the fact that as late as 1926 the figures of illiterates over fifteen years of age were given as 71.4 per cent in Asian Russia, and 44.5 per cent in European Russia,[6] the magnitude of the Soviet achievement seems impressive by any standard. However, one passage will suffice to show that the process was not accomplished without considerable tensions:

In November 1929, eighth- and ninth-grade students were taken from their studies and sent into rural areas on a "culture campaign" to "liquidate illiteracy." Each of these "soldiers of culture" was assigned twenty or twenty-five illiterate peasants, to whom he had to teach reading and writing for three months. This broadly conceived measure did not yield the expected results. It failed because the "teachers" were inexperienced and often quite helpless, and because the "students" sabotaged the studies, regarding them as a measure preparatory to collectivization.[7]

Some such tensions must persist even today. As a result, international sources judge the Soviet Union at present to have between 5 and 10 per cent of adult illiteracy, although some of it may be due to the 1940 territorial annexations.[8] Also in the case of ethnic minorities, literacy figures refer to their national languages, for some of which an alphabet was only created two decades ago and who, being sometimes slower to learn Russian, cut themselves off from literacy in any real sense. Finally, there

[3] A. Inkeles, *Public Opinion in Soviet Russia* (rev. ed., Cambridge, Mass., 1958), 323.

[4] UNESCO, *World Illiteracy at Mid-Century* (Paris, 1957), 17.

[5] *Periodicheskaia pechat' SSSR, 1917–1949. Zhurnali, trudi i biulleteni po kul'turnomu stroitel'stva, narodnomu obrazovaniiu i prosveshcheniiu* (Moscow, 1956), 9–11.

[6] UNESCO, 118.

[7] D. Samarin, in G. Kline, ed., *Soviet Education* (New York, 1957), 29.

[8] UNESCO, 17.

are no available figures on semiliteracy and lapses into illiteracy, the commonplace stumbling block of collectors of illiteracy statistics, no doubt applicable also to the Soviet situation. Even simple literacy legislation can sometimes be defied, it seems, with impunity.

Coupled with the attempt to tackle adult educational problems, there were the provisions for education of young people. At all levels, preschool, primary, secondary, and higher, the authorities have launched upon programs of expansion. The employment of a large number of working mothers necessitated, first of all, an expansion of preschool education. In 1955, more than five million children under seven years of age attended some sort of school. Between 1928 and 1955, those in nursery schools increased from 62,000 to 906,000; those in kindergarten from 130,000 to 1,713,000.[9] Preschool education thus made a steady if somewhat checkered progress. It started its growth soon after the revolution and made headway until 1936. At that time it began to decline. This decline applied particularly to the countryside and continued until 1953, when a new campaign was launched to set matters right. To the present time the situation has not, however, substantially improved. Kindergartens are still available only to a fraction of the age group. The major causes of this are, of course, financial and administrative. But even in this area we cannot entirely ignore the obstacles presented by the population. One cannot escape a sense of similarity between explanations of slow progress adduced in 1927, when:

people were afraid not that their children would be badly treated, but, on the contrary, that they would be treated too well, spoilt and made unfit for eternity. They were also afraid that their children's crosses would be taken from them, that they "would be made godless" and that the family would be broken up.[10]

and those given in 1953:

The nature of agricultural work makes permanent kindergartens appear less necessary, and the majority of collective farms have merely organized seasonal playgrounds during the summer. As can be well imagined, the educational work carried on in these playgrounds is often of a very low standard, if indeed it is carried on at all.[11]

In spite of centralization, the attitudes of the people seem to count in this area, as everywhere else, in contributing to a determination of precisely what progress is achieved.

In the area of compulsory education a more successful advance took place. At the level of primary and secondary education, after an initial decade of detours and experimentation, a unified ten-year school has solidly emerged. This "school of general education" is being steadily

---

[9] U.S. Office of Education, *Education in the USSR* (Washington, 1957), 40, 42.
[10] D. Meek, *Soviet Youth: Some Achievements and Problems* (London, 1957), 4.
[11] Meek, 9.

expanded. By 1950, final declarations of having accomplished universal seven-year education (first planned for 1937) began to appear. By 1956, with some qualifications, education for all until the age of fourteen had become a fact. Secondary education for all was to follow by 1960. The number of schools between 1922–23 and 1955–56 (after allowance has been made for the 1939 increase of territory) has exactly doubled to a figure of 213,000. The number of pupils for the same period (though not weighted for population increase) more than quadrupled, to a figure of about thirty million.[12] The provision of educational opportunities of this magnitude is certainly a significant achievement.[13]

Similar advances were pressed for and, it seems, attained in higher education. At the time of the revolution there were some ninety institutions of higher learning in all Russia. Moscow alone now possesses that many. There are now 1,867,000 students attending Soviet institutions as full-time or correspondence students, as against an average of 200,000 in the first decade of the Soviet regime. American sources, even more than Soviet, have lately fully publicized this sector of expansion. The Soviet Union, after reorganization and consolidation of some types of teachers' colleges, now has some 770 institutions of higher learning, of which 40 are universities.

It is obviously in the interest of the regime to expand educational opportunities as rapidly as possible. But in this area, as in all others, considerable difficulties intervene. In the primary sector, the compulsory seven-year attendance has shown itself to be a persistent headache. In a study published in France, I. and N. Lazarévitch include ten pages of quotations from the Soviet press indicating substantial nonattendance in various regions between 1948 and 1953.[14] A. Korol, to whom we owe an exhaustive account of Soviet education, describes the situation after 1954 as being characterized by "substantial lapses here and there."[15] The accounts of such lapses continue to appear in the Soviet press without interruption.[16] There must also be some significance in the fact that only 5 per cent of primary schools contain more than eighty pupils.[17] Obvious building difficulties, too, cannot be ignored. Their shortage has been

[12] Kul'turnoe stroitel'stvo (Moscow, 1956), 76.

[13] For comparison with the United States, see N. DeWitt, "Basic Comparative Data on Soviet and American Education," Comparative Education Review, II (June 1958), 9–11.

[14] I. and N. Lazarévitch, L'Ecole soviétique (Paris, 1954), 48–58.

[15] A. Korol, Soviet Education for Science and Technology (Cambridge, Mass., 1957), 3.

[16] For instance: "Can we really be reconciled to the fact that several thousand children of school age were not in school in the republic in 1956?" T. Turgunov, Sovetskaia Kirgiziia (July 25, 1957), 2, in Current Digest of Soviet Press (September 11, 1957), 29.

[17] I. Z. Kaganovich, Ocherk razvitiia statistiki shkol'nogo obrazovaniia v SSSR (Moscow, 1957), 88.

such that the length of the school day was affected. In the words of N. Goncharov, substantiated by other official sources, "we are still compelled to have two and sometimes three shifts to accommodate the 29 million school children from seven to seventeen in attendance." [18] Many schools continue to use buildings rented from other enterprises, and even the newest schools, and school furnishings are considerably below Western standards.

Universal secondary-school attendance, up to the age of seventeen, had been originally hoped for by 1960. But here as elsewhere the achievements have lingered behind the promises. There is no point in discussing the fulfillment of the latter, since the proposals made by Khrushchev in the second half of 1958 resulted in the curtailment of secondary education to eight years. An obvious and substantial increase of numbers at the senior secondary level has nonetheless taken place.[19] It is enough, however, to note the phrases "as a whole" and "in the main" upon which the official spokesmen had fallen when describing the hopes of the program in 1957:

During 1951–55 the transition to universal ten-year schooling from the age of seven to sixteen or seventeen was achieved as a whole in the capitals of the republics and in large cities and regional, territorial and industrial centers. At the present time, the organs of public education are confronted with the task of effecting universal ten-year education in the main in the remaining towns and rural localities by 1960. This task is being accomplished.[20]

The weak spots of a policy of expansion so vigorously pursued cannot be explained merely by inefficiences of administration. More relevant answers must be sought in the climate of opinion of the people. On the whole the program of expansion, with its promise of enlightenment and career, did enlist the enthusiastic support of the Soviet masses. A reader of official discussions, refugee accounts, and reports by visitors is invariably struck by the atmosphere of universal fervor and activity. But even though expansion is the one phase of the educational scene on which the government and the people agree, the program has its problems, which can be traced to the existence of two important groups. Instead of a clear-cut educational policy, ideally conceived and carried through without obstacles, we find a school program faced with those who want to ignore it and those who find it inadequate. Absenteeism, apathy and hostility to teachers and education, have not been entirely eliminated in spite of meticulous planning. On the other side, the enthusiastic demands for more educational opportunity tend to outrun the need for edu-

[18] N. Goncharov, "The Soviet Public Schools," USSR (illustrated monthly), no. 13 (1957) 8.

[19] See G. Z. F. Bereday, "Recent Developments in the Soviet Schools, Part II," Comparative Education Review, I (October 1957), 16–17.

[20] L. Dubrovina, in The Times Educational Supplement (December 6, 1957), 1551.

cated top-level men and the government's means (in terms of buildings, teachers, and equipment) to satisfy mass ambitions. That the first group is diminishing while the second is increasing can be taken as a measure of Soviet efforts and successes. These problems nevertheless exist and as such illustrate the difficulties incurred in systems in which educational policy is not a simple index of local energy.

The history of Soviet education is partly the story of a continuous battle of the regime against the apathy and recalcitrance of the masses. The peasant, from the cunning villager who outwits his social superiors in the old folktales to Arthur Koestler's prisoner who refuses medical injections offered by the government, presented the earliest obstacle to speedy implementation of policy. Later, in the period of political terror, there was also some reluctance to study since too much education bestowed onerous (and dangerous) responsibilities. To this attitude there now have been added economic overtones. They are, perhaps, best illustrated by a comment of a young *nibonicho* worker:

I have already bought an accordion in the secondhand store and soon I'll get a motorcycle. That's enough for me. I pull down nearly 1000 rubles a month. But the main thing is that I do my work and when I finish I am free. Studying means getting stuck on a stipend of 300 a month at best. That is, if you do well. And you become an engineer and are appointed a chief. The money is about the same as I am making now and the responsibility is enough to send you to the grave. Why should I? No possible reason. Ridiculous.[21]

Soviet educational authorities have thus been unable to free themselves from people who drag their feet, whether actively or passively. But it is probably true to say that the majority of the people threaten the regime with an opposite attitude. The respect for culture and an idealistic quest for learning have characterized the Russians even in the pre-Soviet era. More important, the almost overnight creation of new jobs for which the modern state had to find men with training introduced a tremendous career pressure for education. The transition from rural to city life exercises in all cultures a powerful attraction to youth of ambition. Rural youth crowd into cities and, combined with the urban youth and their parents, create powerful demands for more educational opportunity.

The result has been vitiating. Beset by shortages in buildings, undertrained teaching staffs, and immediate need for manpower, the authorities are forced to limit the pressure by pushing up standards of selectivity. But this too is a double-edge sword. There have recently been medical protests which forced the authorities to abolish a number of competitive examinations and to soften others in the interest of the health of the pupils. The false grading of pupils to enable them to pass has become so obvious

[21] Lev Kassil, *Literaturnaia gazeta* (May 25, 1957), 2, in *Current Digest of Soviet Press* (August 14, 1957), 12. "On ne verit ni v boga ni v chorta" is reported to be the source of a new term for the young cynics of the Khrushchev era.

as to have worked itself into Dudintsev's fiction.[22] The pressure for admission to overcrowded universities and colleges has reached notorious proportions.[23] A recent news item reports the dismissal of several university officials for altering entrance records so as to enable students to enroll without complying with the regulations requiring health and two-year labor certificates as prerequisites of admission.[24] It is, indeed, quite a striking spectacle to see the regime, intent on pioneering expanded education, having to fight both advance-guard and rear-guard action with its people. The efforts of the government have given this advance a sense of direction, but it is the combined attitudes of the people that dictate the actual rate of advance. It is clear that between the two the school acts merely as a shock absorber.

III

The character of the schools is even more clearly illustrated by the second example — the impact of official government and unofficial popular pressure upon the curriculum. In particular, two aspects of instruction, the issue of the unity of organization and the history of methods, will serve to show the confluence and divergence between the planning and execution of government directives.

Before examining the impact of progressivism and formalism, it is relevant to remember the postulate of one unified school system which the original Soviet theory seemed to imply. The ideal of a single ladder of education for all persists as an educational theme. In fact, Soviet and American practices are closer to this theme than the practices of any other countries. Not only were all citizens to be educated in common schools, but they were to be educated by and large in the same type of schools. This led to the basic design of a ten-year school extending from ages seven to seventeen, to embody eventually the entire age group. Herein we may also find the explanation for only five branches of learning in higher education. In technicums and higher institutions, at which professional diversification was inevitable and has in fact reached exaggerated proportions, steps have recently been taken to reduce the number of specialists and of faculties within them.

On the surface this policy has succeeded admirably well:

In Moscow or Irkutsk, Russians or Buryats, boys or girls in corresponding grades follow the same curriculum prescribed by the Ministry of Public Education and study identical subjects, following uniform syllabi and, except for the language in which they are written, identical "approved" textbooks. Thus in theory, each intermediate level (elementary, after 4 years at age 11; "incomplete secondary," after 3 more years, at age 14) and the terminal level, after graduation from the

[22] V. Dudintsev, *Not By Bread Alone* (New York, 1957), 22.
[23] G. Z. F. Bereday, "Recent Developments in the Soviet Schools, Part I," *Comparative Education Review,* I (June 1957), 4–7.
[24] *New York Times,* December 29, 1957.

tenth grade at age 17, are all clearly definable as to the scope and subjects of instruction they imply.[25]

The bulk of the school population today studies in institutions that are as identical in their organization as possible. Even in the sector of special schools, the authorities tend to move toward reintegration with the general system as soon as they have fulfilled their special mission. The disappearance of the *Rabfaks,* the reintegration of the two-year teachers' institutes into the full four-year pedagogical institutes, and the occasional reference to the temporary nature of labor-reserve schools[26] supply instances of this general tendency.

But it is one of the major tenets of modern educational theory that a system catering to vast masses of population cannot withstand pressures for a great variety of offerings. In confirmation of this, the basic school design became from the beginning the subject of persistent demand for greater diversification. In a system of totalitarian education people cannot, of course, create private schools, although cases of private tutoring to supplement official training have occasionally been reported. But through various agencies of public administration certain interest groups have succeeded in carving out of the main trunk of education special-purpose schools particularly suited to their needs. Furthermore, they can exercise steady and intangible pressure to force the government itself to recognize the need for diversified offerings. These two tendencies have long been at work to change the profile of Soviet education.

With the advance of universal secondary education, one may predict that the senior secondary school, hitherto planned as comprehensive, will be subject to the pressures to compartmentalize. Already there is impressive evidence of experimentation in this direction.[27] Soviet psychologists have been increasingly pressing for a curriculum adapted to individual differences, and thus likely to secure the conditions for the optimum development of every child.[28] It is quite likely that the expansion in the number of technicums, conceived as alternatives to senior secondary schools, will continue more rapidly. At least it appears that the authorities are determined not to have these converted into postsecondary schools, although the latest regulations provide for entry (with different examinations) for both the graduates of the seven-year and the ten-year schools.[29]

---

[25] Korol, 1, 2.

[26] For instance, in the report of William Benton, "The Voice of the Kremlin," *Britannica Book of the Year, 1956* (pages unnumbered).

[27] W. K. Medlin, "Soviet Pedagogical Academy and the New School Plans," *Comparative Education Review,* II (October 1958), 12–14. These reforms are also discussed in the report of the United States Office of Education delegation to the Soviet Union, *Soviet Commitment to Education* (Washington, D. C., 1959).

[28] A. A. Smirnov, "School Success and Related Problems of Psychology," *International Review of Education,* III (1957), 320.

[29] *Spravochnik dlia postupaiushchikh v srednye spetsialnye uchebnye zavedeniia* (Moscow, 1957), 15–20, 23–42.

Party, military, and special technical or professional schools, such as ballet, schools of art and music, and the experimental schools of the Academy of Pedagogical Sciences, also come under the heading of diversification accepted by the government as inevitable and useful. Like the recently created boarding schools, they obviously serve legitimate interests in which the state has a significant stake. But it is interesting to visit them and to examine their student composition. One sees how far over the years they have become the means of supplying better training, as distinct from simply different training, to special groups and which, under the guise of special service, give privileged treatment to privileged children.[30] Even the boarding schools which do not now seem to have an elite character, though originally highly suspect,[31] have potentialities to acquire such a character in time if their physical plants and the training offered prove themselves to be of an attractively superior quality.

More significant than the special-purpose schools are the schools created by specific institutions. These are not necessarily vocational schools. Indeed, several ministries and single plants operate trade schools to ensure the supply of sorely needed skills for which there is a never-ending competition between various agencies of production. But often they run or patronize, instead, schools of a general type sponsored in order to ensure good education for the children of their employees. Thus, the Suvorov and Nakhimov officers' schools and railway schools seem to be restricted to children of officers and railway workers, respectively.[32] Cases of factories taking under their patronage specific public schools and obtaining privileged treatment for the children of their employees have also been reported.

But perhaps the schools for defective and delinquent children deserve the greatest attention as proof of the pressures for diversification. A social theory based on work for rapid progress and on subordination of individual welfare to that of society was likely, in spite of professions of over-all altruistic aims, to produce harsh rules for the education of marginally useful children. Certainly rules resulting in long hours of study and strict examinations made themselves felt as soon as the initial period of experimentation gave way to an established school order. In the field of delinquency the same rules found expression in the provisions of the law which, contrary to Western practice, regard criminals over the age of fourteen, and in some cases over twelve, not as juveniles but as adults.[33]

---

[30] G. Z. F. Bereday, "Class Tensions in Soviet Education," in G. Z. F. Bereday and J. Pennar, eds., *The Politics of Soviet Education* (New York, 1960).

[31] G. Z. F. Bereday, "Recent Developments in the Soviet Schools, Part II," *Comparative Education Review*, I (October 1957), 14–15.

[32] A. Inkeles, "Social Stratification and Mobility in Soviet Russia," in R. Bendix and S. M. Lipset, eds., *Class, Status and Power* (Glencoe, 1953), 619.

[33] W. W. Kulski, *The Soviet Regime: Communism in Practice* (Syracuse, 1950), 267.

In the area of "defectology" this was translated into the theory that the problem of rehabilitation is primarily the problem of rendering the handicapped fit and skillful enough to participate in industrial production. Hence we find a scornful reference to bourgeois "idealistic theories and religious-philanthropic principles" and concentration instead on "socialist humanism." [34] By and large the trend of official Soviet theory has been to refuse to regard special education as a mere problem of caretaking. Only the needs of the expanding economy and the occasional propaganda value seemed to justify efforts in this direction. But in this area, too, the pressures of the population and of inspired individuals exercised a steady modifying influence.

The figure of A. S. Makarenko looms large in the history of Soviet education for delinquents. It is well known that until after his death his efforts were disparaged and his theories disputed. Only very slowly have his contentions gained ascendency: that education of delinquents, as indeed all education, must begin with the individual, that it must match the demands on him by respect for him, that the vision of personal happiness is an indispensable educational incentive, and that the group must support the individual in order to command his allegiance. Such propositions for reclaiming delinquents in a system in which law violators were regarded as antisocial elements fit only for elimination naturally could not easily win acceptance. But the success of Makarenko's work with delinquents, coupled with the failure in other similar establishments in the twenties, has proved to be an opening wedge. As a result, *detskie domy* grew in number and respectability. Moreover, Makarenko's ideas began to penetrate other forms of school practice. For instance, the new boarding schools are experimenting with his idea of vertical grouping of children into all-age "collectives." [35] Most of Makarenko's works are now available in English.[36] Their arguments and convictions are a testimony to the potential strength of individual opinions on the official colossus.

The expansion of special education for the physically defective might also be interpreted as a result of the impact of popular opinion. Thanks to it a growing network of special schools for the blind, deaf, and mentally retarded is making its appearance. Model schools such as these are now pointed to with pride as examples of official achievements, but remarkably less is said about the actual saturation of the country by them. The official position still is that these schools exist for those children who can demonstrate ability to *improve*. "If after three years at a special school the pupil has shown no progress, he either is to be returned to his parents or sent to

[34] "Vospitanie i obuchenie anormal'nykh detei," *Uchitel'skaia gazeta* (November 28, 1957), 2.

[35] O. S. Kei and N. P. Zubachev, "Opyt organizatsii pervichnogo detskogo kollektiva v shkole-internate," *Sovetskaia pedagogika* (February 1957), 22–31.

[36] A. S. Makarenko, *Learning to Live* (Moscow, 1953); *The Road to Life* (3 vols.; Moscow, 1955); and *A Book for Parents* (Moscow, n. d.).

a special home." [37] Little is known about the fate or care of such rejects. There is increasing information on medical activities and treatment, but as yet not enough educational research to determine the degree of over-all improvement. The best guess is that the climate of popular opinion is increasingly successful in emphasizing the original humanitarianism promised by the regime in theory but minimized in practice.

The history of the Soviet curriculum, no less than the struggle for diversity, reflects the conflict of values in Communist education. On one hand, the collectivistic school obviously demands and exacts vigorous efforts. On the other hand, its vast and expanding ramifications inevitably bring about fresh relaxations and dilutions. Every student of Soviet education is familiar with this perennial dichotomy. The official Soviet endeavors have always concentrated on ensuring the highest possible level of learning. In practice, in spite of unusually careful legislation and inspection, they have at several points been constrained to accept much less than perfection.

The first well-known effort of the Soviet curriculum to elicit maximum results was made wholly in the progressive direction. The traditional curriculum inherited from Tsarist times was officially swept away in favor of "complex themes." The present wave of hostility against progressive ideas or, perhaps more properly, against their abuse has tended to obscure the fact that in choosing progressivism, the early Soviet leaders did not simply indulge in whims of extreme liberalism. They earnestly hoped, by reorganizing traditional subject methods, to break with the dead weight of the

Nature	Work	Society	Year of studies
Seasons, elements of physical geography.	Life and work of a family in the village or in the city.	The family as a social unit in relation to school.	1
Air, water, sun. Domestic uses of vegetation and animals.	Life and work of the village or of the urban precinct in which the students live.	Social institutions of the village or of the city.	2
Elementary notions of physics, chemistry, agriculture, industry, mines, means of transportation.	The economy of the region.	Present and past institutions of the region.	3
Geography of the USSR and other countries.	Economy of the USSR and other countries.	Political and social regime of the USSR and other countries in the past.	4

[37] U.S. Office of Education, *Education in the USSR* (1957), 106.

past and to ensure the maximum of creative learning. There is certainly thought and system in the general plan of studies of that period as reported by Luigi Volpicelli.[38]

The progressive system of training might well have proven logical and effective in the long run. Instead, it has failed to establish itself, although many other features of Russian life were at the same time radically and successfully transformed. Its eclipse must be partly attributed to the resistance of public opinion. Old teaching methods were persisted in, especially by conservative teachers and the more obscure communities. There was a steadily mounting pressure in favor of "solid" training. The central tenet of progressivism is, of course, that people are inherently good and that, given opportunity, they will develop for the best. But, in practice, its application has shown that knowledge is simply power which both good and evil pupils can apply for ends of their own. The appearance of the undesirable by-products of progressivism, the vocal and yet unlearned and personally disorganized students, has alienated both the Soviet public and publics elsewhere against the central idea. In addition, forced industrialization rendered paramount the need for good and clearly definable training of the "cadres." In the circumstances, the scheme never had a chance to prove itself fully workable. Thus, in a spectacular and probably not universally palatable reversal, the Soviet state had to throw its weight on the side of the traditional type of education. Stalin's accession, his new methods of government, and his actual decision in the matter are given as the immediate causes of this change.[39] But in a deeper sense, such arbitrary action only confirms the fact that under a progressive system people were found too undisciplined to do the official bidding. Progressivism was defeated not only because it failed to force strong subject-matter instruction; it was banished also because it failed to teach people to obey.

But the human situation also frustrated the new formal educational efforts. This is something that Western observers are only now beginning to admit or realize. Armed by the support and directives of the state, the school immediately became a giant tester and grader. It became a stern and discriminating sieve. It became an originator of tensions. As such, it could not elicit an undue show of enthusiasm from the population.

First, the selective function of education embroiled it again with the parents, on the one side ambitious for their children's preferment, and on the other pressed by the school to punish severely all lapses from industry.[40] Second, as descriptions and paintings of school life abundantly indicate, education became a scene of formidable social frustrations. The

---

[38] L. Volpicelli, *L'Évolution de la pedagogie soviétique* (Neuchatel, 1954), 79.

[39] R. Widmayer, "The Communist Party and the Soviet Schools, 1917–1937," (unpublished dissertation, Harvard University, 1952), 436.

[40] A. Herzer, *Bolschevismus und Menschenbildung* (Hamburg, 1951), 105.

children, often driven to get ahead, became victims of the necessity to get good grades. This has turned them into jittery crammers. It has also led to the "percentomania" of teachers anxious to see the majority of their pupils succeed. Third, formalistic training immediately projected school life into the realm of recitation and theory, with all the concommitant loss of touch with practicality which such methods are now known to imply. Sometimes even the location of the schools bears little relation to their function, a fact which a simple example given by Khrushchev will serve to illustrate:

Moscow is the seat of three oceanographic and marine research institutions — the Marine Hydro-Physical Institute, the Institute of Oceanology of the USSR Academy of Sciences, and the Institute of Oceanography of the Hydro-Meteorological Service, and two mining institutes — one under the USSR Academy of Sciences and the other under the Ministry of Coal Industry. Isn't it a bit too much for the Moscow Sea and the Vorobyovi Hill? (Laughter, applause.)[41]

Fourth, the problem of sluggishness most bitterly complained of under progressivism has not been solved under formalism. This is commonplace knowledge to pedagogues, as stated humorously by a Soviet educator to a recent Scottish visitor:

I asked him [the Soviet headmaster], "But what happens if a boy persists in laziness?" He answered with a twinkle, "Mr. Kinloch, boys are boys all the world over, and in Russia, as I am sure even in Scotland, the persistently lazy boy can always triumph over the teacher." He was a very human headmaster.[42]

Levity aside, poor school discipline, juvenile delinquency and lack of political dedication are as real and as difficult to solve in the Soviet schools today as they were thirty years ago. Even the most carefully planned school policy has been unable to remove these now well-recognized stumbling blocks of formalism.

Rigid subject training thus has been declared once more a failure. The exigencies of practice have now forced a modification of the official attitude. At present we have witnessed the return of politechnization in the curriculums at secondary as well as at higher levels. There has been an increase of hours spent on handwork, practical work in training-experimental plots, production practice in factories and farms, even the study of politechnization as a subject.[43] Examination procedures, methods of recruitment and graduation, work-load requirements, and ratio of lectures to seminars have undergone a substantial review and revision. Moreover,

[41] N. S. Khrushchev, "Report of the Central Committee of the Communist Party of the Soviet Union to the Twentieth Party Congress" (Moscow, 1956), 102.

[42] J. L. Kinloch, "Education in USSR: III," *Scottish Educational Journal* (July 1, 1955), 435.

[43] Summarized in the report "Union of Soviet Socialist Republics. Educational Progress in 1955–56," *International Yearbook of Education* (Geneva, 1956), 380.

the whole spirit of instruction has been vigorously attacked. Recently the Deputy Minister of Higher Education wrote:

At present our higher educational institutions use the system of instruction and the teaching methods established back in the 1930's. For some directors in higher schools this system of precise regulation of the entire educational process is very convenient: everything is outlined and written down in advance; everything is provided for by the study plans and instruction. In other words, there is no need to be particularly concerned about the life of a higher educational institution because it has been standardized by instructions "from above." [44]

With American controversies in mind it is instructive and somewhat amusing to see the hesitating steps of the Soviet regime caught, as the donkey in the Polish fable, between the oats of high scholarly standards and the hay of practical socialist construction.

IV

No educational legislation can succeed unilaterally. It is clear that in theoretical perspective the official educational policy has exhibited continuity of purpose. But in practical application the desires of the people have brought about serious discontinuities. Whereas the government always intended to pursue a steady course, it found itself embracing or implementing quite divergent policies. The problems of the structural expansion of education and its curriculum have illustrated the basic design and the numerous deviations from it. They supply comparative documentation about an educational model in which, contrary to many pronouncements, the school has not become a one-sided source of indoctrination, but has instead been reduced to the function of mediator.

Categories other than organization and curriculum would confirm the contention that the totalitarian school is never as totalitarian as its blueprints. It is obvious how keenly Soviet authorities want to teach political indoctrination. Even at the infant level, in spite of advances in Soviet pedagogy, they still do not hesitate to instill the party line.[45] Yet, though no one can wholly escape, people continue ingeniously to resist official pressure. They avoid politically slanted higher schools.[46] They seem on the whole unconcerned about the classroom downgrading of Stalin.[47] In

[44] M. A. Prokof'ev, *Vestnik vysshei shkoly* (August 1957), 3–4, trans. in *Current Digest of Soviet Press* (October 16, 1957), 9.

[45] An Indian visitor was recently confronted in a kindergarten by a group of children, ages three to seven, who "sung the songs of welcome to us, and songs expressive of their desire to see Peace established in the whole world." K. A. Subramania Iyer, "Education in the Soviet Union," *Indian Education* (Spring 1955), 15.

[46] S. Banbula, *Das neuzeitliche Erziehungswesen in Sowjetrussland und in den Vereinigten Staaten Nordamerikas. Ein Vergleich* (Zurich, 1956), 82.

[47] Children are now taught that Stalin was "excessively rude, showing his intolerance, his brutality, and his abuse of power," and that his actions led to "the most cruel repression, violating all norms or revolutionary legality." See K. S. Davies, "The Stalin Generation," *Journal of Education* (July 1956), 293. Compare this with the contents of G. S. Counts and N. P. Lodge (trans.), *I Want To Be Like Stalin* (New York, 1947).

1957 there were even signs of questioning of the wisdom of official leadership.[48] It is similarly obvious how keenly and how successfully Soviet education has emphasized science. Its role — although greatly exaggerated in the United States,[49] and although every subject not classed as "arts" is counted as "science" in the Soviet Union[50] — is still said to be of paramount importance to the expanding national industry.[51] Highly successful examples of Soviet science teaching are now readily available in Korol's book and elsewhere.[52] Yet Russian pride in their achievements in space and Western publicity notwithstanding, several recent Soviet pronouncements seemed to emphasize training in arts instead of science. Women in particular are beginning in larger numbers to select arts courses rather than science. Interest in arts and literature is a deep tradition with the Russian people, and its fervent continuance must contribute to the exercise of a counterbalance against the policies of a government dedicated one-sidedly to rapid scientific progress.

However, one problem must be watched as a potential means of modification of the present analysis. This problem is related to the general situation in the schools and centers on the fate of the development of Soviet teaching as an independent profession. Such a development would imbue the teachers with a sense of separateness and a sense of responsibility for education, independent of the government as well as of the governed. Professional loyalties, transcending patriotic and human loyalties, could be developed by teachers, and they could come to see themselves not as servants of the state, not as an occupational equivalent to other callings, but as autonomous agents. The school in their hands might thus become a third factor capable of molding educational policy, instead of a mere prism reflecting the official and popular endeavors. There are signs that might be interpreted as forerunners of such a transformation. But the appearance of an independent professional force would be the sign of the eclipse of the governmental supremacy. We would then no longer be able to speak of Soviet education as possessing the continuity with which the Communist revolution has invested it.

[48] See "The Ferment Among Soviet Youth," *Soviet Survey*, no. 12 (February 1957), 1–16.

[49] See G. Z. F. Bereday, "American and Soviet Scientific Potential," *Social Problems*, IV (January 1957), 208–219.

[50] John McLeish, "The Soviet Society for the Dissemination of Political and Scientific Knowledge," *Fundamental and Adult Education*, VII (October 1955), 157.

[51] A. F. Shalin, "Technical Education in USSR," *Yearbook of Education* (1956), 110.

[52] See, for instance, on chemistry, S. G. Sciapovalenko, "Sullo studio nella scuola media dei fondamenti dell'industria chimica moderna," in L. Volpicelli, ed., "La Scuola e la pedagogia sovietica," *Problemi della pedagogia* (July–October 1956).

LITERARY AND HISTORICAL SCHOLARSHIP

HERBERT E. BOWMAN

I

The line of development in Russian literary and historical scholarship during the past one hundred years follows the pattern of a rising and falling curve. The curve is neither smooth nor symmetrical, and of course it does not begin from zero in 1861 or fall to zero in 1958. But the general line is an upward movement from 1861 on into the twentieth century and until the decade of the twenties, after which the movement of the graph is generally downward. In this it follows the progress of Russian cultural existence, as scholarship in the humanities can probably always be expected to do. Coming late into modern consciousness, Russian intellectual life exploded into a profuse flowering in a very short time; but seldom has any culture exhibited the suddenness with which Russian vitality in the humanities was overtaken by sterility. It may be possible for the physical and natural sciences to remain relatively free of binding ties with the inner life of a nation. However, such areas as literary criticism and historiography are bound to reflect the sense of life that pervades a national culture, for they are essentially expressions of opinion, of attitude, of outlook on human affairs. If, for example, the Soviet Union had produced a great literature, we would surely be forced to revise our judgment of the Soviet world.

A comparison of Russian achievement in literary scholarship, on the one hand, and historical scholarship, on the other, would probably have to be made in favor of the field of history. Russian and Soviet intellectual life has been marked by a dynamism of concern for the problems of historical existence, of the historical destiny of Russia, of the role that Russia has played and is to play in the world. One of the basic appeals of Marxism for the Russian intellectual is that it provided a key to the interpretation of historical fate and historical process. Certainly other modern cultures have been concerned with devising a philosophy of history; but seldom has this interest been pursued with more life-and-death urgency. And of course the cataclysmic nature of historical events in the Russia of the last hundred years makes amply appropriate such intellectual concern with the realities of history.

Especially within the circumstances of Russian historical existence in the modern period, it would be natural to expect that Russian historical writing would be chiefly devoted to the history of Russia itself. But Russian achievement in non-Russian historiography has also been considerable. Many eminent Russian students of non-Russian historical subjects could be named. Paul Vinogradov, a distinguished scholar in English medieval history, attained something like the ultimate in recognition by becoming a professor of English institutions at Oxford. In the same class belong Michael Rostovtzeff in Greco-Roman history, Vasilii Vasilevsky in Byzantine history, and Maxime Kovalevsky in European medieval history. Perhaps no country in Europe outside of France itself has devoted so much scholarship to the French Revolution and its intellectual backgrounds. A Russian historian has claimed that the Russian scholar, by his distance from Europe, has the advantage of a greater objectivity.[1]

Russian literary history and criticism is perhaps a lesser achievement. The comparison with the scholarly study of Russian literature carried on outside of Russia is interesting. Perhaps final judgment on such a comparison should be suspended; perhaps one could compromise by deciding that the best general history of Russian literature is the history of Prince D. S. Mirsky, who might be claimed by both Russian and English intellectual life.[2] As for Russian literary scholarship, for all its accomplishments, it has hardly been worthy of the great literature that has lain at its disposal. Perhaps the chief blame must be given to the fact that Russian literary criticism was from its beginnings involved in a tradition of "civic" or "social" criticism, which by the very seriousness of its concern for the work of literary art tended to encumber the flight of imaginative aesthetic criticism. Of course one can find aesthetic perceptivity and imaginative scholarship in modern Russian criticism; but the examples are scattered. Nineteenth-century social criticism joins forces with Soviet literary policy in so dominating the field of literary scholarship that the finest Russian critics remain a relatively obscure minority.

Yet for all the fluctuations and inadequacies that might be detected, Russian literary and historical scholarship during the past century has surely lived through its period of greatest achievement. If the preceding statement carries a suggestion of an obituary notice, it is probably fitting. There is a good chance that the period from the middle of the nineteenth century until approximately 1930 will stand for a long time to come as the golden age of Russian literary and historical scholarship. Yet even today, in a period of far less achievement, Soviet scholarship in these fields does at least continue to display the characteristic that has always constituted the distinction of modern Russian intellectual life in the humanities:

---

[1] V. Butenko, "La Science de l'histoire moderne en Russie," *Le Monde slave*, II (1926), 120.

[2] D. S. Mirsky, *A History of Russian Literature from the Earliest Times to the Death of Dostoyevsky* [1881] (New York, 1927); and *Contemporary Russian Literature, 1881–1925* (New York, 1926).

namely, its close engagement with the problems of contemporary Russian society. Russian originality in these fields has always been an originality of spirit even more than an originality of mind — a distinctive force of motivation more than a distinctive content of thought. So great has this intellectual and moral dynamism been, in fact, that it has constantly threatened to destroy the precarious structure of objective and imaginative scholarship. Literary scholarship in particular suffers at the hands of the critic who insists upon taking a moral or a moralistic stance. The writing of history also probably suffers from too much moral fervor. And yet it is precisely this highly charged moral fervor that seems a special mark of Russian intellectual life, a world into which the non-Russian student enters as into an arena.

II

Both literary and historical studies, from the time of their modern beginnings in the beginning of the nineteenth century, were motivated in Russia by the drives inherent in a developing national consciousness. The beginnings of modern Russian historiography lie partly, it is true, in Germanic scholarship with its ideal of vast documentation. But there is another and more natively Russian foundation of Russian historiography: that represented by the first "Philosophic Letter" (1836) of Peter Chaadaev. The questions that Chaadaev raised, questions of Russia's destiny in the world, were soon to be elaborated into a great intellectual controversy that provided a major stimulus to nineteenth-century historical thought in Russia — the quarrel between Slavophile and Westerner. Is Russia part of the Western world or not? Has Russian society developed through the same historical stages as Western society or not? What special contribution to world history is Russia called to make? In short, what is the nature of Russia's historical destiny? These are the vast fundamental questions that moved and continue to move modern Russian historiography.

Literature and literary scholarship shared in this motivation kindled by national self-criticism. In the literary field the argument between Slavophile and Westerner did not occupy the central position, but the major concern nevertheless was still a concern with the national life and its destiny. Here the questions became: How does Russian literature represent Russian society? Have we a great literature or not — since art, as Herder, Schelling, and Hegel had shown, is the articulation of national culture? What is the role of literature in the developing national consciousness? These are the questions that stimulated Russian literary criticism from its modern beginnings; indeed, they remain the underlying questions today.

By the second half of the nineteenth century, Russian literary and historical scholarship was well launched in the main directions it was to follow for a number of decades. Scholarly activity had already been begun and major work had already been done in the preceding half century — for example, by Belinsky in literary criticism and by Karamzin in historiography. By 1861, gathering energies in both activities were beginning to find mature expression. The date is significant as marking the time of new freedoms in Russian life — and freedom to express itself was now a chief need of Russian scholarship. The new freedom was seriously qualified, to be sure, and the decades ahead would bring periodic reversions to the oppressive rule of Nicholas I. Thus the reforms that marked the beginning of the reign of Alexander II included more independence for university administration and faculty and larger salaries; but by the eighties an academic career of university teaching was attracting very few, for familiar reasons: oppressive supervision and poor salaries. One does not have to wait until the Soviet period to find examples of scholars in trouble with the authorities; more than one historian working in the later nineteenth century had his career seriously disrupted or frustrated by official disapproval. Yet the decades between the 1860's and the 1920's constitute a period when intellectual freedom in Russia was as broad as it would ever be. At the same time, both historical and literary scholarship had new materials to exploit: history could profit by the maturing national self-consciousness, and literary criticism could find in the new great age of Russian literature a rich accumulation of materials for study. As the century moved toward its end, both these conditions continued to prevail, and with increasing force. Historians coming into prominence after 1861 had the advantage of relative maturity: they could look back on an old feudal society that was passing, and they could also look back upon an old historiography that had been too much under the spell of Hegelianism and too much occupied with the everlasting Slavophile-Westerner debate. As for the field of literature, 1861 is as good a date as any for the beginning of the major phase; by the end of the century the literary historian Vengerov could write that Russian literature of the second half of the century had not only surpassed the achievement of any Western European country, but that in Russia literary achievement had surpassed all other areas of Russian cultural accomplishment.[3] The result is that the annals of Russian historical and literary scholarship during these years are filled with great names and great works.

For purposes of description, it would be simpler to take historiography and literary criticism separately. But if they are considered together, one can make an interesting discovery: namely, that they both move toward the same goal, the best name for which is scientific method (in the broadest meaning of the phrase). The greatest material riches in both fields consist of individual monographs, an impressive accumulation of distin-

[3] S. A. Vengerov, *Osnovnye cherty istorii noveishei russkoi literatury* (St. Petersburg, 1899), 5–6.

guished separate studies. But moving through this activity of producing more and more critical and historical studies runs a mounting drive toward scientific synthesis. In history, that effort found its culmination in Marxism. In literary criticism the same effort culminated in Formalism. Marxism and Formalism may be unhappy bedfellows, but the interesting fact remains that each of them represents a similar effort to be done with old ideological arguments and to strive for a purity of scientific objectivity. The "slap in the face" of the older social, civic, and utilitarian criticism that Formalism represented is a gesture of the same sort as Pokrovsky's repudiation of all Russian historiography coming before him. To cite Pokrovsky as an exponent of scientific method may seem questionable, especially since he was as effective as any single scholar could be in destroying the edifice of prerevolutionary historical science in Russia, which had been moving more and more progressively toward the goal of universality. Yet the emergence of Marxism in Russian historiography can still be seen as a final destination of the drive toward system in the writing of history.

In their increasingly lively pursuit of synthesis, both historical and literary scholarship of the prerevolutionary period is filled with ambitious projects of wide scope. In the field of history, big studies are undertaken — and usually left unfinished. One has the impression that anything under five volumes is only an "essay" (*opyt*) or a "sketch" (*ocherk*) — as witness Ikonnikov's essays on Russian historiography in two massive volumes[4] and Miliukov's sketches of Russian culture in three volumes.[5] Among the producers of mammoth works are numbered some of the most distinguished historians of the era after 1861. A leading example is Sergei Solov'ev with his twenty-nine-volume "History of Russia from the Earliest Times." [6] — death prevented the author from bringing it up to the nineteenth century. A similar example is Nicholas Kostomarov, whose "monographs and researches" fill twenty volumes.[7] A similar ambitiousness marks literary history in the era after 1861, but it takes a qualitative form. The works of literary scholarship are not so enormous in size, but they are broad in scope, assuming as a necessary part of their jurisdiction the whole history of society.

III

The large size of many historical works of the prerevolutionary period is partly the expression of the effort of Russian historical writing to make its outlook more and more inclusive. Increasingly throughout the latter half of the nineteenth century and into the twentieth, Russian historical

[4] V. S. Ikonnikov, *Opyt russkoi istoriografii* (2 vols.; Kiev, 1891–1908).
[5] P. N. Miliukov, *Ocherki po istorii russkoi kul'tury* (3 vols.; St. Petersburg, 1896–1903).
[6] S. M. Solov'ev, *Istoriia Rossii s drevneishikh vremen* (St. Petersburg, 1851–1879).
[7] N. I. Kostomarov, *Monografii i issledovaniia* (St. Petersburg, 1868–1889).

writing was concerned with elaborating a conception of a total moving structure of institutional life. Russian historiography from 1861 until the revolution is thus marked by an increasingly sociological orientation, a broadening of view to include all aspects of the national life, and a search for what it hoped could be established as laws of societal evolution. Into this context it was easy for Marxism to move, although Marxism imposed a doctrine upon a historical science that had been free to search for observable patterns.

In its move toward a conception of society as a total moving organism Russian historiography of the later nineteenth century corrected two major deficiencies in previous Russian historical writing: (1) an exaggerated veneration, learned partly from German historical scholarship, for facts and the accumulation of facts; and (2) an overvaluation of the higher strata of Russian society, of the state, of the tsar, as well as of the Great Russian people, in shaping the national history. As Russian historical writing developed, it made progress in transcending its earlier factualism in favor of historical synthesis, and in that synthesis it worked to include all the social strata and all the ethnic elements that had helped to shape the national history. Veneration for facts is hardly a fault in a historian, and the amassing of facts without adequate interpretation which marks much of nineteenth-century historical scholarship in Russia at least served the purpose of providing the materials from which history could be written. (Perhaps the writing of history should always begin with the gathering of too many facts.) The second limitation mentioned above, that of a tsar-centered, state-centered, Great-Russian-centered history, is not only a serious fault but one that is not corrected easily. If a film of modern Russian historiography could be opened with a scene of Karamzin composing his "History of the Russian State" and handing pages of his manuscript to Alexander I for approval, it would have to end with the picture of the Soviet historian as a state employee.

The first great step in expanding the view of the Russian historian was to move from writing histories of the Russian state to writing histories of the Russian people. This was a shift that was not long in coming, since many of the dominant ideological camps of nineteenth-century Russia had their reasons for favoring an emphasis upon the people: not only the Slavophiles and the populists, but also the radical Westernizing intelligentsia, and then the school of liberal Westerners, which provided the leading writers of Russian history. Slavophilism had provided the first major support for the claim of the common people to a place in Russian history, and it was the ranks of the Slavophiles that produced in Ivan Beliaev one of the first academic historians to take up the cause of the peasants.[8] This emphasis was further extended by later historians — for example, Shchapov, of populist tendencies, who not only continued

[8] For example in *Krest'iane na Rusi* (1859).

to argue for the importance of the peasant in Russian history, but who sought the physical and anthropological bases of a historical process that had been too much assigned to the "leaders." The radical intelligentsia, on the other hand, who had other reasons for arguing in support of the people, joined forces with conservative Slavophile sentiment in decrying the absence of the peasant from the annals of Russian history. Of course this radical stream of thought could have no place in the academy, and it was interested in publicizing an ideology rather than in scholarship; but a writer like Chernyshevsky certainly represents a correction of that voicelessness of the people that mars the work of a historian like Karamzin. In the strict annals of history writing it is the historians of liberal tendency who made the greatest contribution to this widening of the base of history. Major historians of the later nineteenth century like Solov'ev, Kavelin, Kliuchevsky, Semevsky, Miliukov, all gave due weight to the importance of the common people, not so much out of motives of political ideology as because a broad conception of Russian history seemed by this time impossible without a scholarly reckoning with the existence of the popular masses.

Recognition of the role of the people was sure to come in Russian historical scholarship: almost every major intellectual influence of the nineteenth century favored it. Much less inevitable was the qualification of a predominant Great Russian bias. This was a much more complex problem. A problem, indeed, that never was solved: certain promising lines of development were just being laid out when the revolution reversed the trend, until today the glorification of the Great Russian people seems almost the main task of the Soviet historian.

The widening of historical vision beyond the Great Russian capitals was greatly forwarded by historians of Ukrainian or other non-Great Russian origin, who by reason of their ethnic origins could feel the bias in Russian historiography. Kostomarov, Shchapov, and Hrushevsky are three important scholars who might be taken as representatives in this connection, Shchapov being of partly Buriat origin and the other two Ukrainian. Such scholars were simply insisting upon the evident fact that Russian history did not always proceed upon a schedule drawn up in Moscow or St. Petersburg — but it was an insistence that did not always make them popular, when even a historian of the stature of Solov'ev still carried the mark of Russian messianism. Purely patriotic conceptions of Russian history might be relatively easy to outgrow, as the best of Russian historians did succeed in outgrowing them; but the emphasis upon the Great Russian people, who after all occupied the center of the historical stage, was not an emphasis easy to change.

One promising school of thought, passing beyond the particular contributions of historians of minority origins and building toward a new geopolitics of Russian history, was Eurasianism. As the name implies, this conception of Russian history was based on a conception of Russia as belonging to both Europe and Asia but representing an entity in itself, distinct from both Europe and Asia. This school of thought not only brought a centrifugal influence to bear upon the standard Great Russian bias, but it broadened Russian history by placing it within the mainstream of Eurasian and universal history. But Eurasianism remained more a conceptual frame of reference than a consolidated school of historiography, and like all the promising tendencies of prerevolutionary historiography it was fated to receive little encouragement when the Soviet period really got under way.

IV

Just as historical scholarship made great advances toward broadening its outlook and establishing itself upon a sound scientific basis, so also literary scholarship of these years showed increasing promise of intellectual fulfillment. One might question whether that fulfillment ever came. By the twentieth century many new starts were made in the study of the craft of poetry and prose, but perhaps it must still be concluded that Russian literary scholarship continued to find its chief claim to originality in the distinctive character of social criticism. This is not a critical tradition that makes for superior criticism. But it has been the dominant Russian tradition, and one that has finally come into a kind of official beatification in the Soviet Union.

By the middle of the nineteenth century the social or civic tradition in the criticism of literature was already under full sail. Especially in its formative period, this tradition was carried on most vigorously by members of the radical intelligentsia, writing mostly for the "fat journals," working outside of academic institutions. Chernyshevsky, Dobroliubov, Pisarev — the names are sufficient to recall the flavor of that school of literary journalism, which aimed deliberately at what Pisarev called "the destruction of aesthetics" — and succeeded better than even Pisarev might have wished. One of the principal tenets of this school of criticism was that literary work is never to be considered as a thing of value for its own sake, for the great art of literature is thereby belittled into an effete and trivial hobby; the work of literary art must be judged mainly by its power to express and to transform the national life of Russia. Thus literary criticism included in its province the interpretation of the condition of the national life, and literary criticism as a result became something like a philosophy of society. One would naturally expect that the more radical opinions of the intelligentsia would not be adopted widely in the Russian university world; but at the same time their emphasis upon the social and cultural context of the literary work was sure to be congenial to the professorial mind. And the fact is that the writing of Russian literary history, both in and out of academic circles, came almost entirely under the influence of social criticism. Not only were important studies made of the heroes of social criticism, as in Pypin's study of Belinsky[9] and Steklov's study of Chernyshevsky;[10] but literary history became predominantly a history of social and political ideas, and a history for the most part unfriendly to the older culture of Russia. As for old Russian literature, it remained mostly a subject of more or less obscure academic interest.

Although limited in outlook, this social-history school of literary scholarship contributed many substantial studies, both of individual figures and of general periods, chiefly modern. Thus Skabichevsky's history of Russian literature from 1848 to 1890[11] or Ovsianiko-Kulikovsky's history of Russian literature of the nineteenth century[12] still remain useful to the student of Russian literature.

While many works of a popular and publicist nature were being produced in the field of literary history, the cultivation of what might be called a science of literature was being quietly carried on in the academic world. Specialists in such subjects as Russian folklore, Slavic linguistics, and comparative literature numbered among their more illustrious members such names as Buslaev, Potebnia, and Veselovsky, whose major work was done in the second half of the nineteenth century. Thus when the great age of the novel gave place to an age of poetry at the turn of the century, and interest grew in the technical and thematic analysis of the work of art as an end in itself, a certain foundation had already been laid for technical literary analysis. The efflorescence of Symbolism at the turn of the century, to be followed by such schools of poetry as Acmeism, Futurism, and Imagism, had the effect of bringing to the center of the literary stage the work of technical analysis that had remained a largely academic pursuit in the nineteenth century. This movement toward new emphasis upon the specifically literary character of the literary work, as opposed to the older school of social criticism, was a movement of many currents, which emptied into a mainstream called Formalism. The name is partly ironic, having been caught and used by the "Formalists" after it had been thrown at them by their literary opponents. But the name does serve to suggest a cult of the analysis of literary form which fought to replace the older cult of ideology.

Formalism was part of an effort in Russian literary scholarship to create something like a "science of literature"[13] — a term, like "theory

[9] A. N. Pypin, *Belinsky, ego zhizn' i perepiska* (St. Petersburg, 1876).

[10] I. M. Steklov, *N. G. Chernyshevsky, ego zhizn' i deiatel'nost', 1828–1889* (2 vols.; 2nd ed., Moscow, 1928).

[11] A. M. Skabichevsy, *Istoriia noveishei russkoi literatury 1848–1890 gg.* (St. Petersburg, 1891).

[12] D. Ovsianiko-Kulikovsky, *Istoriia russkoi literatury XIX veka* (5 vols.; Moscow, 1911).

[13] In Russian, *literaturovedenie*. Cf. *Literaturwissenschaft*.

of literature," that comes into increasing use at this time — which would transcend the merely personal or partisan opinions of the older criticism. It aspired to greater technical knowledge of the materials of literature, both Russian and comparative. It was thus disposed to receive assistance from academic scholarship in such fields as linguistics and classical philology. By their special interest in poetics, Formalist students made valuable contributions not only to the study of Russian verse in its technical aspects but to the study of "classical" Russian poets like Pushkin, who had been conspicuously neglected or crudely interpreted by nineteenth-century criticism.

Formalism in its major intention thus represents an emphasis that could not help but invigorate Russian criticism, too long given over to critics with too many extraliterary interests and missions. It also represents a welcome renewal of interest in poetry and poetics, subjects much neglected heretofore. In its total effect, therefore, Russian Formalism brought a rich fertilization into the study of literature. But at the same time it exhibited weaknesses and extravagances. This sophisticated refusal to avoid looking for meaning in the work of literary art, in favor of analyzing linguistic and stylistic devices, is one-sided. The literary artist is, or should be, a craftsman in language; but he is also, or should be, saying something. The danger of "formal" analysis always is that it will pay such meticulous attention to how the author is talking that it will neglect to listen to what he is saying. Russian Formalism suffered from this fault, partly no doubt in extreme reaction against the opposite fault among the social critics of looking only for literary messages. A fully mature literary criticism would be one that managed to combine both concerns, and in fact to see them as one single concern. This ultimate maturity was doubtless promised for the future to Russian literary scholarship, if the free evolution of literary study had been allowed to continue. Already in the twenties, just before its demise, Formalism could be observed, especially in Zhirmunsky and Tynianov, and even Eikhenbaum, reaching beyond its original concentration upon technique into a broadening interest in the nonliterary realities surrounding and affecting the work of literary art. But with the consolidation of Soviet literary policy, free evolution was replaced by doctrine. Social criticism and Formalism are the thesis and antithesis; but the world of Russian literary scholarship still awaits a synthesis.

v

With the advent of the revolution, Russian scholarship was not abruptly diverted from its course. In fact, the main tendencies of the prerevolutionary period continued to work themselves out for at least a decade. Formalism, indeed, had its heyday in the early twenties. In the field of history, Platonov might serve as an example of a distinguished prerevolutionary historian joining the ranks of the Soviet intelligentsia by becoming director of the archives and library of the Academy of Sciences and continuing publication of monographs based on his earlier research. That is not to say that scholarship was not seriously affected by the bleak years of the Civil War and War Communism, as well as by the application of official policy in intellectual affairs.

Even in the more drastic changes of intellectual direction brought by the Soviet period it is, of course, possible to see revivals of traditional tendencies. The whole temper and outlook of Soviet literary criticism, for example, is partly a culmination of the traditions of the radical intelligentsia of the nineteenth century. And if the effort is made to give literary scholarship a systematically Marxist orientation, that effort too had been already started in the preceding century, especially with the writings of Plekhanov. Similarly Pokrovsky, whose school rose into ascendancy in the field of history in the twenties, was already a well-established historian before the revolution.

What gradually emerged as new or distinctive in scholarship in the Soviet period was on the whole a decline from the past. Scholarship, a precarious structure under the best circumstances, cannot endure the pressures of ulterior motives. Soviet policy is intent upon turning scholars into publicists and upon using the materials of literary and historical scholarship to buttress ideological or political platforms, as if scholarship had not ultimate reason for being except utility. And since the Soviet scholar is an employee of the state, he cannot work independently of official policy, even in his efforts to circumvent it.

The lengths to which the distortion of scholarship by political programs has been carried in the Soviet Union can shock even the well informed, and documentation would only be tiresome. From the time of the early thirties until the present, the fact is that nothing is done in the field of literary and historical scholarship that does not in some way serve state policy. Even the relaxation of controls, as during World War II, can still serve policy. Soviet literary criticism, for example, has long debated such terms as Socialist Realism and later abstruse concepts, equally amorphous, like *ideinost'* and *partiinost'*. But when all is said and done, there is no mystery about these doctrines: for practical purposes, they simply serve as abstract cover names for the dictates of party policy. Nothing reveals this more dramatically than the sudden shifts in party policy, always followed by equally sudden and parallel shifts in literary criticism.

The situation in this regard has clearly worsened as the Soviet period has proceeded. But the roots of the trouble were always there, for they lie in fundamental attitudes characteristic of Communist leadership from the beginning. Even a thoughtful book like Trotsky's *Literature and Revolution,* published in 1924, can be taken as an unfavorable omen: too serious an interest in literature on the part of leading officials does not promise well for literary freedom. Of course the party leadership is not only interested in the intellectual situation but constitutes the first authority on every fundamental intellectual question. Nicholas I may have kept an eye on writers, but at least he did not write books on linguistics.

Partly because of the poverty of Soviet literature, literary scholarship of the Soviet period has done its best work on prerevolutionary subjects. In criticism, this has meant a revival of the social critics of radical bent, beginning with Belinsky. Such figures have been studied and their works published, always with appropriate interpretations and frequently with quiet omissions, but nevertheless in useful editions. Similarly the classics of nineteenth-century Russian literature have been widely published and many materials published about classic authors. Certain major authors may be commended for extraneous or distorted reasons: thus Pushkin may be glorified as a rebel against oppression or a poet of the Russian folk, or Tolstoy as a partisan of the Russian people. Other less acceptable authors, Dostoevsky especially, are the subject of deviously fluctuating policy.

Dostoevsky is the prime example of a dilemma in Russian literary scholarship. Dostoevsky is a major Russian author, and so he must be glorified; but the heart and soul of Dostoevsky's work contradicts basic assumptions of Soviet doctrine. Such a subject calls for considerable astuteness in interpretation. The result is that scholarship on Dostoevsky at times has simply languished, as during the thirties and during the period of Zhdanovism after World War II. But this is not the favored solution; such an outstanding example of Great Russian genius is simply too precious to neglect. Yet one could suspect that Soviet critics would be happier if Dostoevsky had never existed. A Great Russian author of the first magnitude who seems alien to the Soviet *Weltanschauung* — this is a great disaster.

Dostoevsky may be the most striking example of the difficulties that nineteenth-century Russian literature can present to the Soviet scholar. But the difficulty is far more general than one hard case. The fact is that the Soviet outlook, especially in its optimistic view of man and society, is alien to the spirit of many of the greatest works of Russian literature. Dostoevsky is only the most striking example; but Pushkin, Gogol, Lermontov, Goncharov, Turgenev, Tolstoy — these are only some of the most distinguished names of writers who would find unacceptable the predominant official Soviet attitudes toward the nature of man and society. That Soviet scholars manage to rehabilitate these nineteenth-century greats for their own purposes proves little but the dexterity of Soviet scholars.

As for contribution to theory or methods in the literary field, Soviet scholarship was never very promising. First of all, Marxism is devoid of an aesthetic, and it is probably hopeless to try to evolve one from it. As if that were not bad enough, by the time Soviet controls became firmly consolidated it was no longer Marxism but simply party policy that the scholar and critic had to reckon with. The ultimate result of such a situation is that scholarship simply has no history; only the party has a history.

For history itself as a field of scholarship, in contrast to literary scholarship, it might reasonably have been expected that the Soviet period would bring a brilliant development. After all, the Communist revolution was by nature a revaluation of history, at least of the history of Russia; and one of the important claims of Marxism is that it represents a philosophy of history. Indeed one of the unique features of Soviet society is that it is a society consciously planned to operate in conformity to a system of historical goals and principles, however vaguely defined. Those large questions of Russian national destiny and "world-historical" role that nineteenth-century Russian thought had raised so anxiously became in the Soviet period the decisive motivation of practical national policy. In such circumstances it goes without saying that the study of history cannot remain a matter of only academic interest. As a result historiography has been one of the liveliest arts of Soviet scholarship. But in the last analysis the writing of history in the Soviet Union is interesting mostly as a lively demonstration of ideological and political controls, and their evasion. For the immediacy of official concern that gives the study of history a vigorous sense of relevance also imposes a vigorous regulation. Perhaps no activity is more important to the ruling authority in a totalitarian society than the interpretation of historical fact. In the Soviet Union the past must be rehabilitated not only for the purpose of vindicating the ruling party and its current leadership, but also for the purpose of vindicating Marxism. Toward the former end the history of the revolution and of the party has had to be rewritten frequently; toward the latter end the history of Russia and of the world must ultimately be rewritten. Unfortunately for the Soviet historian, the supreme fact of Russian history for him — the revolution — contradicts Marx. But this is only one example of the enormous difficulties under which the Soviet historian is forced to work.

The Soviet historian's necessity of reconciling his work at every turn with current ideological and political purposes forces every Soviet historical work to lead a double life: as a description of historical fact and as a revelation of party policy. Its latter function may be revealed in devious ways: for example, the choice of topic may tell more than anything said about the topic. So also the absence of studies may be revealing — as, for example, the reduction almost to nothing just after the revolution of the distinguished prerevolutionary Russian scholarship in church history.

The impact of the revolution upon Russian historical writing was immediately discernible in the rapid rise to dominance of the school of Pokrovsky. The revolution called for a Marxist interpretation of history with at least more urgency than it called for a Marxist interpretation of literature. Yet, as in the field of literary scholarship and criticism, Russian historiography in the twenties still remained relatively free and varied, with non-Marxist historians continuing to occupy important positions. But by the end of the 1920's the school of Pokrovsky, with its emphasis on the universal application of the doctrine of historical materialism and with its disparagement of the prerevolutionary Russian national past, had won the field. The fact that soon after his death in 1932 Pokrovsky was officially repudiated does not alter his importance as a figurehead of the rapid installation of ideological control in the field of historical writing. In the crucial turning point of the early thirties, the demise of Pokrovsky might be compared to the demise of RAPP as signifying the move from a more particularistic authoritarianism to a more centralized control.

Following the consolidation of centralized control that marked Soviet life in all areas after the First Five Year Plan, historical scholarship in the Soviet Union, like literary criticism, moved down a rather steep path of decline. The reinforcement of control as such is probably not the primary cause of this decline, but rather the goals which historical writing was now forced to serve — all clustered about the central goal of national self-glorification. All the advances that had been made in the past hundred years in developing away from nationalistic history toward the application of objective scientific method now seem swept away in a kind of reversion to early beginnings. The tendency to attach excessive importance to the role of the state and of the Great Russian people, which historiography of the past generation had been working to qualify, now assumes a more active role than ever before.

The effort of the school of Pokrovsky to interpret history in terms of impersonal economic forces rather than national individuality, and its tendency to take a negative view of the Russian past, obviously had no place in the new program of Great Russian nationalism. In this radical about-face of the early thirties there are inherent, it would seem, certain advantages for the art of historiography. The national past in its historical individuality must at least be recognized and respected if it is to be written about at all. And it is true that the nationalistic emphasis of the thirties, further strengthened by the war, produced numerous studies of Russian historical personalities that the impersonalism of Pokrovsky had deliberately obliterated. But the advantages of renewed interest in the Russian past were more than balanced by the tremendous damage to the science of history inflicted by the cult of national self-glorification. Now even the glorification of socialism, which it is a chief task of Soviet history to teach, comes to be used as a demonstration of the superiority of the Russian people, since they are the first people in the world to have achieved a socialist society. The historical assessment of foreign influences in Russian history, which prerevolutionary historiography had worked to build up, now becomes the crime of "cosmopolitanism." In this spirit Norman and Byzantine influences in early Russian history are, for example, systematically discounted — not for reasons of respect for historical evidence but for reasons of strategy.

Thus in both literary and historical scholarship the revolution has succeeded even beyond its conscious intention in repudiating the best of the Russian past. The party in power, by its very effort to make scholarship serve a useful purpose, has disappointed the great promise of humanistic scholarship in Russia.

SCHOLARSHIP IN THE NATURAL SCIENCES

NICHOLAS DeWITT

I

The words "scholarship" and "natural sciences" are commonly used with reassuring definiteness, and yet the meaning of each, and particularly in combination, is often ambiguous. The seemingly precise term "natural sciences" is like a rubber band which may be contracted or stretched at will. It can be all-embracing — as broad as the German *Naturwissenschaft* or its Russian countepart *estestvoznanie* can make it — or very narrow, limited to physics and chemistry as is also sometimes done. If the broad definition is accepted, then it has to be stretched even further to include mathematics ("the logic and the symbolic language of science") and the applied natural sciences, such as engineering, medicine, and the like. Stretching the definitional bounds has its immediate advantage in the discussion of historical trends, and hence the unrestricted *estestvoznanie* (including mathematics and the applied arts) has been favored for this chapter.

In regard to scholarship, the problem is not solved so easily. To begin with, the word "scholarship" is commonly used to designate only the demonstrable act of having acquired certain knowledge without reference to the process of its acquisition. In dictionary terms, however, "scholarship" is defined as synonymous with both "knowledge" and "learning." It is obvious that learning is a process and that knowledge is a product obtained by studying or from instruction and is the result of a process.

This process may be theoretical or experimental, or both, and it is often referred to simply as "research," particularly in the field of the natural sciences. The question arises when we speak of "scholarship" in the natural sciences (or in any other field) as to whether we are concerned with the product or the process and how we can make a meaningful separation in order to distinguish the two.

D. I. Mendeleev's system of periodic elements or N. I. Lobachevsky's non-Euclidian geometry, V. I. Veksler's autophasing principle (for cyclotrons), or the BESM digital computer are all, though quite distinct in their substance, "products." There are many other products of this type, and all of them in combination represent a specific item in our applied and theoretical knowledge. Yet each one of these products was obtained through a certain creative process, which in turn may have been significantly conditioned by social, political, and economic factors. The process of creative research is an individual act carried out by a single person or a plurality. In reference to the existing body of knowledge, new "products," theories, and experimental findings may be irrational. In science the new rationale thus introduced has to meet the criteria of logical consistency in respect to itself. Consequently, the essential point is that while the individual steps in the creative "research" process (particularly the logical steps of abstraction, analysis, and synthesis) may be the same for different individuals, diverse localities, and distinct points in time, because of the impact of external factors (such as dogmatic systems) the product may be of better or worse quality or may even not emerge at all. It is just like baking a loaf of bread — the ingredients and process are constant and yet the oven temperature may burn it to a frazzle.

The difficulty here, of course, is how to present in the most general terms the nature of the problem with which this essay is designed to deal. Which is it going to be: the product, the process, or the factors which condition the process and in this way affect the product? The interrelation of science and society — and this, I believe, is the main topic of our concern here in studying the historical trends accounting for the transformation of Russian society in the last hundred years — can be most meaningfully approached by studying the process, and particularly the factors which condition it, rather than the products. An immediate objection to this approach may be raised, for the existing products and the contemporary internal state of the separate disciplines cannot be overlooked, and thus the substantive content of a given field of science conditions further steps of development.

It should be added hastily, therefore, that if we were concerned not with the interrelation of science and society but rather with the substantive indexes of science, or the qualitative evaluations of a certain level of accomplishment at some specific point in time, or even with the dynamics of the accumulation of theoretical and applied knowledge — for all this we would have to turn primarily to products. Actually there is a circular process involved. The "products" of scientific research per se or through their embodiment in technological by-products affect the social structures. It is indeed true, as Bertrand Russell has said, that the natural sciences exercise a powerful impact upon social organization, which in turn cause political change.[1] But if we are to break the chain of interrelationships and dependencies, I think this break should come, if for no better reason than for the sake of analytical convenience, at the level of factors affecting the process of scholarship or research. Thus, in speaking about trends in scientific research in Russia during the last hundred years, this essay will be concerned primarily with those factors which may have had their impact upon the process of creative scholarship in the fields of the natural sciences.

In following this approach I do not want inadvertently to open a Pandora's box and plunge exclusively, as James B. Conant remarked in *On Understanding Science,* into the discussion of "the interconnection between science and society, about which so much has been said in recent years by our Marxist friends."[2] We are concerned with such interconnection, but we should be more than wary of accepting it in terms of a one-way-street determinism. What Marx and Engels did not accomplish by their economic overdeterminism, the party theologians of *Voprosy filosofii* in Russia and some of their Western intellectual cousins succeeded in doing — namely, almost strangling the historiography and sociology of science. Stripped bare, Marxian analytical categories of the "superstructure" and the "base" offer little help in explaining the factors affecting the processes of creative scientific research and the development of technology as its extension. There are a variety of causal factors, at times autonomous, which affect the process of scholarship and which cannot be squeezed even by the most daring manipulation into two predetermined analytical categories.

Investigations in the natural sciences are indeed by and large manifestations of intellectual activity. As is well known, Marxist definitions regard "all intellectual activity as a part of a superstructure of social development taken as a whole."[3] Scholarship in the natural sciences belongs there too, by definition, but at the same time the natural sciences as an indispensable tool in the creation of the technical means of production form a part of the "base." At least in Marxian dialectics we have this conceptual problem at hand with which Soviet theoreticians attempt

[1] B. Russell, *The Impact of Science on Society* (New York, 1951), 3.
[2] J. B. Conant, *On Understanding Science* (Cambridge, Mass., 1947), 18.
[3] P. E. Mosely, "Freedom of Artistic Expression and Scientific Inquiry in Russia," *Annals of the American Academy of Political and Social Science,* CC (November 1938), 254.

to struggle on occasion. In order to get out of this muddle, the Soviet academician S. G. Strumilin proposed in 1951 "not to assign all that science deals with to the category of superstructures" and to exempt the natural sciences from the superstructure. Since science plays the role of a productive force (through its "embodiment" in the technical means of production) it should be viewed as a "natural resource" and thus one of the primary factors in production.[4] This was an obvious heresy, and the party theologians immediately condemned it. Shortly thereafter Strumilin had to reverse his position and to recognize sheepishly that "it would be totally erroneous to recognize scientific thought as a primary source of technical progress"; science was *not* a productive force, and so on and on.[5] It is very doubtful that much insight can be gained by following Soviet "theoretical" arguments as to the causal factors of the scientific-research activity in Russia. In fact, as will become apparent below, in the nineteenth century the meager Russian base was out of kilter with the flourishing intellectual superstructure.

II

The natural sciences and technology in Russia, their development and interrelation with the world's scientific and technological progress, and their interdependence with the social and political institutions of Russia — this is a vast, important, though highly neglected, subject. Although some work has been done in regard to the substantive aspects of science and its interrelations with Communist ideology and politics during the Soviet era,[6] no integrated studies with historical retrospect have appeared as yet. The difficulties in handling this perplexing subject are not indigenous to American scholars of Soviet Russia. Even in the Soviet Union itself, up to the present time, there are no integrated surveys of the development of the natural sciences and technology, although there has been enormous activity in this field.

Prior to the mid-1930's a number of histories of the Academy of Sciences appeared, but the Academy's effort to do research on the history of the natural sciences in Russia at large is of more recent origin. In 1938 at the Academy of Sciences, the Commission on the History of the Academy was reconstituted so as to give it the broader task of investigat-

[4] S. G. Strumilin, "Nauka v svete ucheniia I. V. Stalina o bazise i nadstroike," *Izvestiia Akademii Nauk: Otdelenie Ekonomiki i Prava,* no. 4 (1951), 287–288.

[5] S. G. Strumilin, "Nauka i razvitie proizvoditel'nykh sil," *Voprosy filosofii,* no. 3 (1954), 46, 51–52.

[6] E. Ashby, *A Scientist in Russia* (New York, 1947); C. Zirkle, ed., *Soviet Science* (Washington, 1952); A. Vucinich, *The Soviet Academy of Sciences* (Stanford, 1956); Arnold Buchholz, *Ideologie und Forschung in der Sowjetschen Naturwissenschaft* (Stuttgart, 1953); B. Moore, Jr., *Terror and Progress: USSR* (Cambridge, Mass., 1954).

ing the role of the Academy in developing Russian science.[7] During World War II, in 1942–1944, half a dozen commissions emerged, each of which dealt separately with the history of a given field of science (such as biological, engineering, physical-mathematical, or chemical science). In addition, in 1944 under the Division of History of the Academy of Sciences of the USSR, an Institute of the History of Natural Sciences (under the direction of K. S. Koshtoiants) was formed, and it is rumored that Stalin personally was instrumental in organizing it. I am inclined to believe that the mushrooming activity in this field by the Academy in the 1940's was promoted to a great extent by political motivation and party edicts. But at the same time it would not have made such startling headway if it were not one of the pet projects of S. I. Vavilov, then the president of the Academy (until 1951), who was not merely an outstanding physicist but had for years advocated research into the history of Russian science. In this case, as in many others, personalities count and Vavilov had many helping hands among Soviet academicians, for interest in the history of science has always existed among Russian scientists. It should be added that for some of the ardent promoters this also meant "an easy kill" as far as the reward of advanced degrees was concerned. The latter may particularly account for the volume of mediocre dissertations which one finds aimed at a historical slant.

In the fall of 1953 the Institute of the History of Natural Sciences was transferred directly under the jurisdiction of the Presidium of the Academy of Sciences, and all commissions were incorporated into its structure (as well as the renowned Lomonosov Museum [formerly *Kunstkamera*] and another natural history museum). This newly reconstituted establishment was named the Institute for History of Natural Science and Technology (at first headed by A. M. Samarin, and since early 1957 by N. A. Figurovsky).[8] These original commissions and the Institute were designated to study the history of science in Russia from the point of view of demonstrating the gains of "native science" (*otechestvennoi nauki*). The strength of this expression, *scientia patriae*, has no English equivalent. Their activities resulted in a veritable downpour of publications. In addition to books, pamphlets, and articles in regular Academy publications, the monthly *Nauka i zhizn'* (Science and Life) was designated to propagandize this attitude at the popular level.

During the decade 1941–1951 alone it was reported that some eight

---

[7] For a discussion of the role of the Academy as a leader, see, for example, Akademiia Nauk SSSR, *Ocherki po istorii Akademii Nauk* (Moscow, 1945), in five parts: biological, chemical, linguistic, historical, and physical-mathematical sciences.

[8] For more details, see Akademiia Nauk SSSR, *220 let Akademiia Nauk SSSR* (Moscow, 1945); *Vestnik Akademiia Nauk* (to be referred to hereafter as *VAN*), no. 4 (1954), 88, no. 10 (1953), 109, no. 3 (1957), 18; and Vucinich, *The Soviet Academy of Sciences*. *passim*.

hundred books and thirty-five hundred articles concerning the history of science in Russia, the majority with distinct emphasis on achievements (*dostizheniia*) of native scientists, appeared.[9] Significant portions of the annual general assemblies of the Academy in the 1940's, as well as special conferences, were devoted to the history of "native" Russian science. Directives were issued and special research projects were organized to establish claims to priority of discoveries and research of Russian scientists. The famous general assembly in 1949 (January 5–11) was devoted exclusively to "problems of the history of native science."[10] But even prior to this growing activity, a large number of pamphlets, books, and articles had appeared.[11]

What kind of information do they present? The majority of these publications deal with the biographies of outstanding Russian scientists,[12] certain discoveries or surveys of the development of narrow specific branches of science and technology.[13] They are very rich in detail, descriptions, and personalia. But an integrated survey which would discuss general trends, the interrelations of different branches of science and technology in Russia proper, and their ties with world science and technology has still not been produced.

The first and the only integrated effort of this type is currently in progress at the Institute of History of Natural Sciences and Technology of the Academy, which has recently published the first volume of a "History of the Natural Sciences in Russia."[14] The second volume, dealing with the second half of the nineteenth century and the prerevolutionary twentieth century, is scheduled to appear in the "near future." The history of natural sciences during the Soviet era is contemplated, then, as a separate publication without any indication as to the probable date of appearance. It is the first Russian attempt to do such integrated work, and the published volume deals with the period prior to 1861. But in reading this prehistory of modern science in Russia in a magnificent edition prepared by some twenty outstanding Russian authorities, with

[9] *VAN*, no. 5 (1953), 12.

[10] Akademiia Nauk, *Voprosy istorii Otechestvennoi Nauki* (Moscow, 1949).

[11] Perhaps the most complete (though somewhat out-of-date) bibliography can be found in S. I. Vavilov, ed., *Trudy Instituta Istorii Estestvoznaniia* (Moscow, 1947), I, 457–535 (summary bibliography).

[12] A useful short-cut in dealing with brief biographical data can be found by consulting the two-volume reference: S. I. Vavilov, ed., *Liudi Russkoi Nauki* (Moscow, 1948). Otherwise, there are several hundred books dealing with biographies of individual scientists.

[13] The interested reader should start exploring this vast material by consulting first the three main sources: Akademiia Nauk, *Trudy Instituta Istorii Estestvoznaniia* (5 vols.; Moscow, 1947–1951); Akademiia Nauk, *Trudy Instituta Istorii Estestvoznaniia i Tekhniki*, to date 15 vols.; *Uchenye Zapiski Moskovskogo Gosudarstvennogo Universiteta*, various issues, especially during the years 1947–1949.

[14] Akademiia Nauk SSSR, Institut Istorii Estestvoznaniia i Tekhniki (N. A. Figurovsky, ed.), *Istoriia Estestvoznaniia v Rossii* (Moscow, 1957), I, parts 1 and 2.

the aid of a very substantial staff, I could not suppress the feeling that even if we had the second volume (for the period 1861–1917) at our disposal, the pastures would still remain greener elsewhere.

Despite heavy bias (and occasional forgery), however, the second volume summarizing the Academy's work, dealing for over a decade with the history of science in Russia, will be unique, for it must be admitted that today the Soviet Union is the only country in the world extensively preoccupied with the historiography of science and technology. I doubt that for the last hundred years of scientific and technological development we will find an adequate study for any country. At least I have not been able to find one which was broad enough to discuss general trends, and not specifics of scientific hypothesis, discoveries, or the personalities of scientists. This entire area of studies seems to be a wide-open field. The objection might be raised at this point that the subject matter of science is such that one cannot dispense with specifics and that all the trivia count. While in historical retrospect certain things may seem trivial, they may have been the moving vehicle of scientific discovery. Perhaps this is so, and yet generalizations are in order and they are to be viewed as "trends" for present purposes. Continuity or change in respect to one specific aspect or development over time will therefore be called a trend.

III

Keeping in mind that the term "trend" is and should be used advisedly, for it does not necessarily imply continuity or uniformity of certain developments, what are the trends that a number of Soviet studies of "native science" are trying to ascertain? There are two main ones in evidence in all these studies, and this applies also to the new magnum opus, "History of the Natural Sciences in Russia." First, they perpetrate and promote the view of unadulterated nationalism and chauvinism as far as scientific discoveries and theories are concerned. Occasional lip service is paid to Western science, but the theme of priority of Russian science is ubiquitous. The point which is being argued is that any Russian scientist, past or present, had a Russian precursor.

It would be easy to shrug this off if this argumentation was not relevant for our understanding of one of the real trends in the process of natural-science scholarship. Throughout the centuries, many scientific theories and discoveries were made because the people who made them were skeptics and did not accept as "truth" the postulates of their predecessors. This was universally true, and was true in Russia in the nineteenth and early twentieth centuries. The body of scientific thought was universal and international and was openly questioned, no matter which source or whose authority. Organized skepticism is the moving vehicle of scientific progress. However, during the last two decades in particular, Soviet science has not followed this maxim of scientific inquiry. The quite deliberate manipulation and marshaling of facts has been under way in the search for "native ancestry" for scientific theories, discoveries, and inventions. If this is a factor entering into the mental process in the course of creative research, then it can result in very unfortunate effects upon scholarship in the natural sciences. I believe the trend for which the Academy has been busily searching for the last two decades has imposed limitations and chains on Soviet scholarship which never before existed in the eighty years since 1861. This is a fundamental trend, the assessment of which can be rendered by Whitehead's apothegm: "A science which hesitates to forget its founders is lost."

The second main trend which the Soviet studies of the history of the natural sciences are trying to prove is the thesis that the process of scientific inquiry progresses to higher levels in successive stages, from "primitive materialism" to "chaotic" and "nonsystematic," "natural-historical materialism" (*estestvenno-istoricheskii materializm*), on to organized, conscious, and orderly philosophical "dialectical materialism." [15] Archives and the writings of most prerevolutionary scientists are gone over with a fine-tooth comb in order to find even the vaguest hints of "materialism" as a belief. In its dogmatic essence it is related to an "ancestry search" though it is carried out with far greater vigor. The pilot light, of course, is Lenin's statement of 1911 that physics was undergoing labor pains because dialectical materialism as the sole philosophical foundation of modern physics (and science at large) was being born.[16] This official ideology may be even more constrictive to the process of scientific inquiry and organized skepticism than the ancestry search. The indoctrination of Russian science with dialectical materialism as a method of scientific inquiry has been progressing with great intensity for about three decades (since the late 1920's), and it again represents a reversal of the real trend which prevailed in the prerevolutionary period and which is characterized by a lack of unifying ideological orthodoxy. In regard to both these developments, the strait jacket of national ancestry and the dogmatic prescriptions concerning the philosophy of science and its methods, though they may at times not be taken very seriously by some practicing scientists, nevertheless constitute a hindrance and serve as an artificial restraint upon creative scholarship as far as science at large is concerned.

Both these trends — the attempt to reorient science along national lines and the forceful persuasion to accept dialectical materialism as the method of science — serve as the foundation of a third trend. This is

---

[15] Among a number of works on this topic, see the outstanding example, A. A. Maksimov (corresponding member of the Academy of Sciences), *Ocherki po istorii bor'by za materializm v Russkom Estestvoznanii* (Moscow, 1947). Volume imprimatur of the Institute of Philosophy of the Academy of Sciences of the USSR.

[16] V. I. Lenin, *Sochineniia*, XIV, 299.

the over-all ideological creed and political conformity which are being promoted by the Soviet regime. These were not fostered by the pre-revolutionary government in Russia and represent a new departure in the Soviet period. Russian science of the prerevolutionary era is characterized by its tendency to dissent; and although the Tsarist regime was at times hostile to this, it did not enforce a unified dogmatic creed. While there are undoubtedly conflicts on a philosophical plane which may be resolved (or neglected at times), it is essential to realize the fact that since the mid-1930's, and especially in the 1940's, ideological and political factors had their impact also upon institutional arrangements. Professor Mosely observed over twenty years ago that "politicians, but slightly acquainted with complex problems which are being worked out along the frontiers of knowledge, attempt crudely and arbitrarily to define the channels and goals of human thought." [17] It was not only the philosophical plane but the substantive part of research that was affected via institutional channels. In a number of instances arbitrariness was introduced because scientific charlatans had the political power to manipulate the direction of research. This did not happen in all areas of research, but there are a number of well-publicized instances (notably Lysenko's genetics) which reveal the possible extent of damage to scholarly pursuits resulting from this politically oriented arbitrariness.

Consequently, it was, and still is, feared that:

such a hamstrung species of science is not likely to advance the frontier of general knowledge very far. Over a short period of time, extreme specialization, based on intensive work and also on the general advances borrowed from countries with a relatively broad scientific freedom, may give striking and valuable results. In the long run, and especially if cut off from like activities in other countries by deliberate self-isolation, this policy is likely to result in intellectual sterility. Such restriction of freedom in abstract science will ultimately affect unfavorably the development of practical knowledge.[18]

Obviously the severity of such an impact may vary from field to field, and the time factor becomes an all-important criterion. It is being argued (in view of the demonstrations of some recent Soviet advances in science and technology — from atomic energy developments to the sputniks) that we are now still dealing with short-run developments, and as far as the long-run impact is concerned, only time will tell.

While it is essential to keep these trends in mind as the guide rails of the evolution of scholarship in the natural sciences in Tsarist and Soviet Russia, the question which remains unanswered is how an individual Soviet scientist feels about them. We have very meager clues, but during the brief period of the thaw in 1956 some revealing stories came out. One of them, told by a well-known Soviet writer, Valentin

[17] Mosely, 20.
[18] Mosely, 20.

Kaverin, in his novel "Search and Hope," makes most worthwhile reading:

In the postwar years we had posed before us the strange task of proving that our medical science [the story specifically deals with the invention of penicillin] was developing with unusual speed, or at least with a faster rate than the developing of science in other countries and in the world at large. It has been asserted in books and articles, in movies and plays, that all the major discoveries of the nineteenth and twentieth centuries were made by us. Yes, by us alone and nobody else. And in making this claim, while defending this invented, imaginary priority, it has gone unnoticed that we are losing the real advances obtained through agonizingly hard work and search. There are dozens of reasons why we were losing this real priority, but the main one among them was that no one of us had the right to share his discoveries even with the neighboring laboratory.

Oh, this secrecy and gloom which prevented us from seeing one another! Even now as I write these lines in 1956, we still have not called quits to this ignorant nonsense, mysterious rubbish around which we have built barbed-wire fences and which was stored after hours in sealed-for-security safes. There were many "wise guys" who had absolutely no place in medical science, who received high titles under the protective cover of this artificial secrecy, without which — strangely enough — we could neither work nor live.

This imaginary, artificially invented science required artificial invigoration as well, and to accomplish this, wide debates were organized in order to show off to the entire world the sparkle of our creativity, the clash of our creative minds. But even under this most artificial light, there appeared in full view only the shabby decorations of dogmatism, ready-made concepts, and prompted thoughts.

Of course this was the victory of Kramov [a Soviet scientist-bureaucrat with party affiliation and backing]. It was a victory, the evil consequences of which he himself could not have foreseen.[19]

Where there is light like this, there may also be hope. Perhaps the chains on the process of creative scholarship stemming from national-traditional, ideological, and political sources only look strong; underneath them there may be an undercurrent of healthy "organized skepticism." When Soviet intellectuals and scientists are told that "whatever cult there might be . . . wherever there is a cult, scientific thought must retreat before blind faith, creativity must submit to dogma and popular opinion to the rule of arbitrariness,"[20] it contains at least the realization of the predicament that confronts creative activity in the Soviet Union. And the realization of a predicament is a healthy sign in itself.

This discussion may be summed up as follows. In prerevolutionary Russia, creative intellectual activity and scholarship in the natural sciences were not subjected to the influences of one unifying and official ideology. The attitude of the state was one of indifference or, at times, of suspicious hostility. The concept of "native ancestry" was not held in

[19] V. Kaverin, *Poiski i nadezhdy* (a novel, third part of the trilogy "Open Book"), in M. I. Alger et al., eds., *Literaturnaia Moskva: sbornik vtoroi* (Moscow, 1956), 277–278.

[20] A. Kron, "Zametki pisatelia," *Literaturnaia Moskva*, 780.

a position of authority. During the period of the 1920's, which can be characterized by the so-called proletarianization scheme (namely, trying to point out the proletarian origins of intellectual activity and its participants) and a campaign of "withering away of the differences between mental and physical labor," Russian science and scientists occupied an ambiguous and uncertain position. This period of the 1920's might be called a transitional one, during which the natural sciences gained some recognition and state support but still retained freedom in the sense of neutrality and noninterference. Since about the mid-1930's, the period of active conversion has begun to take place, the net result of which cannot yet be fully appraised.

IV

Another trend in the development of science and technology in Russia which ought to be singled out is the interaction of applied and theoretical science. It appears to me to be of primary significance that Russian scientific development, particularly at the end of the nineteenth century, proceeded largely without the blend of pure and applied research. It appears characteristic for the Tsarist and Soviet scientific and research effort that there has been and still is a differential and conflicting level of pure and applied knowledge.

It is a well-recognized fact that continuous interdependence of abstract (theoretical) and applied knowledge (inventions and technology) is essential for the progress of both in the natural-science fields. They are but two manifestations of the unified human effort to reach higher levels of understanding and the mastery of nature. To divorce one from the other, to explain or justify one at the expense of the other, or to promote one while neglecting the other is bound to result in conflict. This conflict manifests itself first in the lags which accompany the process of introducing inventions and innovations and, second, particularly in the ways in which a body of applied knowledge is advanced and modified by internal, indigenous theoretical research, rather than by external, imported inventions, equipment, and techniques. The conflicting level of theoretical and applied advances, or conflict in the states of knowledge, results in gaps and particularly in qualitative unevenness. Obviously, these problems are universal in nature, but the enormous differential which is observable in the state of pure knowledge and applied research, in the body of theoretical knowledge and its application to industry and technology, in prerevolutionary Russia and still present in the Soviet Union represents, to my mind, a quite striking and unique historical trend.

The crucial factor indispensable for the understanding of the nature of this paradox of flourishing theoretical science versus the lack of its application is that in the second half of the nineteenth century in Russia there was hardly any industrial or technological foundation to which to apply the rich theoretical findings of natural science. In Russia at that time there was a virtual lack of what Soviet historians now commonly call a "broad material and technical base." This term, as already mentioned, originates in Marxist analysis, but in this case it simply meant that Russian industry was very weak. Technologically, it was uniquely static and backward as compared with the rapidly developing industry and technology in the West. Furthermore, there was for the most part an ominous lack of contact (and at times even antagonism) between those who were in theoretical research and those who had anything to do with entrepreneurial and innovating activity. In short, the flourishing of the natural sciences in the second half of the nineteenth century in Russia was not paralleled by a technological and industrial upswing.

During the period of industrial expansion of the 1890's and the 1900's the technology which was introduced into Russian industry came, by and large, from the West; and again native scientific research played a relatively minor role in the solution of applied problems of technology. For about twelve years after the revolution of 1917 the Soviet Union's stagnant industry, and the economy at large, was not conducive to any technological change. In the 1930's the advent of the era of forced industrialization opened up a new chapter in the interrelation of applied and theoretical pursuits. Now science was being compelled to become applied. New institutional arrangements were rapidly shaped to foster these applied pursuits. But again the applied-research pursuits were still generally oriented toward the modification and adaptation of technology, processes, models, specifications, and so on, which again were of foreign origin. The older generation of Russian scientists, although paying increasing lip service to applied needs, remained largely outside this process of integration and continued with some difficulties the abstract theoretical orientation of past decades. It is only in recent years (since the late 1940's), as the new generation of Soviet-educated scientists begins to come to the fore, that we start to observe a more genuine and natural blending of applied and theoretical research. This blending has many signs of carrying applied-research pursuits into a dominant position, but it is too early to tell whether it will arrive at the point where applied tasks completely overshadow theory.

Perhaps some examples will help to illustrate these tendencies. First and very obvious is the role played by mathematics in Russia. Euler and Lobachevsky are long-revered ancestors in this field. Chebyshev, Markov, Liapunov, Khinchin, Kholmogorov, and many others are world-renowned for their contributions in theoretical and applied mathematics. The reliance on mathematics in the applied sciences in Russia is enormous, which in effect gives the applied sciences an added theoretical slant. And yet since A. N. Krylov invented a simple type of analogue computer for solving differential equations in 1911, it took four decades for analogue computers (of S. I. Bruk) to appear in Russia (after World War II). Despite a score of excellent mathematicians in the field, the technical aspects of digital-computer technology in the Soviet Union are still very weak.

In aerodynamics and related fields the work of N. E. Zhukovsky, the father of Russian aviation, and S. A. Chaplygin before the revolution was carried out exclusively in theoretical terms. In fact, until the 1930's we cannot even speak of an aircraft industry in Russia.

To some extent, foreign influence on Russian industry before World War I is a factor in divergence of the theoretical and applied effort. A good example (as discussed by V. N. Ipatyev) is the absence of a dye-manufacturing industry in Russia while the development of organic chemistry was fully capable of creating and supporting it.

Another striking historical example will illustrate the point. M. C. Danilovo-Dobrovolsky was indeed the inventor of an asynchronous motor and originator of AC (alternating current) three-phase electric power technology in 1888–1891. However, because the world was then mostly concerned with DC (direct current) — in fact, Thomas Edison was at first radically opposed to AC-technology, erroneously fearing its inefficiency — Russian administrators and industrialists were not impressed. Danilovo-Dobrovolsky, after demonstration exhibits in Germany, sold some of his inventions there. The advantages of AC-technology were recognized and conversion to AC-technology proceeded rapidly. Meanwhile, in Russia proper, industry in the 1890's was largely geared to DC-technology and most of the power stations (primarily local) used imported DC equipment. Thus "stuck with it," the wide reliance on DC-technology continued into the 1920's, subsequently causing severe handicaps to industrialization (and Goelro plans).

A similar situation prevailed in electronics. A. A. Eikhenvald's theoretical investigations (in 1901–1905) laid the foundation for modern electronics. A. G. Stoletov discovered photoeffect in 1889. I. E. Tamm and S. P. Shubin were the first to work out the quantum theory of photoeffects (in 1931). And yet in the mid-1930's, Soviet industry was importing, and then finally buying patents, plant, and equipment for, simple electron tubes from RCA.

It might be convenient to conclude these examples by mentioning the fact that the foundations of sputnik technology were mathematically derived by K. E. Tsiolkovsky in 1903.

Related to this applied versus theoretical research is another development in Russian science which has been very prominent in the last hundred years: the trend of descriptive studies. K. A. Timiriazev once stated that "it is not the accumulation of an endless series of numbers from meteorological bulletins, but the discovery of the laws of mathematical thought; it is not the descriptions of fauna and flora, but the discovery of the laws of the evolution of organisms; it is not the description of the many riches of our country, but the formulation of the laws of chemistry — these are the principles which guided the historical development of Russian science and offered it equality with and at times supremacy over World Science." [21] We may qualify what the Russian natural sciences are noted for, but it is indisputable that in this passage Timiriazev touches upon one of the fundamental trends in Russian research during the last hundred years.

These are the so-called group-research projects such as are found in astronomy (for example, V. Ia. Struve's star catalogues), geology, meteorology, geobotanics, plant and animal ecology, and so on. All these studies are primarily descriptive in nature. Ever since K. M. Ber's "History of the Animal World" (1828–1837) to the current fifteen-volume set of "Flora of the USSR," the Russians have been keen on meticulous, detailed, and descriptive surveys of nature, from stars to seaweed. These systematic survey projects were conducted by a large number of scientists, and at times individual projects span decades. These projects were especially prominent between 1850 and 1880 and throughout the Soviet era. (Actually, the formation of KEPS — Commission on Productive Resources of Russia — in 1915 gave renewed stimulus to this activity, especially in geology.) Whether these activities are to be considered "creative research" can be openly disputed, but the fact remains that they provide an indispensable foundation for the general development of scientific research activity in many fields of the natural sciences.

V

Another general trend is the very process of the development of science during the last one hundred years. Some historians call this period (particularly since about 1870) the age of imperialism and world conflict. But whatever the outward manifestations may be, man entered the age of science and technology just about one hundred years ago. Most modern conveniences, almost every device or gadget, tool, medium of communication and transportation — all are products of these last one hundred years. Reinforced concrete and the Bessemer process are slightly more than a century old. Lenoir's combustion engine is not even one hundred years of age. Thomas Davenport's invention of the electric generator was made just about one hundred years ago. And when we look at a radio, an airplane, or a plastic pen — they are the products of this century. It was in 1869 that Mendeleev formulated his periodic law of elements, and we are still adding elements to the empty spaces in the periodic table.

[21] K. A. Timiriazev, *Sochineniia* (Moscow, 1938), V, 142.

It is the relative youth of modern science and technology which has to be remembered in speaking about trends. The end of the nineteenth and first half of the twentieth century brought about the development of science in breadth and in depth. The role of the individual as a vehicle of theoretical discovery still remains strong, although on the experimental scale it gives way in many fields to organized research. It is characteristic of scientific research during this period that, on the one hand, there is a continuing process of differentiation of fields and differentiation within each field, and, on the other, the interpenetration of distinct disciplines which results in the establishment of interdisciplinary fields. The process of differentiation resulted in a greater need for coordination and cooperation in research. In order to solve a problem, diverse groups of research scientists are brought together, and consequently scientific experimentation has lost its individual orientation and has begun to require the participation of large numbers of scientists (and also of supporting staffs). The process of experimentation is being applied more frequently and with the wider utilization of various technical means of increasing complexity and precision. To process a wide range of experimental data, greater reliance is placed on mathematical (and statistical) generalizations. And to facilitate the recording and processing of data, automatization (from automatic measuring and registering devices to computing technology) of research is gradually being introduced and perfected. In this setting empirical verification of scientific discoveries or theories is being sought, particularly in the physical and biological sciences.

These are the general trends in scientific research over the last hundred years and particularly since the turn of this century. They are evident in all countries and are universally recognized, and the developments in Russia do not represent an exception. What is different and distinct, however, is the role of institutional arrangements, but before we discuss them another development must be pointed out.

Education and science in Russia from their very institutional inception (let us say from the time of the opening of the Academy of Sciences under Catherine I in 1725) have been the business of the state. Originally teaching and research were blended together, but even after they were divorced (at the Academy in 1747) and universities began to emerge (particularly in the early nineteenth century), it was the state which operated them, and the academicians, adjuncts, professors, and researchers were all civil servants confirmed, if in most instances not actually chosen, in their positions by imperial administrators. For more than two centuries, teaching in universities and research were carried on by civil servants; and the changes in employment arrangements in the sphere of education and research which have occurred during the Soviet era are a continuation of the existing trend and not an entirely new departure.

The growth in complexity, specialization, and coordination of research functions resulted in the enormous expansion of research personnel and institutions. In terms of research and teaching personnel, Russia had perhaps several hundred people (certainly less than 1,000) in 1861. In 1913 there were about 10,000 teachers and researchers in higher education, in various institutions of research and industrial laboratories, of whom about 4,200 were classified as research personnel.[22] In 1940 there were already 98,000 in higher-education teaching and research, and in research alone about 26,000. And in 1956 there were 240,000 in teaching and research, of whom 106,000 were performing research only.[23] These figures refer to all fields of research, among which all natural-science and applied-science fields account for about one half to two thirds of the total personnel. In terms of institutions performing research functions during the last fifty years in Russia and the Soviet Union, their number has grown from several dozen to 2,800. This formidable numerical growth was accompanied by institutional rearrangements which resulted in the multiplicity of hierarchical pyramids of control and subordination over individual institutions and the personnel within them. In the course of the late nineteenth century, individual centers of research and their organizational pyramids remained autonomous and uncoordinated. The new development of the Soviet era (particularly since the 1930's) is the centralization of control over the hierarchical structures in the hands of a few coordinating boards.

In the eighteenth and early nineteenth centuries the Academy of Sciences could be used synonymously with the seat of Russian science and research. During the first quarter of the nineteenth century the universities began to assume a growing role as seats of learning and at times even research. The emergence of learned societies (such as the Moscow Society of Natural Experimenters — MOIP since 1803) also contributed to diversification, and they began to play an important role (in fact the MOIP contrasted itself to St. Petersburg's Imperial Academy as being the "Moscow Academy"). In the eighteenth century the Academy was dominated by foreigners who were brought by the crown from abroad. Discontent with such a situation was voiced quite frequently. Not until the 1860's, however, and particularly during the 1870's and 1880's and the revolt of the Russians against foreign-born members of the Academy (particularly Germans), did it reach its climax. The clashes often centered around elections and appointments which eventually resulted in the easing out of the "foreigners"; by the late 1890's there was a pronounced Russification of the Academy.

During the last half of the nineteenth century the Academy lost its footing as the seat of learning and research, and the majority of scientific discoveries were made in the universities. In physics, mathematics, and

[22] A. Beilin, *Kadry spetsialistov SSSR* (Moscow, 1935), 257.
[23] TsSU, *Narodnoe khoziaistvo SSSR: 1956* (Moscow, 1957), 257.

chemistry, the world-renowned names of Russian theoretical scientists and experimenters were associated with the universities. The end of the nineteenth century up to the time of the revolution is the period of shift of research (particularly in physics) to Russian universities. It was at the end of this period that large-scale experimental research (such as Lebedev's physical institute) began to be established.

On the eve of World War I we begin to notice a shift to specialized research establishments, and, after an interruption caused by the chaos of the 1920's, this trend continues up to the present. In the last few years, however, there have been renewed attempts to widen the research base so as to pass on some of the specialized research tasks, personnel, and research equipment to universities and certain select engineering schools. Little headway has been made so far, but the attempt to reintegrate teaching and research is currently in progress. This would represent, therefore, a reversal of the tendency over the last four decades (particularly since the late 1920's) when specialized research tasks were being carried out in Russia primarily in research institutes not directly connected with teaching facilities or universities. These research institutes are run in technological (and at times in theoretical) fields by various economic ministries and especially by the Academy of Sciences of the USSR, as well as other regional and specialized academies. At the same time, the Academy of Sciences of the USSR has emerged as the leading coordinator of research.

In describing these developments, it is important to note that the shift of the research burden and theoretical investigations from the Academy to the universities in the late nineteenth and early twentieth centuries happens to coincide with the "Golden Age" of Russian science. The resurgence of the Academy to a position of leadership, coordination, and planning in the Soviet era has taken place at a time when organized massive research has begun to supplant individual effort and when technical means (including automatics) have become paramount attributes of the research effort. It must also be emphasized that in the last two decades the Academy has been operating in new circumstances. In addition to its main function as the central, gigantic clearinghouse of research which is assigned to it by the Soviet government, it had also to deal with the changing nature of the process of scientific research.

It is important to recognize that the emergence of the Academy as the coordinator of research has created new problems. The Academy is run largely by scientists themselves, but the political orientation and lack of autonomy causing arbitrariness in decision-making procedures in a number of instances have played havoc with its function. This has been discussed earlier, but at the same time the advantages in applied-research fields, as well as the mass-experimentation (such as nuclear research) research of institutions of the Academy type, are not to be denied. The disadvantage of centralized coordination may lie in the area of decisions and choice of projects which are selected in accordance with certain planners' preferences, a function which in turn may or may not foster the development of the pioneering fields of science. The advantage may consist mainly in the ability to concentrate research and experimentation effort in a chosen field. This undoubtedly results in great unevenness of research effort among diverse fields of science.

This discussion immediately points up another development. In the second half of the nineteenth century, research in the natural sciences was centered around an individual scholar and a small group of immediate associates or aides. By the mid-1930's in Russia we begin to deal mainly with institutions of research, employing hundreds of research scientists grouped under or aligned with some "name" scientist. The depersonalization of research effort, particularly the experimental part of it, does not, however, replace the individual's research ideas or scientific theories. But in regard to the latter, the centralization of coordination and planning of research have their pronounced negative effect, for though widening the base (in terms of facilities and personnel) in one organization, the pyramidal institutional structure stifles individual initiative and independence of thought and research action. All this, it seems to me, has resulted in the trend of having a smaller number of outstanding researchers at the top than would be the case without centralization. In the second half of the nineteenth century Russia appeared to have larger numbers of outstanding scholars in the natural sciences in relation to the over-all base than it has today. This is generally true, of course, for all countries, but the first-echelon scientists seem to be rarer in the Soviet Union in relation to the total numbers engaged in research than is the case in the West. The fundamental problem of the relation of individual effort within the framework of organized research is a general one in modern science, and the Soviet Union does not seem to have any specific solutions of its own.

Directly related to this is the problem of "schools," in the sense of groups of scientists working in the same field and following the direction of research originating in a given institution. In tracing scientific schools, it is sufficient to point out two, the Moscow and St. Petersburg-Leningrad schools in mathematics (especially the theory of probability).[24] In organic chemistry there was and continues to be a Kazan University school; there is the Vernadsky school of geochemistry, and so forth.

Related to the problem of individual versus organized research is also the trend in international contacts on the part of Russian scientists. It is very important to recall that in the prerevolutionary period promising university graduates were sent to study abroad. Soviet his-

---

[24] A detailed discussion may be found in B. V. Gnedenko, "Razvitie teorii veroiatnosti v Rossii," *Trudy Instituta Istorii Estestvoznaniia* (Moscow, 1948), II, 390–425.

torians of science try to belittle the importance of these studies by stating that their contribution should be disregarded since people who went abroad "went there not necessarily for study." [25] It is said that assigning significance to foreign studies of Russian scientists leads to the "malicious lie" spread by "bourgeois historians" that there are "foreign roots" in Russian science. It is not the problem of foreign roots, but the stimulus caused to scholarly pursuits through these foreign contacts.

It is true that Heidelberg, Berlin, and Paris were common meeting places of Russian natural scientists in the second half of the nineteenth century. D. I. Mendeleev, K. A. Timiriazev, Sofiia Kovalevskaia (mathematician, inventor of the gyroscope), among many others, studied at Heidelberg. I. I. Mechnikov spent many years in Rome and Paris (in fact, the Nobel Prize for bacteriological research was awarded not for his work in Russia, but for that done at the Pasteur Institute in Paris). I. P. Pavlov spent two years abroad. A. G. Stoletov, the father of Russian physics (discoverer of electrical discharge and photoelectricity), was Kirchhoff's pupil in Heidelberg, and later studied in Berlin and Paris. P. N. Lebedev was August Kund's pupil in Strasbourg and later did research in Berlin. N. S. Kurnakov (who established the school of physical-chemical analysis) spent years in Freiburg. Zhukovsky, Chaplygin, Umov, Williams, Vvedensky, and many others studied abroad. In addition to actual work abroad, it is important to mention that there were frequent contacts by Russian researchers and inventors with foreign firms, especially because many patents were filed abroad (particularly in Paris).

After the revolution, there were still opportunities, though greatly restricted, for foreign study and travel, but the Kapitsa incident (1935) marks the terminal point of these practices. For some twenty years thereafter, foreign study was absolutely taboo. At present there are very timid steps to resume such foreign study and travel abroad, but the path of their development still remains uncertain.

Partly in order to substitute for the lack of personal opportunities for foreign study, but largely because of the necessity to provide a flow of increasing information required in day-to-day research, in the last two decades and particularly in the postwar period the Soviet Union has embarked upon information-processing and -dissemination programs on a grandiose scale. The State Scientific Library and the Academy's Institute of Scientific Information are rendering many services to the community of Soviet research scientists. This information-processing and reference service performed by separate bodies represent a new departure in the research setting.

The role of the scientist in society is of crucial importance in creating an understanding of his activity. During the last century and a half one

[25] N. A. Figurovsky, "Zadachi sovetskikh istorikov khimii," *Trudy Instituta Istorii Estestvoznaniia* (Moscow, 1949), III, 42.

of the fundamental links with society which Russian scientists have tried to develop was their mission to popularize science. This task is explicit in the edicts of the Academy since the beginning of the nineteenth century. And when Lenin (in 1920) called on the Academy to broaden this task, it was just a reaffirmation of the traditional orientation. Today these activities are conducted on a scale unmatched by any other country, and they are responsible to a great degree for preserving the prestige of scientists and a significant force in mobilizing public support. Of course the circumstances and the causal factors have altered, but the missional function of the Russian popularizers of knowledge in general and science in particular has paid dividends.

VI

I would like to conclude by saying that the foregoing discussion has intended merely to focus attention on certain trends which have to be explored further and to point out by default that there are still many other trends which have not even been mentioned. But since some summary is in order, we might say that the distinguishing mark of the Soviet era as compared with the nineteenth century is the planning aspect of scientific research. This Soviet planning of science is alleged to be currently guided by its task-orientedness (*tseleustremlennoe planirovanie*).[26] It is often said that the absence of competition and pressure of vested interests is the main advantage of Soviet advances in developing science and technology. Khrushchev was recently reported as saying that Soviet science has an inherent superiority and will be in the lead in times to come. This will take place because of the planning of the socialist system and of the method of dialectical materialism which is the most progressive force propelling socialist science forward. Many of us may quarrel with this. The achievements of Soviet science and technology have occurred "not because of the alliance between Soviet physical science and dialectical materialism, but in spite of the entanglement of science with ideology."[27]

Recently I had an opportunity to talk with an outstanding Soviet scientist who visited the United States. I asked him what he believed was the main problem for the creative development of science in the Soviet Union. His thoughtful answer was: "In the Soviet Union today there are necessary but not sufficient conditions for the development of creative research." He continued: "If you know the Bible, always remember that for progress, not only in science but for all mankind, one Thomas is worth more than the eleven other apostles combined."

[26] A. Blagonravov, "Plan i nauka," *Izvestiia*, February 7, 1958.
[27] G. Wetter, "Dialectical Materialism and Natural Science," *Soviet Survey*, no. 23 (January–March 1958), 59. See also, G. Wetter, *Der dialektische Materialismus* Freiburg, 1952), esp. 341–379.

This has a familiar ring. Sacrifice and dedication to science on the part of the individual, despite the imposition of control and the restraints of political ideology and planners' priorities, still remain the main force behind scholarship in the Soviet Union. This was the case in the past, and it is true today. This is perhaps the real source of vitality in present Soviet science. "I will not tell a long story, one of many about Great Science, in which those who are generous win and those who are niggardly lose, for in Great Science nothing can be accomplished with less than the work of an entire life." [28] To this Valentin Kaverin adds — "even if the price one pays is his own life." Fortunately for world science and human progress, the work goes on.

CHURCH AND STATE

JOHN S. CURTISS

I

The Russian Orthodox Church today enjoys the distinction of being the only institution of the old regime that has survived, virtually intact, after forty years of Soviet rule. It is the only institution in the USSR that professes aims basically incompatible with those of the Soviet regime. It seems safe to say that no member of its hierarchy is a Communist. Thus the Russian church is like Abbe Sieyès, who, when asked what he had done during the Reign of Terror of 1793–1794, answered: "I lived." That the church can give the same answer indicates that it has great vitality and adaptability.

In 1861 and for nearly six decades thereafter, the Russian Orthodox Church was the national church of the Russian Empire. At its head was the tsar, "the Anointed of God." According to official practice, a Russian was automatically Orthodox from birth and an Orthodox believer to all intents and purposes was Russian. The government grudgingly made exceptions in the case of the Old Believers (an offshoot of Orthodoxy) and to some degree regarding the "sectarians," who were close to the Protestants in outlook. But on the whole, in the eyes of the government "Russian" and "Orthodox" were synonymous.

This official church enjoyed special privileges. In the Council of Ministers the Over Procurator represented its views. In the provinces, the local bishops might appoint clerical members to attend the meetings of the zemstvos and the town governments. In addition, the officials of the

[28] Kaverin, 284.

civil government were required to protect the interests of the Orthodox church and defend it against attack.[1] Furthermore, the Code of Laws provided that monasteries and parish churches should have tracts of land. Not all cloisters and churches, however, were so endowed; but for many of those that were not, and for the bishops, the government provided salaries and other subsidies. It should be noted that the government also paid salaries of Protestant, Roman Catholic, and other recognized clergy; but the Russian church received far more than the others.[2]

Probably more important was the monopoly of religious propaganda that the Russian church enjoyed. While it freely published religious literature, thanks to its right of censorship it banned theological writings that it regarded as dangerous to its interests.[3] It alone could establish parochial schools among the Orthodox, and its clergy gave religious instruction to the Russian pupils in all schools, public and private.[4] And finally, only the Orthodox church could carry on missionary work and win converts, both among Russians and non-Russians. This rule even extended to the children of mixed marriages, who by law had to receive an Orthodox upbringing.[5]

Along with government favors to the church went government control. While in theory the Most Holy Synod governed the ecclesiastical body, in reality it was subservient to the Over Procurator, a lay appointee of the tsar. At his suggestion the tsar named hierarchs to the Synod or dismissed them, and appointed, promoted, demoted, or transferred bishops. Moreover, the Over Procurator dominated the lay officials of the dioceses, who, headed by the secretaries of the consistories, were the real power in the episcopal sees.[6] Least of all did the parish priests possess independence. Often the bishop of the diocese snubbed and humbled them, while the diocesan consistory, dominated by the secretary — a little Over Procurator — watched, promoted, or harassed them in various ways.[7]

The chief function of this official church, of course, was the saving of

---

[1] T. V. Barsov, *Sbornik deistvuiushchikh i rukovodstvennykh tserkovnykh i tserkovno-grazhdanskikh postanovlenii po vedomstvu pravoslavnago ispovedeniia* (St. Petersburg, 1885), 13; *Svod zakonov rossiiskoi imperii* (21 vols.; St. Petersburg, 1857), II, "Polozhenie o gubernskikh i uezdnykh zemskikh uchrezhdeniiakh," secs. 56–57, and "Obshchee uchrezhdenie gubernskoe," secs. 298–299.

[2] *Svod zokonov*, X, pt. 2, "Zakony mezhevye," secs. 347–356; *Smeta dokhodov i raskhodov vedomstva sviateishago sinoda na 1913 g.* (St. Petersburg, 1912), lviii–lix.

[3] *Svod zakonov*, XIV, "Ustav o tsenzure i pechati," sec. 293.

[4] *Svod zakonov*, XI pt. 1, "Svod ustavov uchennykh uchrezhdenii i uchebnykh zavedenii," secs. 1476 (supplement), 1699 (sup.), 1823 (sup.), 3124, 3476.

[5] *Svod zakonov*, XI, pt. 1, "Ustavy dukhovnykh del inostrannykh ispovedanii," sec. 4.

[6] Sviateishii Sinod, *Otzyvy eparkhial'nykh arkhiereev po voprosu o tserkovnoi reforme* (3 vols.; St. Petersburg, 1906), I, 219, and III, 385; Barsov, 11–12.

[7] Sv. Sinod, *Ustav dukhovnykh konsistorii* (St. Petersburg, 1883), secs. 148 and 153; Sv. Sinod, *Otzyvy*, III, 53.

souls. Certainly there must have been many devoted pastors who performed this function with zeal. On the whole, however, the Russian church did not excel in evangelical fervor, but rather stressed liturgical observance. It also did not accomplish much in the fields of charity or education.[8]

As a state church, Orthodoxy had a second function: that of rendering unto Caesar, which it did in a variety of ways. Through catechisms, sermons, proclamations, and personal admonition the clergy sought to make their flocks obedient to the tsar and slow to listen to his enemies, against whom the church publicly hurled its anathemas. The Over Procurators consistently employed the whole ecclesiastical machinery for this purpose, and most of the clergy obeyed orders. Especially under Pobedonostsev, Over Procurator for twenty-five years under the last two tsars, the church organization gave strong support to the imperial regime.[9]

But while the church appeared to be strong and influential, it was not without weaknesses. For one thing, its influence upon the minds of the Russian people declined during the nineteenth century. Many prelates ruefully admitted that the intelligentsia was largely lost to the church,[10] while the growing class of factory workers was less devout than its ancestors had been. The peasantry had not turned away from the church, but even they were not in full harmony with it. Many of them mechanically observed its rules and attended its ceremonies without real comprehension of Christian doctrine.[11] Pobedonostsev himself wrote that often peasants did not understand the words of prayers that they uttered. In addition, many were gradually coming to feel that the powerful and the wealthy dominated the hierarchy and used it for their purposes. To be sure, there were occasional clerics who expressed views contrarary to the wishes of the Over Procurator and the leading hierarchs. Nevertheless, by 1900 some of the peasants had become convinced that the Orthodox church supported the interests of the landowners rather than theirs.[12]

Furthermore, there was dissension in the ranks of the clergy. The parish priests — the "white clergy" — felt that they were in an inferior position to the monastics, since the married state of the priests made them ineligible to become bishops. The prelates, who were monastics and enjoyed some prestige, often looked down on the priests and occasionally treated

[8] Sv. Sinod, *Otzyvy*, III, 53; also supplement, 45–46.
[9] P. Smirnov, *Nastavlenie v zakone bozhem* (St. Petersburg, 1895), 133–135; *Svod zakonov*, I, pt. 1, "Svod osnovnykh gosudarstvennykh zakonov," secs. 4, 55, 56; I. V. Preobrazhensky, ed., *Tserkovnaia reforma: sbornik statei dukhovnoi i svetskoi pechati po voprosu o reforme* (St. Petersburg, 1905), 39–52.
[10] *Bogoslovskii vestnik* (May 1906), 35–37.
[11] *Tserkovnyia vedomosti* (April 29, 1906), 1018; Sv. Sinod, *Otzyvy*, III, 451.
[12] Protohierarch F. I. Iankovsky, "O preobrazovanii russkoi pravoslavnoi tserkvi," *Khristianskoe chtenie* (November 1906), 628; Sv. Sinod, *Otzyvy*, III, 33.

them haughtily. For these reasons the parish clergy tended to feel bitter hostility toward monastics in general and toward bishops in particular.[13]

Subservience to the bishops tended to engender in the parish clergy a feeling of hopelessness and apathy. This seed often fell on fertile ground, since many of the priests, whose fathers had been pastors before them, had had no desire to take the cloth but had accepted a theological training because they lacked funds for a secular education. Over and over the bishops and the church press emphasized that the theological students were often sullen, if not rebellious, prone to socialist ideas, and opposed to the teachings of the church.[14] Once installed in their parishes, some of them sought relief in alcohol, and a drunken priest was no rarity in the villages. Others became immersed in the details of rural life, devoting themselves to farming and quarreling with peasants about their lands, the fees for performing services, and other petty matters.[15] Certainly not all of the clergy suffered from these failings, and there must have been many who were sincere and dedicated pastors. Nevertheless, the priest did not enjoy much esteem in Russian society, and the strength of the Old Believers and the sectarians indicates that the official church had been found wanting by a considerable part of the people.

In the revolution of 1905 the Russian church played a definite role. The Synod, which hailed the conflict with Japan as a holy war, charged that the unrest that led to the massacre of Bloody Sunday had been inspired by Japanese money and warned the masses against dangerous agitators.[16] Throughout 1905 the Synod supported the embattled government, although it mildly rebuked some of the most reactionary bishops. The official church journals and most of the diocesan periodicals expressed strong conservative views.[17] In addition, the ecclesiastical authorities printed thousands of leaflets and brochures for mass distribution, warning against godless socialist ideas and upholding the state order.[18] Likewise, most of the bishops took a definitely conservative position, defending the regime against attacks of the liberative movement. Liberal priests suffered various ecclesiastical punishments,[19] while those who zealously supported the autocracy received generous rewards. Some of the prelates gave open support to the vehemently anti-Semitic Union of the Russian People,[20]

---

[13] *Grazhdanin* (September 9, 1905), as quoted in V. V. Rozanov, *Okolo tserkovnykh sten* (2 vols.; St. Petersburg, 1906), II, 196.

[14] *Tserk. ved.* (January 27, 1907), 137.

[15] Sv. Sinod, *Vsepoddanneishii otchet ober-prokurora sviateishago sinoda po vedomstvu pravoslavnago ispovedaniia* (September 7, 1902), 48; *Tserk. ved.* (September 7, 1902), 1234; *Vera i razum* (January 1906), 31–32.

[16] *Tserk. ved.* (January 15, 1905), official part, supplement.

[17] *Tserk. ved.* (January 29, 1905), official part, 42; (March 5, 1905), official part, 72–73; (December 3, 1905), 2110.

[18] Sv. Sinod, *Vsepoddanneishii otchet* (1905–1907), 122.

[19] *Tserk. ved.* (January 7, 1906), official part, 6–7.

[20] Sv. Sinod (1906), portfolio 775, sheets 1–36.

whose banners were stained with the blood of victims of pogroms, with Archbishop Antonii Khrapovitsky and Metropolitan Vladimir of Moscow in the forefront of the reactionary agitation.[21]

Under such leadership, probably the majority of the Orthodox priests supported the government. They attacked radicals and liberals and admonished peasants and mutinous soldiers to submit to the authorities, in some instances with much success. Long lists of priests received decorations and other rewards from a grateful government.[22]

For a time liberal tendencies appeared among the clergy. A few of the church periodicals were quite progressive, and several diocesan or informal gatherings of clergy adopted resolutions supporting the liberation movement and criticizing the bishops and the church authorities. A few priests even led groups of rebellious peasants, and one died of gunshot wounds.[23] Others, less extreme in their views, nonetheless incurred the wrath of the church authorities and were punished, perhaps to the number of several hundred. In the First and Second Dumas there were small groups of priests among the deputies, who infuriated the Synod and the Over Procurator by strong utterances in behalf of the masses and against the government. Those who refused to recant received strong punishment.[24]

Another sign of ferment in the church was the movement for ecclesiastical reform, centered around the proposal to call a church council or *Sobor*. This scheme enlisted the support of both conservatives and liberals, with the latter going much farther in the direction of a more democratic system for the church. After a promising start, however, the movement faded out, resulting in little more than a lengthy committee report.[25]

Thus the Russian Orthodox Church came through the first revolution unchanged. Nothing happened between 1906 and the First World War to alter its condition for the better. The leaders of the church continued to support the autocracy and fulminated against the mildest of opposition tendencies. Both the Third and the Fourth Dumas had over forty ecclesiastical members; unlike the priests in the first two Dumas, those in the later Dumas were almost entirely conservatives or reactionaries.[26] Many

---

[21] *Krasnyi arkhiv*, no. 31 (1928), 207–208; *Moskovskiia vedomosti* (October 16, 1906).

[22] Sv. Sinod, Chancellery of the Over Procurator (1908), portfolio 47, sheets 1–5, 42, 50–52.

[23] M. N. Pokrovsky, ed., *1905 — materialy i dokumenty* (8 vols.; Moscow, 1925–1928), V-1, 5–6, 48, 139, 271, 480–481, 482, 581, 607, 667.

[24] *Tserk. ved.* (May 12, 1907), official part, 200; (June 2, 1907), official part, 220–221.

[25] N. V. Ognev, *Na poroge reform russkoi tserkvi i dukhovenstva* (St. Petersburg, 1907), 12–16; N. D. Kuznetsov, *Preobrazovanie v russkoi tserkvi* (Moscow, 1906), 7–10, 26–63; Preobrazhensky, *Tserkovnaia reforma*, 1–47, 87–88, 422.

[26] Gosudarstvennaia Duma, *Ukazatel' k stenograficheskim otchetam* (St. Petersburg, 1908), Third Duma, Session 1, 13–18; (1913), Fourth Duma, Session 1, 19–24.

high ecclesiastics as before gave utterance to vehement anti-Semitism, which reached its high point in the trial of Mendel Beilis for ritual murder in 1913.[27] In addition to these failings, by 1911 the corrupting influence of Rasputin had penetrated the ruling circles of the church.[28] At lower levels the growing difficulty of filling pastoral vacancies boded no good.[29]

During the First World War the church strongly supported the Russian arms by proclamations to army and public and by sending famous ikons and ardent preachers to inspire the troops.[30] After the first flush of enthusiasm, however, the church took a less active role in upholding morale. From 1915 on the influence of Rasputin increased. Prelates in his good graces received preferment, and his henchman, Metropolitan Pitirim of Petrograd, was active in the disgraceful high politics of the times.[31] Many voices spoke out against the sad state of the church: the priests in the Fourth Duma, several moderate conservatives devoted to Orthodoxy, and the press of various shades of opinion. But to the end the church remained fettered to the government. At the very last moment several reactionary church leaders urged the people to rally around the banner bearing the device: "For faith, tsar, and fatherland!" [32]

II

When, in spite of the urgings of the church, the people rose in the February Revolution to overthrow the tsar, the Russian church took no action. In general, the clergy were passive. A few priests tried to incite the people against the new regime; very few spoke in favor of it. The Synod remained as before, until the new Over Procurator ousted its Rasputinite members and replaced them with more reputable churchmen.[33] A grant of autonomy to the church soon followed, as the Provisional Government had no wish to dominate it.

After the first shock had worn off, liberal tendencies appeared among the clergy. In Petrograd several progressive priests took the lead in forming a League of Democratic Clergy and Laymen, with a program of mild

[27] P. E. Shchegolov, ed., *Padenie tsarskogo rezhima* (7 vols.; Moscow-Leningrad, 1925–27), II, 395.
[28] Shchegolov, IV, 505; *Krasnyi arkhiv*, no. 31 (1928), 211–212.
[29] *Tserk. ved.* (September 27, 1908), 1917–1921.
[30] *Tserk. ved.* (July 26, 1914), official part, 346–348; (August 2, 1914), official part, 350; (August 23, 1914), 1541; (September 1, 1914), 1545–1552. Also I. V. Proebrazhensky, *Velicheishaia iz velikikh voin za pravdu bozhiiu* (Petrograd, 1916), 7–71.
[31] Gos. Duma, *Stenograficheskie otchety* (Petrograd, 191–), Fourth Duma, Session 5, col. 39; N. D. Zhevakhov, *Vospominaniia tovarishcha ober-prokurora* (2 vols.; Munich, 1923), I, 189–190.
[32] *Moskovskiia tserkovnyia vedomosti*, no. 3–4 (1917), quoted in B. Kandidov, *Tserkov' i fevral'skaia revoliutsiia* (Moscow, 1934), 16–17.
[33] Protopresviter Georgii Shavel'sky, "Tserkov' i revoliutsiia," *Russkaia mysl'* (April 1922), 111–112; A. V. Kartashev, "Revoliutsiia i sobor 1917–1918 gg.," *Bogoslovskaia mysl'* (1942), 78–81.

socialism.[34] Similar groups sprang up in some of the provincial cities. In addition, in the spring of 1917 several diocesan congresses of clergy passed resolutions favoring liberalism and strongly attacking unpopular bishops. In a few places the clergy ousted hated prelates.[35] This flare of liberalism soon passed, however, and the clergy reverted to more traditional ways.

As the Provisional Government continued to push the war, the Synod and the clergy gave firm support. The church distributed masses of propaganda leaflets, issued appeals to the people to be read in the churches, and ordered special *Te Deums* asking for victory. Numerous sermons urged the laymen to give ardent support to the war, while popular preachers made speaking tours along the fighting fronts to inspire the troops.[36] Like the government, the church favored peace only after victory.

But although the church supported the government's war policy, it soon quarreled with the new regime over the nationalizing of the parochial schools and the ending of compulsory religious instruction.[37] By midsummer the churchmen were increasingly concerned over threats to their interests not only from the Provisional Government, but even more from the growing radicalism of the masses. Frightened by the huge demonstrations of the July Days, the Synod spoke out strongly against the Bolsheviks and asked nation-wide prayers against civil strife. It also urged the church to support effective military discipline and advocated the distribution of leaflets opposing socialist ideas.[38] The clergy turned increasingly to participation in politics, giving their support to the relatively conservative Cadet Party.[39]

Beginning with August 12, 1917, church life centered in the All-Russian Sobor — the first such council since 1681. It was in part an elected body, but the presence of all the bishops ensured the predominance of the conservative upper clergy. The lay members came chiefly from the nobility, the army, and the bureaucracy.[40] While the Sobor was called to deal with purely church problems, from the first the members felt the need to save Russia from disaster. To accomplish this, the Sobor issued solemn appeals to the troops and to the Russian people, warning them against radical tempters.[41] When General Kornilov attempted to overthrow the Provi-

[34] *Vserossiiskii tserkovno-obshchestvennyi vestnik* (April 15, 1917); *Rech'* (March 25, 1917).

[35] Shavel'sky, 108; *Deianiia sviashchennago sobora pravoslavnoi rossiiskoi tserkvi* (15 vols.; Moscow, 1918–1919), II (Vyp. 2), 103.

[36] *Vser. Ts.-Ob. vestnik*, no. 28 (1917), quoted in Kandidov, 57–62.

[37] Kartashev, 84–85; A. I. Vvedensky, *Tserkov' i gosudarstvo* (Moscow, 1923), 64–66.

[38] Vvedensky, 51–53; *Tserk. ved.* (July 22, 1917), 231–233, and (August 19, 1917), 263–264; Kandidov, 80–84.

[39] Kandidov, 43–45, 75.

[40] *Deianiia sv. sobora*, I (Vyp. 1), 60–133.

[41] *Deianiia sv. sobora*, I (Vyp. 2), 25–67; *Tserk. ved.* (September 30, 1917), 311–313, 327–330.

sional Government and set up a military dictatorship, the Sobor sent him a message asking God's blessing on his efforts. Only the fact that Kornilov's coup failed so quickly prevented the Sobor from committing itself strongly in his favor. Nevertheless, in other ways it made clear its sympathy with the fiery general.[42]

After Kornilov's failure, the members of the Sobor felt sure that Russia could escape calamity only if they should elect a Patriarch to lead the people. After repeated proclamations and appeals had failed to win the masses away from the Bolsheviks and, because of the dangerous time, the churchmen had to abandon a projected religious procession around the Kremlin to confound the foe,[43] in October 1917 the Sobor took up the matter. The debate on the revival of the Patriarchate ended with the driving out of the more liberal members, who feared that ecclesiastical absolutism would result. Finally, while revolutionary fighting was still in progress in Moscow, the Sobor voted to restore this office, and to the sound of cannon Metropolitan Tikhon of Moscow was elected as the first Russian Patriarch since 1700.[44] The leaders of the Sobor had to ask the victorious Bolsheviks for permission to hold the installation ceremony in the Kremlin — which the victors readily granted.[45] In spite of this, however, the heads of the church refused to accept the new regime, which they regarded as a passing episode. When the Soviet leaders began peace talks with the Germans, the Sobor appealed to the people not to countenance this betrayal of their Orthodox brethren.[46] Although Lenin and his fellows were hostile to religion and to the Russian church, they did not, however, arrest the Patriarch or close the Sobor.

III

Soviet antireligious feeling stemmed from Karl Marx, who had termed religion the "opium of the people" — an anodyne for their sufferings. Lenin also held that religion tended to make people submissive under oppression, seeking salvation in a future life rather than on earth. He specifically attacked the Russian church as being hand in glove with the oppressors, but he also termed the faith of the Tolstoyans, with their stress on nonresistance to evil, a "new, purified poison for the masses."[47] On the other hand, he warned that religion was a minor problem and should

---

[42]*Deianiia sv. sobora*, I (Vyp. 2), 48–49, 74; Vvedensky, 98–99; B. V. Titlinov, *Tserkov' vo vremia revoliutsii* (Petrograd, 1924), 70.
    [43] *Deianiia sv. sobora*, II (Vyp. 1), 275, 335–336, 402–403; *Birzhevyia vedomosti* (October 20, 1917).
    [44] *Deianiia sv. sobora*, III, 1–2, 9–10, 38–41, 52–56, 107–109.
    [45] *Deianiia sv. sobora*, III, 129.
    [46] *Deianiia sv. sobora*, IV (Vyp. 1), 138–139.
    [47] V. I. Lenin, *Sochineniia* (3rd ed.; 30 vols., Leningrad, 1935–1937), IV, 353–354; XIV, 76 and 402.

not become the primary target, lest good proletarians turn against the revolution because of insult to their faith.[48]

Guided by these precepts, the Soviet government made no direct attack on the church, but rather reduced its strength by flanking movements. The nationalization of land expressly included that of the church, thus reducing its economic position. Another decree took over parochial as well as other schools; and a third ordered that records of births, marriages, and deaths should be kept by the government, not the clergy. Finally, the decree of February 5, 1918, provided for separation of church and state. This measure, which completely secularized the state and made religion a private matter, provided for the nationalization of the churches and monasteries and their contents, irrespective of denomination, and deprived the church of all subsidies. Even this sweeping measure, however, made no effort to close churches *en masse*, for it made provision for turning the nationalized parish churches over to groups of believers who would assume responsibility for them.[49]

Unfortunately, along with these official measures there occurred a number of unofficial outrages against churchmen and church property. A considerable number of priests suffered arrest and even murder at the hands of supporters of the Soviet regime, and Metropolitan Vladimir of Kiev was dragged from his monastery quarters and murdered by cutthroats. Soviet sources tell of bands of Red Guards that invaded churches during services, smoking cigarettes and wearing caps; some even fired shots at ikons. Occasionally fanatically atheistic soldiers confiscated church vestments and cut them up to make banners or put them to other profane uses. The Soviet authorities strongly condemned such deeds,[50] but to angry churchmen these acts were no less offensive because they were unsanctioned.

The fury of the churchmen soon led to active resistance. After Soviet officials had taken over the Synod's printing plant and closed two chapels in government buildings, the Sobor issued a solemn warning against sacrilege. In January 1918, when an official, backed by Red Guards, tried to take over a great monastery in Petrograd, monks rang the bells to summon the believers, who drove out the Red forces; a monk was killed in the melee.[51] A week later Metropolitan Veniamin organized a religious procession through the streets, with hundreds of thousands of impassioned believers chanting hymns and attacking the disrespectful. The Metropolitan in a strong sermon urged his followers to unite around their clergy

---

[48] *Lenin*, XIV, 72, 75.

[49] RSFSR, *Sobranie uzakonenii i rasporiazhenii raboche-krest'ianskogo pravitel'stva*, no. 18 (1918), 272–273.

[50] Titlinov, 130; *Revoliutsiia i tserkov'*, no. 2 (1919), 38–39; P. V. Gidulianov, ed., *Otdelenie tserkvi ot gosudarstva* (Moscow, 1924), 371.

[51] *Deianiia sv. sobora*, IV (Vyp. 1), 8–9, 57–59.

in defense of the faith and ordered the reading of a message from Patriarch Tikhon pronouncing anathema on enemies of the church, whom he threatened with the fires of hell for their satanic deeds.[52] The churchmen apparently believed that the Soviet officials would use force to suppress this demonstration and probably hoped that the populace would fight back against the godless powers. But the authorities realized the danger and took pains to distribute leaflets warning against attacks on the marchers. As a result, the occasion passed without violence.[53]

In the meantime, the Sobor in Moscow had approved the Patriarch's anathema and drafted a message of its own concerning the separation of church and state. During the debate the Sobor heard many vehement speeches, of which the most outspoken was that of Dean Vostokov, who, amid much applause, charged: "We have cast down the Tsar and subjected ourselves to Jews." He continued: "The only salvation for the Russian people is an Orthodox, Russian, wise Tsar." [54] A message of the Sobor termed the separation of church and state an attack on the church and urged the faithful to be ready to fight against "the dark deeds of the sons of destruction" in defense of their sacred things. Another proclamation called the people to unite to defend their churches, lest they fall into the hands of the ungodly. "Better to shed one's blood and gain a martyr's crown than to turn the Orthodox faith over to its foes for abuse." [55]

The churchmen continued to carry the fight to the enemy. On March 18, 1918, Patriarch Tikhon condemned the Treaty of Brest-Litovsk for having surrendered millions of Orthodox believers to the enemy.[56] Religious processions through the streets challenged the Soviet authorities, including one to the Red Square in Moscow, where the Patriarch called on the people to go to their Golgotha.[57] Fearing that the government would arrest and execute him, the leaders of the Sobor organized brotherhoods to defend his person night and day.[58] Quantities of leaflets were distributed, condemning the Bolsheviks as sons of Antichrist and calling on the people to defend their holy faith. In some provincial cities these efforts led to outbreaks of violence.[59] Another defiance of the authorities was a solemn requiem for the slain Nicholas II and his family, which the Patriarch and the Sobor performed shortly after the execution.[60] When the Sobor dissolved in August 1918, the Patriarch continued his opposition.

---

[52] *Deianiia sv. sobora,* IV (Vyp. 1), 59–60; Vvedensky, 114–116.
[53] *Deianiia sv. sobora,* IV (Vyp. 1), 59–60.
[54] *Deianiia sv. sobora,* IV (Vyp. 1), 43–44.
[55] *Deianiia sv. sobora,* IV (Vyp. 1), 71–73.
[56] Titlinov, 120–121.
[57] *Deianiia sv. sobora,* as cited in Vvedensky, 150, 183–187, 191, 193; Titlinov, 122.
[58] Vvedensky, 202–207; G. P. Fedotov, *The Russian Church since the Revolution* (New York, 1928), 24; Titlinov, 125–126.
[59] Titlinov, 127; Fedotov, 24; *Deianiia sv. sobora,* as cited in Vvedensky, 194–195.
[60] *Tserkovnyia vedomosti izdaemyia pri vysshem russkom tserkovnom upravlenii zagranitsei,* Sremski Karlovsty, Yugoslavia, no. 9–19 (1925), 20–21.

In October 1918, he charged the government with all the evils then afflicting the people and warned the commissars that they who had taken up the sword would perish by the sword.[61] The government merely put the Patriarch under house arrest for a time. Many of the lesser clergy also continued to combat the Soviet regime during 1918. But these efforts failed to arouse a great upsurge of religious feeling leading to the overthrow of the Bolsheviks, and during 1919 the Soviet regime was able to pursue its policy regarding the church.

On the whole, the Soviet measures were not spectacular. The nationalization of church property, including parish funds and investments, went steadily forward, and the government easily took over the civil record books. The authorities closed a few parish churches, which they chiefly converted into schools,[62] but religious observance continued in most parishes without interference. On the other hand, the Soviet regime forbade religious education of the young in the churches and permitted it only in private homes.[63] Far from striking sensational blows at the church, the Soviet leaders warned urgently against outrageous actions against religious faith and insults to believers. Lenin gave a striking example of moderation at Easter 1919 by releasing the patriarch and several other hierarchs from arrest.[64]

Not all of the hostile clergy got off so lightly. During the Civil War the Soviet police shot some of the most incendiary of the ecclesiastical agitators, but the number of such executions apparently was not large. Other hostile clerics were arrested or exiled, most of them obtaining their release at the end of the Civil War.[65] On the whole, the government seems to have been rather mild in its treatment of the clergy.

Toward the monasteries and convents, however, the Red leaders were unrelenting and demonstrative. The government seized almost all the cloisters and ousted the monastics, putting the buildings to use as hospitals, schools, or asylums.[66] Moreover, when inventorying the contents of the monasteries the commissars laid bare sensational frauds concerning relics of the saints, which permitted them to strike at the prestige of the church by making the most of these scandals.[67]

[61] S. V. Troitsky, *Chto sdelal Patriarkh Tikhon dlia tserkvi i rodiny* (Odessa, 1919), 13; A. Rozhdestvensky, *His Holiness Tikhon, Patriarch of All the Russias* (London, 1923), 22.

[62] *Revol. i tserkov'*, no. 6–8 (1919), 113–114; no. 9–12 (1922), 106.

[63] RSFSR, *Sobranie uzak. i rasp. pravital'stva*, no. 18 (1918), 272–273; RSFSR, *Sistematicheskii sbornik vazhneishikh dekretov, 1917–1920* (Moscow, 1921), 20–21. P. V. Gidulianov and P. Krasikov, eds., *Tserkov' i gosudarstvo po zakonodatel'stvu RSFSR* (Moscow, 1923), 27–28.

[64] *Izvestiia*, no. 84 (April 18, 1919); *Revol. i tserkov'*, no. 1 (1919), 8–9; Fedotov, 42–43.

[65] *Tserk. ved. . . . Zagran.*, no. 13–14 (1923), 10; *Ezhenedel'nik chrezvychainnykh komissii* (October 20, 1918), 20–21; *Revol. i tserkov'*, no. 6–8 (1919), 100–101.

[66] *Revol. i tserkov'*, no. 9–12 (1920), 83–84.

[67] *Revol. i tserkov'*, no. 1 (1919), 42; no. 6–8 (1919), 124–125; no. 9–12 (1920), 72–82.

But while the Soviet authorities behaved relatively mildly toward the church, many churchmen continued their opposition to the Red government by supporting the Whites. Prelates and priests in anti-Soviet territory urged the people to enroll in the White armies, blessed their banners, and condemned the Bolsheviks as bloodthirsty monsters accursed of God. Ecclesiastics gave warm approval to such White leaders as Kolchak, Denikin, and Wrangel and sought to stimulate the loyalty of the people toward them. The clergy performed *Te Deums* asking victory for the White armies and published printed matter attacking the Communists and sometimes the Jews allegedly identified with them. Some of the priests served as chaplains with the anti-Soviet armies, raising their voices to inspire the White troops to valiant deeds.[68] Finally, on several occasions the clergy in anti-Soviet areas sent out appeals to Christians of other lands, urging them to support the White armies against the godless Reds.[69]

After the Red army had won the Civil War, an uneasy truce existed between the Soviet government and the Russian Orthodox Church. The famine of 1921, however, soon brought fresh conflict. When the government asked for contributions for the victims, the church grudgingly donated a small part of its holdings of precious metals.[70] Early in 1922 the government, not satisfied with the church's gifts, decided to take a large part of the church plate for relief.[71] Patriarch Tikhon termed this sacrilege and ordered the clergy not to permit it.[72] At almost the same time the Karlovatsky Sobor, a gathering of émigré prelates and laymen in Yugoslavia, urged that no aid should go to Russia in order that the famine might cause the Soviet regime to collapse.[73] Disorders broke out in several Russian cities when Soviet officials attempted to seize the church treasure, resulting in loss of life. The government, apparently feeling that the Patriarch and the émigré churchmen were acting in harmony against it, struck ruthlessly, trying and executing a number of clergy involved, among them Metropolitan Veniamin of Petrograd.[74] Finally, Patriarch Tikhon himself was arrested and held for trial, and many observers expected that his excution on charges of counterrevolution would follow.[75]

[68] *Tobol'skiia eparkhial'nyia vedomosti*, no. 34 (December 28, 1918), 321–322; *New York Times* (February 15, 1919); L. A. Krol', *Za tri goda* (Vladivostok, 1921), 195–196; A. I. Denikin, *Ocherki russkoi smuty* (5 vols.; Paris, 1921–1926), II, 204, 206, 261, and IV, 234–235; *Kubanskii tserkovnyi vestnik*, no. 22–23 (1919), 339–343.
[69] *The Times* (February 15, 1919, September 9, 1919).
[70] Titlinov, 184.
[71] *Izvestiia* (February 24, 1922, February 26, 1922).
[72] A. A. Valentinov, ed., *Chernaia kniga* (*shturm nebes'*) (Paris, 1925), 253–254.
[73] *Deianniia russkago vsegranichnago tserkovnago sobora* (Sremski Karlovtsy, Yugoslavia, 1922), 3, 8–14, 24–28, 37–38, 48–52, 151–156; *Tserk. ved. . . . Zagran.*, no. 3 (1922), 2–4.
[74] *Izvestiia* (March 28, 1922, April 4, 1922, April 28, 1922, May 6, 1922, August 13, 1922); *Pravda* (September 7, 1922, July 27, 1922).
[75] *Izvestiia* (May 7, 1922, May 9, 1922).

At this juncture a handful of priests who had been liberal before 1917 persuaded the Patriarch to give them limited and temporary power over the administration of the church.[76] With tacit Soviet support the priests, headed by Dean A. Vvedensky and Father Krasnitsky, and aided by two bishops, set up a Temporary Higher Administration of the Church. Calling themselves the Living Church, they purged the hierarchy of bishops hostile to the Soviet regime, consecrated some priests as bishops, and declared Patriach Tikhon deposed. The new heads of the church sent many prelates into exile and received the support of many priests and some of the bishops.[77] Their sway proved to be brief, however.

The release of the Patriarch in 1923 struck a mortal blow at the Living Church. The government had actually issued tickets of admission to his trial, but suddenly it announced that he had admitted his guilt and repented of his misdeeds.[78] Upon his release he took over control of the church and received the enthusiastic support of most of the believers, who deserted the Living Church in droves. The latter organization survived for years, in gravely weakened form, but although the Patriarch had signed a statement admitting his guilt and renouncing hostility to the Soviet regime,[79] he failed to persuade his followers to become reconciled with the government. The two groups of clergy, with the approval of the government, made several efforts to unite and reach a *modus vivendi* with the Soviet regime,[80] but all attempts ended in failure.[81] The patriarchal church remained hostile to the government, although when Patriarch Tikhon died in 1925 he left a testament calling on his followers to cease their opposition to the Soviet order and to support it loyally.[82]

With the church remaining hostile, the government sought to compel reconciliation by arresting all the hierarchs who sought to function as Locum Tenens, thus depriving the church of central leadership.[83] Finally, in 1927, after several arrests and long negotiations Metropolitan Sergii of Nizhni Novgorod, an elderly and revered prelate, announced that he had reached agreement with the government and would be permitted to set up a central administration of the church.[84] He called on all believers

---

[76] *Tserk. Vied. . . . Zagran.*, no. 11–12 (1922), 1–2; *Vestnik sviashchennogo sinoda pravoslavnoi rossiiskoi tserkvi*, no. 2 (1925), 18.

[77] *Pravda* (May 21, 1922); *Izvestiia* (May 20, 1922, July 11, 1922, August 12, 1922); *Pravda* (August 17, 1922).

[78] *Izvestiia* (June 27 and June 28, 1923).

[79] *Izvestiia* (July 6, 1923).

[80] Troitsky, 25; I. Stratonov, *Russkaia tserkovnaia smuta* (Berlin, 1932), 98–99; *Vestnik sv. sinoda*, no. 4 (1927), 16, 23–24; *Izvestiia* (July 5, 1924, July 10, 1924).

[81] P. N. Miliukov, *Outlines of Russian Culture* (3 vols.; Philadelphia, 1942), I, 186.

[82] *Izvestiia* (April 15, 1925).

[83] Stratonov, 129–30; Miliukov, I, 191; *Tserk. ved. . . . Zagran.*, no. 5–6 (March 1926), 6–7; (May 1926), 6; (June 1926), 32; (December 1926), 9; Fedotov, 75.

[84] Stratonov, 175–176.

to renounce hostility to the regime and ordered prayers for the Soviet leaders.[85] Thus the government had obtained its desired compromise with the church — a compromise that has endured down to the present.

IV

But while the church was now at peace with the government, it encountered a rising tide of antireligious propaganda. During the early years the Communist Party had been too busy to carry on any but the most rudimentary antireligious work. From 1922 on, however, antireligious periodicals began to appear and an organized movement known as the League of Militant Godless started a drive against religion.[86] At first the efforts were crude and insulting parodies of various faiths, but as time went on the movement grew and the methods became more skillful, making effective use of science to stress materialism and combat "superstition." [87] By the end of 1928 there were nearly half a million members of the League of Militant Godless.[88]

During the First Five Year Plan the attack on the church grew in intensity. The church lost the right of religious propaganda, and various restrictions and discriminatory taxation made the lives of the clergy difficult. A few priests were shot for hoarding silver coins.[89] The League of Militant Godless grew very rapidly and pushed a frenzied drive to get the people to destroy their ikons and to close churches. Collective farms voted to call themselves godless.[90] But in winning these successes the Godless had often gravely alienated the peasants. Hence in March 1930, the Communist Party issued a warning against arbitrary closing of churches and outraging the feelings of the peasants.[91] After this, the antireligious work became less aggressive, although the League of Militant Godless reached a peak of nearly six million members in 1932.[92]

Even before the end of the First Five Year Plan the antireligious drive began to slacken. Now that the collectivization of agriculture had suc-

[85] *Izvestiia* (August 19, 1927).

[86] *VKP (b) v rezoliutsiiakh i resheniiakh s"ezdov, konferentsii i plenumov TsK* (2 vols.; Moscow, 1933–1936), I, 618–620; M. Enisherlov, ed., *Voinstvuiushee bezbozhie v SSSR za 15 let* (Moscow, 1932), 285–286; 413–417, 326, 344–345; *Antireligioznik* (July 1929), 112.

[87] *Izvestiia* (January 10, 1923); *Antireligioznaia propaganda. K postanovke raboty* (Kharkov, 1925), 7; Enisherlov, 305–306, 390–394; I. V. Stepanov, *Kak vesti antireligioznuiu propagandu v derevne* (Leningrad, 1930).

[88] Enisherlov, 344–45.

[89] N. Orleansky, compiler, *Zakon o religioznykh ob'edineniiakh RSFSR . . .* (Moscow, 1930), 6–12, 25; *Konstitutsiia Soiuza SSR i soiuznykh respublik* (Moscow, 1932), 22; *Izvestiia* (February 24, 1931, December 21, 1930); *Pravda* (September 9, 1930).

[90] Enisherlov, 296–98, 309–10; *Antireligioznik*, no. 1 (1931), 40, no. 3 (1930), 6–7; E. Iaroslavsky, *Razvernutym frontom* (Moscow, 1929), 48–49, 62–64; *Pravda* (January 15, 1930, January 19, 1930).

[91] *Pravda* (March 15, 1930); *VKP (b) v rezoliutsiiakh*, II, 404, 662–663.

[92] *Antireligioznik*, no. 8–9 (1930), 101.

ceeded, the promotion of atheism seemed less vital and the ranks of the Godless dwindled.[93] Nevertheless, the church also declined. Many peasants had concluded that religion was old-fashioned, while the schools sought to give the children an atheistic outlook. On the whole, the older people kept their faith, but support for the churches lessened and more and more priests renounced the cloth.[94]

Possibly in part because of the decline of the church, in 1936 the status of the clergy improved. Stalin himself sponsored a passage in the new constitution giving them the right to vote and hold office, which meant equality with other citizens,[95] including the right to unrestricted education of their children. The income-tax laws were changed to put the clergy on the same footing with doctors and lawyers.[96] Furthermore, Stalin banned Demian Bednyi's play *Bogatyri* because it burlesqued the introduction of Christianity into Russia in the tenth century, when — so Stalin declared — this faith was a progressive and civilizing influence. During these years Soviet writers portrayed churchmen of ancient times as staunch patriots who had inspired the Russians to fight against invaders.[97] It is worthy of note that apparently only a few ecclesiastics met death during the great purges of 1937 and 1938, although many Communists — political leaders, diplomats, industrialists, army men — suffered punishment. Somewhat paradoxically, however, the Godless movement, which had been in the doldrums, recovered between 1937 and 1941 to a total membership of almost three and one half million members.[98] Nevertheless, although the Godless periodicals rejoiced that the number of churches had greatly declined and that the Orthodox church was having difficulty in finding priests, gone was the easy optimism of early years. The Godless leaders warned that "religion is very long-lived" and that only by skillful, persistent atheist propaganda over at least another decade could they hope to eradicate it.[99]

When the German armies attacked the USSR in June 1941, both

[93] *Bezbozhnik* (July 30, 1931, October 25, 1931, January 24, 1932); *Antireligioznik,* no. 22 (1933), 27–28; no. 14 (1932), 36; *Izvestiia* (December 24, 1930); *Komsomolskaia pravda* (December 24, 1930, April 4, 1931, April 12, 1931).

[94] *Antireligioznik,* no. 8–9 (1930), 101, no. 10 (1932), 49–52, no. 3 (1933), 14; Paul B. Anderson, *Russia's Religious Future* (London, 1935), 19, 41–43; *Pod znamenem marksizma,* no. 3 (1931), 48.

[95] *Konstitutsiia soiuza sovetskikh sotsialisticheskikh respublik* (Moscow, 1938), arts. 135–136, 124; E. E. Iaroslavsky, *Stalinskaia konstitutsiia i vopros o religii* (Moscow, 1936), 4–6; I. V. Stalin, *O proekte konstitutsii soiuza SSR* (Moscow, 1949), 32–34.

[96] K. N. Plotnikov, *Biudzhet sotsialisticheskogo gosudarstva* (Moscow, 1948), 280.

[97] Vsesoiuznyi Komitet po Delam Iskusstv, *Protiv fal'sifikatsii narodnogo proshlogo* (Moscow, 1937), 3–13.

[98] *Bezbozhnik* (April 6, 1941).

[99] *Antireligioznik,* no. 4 (1935), 11–13, no. 6 (1935), 2; *Pravda* (February 5, 1938); F. N. Oleshchuk, *O preodolenii religioznykh perezhitkov* (Moscow, 1941), 12–17; *Bol'shevik,* no. 7–8 (1941), 119; E. E. Iaroslavsky, *Kommunizm i religiia* (Moscow, 1931), 3–21; *Antireligioznik,* no. 3 (1934), 38.

church and government strongly supported the agreement made in 1927. At the very outset the acting Patriarch reminded the faithful of the patriotic deeds of their ancestors and blessed all Orthodox fighting "in defense of the sacred frontiers of our fatherland." Similar appeals were made by other hierarchs. In addition, Metropolitan Sergii sent encouraging messages to the guerrillas behind the German lines and condemned those who collaborated with the enemy.[100] He also set an example for his flock by contributing substantial sums for the construction of a unit of tanks.[101] His patriotic zeal reached its climax, however, in his message to Stalin on November 1942, terming him the "divinely anointed leader" of the nation and asking God's blessing for his "great deeds for the fatherland." [102] The Synod also supported the government by excommunicating four Orthodox hierarchs who collaborated with the Germans in the occupied areas.[103]

The government of the USSR cordially reciprocated. Antireligious propaganda ceased almost immediately when war came. In Moscow in 1942 the authorities lifted the curfew on Easter eve so that the faithful might attend midnight services, and in 1943 they released the miraculous ikon of the Iverian Virgin for worship by the people.[104] Also the government named Metropolitan Nikolai of Kiev to an official commission investigating German outrages — the first such appointment since the famine of 1922.[105] Most important of all, however, was the restoration of the Patriarchate encouraged by Stalin in 1943. He, together with Molotov, received Metropolitans Sergii and Nikolai in the Kremlin and gave them permission to hold a Sobor to elect another Patriarch.[106]

As a result, on September 7, 1943, a Sobor of nineteen bishops met and elected Metropolitan Sergii as the second Patriarch since 1700 and named a Synod. The Sobor also voted thanks to the government for its attention to the church's needs and urged all Christians to unite against Hitlerism.[107] The publication of the *Journal of the Moscow Patriarchate* after a lapse of ten years further marked the government's benevolence, as did the visit of the Archbishop of York as a guest of the Patriarch. It is remarkable that this historic event happened under the godless regime, for under the Orthodox tsars no Anglican archbishop had ever come to Russia.[108]

The government continued to display favor toward the Orthodox

[100] *Pravda o religii v Rossii* (Moscow, 1942), 15–17, 83–86, 98–111; *Patriarkh Sergii i ego dukhovnogo nasledstvo* (Moscow, 1947), 90.

[101] *Pravda o religii v Rossii*, 168.

[102] *New York Times* (November 10, 1942).

[103] *Pravda o religii*, 129–42; *Patriarkh Sergii i ego dukhovnogo nasledstvo*, 89.

[104] *New York Times* (October 6 and 7, 1941, August 5, 1943); N. S. Timasheff in W. Gurian, ed., *The Soviet Union* (Notre Dame, 1951), 184; *Pravda o religii*, p. 216.

[105] *Soviet War Documents* (Washington, 1943), 155–57.

[106] *Izvestiia* (September 5, 1943).

[107] *Zhurnal Moskovskoi Patriarkhii*, no. 1 (1943), 5–6, 21.

[108] *Zhurnal Moskovskoi Patriarkhii*, no. 2 (1943), 18–23.

church. G. G. Karpov, named head of the cabinet's Council for Affairs of the Orthodox Church, proved zealous in aiding the church to rebuild damaged buildings and to open seminaries and helped in securing permission for organized religious instruction to children.[109] Patriarch Sergii succeeded in bringing into his fold the remnants of the Living Church and the Orthodox clergy of Carpatho-Ukraine, and re-established communion with the Orthodox church of Georgia, doubtless with the encouragement of the government.[110] The latter openly showed its benevolence by awarding medals "For the Defense of Leningrad" and "For the Defense of Moscow" to groups of ecclesiastics.[111]

As before, the churchmen rendered service to the government, by contributions of over 150 million rubles, in addition to hailing triumphs and inspiring the people to work and fight for victory. On November 7, 1943, after the recovery of Kiev, Patriarch Sergii prayed for "our divinely protected land, and for its authorities, headed by its God-given leader." [112] And in 1944 Metropolitan Alexii of Leningrad, Sergii's successor, assured Stalin he and his flock all bore deep love for the Soviet leader.[113] The churchmen also served the state by appealing to the Orthodox believers of Rumania, Greece, and Bulgaria to throw off the domination of Hitler. Even Patriarch Sergii's denial of the Pope's claim to be God's vicar[114] doubtless was pleasing to the Soviet government, which was also critical of the papacy.[115]

After the death of Patriarch Sergii in May 1944, Metropolitan Alexii of Leningrad, who became Locum Tenens, called a new Sobor in Moscow in January 1945. This gala event stressed the importance of Russian Orthodoxy, since, in addition to Russian clergy, two of the Eastern Patriarchs and the Patriarch of Georgia attended, as well representatives of two other Eastern Patriarchs and of the Serbian and Rumanian churches. The Soviet government provided transportation for the visitors, and lavish ceremonies took place after the election of Metropolitan Alexii as Patriarch. The Sobor voted gratitude to the government and praise for Stalin. It also issued a message "to the people of the whole world," denouncing Hitleriate Germany and accusing the papacy of sympathy with fascist doctrines.[116]

---

[109] *Zhurnal Moskovskoi Patriarkhii,* no. 3 (1945), 22–24; no. 7 (1944), 10–18; *New York Times* (August 11 and 12, 1944); *Christian Science Monitor* (September 30, 1944).

[110] *Zh. Mosk. Pat.,* no. 3 (1943), 8–9; no. 3 (1944), 6–10; no. 4 (1944), 9; no. 1 (1945), 7–8.

[111] *Soviet War News* (October 19, 1943); *Russkii golos* (October 11, 1944).

[112] *Zh. Mosk. Pat.,* no. 10 (1944), 3; no. 1 (1943), 9–13; no. 4 (1943), 13–14.

[113] *Patriarkh Sergii,* 135–36.

[114] *Patriarkh Sergii,* 90; *Zh. Mosk. Pat.,* no. 9 (1944), 3–5.

[115] *Zh. Mosk. Pat.,* no. 2 (1944), 13–18.

[116] *Patriarkh Sergii,* 322–31; *Zh. Mosk. Pat.,* no. 2 (1945), 10–11; no. 3 (1945), 27–32; *Izvestiia* (February 4 and 10, 1945).

After the Sobor of 1945 the Russian church continued to support the Soviet government with words of praise, gratitude toward Stalin, and services of thanksgiving for victory. The Patriarch told a reporter from *Izvestiia* that the church had contributed over three million rubles to the government and, above all, had demonstrated to all the world "its complete unity with the government." [117] It also continued its hostility to the Vatican on political and theological grounds[118] and strengthened its ties with the Serbian and especially with the Bulgarian Orthodox churches.[119] It likewise succeeded in regaining control of the Russian monasteries in Palestine and improved its relations with the Patriarch of Antioch.[121]

But while the church was thus gaining in strength and importance, toward the end of the war a revival of mild antireligious activity became evident. It was called "scientific and enlightening propaganda," with no mention of religion or the church, but its announced purpose of overcoming survivals of "ignorance, superstition, and prejudice" [121] boded no good for the church.

During the war Karpov expressly stated that the government's favor was not a temporary thing, but had resulted from the church's attitude toward the Soviet state before and during the war. This policy did not end with the war. In 1946 Patriarch Alexii received the Order of the Red Banner for his work during the war, and in 1947 war medals were bestowed on groups of clergy of several dioceses.[122] In the postwar years the government made possible the rebuilding or repair of many damaged churches, so that by 1948 Karpov reported that the functioning churches numbered more than 22,000,[123] or about one half of the number of parish churches in 1917. The number of bishops and archbishops grew, and the churches were filled on festival days. Moreover, the church and its clergy appeared to be in comfortable financial circumstances. A great expansion of theological education took place, so that by 1955 there were nine seminaries and two theological academies for higher education.[124]

The Russian church also continued to grow in strength through new acquisitions. In 1946 some five million Uniats of the Western Ukraine renounced the jurisdiction of the papacy and rejoined the Orthodox church after some four hundred fifty years.[125] A somewhat similar development

[117] *Zh. Mosk. Pat.*, no. 5 (1945), 3; *Izvestiia* (May 12, 1945).
[118] *Zh. Mosk. Pat.*, no. 4 (1945), 7–9, 19–21; no. 5 (1945), 36–43.
[119] *Izvestiia* (April 13, 1945); *Zh. Mosk. Pat.*, no. 10 (1944), 6–7; no. 5 (1945), 19–26.
[120] *New York Times* (May 9, 1944); *Izvestiia* (December 14, 1944).
[121] *Propagandist*, no. 18 (1944), 1–5; *Izvestiia* (December 14, 1944).
[122] *New York Times* (August 18, 1946); *Zh. Mosk. Pat.*, no. 2 (1947), 37, no. 4 (1947), 37.
[123] *USSR Information Bulletin* (January 28, 1949), 54–56.
[124] *Russkii golos* (December 1, 1946); *Zh. Mosk. Pat.*, no. 6 (1947), nos. 1, 2, 7 (1948).
[125] *Patriarkh Sergii*, 372–73; see also J. B. Barron and H. M. Waddams, eds., *Communism and the Churches* (New York, 1950), 29.

occurred in Carpatho-Ukraine, where, after intensive Orthodox missionary work, the Uniats came back into the fold.[126] The Vatican has charged that these changes were the result of Soviet intimidation; the Orthodox spokesmen admit that Uniat leaders were arrested after the war, but claim that the arrests were made because they had actively collaborated with the Germans.[127] It has not proved possible to determine the facts of the case.

That the Soviet government is not adverse to the Russian church's claims to leadership of the whole Orthodox world was shown by the great church anniversary celebration in 1948. The heads of all the Orthodox churches of Eastern Europe and the Levant or their representatives were present, so that the gathering resembled an ecumenical council.[128] Indeed, Patriarch Alexii sought to have it function as one by supporting the position of the Russian church and condemning the papacy and criticizing the Protestant churches. To his annoyance, however, the Patriarch of Constantinople objected, so that the Russian Patriarch has not been able to assume full primacy in the Orthodox world. Relations between the two Patriarchs have remained strained.[129]

Since the end of the war the Russian church has extended its influence by visits to churchmen in Western Europe and in eastern Mediterranean lands, as well as by entertaining visiting church dignitaries. In addition, it has supported Soviet foreign policy. It has consistently charged the United States and other Western powers with aggressive intent and has taken an active part in Soviet peace campaigns.[130] The Patriarch and his Synod protested to the United Nations against alleged American aggression in Korea and the bombing of peaceful civilians.[131] It strongly supported Stalin until his death and has continued its cooperation with the Soviet government, condemning American atomic armaments and urging peaceful coexistence.[132]

In spite of this harmony of views, however, antireligious propaganda has continued unabated since 1945, although not in the strident tones of earlier years. Above all, strenuous efforts to educate the young along atheistic lines have become more explicit, with the Komsomol claiming that a youth cannot be an effective and progressive citizen while clinging to outmoded superstitions.[133] Probably this campaign has had some effect.

[126] *Zh. Mosk. Pat.*, no. 10 (1949), 6–10.
[127] *New York Times* (March 7, 13, 19, and April 15, 1946).
[128] Gurian, 161–62; *Zh. Mosk Pat.* (1948), special number; no. 8 (1949), 14–28.
[129] *Zh. Mosk. Pat.* (1948), special number, 35–37, 66.
[130] *Zh. Mosk. Pat.* (1948–1957), *passim.*
[131] *Zh. Mosk. Pat.*, no. 8 (1950), 5–7.
[132] *Zh. Mosk. Pat.* (1953–1957), *passim.*
[133] *Komsomol'skaia pravda* (October 18, 1947, March 31, 1949); *Narodnoe obrazovanie*, no. 4 (1949), 18–21, 25; *Uchitel'skaia gazeta* (June 10, 1948, November 26, 1949); *Bol'shevik*, no. 11 (1948), 36.

V

In retrospect, the Russian Orthodox Church seems to have endured remarkably well under Soviet rule, in spite of its earlier identification with the imperial regime. The church is probably in better condition than at any time since 1917. There has been a considerable religious revival since 1941, so that the church again has half as many active parishes as before the revolution. While its support comes chiefly from older people, it seems to have been able to attract younger members to replenish its congregations. Certainly the hopes of the Godless for its speedy demise have been disappointed.

On the other hand, at least half of the Soviet population has broken with religion — a tremendous decline in the faith. In part this has undoubtedly resulted from official Soviet policy, which has been remarkably skillful. In the early years it avoided a head-on clash, while reducing the church's strength through indirect measures. When Patriarch Tikhon failed to persuade his followers to adopt his changed attitude, the Soviet authorities finally secured a relatively harmonious arrangement with Metropolitan Sergii, which has continued down to the present. The government has bestowed favors on the church, so that in some respects its position is excellent. Nevertheless, antireligious propaganda has continued, except during the war, and is still strong. This apparently paradoxical policy is understandable only if one realizes that the Communist leaders follow both a long-term and a short-term program. The short-term aims call for support of the Orthodox church and use of its influence to further Soviet policy. The long-range program, which is consistently followed, calls for the full elimination of religion in the USSR. There is no reason to expect any change in these policies.

Another set of reasons for the decline of religion in the Soviet Union is not peculiar to that country alone. The increase in public amusements, such as motion pictures, television, libraries, and a massive sports program, has undoubtedly cut church attendance. The development of a more modern way of life, with its great stress on science and technology, has helped to undermine some of the authority of the Russian church, which was adapted to a simpler society. The state has taken over all social functions, so that the church has little to offer the people except divine worship. Moreover, the influence of Soviet life is materialistic and secular, and it is neither fashionable nor advantageous to be a church member. In spite of this, there has been a religious revival since 1941. Perhaps the best explanation of this may be that it is a result of the horrors and suffering of the war and the consequent hardships of the postwar period. If that is the case, then improvement in the lot of the people should lessen the quest of the people for religious consolation. As the standard of living rises, the church may again decline.

There appears to be little reason to expect that the Russian church will be actively hostile to the Soviet regime. During the 1920's, when the church was still strong and the regime was weak, it tried this, only to fail. Since then it has strongly supported the government. The whole tradition of the Russian church has been acceptance of the civil power rather than ecclesiastical supremacy, and when it proved impossible to fight the Soviet authorities, the church reverted to this tradition. During the 1930's the Soviet leaders realized the loyalty of the church, and the church repaid this trust with convincing support against Hitler from the first moment of the war in 1941. In the light of these facts, it seems likely that the church will not turn against the Soviet regime.

Thus, a survey of relations between the Russian Orthodox Church and the state since 1861 makes it seem likely that in the next decades these relations will, as before, remain harmonious, except that antireligious propaganda will continue. While the Russian church will probably remain strong, it may experience a slow decline during this period.

THE INNER LIFE OF THE RUSSIAN ORTHODOX CHURCH

NICHOLAS S. TIMASHEFF

The inner life of the religious organizations, especially of the Russian Orthodox Church, is beyond doubt the segment of Russian culture where change since 1861 has been smaller than anywhere else, and this despite the tremendous change in the state-church relations (which remain outside the scope of this chapter). Of course, today the scope of activities carried out in the framework of the Russian Orthodox Church is much narrower than it was from 1861 to 1917. But no new activities have been added, and those which were present before the revolution and still exist today are almost identical in form and content.

A separate description of these activities before and after the revolution would be tediously repetitious. This essay therefore concentrates on the inner life of the Russian Orthodox Church as it is today, with further statements about the partial difference between now and then. There is an additional reason for choosing this plan. Before the revolution, among investigators of Russian church life, both foreign and Russian (except spokesmen of the church and the government), the opinion was strongly represented that the Russian Orthodox Church was almost a dead body, attached and subordinate to the imperial government. This opinion never could be proven, but neither was it easy to refute it. If the opinion were correct, any inner life of the church would have stopped shortly after the October Revolution; such was definitely the expectation of the new rulers of Russia. But undeniable facts which could be observed and recorded during the past forty years demonstrate that the church is alive. Anticipating more detailed statements, let me quote the conclusion to the report of the Quakers who visited Russia in 1955:

We see the Russian Orthodox Church as a living force capable of great good and offering some promise of influencing the future development of Soviet society. In any event, we found it in anything but the moribund state in which most Westerners assume it to be.[1]

The conclusion is obvious: if the Russian church is alive today, it was alive before the revolution, and the controversial past can be best reconstructed on the basis of the data based on the present.

I

The survey of the inner life of the Russian Orthodox Church today with occasional excursions into the past must be preceded by a few statements about the structure of the framework in which the activities under study were and are being carried out. Since time immemorial, the Russian Orthodox Church has been the established church of Russia to which the vast majority (about 70 per cent) of the population officially belonged; the actual figure was somewhat smaller because of defections among the intellectuals and the industrial workers. After Peter the Great, the church was headed by a Holy Synod, an assembly of bishops designated by the government. In 1914, the church was divided into 64 dioceses, with 130 bishops and about 50,000 priests. The church encompassed more than 900 monasteries and convents, with 80,000 monks and nuns. It maintained four theological academies and 58 seminaries for the training of priests. Moreover, it controlled a network of parochial schools granting primary education to three million children. It also fostered an impressive number of publications, periodical and nonperiodical.[2]

The dark spot in the picture was "the withdrawal of the intellectuals," accentuated since the 1860's. But early in the twentieth century the tide turned; there began a back-to-church movement led by such men as P. Struve, N. Berdiaev, S. Bulgakov, and S. Frank. In the early 1900's, brilliant debates on religious topics could be heard in the Religious Philosophical Society, with the participation of both clergymen and laymen.

---

[1] *Meeting the Russians* (Philadelphia, 1956), 79.
[2] The data on the Russian Orthodox Church before the revolution have been compiled from the *Otchety Ober-Prokurora Sviateishego Synoda*, for the years 1909 and 1910, the last published.

Within the church itself, there arose a group of liberal priests who longed for a renovation (not reformation) of the church.[3]

The Provisional Government granted the church the right of self-determination. The National Convention (Sobor) of 1917–1918 repealed the Petrinian reform and went back to the monocratic organization which the majority of the Eastern churches had had throughout their history. The Sobor decreed two reforms deviating both from the Petrinian and the Muscovite style. It placed between the central church government and the dioceses twenty-odd metropolitan districts and granted the parishes a democratic organization. But the October Revolution put the very existence and survival of the church in question, since it forbade religious education to be given to persons below the age of eighteen, nationalized church property, and deprived the latter of legal status. Only "groups of twenty believers" were recognized and entitled to run individual church buildings. On the unofficial level, the structure survived but was badly shaken. The metropolitan districts were *de facto* abolished when regular communication between the levels became impossible because of persecution; they were not restored when persecution gave way to compromise. The democratization of the parishes was curbed at the Sobor of 1945; this probably was part of the price the church paid for receiving official status.

Today the structure consists of the three canonically essential levels: the national church headed by the Patriarch and a Synod of bishops; the dioceses whose heads bear the title of metropolitans, archbishops, and bishops (but are equal in rights and duties); and the parishes which are said to number twenty to twenty-five thousand.

During the first few years after the revolution, the church, despite all limitations and deprivations, fostered charitable and cultural activities, through fraternities and sororities. Such institutions were known in pre-revolutionary days but suddenly became more numerous and vigorous. These activities were curbed during the first wave of persecution, 1922–1924, but revived during the truce of 1925–1929. Cultural activities (short of formal religious instruction) received a tremendous impetus. During these years, the Soviet press mentioned the existence of a youth organization called Khristomol, in opposition to the Komsomol; in some dioceses, the former was larger than the latter. In 1929, all these activities were abruptly terminated by a decree explicitly prohibiting them. Since then they have not revived, at least on a large scale.[4]

II

Now let us turn to the activities performed by the Russian Orthodox Church in our day. The central church government takes care of all

[3] On these movements see V. Weidlé, *Russia Absent and Present* (New York, 1952), 80–90.
[4] N. S. Timasheff, *Religion in Soviet Russia* (New York, 1942), 59, 62.

questions of faith and church order. Not much is known about this activity but all symptoms point in one direction, ultraconservatism and antimodernism. The sermons published during the past fourteen years in the *Journal of the Moscow Patriarchate* and the rare publications treat problems of theology, Christian ethics, rites, and so on exactly as was the case some fifty years ago. The Patriarchate insists on keeping the old Julian calendar, despite the fact that in 1918 the Soviet government shifted to the Gregorian and that an all-Orthodox conference held in Moscow in 1948 advised the individual churches to use the calendar adopted by the respective governments, though continuing to calculate the date of Easter according to rules established in the fourth century by the Church of Alexandria. On many occasions the Patriarch has enjoined the bishops and priests strictly to follow the ancient rules concerning divine service and admonished the flock to comply with the church rules concerning fasting. In 1955, the Patriarch directed the clergy and the flock to avoid exaggerated decoration of the churches; emphasis should be laid on cleanliness and conformity with the traditional style; there should be not too much electrical light; living flowers should never be brought on the altar; the choirs should preferably choose ancient and austere motifs.[5]

Another major function of the central church government is that of supplying the total structure with trained priests. After fifteen years of interruption, the training of priests has been resumed in eight seminaries and two academies, the latter being conducted on a substantially higher level than the former. According to information available, the inner order of these institutions is almost of the monastic type, and the curriculum is similar to the prerevolutionary one. Of course, the students have to study the Soviet constitution; lately, the teaching of philosophy has been substantially curbed. On the other hand, the students of the academies are sometimes granted the opportunity to attend good plays in the theaters and are enjoined to participate in excursions to museums, under the guidance of instructors; this is a conspicuous innovation. The teaching staff consists partly of persons trained before the closing down of theological schools (in 1927) and of graduates of schools located outside Russia (Warsaw, Paris, Sofia, Harbin); recently, a few graduates of the two academies functioning on Soviet soil have been appointed to teaching positions. The number of applicants for enrollment (who must carry recommendations of their parish priests) is larger than the number of vacancies. But the number of graduates is lower than needed to replace those who die or quit. Therefore, the Leningrad Academy has organized correspondence courses, and in some dioceses short courses are organized to prepare for priesthood persons already familiar with divine service and

[5] *Zhurnal Moskovskogo Patriarkhata* (hereafter cited as *Zhurnal*), no. 2 (1955).

the Holy Writ; these again are innovations.[6] Unfortunately, no figures are available. Information collected by recent visitors to Russia makes it seem probable that no more than five hundred graduate each year from the regular schools, though one thousand are needed to maintain the clerical staff on the present level.[7]

Little is known about the functions of the dioceses. Of course, supervision of the activities on the parish level is their main responsibility. Since the official recognition of the church, this activity has been resumed. Initially, it was carried out mainly by correspondence, by invitation of individual priests to the diocesan see, and through the intermediary of archpriests — that is, older priests designated by the bishops to guide their younger colleagues and to check their activity. Since 1955, the *Journal of the Moscow Patriarchate* has started publishing reports about visitation of parishes by the bishops, which was quite common prior to the revolution. These reports show the bishops going occasionally to remote villages and finding there large crowds gathering from vast areas.

The main function of the church as a whole is to provide the believers with divine service, especially the sacraments and certain essential rites. This activity, common to all religious denominations, has always been emphasized by the Eastern churches. The function is, naturally, carried out on the parish level. Since the reconstruction of the church during the war and its aftermath, divine service is regularly going on in thousands of churches. On weekdays, attendance is small. But, as testified both by the *Journal* and by foreign visitors, on big holidays and on special occasions, such as the visit of a bishop, churches are often jammed. When, for instance, in June 1955, the Quaker delegation attended a Mass in one of the largest churches in Moscow, Metropolitan Nicholas of Krutitsy was officiating. The service was long and ceremonial — the congregation numbered about five thousand persons.[8]

Mrs. Henrietta Bower, in Moscow to study Soviet children's films, and who, incidentally, was shown the way to a Russian church by a senior army officer, reports: "On Sundays, the churches are tightly jammed. I had the greatest difficulty in edging and elbowing my way, inside the cathedral, to a point where I could catch a glimpse at three priests chanting the Mass. The churches I visited on weekdays were comfortably full." [9]

Harry Schwartz who visited Russia in the fall of 1955 relates his impressions as follows:

[6] *Zhurnal,* no. 10 (1949), no. 3 (1950), no. 11 (1951), nos. 2 and 3 (1955), no. 11 (1956).
[7] Henrietta Bower, "God's Underground in Russia," *Christian Herald* (November 1954), 20ff.
[8] *Meeting the Russians,* 71.
[9] Bower, 20ff.

A Sunday visit to a typical church finds it well filled with a congregation made up more than half of old women. . . . A better idea of the hold of religion is given when one attends a church on a special holiday. On such occasions, people come in large masses. There are many children, soldiers, men and women in the prime of life. One can see parents leading their toddlers to sacred relics to kiss them. An atmosphere of profound devotion and joy in worship predominates.[10]

The crowds seen in the churches are, so to speak, samples from a universe formed of the totality of the believers belonging to the Russian Orthodox Church. Unfortunately, the size of the universe is unknown, not only to students of Russian church affairs but probably also to the heads of the church and the government. Only estimates are possible. In conversations with a delegation of American churchmen to Russia in March 1956, Metropolitan Nicholas of Krutitsy, the second-ranking person in the Russian Orthodox Church, agreed with a suggested estimate of fifty million.[11] One year earlier, the present writer reached conclusions pointing to a similar figure by comparing the number of bishops and parishes today and in 1913 and assuming that the ratio of bishops and parishes to the number of believers was the same.[12]

Who are the believers? There is no doubt that the bulk is formed by middle-aged and older persons. But, according to numerous testimonies of eyewitnesses and statements of the Soviet press, children and younger persons may also be seen at the churches. During the acute antireligious campaign of 1954, one could read in *Pravda* that in many villages children continue to parade through the streets at Christmas time singing carols and reciting prayers, and that even in Moscow many children attend church. In a more general form, the *Komsomolskaia pravda* wrote: "Many boys and girls believe in miracles; they attend services organized by various denominations; they often consider it necessary to consolidate their marital happiness by church weddings and to have their children baptized." [13]

An extremely important fact has been recently reported by John Lawrence, a Baptist observer who has visited the Soviet Union many times. Of course, he says, "a great part of the congregations are old or middle-aged, but they are not older now than they were thirteen years ago when I began to observe such things." He explains this fact by a kind of religious cycle: most of the children are taught to say their prayers in the family, but when they go to school they come under atheist influ-

[10] Harry Schwartz, *New York Times* (November 9, 1955).
[11] Paul Anderson, *Christian Century* (April 19, 1956).
[12] N. S. Timasheff, "Urbanization, Operation Anti-Religion and the Decline of Religion in the USSR," *American Slavic and East European Review*, XIV (April 1955), 234–235.
[13] *Pravda* (August 4, 1954); *Komsomol'skaia pravda* (August 6, 1954).

ence and most of them break with the church before they are eighteen. But later on many find the way back into the church.[14]

As to the class membership of the believers, the bulk are peasants who still form half of the total population. But there are believers also among industrial workers and intellectuals. The persistence of religion among industrial workers is confirmed by information published in the *Journal* about the visits by bishops to such industrial centers as Shakhty and Magnitogorsk. The latter is an entirely new center, so that the church visited must have been built rather recently. New churches are reported to have been built in such industrial centers as Ivanovo and Anzhero-Sudzhensk (in Siberia), and existing ones to have been repaired in such large cities as Rostov, Saratov, and Kishinev.

Concerning the participation of the intellectuals, the following statements of the Soviet press are revealing: "Among people participating in the celebration of religious holidays one often finds doctors, engineers, labor-union activists. The majority come simply because they have been invited by friends; but they consider it proper to accept invitations to serve as godfathers or to attend at a church wedding or funeral." [15] Around "the holy spring at Glinkovo" (of which more will be said later), a Soviet newspaperman could identify an assistant principal of a technicum, an engineer, a senior research assistant at the Moscow University and his wife, a student of the Institute of Foreign Languages, as well as the head of an office that forms a part of the ministry of capital construction.[16]

The attraction of the church does not stop even at the gates of the party and the Komsomol, despite the obligation imposed on the members to adhere to the atheist philosophy of Marxism. Members of the two organizations often participate in the mammoth celebrations of local church holidays. During the antireligious campaign, *Pravda* acknowledged that even local party officers let their babies be baptized, commonly at night to avoid public attention.[17]

III

What is the value which exerts the strongest attraction toward the Russian Orthodox Church? There is no doubt that it is the divine service itself which people have learned to love in the course of an ancient tradition. They like the icons, the ceremonial movements, the sacramental invocations, and, above all, the beautiful church songs. The beauty and order found in the churches, in contrast to the ugliness and disorderliness of local "cultural institutions" of the Soviets, is often striking.

[14] John Lawrence, "Here Are Facts about Russian Protestants," *Eternity* (November 1955), 8ff.
[15] *Trud* (June 28, 1954).
[16] *Trud* (July 25, 1954).
[17] *Pravda* (August 4, 1954).

The church definitely wins out over the atheist state in the wedding ceremony. Recently, this telling story was published. Two young people, contrary to the advice of their parents, decided to get married in the office for the registration of births, deaths, marriages, and divorces. They entered the office; it was dark and damp, and there was a pronounced smell of mice. The officer in charge, a girl, did not conceal that she hated to work under these conditions. As if to corroborate her complaint, a mouse climbed over a filing cabinet; the girl hurled a paper weight at it from the desk. The young couple had to wait for two hours. When their turn seemed to have come, a new visitor appeared and the officer shouted: "Wait a moment, I must first register a death." The marriage was finally registered, but the young people were so disgusted that the next day they went to the church and had a beautiful church wedding. They were accompanied by several young boys.[18]

There is one more interesting and important symptom of the survival of religion among the masses of peasants. The practice is not actually religious and is frowned upon by many clergymen; but it flows from the religious sentiment as shaped by an age-old tradition. This is the extravagant celebration of the days of the patron saint of a church, a phenomenon which was quite common before the revolution and which, by the way, is described along similar lines with respect to southern Italy and Spain. Reports published during the antireligious campaign of 1954 show that the customs in question have not been uprooted by the years of Communist dominance. Here are a few instances.

In Sergievo, a village twenty miles from Vologda, a reporter sent by the *Komsomol'skaia pravda* could not find anyone working in the fields of the collective farm, not even the chairman or the secretary of the Komsomol organization. He asked an old man where they were. The latter looked quite astonished: "But do you not know? This is the day when everybody worships the Tikhvinskaia icon of the Blessed Virgin to which our church is dedicated." Finally, the reporter found a militiaman who looked quite tired. "Believe me or not," he said, "this has been my fifth sleepless night, so large have been the crowds." He continued: "A few days ago, in the Soviet farm Dikoe, the people have celebrated the St. John the Baptist day; a few days later, they will gather in the village of Dulepovo, to celebrate the Sts. Peter and Paul day." Finally, the secretary of the Komsomol organization showed up, and with her a number of rank-and-file members. The reporter thought that maybe they had come to explain to the people how disgusting their conduct was and to persuade them to go home and resume working. But the girl said emphatically: "It would be useless; nobody would go to work on such a day; such is the old tradition, and nobody can break it." [19]

[18] *Turkmenistanskaia iskra* (April 2, 1954).
[19] *Komsomol'skaia pravda* (July 29, 1954).

This story appeared in 1955. A reporter visited the kolkhoz Roscha, in the Vologda oblast, but could see nobody in the fields. Women were busy preparing food for a festival and men were bringing up from the cellars barrels of alcoholic beverages. This was the eve of Ascension, and Ascension was the local church's holiday. The visitor was told that for several days nobody would be working for the farm, since permission to stay home had been granted to everybody. The reason was very simple. The chairman of the kolkhoz and the local party organizers were walking from home to home enjoying food and drinks. The visitor continued his investigation and learned that similar mores prevailed throughout the whole region. He was told that at the St. Nicholas day the village had been honored by the visit of the chairman of the local executive committee accompanied by several aides. They spent four days celebrating with the peasants and seemed to have been very pleased.[20]

Such celebrations cannot be considered as taking place within the framework of the church; but they are functionally linked with church activities since the festival always begins by a solemn Mass, often celebrated by several priests and attended by large crowds.

Let us now return to the liturgic activities of the church and examine some of its phases. For the believer, the climax is reached when he receives Holy Communion. According to a recent statement, it is typical for an average church to have ten or more communicants on regular Sunday Masses, while at Lent there are several hundreds.[21] In the cathedrals during Lent, many priests have to officiate simultaneously. Nevertheless, it takes hours before the last man is satisfied; the communicants are very patient.[22]

Since in the Russian church Communion must be immediately preceded by confession, difficulties arise. The traditional manner of confession is private but, reluctantly, the clergy had to recur to group confession; then, the priest says aloud the ritual prayers and exhorts those present to confess to the Lord their sins. This is done silently. In 1955, this practice was condemned by the Patriarch. But since not enough priests were available to execute the order and return to private confession, a compromise has arisen. The priest reads the prayers and enumerates the common sins; the worshippers confess silently but absolution is given to each separately, and everyone is enjoined to tell the priest one's sins not comprised in the list.[23]

Many recent visitors from the outside report that baptism of children is widespread, church weddings fashionable, and religious funerals quite

[20] Krokodil (July 1955). This satirical periodical often conveys important information otherwise unavailable.
[21] Zhurnal, no. 2 (1957).
[22] C. Shevich, in Vestnik zapadno-evropeiskogo ekzarkhata [Paris] (May, 1947).
[23] Zhurnal, no. 4 (1956).

common.[24] Babies are often baptised in groups, a practice formerly unknown. Attending such ceremonies must be a startling experience to judge from the following testimony by Mrs. Bower:

We stood in a large chapel, with a great font in the center. Bending over it stood a priest; around him, in a great circle, were about seventy young couples, some of them with lighted candles, chanting hymns. On each side of the wall, there were tables where babies were being stripped for baptism by immersion. . . . It was quite impossible not to be overwhelmed by the atmosphere of devotion and faith which filled the chapel.[25]

A similar scene was observed by the American delegation of churchmen to Russia in March 1956, in Udelnaia, a suburb of Leningrad. Twelve children were baptized in their presence, but the visitors were told that sixty more had been baptized before their arrival. One of the members of the delegation, Mr. Parlan, states: "The sponsors stood quietly by taking vows in the ceremony as solemn as the coronation of a King." [26]

In addition to the regular divine service, the Russian Orthodox Church offers the believers the opportunity to satisfy their religious needs on a higher level, by pilgrimages to monasteries and shrines with relics of saints, commonly located in monasteries. During the period of persecution, monasteries and convents were disbanded, although some found a way to survive underground. With the reconstruction of the church, some of the monasteries reappeared. Immediately after the end of the war, ninety such institutions were said to exist; sixty-nine were reported to exist in 1956.[27] Of the monasteries, two, the Troitsky-Sergievsky in the region of Moscow and the Kievo-Pechersky in Kiev, exert the greatest attraction.

Harrison Salisbury, for several years the representative of the *New York Times* in Moscow, gives an interesting account of his Easter visit to the Troitsky-Sergievsky Monastery: "Thousands of believers and spectators jammed the great monastery enclosure and the three cathedrals. Hundreds of believers formed lines waiting for priests to bless their Easter cakes. The great onion-shaped towers of the churches, freshly painted and spattered with golden stars, gleamed against a brilliant April sun." In the book reproducing his observations made during the sojourn in Russia, he adds that in each year of the six during which he paid visits to the monastery, there came more pilgrims, and that finally twenty-

[24] Frank Rounds, *Window on Red Square* (Boston, 1953), 81; E. Stevens, *This Is Russia, Uncensored* (New York, 1950), 114; J. Lawrence in *The Listener* (June 30, 1955); Dr. Heinemann, president of the All-German Synod of the Evangelical Churches, as quoted by Ivan Bilibin, "Religion in the USSR," *The New Leader* (November 1, 1954).
[25] Bower, 20ff.
[26] Anderson; Parlan's statement appeared in the *New York World-Telegram and Sun* (April 2, 1956).
[27] Anderson.

five to thirty thousand people gathered inside the monastery walls.[28] As seen from yearly accounts in the *Journal*, approximately the same number of pilgrims attend on July 18, St. Sergius's day. Quite recently, a note appeared in the *Journal* reporting that two new chapels had been added because of the overwhelming number of pilgrims and that special prayers before the relics of St. Sergius were said all day without interruption.[29]

In 1955, the Kievo-Pechersky Monastery was visited by Father Bissonnette. Here are excerpts from his account:

When we reached the caves we saw a group of pilgrims straight out of Dostoevsky. A hundred or more were sitting against a wall. They had pitiful bundles of clothes at their feet. We found that some had come from even farther than we (Moscow). . . . We moved to the entrance of the monastery following a line of persons going into the caves with a young monk as a lead. He indicated the final resting places of the founders of the monastery, Sts. Theodore and Anthony. . . . The persons in the group kissed the glass above their heads many times and crossed themselves continuously muttering prayers. . . . There could be no doubt about the sincerity of their religion.[30]

Pilgrims, however, go not only to monasteries and shrines. Sometimes they choose as goals places to which the church does not ascribe any significance; and still they are moved by intensive religious feeling. Two recent cases are of great interest.

The article in the *Komsomol'skaia pravda* which signalized the beginning of the antireligious campaign stated that in the rural parts of the province of Gorki, people, young and old, continue to believe in a legend connected with Lake Svetoiar, located in one of the regions of the province. According to the legend, the lake was formed by God's will during the Tatar invasion, on the location of the God-loving city of Kitezh which sank to its bottom, all church bells ringing, to escape desecration and to reappear when Holy Russia would be alive again. Now, it was stated, the people were asserting that believers, after long and intensive prayers, could see the city with its churches in the waters of the lake. Half a year later, another Soviet paper returned to the legend and its acceptance by the population. On the eve of the holiday of the Vladimirskaia icon of the Blessed Virgin, pilgrims arrived from Gorki, Arzamas, Kostroma, Kirovsk, and so on. Among them there were many youths. When asked why they had come, some answered that they had made a vow to make the pilgrimage if they passed their examinations.[31]

A newspaperman heard from a Soviet functionary of fairly high rank that in Glinkovo, near Moscow, there was a spring of water which had the miraculous power to cure many diseases. One Sunday the reporter

[28] *New York Times* (April 30, 1951); *American in Russia* (New York, 1955), 303.
[29] *Zhurnal,* no. 2 (1957).
[30] *New York Times* (August 3, 1955).
[31] *Komsomol'skaia pravda* (December 18, 1953); *Uchitel'skaia gazeta* (July 28, 1954).

went to the spring. On a hill he saw a long line of women with bottles for the water; many of them were chanting hymns. In a pond toward which the "holy water" flowed, quite a few older men and women were bathing. The reporter stood long enough to observe many cars coming, with doctors, students, and engineers as passengers. They asserted that the Glinkovo water really helped while doctors often did not.[32]

However, the bulk of religious exercises are still carried out in the framework of the church. The believers fully support the church which, naturally, is no longer supported by the government, while the big endowments which played a large part in the church budget before the revolution were nationalized in 1918. Now the believers have to give enough to provide the personnel — the priests, the bishops, the members of the diocesan administration, and the central church government — with means of subsistence and to maintain the church buildings and the monasteries. They do this by voluntary donations and by buying, in large amounts, tapers priced (as has always been the case) many times above the cost. A priest's average income is said to be 50 per cent higher than that of a skilled worker.[33]

But the believers do more than support the personnel and the existing establishment. Almost every issue of the *Journal* mentions cases of conse- cration of newly built, reconstructed, enlarged, or redecorated churches. It is interesting that this activity did not slow down even during the year 1954, when the acute antireligious campaign was going on. During that year, the cathedral in Vladimir was renovated as well as those in Irkutsk and Zhitomir. Substantial repairs were carried out in churches in the dioceses of Chernovtsy, Novosibirsk, Leningrad, Pskov, Volyn, and Riazan. In 1955, among other activities, a convent was rebuilt in the Chernigov diocese, and the church on Pushkin's estate (Mikhailovskoe) was renovated. In 1956, again among other things, in the Molotov diocese (now probably Perm) a church building was moved from an area to be flooded as the consequence of the construction of a dam. In the Tula, diocese a church was built in place of an older one on the Kulikovo Pole, the battlefield between Russians and Tatars in 1380. In the early issues of the *Journal* for 1957, general repairs of churches are reported from the dioceses of Kaluga, Staraia Russa, and Odessa. It is sometimes empha- sized that all these works have been performed by the parishioners, sometimes aided by collections in neighboring parishes and dioceses. It must be noted that large-scale work aiming at the restoration of church buildings of exceptional architectural value is carried out by the Soviet government. As a rule, such buildings are treated as historical monu- ments and are not open for worship. But the majestic cathedrals in the

[32] *Trud* (July 25, 1954).
[33] Bilibin.

Troitsky-Sergievsky Monastery have been beautifully restored by the government and are open to the public, as has been mentioned above.

IV

Concluding this survey, one may assert that there is genuine life in the Russian Orthodox Church — continuous interaction engendered by the religious aspirations of millions of believers who obviously find in the church what they want and what they are accustomed to. The scope of this inner life is extremely limited, being confined to the celebration of divine service, the maintenance of monasteries, and the training of priests. There is neither organized religious education of the young generation nor any kind of social work, while, prior to the revolution, such activities were well developed. During the 1956 exchange of views between the Russian and American churchmen, the question of the "mission of the churches" was vividly discussed. The Russian delegates stubbornly emphasized worship, pastoral visitation, confession, and communion as the very mission of the church. One of the delegates said: "The only true interpretation of religious life is the church itself. Sermons, confession, special services in the homes are sufficient. No amount of literature can give what example offers." [34] Before the revolution, the view of the mission of the church was broader.

Being limited in scope, the inner life of the church is intensive, as seen from the data on church attendance, baptism, confession, communion, and pilgrimages. On the part of the believers, participation means sacrifice, material and social, since churchgoers expose themselves to the discrimination inherent in the political structure of the Soviet Union. While the Soviet government officially is religiously neutral, the Communist Party is not and, as is so well known, all important positions are reserved for members of the party.

The thesis asserted at the beginning of this chapter seems to be substantiated by evidence: in the church, and around the church, a part of old Russia has survived, within the context of a complete social and cultural change. The believers form a much smaller percentage of the total population than was the case before the revolution; but those who are believers want to actualize their faith in the framework of a structure and in forms which faithfully reproduce the past. The tenacity of the tradition was once again proven during the difficult year 1954 when it compelled the leadership to abandon the attempt to accelerate the decline of religion in the society under their rule.

[34] Anderson.

SUMMARY AND REVIEW

SIDNEY HARCAVE

I

The foregoing studies of the church, the school, and the republic of scholarship must raise — as do all explorations — at least as many questions as they settle. If the exhaustion of a field of inquiry were the only measure of progress, we would have to say that there has never been any intellectual progress. But, of course, that is not the case; progress is measured by the extension of a field of inquiry, by the uncovering of complexities. And the investigations considered here have certainly opened paths that invite us and sharpen our anticipation of the inquiries to come.

Although the fields of education, scholarship, and religion, taken together, do not constitute a discrete element of Russian society, they are closely enough allied to justify collective consideration. In the preceding discussions it has been demonstrated, for example, that a common and major agent of change in these fields has been the state. Herbert Bowman's suggestion for a motion-picture script of modern Russian historiography emphasizes the point quite well.

George Bereday draws a compelling analogy between social and physical changes when he speaks of change in educational values as resulting from two forces, the state and the people. Those two forces have been opposed so frequently that it is regretfully tempting to regard their opposition as an enduring characteristic. But the temptation must be fought, particularly in view of the strength of the traditional Russian tendency to idealize elemental forces in society and to denigrate the pressures exerted by the state. One may feel himself safely on the side of the angels by arguing that the good in Russian religion, scholarship, and education has come from the people, and the evil from the state. Certainly, examples in support of that argument are not difficult to find. As Bowman has shown, Russian historians did their best work when they were reasonably free from state interference and not when a Karamzin or a Pokrovsky was in the saddle.

The state, however, must be credited with helping to provide (often with little popular support) the environment in which the church, the schools, and scholarship could develop. Instances of that are many and outstanding. St. Vladimir made Christianity the religion of his land (had there been a Gallup Poll at the time, he might have hesitated — though I doubt it). Peter the Great must be given some credit for helping to establish the necessary preconditions for historical scholarship. And one finds it difficult to conceive of an extensive school system in Russia without the social base made possible by the reforms of Alexander II.

Change, at whatever level, requires leadership. To illustrate this relationship I suggest the concept of a continuum, at one end of which is change imposed from above by one man receiving little public encouragement (the abolition of the Patriarchate by Peter, for example), and at the other end of which is unorganized mass pressure (well illustrated by Bereday's reference to the modification of school standards). There are an infinite number of gradations between the two extremes of this continuum, but the contrast between the extremes is too often obscured by what lies between.

The case of the Russian Orthodox Church offers a striking example of the interaction of state and people. John Curtiss and Nicholas Timasheff agree that the church has suffered less change in the last century than any other of the Russian institutions, and they agree that its resilience has been particularly marked in the last forty years. But they differ in their explanations of the reasons for its survival — perhaps because Curtiss is concerned with the church as an organization, while Timasheff is concerned with it as the outer shell of the life of faith.

Curtiss finds that the church has endured partly because of its own prudence, its fine perception of what has to be rendered unto Caesar and when the rendering is necessary; and partly because of the prudence of the Soviet state, dictating its acceptance of the church's offer of peace in the knowledge that it cannot destroy the church at once but must do so piecemeal. From Curtiss' findings, it is only one step to Timasheff's explanation that the church could not be destroyed because of the powerful hold that religion has had, and continues to have, on a large number of the Russian people. The two explanations differ but do not clash; in fact, they complement each other. At the same time, they raise some questions that I can, as a matter of prerogative, put forth but that I cannot, as a matter of fact, answer.

The inner life of the church as described by Timasheff can be equated, I think, with religiosity. Considering this aspect of it, he has refuted the allegation that the church before the revolution was "a dead body, attached and subordinate to the imperial government"; and he has shown that a considerable proportion of the Russian people have remained firm in their faith and devoted to the church and its rituals. In doing so, he has demonstrated the vitality of the church; but the vitality to which he points is expressed almost exclusively in connection with the function of the saving of souls. If one is concerned only with the manner in which the church views its duties, there would be no need to go further; but the historians (and others, I suspect) are concerned also with the influence that the church exerts upon society. The most economical way of suggesting the chief problem that occurs to me in this connection is to repeat B. H. Sumner's statement that "what the church most needed, a Leo XIII, it could not produce; it was given instead a Pius IX — Pobedonostsev." [1] To ask why the Russian Orthodox Church produced no Leo XIII may be uncanonical from the point of view of historiography: the Russian Orthodox Church, of course, has followed its own course of development, and that has not been the course of the Roman Catholic Church. But it is canonical, I believe, to measure the Russian Orthodox Church on the scale of its own history. There have been, at times, significant stirrings within the Orthodox Church, but few of them have been discernible in the last half century, a period that might have been expected to have an impact on the church. Of course, there have been some reflex actions; some rather minor shifts in emphasis have been noted in recent theological writings. [2] However, though we may not follow Eliot completely when he says that the church can "sleep and feed at once," we might justifiably modify the idea only by replacing "sleep" with "be in a torpor."

If the fact of torpor is admitted, to find an explanation for it might require a study of the church outside the control of the Russian state as well as under it. Did the Orthodox Church exhibit the same traits under German occupation as it did under Tsarist rule? Has it exhibited the same traits in emigration as under Communist rule? The investigation should go even further: to compare the behavior of the Russian Orthodox Church with that of other branches of Eastern Orthodoxy, to discover whether it is in the culture of Russia or that of Eastern Christendom that the answers to our questions will be found.

Returning to the fact of the survival of the Orthodox Church in Russia, it may be asked whether or not the cost of survival has been excessive. The cost I have in mind is entailed in the subordination of the church to the state. If the sacerdotal function is the only one with which we deal, there is no problem of cost since, as long as the church continues the care of souls, it is rendering unto God the things that are God's, and the cost of what is rendered unto Caesar is irrelevant. But if other functions are considered — say, such functions as the exertion of moral influence — a rather high cost must be entered on the debit side. Moreover, the state also must be counted the poorer. The Tsarist state may well have lost much, morally and otherwise, by having a docile church. And the Soviet state, in time, may find that a weak and subordinate church can outlive a powerful and superordinate state.

[1] B. H. Sumner, *A Short History of Russia* (New York, 1943), 185.
[2] D. Konstantinov, "K razvitiiu pravoslavnoi bogoslovskoi mysli v SSSR," *Vestnik Instituta po Izucheniiu SSSR*, no. 3 (1957), 80–89.

In contrast to the church, the Russian educational system has been profoundly modified both as to structure and as to values, a fact pointed out most effectively by Bereday. The reason is obvious: the church, in the eyes of the present regime, is an instrument for the conservation of the old and continues on sufferance; the school, on the other hand, is an instrument of change and is cherished.

Though the educational system has been marked by modification, in at least one respect there has been continuity — that is, in quantitative growth. There is no doubt that the rate of growth has increased under the Soviet regime, but it must not be forgotten that the Russian educational system before 1914 was not only expanding but also accelerating in its rate of expansion. Growth, in this area, was just another expression of the interaction of state and people. In the Tsarist period, it was the state that provided major impetus for the development of secondary and higher education; and popular pressure provided the impetus for that of the primary schools. The primary-education law of 1908, for instance, was more the result of pressure from below than of initiative from above. Now, in the Soviet period, the often-conflicting ambitions of the leaders and of the led have occasioned strain, as Bereday indicates; but the result, nonetheless, has been growth in educational facilities.

Bereday states that the interaction of the state's pushing and the people's pulling has also reshaped educational policy. He is so bold as to suggest that it is not impossible for an independent teaching profession to emerge. But he would agree, I think, that there are limits even to flights of imagination; one finds it difficult to envisage a situation in which, as a result of popular pressure, the course in Marxism-Leninism, or some equivalent, is dropped as a requirement in favor of, let us say, the history of religion. Soviet educational policy is less responsive to the public will than our own is.

The theme of interaction of state and people or state and society can be followed also in our consideration of Russian scholarship, both in the natural sciences and in the field of letters. The initial impression is that as the state giveth, so the state taketh away. The state helped originally to create the environment in which scholarship could develop; but it has often helped (more often under the Soviet than under the Tsarist regime) to poison the atmosphere in which scholars worked.

The fact of the persistence of scholarly traditions seems to be the work of a kind of "invisible hand," perhaps the hand of selfishness, prompting the state to seek the fruits of scholarly effort and prompting the scholar and scientist to accept the benefits of state support. The common interests have ensured quantitative growth; the opposing interests (here Adam Smith is of no help) have hindered the achievement of optimum results.

Neither Bowman nor DeWitt appears to be a determinist; each seems to believe in the efficacy of the human will and to argue, from this belief, that the Russian scholar as well as the scientist have a will toward quality that persists despite adverse societal conditions. They would agree that favorable conditions will encourage quality. In this connection, one cannot doubt that the trend toward strengthening the research activities of the universities, observed by DeWitt, will encourage better quality. To be sure, there have been periods in the past, in Western Europe, when the best work in science and in the field of letters was done outside the universities. On the other hand, it appears that the conditions of work in the Soviet research institutes are less favorable to disinterested scholarship than the academic atmosphere in the universities, restricted as it is.

II

A general question, somewhat tangential but nevertheless pertinent, suggested by the foregoing essays is whether or not a discernible interrelationship among the institutions that they consider and between them and Russian culture as a whole has been or can be demonstrated. What I have in mind is suggested by George Murdock's assertion that "the elements of a given culture tend to form a consistent and integrated whole." [3] It is an idea emphasized by Harvard's Russian Research Center, with its charter to employ sociological, anthropological, and psychological approaches to Russian studies.

The model of a culture the elements of which are "consistent and integrated" is one that is in a state of equilibrium, one in which the forces at work are autochthonous and elemental, and one that has had little contact with other cultures. But the culture with which we are dealing, the Russian, has not been in a state of equilibrium; many of the major forces have been neither autochthonous nor elemental; and it has been subject to significant external cultural influences.

The operative word in Murdock's statement is "tend." I suggest that — if not now, then in the future — it may be profitable to determine whether or not there have been tendencies toward integration and consistencies among the fields that we have been examining. The result would not only advance our understanding of Russian culture but would also serve to test the validity of what is an accepted postulate among social scientists.

Of course, consistency and integration may take many forms. In a Marxist universe they may take the form of "base" and "superstructure." In the universe of an anthropologist (perhaps I should say some anthropologists), they may take the form of "structure" and "design." Whatever the accepted form, it seems obvious from our essays that there has not been a high degree of consistency or integration among the Russian

[3] George P. Murdock, "The Cross-Cultural Survey," *American Sociological Review*, V (June 1940), 368.

institutions of religion, scholarship, and education. Given the facts of Russian history in the past three — and more particularly in the past one hundred — years, this is not unexpected. Some conditions, however, we might expect: for example, mutual reinforcement of values shared by church and school or by school and scholar, or a tendency toward change or accommodation when values are antagonistic, as in the case between church and school today.

The studies of Bereday as well as those of DeWitt and Bowman have shown a predominantly secular trend in school and academic growth in the past century; as they indicate, a quasi-scientific creed has been challenging a supernatural one. That being the case, how has the church attempted to accommodate itself to the challenge? The latitudinarian tradition of the Russian Orthodox Church, which has been the subject of much comment, explains much; but, when the church has become a target for persistent challenge and threat, one might expect its reaction to be other than tolerance. What kind of reaction, then? Modernism, perhaps, or fundamentalism, or a tendency to assimilate (I am not thinking in terms of extremities such as the development of drive-in churches, but of efforts such as those of the Catholic Church, which has demonstrated an ability to work closely with scientists). One might look, too, for evidence of accommodation on the part of the Soviet school system if its offering of spiritual values continues, as Timasheff has shown, to leave many of the new generation cold.

If investigation does not show even a tendency toward consistency and integration, there may be a variety of explanations: it may be that the initial postulate is unacceptable or that "Russian culture" as the universe of discourse is sometimes too confining. Kluckhohn and Murray have put it this way:

In distinguishing group-membership determinants, one must usually take account of a concentric order of social groups to which the individual belongs, ranging from large national or international groups down to small local units.[4]

The number of groups to which a Russian may be said to belong is many: Christian, Western European, Asiatic (says Karl Wittfogel), Slav, Byzantine, Eastern European, and human. Therefore, it seems logical to suggest that, for further explanation of the characteristics of the Russian Orthodox Church, it is pertinent to deal with the Eastern Orthodox as well as with the Russian environment. And, for an examination of the values that have helped to set the tone of the schoolroom, laboratory, and scholar's study, it is pertinent to include Russia in a culture area that embraces Western Europe.

[4] Clyde Kluckhohn and Henry A. Murray, "Personality Formation: the Determinants," in *Personality in Nature, Society, and Culture*, Kluckhohn and Murray, eds. (New York, 1953), 57.

FAMILY, YOUTH, AND HUMAN WELFARE

PART FIVE

FAMILY, YOUTH, AND HUMAN WELFARE

THE FAMILY AND SOCIAL CHANGE

KENT GEIGER

In an assessment of the place of the family in the transformation of Russian society three questions come immediately to mind. How has the family changed? What have been the sources of change? To what further developments have changes within the family led? The answers to these questions, even if tentative and incomplete, furnish a basis for some of the more specialized topics taken up by other contributors to the present volume as well as suggesting further inquiry into such interesting matters as the philosophy of the Soviet regime in dealing with family problems and the future role of the family in a collectivist society. In view of the dearth of studies of primary group relations in Russia, the reader will understand that to deal with the family even in the most general fashion it has been necessary to place considerable reliance on work done by investigators concerned with societies other than the USSR, especially that which has aimed at the construction of a general model of the relations between family and total social system.[1]

I am most grateful to Ezra F. Vogel for suggestions and criticisms made of an early draft of this chapter.

[1] Representative recent works in English are: Nels Anderson, ed., *Studies of the Family* (Tübingen, 1956); Kingsley Davis, "The Sociology of Parent-Youth Conflict," *American Sociological Review*, V (1940), 523–534; Erik H. Erikson, *Childhood and Society* (New York, 1950); Reuben Hill, *Families Under Stress* (New York, 1949); Marion J. Levy, Jr., *The Family Revolution in Modern China* (Cambridge, Mass., 1949); William F. Ogburn and Clark Tibbitts, "The Family and Its Functions," *Recent Trends in the United States* (New York, 1933), ch. 13; William F. Ogburn and Meyer F. Nimkoff, *Technology and the Changing Family* (Boston, 1955); Talcott Parsons, "The Kinship System of the Contemporary United States," *American Anthropologist*, XLV (1943), 22–38; Gideon Sjoberg, "Familial Organization in the Pre-industrial City," *Marriage and Family Living*, XVIII (1956), 30–36; Robin L. Williams, Jr., *American Society: A Sociological Interpretation* (New York, 1951); and Carle C. Zimmerman, *Family and Civilization* (New York, 1948). A few studies dealing in part with patterns of change in the Soviet family are available: Kent Geiger and Alex Inkeles, "The Family in the U.S.S.R.," *Marriage and Family Living*, XVI (1954), 397–404; Mary Matossian, "Soviet Armenia After Stalin," *The Armenian Review*, IX (1956), 3–11; Richard Pipes, "Muslims of Soviet Central Asia: Trends and Prospects," *Middle East Journal*, IX (1955), 147–162, 259–308; and Alice S. Rossi, "Generational Differences in the Soviet Union," Project on the Soviet Social System (Cambridge, Mass., 1954). Within the past five years two doctoral dissertations dealing with Soviet family life have been completed. They are: Kent Geiger, "The Urban Slavic Family and the Soviet System," Harvard, 1955, and Malte Bischof, "Die Struktur und die Wandlung der Sowjetischen Familie (um 1950)," Hamburg, 1956.

I

One hundred years ago the ancestors of the population now controlled by the USSR lived under many different subcultures. There were three great sources of variation. The first was that of residence; the population consisted of a small proportion, perhaps one tenth of the total, who lived in urban areas while the great mass of people lived off the land as agriculturalists and nomads. A second mode of variation was that of ethnic and national subgroupings; the political boundaries of Tsarist Russia included a wide diversity of peoples with quite dissimilar histories and social systems. Finally, analysis of the social patterns of the pre-Soviet population calls for distinctions made along the dimension of economic position and prestige.

Hence, there was great variety in patterns of family life. There were Great Russian peasant families, tied to the household work economy and the mir, sometimes consisting of many more than two nuclear or conjugal units, patrilocal, and living under the hegemony of a patriarch or *bol'shak*. There were many smaller peasant families in the Ukraine with land held in hereditary tenure. In the cities there were families of workers, merchants, and titled nobility. The Jewish family hung on to a precarious existence in the ghettos within the Pale. The Kazakh roamed the steppes, often with several wives, and in close bond with a larger patrilineal clan. And so on. For this era of Russian history, and at the level of institutional description, the sociologist's generalizations must defer to the ethnographer's portrayal of cultural diversity.

By contrast, at the present time subcultural differences have diminished considerably. As in other modern societies, the trend is toward similarity in family patterns, so the family in the USSR is much more a homogeneous unit than formerly. This is due primarily to the emergence of conditions associated with an urban industrial economy, but can also be attributed to the development of mass education and communication, increasing centralization of political control, the Russification and sovietization policies of the Tsarist and Soviet governments respectively, and the social leveling brought by the abolition of private property and other developments associated with the revolution.

In spite of the fact that the starting points of a century ago were in many respects quite different, certain other general changes are apparent. The family in the contemporary Soviet Union is smaller in size than that of earlier times. As an over-all statistical generalization this is unquestionable if for no other reason than the fact that such a large proportion of the population has become urbanized. But other conditions, not all from the Soviet period, have lent a hand. The Stolypin land-reform policies, for instance, further encouraged among the peasantry the desire to live in simple nuclear families that had been initiated earlier by the emancipation of the serfs. The land policy followed by the Soviet government under the NEP and also after collectivization continued the trend.[2]

On the other hand, the transformation of the family from a large to a smaller unit has been slowed down by another group of circumstances. Under the conditions of Soviet family life it has been advantageous to have someone other than the gainfully employable take responsibility for the care of young children and the management of household affairs. Soviet married women frequently must work to help support the family, and thus adult relatives, especially older females, are usually welcome additions to the nuclear group of husband, wife, and minor children.

A smaller family comes about not only through the break-up of previously larger joint and extended families, but also through a basic change in birth rate. The available evidence shows that the Soviet birth rate has been lower than that of prerevolutionary society and that it has continued to decline within the Soviet period itself.[3] This is due to urbanization and hard living conditions, particularly the housing shortage which has characterized Soviet cities since the start of the Plan era. Since the Second World War the sex imbalance resulting from wartime population losses has sharpened the trend.

Other trends in the social structure of the family are not unrelated to its diminution in size. On the average, interpersonal relations between husband and wife a century ago were markedly asymmetrical. The man was legally and traditionally the master of the household and of his wife. There was a strong male sex preference whereby the birth of a son was cause for rejoicing, while that of a daughter was often seen as a misfortune. Among the peasantry the submissive feminine sex role was enhanced by the custom of patrilocal residence. However, the complex of behavior and ideas known as the emancipation of women has taken strong hold in Russia, and particularly among the peasantry and Moslem nationalities has constituted a radical departure from traditional family norms. Social equality between the sexes has not been achieved in practice; even today there is substantial evidence that older customs often prevail. But wife beating and other forms of male tyranny, and, among the Moslem population, polygamy and the bride price are now not only illegal but looked upon by the great bulk of the Soviet population as archaisms.

The trend toward a more equal distribution of authority within the family has included the relationship between parents and children. The rapid changes in the larger society, which are picked up more rapidly by

[2] Lazar Volin, "The Peasant and Household Under the *Mir* and *Kolkhoz* in Modern Russian History," in Caroline F. Ware, ed., *The Cultural Approach to History* (New York, 1940), 125–139. Under collectivization the provision that each kolkhoz family have a private plot of its own has been a crucial factor.

[3] See Warren W. Eason's chapter on "Population Changes" above.

young persons than by old, and the government's emphasis on the prerogatives of youth have been especially important in supporting the status
and influence of children in the family. The abolition of the private ownership of productive property is also a contributory factor. As Engels emphasized, the vested interest of ownership and control does not easily mesh
with equal distribution of power among the different members of the
family.[4]

In the realm of general values and roles there have also been changes.
Industrialization in Russia has brought with it a voracious demand for
technical specialists, and skilled labor has been set at a premium price
since the beginning of the five-year plans. This fact, when taken with
certain institutional arrangements which serve to accentuate the pattern
in the popular image,[5] has called forth a new outlook in the Soviet people
toward the concept of a personal career. This is expressed clearly within
the family, most concretely in terms of the aspirations of parents for their
children. Thus, an important new emphasis in the value structure of the
family involves the attachment of importance — one might even say
reverence — to educational training and to mobility within one's chosen
field of occupational specialization. It should also be noted that parental
aspirations for children in this regard are much less differentiated by sex
than was the case in earlier years.

From the point of view of the individual living in a family there has
been a most important shift in the general pattern of expectation governing his behavior in relation to other family members. The right of the individual to select and pursue his own personal goals has increased in strength,
as has the obligation of the other members of his family not to interfere in
such pursuit. In other words, the claims of the family upon its individual
members have become more flexible and even residual, for, as will be
seen in a moment, many activities formerly carried out by the family as
a unitary group or by the individual family in conjunction with other
members of the larger kin group are now performed in social contexts
rather completely segregated from the family.

To summarize the preceding, the family as a social institution is today
more homogeneous in structure, smaller, more equalitarian, more committed to striving for formal education and occupational mobility, and
more "individualistic" than the family of the last century. Such developments as these imply a number of corollary patterns. The requirement of
compatible personalities, the expectation of a uniquely intimate relationship, and the feeling of love have all come increasingly to characterize

[4] Friedrich Engels, *The Origins of the Family, Private Property and the State*
(New York, 1942), ch. 2.
[5] For example, a steeply graduated wage and salary scale and the abolition of
private property ownership, which means, as a refugee respondent remarked, "In
the Soviet Union there is no capital but education."

marriage. The marriage arranged by parents or by go-betweens has given way to one based upon interpersonal attraction and the free choice of the individuals directly concerned. Even the custom of requesting parental consent has vanished or decreased greatly in significance.

While statistical data on changes in the frequency of divorce over time are not available, there is little doubt but that the trend over the century has been toward an increase. As has been often observed, the freedom of the individual to enter into a marital union of his own choice and in pursuit of his own happiness implies freedom to dissolve the union if it is not successful. However, the legal, financial, and ideological pressures exerted by the regime against divorce from the mid-thirties until the present have restricted its frequency of occurrence and so forestalled the development of a closer equivalence in the right to marry and the right to divorce.

In the family of the last century religious beliefs and practices played a prominent role. In the family of today such ideas and supporting ritual are much less prominent and, to the extent that they survive at all, are found chiefly among the older and less urbanized elements of the population. During much of the Soviet era the profession and practice of religion has been dangerous, and during all of the Soviet era it has been inconvenient, an obstacle, for example, to full access to educational opportunity and to occupational advancement. Although the sources of information on this subject are far from unanimous,[6] it is the judgment of this writer that religion in most Soviet families is a dead issue.

If one conceives of the family as one among several institutions and orders of the total social system, it is possible to distinguish still other shifts in its position and role. Of these three are particularly important: the family's "loss of functions," its separation from traditional solidary groupings, and its increased permeability to external sources of influence.

The trend whereby many activities previously carried on by family members in common as a group are given up and relegated to other social organizations and agencies occurs everywhere in industrial societies and has been aptly described as the family's loss of functions. The most important of these is that of productive work; work in the Soviet Union is almost always carried on in large-scale, highly organized enterprises, and there is virtually no household economy remaining. The closest approximation

---

[6] By and large, personal predilections seem to play a very substantial role in determining the direction in which the Soviet people are perceived as moving in respect to religious sentiment. Religious personages and delegations, for instance, are more likely to report survivals or revivals of religious sentiment than are lay representatives. Among the few scholarly investigators who report an increase in the strength of religious sentiment are Ivan D. London and Nikolai P. Poltoratzky in "Contemporary Religious Sentiment in the Soviet Union," *Psychological Reports*, III (1957), 113–130. They conclude that "religious sentiment is not only widespread among the Soviet younger generation, but on the increase" (128).

is found in the private plot of the peasant farmer, but even here the main work responsibilities of the family members lie with a larger economic unit, the collective or state farm.

In addition to work, the family in the USSR has lost other functions. The following activities are at present taken over entirely or in part by outside social establishments: the care of persons who are seriously ill or otherwise handicapped, the holding and management of productive property, the education and much of the socialization of young children, recreation, and control over the deviant behavior of members. Much of this can perhaps be said of the family in any modern society, but in the USSR the provision of a wide range of welfare services, the organization of youth groups, the development of communal facilities such as dining halls, workers' clubs, rest homes, nurseries for babies, and great ideological emphasis on the superiority of collective over private life have served to push the pattern quite far in the direction of an extreme transfer out of the family of activities which were formerly its concern. To students of Western family life it is quite surprising, for instance, to find that in the USSR the family vacation is by no means the only respectable way to spend one's respite from work responsibilities. Soviet married persons regularly and apparently with small regret take vacations at separate places and times from their families.

From all this it is seen that the family has become a more highly specialized institution. It is a voluntary group formed on the basis of individual preferences and held together basically by affiliative needs and the advantages offered by a rudimentary division of labor in the pursuit of daily sustenance activities. Contributions still made to Soviet society include reproduction, the socialization of children, and aid in the maintenance of proper motivational orientations on the part of adults. From the point of view of the individual Soviet citizen it is most important that in the family he is provided with a set of relatively fixed and close social relationships. These afford him acceptance as a person and some gratification of his idiosyncratic and unsocialized needs, and ultimately augment his psychological security.

The family's loss of functions goes hand in hand with a marked increase in the separation of the family from a situation in which it maintains a fixed position as a unit in larger solidary groupings. This is because an urban industrial economy requires a large element of labor mobility; the worker must go to the factory or office wherever the job opportunity exists. Thus urban industrialism greatly increases the phenomenon of residential mobility. Such mobility is engaged in essentially by small family units, which therefore tend to be distributed ecologically in a fashion primarily responsive to the opportunities of the labor market. In consequence, an important effect of the dynamic Soviet industrial economy on the nuclear family has been to enhance greatly its isolation from larger diffuse solidarities based on kinship, on permanent residential proximity, and on ethnic, religious, or national identity. The family has become a more "unconnected" and independent unit. This fact has in turn some corollary implications, for the individual family thereby is released from the demands of and obligations to these larger solidarities, and can carry on in a fashion designed to afford maximum satisfaction of the needs of its members. But at the same time the looseness of the bonds between the small nuclear family and these larger solidary groups deprives the family of their social support and of the controlling influences which they exert. The other side of the coin of freedom is social isolation. Furthermore, there is little evidence that new informal solidary groups, such as social classes, have appeared.[7]

The above account leads into the final major shift in the role of the family in the larger Soviet system. By virtue of its loss of functions and increasing lack of connection with the traditional solidary groupings, the family has become more likely to adapt to external social influences. Analysis of the specific mechanisms by which such influences penetrate should not overlook the strategic role of the family's children; they frequently serve as the mouthpiece of emergent conditions and requirements in the larger society.[8] On the other hand, if one accepts the "loss of functions" as an accurate characterization of fact, then the decrease in the ability of the family to withstand external influence is virtually a tautological proposition, for a large part of the content of familial values and role expectations deals with behavior and attitude pertaining to the external — occupational, educational, recreational, political — activities and concerns of the family member. These constitute diffuse role obligations for the other family members, that is, they are obliged to let him "do as he will" unless they can show that this is patently harmful or inappropriate for any other family member or the family as a whole. Therefore, the conditions which govern behavior and attitudinal orientation in these external contexts are easily recognized by all as compelling and quickly permitted to influence the normative structure of family life.

II

The trends described above take on added significance in the intricacies of contemporary Soviet social development when they are seen as responsible for consequences elsewhere in the social system as well as for additional patterns emerging within the family itself. In this section and the next I shall suggest a few ramifications in Soviet society of some

[7] See Robert A. Feldmesser's chapter on "Social Classes and Political Structure" above.

[8] These features of family life in Soviet Russia are discussed at greater length and with special reference to the intergenerational transmission of political attitudes in Kent Geiger, "Changing Political Attitudes in Totalitarian Society: A Case Study of the Role of the Family," World Politics, VIII (1956), 187–205.

of the trends outlined above. It should be understood that a good part of what is to follow in this section must be regarded as hypothetical. This is not to say that the statements below are simply matters of opinion, but rather that they are for the most part not susceptible to rigorous documentation or test, and thus must rest essentially on theoretical considerations.

Increased homogeneity of family social structure signifies that size and membership composition, general values and roles, modes of relatedness to other institutions and groups, and sources of tension of families in the USSR are becoming more similar. This leads in turn to some interesting developments. First, it implies an increase in intergroup contacts and probable decline in intergroup tensions between peasantry and urbanites, among the various Soviet nationalities, and among social classes. Homogeneity of family patterns breeds a broad similarity of personal aspirations, attitudes, tastes, and leads to the emergence of an easier tolerance of the ascribed characteristics associated with persons in other membership groups. Changes on the level of family patterns therefore make a modest contribution to a decrease in ethnic and class prejudice and other forms of group antagonism in Soviet society. If information about the social activities of the Soviet population classified according to different subcultural groupings were available, it would probably show a noticeable rise in intermarriage rates and other signs of the gradual assimilation of minority patterns into one central and dominant way of life.

Another result of the movement toward family homogenization is an increase in the degree of utilization of resources of human talent. From the point of view of the individual, similarity of family structure helps to reduce the subcultural barriers to equal opportunity and social mobility. From the point of view of society, if a mechanical analogy may be used, the parts have become more interchangeable, and so the machine works more efficiently.

The most permanent and thoroughgoing focus of the trend toward equalitarianism is in the relationship between husband and wife. The change has been toward more status and freedom for women and toward more constraint exercised by the other family members over the behavior of men. The transfer of personal authority from husband to wife is probably a source of some personal frustration and uncertainty to both parties insofar as it represents for many a shift from social patterns internalized earlier in the life cycle. In the beginning years of a contemporary Soviet marriage there is likely to be little consensus in regard to the rightful distribution of personal power. The result is doubtless a tendency for personal qualities and abilities to play a more important role than in most societies in determining which, if any, member of the particular family will be generally recognized as the dominant person.

Prior work on the relationship of social status to the mode of expressing aggression would lead us also to expect that the shift in authority between husband and wife would lead to some convergence in suicide and homicide rates. We might anticipate that in the USSR suicide rates for women are increasing at a faster pace, or decreasing at a slower pace, than are those of men. Similarly, we might predict that homicide is coming to be a relatively more frequent mode of expressing aggression for men and relatively less likely to be chosen by women.[9]

It is interesting to raise the question here of whether the development of familial equalitarianism affects the political orientation of the Soviet citizen. In a broad way the modes of relatedness nurtured within the family probably reflect in some degree the expectations governing the individual's other social relationships. But they apply in the main to face-to-face behavior. Expectations of right and wrong in respect to more complex social operations are developed elsewhere, particularly in the schools. Moreover, as we have seen, a prominent motif in the pattern of change of the family has been its loss of functions. Among those lost is the function of directly controlling the behavior of family members in a variety of task-oriented social contexts. This is one of the reasons why it has been possible for the family to become more democratic, and it suggests why the Soviet person may come to feel that even on the person-to-person level a notable difference between the social atmosphere of his family life, intimate and equalitarian, and the authoritarian atmosphere of the larger society is part of the rightful order of things. Aside from the intrinsic difficulty of the individual's having to come to terms with institutional differentiation in modern society, I see no reason to conclude that a democratic family and an authoritarian government are incompatible. In fact, it is possible to argue that democracy in the Soviet family actually serves the purpose of the regime by implying a less active role in transmitting parental values to children.[10]

An important pattern associated with the changing shape of the family is found in the heightened valuation placed on personal achievement in opportunities connected with the family member's external roles. One of

[9] Andrew F. Henry and James F. Short, Jr., *Suicide and Homicide* (Glencoe, 1954). The authors develop and test in this book a general theory of the directions in which aggressive feelings are expressed. One of the key propositions is that suicide, or aggression directed inwardly, varies directly with social status and that homicide, or aggression directed outwardly, varies inversely with status.

[10] Consider the following: "A democratic parent role implies a great permissiveness on the part of the parent to allow his child to develop in directions of his own choosing. . . . If their parents are less apt to impose their ideals and goals upon their youngsters but tend to a greater extent than their predecessors in early decades to play a passive or largely supportive role toward whatever the [child's] own wishes for his future might be, this leaves open the possibility that the ideals and goals which Soviet young people develop will be derived from their exposure to the Soviet outside world rather than from their families — and this is precisely what the regime has wanted Soviet parents to do. The consequences can be more rapid sovietization of the present generation of Soviet children than took place in the past generation." Rossi, 62–63.

the results is quite apparent and positive in its consequences for the total system. Within the structure of opportunities and rewards provided, the material and psychological welfare of the individual is closely tied to his level of performance in educational and occupational roles. This generates a tremendous compulsive force analogous to the achievement ethic of American society and calls forth the most energetic efforts of the population.

However, the achievement motive also has some unhappy consequences. Personal autonomy, the chance to make of one's life what one will, in a society offering a rich proliferation of achieved statuses is for the individual far from a comfortable state of affairs; in fact it often involves considerable psychological strain.[11] Our knowledge of reactions to psychological strain tells us that we may expect a number of patterns of response, but that they are likely to include some which are focused directly on the complex of normative expectations giving rise to the difficulty.[12] Thus, it is instructive to search for patterned evasions or distortions of the highly mobilized and productive state in which Soviet citizens are encouraged to live by their life conditions and their rulers.

Two ways in which the pressure of personal achievement is mediated within the family into newly appearing structural features can be visualized. The first involves a contrast between the two spouses in regard to the direction in which effort is expended; complete dedication to the order of performance expected of the ideal Soviet citizen on the part of both husband and wife would seem to be unlikely. This is true not only because much is expected, but because it would serve as grounds for completely vacating the role of social-emotional leadership within the family. A much more likely development would consist of a distinct, thorough specialization, in which the efforts of one spouse, usually the man, are balanced by a relinquishment of any claim to the assumption of "socially optimum" occupational or political responsibilities on the part of the other. In all probability this is one of the reasons why so little is heard or known about the wives of prominent Soviet men; they are complementary to their hard-driving husbands in the sense that their energy is oriented toward supporting the internal emotional life of their families, to which their husbands are able to contribute little. Such an arrangement is in general not deemed newsworthy, but would also not be entirely suitable for public exhibition in the Soviet system because of the ideological premium placed upon equal participation by women in the affairs of society. How this kind of pattern fits into the psychological

[11] Erich Fromm, *Escape From Freedom* (New York, 1941). See also Ralph Linton, *The Study of Man* (New York, 1936), 131: "Membership in a rigidly organized society may deprive the individual of opportunities to exercise his particular gifts, but it gives him an emotional security which is almost unknown among ourselves."

[12] A theoretical formulation of the socially patterned reactions to psychological strain may be found in Talcott Parsons, *The Social System* (Glencoe, 1950), 256–267.

make-up of Soviet women is an interesting question. In any event, it works at cross-purposes with a salient motif in the Soviet conception of the ideal role of women.

A second mode of response to the imperative of individual achievement is connected with the difficulty of internalizing it as a personal motivational orientation. Because of this, the transition from child to adult in such a society is an especially hard one, and typically involves disturbance in the relationship of children to parents. The parents transmit an image of the opportunities and requirements of society to their children, and in the process of socialization they come to symbolize both the authority of society and the fact that the child ought to grow up to assume the responsibilities of adulthood. The fusing of these two aspects of the parental role, together with another set of factors to be discussed below, leads with regularity to the appearance of feelings of rebellion against parental authority and a strong desire for personal autonomy. This in turn acts as a force tending to drive the adolescent child away from close association with his parents and into outside activities.

Involvement in extrafamilial activities for adolescents is available in the regime-sponsored Soviet youth organizations. In terms of the development of personal independence from parental ties the Soviet youth organizations probably play a vital role. To some extent, however, participation in them represents to the individual young person only a partial declaration of personal independence and often seems stigmatized with the stamp of legitimate authority. For young people who have a deep need for personal autonomy, an unofficial and sometimes delinquent youth culture serves as a device for severing dependency ties with parents. The main values of such a subculture often stand in contrast with those championed in the Pioneer and Komsomol organizations, and evidently constitute a source of uneasiness to the Soviet leaders.[13] The management of this phenomenon is an unsolved problem for the Soviet Union as for other societies, although a partial solution is achieved by imposing severe punishment for the more serious forms of deviance.

This troublesome complex of patterns is buttressed by still other considerations. The different positions in the life cycle of parents and children imply a differential ability to keep up with external trends and demands. Age brings its psychological rigidities as well as its physiological problems. Consequently, a typical feature of Soviet family life has been a discrepancy between the generations in values, attitudes, and modes of behavior. The rapidity of change in economic and political affairs tends to mold each age group into a distinctive subculture, and estranges it from

---

[13] Allen Kassof, "Youth vs. the Regime: Conflict in Values," *Problems of Communism*, VI (1957), 15–23; Mark G. Field, "Alcoholism, Crime and Delinquency in Soviet Society," *Social Problems*, III (1955), 100–109; S. V. Utechin and P. Utechin, "Patterns of Nonconformity," *Problems of Communism*, VI (1957), 23–29.

both the older and the younger generations. This is reflected within the family in the form of parent-youth conflict or other responses to interpersonal tension such as mutual avoidance or lack of communicativeness, and, as depicted above, is helped along by the growth of the individualistic achievement motive and the regime's generous provision of collective activities outside the family.

III

The reader will recall from previous pages that the family has lost many of its earlier functions, has become separated from the influence of the larger kinship group, the local community, and other of the society's traditional solidary groupings, and has become more flexible or adaptable to newly developing economic and political conditions. Some of the implications of these changes in the relation of the family to the larger society deserve further discussion.

In the first place, the family is quite clearly a compliant type of group. This is because of its lack of connection with larger social groups which could support it in opposition to external forces and because it is no longer a production unit. The provision for the family of food, clothing, housing, and other necessities and luxuries is dependent on performances taking place outside the family. And in Soviet society a very considerable political orthodoxy has been a prime requirement for successful performance in educational and occupational organizations. In brief, the family has become economically dependent, and in a totalitarian system this has also meant political helplessness. It has lost a considerable amount of its power to act as a corporate group in influencing the behavior of its members in outside activities or to maintain and transmit its values and role structure over time. Thus it can be said that the family is less able to act as a source of opposition to the ruling regime than it was in former times. Even those cases where a family member was arrested for political reasons, a not infrequent occurrence during several eras in Soviet history, did not always lead to political disaffection on the part of the entire family. In effect, then, this change in the role of the family has shortened the link between totalitarian government and the Soviet individual and facilitated his political indoctrination.

A final question of widespread interest concerns the interaction between family and regime and its reflection in popular psychology. Little can be said in this brief discussion about the role of the Soviet regime in actively shaping the patterns of family life. But it can at least be stated that the official view has carried a strain of hostility toward the family.

In the early postrevolutionary years the family was apt to be seen as a repository of all the traits associated with the old regime — interest in accumulating property, religiosity, the so-called domestic slavery of women, and such — and at times this led to the prophecy or wish that the family would wither away. In later years the party made official peace with the family, accepted it as a basic unit of socialist society, and supported it with specific measures.[14]

At the same time, since the family is a private group not directly accessible to political control and since, as we have seen, one of its important functions has come to be that of supporting the individual personality by catering to certain aspects of its uniqueness, it is not difficult to see how a sense of its incompatability with the spirit of collectivism would linger on. Moreover, since the start of the Plan era a new source of antagonism has appeared. The rulers of Soviet society are nothing if not ambitious and have set their people a series of most difficult tasks to perform. This has seemed to crowd the family out from among the institutions whose contribution to the attainment of such goals as "socialist construction" is more readily apparent.

As a result, many in the population who have identified deeply with the cause of Communist Party and Soviet government have also developed an ambivalent feeling toward the family. It is too closely and exclusively associated with personal needs rather than with the social concerns of higher priority. Therefore, in the psychology of contemporary family living in the collectivist USSR, the family group has an aura of illegitimacy about it. The well-indoctrinated Soviet citizen often may have a semiconscious but nagging feeling that the family and his interest in it are not entirely meritorious, and may even have some degree of intolerance for tenderness, play, and other forms of personal spontaneity.

THE STRONG-WOMAN MOTIF

VERA SANDOMIRSKY DUNHAM

The mold for a hero differs from that of the heroine in Russia as elsewhere. In spite of the theory of the "absolute equality" of the sexes, the Soviet novel testifies to this fact. Not only is the mold different, but the large number of artistically convincing heroines stands in contrast with the stilted heroes. The relaxed, nonneurotic quality of feminine strength echoes the nineteenth-century literary tradition.

After indicating the difference between the current Soviet literary hero and heroine, we shall look at some highlights of the literary tradition

[14] A documentary record of this may be found in Rudolf Schlesinger, *The Family in the U.S.S.R.* (London, 1949) — esp. part III, "New Trends After the Stabilization of Soviet Society." See also William Petersen, "The Evolution of Soviet Family Policy," *Problems of Communism*, V (1956), 29–35.

and emphasize one pattern in it — the strength of the woman in the face of the weakness or the one-sidedness of the man. Thereafter, I shall illustrate the inclination toward feminine imagery in the literary expression of nationalism. For traces of *Matushka-Rus'* symbolism as well as the strong-woman motif are present in the "new woman."

Except for the fiction of the early 1920's and the permissive war years, the new woman was to a large extent only a model. The high gloss (*lakirovka*) of socialist realism during the Stalinist period permitted a limited view of human problems. Class tensions and family conflict were tabooed. The absence of a realistic portrayal of the family obscured the woman even more than the man. Fiction placed her primarily in the factory, office, or MTS, and heavily moralized the excellence and superiority of the Soviet family. Dispelling the monotony of socialist optimism, the marital-conflict theme emerged in post-Stalin novels. (The problem of Soviet marriage as it reflects unresolved larger tensions warrants an examination beyond the scope of this chapter.) The new woman, strong both by Soviet definition and by the nineteenth-century literary tradition, brings sharpness and urgency to the marital conflict. As a result, the conflict can be revealed more clearly in its social meaning.

I

The glorification of women in current Soviet fiction is more convincing than that of men. The heroine, in contrast to the hero, shows consistently fullness of character: *tsel'nost'*. It is a multifaceted character of wide range, encompassing positive qualities such as selflessness, endurance, generosity, ability to adjust to stress, ability to solve immediate problems. One of the foremost properties of *tsel'nost'*, a term much less fuzzy than "wholeness," is unselfconsciousness. Moreover, in contrast to the man, the woman represents strength which is derived from an ability to relate actively to society, to the collective, to the family.[1] To use a literary allusion dear to Russians, she represents a sort of Karataevism, a state of blissful communion with others.

Male heroes who are a literary success are strikingly few.[2] If they are successful, they are narrower than women and stand for the extension of one positive quality. Their ties with the collective are more self-conscious, more "planned," and their relationship to the family is frequently more strained. Their strength is directed toward self-assertion. Even though the

---

[1] Socialist realism under Stalin disclosed *tsel'nost'* primarily in the "new" man. I am emphasizing merely the mediocre *literary success* of this effort. In periods of strict controls, only men *qua* villains seem to score any life-likeness, whereas portrayal of heroines is a more gratifying task whatever the period.

[2] There is no worthy replacement to date for Ostrovsky's metallic and uncomfortable hero of the thirties, Pavel Korchagin in *How Steel Was Tempered* (1934). Suffice to compare him with the cardboard superman in B. Polevoi's extolled *The Story of a Real Man* (1947).

days of revolutionary martyrdom are but a memory, asceticism is still apparent with the frequent admixture of *nadryv*, of "crackedness."[3] Masculine heroics are based on long-term planning whereas the heroine's efforts are more frequently oriented toward the present. Thus, she is much less lonely than the hero, who is not only lonelier but "future-bound."

Post-Stalin heroes, both men and women, having become lifelike due to political exigencies, reveal more fully the difference in expected behavior of positive fictional characters according to sex.[4] The demands placed on all positive characters are paradoxical, calling for simultaneous demonstration of pride and humility, authoritarian posture and identification with the collective. This is theory. Nevertheless, even in relation to theory, fictional characters must pay attention to the correct emphasis which varies according to sex. If a woman becomes overly self-conscious and driving, particularly when coping with a marital conflict, she commits an error.[5] If the man in his more taxing role upsets the balance between self-assertion (which is the same as self-negation in the difficult language of masculine heroics) and undue craving for the supportiveness of the collective or the family, he too errs.[6]

II

Perhaps Pushkin might have done better had he called his poem by the name of Tatiana, and not Onegin, since she is undeniably its protagonist. [Dostoevsky]

Whatever literary motifs may have been suppressed by controls from above and expediency from below, the "new woman," particularly in the

[3] Strictness or relaxation of controls can be measured by the degree of *nadryv* permissible in a hero. A characteristic repression under Zhdanovism was the suspension of the publication of Iu. German's "Lieutenant Colonel of the Medical Corps," *Zvezda*, I (1949), because of the somewhat neurotic traits of the hero.

[4] The hapless engineer Lopatkin in V. Dudintsev's *Not By Bread Alone* (1956), is an isolate of a stubborness not to be found since the twenties. He might be compared with a fashionable current heroine, Nastia, the childlike "improbable agronomist" in G. Nikolaeva's *Story of an MTS Director and of the Chief Agronomist* (1954). She is just as strong and as stubborn. But free of bitterness and solitary brooding, she easily takes roots in the collective. Nastia is part and parcel of *narod* whereas Lopatkin is not.

[5] The leading revolutionary heroine of the twenties is Dasha Chumalova in F. Gladkov's *Cement* (1927). Evaluation of her has drastically changed. A true leather-jacket new woman, she had destroyed her marriage and abandoned her child to an early death in a *detdom*. This was her revolt against old ways. She was the very incarnation of woman's new cause. Whereas such one-sided onslaught on *tsel'nost'* was glorified at the time, Dasha's attitude today is not only heretical but downright incomprehensible in the framework of current values.

[6] Some of the novels spelling out in detail the marital conflict in the urban professional setting are: A. Koptiaeva, *Comrade Anna* (1946) and *Ivan Ivanovich* (1948); V. Vasilevskaia, *When There Shall Be Light* (1946); A. Chakovsky, *Days of Peace* (1947); V. Panova, *Kruzhilikha* (1947); V. Dobrovol'sky, *Zhenia Maslova* (1950); V. Kochetov, *Zhurbiny* (1952); A. Arbuzov, *Years of Wandering* (1954) [drama]. Those dealing with the same problem in the kolkhoz setting are: V. Panova, *The Clear Shore* (1950); E. Mal'tsev, *From the Very Heart* (1948); G. Nikolaeva, *Harvest* (1950); G. Medynsky, *Mar'ia* (1948); S. Voronin, *Unnecessary Fame* (1956).

last decade, manages to preserve some connections with the classical heroine.

"Russian womanhood" is remarkable in that it is a perceptible motif. It extols the coherence and strength of the woman in a historical sequence and in divergent class settings, collecting more similarities than differences. By contrast it is impossible to speak as emphatically of a binding motif extolling the heroism of men. Even the spirit of the folk epic occasionally hints at the limitations imposed by culture on masculine strength. One of the favorite heroes, Ilia Muromez, starts out by being paralyzed for thirty years, and when the daredevil Alesha Popovich boasts in promethean rebellion, challenging the supernatural power, the host of epic warriors turn one by one to stone.

The historical sequence of active masculine heroism — Nevsky, Donskoy, Tsars Ivan and Peter, the Razin rebels, the Suvorov generals — left relatively little impact on purely imaginate literature. Tolstoy's rendition of Kutuzov as a quasi-Buddhist illustrates this contention. It is curious that a novel about Maiakovsky has not been written, an influential new man who represented such a close fit between his own personality and values of militant masculinity. It is even more curious that Pasternak, dedicating to him so far the only appropriate necrologue, expressed the conviction that this strong man was extraordinarily unique and, in a sense, lonely:

this man was, to tell the truth, perhaps the only fitting citizen in the new state. In his blood alone the newness of the times was climatic. He was strange with the strangeness of the epoch which was only half realized. I started recalling the traits of his character, his independence, in many respects entirely unique.[7]

This is tangential evidence that strength is more easily perceived, accepted, and extolled in a woman.

From Pushkin's Tatiana — and even from the less colorful Lusen'ka Kruziferskaia, who represents the initial moment of emancipation better than Pushkin's privileged heroine — the drive to realize human potentialities was restated as "Russianness" in Turgenev's and Goncharov's young women, in Nekrasov's Decembrist countesses, in Tolstoy's Natasha. One usually accounts for the "communality" of the Russian *Entwicklungsroman* of the midcentury by the postulates of Russian realism — essentially dedication to social problems and dislike of introspection. Whatever the reason, the alliance of the heroines is striking.

The strong-woman motif finds no parallel in a series of male counterparts, who, to begin with, frequently stand for ideas. The heroine preempts the hero's place. She might even personify a reproach against the restlessness, escapism, and narrowness found in the Onegins, Chatskys, Pechorins, Beltovs, Raiskys.[8] Strong men seem to be punished for their

[7] B. Pasternak, *Safe Conduct* (Leningrad, 1931), 128.
[8] Pushkin calls it spleen; Turgenev's term is Hamletism.

masculinity and self-assertion with early death. This is the case with Bazarov, Insarov, Bolkonsky. The longevity and softness of the slumbering Oblomov, the giant of low vitality, makes the point.

Weidlé's observation of the relative absence of the strong-man ideal in Russian culture is, thus, demonstrable in fiction.[9] Men *qua* men are disappointing. Oblomov is incapable of the simplest salvation offered him by Olga. The technicalities of a wedding are too much for him. Onegin, stronger by far and man that he is, assumes the frustrating posture of brotherly love. The escapist Aleko cannot satisfy his beloved, and that other escapist into exotic realms, Olenin, is entirely unsuccessful in his courtship. Insarov, decidedly masculine, is not much more palpable than Elena's premature widowhood. And the strongest of them all, Rakhmetov, the new man, stiff, stuffy, unreal because he is a superman by political design, posits abstinence as an essential part of his self-definition.[10] It is the lean soil on which masculine heroism grows, revolutionary soil at that.

The singularly non-Victorian heroine gives herself spontaneously and, if need be, commits adultery for the sake of full participation. Tatiana's dream marks the acceptance of Onegin's dangerously evasive reality and her strength is expressed in that frustrating surrender. Turgenev's Elena also stands for readiness. It is the virtuous man who hesitates. The urgency with which revolutionary Insarov, stricken by disease, chases her away from his bedside is unintentionally comical.[11] Goncharov's proud Vera gives herself without ado to the questionable Volokhov. Even the conservative Goncharov interprets her act as a necessary step toward maturity, giving it a meaning beyond the personal boundaries of one fictional character.[12] The very motif of the strong woman makes it possible to mention Ostrovsky's untutored, primitive Katerina side by side with the

[9] "Woman, in the course of the last century, won her important position in Russian life, not by fighting for it, as she did in the Anglo-Saxon countries, but as a result of a man's coming to see her, more than elsewhere, as a human person equal in value to himself, rather than as a mere instrument of pleasure or an object of utility. The cult of force and the strong man never went further in Russia than its purely infantile and harmless stage." W. Weidlé, *Russia: Absent and Present* (New York, 1952), 145.

[10] When the young woman with whom he is in love proposes to him (the woman as aggressor), his reply is rejection of marriage and of a love affair as well: "No, I can't accept this either . . . I must crush love in me. My love to you would tie my hands. It's not going to be easy to do it for they are already tied. But I will untie them. I must not love." N. Chernyshevsky, "What is to be Done?" *Izbrannye sochineniia* (Moscow, 1950), 123.

[11] The loyal friend, Bersenev, suggests that ailing Insarov might die from the sight of his beloved.

[12] "Not Vera, not an individual . . . but the Russian woman fell as a sacrifice in the struggle of the old life with the new. She did not want to live blindly according to directions from her elders. She knew what was dead in the old forms of life and she craved for a long time, she searched for fresh, spiritual meanings. She consciously wanted to find and to espouse the new *truth*, retaining, however, that which was strong, basic, and best in the old ways. She did not want destruction but renewal." I. Goncharov, "Better Later Than Never," critical remarks, *Polnoe sobranie sochinenii* (St. Petersburg, 1899), I, 68–69.

refined gentlewomen. He presents her as a result of an oppressive milieu, of the heavy and cruel *kupechestvo*. But the important thing is that Katerina acts when driven toward fulfillment. Having enacted the storm of her life, she leaves her weak husband to his desolation and in envy of her courage. Her lover likewise is weak while in contrast Katerina's strength is monumental. Her suicide may seem melodramatic today, but the words to her lover are not:

don't feel sorry for me. No one is responsible. I myself wanted it that way. Don't feel sorry, go ahead ruin me! Let them all know. Let them all see what I am doing. . . . If for your sake, the fear of sin didn't stop me, why should I fear the judgment of people? [13]

No matter how limited Dobroliubov's literary sensitivity may seem today, he was an expert in the Russian skill of politicizing literary characters. If Goncharov saw in Vera's challenge to convention a search for the new experience, Dobroliubov goes further. He sees a relationship between the expression of love and rebellion against the status quo. He transforms love and the inferior position of the woman into a revolutionary mission to dispell Russian "darkness." [14] Moreover, he strongly feels the absence of a masculine hero. It was meaningful to him that Turgenev chose a foreigner to fill that role.

Now everybody waits, everybody hopes . . . in literature there shall appear a vividly drawn figure of a Russian Insarov. We won't have to wait for him too long.[15]

In a sense, Dobroliubov is still waiting.

It would be incorrect to say that only the "left" pre-empted the "feminine question" for revolutionary purposes. Dostoevsky, the cantakerous pamphleteer of reaction, incessantly praised the superiority of the Russian woman. He condemned men for corrupt materialism and saw the idealistic spirit preserved only in women.[16]

---

[13] A. Ostrovsky, "The Storm," *Polnoe sobranie sochinenii* (Moscow, 1950), II, 248.

[14] "The strong, whole (*tsel'nii*) Russian character appears in Ostrovsky in the feminine type. . . . It is known that extremes engender extremes and that the strongest protest is that which finally rises from the breast of the weakest and most patient . . . in the family who but the woman suffers most under the burden of tyranny? . . . The woman who wishes to go to the end in her protest against subjugation and tyranny perpetrated by the elders in the Russian family must be filled with heroic selflessness, must have courage for everything and be ready for everything." N. Dobroliubov, "Ray of Light in the Dark Kingdom," *Polnoe sobranie sochinenii* (Moscow, 1945), II, 348.

[15] "When Will the Real Day Come?" *Polnoe sobranie sochinenii*, II, 240.

[16] ". . . I wish to add one more word about the Russian woman. I have already stated that in her resides our only great hope, one of the pledges of our revival. The regeneration of the Russian woman during the last twenty years has proved unmistakable. The rise in her quests have been lofty, candid and fearless . . . the Russian man has become terribly addicted to the debauch of acquisition, cynicism and materialism. But the woman has remained much more faithful to the pure worship of the idea, to the duty of serving the idea." F. Dostoevsky, May 1876, *The Diary of*

The courage to involve oneself fully was seen in its connection with the feminine ability to love and to act. The nuptial scene in *On the Eve* is a motto for many novels. Insarov warns Elena of the hardships ahead: exile, poverty, humiliation. To all this she replies:

"I know. I know everything. . . . I love you."
"Welcome, then, my wife in front of the people and in front of God!" [17]

Elena knows. But Nekrasov's countess, Volkonskaia, does not. A bride at eighteen, raised in the greenhouse of the Pushkin era, she has no notion of her husband's political activities. She hardly knows him. When he is arrested, unquestioning loyalty determines her martyrdom — in her mind, he cannot be dishonorable. Martyrdom is appealing to the Nekrasov generation especially when it is childlike and innocent.[18] The countess acts through love and compassion. Planned abstinence and self-sacrifice are foreign to her. She leaves her child and her way of life behind. When she joins her husband in a Siberian mine, she kneels before him and kisses his chains. Astonishing at it may seem, this romantic narrative has never been considered sentimental. This is germane to the argument of the extra-literariness of the motif. Nekrasov measures integrity in terms of commitment to primary loyalty in the face of threats, both intrinsic and extrinsic.[19] If there is anything this young woman knows it is that the state, the tsar, the mighty are wrong. Her loyalty is of an ecstatic nature, and her strength rests in love.

It is notable that the "strong man" is reluctant to enter into primary loyalties. Chernyshevsky spelled out the program of abstinence for his bristling radical. Innocence, generosity, spotaneity, essential ingredients of *tsel'nost'*, are not Rakhmetov's qualities. He has no drives — he is all brain. Chernyshevsky's literary talent is of lesser importance here than the

---

a Writer (New York, 1954), I, 340. ". . . 'barbaric' Russia will show what a place she will allot to the 'little mother,' 'little sister,' that self-renouncing martyr for the Russian man." Dostoevsky, September 1877, II, 846.

[17] I. Turgenev, "On the Eve," *Polnoe sobranie sochinenii* (St. Petersburg, 1898), II, 309–310. There is a variant of this scene in *Senilia*. In the poem "The Threshold" the test of awareness for the revolutionary self-sacrifice is dramatized. In a crescendo of terror which lies ahead, the "Russian young girl," who could have been Figner, Breshkovskaia, or Perovskaia, is forewarned of loneliness, hatred, prison, sickness, death, loss of identity, and ultimately even of loss of faith. She enters, both a "fool" and a "saint." *Sobranie sochinenii* (Moscow, 1956), VIII, 478–479. The poem somehow could not have featured a young man.

[18] As a parallel in Soviet literature, war patriotism found its most flamboyant expression in the martydom of the adolescent Zoia Kosmodemianskaia.

[19] On the Soviet scene, after many years of hibernation, this critical pattern of interpersonal relations has been brought to light again. The external motivation was the Beria affair. A. Korneichuk was one of the first to respond with precise specifications in hand. In "Wings" (1954), a party official fails to act when his innocent wife is arrested. He was well trained to believe that the secret police cannot be wrong. In the scene, for the sake of which the play was written, the estranged wife accuses him of treason against faith in human beings, against primary loyalties, for the first time considered higher than the state. Here too love was betrayed.

continuity of the idea of the truly strong man who can be strong only as an ascetic revolutionary.

Gorky's victim of 1905, the revolutionary Pavel, admonishes an underground comrade against marriage: "You shall live for the sake of a piece of bread, for your children, for your house; and you shall both be lost to the cause. Both!" [20] The same comrade explains to Pavel's mother why it is impossible for Pavel to marry the girl he loves: "He loves her and she loves him. That's true. But they will never get married, never! She would like to. But Pavel does not." The mother's comment fixes the sacrificial quality of abstinence typical of male heroes: "Yes. Is that the way it is? People deny themselves." [21]

The denial of love is an essential attribute of the revolutionary man who fears dissipation of strength, diffusion, submersion in *autrui*. Rakhmetov's Bolshevik progeny indeed donned the garb of the new monk, be it Fadeev's Levinson, Ehrenburg's Kurbov, Leonov's Kurilov, Sholokhov's Davydov, or Ostrovsky's Korchagin. [22]

Of course, the heroines of the twenties were dressed in leather jackets accordingly. But abstinence was not as binding on them. Liubov' Iarovaia[23] was a married woman and came to the revolution inspired by womanly love. Promiscuous Virineia[24] found the revolutionary road only when purified through real love. Characteristically the new freedom of the woman entailed sexual liberties. Dasha Chumalova, the prototype of the new woman, destroyed the old forms of marriage rather tragically. But she prepared herself for "newness" partially through extramarital experiences.

[20] M. Gorky, "Mother," *Sobranie sochinenii* (Berlin, 1923), VII, 36.

[21] "Mother," p. 78.

[22] The glib Ehrenburg, who likes to dot his heavily symbolical *i*'s, not only has his idealistic Cheka man born as a sordid surprise to a prostitute, but has him commit suicide after he loses his virginity in a bawdy house: *Life and Death of Nikolai Kurbov* (1923). In Sholokhov's objective document on the travails of collectivization, Davydov is indecently assailed by the village women when he first begins his mission and later, in a gory scene, is beaten by them. This is a motif which sustains not only the economic resistance of the peasant woman but the existential threat to a man: *Virgin Soil* (1931).

[23] The heroine of K. Trenev's acclaimed revolutionary drama by the same name, 1924.

[24] When it was still permitted to tell the story of the revolution in somber tones of sensationalism, L. Seifullina's Virineia, an "unawakened" victim of the bestial prerevolutionary peasant milieu and thus a modern and much abused Katerina, manages to preserve her integrity and awaken to the new because she is strong. This author also liked dotted *i*'s. The heroine's pride first grows out of the confrontation with the impotence of her lover. The praise of this canonized heroine has the familiar ring of the traditional glorification of feminine strength as being especially true and real. One might gather from these overstatements that masculine strength can never be quite that. "One feels in Virinei's each word and action a true strength, rich but dormant, undeveloped abilities. This is not simply a beaten down peasant woman . . . O, no, Virineia cannot be bent . . . she is strong. . . . She will rather perish than give in." D. D. Furmanov, *Sochineniia* (Moscow, 1952), III, 266.

The point, however, is this: in spite of numerous treatises on the "New Hero in Literature," the anachronistic revolutionary monk has not been successfully replaced by a more relaxed, wholesome heroic personality. Dudintsev's inventor is effective not because he fits the proclaimed current life of plenty but because he resembles the stubbornly narrow hero of the twenties. The "revolutionary" state of the new woman, by contrast, was short-lived. The success of the literary heroine today is based on echoing the old motif of feminine many-sidedness, not the innovations of sovietism. When puritanism descended on Soviet literature, it inhibited the interest in intimate personal relationships and diluted the differentiation between feminine and masculine heroics. But some connections with the traditional motifs remained. For instance, the painfully ineffective manner in which heroes pay court in most Soviet novels is partly an idealization of chastity and partly a lasting reflex of masculine inadequacy.

At this point, it would be unwise to relate fiction, which emphasizes the one-sided man, too closely to the political situation. In the face of radicalism and Bolshevik achievements, how can one doubt the impact of strong men? Perhaps literature merely illustrates the Russian predisposition toward cultural dichotomies and counteracts politics by failing to idealize the strong man *successfully* and *consistently*. It should suffice to say, however, that the ideal of *tsel'nost'* is more fully expressed in the feminine figure in which tensions are more credibly resolved. Oblomov can do only one thing: submit. Raskolnikov's cerebration, far from being submissive, represents also only one state: alienation. The split in Raskolnikov, as the name implies, describes him fully. He indeed stands in contrast to *tsel'nost'*. In Russian fiction, only a man can be so split. To be sure, only a man can be a Prince Myshkin. The Idiot's impotence, Raskolnikov's alienation, Oblomov's phlegma, all are unthinkable in a heroine.

III

I am like a child in its mother's womb, reluctant to be born. I am warm enough here. [Vasily Rozanov]

G. Fedotov remarked that love of country in any nation is conceived in terms of a motherly, feminine image.[25] In this respect, the Russian inclination is to exaggerate this maxim. The organizing, orderly "o" of *otechestvo* (or the paternal "p" of *patria*) pertains to abstraction and is foreign to the core of patriotism expressed in popular as well as in esoteric poetry.

Rus', a feminine principle, is inseparable from *Matushka*. Emotions of nationalism are articulated in grandiose feminine-kinship images. It cannot be accidental that Goncharov endowed his despotic and irresistible *ba-*

---

[25] "Dlia vsiakogo naroda stikhiia rodiny, kak stikhiia materinskaia iavliaetsia v zhenskom like," *Novyi grad* (New York, 1952), 291.

bushka, one of the broadest, most typical characters in Russian fiction, with positive and enduring nationalism. He created a monument as Russian as Oblomov, and not at all dissimilar. One might suspect that *babushka* turned out to be so strong primarily because she was a woman. Raisky, one more superfluous man, salvages from his peregrinations through Europe only one invigorating sensation: his longing for home.

Behind him stood all the time his three figures and warmly beckoned him: his Pera, his Marfin'ka, *babushka.* And behind them stood and beckoned more compellingly than they one other gigantic figure, that other great *babushka* — Russia.[26]

But the symbol of *Matushka-Rus'* grew from another source as well. The alternative to Goncharov's stately image is the image of suffering. One might recall Garshin's interpretation of the captive fanatic Boiarynia Morozova, Avvakum's great friend, as she was painted by Surikov. The fiercely stubborn folk heroine who went "to the end," who would have let her son be torn by bloodhounds rather than deny her faith and who indeed died in prison of starvation, evoked in Garshin less praise for her heroic deed than for her "creative love" and enormous potentialities.[27]

Nekrasov, Dostoevsky, and Blok, as unrelated as they may have been, perceived in the Russian misery of the woman a vital source of national salvation. In their own way, they assisted the transfiguration of humiliation into strength.

but don't tell me that I don't know the people! I know them: from them I received the image of Christ into my heart once more . . . but let us admit that our people are sinful, let their image be bestial: *"Syn na materi ekhal, moloda zhena na pristiazhechke"* — This song must surely have come from some truth.[28]

In the sexual image of the riding son, the bestiality is masculine. Whipped by the landlord and beaten by the husband, the woman was possessed and insulted. This dark and vivid sexual motif appears in Nekrasov's and Ostrovsky's genre pictures, in Dostoevsky's *fin de siècle* rapes, in Gorky's and Sholokhov's more sociological "folk" scenes.

A compensatory motif of cruelty in the feminine incarnation gained parallel momentum. Dostoevsky's fatal women are not the only examples.

---

[26] I. Goncharov, "The Precipice," *Polnoe sobranie sochinenii* (St. Petersburg, 1899), X, 319.

[27] "What is this remarkable sacrifice? For the sake of what is it being made? Her drive was great but there was no outlet. There was no living life which could have opened its arms to Fedos'ia Prokop'evna, a life to which she could have given her creative [*deiatel'naia*] love, passion, energy, selflessness. . . . She ended her life not giving in an iota." V. Garshin, "Notes About Exhibitions," *Sochineniia* (Moscow, 1955), 360.

[28] F. Dostoevsky, *The Diary of a Writer* (1st ed., 1877; Berlin, 1922), 605 (I use the Russian text because I find Brasol's translation of this passage inadequate).

Feminine despotism reached orgiastic frenzy on a firmer national basis and with less psychological complications in Ostrovsky's lady-Tartars — Ulanbekova, Murzavezkaia, Gurmyzhskaia, in Turgenev's mother — the aristocrats; in Leskov's logical tigress of the Mzensk merchant district; and, in the peasant *Power of Darkness,* in Tolstoy's monstrous women. The reversal of the theme added spice to the martyrdom of the woman. Even in perversion she proved stronger.

Strength in cruelty, however, was only a foil. One turns to Nekrasov for the straightforward intensity of nationalism which he expressed in the image of the suffering peasant woman. A young peasant woman is publicly lashed. She utters not a sigh. The poet sees dignity in her, not humiliation.[29] A fish had swallowed the key which was to open the gates of paradise for the hard-working, beaten-down peasant woman; even God forgot the whereabouts of that fish.[30] Just the same, the peasant woman is a queen:

> Est' zhenshchiny v russkikh selen'iakh
> S pokoinoiu vazhnost'iu liz
> S krasivoiu siloi v dvizhen'iakh,
> S pokhodkoi, so vzgliadom zariz . . .
> V igre — ee konnyi ne slovit,
> V bede — ne srobeet, spaset;
> Konia na skaku ostanovit,
> V goriashchuiu izby voidet.[31]

The amazon is entrenched in the literary tradition. She was glorified with special fervor during the last war and even more lovingly in the poetry of postwar melancholy. Something of Nekrasov is echoed in Aliger's hymn to widowhood, national in mood.

> Widows don't wear mourning,
> Do not cry in front of others,
> Do not hide their eyes in the morning,
> Do not throw their moans to the winds.
> Lips pressed drier,
> Voice choked lower,
> Singed hearts have nothing to fear . . .
> For Russian Women, widows,
> Who have looked at death,
> Who came through alive
> With an unriddled strength,
> For them in Russia
> We must find a new name.[32]

[29] V. Nekrasov, "Last Night . . . ," *Polnoe sobranie sochinenii* (Moscow, 1938), I, 50.

[30] Nekrasov, "Who Lives Well in Russia," II, 316.

[31] Nekrasov, "Moroz Krasnyi–Nos," II, 168.

[32] M. Aliger, "New Name," *Znamia,* no. i (1945), 63.

The remarkable Leningrad cycles also leaned on Nekrasov's patriotic language with its feminine imagery. In the guilt for the suffering of the Russian woman there was clearly discernible the hope that her traditional strength might contribute to a humanistic transformation of Soviet society.

Two peculiar poetic exclamations hint at the richness of the feminine national theme — one, ecstatic, and the other, mannered sobriety. Both are equally romantic, both stemming from the period of revaluation of values. When Blok abandoned his ethereal deity and his eerily urban "stranger," he found his last love. Perhaps no one before him brought to Russian nationalism such a tense and erotic note. He remained faithful to his debauched and saintly lover: "O, Rus' moia! Zhena moia!" [33] It is hard to say who was more "Russian" in the prerevolutionary twilight, Blok or Rozanov. The latter's eroticism was expressed in "contrary" aphoristic diction, perhaps less translatable than that of Blok: "The *real* Russian was reared not at all in universities, but by kind, illiterate nurse-maids." [34] Weidlé observes that only a Russian could have said: "I am like a child in its mother's womb, reluctant to be born. I am warm enough here." [35] This quote lends itself to a great deal of interpretation. Weidlé relates this aphorism to the strength of the Russian family nexus. One might suggest that the Russian masculinity is reluctant to detach itself from the shelter of the feminine principle, the mood in which so much national poetry was written. Nekrasov's lines

> Ty i ubogaia,
> Ty i obil'naia,
> Ty i moguchaia,
> Ty i bessil'naia
> Matushka-Rus' [36]

couple poverty and richness, strength and weakness, contradictions which abound in Russian poetry. If the motif of feminine strength is at all convincing, *obil'naia* and *moguchaia* relate to the feminine ideal of national consciousness, whereas the other face of *Matushka-Rus'*, *ubogaia* and *bessil'naia*, illuminates the cherished meek heroes, Prince Myshkin and Ilia Oblomov.

---

[33] . . . O, Rus' moia! Zhena moia! Do boli
    Nam iasen dolgii put'
Nash put' — streloi tatarskoi drevnei voli
    Pronzil nam grud'
Nash put' — stepnoi, nash put' — v toske
       bezbreshnoi
V tvoei toske, o Rus'. . . .
    A. Blok, "On the Field of Kulikovo," *Stikhotvoreniia* (Berlin, 1923), III, 273.
[34] V. Rozanov, *Fallen Leaves* (Berlin, 1923), 450.
[35] V. Rozanov, *Uedinennoe* (1912), cited in Weidlé, 149.
[36] *Moroz Krasnyi–Nos*, cited in Weidlé, 168.

IV

[Cartoon depicting a middle-aged prosperous beau being asked by a langorous
  lady-friend:]
"Do you love children?"
"Of course. I always pay alimony on time." [March 16, 1958, Gospolitizdat
  Leaf Calendar]

In the beginning of post-Stalin literary reforms the Soviet writer was
invited to take a look at the private world of the citizen, his love life, his
family. The report was somewhat on the gloomy side, especially when
introducing the abandoned woman.

> Glasses are washed clean and sparkle.
> You mirror yourself in them and feel young.
> Floors are waxed. And the children are fed.
> Thank God, no worse than in other families.
>
> Thank God, we live well and don't grieve.
> Quietly, peacefully we live . . .
> No worse than the others who have a husband.
> Perhaps, better than with him.
>
> Can a house be kept as clean with a man?
> He smoked so much. . . . Our house now
> Smells of wax, of dry herbs,
> Of March air when the door is ajar. . . .
>
> Rusty drops slowly bore holes
> Into the damp, grey snow.
> The air, light, bitter and bright,
> Sometimes chokes my throat.[37]

The topic of the broken family has become widespread. The abandoned
woman keeps the family together. The dignity of her bitterness is suggested, as well as a new sophistication in approaching human problems.
In another poem, equally autumnal and melancholy, but with more of a
story, the husband returns to the poet's "taciturn neighbor Varia." This
return is different from the reunion at the end of the war, a juxtaposition
indicating the double indemnity of the present-day family, first war-torn
and, later, submitted to new stresses.

> He quietly, guiltily knocked at her door,
> After leaving the house of his second wife.
> Varia dried her hands on her apron
> And calmly opened the door.
> She saw him and clasped her throat
> And didn't lead him in at once. . . .

But the celebration à la russe is on anyway, with neighbors, clinking
glasses, and accordion.

[37] Ia. Neiman, "Abandoned Woman," *Literaturnaia Moskva*, II (1956), 296.

> But I thought that Varia was strong,
> Strong in hiding pain and bitterness,
> I thought she would not forgive, for once,
> That which I keep forgiving.

Only ten years ago, concern with the marital conflict was frequently interpreted as heretical predilection for the "untypical." Now, typically enough, the author is in the thick of it and feels something strained, sad and morally wrong about the festivity in full swing.

> I waited for Varia to proudly rise,
> To cross her arms in majesty,
> To look at him with burning eyes,
> To tell this stranger: "Go away!"

Varia does no such thing. She sits at the man's side in her new dress and smiles serenely as if she had never cried. What is more, she dances.

> Tonight that other one is crying
> Of whom he had grown tired.
> As if winds don't howl out there
> And break young trees.
> The children of that other wife
> Are fatherless, in turn.

And the man, to the poet's irritation, sits entirely unconcerned

> and eats, jokes, and toasts his guests.
> This time, a year or half of one, perhaps,
> He won't grow tired of Varia.[38]

The poem ends on a note typical of current realism, not exactly socialist. Taciturn neighbor Varia is exonerated. Love might not return. In fact, Varia dances so hard to bid it farewell. The gesture of acquiescence and forgiveness is selfless and supportive of the family. The new woman in fiction, from 1917 to the present day, grew increasingly more expert in crossing her arms majestically and saying "out!" Those who have done so are legion, led in that first contingent of revolutionary heroines by Liubov' Iarovaia and Dasha Chumalova. The solution found by the contemporary woman is extolled with much less fanfare. The alternative of compromise is newer than the intransigence of the pioneer new woman. As far as the man is concerned, he remains a heel and a weakling.

In the fashionable somber key, a poem entitled "The Foundling" deals with the return of a soldier after four years of war. The peasant hut is scrubbed clean, the table is neatly set, the pancake dough is on the point of running over. But the house is empty. Perplexed, the man stoops to fetch a smoldering piece of coal out of the stove for his cigarette. That is when he notices that from under the oven something is staring at him. It is a little girl of three, her eyes brimful of tears.

[38] M. Agashina, "Varia," *Stikhi 1955 goda* (Moscow, 1956), 5–7.

What is your name?
           Alenushka.
Whose daughter are you?
           She doesn't say.
           Finally —
           Nobody's.
Mother found me by the brook
Behind the faraway field
Under the white birchtree.
And where is mother?
    She is hiding in the rye.
    She is afraid you will kill us.[39]

The satirical approach is even more somber. The heretofore stubbornly glorified monolith of the Soviet family is being mocked with a touch of cynicism. Thus, two little girls play "mothers" in front of their house:

First Girl (rocking a doll):
    Lullaby, baby, lullaby.
    Daddy loves his little girl. . . .
    Daddy! That's no way to play!
    Why do you sit there alone?
Second Girl:
    Because — listen to me!
    I was father yesterday!
    It bores me.
First Girl:
    But you can stay where you are
    And still play our daddy!
    Is it difficult
    To ask about your child
    Once in a while?
           (rocks her doll)
    Lullaby, baby, lullaby.
    Daddy loves his little girl.
    Soon he will come home. . . .
Second Girl:
    No, you live alone!
First Girl:
    And where is daddy?
Second Girl:
    I left you.
    I went with the new auntie.
           (exits)
First Girl (to her doll):
    Lullaby, baby, lullaby.
    Daddy left his little girl.
    I provide you all alone.
    With oranges, with vitamins.[40]

[39] M. Zenkevich, *Oktiabr'*, II (1955), 39.
[40] A. Barto, "Playing Grownups," *Den' poezii* (Moscow, 1956), 10.

The order to depict love instead of work resulted in an abundance of revelations. The family tragedy is becoming an open theme, and the marital conflict is explored with such verve that satire no longer sounds startling. The little provider of oranges and vitamins would have seemed blasphemous if not bolstered by so many variations. Repressive machinery is in full gear to counteract the overexposure. But, as always, it is too late. The above fragments suggest how much heavier the responsibility for the family weighs on the woman than on the man. This is not peculiar to the Russian or Soviet situation. What concerns us is the vehemence of the discovery. After the revolution the new social order had liberated the woman sufficiently to impose on her a double duty: she holds a job like a man and takes care of the family. This is a standing contract. But new pressures are also evolving. As literature recorded, the young woman who was capable of becoming "new" brought all her strength to the revolution. She learned to write and read and many other lessons of discipline and self-denial. She prepared to compete in education, skill, and political righteousness with the man. She wore the black leather jacket for quite a while. And for quite a while, at least in literature, she let the state care for her children according to the blueprint. And then it happened that the loosening of the family nexus, its bolshevization, with easy divorce, abortion, promiscuity, and cynicism turned out to be beyond her endurance.

In an amusing story of the late twenties, the strength of the family is quite evident in spite of bolshevization. A militant student conducts a discussion with factory women on "The Woman in the USSR and Abroad." The zealot questions a mousy participant, known as a *bessoznatel'naia*:

"Tell us, what is the main tool of enslavement of the woman?"
"What is the main enslavement of the woman?" she repeated somewhat slyly.
"Well, if her husband drinks and if there is no plenty, that would be then the main enslavement of the woman."
"That's not it, not it at all!" Sonia shot back. "It's private property!" [41]

Matushka-Rus' rebelled. The inversion of public and private values did not quite work out as far as she was concerned. Out of her commitment to the importance of personalism, the family was rebuilt. Maybe the war was not as damaging to the family as the early bolshevization had been because of the counterforce of soldarity in a national crisis. But it was injurious enough indirectly to cause marital tensions in the postwar period which is a period of adjustment and, therefore, of weakened solidarity.

I shall illustrate below some patterns in the marital conflict in which the woman emerges as the strong figure. Her strength is an expectation deriving partially from Soviet ideology and more substantially, perhaps,

---

[41] M. Kolosov, "Individual Education," *Oktiabr'*, no. 3 (1929), 5–6.

from the literary tradition. In contrast to the man, she is expected to be decisive and selfless — either in defending her pride or in swallowing it. Either course is extolled as long as it represents *tsel'nost'*.

v

Everything little by little takes shape. [Vera Panova]

The attribution of special strength to the Russian family has become a fashionable, if not uncontroversial, cornerstone in the study of Russian culture.[42] Though a sociological examination may not bear out this contention, its existence in literature is undeniable.[43]

If a strong family is a shelter from totalitarian excesses, the demands and expectations placed on it are so marked that internal pressures are created. In addition, war and its aftermath produce new strains in interpersonal relations. The resultant marital conflict provides one pattern of interaction to which the motif of the strong woman brings poignancy. Without that catalytic agent, the conflict would not have been quite so sharply presented.[44] Though there is continuity in the strong-woman motif, her strength begins to show vulnerable spots in the postwar period. When the woman transgresses in any form of self-exaggeration, it is judged as particularly reprehensible. A corollary change is perceptible in the new courtesies allotted the man. For instance, the topic of masculine loneliness is treated with new interest.[45]

[42] In reaction to Weidlé's perceptive argument on "the family connection," 130–134, V. Varshavsky has this to say: "Having highly exaggerated . . . the importance of the family principle in the life of the Russian people — while reading this chapter it seems all the time that the author speaks of China and not of Russia — Weidlé sees precisely in this state of being dissolved in the natural force of familyness (*semeistvennost'*) the cause of the Russian's indifference toward western concern with juridical safeguards." *The Unnoticed Generation* (New York, 1956), 384.

[43] "We love the sanctity of the family when it is in reality holy, and not because the state is solidly founded upon it." Dostoevsky, 237. I am sure that it could be demonstrated that the word *sanctity* was for the first time seriously uttered in "Sovietese" in the family context.

[44] The postwar family drama is well told in Vassilevskaia's "When There Shall Be Light," *Zvezda*, no. 12 (1946). A shell-shocked veteran returns to a superpositive wife who is incapable of lending him moral support during his painful readjustment: "they had nothing to talk about. Their paths no longer met." Her disdain, war trauma or not, toward his introspection and reluctance to jump at once into future-bound work arouses hatred in him. "What is it exactly that you want from me today?" he asked in a piercing whisper. "I don't want anything from you neither today nor any other day." An old painter who is close to them both finally has the courage to warn the amazon that he is sorry not for her but for him. "So it's me then? I am responsible?" — "I don't know who is responsible, I am not a judge . . . but he must be helped, he must be helped under any circumstances. . . ."

[45] The Lopatkin type of isolates preceded Dudintsev's *Not By Bread Alone*, but a portrait of fullest length is there. He appears in a younger, more concise, and poignant version in D. Granin's short story "One's Own Opinion" (which recently produced indignation in official circles), *Novyi mir*, no. 8 (1956). Another idealist, another frustrated engineer, has all the telling attributes of un-*tsel'nost'*. His face is "pale," his voice "thin," "his dry lips moved without producing a sound," "he defends

But these were not granted without a struggle. In the early Stalinist period, the male hero, harrassed by external pressures and by internal self-doubt, was seldom a match for the buxom heroine. When there was a marital clash, in the Stalinist literary manner, the husband, who at best was only good, cut a sorry figure. When the latter is recently confronted with the uncompromising woman of the Stalinist version, his weakness for the first time evokes sympathy.[46] The vague disapprobation toward the amazon differentiates the strong-woman motif in the current novel from previous periods. It is to a certain extent a result of normalizing the achieved status of the emancipated woman, and behind this process stands a long literary development.

The drive for a social change, beginning in the 1850's, gained momentum in the 1880's and lasted through the turn of the century. In the emancipation of woman, it found an effective way to express itself. In periods of political repression, the searching, restless, "civic" writer — whether left or right — was particularly addicted to self-laceration in that he viewed the state of the nation, and indeed of the stable social order, as one of oppressive stagnation. The parasitical *chinovnik*, the lazy *barin*, the ineffectual *intelligent* — all male figures — characterized the age of the decline of autocracy, a corollary of which was the inferior status of the woman. Frustration blossoming in the repressive periods rekindled the need to romanticize the bizarre and dynamic. Emancipation of the woman was one such motif. But the hope is more appealing and, in a literary nonphotographic sense, more real than the actual attainment of social gains.

The dream was strong. It grew with the revolutionary drive in the first two decades of our century. When it coincided with the dissolution of

---

truth awkwardly" and "in despair." His colleagues and superiors take him for a "hallucinating maniac." For a poetic version of the *lonely* road on the search for truth entered by a disillusioned young man, see E. Evtushenko's remarkable "Station Winter," *Oktiabr'*, no. 10 (1956).

[46] The discrepancy between intent of the author to extol the strong woman and the resulting sympathy for the husband who craves marital warmth is apparent in A. Chakovsky's "Days of Peace," *Zvezda*, no. 9 (1947). The husband just demobilized reacts to his wife's militant, stepped-up demands: "I hope you don't think that I don't understand postwar tasks. You may rest assured that even during the war I knew perfectly well that there will be no respite and that there cannot be any. All this is elementary. But I am speaking of something else. I am speaking of life on the very brink which you preach and which you practice. . . . You need some sort of superwork . . . which takes away all one's life without remnants." Later, he pleads with her: "Let's be grateful for what we have. In the past they would have said, don't invite the wrath of God. . . . Don't you remember those without a family, without shelter? Don't you remember those who have lost their happiness in the struggle for the happiness of all? But we, we have found our happiness. Isn't this enough?" This to her is *uspokoennost'*, retreat, weakness. Enraged, she replies: "It's not enough, do you understand, it's not enough! What you are talking about is happiness, but it is small, dried up, as if it were in a can. I always wanted something bigger . . . and I want you to get cured of your disease, of your sleepy life!"

the old social forms, the fictional woman was permitted, while she was acting in her renaissance, to hold a very colorful place in the epic of the revolution. The attractive luster of the motif, however, derives from a dark background. Social injustice, from Herzen's *Who is to Blame?* to Ostrovsky's *Storm,* provided it in the nineteenth century. The spasms of 1905, the bloodshed of the revolution, the Civil War and the Second World War maintained it periodically in the twentieth.

With the stability of the new social order, fiction was assigned the more relaxed task of merely demonstrating the social position attained by the woman. The dynamics of the thrust came to a standstill and much of the romanticism faded. Feminine *tsel'nost'* in a significant portion of current fiction is interpreted as no longer to be used for further competition with the man but in the more traditional direction of strengthening the family which had indeed suffered from these liberties.

There now emerges a tendency to de-emphasize woman's emancipation. This is one pattern in postwar difficulties. Since the marital conflict is frequently determined by larger social issues, it has become one sounding board for the system's current self-examination. In the Stalinist era, the woman won the moral victory in a happy ending. At the present time the finale is less standardized.[47]

Marital themes[48] are abundant and the domestic genre scenes are quite unrosy. The problem of postwar adjustment was added to the older tension in the family — lack of time for personal life.[49] Promiscuity, tabooed during the long period of "conflictlessness," has come to the fore.[50] Though remilitarized critics rave and rant against the new pessimistic tendencies, the topic of defective morality looms large and perilous. With a note of nonideological compassion, a poet speaks to a seduced girl:

[47] For every literary motif which seems to significantly reflect the pattern of evolving interpersonal relations, there are various counterpatterns. Although the number complicates readings of Soviet life, it also testifies to the veracity of each pattern; more patterns, more truth, as it were. It could be easily demonstrated that literary motifs, problems, and solutions multiply in periods of relaxation. The task, therefore, should be the tracing of continuity in each pattern.

[48] *ZAGS-ovskaia tematika:* a derogatory term used by purist critics who rather would have remained at the lathe or in the MTS.

[49] One might say that classical examples of the drama of neglected wives are represented in V. Panova's *Kruzhilikha,* where Listopad, a truly full-blooded managerial tycoon, has no time so much as to take notice of his childbride's suicidal despondency; in A. Koptiaeva's *Ivan Ivanovich,* where an even more admirable but similarly overworked surgeon is divorced by his wife in retaliation for his neglect to assist her spiritual and political growth; in V. Dobrovol'sky's *Zhenia Maslova,* where the marital conflict of a harrassed husband and frustrated wife is played out in a veritable hatred.

[50] O. Djigurda's "Steamship Kakhetiia," *Znamia,* no. 1 (1945), having produced a great deal of discussion, remains one of the most honest documents on the loosening of the moral fiber under the impact of war. In his long family novel *Zhurbiny* (1952), V. Kochetov, in a prethaw mood, drew the first full-length portrait of a promiscuous villain. For interesting variations of that type in officers' uniforms, see L. Zaitsev and G. Skul'sky, *In a Distant Harbor* (1954) and V. Komissarov, *The Lieutenant of the Guards* (1955).

> . . . once you were longing for tenderness
> Trusting that it will last forever.
> No one is given the power to judge you,
> You lonely one.[51]

And the seducer? He is common enough to be encountered in another poem:

> May he always be successful,
> The diligent family head.
> He never disobeys orders,
> He is a pleasant colleague,
> An honest man without doubt.[52]

To compensate for the damages inflicted by the middle-class Casanova on family stability, the new balance in feminine virtue is shifting emphasis from advancements in the public sphere toward family preservation. The man is not always the transgressor, however. The pattern featuring the woman's exaggerated self-assertion reveals the other major danger to marriage.

In the public as in the private setting, complications of correct behavior are still wearisome because the demands continue to be paradoxical. Although the major responsibility for the family falls on the woman and the value of a strong family is self-evident, woman's fulfillment in domesticity is still frowned upon by the system.[53] In the lower classes, it is an economic impossibility to be only a housewife. The upper-class housewife is excluded from the lofty literary sphere and is only occasionally material for satire. Thus, the positive woman must work with dedication. She must constantly grow. Recent growth has become a most complicated process. She must be able to be the equal of the man in competence, efficiency, and self-sacrifice to collective goals. But even the best, if married — and a spinster is not eligible for the positve role — must be conscious of the superiority of the man. He is *primus inter pares,* no matter what his limitations.[54]

The new deference to the man, however, may under no circumstances arrest the competition between husband and wife for ascent toward never-attainable perfection. The mature woman carries the greater responsibility

---

[51] N. Grigorieva "Lonely Person," as quoted in *Posev* (July 28, 1957).

[52] E. Kotliar, "Once," as quoted by V. Zhuravlev, *Izvestiia* (September 3, 1957).

[53] A woman who does not work serves food to her husband:

> You don't seem at all a khoziaika,
> Like a waitress you stand before him.
> You are not glad of his compliments,
> A bitter smile is your reply . . .

A. Romanov, "Housewife," *Stikhi 1955 goda* (Moscow, 1956), 218.

[54] The proud and successful lady engineer in Panova's novel expresses her *tsel'nost'* by accepting her mate's superiority. She knows that he "will sacrifice nothing for love. He will make no concessions. . . . It will be only she who will sacrifice, concede, acquiesce, and wait." (Moscow, 1950, 228.)

for a successful marriage in the following somewhat preternatural way. She must never fall prey to complacency. She is obliged to improve herself constantly and to strive for heights of achievement and status. But — not too much. Margarita Aliger gave a subtle account of difficulties intrinsic in the "new" Russian marriage. The poem, based on experience, not on theory, suggests softly and persuasively the difficulty in the woman's role of defending her rights:

> My gay freedom almost
> Succumbed under your weight.
> I was almost forced to kneel.

But submitting in the end, rights or no rights, she assumes the role of an auxiliary to the man: "when you decide to carry his destiny not as a burden of the cross . . . when you decide . . . to answer for everything, then, call yourself a wife." [55]

The woman's success must not threaten the male ego. She saved the economy of the country during the war. However, her armor had to be laid down when the man returned. She did not always have to give up her status-gratifying job, but her attitude had to become more humble.[56] In this double posture, she spurns him on should he show a trace of indolence. He must do the same for her. But here, the woman more than the man must know where to stop. The woman must keep deciding between occupational drives and sacrifices for the sake of mellowing marital strains. In regard to marriage, she must remain a paragon of purity. She must show stoicism in the face of the man's unfaithfulness and compensate for his transgressions. For her, the difficult decision is between forgiving the erring husband or casting him out. If she sins herself, she must confess. All these are manifestations of her traditional *tsel'nost'*.

Recently, contradictory notes of new harshness and of new warmth

[55] M. Aliger, "Your Victory," *Znamia*, no. 11 (1946), 23.

[56] In a kolkhoz novel, of which there could be none more typical, the heroine, a simple peasant woman, ascends by trial and error to highest social usefulness during the war. When her equally positive husband returns, she is the kolkhoz chairman, and one above reproach since she combines adequately authoritarianism and humility. But she fails to recognize the destructive frustration of jealousy with which her husband reacts to her ascent. She is his boss. The marital conflict develops to a point where the *raikomsek* intervenes: "you don't understand your Semion. . . . You have lived all your life with him but you failed to understand him. He has a soul, a big soul. He and you are a pair. And just any kind of work should suffice him?" G. Medynsky, *Mar'ia* (Moscow, 1950), 278. The clash between the theory of sex equality and the practice of sharp status differentiation is particularly painful in rural life. It is enhanced by driving women. One of them, competent and driving, permits success to go to her head and so destroys her marriage. From a milkmaid, she rises to kolkhoz chairmanship and is elected deputy to the Supereme Soviet. Her veteran husband, thus handicapped in his career, remains a brigadier. With best intentions he warns her that she might have bitten off too much. She replies: "Don't have fears on my account. And don't throw shadow on my sunshine. Your hour will come and you will rise some day — But I haven't fallen yet, Katia — said Malakhov sternly." S. Voronin, "Unnecessary Fame," *Neva*, no. 5 (1955), 23.

toward human problems have become more frequent. Empathy has replaced dogma in the literary treatment of the hard lot of the working woman. As already illustrated, she might run in terror from her husband's retaliation for a wartime blue-eyed "foundling." But she returns to her door, mute, pale, strong — always strong. Another young mother broke her back in war work, gave her children the black bread of survival, saved the family. During the hard and lonely years she once did not withstand the need for masculine tenderness. She was not ashamed for what had happened, but her chastity makes her tell everything to her returning veteran husband. Though no saint himself in regard to marital faithfulness, he leaves this family of everyman in an outburst of brutality.[57] And here is a soldier's wife, an unskilled laborer with hardly four years of grammar school. She is a beautiful woman, warm and strong, efficient and modest, the type in whom Nekrasov saw a queen. She is the "other woman" whom a wounded evacuated soldier loves. Absorbed in his happiness, he is shocked by the sudden message that her husband is asking if she will take him back now that he had become a war amputee. Taking the way of self-sacrifice, she forces her lover's departure.

It's impossible, impossible. Your children are waiting, the fifth year they are waiting for you. And my man is coming without an arm. Where should I put him? And where should I put my conscience? We must act like human beings.[58]

They meet once more. On a visit to his region, she sends for him. In contrast to the man this woman's strength is not narrow and repressive. For her morality is turned to fully living the predestined. The brief reunion is anguished. She is nursing her infant, and the man is gripped with jealousy. But she is calm with her neat flaxen braid adorning her head:

There is nothing we can do. It's hard, but we will get over it. You look well, suntanned, healthy. And yours, how are they?
All right.
My man, he is a watchman now. He got used to the job. He is in our plant. At the entrance gate. Everything little by little takes shape.[59]

The last words are said — as they must be — by a woman. She is not particularly "new." But she characterizes a newer pattern in the portrayal of personal life where the place of the driving revolutionary woman is now questioned. Her commitment to the family is apolitical. The man would not have returned. Whether this illustrates a quantitatively demonstrable difference in reaction to stress between men and women or whether this difference holds for any society is less important than the

[57] A moving short story by the late A. Platonov, "Ivanov's Family," *Novyi mir*, no. 10–11 (1946).
[58] V. Panova, "Clear Shore" (Moscow, 1950), 78.
[59] "Clear Shore," 189.

meaning of an old literary tradition, out of which this woman's family supportiveness was born. The role of preserving has been assigned to the woman long ago and seems, in the long run, to be more binding than any "new" posture. "Everything little by little takes shape" in the postwar family. The hopeful outcome rests with the resiliency of such a woman.

As stated, the strong character of the Russian woman has brought the current marital conflict into sharp focus. The marital conflict, beyond its importance in revealing larger problems of Soviet life, is a reminder that Russian literature insists on the lack of unity between heroines and heroes.[60] The antimony between the many-sidedness of women and the one-sidedness of men was the primary theme of this essay. If there is any connection between the literary image of the woman and reality, her qualities might have a bearing on the stability of the Soviet system as a diffused, resilient, supportive force.

VI

The prevalence of strong women over strong men in a hundred years of literature is not a statistical fact. Each fictional character carries the author's imprint. Some life patterns of the great writers, however, seemed to work against the illumination of masculine heroism.[61] One's attention must not be focused on the possible personal reasons why a Turgenev or a Goncharov was disinclined or unable to create a truly heroic male character but rather on the fact that, given this incapacity, the result in their readings of life had so much in common. The intranovel connection between the escapists and the meek — between Aleko and Pechorin or between Rudin, Oblomov, and Myshkin — exists. Fiction, the meeting place of the personal and societal, determines that the individuality of the protagonists be as real as that which connects their consecutive generational characteristics.

Similarly, the motif of the strong woman *is* a reality, just as much as a trend, unifying discrete manifestations, can be real. If, again, existential accidents happened to contribute to it, so did the sources of culture.[62] This hypothetical base must be distinguished from a historical continuity. Fiction of social concern was inclined to paint a dark picture

[60] Unlike, for instance, the characterological homogeneity of Greek heroes or heroines or those of French classicism.

[61] Gogol's self-conscious bachelordom; Lermontov's early death permitting no possible alternative to Pechorin's bristling, youthful "negative" romanticism; Turgenev's traumatic encounter with tryannical women, his mother and Viardot; Goncharov's own Oblomovism; Dostoevsky's attachment to demoniacal Suslova; and so on.

[62] Among them the feminine fertility of the idea of *pochennichestvo;* the kenotic recension of Christianity out of which Dostoevsky's saved were born (Zossima, Aliosha, Myshkin) and, perhaps, also Oblomov, Karataev, Kutuzov; the idealization of the ecumenical spirit, mirrored and narrowed in the fervor for the family which was matriarchal in spirit, if not in form; the poetic need itself to express nationalism in feminine symbols.

of contemporary society, much darker than might have been realistically warranted. The black tone was added by the intelligentsia's need to be tormented. The emancipation of the suffering woman, one force directed against the prevailing listlessness, was strengthened by the traditional idealization of the feminine principle. The strong woman became activized and historical. She is so now.

In the post-Stalin period, marked by the system's complex rationalizations, the literary elaboration upon the achievements of the new woman continues. But answers as to her function and aspirations begin to vary considerably. There emerges the realization that the final goal is not displacement of the man. Thus, the emancipation of the woman and its problems is still a dramtic theme in Soviet society, particularly in regard to the peasant class. It is no accident — and not only because agriculture is the least solved problem — that the peasant novel is more voluminous than the urban, and more lively. In it, social change is best portrayed in the motif of the forever "growing" woman.

An attempt was made here to discuss not so much the continuity of this motif as the Russian version of the idea of strength imbedded in it. The famous Russian "oneness," the highest value, even if largely incommunicable, is stubbornly placed in the hands of the idealized woman. What is it? A defeatingly eclectic notion, it seems to be above all a resourceful, patient, resilient stability. It is also a revulsion against introspection, self-consciousness, skepticism. Therefore, it is immediate relatedness and responsibility to the family and the people.

As a matter for future examination, it may be suggested that literature, seen as a whole, seems to interpret the development of modern Russia through the interplay of three national types: the Radical;[63] the Passive;[64] and the third type, somewhat overlooked because of the tempting antinomy between the first two, the one which Fedotov has so aptly called the Builder. It is of significance that the literary tradition places the heroic woman on his side.

Perhaps one facet of social stability might be seen in the relationship of these three literary types today. Rakhmetovism, the goal-directed political force, "masculine" and "Western" in meaning, presses down on the by-products of "Eastern" Oblomovism. The latter, as we tried to point out, is not so much a dialectical opposite to the ideal of strength but one of its corollaries: enormous and, in Western eyes, absurd patience. But the third force, that of the Builder, makes the system viable. It supports

[63] Alesha Popovich, Sten'ka Razin, Bazarov, Rakhmetov, the Possessed and their Bolshevik procreation.

[64] Immovable Ilia Muromez; sleepy Kutuzov; Karataev whose life "had no meaning as a separate life"; Zossima who knew "particularly that you cannot be a judge of any one"; Myshkin who lost his mind through compassion; Oblomov who accepts the world but only if protected by the strongest Russian armor, his sheltering *khalat;* the internal Soviet emigration.

the relationship of opposites as it represents a compensatory ability to adjust; it is that facet of the Russian character which is resilient, soothing, cushioning. This force has been transcribed best in the feminine character.

YOUTH ORGANIZATIONS AND THE ADJUSTMENT OF SOVIET ADOLESCENTS

ALLEN KASSOF

I

Almost from its very inception the Soviet regime has sought to influence the adjustment of new generations to adult life. For the first time a modern state attempted to establish direct, centralized control over this complex and subtle process. The Soviet youth organizations — the Komsomol and the Pioneers — were assigned a key place in this effort. Today, their program for youth reflects some of the continuing problems involved in the rapid transformation of Russian society into an industrial order, and suggests how that transformation is creating new dilemmas in the Soviet system.

The general problem of adolescent adjustment in Soviet society is not fundamentally different from that found in other societies which are undergoing or have undergone industrialization. The twin processes of urbanization and industrialization have entailed the breakdown of traditional communal arrangements for training and placing the young. Though the family retained many of its original functions in infant socialization, new and specialized institutions were required in connection with the training of older children for adult roles in a bureaucratic system with its minute division of labor, novel human relationships, and rapid social change.[1]

If some of the issues faced by Russian society are thus common ones, the Soviet regime's response to them has been extraordinary. Rather than permit an unguided development of the requisite institutional changes, the Soviet leaders were determined to employ their own blueprint. An organized frontal attack was launched, which involved the creation of an official youth program unparalled in scope and vigor. This is to be explained in part by the high priority which the regime assigns to rigid control over the system's human resources. In addition, the very rapidity

[1] For a general discussion of the integration of new generations in various types of societies, see S. N. Eisenstadt, *From Generation to Generation, Age Groups and Social Structure* (Glencoe, 1956).

of industrialization beginning with the First Five Year Plan required that the rising generations be imbued with those attitudes which would make them not only willing but eager and able to assume the burdens and hardships of forced economic growth and the expansion of Soviet power.

The official line now proclaimed by Soviet psychologists and pedagogues, as well as by party spokesmen, is that the creation of a "classless" society has solved all problems of youth adjustment.[2] Evidence to the contrary is ascribed to "survivals of capitalism" in the psychology of backward elements among the population. The Soviet youth, we are told, grows up in an environment so benign, so free from conflict, so charged with high idealism, that becoming an adjusted, happy adult (who behaves in line with the official values) is automatic and inevitable. The very insistence with which such claims are made is perhaps reason enough to question their accuracy, and in fact the actual functioning of the youth program indicates that Soviet officials place little stock in their own assertions. Far from relying on spontaneous and individual patterns of adjustment, the Soviet system subjects adolescents to a program of intensive and organized influences, calculated to produce the "right" kinds of adults — the New Men of the Soviet era.

How does the regime, through its youth organizations, pursue these ambitious goals? Is there any way of gauging its success? For the present, any evaluation of the program must be highly tentative because of the lack of extensive source materials and Soviet reluctance to publicize any but positive reports about the youth organizations. Nevertheless, a good general picture of the Soviet attempt to control the adjustment of new generations can be drawn from available information.

II

The role of the youth organizations in political indoctrination and in providing fresh reserves of the faithful for service in the party is well known and needs no elaboration here.[3] Less familiar, although in many respects even more important, are the intended functions of these organizations in the over-all preparation of Soviet youth for adult life. Once viewed as elite groups of politically active youth, they have become mass organizations. By 1957, the Komsomol had 18.5 million members.[4] In 1953, Pioneer membership reached 18 million,[5] and no doubt the figure will rise in the future. Only a few years after the war, the claim could be made that "by now, it is difficult to find a school without a

[2] Cf. T. P. Simson, *Detskaia nervnost', ee preduprezhdenie i lechenie* (Moscow, 1949), 3; N. D. Levitov, *Psikhologiia starshego shkol'nika* (Moscow, 1955), 4.

[3] Cf. Merle Fainsod, *How Russia is Ruled* (Cambridge, Mass., 1953), ch. 9.

[4] *Komsomol'skaia pravda* (July 25, 1957), 1.

[5] *Bol'shaia sovetskaia entsiklopediia* (2nd ed.; Moscow, 1955), XXXIII, 55.

Pioneer unit of some kind." [6] Indeed, recent proposals that problems of apathy in the Komsomol should be attacked by returning to an earlier policy of restricting membership to the "most active elements" met with a sharp rebuke from Komsomol authorities, who insisted that the youth movement must ever expand its influence and that large reductions in membership would be inconsistent with the fundamental purposes of the program.[7]

Exercising an absolute monopoly over organized youth activities in the Soviet Union, the Komsomol and Pioneers even influence many young people who are not officially enrolled in the groups. The extracurricular life of the schools consists either of Komsomol-Pioneer activities as such, or it is under the control of these organizations. This is also true of such important nonschool activities as summer camps, which operate under Komsomol supervision.

The age spread of the youth organizations is wide. The Octobrists, a junior division of the Pioneers, includes members from seven through nine years of age, while Pioneer membership begins at ten and continues through fourteen. The Komsomol accepts members from fifteen through twenty-seven. A child joining the the youth organizations as soon as he is eligible can be a member for twenty-one years, not counting those venerable youths (many of them, paid officials in the Komsomol apparatus) who maintain membership well beyond the usual age limits. Since this chapter is concerned with adolescents, the focus is on the intermediate age range — from the beginning of Pioneer membership to the final year of Komsomol affiliation in the ten-year school at about age seventeen or eighteen. While this grouping includes preadolescents as well as adolescents, the continuity of the program in which they are involved makes it convenient to consider them together.[8]

If these are formative and impressionable years by our standards, they are more so by the conventions of Soviet psychology. Unlike certain psychological theories currently popular in the West, which emphasize the critical importance of the preschool years in basic personality formation, the Soviet youth program rests on the assumption that fundamental developments in personality can be brought about at a much later age.[9] The sixteen-year-old *Komsomolets*, for example, is considered to be virtually raw material in spite of what may already have taken place in his life. Provided that he is subjected to "correct" influences that are suf-

[6] *Pionerskaia organizatsiia imeni V. I. Lenina, posobie dlia pedagogicheskikh uchilishch* (Moscow, 1950), 9.

[7] *Komsomol'skaia pravda* (March 21, 1957), 2.

[8] The Soviet definition of adolescent is narrower than ours, usually referring to children from eleven to fourteen years of age.

[9] Raymond A. Bauer, *The New Man in Soviet Psychology* (Cambridge, Mass., 1952), 150.

ficiently intensive and consistent, he is still regarded as an appropriate
target for Soviet personality training. Such a conception enhances the
importance which is assigned to the youth organizations. Their official
role is not simply one of providing approved spare-time activities for
Soviet youngsters, but of profoundly influencing their psychological functioning and, accordingly, their adjustment to Soviet society.

III

Another chapter in this volume discusses those qualities of character
which the Soviet regime wants its youth to possess (Ralph T. Fisher, Jr.,
"The Soviet Model of the Ideal Youth"). There is thus no need to catalogue all of the official virtues. Rather, I have chosen for more detailed
examination certain aspects of the Komsomol-Pioneer program which
receive the main emphasis in the youth-organization literature itself and
which will illustrate the basic patterns of adjustment which the organizations are trying to foster.[10]

Political loyalty. The demand for political loyalty is perhaps most
familiar to us and need be mentioned only briefly. Every Soviet child
is expected to learn to identify the interests of party and state as his own,
and to maintain this positive orientation throughout his adult life. The
entire paraphernalia of totalitarian persuasion, from the patriotic songs
of the Pioneers to Communist Party hagiology, is thrown into action in the
youth organizations. Pavlik Morozov, the child-hero of the 1930's who
won notoriety by denouncing his father to the authorities as an enemy
of the people, still retains his place in the official hall of fame side by
side with other model young citizens in whose lives the call of the party
took precedence over all else. The drumfire of slogans, the neat and
inevitable interpretations of Soviet history, the glowing prospects for a
future of plenty, the dogma of the superiority of all that is Soviet Russian,
all continue unabated. And necessarily so, from the point of view of the
regime. The arrival of each new generation renews the endless task of
closing the ranks. As the revolution, with its binding mystique and motive
elan recedes further and further into the past, the regime seeks through
its torrent of words and images to instill in youth so strong a faith in the

---

[10] Materials on the youth organizations are scattered in a large number of sources,
many of them too superficial to be useful in research. The following description of
the Komsomol-Pioneer program is based on a number of the more informative volumes
available: P. N. Shimbirev and I. T. Ogorodnikov, *Pedagogika, uchebnik dlia
pedagogicheskikh institutov* (Moscow, 1954); I. Davydov, *O bodrykh i vynoslivikh:
iz zapisok nachal'nika pionerskogo lageria* (Moscow, 1955); V. G. Iakovlev, *Izuchenie
pionerskoi raboty v shkole* (Moscow, 1956); *Vozhatye o svoei rabote* (Moscow,
1956); and the following volumes issued by Akademiia Pedagogicheskikh Nauk
RSFSR, Moscow, Institut Teorii i Istorii Pedagogiki: V. G. Iakovlev and V. S. Aransky,
Ob oluchshenii pionerskoi raboty v shkole (1955); *Klassnye rukovoditeli o svoei
rabote s pionerami i komsomol'tsami, sbornik statei* (1955); *Zveno iunikh pionerov*
(1956).

present system and its leaders that an awareness of alternatives shall be screened out.

Work and productivity. The demands for political loyalty are rivaled, and in some respects surpassed, by the emphasis on work and productivity. If historical circumstances have deprived Russia of the presumed influences of the Protestant Ethic, the Soviets are determined to create a substitute, complete with the moral overtones:

For us, work is one of the highest moral qualities and values. We should shape the active member of the collective of toilers, and only the person who is a laboring person, who makes the goal of his life labor for the good of the motherland, can be such a member.[11]

As soon as he becomes a Pioneer, the Soviet child is involved in a program aimed at teaching him the sacredness of work and respect for its products. At meetings of his Pioneer unit, he hears stories about the production heroes of the Soviet economy: the Stakhanovites and pace setters, the rationalizers and innovators of industry and agriculture. Trips are arranged to farms and factories so that Pioneers may witness the "glorious toil" in which they will soon be engaged. Outstanding workers visit their meetings to imbue them with enthusiasm for the workaday world, and to tell them that they must emulate and surpass the outstanding achievements of present-day heroes.

Pioneers are supposed to learn that no task — no matter how mean or personally unrewarding — is beneath the dignity of Soviet man. The only standard to be applied is whether the effort makes a positive contribution to the general cause. The basis of the happy Soviet life, Pioneers are told, is to produce to the limit of one's capacities — and even beyond them if the party demands it. True, the life of plenty will come someday, but only after long effort and sacrifice by all. The real Soviet man is concerned with production, not with consumption. Not to produce, or to be motivated by self-gain, is evidence of hostile, un-Soviet attitudes.

A key element in the Soviet program is the belief that children best learn to value the importance of work by working themselves, beginning at the earliest practical age. Parents of young children are reminded to give them household chores to accustom them to work. In the Pioneers, members are supposed to develop appropriate attitudes by participation in group work activities. For the youngest members, the projects may be no more demanding than a regular responsibility to help the teacher clean and maintain the classroom. But as they grow older, Pioneers are pushed more and more into tasks of greater responsibility until, for the older members, an entire school unit may be assigned to a collective farm for summer work.

The work projects are not simply suggestions. Pioneer handbooks

[11] Shimbirev and Ogorodnikov, 252.

prescribe a routine system of checking to see whether members have properly completed their tasks. Adult leaders (usually older Komsomol members assigned by the local organization) initiate the assignments and oversee their fulfillment. For Pioneers who refuse to carry out their assignments or who are otherwise uncooperative, elaborate "corrective" measures are indicated.

The work program is taken quite seriously by youth-organization workers, to judge from their past record. They have more than once been criticized for being so zealous in putting the Pioneers to work that insufficient time and energy were left for routine school tasks. One result of this eagerness is that most Pioneer activities have been administratively subordinated to the schools in order to promote a more balanced program. Nevertheless, work projects continue as a fundamental part of the Pioneer program. In fact, it is intended that Pioneer membership should enhance the quality of schoolwork, for the admonition to the Pioneer that he must study seriously and intensively is part of the work-program approach.

In addition to developing positive attitudes toward work as such, the Pioneer is expected to participate in one or more specialized clubs or circles which are established to promote interest in gaining skills and habits essential to high-level performance in the adult occupational world. These circles reflect a wide range of industrial and agricultural occupations and include, for example, groups of young naturalists, aviation enthusiasts, physicists, radio builders, electricians, tractor "specialists," automobile repairmen, and mathematicians.

The basic activity of the circles consists of practical work — the construction of models and apparatuses, the study and operation of machines. The [adult] director must demand from members . . . accurate fulfillment of their assignments, careful treatment of instruments, and the economical use of materials. It is essential that young technologists be taught this from the earliest days of their work. In testing out models which they have built, Pioneers experiment with them and try to perfect them. Thus they develop their first habits of rational work.[12]

When Pioneers graduate into the Komsomol the work indoctrination program continues much along the lines described above. The requirements are of course more rigorous and the activities more demanding, but the goals are the same.

In carrying out this program in the youth organizations, the regime hopes to create personal qualities which will be congruent with what it conceives to be the needs of a rapidly growing industrial society and the well-known "tempo" of Soviet life:

[12] *Pionerskaia organizatsiia imeni V. I. Lenina* . . . , 106. A detailed description of this aspect of the Pioneer program is given in Akademiia Pedagogicheskikh Nauk RSFSR, Moscow, Institut Teorii i Istorii Pedagogiki, *Rabota pionerskoi druzhiny v sviazi s zadachami politekhnicheskogo obucheniia* (1954).

In the process of labor itself [Pioneers] develop strength, endurance, patience, assiduousness, practical work abilities, skills, and able hands.

In the process of labor they learn to plan and to utilize time economically, to work rationally and in an organized fashion. They learn persistence and pertinacity in overcoming difficulties which may come up; to strive for the highest possible quality in their work; to be as productive as possible. . . . Work itself serves as the best means to indoctrinate a love of work, to prevent and overcome inertia, passiveness, and laziness.[13]

The collectivization of interpersonal relationships. Another major theme in the youth program has to do with the promotion of officially condoned patterns of informal relationships. Of fundamental importance here is the doctrine of the collective, which holds that acceptable adjustment to Soviet society can be achieved only through participation in a certain kind of group life. In its broadest meaning, a collective is any group of persons bound together by a common occupation or activity — for example, workers in the same shop, or schoolmates. But a mere aggregation of such individuals does not constitute a collective — the opinions of the group must become vitally important to each of its members and in all essential matters the group must act in concert. An individual is properly "collectivized" when he is willing to subordinate his personal desires and wishes to the interests and decisions of the group.

Komsomol and Pioneer units serve as prototypes of the collective for adolescents, in the hope that they will carry through to adult life the patterns learned there. Self-striving and "egoistic" tendencies (classified as survivals of capitalism and inappropriate in a socialist society) are supposed to be replaced by an eagerness to make personal sacrifices for the collective and, through it, for the larger society.

Active participation in the collective is a major criterion of normalcy and social adjustment. "Nervous" children, it is asserted, may be products of insufficient participation in the collective.[14] The prescribed cure is for parents, teachers, and youth-organization leaders to push such children into group activities — much in the manner recommended by some of our own group-oriented practitioners.

The collective is not identical with informal friendship, but has its origins there:

During the younger school age [from about seven to twelve] the social interests of children begin to take form. . . . The children dream of entering the Pioneers. Friendship and comradeship are spread and strengthened. All this creates new grounds [through] . . . the formation of the collective for the social-political and moral development of the children.[15]

The youth collective is regarded as an effective instrument in training only when its persuasive force is properly guided by adult leaders. This

---

[13] *Pionerskaia organizatsiia imeni V. I. Lenina* . . . , 90.
[14] Simson, 37.
[15] Shimbirev and Ogorodnikov, 50.

involves the mobilization of group opinion against recalcitrant members through the powerful sanction of shame.[16] The shaming technique is of particular significance, for in some measure it reveals the reasons behind Soviet emphasis on the youth collective. A Pioneer who finds himself in difficulty — because of poor schoolwork, refusal to carry out a work assignment, lack of adequate participation in the collective, or general uncooperativeness — is first approached by a number of his comrades (at the urging of a teacher or Pioneer leader, if necessary) in the *zveno*. (The *zveno* is the smallest Pioneer unit, consisting of from five to ten members, and is the group in which most Pioneer activities are carried on.) If he fails to respond to their urgings, his case is then brought up before the *otriad*, the next higher membership unit, with some thirty to forty members. Here, his misbehavior is discussed at an open meeting, with the offender present. His faults are recounted, and suggestions made of how he can amend his behavior and atone to the group. If he still fails to respond to the satisfaction of his fellows, the next resort is to the *druzhina*, which includes all the Pioneers in a school, where a similar public discussion takes place. If none of these measures succeeds, the Pioneer can be expelled from the organization, a step which officially brands him as unworthy of the friendship of his peers.

This routine can be combined with other shaming techniques, typically in the form of publicly posted notices in the Pioneer wall newspaper ridiculing the offender. Visitors to Soviet classrooms have reported examples of this practice, complete with imitations of *Krokodil*'s satirical art work accusing one or another Pioneer of offenses ranging from un-Soviet attitudes to inappropriate garb.

A current example of how the regime relies on the collective as a means of control is seen in the Komsomol militia brigades. Members of Komsomol cells are assigned to assist the militia in suppressing youthful rowdyism and hooliganism.[17] When an offender is apprehended, provided his offense is not serious enough to result in immediate arrest, members of the patrol contact an officer in his Komsomol unit and request that its members "rehabilitate" their comrade by discussing his behavior with him informally or at a group meeting. Or, if the subject is not a *Komsomolets*, the suggestion is made to the Komsomol cell at his school or place of employment that the local *aktiv* take him in hand and mobilize public opinion against his antisocial behavior.

Since a strongly internalized psychological susceptibility to social sanctions is one of the most important means of social control in any society, it is not surprising that the youth organizations, by stressing the

[16] For a recent discussion of shame, see Helen Merrell Lynd, *On Shame and the Search for Identity* (New York, 1958).

[17] Cf. *Zaria vostoka* (January 17, 1957), 4; *Trud* (December 12, 1955), 3; *Literaturnaia gazeta* (June 19, 1954), 2.

collective, are trying to implant this pattern among Soviet youth. If they succeed, the regime will have a lever of control over adult behavior far more effective than any type of open coercion. And the device of channeling informal relationships into a quasi-formal collective provides a ready-made context in which to exercise this control. It discourages the development of informal group solidarity and "familiness," while turning natural internal group pressures toward conformity to the service of the state.

IV

These illustrations of how the youth organizations operate suggest how little concerned they are with the personal adjustment of adolescents — in the sense of regard for their individual well-being as an ultimate goal. The inner emotional life of the adolescent is almost never mentioned and, when it is, it is treated primarily as an adjunct to preparation for successful role performance in the adult occupational world. The emotions are regarded as unavoidable evils which distract young people from more important matters and which must be pushed into the background if they cannot be harnessed in the form of joy and enthusiasm for job and system. The Soviet approach toward adolescent adjustment, then, is characterized by an almost total instrumentality.

This is related to more general characteristics of the Soviet system as a totalitarian, industrial society. The need in such a system for political loyalty, for reliable techniques of social control, and for a labor force composed of individuals with the appropriate virtues (punctuality, persistence, efficiency, and the like) are obvious. But there remains the question of why the regime chooses to rely on a program of "planned adjustment" to achieve these ends.

Certainly one major reason is the nature of the characterological resources which the Bolsheviks have inherited from traditional Russian society. The modal personality among Great Russians has been described by Dicks as notably lacking the "whole complex connected with the acquisition and husbanding of property; methodical orderliness, neatness, punctuality and regularity of procedure, habit and protocol." [18] This observation is generally supported by the clinical findings of the Harvard Project on the Soviet Social System concerning the "nonstriving quality of the Russian" and his "dependence and noninstrumentality." [19] The extreme emphasis on work indoctrination in the youth organizations can thus be interpreted as a reaction of the regime to the unsatisfactory state of the human materials with which it has had to work in its industrializa-

[18] Henry V. Dicks, "Observations on Contemporary Russian Behavior," *Human Relations*, V (1952), 140.
[19] Raymond Bauer, Alex Inkeles, and Clyde Kluckhohn, *How the Soviet System Works* (Cambridge, Mass., 1956), 142.

tion drive. And because of the great speed with which industrialization is taking place, the Soviet leadership has been unwilling to wait for basic characterological changes to come about spontaneously. Just as it created a social and economic revolution from above, so too it attempts to create a psychological revolution.

Similar considerations lie behind the great stress on the collective and the shaming devices. The strong needs of typical Russians for "intensive face-to-face relationships" and the fact they are "unthreatened by mutual dependence . . . in the peer group" [20] suggests that the regime is working in receptive soil when it promotes the collective as a major context of social control. But this advantage is considerably reduced or canceled out by the fact that "the Russian is little shamed by . . . performance failures. . . . Thus the Soviet Russian might be expected to be fairly immune to the pressure of shame which the regime imposes on him." [21]

These are examples of the profound discontinuities between certain traditional patterns and the regime's adjustment ideals — discontinuities which the youth program is supposed to erase by its intensive campaign among the adolescents of each new generation.

v

The extent and variety of the measures designed to control adolescent development are impressive. What can be said of the results of this program?

If the question is the very general one of whether Soviet adolescents "adjust" to their society, then the answer of course must be in the affirmative. Here I refer not to the dimension of personal adjustment (the individual's achievement of emotionally satisfying or psychologically adequate accommodation to his social world) but to the effective integration of new generations into an ongoing system. In spite of stresses and strains, Soviet society "works." And it is generally stable, which means that one generation succeeds another in ways which do no great violence to the system.

But this is also a matter of degree. For while adjustment patterns may be adequate from this point of view, it does not necessarily follow that they have taken the lines so assiduously fostered by the regime. In this respect, there is evidence that the youth program is not altogether successful, any more than are our own freer institutional arrangements.

Absolute success of the youth program would consist in so complete an internalization by the population of the official values that Soviet citizens would behave as the regime wants them to without the need for external coercion and would socialize their young in the same manner.

[20] Bauer, Inkeles, and Kluckhohn, 135.
[21] Bauer, Inkeles, and Kluckhohn, 140.

In such hypothetical circumstances, there would no longer be any reason for a youth program. This state of perfect integration is, of course, impossible in the Soviet Union or in any complex society. Nevertheless, one important sign that the youth organizations were achieving some of their goals would be a significant slacking off of emphasis in the areas discussed above and a corresponding transfer of attention to more pressing fronts. In fact, the opposite is the case. An extensive survey of youth-organization literature reveals that each aspect of the program has received redoubled attention in recent years. That so bold an effort should not have had more favorable results demands an explanation.

Surely this is testimony to the holding power of the traditional national character which (from the point of view of the regime) continues to act as a brake on the total transformation of the society. The failure or abandonment of earlier efforts to smash the family left intact the major transmission agency of cultural values and, consequently, a powerful link with the past with which the youth organizations must compete. Yet if the youth program is defeated in the long run, it will not be because of the prerevolutionary heritage — which time itself is bound to erode — but because of the functioning of the Soviet system.

Lack of effectiveness in the youth program can be traced in part to the youth organizations themselves. In broadening their membership coverage, the elan and enthusiasm of what were formerly elite groups have largely disappeared, to be replaced by widespread manifestations of apathy and boredom. Combined with the extensive bureaucratization of youth-organization operations, the effect has been to stifle interest to the point where, for many members, participation at meetings and other group activities is a chore to be avoided. Instead of capitalizing on local interests, organizations frequently use prepared programs from central sources. For many officials, the fulfillment of arbitrary plans (hours of lectures, units of reading in Marxism-Leninism, quotas of membership to be reached, and the like) takes precedence over all else, and the original goal of producing New Men is lost in the routine tasks of running an office headquarters.

Complaints about this situation have become standard in the repertory of youth organization publications, and occupy the attention of higher authorities. At a recent Komsomol congress it was charged that

in many Komsomol organizations work is conducted in an uninteresting way, in a trite manner, and fails to satisfy youth. . . . Some members have lost interest in the organization and lost their attachment to the Komsomol.

There are harmful bureaucratic procedures in the Komsomol. The energies of Komsomol workers and of the *aktivs* are directed not towards concrete, living tasks, or to improving work with members of the Komsomol and [non-Komsomol] youth, but to putting out numerous directives and resolutions, making inquiries and accounts . . . [preparing] papers which no one needs, and holding numerous sessions and conventions. Such a situation . . . gives rise to red tape, confusion, and irresponsibility.[22]

Even if these organizational difficulties were to be overcome — for reasons which I cannot discuss within the scope of this essay, such a development is most unlikely — the youth program would still be faced with far more serious obstacles. This is most clearly shown in the partial failure of work indoctrination.

The booming industrial society of the Soviet Union has created a reward system which is ultimately incompatible with the socialist goal — so fundamental a part of the youth program — of joy in work. While adolescents are told that all work is honorable, the greater advantages (in both social prestige and material terms) associated with skilled and professional occupations seems to impress them more decisively than the official lessons of the youth organizations. This is reflected in the continuing campaign against youthful *bezdel'niki*, or idlers.[23]

The behavior of the *bezdel'niki* is the very antithesis of what the regime hopes to achieve through work indoctrination. In its extreme manifestations, this behavior is displayed by the *stiliag*, an urban type who considers a life of leisure the only worthwhile existence. The *stiliag*'s total rejection of the Soviet ideal of work and production involves, significantly, the adoption of what he conceives to be the leisure symbols of the West: extravagant clothing, the cocktail, jazz records, and even American slang. He scorns the thought of hard work, most of all manual labor, and holds in contempt those who are "taken in" by the "joys" of the workaday world. The Soviet press describes one type:

If he is Boris, he calls himself Bob, and if he is Ivan, he calls himself John. He lives off his parents and "burns" his money in restaurants. Sometimes he is registered as a student but he "despises" cramming and crammers and therefore does not study. He "adores" everything foreign and is ready to give his right arm for a fashionable [phonograph] record.[24]

Another *stiliag*

began working, but the work turned out to be "uninteresting" and his co-workers were "crude" people who lacked "understanding" and "sensitivity." He sent in his resignation. Nobody tried to stop him. Insulted, he returned to the bosom of his family, and . . . [rested] a year or so.[25]

Distasteful to the regime as a symbol of un-Soviet attitudes, of course, the *stiliag* is not typical of the younger generation. But less extreme

[22] *Rezoliutsii i dokumenty XII s"ezda VLKSM* (Moscow, 1954).

[23] A more detailed account of this development is given in the author's "Youth vs. the Regime: Conflict in Values," *Problems of Communism*, VI (May–June 1957), 15–23.

[24] *Komsomol'skaia pravda* (August 11, 1956), 2.

[25] *Komsomol'skaia pravda*, 2.

manifestations of this type are by no means unusual. From various areas of the Soviet Union have come reports that many graduates of the ten-year schools refuse to take ordinary employment upon being turned down for admission to a university.[26] A related phenomenon is the refusal of some university students to accept positions in rural areas where their skills are badly needed but where hardships are great and the amenities of urban life lacking. The situation has prompted the establishment of a new priority system for admission to higher education, favoring those who have proved their worth by spending several years in "productive labor" between graduation from the secondary school and request for admission to university or institute.

The present dilemma stems largely from the gap between ideology and reality — a gap which tends to erode belief among citizens of all ages, but perhaps nowhere so critically as among adolescents. Many of them leave school with high ideals, only to find them at variance with the reward system of the adult world. It may be that such phenomena as the behavior of the *stiliagi* are products of this disillusionment. If so, then the Soviet regime is doing itself a disservice by stressing work indoctrination.

The influence of family attitudes must also be taken into account. Soviet attacks on the *bezdel'niki* have included bitter remarks about parents who tell their children that hard work is beneath their dignity.[27] The director of one summer camp even complained of parental inter-ference in the work program, and reported that prolonged attempts were necessary to convince some mothers that their children would suffer no physical or mental harm from washing floors.[28] Such orientations seem to be most prevalent among privileged strata of the society. Successful individuals, who have been rewarded for their presumed contributions to the Soviet system, may now be socializing their offspring in ways which are fundamentally incongruent with the regime's needs in its continuing program of rapid industrialization.

VI

Whatever failings there may be in the youth program, they have not caused the regime to retreat from its conviction that adjustment patterns can be created from above, or prompted any basic modifica-tions in the Komsomol-Pioneer approach. Instead, steps have been taken to intensify and extend the existing program. Of particular significance

[26] *Izvestiia* (July 1, 1956), 1; *Pravda Ukrainy* (January 23, 1956), 4; *Kazakh-stanskaia pravda* (December 20, 1956), 2; *Bakinskii rabochii* (October 24, 1956), 1; *Sovetskaia Litva* (November 14, 1956), 2; *Sovetskaia Estoniia* (September 25, 1956), 2.

[27] *Komsomol'skaia pravda* (August 15, 1956), 2.

[28] N. P. Zubritsky, *Nash pionerskii lager'* (Moscow, 1956), 7.

was the recent decision to re-establish the Octobrists for children younger than Pioneer age.[29] The Octobrists quietly dropped out of the youth-organization picture before World War II, and almost two decades passed before provisions were once more made for this age group. The revival of this unit suggests that the Soviets see a need to begin working with children at a younger age if the over-all program is to be improved.

A related measure, seemingly intended to reduce the influence of the family, is the intention to establish *shkoly internaty*, or boarding schools, where pupils will live away from home most of the year, and where the youth organizations will be able to work more intensively and with a minimum of outside interference.[30] As the schools are established, priority will be given to the "most impressionable" age groups.[31] Whether such ameliorative measures will bring the youth organizations closer to a realization of their goals remains to be seen.

The elusive nature of planned social change, the danger of unintended consequences of such planning, and the tenaciousness of some pre-Soviet patterns are demonstrated once again in the youth program. At the same time, it would be naive to suggest that there have not been fundamental changes in adjustment patterns as a result of Soviet rule. If nothing else, the society to which Soviet adolescents must adjust has itself undergone vast changes. But the question remains of how effectively this — as other types of social planning — can be created from above. The present Soviet rulers, perhaps less sanguine than their early predecessors about the ease with which new generations can be molded to fit the blueprint of a new social order, are nevertheless determined to continue the effort.

CHANGING ATTITUDES OF RUSSIAN YOUTH

KLAUS MEHNERT

A study of the changing attitudes of Russian youth during the century since 1861 is most conveniently divided into two periods, one before and one after the Bolshevik revolution. Of these two I know the first only by hearsay (from my parents, born in Russia like myself but German subjects, and from their relatives and friends) or from the study of printed materials, such as the numerous memoirs of that time. Only of the second, the Bolshevik phase, do I possess personal knowledge.

[29] *Pravda* (November 30, 1957), 2.
[30] *Uchitel'skaia gazeta* (June 27, 1956), 2.
[31] *Pravda* (June 28, 1956), 2.

I

Let me begin by mentioning twelve groups of youth which one might analyze for this period and by explaining why only one of them will be examined in detail.

1. *Peasants*. Among the young people who lived in Russia after the reform of 1861, the great majority were the children of peasants. On the whole the Russian village at that time, under the impact of the mir tradition and the reform, was rather homogeneous, at least as far as Russia proper was concerned (the *Sibiriak* was different, even more so the agrarian population in the non-Slavic areas): hungry for more land, poor, living in "darkness," influenced by the church and many sects, loyal to their little father, the tsar, and rather suspicious of all plans directed toward their salvation coming from nonpeasants. Although the theme of endless discussions by other social classes and the topic of many literary works, the peasantry as a whole was less understood than misunderstood, the object of all kinds of myths. In itself it was as yet voiceless. The disintegration of the mir caused many young peasants to leave the villages, partly to swell the ranks of the young labor class, partly to roam the country as vagabonds or to form the *Lumpenproletariat* lacking professional training and firm occupation and made known to the world by Maxim Gorky's novels. It was only after the turn of the century that the peasant youth made themselves felt politically: by their reactions to the Russian-Japanese War and to the revolutionary movement of 1905. Both events, closely linked, shook the young peasant generation into some activity which expressed itself by mutinies in the armed forces and by disorders in the villages directed against the landed nobility. These in turn contributed to the agrarian reforms of Stolypin, which led to a new development in the country, too short to change the course of events. Although on the eve of the First World War there existed in the empire 97,838 schools with 6,159,376 pupils,[1] the illiteracy of the village was still overwhelming; this also contributed to the relative inactivity of the peasant population in political affairs.

2. *Nobility*. The sons and daughters of the noble class stood at the other end of the social system. Although in their early youth they frequently grew up in the village side by side with the peasants' children, they later quickly developed in a different direction and met their former playmates only as their lords and masters. Their education was taken care of mainly by special schools in St. Petersburg or by the army. Part of the landed gentry was impoverished by the reform. Their children sought their livelihood in other professions, frequently dissatisfied and nostalgic,

[1] Otto Hoetzsch, *Russland: Eine Einführung auf Grund seiner Geschichte vom Japanischen bis zum Weltkrieg* (Berlin, 1917), 269.

some even revolutionary. Yet on the whole the young nobility formed the backbone of the regime.

3. *Officer corps.* Needless to say, the groups enumerated here overlap to some extent; in particular this is true with respect to the nobility, the officer corps, and the officialdom. During the nineteenth century the officer corps drew its members mainly from the nobility; yet it formed within the noble class a caste of its own, which was partly patterned from early youth by the cadet schools. In general officers kept consciously aloof from politics, considering it below their dignity, and were content to serve loyally their imperial lord. Most of them spent their lives in dull little garrisons with very little intellectual stimulation and mainly artificial excitements. Those at the court, members of the guard regiments, moved in a special circle and were absorbed by the life of the capital. Autocracy and orthodoxy were the two poles around which the officers moved. The situation changed when youth of other social groups entered the officer corps, in particular after the army reforms which followed the disastrous defeats in the war against Japan. The difference between "the line" and "the guards" was now felt more keenly, entry into the guard regiments being mainly reserved to young noblemen, with a good deal of frustration developing among the officers of the line.

4. *Officialdom.* The members of this group ranked from the top men in ministries down to the thwarted little officials in the provinces who were so brilliantly described by the masterful pens of Gogol and Chekhov. They came from very different social strata and had not much in common except for one thing, which, however, was quite important for their mental makeup: they all served the tsar. Their children differed socially and in their attitudes as did they themselves.

5. *Bourgeoisie.* During the first decade or two after the reform, Russia still lacked a bourgeoisie comparable to that of contemporary Western Europe, for it consisted — apart from officials — mainly of tradesmen, some very wealthy indeed, described for example by Ostrovsky and Gorky, and of artisans, who were on the whole a poor lot. There was as yet no rising class of industrialists. It was only toward the end of the century that a Western type of bourgeoisie began to emerge and, in fact, to grow very rapidly. Yet the power of the state and its functionaries was so great that the Russian entrepreneur and his associates did not develop the same spirit of free enterprise as did their Western colleagues. This was felt also among their children. On the whole they were more likely than others to turn to industrial and technical professions, skirting political preoccupations. Being linked rather closely with the most rapidly advancing branch of economic life in Russia, and absorbed by the fascinating task of developing a vast and potentially rich country, they were less inclined than others to spend their time in philosophical or

political discussions. They were also less tortured by the feeling of "uselessness," so characteristic of many young Russians of the upper classes during the decades prior to the revolution. Dissatisfaction within the ranks of the bourgeoisie was more likely to be found among its lower strata, among the *meshchanstvo,* the small tradesmen and artisans, whose youth contributed a good deal to the various revolutionary movements.

6. *Workers.* The young generation of the class which was to play — at least for some years — a most important role in the development of the country was little known and little noticed in the beginning; the class as such was at first very small. Even after the rise of modern industries in Russia, the young workers did not become conspicuous; they were part of their class, sharing its troubles and problems without developing a youth movement of their own. Perhaps one might be reminded of the fact that in Germany too the youth movement in the early years of this century was an accomplishment more of the bourgeoisie than of the proletarian youth.

7. *Priesthood.* A group by themselves were the children of the numerous priests, the *popovichi.* Very many of them spent part of their youth in special seminaries preparing for their fathers' calling. These institutions were among the least enlightened of all Russia, and since many of the priests' sons were above average in intelligence, they were hurt and embittered by the low intellectual standard of their schooling. The most famous of the seminarists (no *popovich* himself), who broke with everything the seminaries stood for, was Joseph Dzhugashvili. But among the revolutionaries there were many more who came from a similar background and who fell from one extreme, backward orthodoxy, into the other, revolution.

The next four groups are somewhat different from those already mentioned since they are not determined primarily by their social standing.

8. *Old Believers.* In Russian intellectual history the schism within the church, which led to the departure of the Old Believers from the church's main body, is an event of considerable consequence. The spiritual opposition of this part of the population to the official church and to the powers by which the church was backed created a curious mentality among the youth of its followers. This may be traced in the story of Herzen's relationship to the Old Believers, in A. Tolstoy's The Road to Calvary (1922), and in the personality and fate of a man like the poet Essenin.

9. *Poles.* Among the numerous nationalities in the Russian Empire, the most active, apart from the Jews, were the Poles. With the exception of those who had made their peace with the Russians, they detested Russian rule and never abandoned hope of liberation. Those of their young generation who were revolutionary-minded were so for different

reasons than were the young Russians, but they too were against the existing regime. Hence there were many cross-connections between them and the Russian radicals.

10. *Jews.* Separated from the masses of the Slavic population by the segregation policy of the Tsarist government as well as by their religion, traditions, and history, and concentrated mainly in the western provinces of the empire, the Jews of Russia were forced to lead a life of their own. They were ever conscious of these elements of their segregation, meeting countless obstacles to their physical and intellectual movement, dissatisfied with the glaring discrepancy between their abilities and aspirations, on the one side, and their chances of advancement, on the other. The most active among their intellectual young people joined the professions of medicine and law — or revolutionary circles. There is a good deal of literary testimony concerning the situation of young Jews in prerevolutionary Russia; perhaps the best known are *The Case of Sergeant Grischa* (1927) by Arnold Zweig, one of the earlier books by Ilya Ehrenburg, *The Stormy Life of Rozik Roitschwanz* (1928), and of course Trotsky's *My Life* (1930).

11. *Foreigners.* The foreign communities in Russia, mainly Germans, British, and French, formed an active element in the economic and scientific, but not in the political, life of the country. (By Germans I mean here not the German farmer settlers along the Volga and in the Ukraine or the Baltic Germans, but the descendants of those Germans who, like my own ancestors, had moved from Germany proper to the cities of Russia.) Most of them had come as artisans, others as tradesmen, scientists, and professional people; many had risen quickly with the young capitalistic system. They were eager to give their children a good education, largely in schools of their own; in 1910 there were in Russia 2,987 foreign schools — mainly German — with 169,229 pupils.[2] They were also anxious to keep their children out of politics, which they willingly left to the Russians. They wanted to be law-abiding inhabitants of Russia (many were also loyal subjects of the tsar), and it was in this spirit that they brought up their young generation. On the whole they were well-to-do, even rich, and their children felt neither oppressed nor limited. Yet the spirit of the time affected them too. My mother, for example, after herself finishing a German school in Moscow, opened there classes for needy Russian children under the influence of sentiments prevalent among her Russian friends. There were of course also radical exceptions; the most famous was young Nikolai Ernestovich Baumann, who was killed during the revolution of 1905. One of the suburbs of Moscow is still named after him, as is one of its higher technical schools.

These eleven groups are not being treated in detail for three reasons. First, a brief essay demands concentration on the chief problems. Second,

[2] Hoetzsch, 267.

there is a distinct lack of research regarding the attitudes of the youth of most of these groups. To be sure, young people of all these categories may be found in the pages of many of Russia's famous literary works, but, although these books are enjoyable and valuable if looked at from the point of view of *belles lettres*, they are not systematic and comprehensive enough to be a source for the historian or sociologist. Finally, the young people of these eleven groups remained on the whole politically irrelevant, being objects rather than subjects of the development — with the exception of those who entered, in one way or another, the last group now to be examined.

12. *Intelligentsia*. This much-discussed section of prerevolutionary Russian youth was to become the breeding ground of almost all the effective political ideas of the period. It was also something of a melting pot, absorbing the sons of all other previously mentioned groups, in turn radiating its influence back into these groups and gradually filling, as it were, the place of a "third estate" left vacant in Russian society up to that time. The spearheads of this group were the students, whom Miliukov called "the barometer of society." [3]

One of the characteristics of the Russian intelligentsia was the fact that, by belonging to it, people from lower social levels were able to rise. This was otherwise a most difficult undertaking in the still rather solidly stratified social system of imperial Russia. By way of the intelligentsia even the descendants of serfs could make their way upward on the social ladder. With the exception of the sons of the upper classes, the students had to work — and starve — their way through the university; among the poorest of them were the *popovichi*. The student who earned his living by giving lessons to the lazy children of a wealthy merchant became a standard feature of Russian literature. But the regime did not like this increasing social mobility; they frowned upon the newcomers and their eagerness to enter into affairs of state. This without doubt contributed to the rapid radicalization of the young intelligentsia, to its lack of sympathy with the realities of political and social life. Many of the young people, who had taken privations upon themselves to obtain a higher education, were thus estranged from the state and its head.

It would be wrong to speak only of sons; there were also many daughters in the intelligentsia. Girls formed a majority among the pupils of the gymnasiums, which in European Russia enrolled 204,610 girls and 84,954 boys in 1910.[4] They also studied in large numbers in teachers' colleges, and there were established, toward the close of the period under discussion, special courses for women. These were in the quality of their teaching not behind the universities, and from them came the well-known *kursistki*.

[3] P. N. Miliukov, *Vospominaniia* (New York, 1955), I, 162.
[4] Hoetzsch, 267.

One source of friction between students and government was the discrepancy between the relatively liberal rules issued for the universities in 1863 in the spirit of the reform and the increasingly reactionary policy of the government. At the time when the rules were promulgated, they threatened no great risk to the state. The young intellectuals were in the great majority of the passive type to be found in Turgenev's *Rudin* (1856) and *On the Eve* (1860). In the latter it is only the foreigner, a Bulgarian, who really knows what he wants, thereby astonishing and fascinating his Russian friends with their habitual lack of decision. Furthermore, the reform had produced much rejoicing among those who had worked for it; some time had to elapse before a new generation grew up which took the reform for granted and demanded to go beyond it. But at first even these, such as Bazarov in Turgenev's *Fathers and Sons* (1862), confined their radicalism mainly to the intellectual field. The new rules for the universities issued by Delianov in 1884 attempted to confine access to higher education to children of "respectable" families.

Nor was the church held in any great esteem among the forward-looking circles of the young generation. In their eyes the church was far too obedient a servant of the state. They considered its priests ridiculous, old-fashioned, dirty, and uneducated, and its higher clergy sinister collaborators of the regime. To quote Stepun: "The intelligentsia in the provinces believed in the temple of science with the same passion with which it hated the church." [5]

The attitudes of the students were also influenced by their opportunities for a career. The profession which was most in need of new blood was that of teaching, both in state and private schools. But the reactionary government demanded not simply teachers but teachers who were politically reliable; the *blagonadezhnost'* of the candidate became an important item. This created resentment against the teaching profession among the most active and gifted of the young generation; among the teachers described in the memoirs of that time there appear many ridiculous, corrupt, or hopeless and resigned people. Still worse was the situation in the elementary schools, which had to fall back frequently on uneducated priests or discharged army sergeants. Young people who went into teaching were thus generally cynics, idealists, or people who did not care and had resigned themselves to the existing conditions.

There was a greater attraction to the study of science, particularly to medicine. Students in these disciplines were known as especially radical. Science came closest to the materialist outlook which was to be found increasingly among the rebellious youth; furthermore, the physicians could look forward to a profession of service to the people to which many of

[5] Fedor Stepun, *Vergangenes und Unvergängliches* (3 vols.; München, 1947–1950), I, 268.

them aspired. The most reliable students — from the point of view of the government — were the law students, who had to assume that their further career was likely to be in the government service.

But whatever branch of knowledge the students might pursue, they were all exceedingly interested in intellectual life in general. This interest was promoted by the fact that in Russia at that time politics and criticism of social conditions were closely linked with literature. In the arts, all modern and modernistic schools of the West had their disciples in Russia.

By the close of the century the intelligentsia had been drawn closer to the political groups which had sprung up at that time; almost all of them were hostile to the existing social and administrative conditions. At first the radical groups had only small bands, almost sects, of followers, and their terrorist acts received attention quite out of proportion with the size of the organizations behind them. Gradually their influence among youth grew stronger. In their "hard core" there was a surprisingly large number of young women. The *Narodniki*, the *Tolstovtsy*, the Anarchists, and finally the Marxists had the largest following, with the revolutionaries gradually gaining the upper hand over the less well-organized liberal reformers (as shown by Dostoevsky in his sinister and prophetic novel *The Possessed*, 1871). The dreadful famine in large parts of the country in 1891–1892 greatly accentuated the political activity among the young intelligentsia; their demonstrations grew larger and better organized, the student strikes more bitter; studies took a second place.

However, it would be wrong to overlook those sections of intellectual youth which entered neither the ranks of the revolutionaries nor of the liberals. There existed groups of stout monarchists, and the various wars in the Balkans helped to arouse dynastic feeling and nationalism, including that of the Pan-Slavic variety. Also there were many who devoted themselves to less romantic and exciting exploits than politics and instead turned soberly toward the economic development of the country. The efficient and self-confident young engineer, geographer, or surveyor is not as infrequent in the Russia of Nicholas II as one might conclude from his modest role in political or literary works. It was particularly toward the new areas of the empire, the south and east, the vast spaces of Tsarist Asia, that these people turned. It is true that there were among them exploiters of the "Tashkent" type, immortalized by Saltykov, but there were also many others who were captivated by the tremendous economic and industrial opportunities which the Russia of Witte offered. The dynamics of construction, so impressively developed and utilized by the Bolsheviks, had their roots in imperial Russia. Industrialization had started with a pace that is often forgotten under the impact of the far more publicized industrialization of the five-year plans. Devotion to the industrial development of the country, which motivated its pioneers, may explain the relative ease with which so many of them turned into willing assistants of Bolshevik reconstruction.

In addition to pioneering, one other field appealed to those young people who were eager to do something for their country without fighting for the overthrow of its regime — in other words, for those who did not despair in their hope for evolution and who believed in the chances of a new reform. These were the many charitable institutions, committees, and organizations which had sprung up since the famine of 1891–1892 and which were to be found almost everywhere after the revolution of 1905–1906. It is true that the government did not look with favor upon them, yet it had to tolerate them and found itself increasingly forced to rely on their cooperation, particularly during the First World War. Much of the endeavor of these groups was directed toward education, believed to be a cure for many ills. Stepun justly says in his memoirs: "The unlimited urge toward education in the youth of Russia awoke toward the close of the nineteenth century and continued up to the outbreak of the war." [6] In fact, this urge had existed much earlier, but it was only now that it affected large numbers of people. There were many touching examples for the belief in the magic power of education and in the limitless ability of man to learn. Friends of mine tell the story of a student, a peasant's son, who lodged with them. His slogan was that the human being can learn whatever he sets his mind to. He drove them crazy by insisting on learning by himself to play the violin for which he obviously possessed no talent whatsoever, only unbounded energy.

Through the many forms of popular education developed during the last two or three decades of the tsars, a growing number of petty-bourgeois youths entered into the intellectual and political life of the country. By no means were all of these drawn into radicalism; many found practical careers for themselves. A colorful picture of their life is painted in Gorky's *The Artamonov Business* (1925). Later, in the days of the Civil War, many of these people were to be found — side by side with the sons of the nobility and the upper bourgeoisie — in the ranks of the Whites.

Gradually the zemstvos, granted in 1864, were to become the centers of most endeavors in the field of education and self-administration. They grew into cradles of democracy, attracting many young people. Their work in the provinces showed many hopeful signs which were absent in the overheated atmosphere of St. Petersburg and Moscow. Unfortunately for it, the regime lacked the ability to absorb these forces, or perhaps one should say it lacked the time to do so. When the war started, it was too late.

The First World War had a tremendous impact on the young generation in many ways: mobilization; patriotism; upsurge of monarchistic

[6] Stepun, I, 307.

sentiments; big and catastrophic battles in East Prussia; long years of trench warfare; frustration and disappointment; realization of inefficiency, graft, and corruption; huge losses among the officers and men; both aversion and sympathy toward the news of revolutionary activities at home; privations; disgusting stories about the court; the slogans for peace and bread; influx of very young people into army units and factories; revolution in the spring of 1917, greeted with joy by the liberal youth and at the same time with dismay because its leaders insisted on continuing the war "to its victorious end"; the spectacular rise of the tiny but compact and vociferous minority of the Bolsheviks; the October Revolution; Brest Litovsk; demobilization; occupation of vast areas by the Germans; breakdown of almost all traditions and values; German revolution; civil war; Allied intervention — a huge story in itself, deeply affecting the younger generation with a desire to get out of the war, to get home, to get land. Youth was without a clear conception of how they would achieve what they wanted, and hence were increasingly willing to listen to the one man who insisted that he knew all the answers and who hammered out, day after day, slogans of impressive simplicity, impressive at least for the many who felt lost in the chaos and reached for the straw held out by Lenin. Before most of them realized what had happened, Lenin was firmly in the saddle.

II

In Soviet books about the country's development since 1917, the history of youth is generally treated as an inherent part of the history of the Komsomol. There is, for example, no section on youth to be found in the *Large Soviet Encyclopedia*, but there are, in its latest edition, seventeen pages on the Komsomol.[7] It is true that to some extent the history of youth and of Komsomol are identical, or at least parallel. Some of the ups and downs of the Komsomol since its official foundation in 1918 are connected with the ups and downs of the political attitudes of Soviet youth. But the parallelism of youth and Komsomol is surely one of the less important aspects of a study of the changing attitudes of the young people of the USSR, and it has been treated elsewhere.[8] There is not much to be gained by entering the problem through this particular opening. Nor would sociology be the proper entry, since "attitudes," with which this essay is concerned, is not primarily a sociological category.

What are the changing attitudes of Soviet youth? The answer to this question is most likely to be found, so it seems, by asking another: atti-

[7] "Vsesoiuznyi leninskii kommunisticheskii soiuz molodezhi," *Bol'shaia sovetskaia entsiklopediia* (2nd ed., Moscow, 1950–58), IX, 330–347.

[8] Klaus Mehnert, *Youth in Soviet Russia* (New York, 1933); Merle Fainsod, "Komsomols: A Study of Youth under Dictatorship," *American Political Science Review*, XLV (March 1951), 18–40.

tudes toward what? By "attitudes," of course, I mean the actual attitudes of youth, not the attitude which party and government try to impose on youth or claim youth to have. The analysis of the young generation's attitude toward a number of phenomena will be attempted: first, by using the fruits of Western research, among which the findings of the Harvard Project on the Soviet Social System merit special mention;[9] second, by taking into account Soviet publications, particularly novels and plays, so admirably analyzed by Gleb Struve;[10] and third, through personal observations, at least for the period 1929–1959 when I spent altogether five years on thirteen visits to the USSR.

School. During the years of revolution and civil war formal education came to a standstill. Nobody cared for it. "Closed! Off to the war!" was the most characteristic, if not the most frequent, signboard on schools. The young people felt as if they were standing on the threshold of the millennium. Who cares about school if a most fantastic paradise is just around the corner? There seemed to be too many more important things to be done, quite apart from the time consumed in search for food or fuel. There is a report of a foreigner who was told that the institutions of higher learning in Petrograd numbered 18,700 students; when he went there, he found only 400 actually taking classes while the rest were scattered all over Russia.[11] Those who stayed in the schools had to work on innumerable *subbotniki* or attend meetings and demonstrations.

The official policy of the men responsible for education coincided largely with this attitude of the young people. Lunacharsky, People's Commissar for Education of the RSFSR from 1917 to 1929, was, one might say without too much exaggeration, more a disciple of Dewey, Kerschensteiner, and even Tolstoy than of Karl Marx. He was in charge when many people actually believed that "the school must wither away." Lenin had said that one should arrange things so that any cook could rule the country; why not let any cook be a professor? The *rabfaki* (special schools for training workers for higher education) were to bring the young proletarians without much ado into the universities; the title of university or institute was most liberally bestowed on many an insignificant school.

Lenin was one of the first to realize that Soviet educators were living in a fool's paradise. He was not impressed by the pilgrimages which enthusiastic pedagogues from the West were then making to Russia. When, in October 1920, Lenin appeared at the Third Congress of the Komsomol, he demanded of youth, which thought about nothing but revolution and civil war, that it should study and study more. He said: "The old school

[9] Raymond A. Bauer, Alex Inkeles, and Clyde Kluckhohn, *How the Soviet System Works* (Cambridge, Mass., 1956).

[10] Gleb Struve, *Geschichte der Sowjetliteratur* (München, 1958), carries the story to 1957.

[11] Luigi Volpicelli, *Die sowjetische Schule* (Heidelberg, 1958), 52.

had its value and use and was the source of much important and practical knowledge; without mastering this, one cannot become a Communist."

But for years things remained unchanged. What school and university were like at that time, one can learn most readily from N. Ognev's famous *Diary of Kostia Riabtsev* (1926) and in Maiakovsky's brilliantly satirical *Bedbug* (1928). It was not by Lenin's insight that the system of Soviet education was changed, but rather by the demands of industrialization. The young people began to realize that, in order to succeed in the reconstruction of the country after the civil war and the NEP, they must obtain usable knowledge. When I visited Russia for the first time after the revolution, in the late summer of 1929, things were just beginning to change. During the three-week railway journey from Vladivostok to Moscow I traveled with a train full of students, some of whom have remained my friends to this day. In their discussions, which mirrored the shift from propaganda to study, one could sense the impending change of the system; a few weeks later the intellectual Lunacharsky was replaced by the general Bubnov. The job of the schools was now — and has remained ever since — to train the "cadres" which, Stalin taught, "decide everything." The demands by industry of *spetsy* of all kinds was almost unlimited, and what was needed were specialists with reliable knowledge. Hence the introduction of examinations, an unheard of thing in the days of Lunacharsky when examinations were considered a reactionary method of oppression and torture of the child's mind and when experiments were made with numerous types of nonformal education. In 1933 the first examinations were held after a gap of fifteen years. The excitement among youth was great. Some complained about the inhuman method, but the majority, it seemed, approved. When talking to a group of youngsters in Moscow at that time, one said to me, while the others nodded: "You know, these examinations are a most remarkable invention. They had an almost miraculous effect on us; ever since we knew that they were coming, we have all worked much harder and learned much more." Bubnov in his decree of April 28, 1933, praised examinations as an "instrument for training the architects of Socialism."

Correspondingly the esteem for teachers and professors increased. Discipline was reintroduced. The chaotic situation which developed when teachers feared the children and children did what they liked was condemned. The old *spetsy* lived through a period of re-evaluation. Symptomatic of this changed attitude was the role of the old engineer Sabelin in the play "The Chimes of the Kremlin" (1941) by the Communist author N. Pogodin; even Lenin bows before Sabelin's superior professional knowledge.

Since then the drive toward knowledge, diplomas, and "qualifications" has increased from year to year. There was perhaps some relapse during the Second World War, when the fighting man was much in demand, but even then the highly technical mode of warfare required the knowl-edgeable specialists. The sputnik rage undoubtedly has made science still more the fashion.

Labor. During the first years after the revolution — with the exception of the NEP, which produced conditions of its own — material incentives for stimulating labor were not much employed. They were contrary to the belief in equality, and they were considered unnecessary in a country where, one hoped, everybody would wish to work because "everything belonged to everybody." Wages were not actually differentiated and most of the time were close to the subsistence level. Instead people proved very ingenious in inventing all kinds of nonmaterial forms of stimulation, all based on Stalin's dictum that labor was a matter of honor.

Somehow the system worked in the beginning. But when, during the First Five Year Plan, large-scale construction moved into the foreground of the party's interest, much more was needed. A break was brought about by Stalin's speech of June 23, 1931, in which he proclaimed differentiation of wages instead of the hitherto existing "equalitarianism" (*uravni-lovka*).[12] In a way the about-face in the wage policy in 1931 can be compared to the introduction of the examinations just mentioned; also the reaction of the young generation, it seemed to me at that time, was similar. There were some, probably in the minority, who exclaimed with Trotsky: "revolution betrayed!" The majority accepted the change as reasonable and proceeded to make the best of it. During the following years the sys-tem of material incentives grew in all directions. It was not only the piece-rate wage which mattered; there were many other material privileges granted to those who worked better than others. The nonmaterial incen-tives were not disregarded, but they definitely took second place. The valuable analysis of the managerial mentality in Joseph S. Berliner's *Factory and Manager in the USSR*[13] shows this in detail in its chapters dealing with the premium system. Most young people took the use of material incentives for granted to such an extent that they saw nothing wrong when even the size of scholarships was made dependent on scho-lastic achievement.

From time to time I did encounter signs of dissatisfaction with the new class system, which was the inevitable result of extreme wage differentia-tion. But these were to be found either in some sensitive writer (for example, Sorin, author of *The Guests*[14]), in those who were at the base of the pyramid, or among the older generation. The young people felt that it depended on them whether they stayed at the bottom or rose to the top.

[12] J. V. Stalin, *Works* (13 vols.; Moscow, 1952–1955), XIII, 59–60.
[13] Joseph S. Berliner, *Factory and Manager in the USSR* (Cambridge, Mass., 1957).
[14] Klaus Mehnert, "An Moskaus literarischer Front," *Osteuropa*, IV (1954), 431–435.

To Westerners, who still believe that the Soviet state retains an urge toward equality, it comes as a surprise to realize that the existing and constantly widening disparity among the various social strata is not resented nearly as much as one would expect. On the whole, one can say, first, that the Soviet state has become a highly differentiated *Leistungsstaat,* almost without parallel in history and, second, that this is taken for granted by the younger generation. Wherever exceptions still exist (for example, in the cast of the special privileges granted to the *alte Kaempfer*), this is considered an anomaly, destined to disappear.

Coupled with material incentives there is the incentive, quite powerful in a certain group of the young generation, to do, with the help of science and technology, big things in a big and potentially extremely rich country. I have found that the spirit comparable to the American "Go West, young man" is more likely to be the stimulus of young people in Russia today than the desire to "Go Communist." However the "Go West" spirit should not be taken literally; in fact there is a strong reluctance to go *v provintsiiu.* The desire to stay in the larger cities is one of the most frequent topics encountered in recent Soviet literature.[15]

Inherent in the changed conception of labor is a changed attitude toward time. While the young Russians at the turn of the century were more or less unaware of the fact that there was such a thing as time, they have now become quite conscious of it. For this the Bolshevik training has been less responsible than the facts of life in an industrialized society with its piece-rate wages.

There exists a group in the young generation which feels differently about labor, time, and the urgency of work. This is the *jeunesse dorée* of the Soviet Union, the sons and daughters of the new upper class, in particular the *stiliagi* (from the word for style). However, it seems to me that the West is making too much of them; they are less representative of Soviet youth and less conspicuous than one might expect from the frequent attacks leveled against them in Soviet publications. But perhaps they are symptomatic of a general restlessness, such as was indicated by some reactions of Soviet youth to the events in Hungary and Poland.

After the revolution new roads were tried out. They were new in comparison with what had been the official policy prior to the revolution but not necessarily in comparison with attitudes existing within the intelligentsia and other sections of Russian youth during the last decades of the tsars. Later a reversal took place, a return to a more traditional attitude. This we have seen by examining the attitudes toward school and labor. Because almost exactly the same is true with regard to the attitudes toward the other phenomena still to be examined, the analysis of them can be briefer.

Social position. During the "revolutionary phase" of the postrevolu-

[15] Klaus Mehnert, "Sowjetbühne und Oberschicht," *Osteuropa,* VI (1956), 13f.

tionary period, the proletarian, with worker's cap and without collar or necktie, was the measure of all things. In the "conservative phase," which began in the middle 1930's, the hero to be emulated was the successful and efficient executive, scientist, or engineer with hat and Western clothes, preferably purchased during a *komandirovka* abroad (the *komandirovka* abroad in itself being a sure sign of success). A poll in Germany revealed some time ago that the most honored profession in the country was that of professor. In the Soviet Union there are no polls of any kind, nor are there likely to be any for a long time to come. If there were, however, they might reveal that in Russia also many young people would like nothing better than some day to be a professor — or an *akademik* with an apartment of his own, a dacha, a car, a driver, and a chambermaid. What the Germans call *Rangordnung*, a sense of rank, has clearly re-emerged in the Soviet Union, and it is not too different from that of other countries on a corresponding level of development. I have even heard people speaking about an absent superior in the third person plural; and in a recent Soviet film, "The Lesson of Life," a crying boy threatens his young adversary: "You wait, my daddy is chief engineer." [16]

Communism. The state of Communism seemed very near in the days of the revolution, when news of uprisings were pouring in from Austria, Hungary, and Germany. Gradually Communism moved into the distant future. How this change of attitude affected the daily lives of the young generation is shown very convincingly in a diary of one of the many youth communes, and in the revealing decision to disband them in 1932.[17] As time went by, youth was sobered and disillusioned. It turned from dreaming to the daily chores. The violence and injustice of the purge era added to the disappointment; the accused "deviators" had had many followers among the younger generation. More disillusionment came — affecting the hopes of millions of young people — when in 1940 tuition fees were introduced for the upper grades of high schools and for the institutions of higher learning. Some years ago, when, in a long talk with a young defector, I tried to discover the earliest origin of his hostility toward the regime, I found that it lay in his bitterness over that decree which had forced him to abandon his studies.

Of the various teachings of Marx and Lenin only one seems to have been fully accepted by the young people of the Soviet Union: Marx's theory on the predetermined course of history which supposedly makes inevitable the road of humanity from feudalism via capitalism and socialism to communism. This to most of them is as self-evident as two times two equaling four. By accepting Marx's doctrine of history they have, of course, also accepted other teachings of his, for example atheism and his view on ownership of the means of production. However, one of the

---

[16] Mehnert in *Osteuropa*, VI (1956), 18f.
[17] Mehnert, *Youth in Soviet Russia*, 163ff, 249ff.

most revealing experiences one can have in the USSR is to ask young people what they think Communism will be like. The answers are blank faces and rather helpless stammerings. They obviously have not given much thought to this question.

Patriotism. The official line of antinationalism was adhered to in the first phase after the revolution, when a strong wave of internationalism swept the younger generation in the wake of the disastrous First World War. But much of this was simply lip service to an official dogma, for even then the flame of the revolution and of the victories against the enemies was nourished at least in part by patriotism. In many a discussion I found also that people critical of, or even hostile to, the Bolshevik regime would rally to its support if a foreigner spoke ill of it. The change-over to patriotism by Stalin in the spring of 1934 was therefore readily accepted by the young generation. The curve of patriotism rose to its peak in the second half of the Second World War, much influenced by Hitler's criminal treatment of the population in the occupied areas. In postwar years, patriotism was decidedly overdone in the ridiculous claims that all important inventions had been made by Russians. The less sophisticated young people accepted these declarations, while others scoffed at them. It may well be that the sputnik success has swelled the ranks of those believing in innate Russian superiority.

The state. The withering away of the school and of the state (as well as of the family) — these were some of the ideas that were accepted in the first phase after the October victory. But gradually these things were discarded. Far from withering away, the state became stronger and stronger, first in fact and then also in theory, with Stalin as chief proponent of the strong state. The strong state — this meant a strong state machine. The more totalitarian the regime became, the bigger and the more powerful grew the state apparatus. The service in this apparatus became a most important profession, which buttressed itself with glittering uniforms and titles reminding the foreign observer of tsarist days. State authority became unchallengeable, except, of course, by the party.

In recent years a feeling has grown abroad that there exists an increasing opposition against the dictatorial state among Russian youth. From my observation, during four visits of altogether seven months since Stalin's death, I would venture to suggest that this assumption should not be overstressed. To be sure, there exists a strong urge among young Russians to enjoy a little more intellectual freedom, but one should not mistake this for a demand for democracy. In fact, among the wishes of young Russians the desire for a change of the state's structure is still far from the top of the list. If they are given — as they were during the last years — a reasonable measure of security from sudden and arbitrary arrest, they are likely to feel, for the time being, that they are quite well off. Probably more time will have to elapse before a drive for democracy in the Western sense will be felt in the Soviet Union. For the present, to use two terms from the predemocratic West, the change-over from absolutism to enlightened absolutism is much appreciated. I also felt that there exists an increased interest in questions of law as well as in the legal profession because, for the first time since the revolution, people feel that law makes some sense, that they are not helpless victims in the clutches of an autocracy which until recently did whatever it liked without regard to law. On the other hand, there was this remark by Khrushchev made in December to a visiting German lawyer: "We have too many lawyers in our country."

Family, elders, tradition. The withering away of the family was at first accepted by the revolutionary-minded young people as part and parcel of the great upheaval. Party and political organizations did their best to loosen family ties in order to wean away the young generation from the influence of its elders. But once the young people began to found their own families, the shoe was on the other foot. The forming of the youth communes and their dissolution is, in its simplicity, an almost classic statement of this change. Hence the young people did not find it difficult to accept the about-face in family legislation during the middle 1930's. There was one exception: at first many were opposed to the abolition of easy abortions, since they had become used to this way out. But after a few years that too was generally accepted as the right thing, even though in individual cases one might still try to circumvent the law.

A similar change occurred in the attitude toward the older generation. From being despised as useless relics of an ancient period, they become objects of sympathy and often admiration. Sometimes, in visiting Soviet schools, I found that an old woman teacher with grey hair and wrinkled face, but young eyes, was the object of general love, frequently mentioned when the children were asked about their favorite teachers. The *akademiki* with reputations from prerevolutionary days, whose pictures with white goatees and rimmed skullcaps are to be found on many a wall, are the object of reverence. In novels they frequently appear to solve seemingly insoluble scientific or human problems, almost like the party secretaries who inevitably perform these duties in Soviet literature.[18]

Traditions too are differently looked at now than in the earlier period. It was impossible to think in the days of Lunacharsky that Soviet schoolchildren would ever wear uniforms as the children of the bourgeoisie had done in the despised schools of the *ancien régime*. Yet today millions of children wear uniforms without ever giving it a second thought.

Religion. The young peoples' greater tolerance toward elders and history includes also a friendlier attitude toward the church (or mosque or synagogue). They are inclined to take it to be part of those quaint and

[18] Klaus Mehnert, *Der Sowjetmensch* (Stuttgart, 1958), 214ff.

not necessarily wicked, in some ways even charming, traditions of the old folks, which do not harm anybody even though there is not much sense in them. It may be that some day young Russians, who are now preoccupied completely with the problems of the physical world, will turn to the metaphysical one. Perhaps some have already done so, but I did not find much evidence of it, at least not among those who come from nonbelieving families.

Sex. Even people who know little about the Soviet Union know all about free love as it was practiced and propounded there in the first chaotic years, many believing that this is still so. But the days when Alexandra Kollontai wrote her *Ways of Love* (1927) have long disappeared. In her biography in the latest edition of the *Large Soviet Encyclopedia* she is described exclusively as a woman with a political and diplomatic career, and no space is devoted to her world-famous writings.[19] In this respect, too, Lenin was ahead of others. It was in a conversation with the German Communist Clara Zetkin that he attacked the "glass of water theory," which compared the performance of the sex act with the drinking of water by a thirsty person. One of the books read most widely by Soviet youth during the late twenties was *The First Girl* by Bogdanov, which showed the disastrous effects of promiscuous love. But even at a time when Soviet authors, under the whip of the five-year plans, were still writing their novels about love's being a stimulus to the tractorist's plan fulfillment, love in its eternal, nonindustrial form had returned to Soviet youth.

With the new family legislation the government threw all its weight on the side of orderliness in sex relations. In literature and public statements, sex was confined almost exclusively to marriage. An almost Victorian prudishness descended on the Soviet empire; the entire atmosphere was desexualized to an extent unimaginable in the West. Literature, plays, movies, television, art galleries, variety shows, magazines — never was anything included to cause sensual excitement. For the foreigner it is difficult to say to what extent young Russians have also become desexualized; he cannot speak of what goes on in the minds of the people he meets. He can only speak of what he sees and hears — or fails to hear. For example, one almost never hears off-color stories (although one does hear a great deal of swearing). German army physicians who came in contact with the Soviet civilian population during the war reported their surprise at the large number of virgins among the unmarried female population.

Again, it seems to me that the occasional stories of orgies among the gilded youth published in the Soviet press should not be overemphasized when one attempts to evaluate the present situation. There is some evidence that the moral situation is least stable in the villages; much of their

---

[19] *Bol'shaia sovetskaia entsiklopediia,* XXII, 12.

male population has been removed, and the women compete for the few remaining men. One can hear stories reminding the listener of Gerhard Hauptmann's fanciful novel *Die Insel der grossen Mutter*.

It may not be considered entirely appropriate to add a few words about alcohol at this point, but it hardly merits a section to itself. There is still a great deal of drunkeness among Russian youth, but it seems to be somewhat decreasing, at least in the ugly form of the desperate *zapoi* which still has its stronghold in the villages. The often mentioned *khuliganstvo* is, of course, usually linked with drinking.

The arts. There was a period when art was considered a silly bourgeois prejudice, acceptable only in the form of propaganda posters or rhymed instructions for the use of electrical motors. This was the time when everybody believed that a man could be a writer if only he made up his mind to be one. I was one of the few foreigners present on the occasion when an official change in attitude was proclaimed. In his speech delivered during the First Soviet Writers' Congress in Moscow in the autumn of 1934, Bukharin quoted in Latin: *Nascuntur poetae*. There was at first an astonished silence and after that a vigorous applause. In the same speech Bukharin praised the definitely antipropagandist poet Pasternak, whose *Doctor Zhivago* has since created a stir throughout the Western world.

One certainly cannot say that the young generation adheres to the slogan of art for art's sake. It accepts the thesis that literature is a social function. But time and again it has shown its dislike for rhymed or fictional propaganda and, in painting, its preference for the genre. Incidentally, interest in nonpropagandistic forms of art and literature is very great among Soviet youth, much greater, one is sorry to say, than among the youth of the West.

The West. As far as the attitude of Soviet youth toward the West is concerned, the rhythm of development differs somewhat from that shown in the above topics. Youth was not anti-Western even in the days of the war against the "interventionists." On the one hand, it believed the Russian revolution to be part of the world revolution and of the stream of Western thought. On the other hand, to many young Russians America was the ideal country of the contemporary world because it was today what Russia would be tomorrow. There was also — and still is — a great deal of respect for the Germans and their ability to work. Many young Russians all through the 1920's and 1930's felt like beginners or barbarians compared with the advanced countries of the West. Few of them believed in the stories of wicked misdeeds, allegedly performed or planned by the West against the welfare of the Russian people. The change came during the Second World War, which showed the German invaders to be as bad or worse than Soviet propaganda had previously painted them and which enormously increased the self-confidence of the younger generation of the USSR. The Communist victory in China added to this feeling. The former inferiority complex changed into overconfidence, stimulated violently by Stalin's and Zhdanov's propaganda.

It was only after Stalin's death that the official line toward the West became more tolerant. Young Russians no longer had to proclaim constantly that they despised the West. Sympathies toward the West, in particular toward Americans, whom they had found during the war to be a friendly, helpful, and big-hearted people, cropped up again. Some lucky ones were allowed to travel abroad. In addition there were many in the occupation forces outside the frontiers of the USSR. Quite a large number had a chance to see foreign books and magazines, and even "live foreigners" in large numbers during the youth festival in August 1957. Apparently Stalin's successors feel somewhat surer of their youth than Stalin did and must have thought that they could afford to allow them contacts with the West. Some foreign visitors at the festival were of the opinion that in this the Kremlin was wrong.

III

If one were to draw curves of the changing attitudes of Soviet youth toward the phenomena examined above, he would find that they are on the whole rather identical. All of them have their peak of newness and experimentation somewhere between the middle 1920's and the early 1930's, and all return after that to a more normal level — in some cases above, in some below, the level of the prerevolutionary period.

In comparing the swing of the pendulum during the pre- and the postrevolutionary periods, one is struck by some similarity in the years following the death of Nicholas I and that of Stalin. In both cases there were reforms, which did away with some of the worst abuses of the preceding regime, and then again a tightening up of the strings of power. Under the rule of Alexander III and Nicholas II this led to an increasingly bitter tension and finally to a life-and-death struggle between the regime and the people, particularly the young generation. Will there be a similar development in the coming years?

THE ORGANIZATION OF WELFARE SERVICES

BERNICE MADISON

Social welfare may be defined as the organized system of social services and institutions, designed to aid individuals and groups to attain satisfying standards of life and health. It aims at personal and social relationships which permit individuals the development of their full capacities and the promotion of their well-being in harmony with the needs of the community. Obviously, such services and institutions cover a wide range of activities, sometimes inextricably interrelated and almost always influencing each other profoundly in form, scope, and function.

This chapter, however, is limited primarily to income-maintenance programs, with only brief discussion of those services whose major objective is to facilitate normal growth in the individual — physical, emotional, and intellectual — toward maximum fulfillment. Poor relief, private charity, mutual aid, and social insurance are considered along with some mention of services to children, the handicapped and disabled, and those experiencing marital difficulties.

I

From 1864, when regulations controlling the zemstvos were promulgated, up to the October Revolution, three systems of economic assistance functioned in Russia: state poor relief, local poor relief, and private charity.[1]

Almost continuously throughout this period, responsibility for the administration of state poor relief was vested in the Ministry of Interior. Its jurisdiction did not extend, however, to assistance issued to members of religious orders, their welfare activities being within the jurisdiction of ecclesiastic authorities. The central government gave over-all direction to poor-relief work and enacted legislation. Where zemstvos and municipal governments had not yet developed, poor relief, exceedingly meager, was centrally administered, either by state agents or through state organs of poor relief (*prikazy*) in existence in each *guberniia* since 1775. In addition, the state created its own charitable institutions under special laws.

Among the latter, the most important were those in the Department of Institutions of the Empress Mariia Feodorovna, founded during the reign of Paul I (1796–1801). Enjoying the patronage of succeeding empresses, the department enlarged its administrative sphere from charitable institutions created directly by members of the royal family to those organized under private initiative and others supported entirely or in part by public funds. To secure increased voluntary support, the wife of Alexander III (1881–1894), devised the scheme of selling ranks (*chin*) to members of the bourgeoisie who wished to become noblemen. As payment, they made donations to charity. The top managerial body was named by the emperor,

---

[1] Special provision existed for veterans and their families. In addition to institutional care, the zemstvos issued to families of breadwinners called to active duty, "supplies in money and kind — amounting to not less than one pud and 28 pounds of flour, ten pounds of groats, and four pounds of salt per month." In 1912 legislation was passed making pensions available for disabled military personnel and for families of dead members of the armed forces. In calculating the amounts of pensions, sharp distinctions were made between officers, NCO's, and enlisted men.

and the head of the department held ministerial rank and a seat in the Council of State. The next in importance were the Imperial Philanthropic Society and the Workhouse Patronage. Both controlled numerous institutions. The former was especially interested in the incurably sick, orphans, children of poor parents, and those needy who had retained partial work ability; the latter concerned itself primarily with furnishing medical care, education, and sheltered work to destitute adults and children and with providing work relief in famine-stricken areas on an emergency basis. Finally, there were the parish patronages for the poor supported largely by public funds from local communities and by private charity.[2]

In 1864 the prikazy were disbanded and administration of local poor relief was taken over by the zemstvos. Their functions included the management of charitable funds and properties and the administration of philanthropic activities themselves. The latter encompassed orphanages and other types of children's institutions, hospitals, homes for the mentally ill, almshouses, workhouses, and correctional institutions — whether established under private auspices or by the zemstvos themselves.

Most of the money needed to carry on these activities came from the interest on capital turned over by the prikazy and from donations, the zemstvos being most reluctant to assign any of their own revenues for public-assistance purposes. The small sums that were allotted varied greatly between communities, from none at all in many of them to 11 per cent of the total budget in a few. Furthermore, the proportion of the budget spent for poor relief — consistently its smallest item — declined steadily, from 5.3 per cent in 1890 to 1.5 per cent in 1913.

The number of almshouses ranged from none in some provinces and districts to twenty-one in others. Actually, the circumstances determining whether or not an almshouse would be established in a given locality were largely fortuitous — availability of private gifts, for example. The almshouses were supposed to care for the destitute, without discriminating against applicants from the lower social classes. In fact, however, the latter were often excluded. As custodial institutions with inadequate facilities, almshouses became dumping grounds for every kind of person who could not be sent off to Siberia or be left to beg on the street: side by side with the old and crippled, there were children, nursing mothers, thieves, moral degenerates, and the infectiously diseased.

Child-caring institutions, although available in most zemstvos, were so insufficient that in rural areas abandoned and orphaned children were more or less left to themselves. In most of them the chronically ill, the handicapped, the epileptic, and the mentally deficient children were kept together with the normal, healthy ones. Orphans were maintained in insti-

[2] Major sources used were: Direction Generale de l'Économie Locale du Ministère de l'Interieur, *L'Assistance publique et privée en Russie* (St. Petersburg, 1906); and O. Imeretinska, *Blagotvoritel'naia Rossiia*, ed. P. E. Lykoshin (St. Petersburg, 1901).

tutions up to a certain age and then were distributed among peasant families paid by the zemstvos for their upkeep. Adoption, although practiced, was infrequent. In 1912 special correctional institutions for children existed in two zemstvos only.

Data for 1912 indicate that in that year forty provincial zemstvos spent more than 4.2 million rubles on various types of aid to the indigent. Although lack of information makes strict comparison impossible, this figure probably represents an expenditure at least five times as great as the amount spent for similar purposes by the prikazy — an increase that occurred over a period of sixty years which included forty-eight years of zemstvo activity. This fact seems to justify, to some extent at least, the claim that the zemstvo released local creative forces and gave new impetus to community effort on behalf of the needy and the helpless.

It may be more meaningful, however, to look at these developments in relation to the then-existing needs. The number of needy in zemstvo provinces in 1912 was estimated to have been more than 1.5 million persons, for each of whom even modestly adequate care would have required an annual expenditure of 200 rubles. Thus, in order to make universal provision at a minimum level, the zemstvos would have had to spend 300 million rubles per year for poor relief instead of the 4.2 million which they did spend. Authoritative writers on this subject felt that while none of the zemstvos could have raised sums of this magnitude for relief of the indigent, they could have done better than they did by assigning for this purpose more than an insignificant proportion of their budgets, by planning and coordination, and by paying more than sporadic attention to the problems involved. As for the proportional decline in the amount spent, it could not be justified by a corresponding decline in need, which did not take place.

In 1870, the municipalities, reorganized, also became local self-governing agencies. In poor relief, however, they accomplished relatively even less than the zemstvos. The institutions supported by them for the most part housed the old, the infirm, the handicapped, and the incurably ill. They also financed some homes for children, establishments where the poor could live rent free, and a few others where free or cheap meals were provided.[3]

The formalities imposed by law placed so many obstacles in the way of private initiative that until 1862 there were only eight charitable organizations functioning regularly in the whole Russian Empire. In that year, the Ministry of Interior was invested with the power to approve the founding of charitable and mutual-aid societies, and shortly after 1890 it issued a series of model regulations and authorized local police chiefs to approve

[3] Major sources used were: Boris Veselovsky, *Istoriia zemstva za 40 let* (St. Petersburg, 1909); and Vladimir Trutovsky, *Sovremennoe zemstvo* (Petrograd, 1915).

the formation of those charitable societies which conformed to one of the several models.

This facilitating move released a flood of activity, so that by 1901 there were 4,800 charitable organizations which assisted nearly three quarters of a million persons. This number, however, included not only those who received economic aid but also those who were given free education and medical care. This relatively extensive provision gave private charity an important place in income-maintenance programs. It also emphasized the failure of state and local efforts to meet existing need: private charity was in fact partly making up for deficiencies in the public sector.

Official sources show that in 1899 the total network of philanthropic organizations — under state, church, zemstvo, municipal, and private auspices — numbered 14,854 with a capital of 405 million rubles. From the fragmentary data at hand, it is not possible to give a full accounting of expenditures, numbers aided, or the kinds of assistance and services offered. It seems clear, however, that a large proportion of the sums spent went for health and education rather than for poor relief per se, although the need for free health and educational services stemmed from poverty to begin with. If the estimate that in 1912 there were more than three million needy persons in Russia provision for whose mere subsistence would have required an annual expenditure of 600 million rubles is accepted, then it is highly probable that these combined efforts fell far short of meeting the need. In fact, the aid given seems to have reached only a part of the poor and was so negligible and sporadic that it could not possibly prevent the ruin of any working class or peasant family faced by sickness, unemployment, or serious natural calamity. The plight of the poverty-stricken was also aggravated by the sharp imbalance between needs and resources that was the universal concomitant of local responsibility: where the need was greatest, the resources to meet it were the meagerest. And then, too, some of the charitable institutions had such an unsavory reputation (homes for illegitimate infants, for instance, were often referred to as "angel factories" by the populace!) that people avoided them unless practically desperate.[4]

These facts go a long way to explain the persistence of widespread begging and vagrancy, apparently defying all measures to curb them, however repressive and cruel, that characterized the Russian scene throughout the period under discussion. In all communities there were many old, handicapped, and sick people who had a clear claim to economic assistance, but who resorted to begging because institutional facilities were insufficient and sometimes frightening and outdoor relief was nonexistent in many places. Given this paucity of resources and the traditional willing-

[4] Narkomat Sotsial'nogo Obespecheniia RSFSR, *Sotsial'noe Obespechenie v RSFSR k desiatoi godovshchine Oktiabria* (Moscow, 1927).

ness of the Russians to give alms, the police could not cope with the hordes of beggars who roamed the streets and the countryside. There were villages whose entire populations lived by begging. Writers dealing with the problem used the words "elemental," "all-enveloping," "endless," "hopeless," and "uncontrollable" to characterize it. Consequently, begging, while officially forbidden, was in fact quietly encouraged for the impotent and tolerated for the able-bodied who slipped by the authorities in charge of law and order. Actually, in some localities there existed lists of legal beggars — lists not permitted by law but set up by administrative fiat. The situation was especially bad in rural areas: if there were no almshouses, the authorities would occasionally board some of the poor with alternate households for varying periods of time; but in most instances nothing was done for them at all.

In Tsarist Russia, one of the earliest methods of protection against the consequences of unemployment was the mutual-aid society which first came into being in 1859; by 1900 there were approximately three hundred such organizations. The original purpose of the workers who joined was to secure themselves and their families, by union, against the consequences of illness, disability, unemployment, and death. Gradually, however, the societies began to consider matters and engage in activities beyond the scope of their original intent, such as the creation of schools and libraries, a shorter working day, regulation of relations with managements, holding periodic congresses, and finally petitioning the government concerning working conditions and setting up strike funds. The transformation of mutual-aid societies into trade unions — often repressed by the Ministry of Interior and the police — was advanced by the spread of the mutual-aid movement among the proletariat of the growing large-scale industry, especially among the metallurgical, textile, and typographical workers. Data for the year 1906–07 concerning 106,463 union members show that they spent on mutual aid slightly more than a ruble per member.[5] It seems clear that this type of help reached a relatively small number of people who needed assistance and that its benefits were insignificant and sporadic.

The earliest social-insurance legislation in Russia, passed in 1861 but inoperative until 1893, sought to give some protection against work-connected illnesses, injuries, and deaths to workers in mining, the railroads, and the Navy Department. It created insurance societies (tovarishchestva) whose revenue was largely derived from an equal tax on employers and workers. The administrative organs — executive committees and control commissions — were composed of representatives from employers, labor, and the state. Both pensions and temporary benefits were

---

[5] Especially pertinent sources were: B. Liubimov, Sotsial'noe strakhovanie v proshlom i nastoiashchem (Moscow, 1925); and Iu. Milonov, Kak voznikli profsoiuzy v Rossii (Moscow, 1929).

exceedingly low, and by 1910 administration for the 22,000 members was still complicated by many practical difficulties.

One of the results of widespread strikes in 1902 was an accident-and-death compensation law passed in 1903 which covered workers in factories, mines, and foundries, and which was subsequently extended to government employees. Its main contribution was that it recognized the professional risk principle; that is, it placed responsibility for accidents resulting because of or during work on the employer. It did not, however, introduce compulsory insurance and was weak from many other points of view: employers, individually accountable, frequently could not or would not pay claims; benefits were denied on grounds of negligence by the worker; administration was entirely in the hands of employers and officials. Railroad workers enjoyed a somewhat more advantageous position since they were represented in the special committees which administered the funds, but even in their case management contributed only one half the amount paid by labor.

As for financial assistance during nonwork-connected illness, no compulsory provision existed until 1912. Voluntary arrangements, however, provided four million rubles for this type of assistance in that year, three fourths of this amount coming from employers and one fourth from workers. Such arrangements were of four kinds: funds into which contributions were made by both employers and workers; commercial insurance purchased by employers; collective agreements which included sickness benefits at the expense of the employer; and funds resulting from fines on workers. Fines could be levied by individual employers, purportedly to maintain discipline, but in fact frequently in order to produce additional revenues for themselves. The law of 1866 curbed some of the worst abuses by requiring that the money, although managed by the employer, be spent only in assistance to workers. Great variations in coverage existed as between provinces, with the highest percentage in those guberniias in which collective agreements were arrived at following the 1905–1906 strikes.

Actually, the revolution of 1905, for the first time in the history of the Russian working-class movement, posed the demand for social insurance as one of the political objectives of the proletariat. Under its pressures, the Tsarist government moved forward with reforms initiated in earlier years, but as reaction set in, the desire to act upon them cooled off. It was not until 1908 that curtailed proposals were presented to the Duma and after four years of deliberation finally became law: the Health and Accident Act of June 23, 1912.

This law covered workers and employees in manufacturing, mining, and foundries, vessels on inland waters, streetcars, and auxiliary railroads. Severe exclusions, however, limited its application to only 23 per cent of the workers and employees active in the labor force at that time. Benefits were available for work-connected accidents, illness, maternity, and death with those for accidents financed by employers, while those for the remaining contingencies came out of contributions by both employers and workers.

For work-connected accidents, administrative organs at the lowest level were the *tovarishchestva* controlled entirely by employers. The next step in the hierarchy led to a provincial authority (*prisutstvie*), composed of worker, employer, and government representatives. This agency supervised the operation of individual societies, on the one hand, and carried out over-all official policy, on the other. The next higher echelon was the Central Social Insurance Council, again made up of workers', employers', and government representatives, whose job it was to determine policy and conduct fair hearings on appeal from the *prisutstvie*. From it appeal could be taken to court which was the final arbiter. For sickness, maternity, and death benefits, the administrative machinery was the sickness fund (*kassa*) in each covered establishment, manned by both workers and employers. From the *kassy* up, the structure was identical with that for the *tovarishchestva*.

The idea of establishing a single central-government agency to operate the whole insurance scheme did not appeal to the lawmakers chiefly because they felt that such an agency would be unable to adapt itself to the variety of conditions in industrial establishments in different localities, and would make impossible active worker participation.

On the whole, the new law was extremely unpopular among the masses of workers and employees, and its administration encountered numerous difficulties. It fell short of workers' expectations in coverage and in the amount and duration of sick benefits. There was also widespread conviction that treating work-connected accidents as ordinary illness during the first thirteen weeks was tantamount to transferring costs from employers to workers, a procedure which could not be justified on practical grounds. The fact that worker contributions made up three fifths of the sickness funds represented a step backward for those groups whose benefits used to be financed by employers prior to 1912. The real merit of the 1912 law was that through the *kassy* it recognized the right of workers to participate in the organization and enforcement of measures concerning their welfare. The importance of embodying this right in law was a victory over those experts, employers, and officials who had maintained that the intellectual level of the Russian worker was too low at that time to permit such participation.[6]

[6] The works most frequently consulted were: three books by V. P. Litvinov-Falinsky, *Otvetstvennost' predprinimatelei za uvech'ia i smert' rabochikh po deistvuiushchim v Rossii zakonam* (1903), *Novyi zakon o voznagrazhdenii uvechnykh rabochikh* (1904), and *Novye zakony o strakhovanii rabochikh* (1912); K. A. Komarovsky, *Strakhovanie rabochikh v Rossii i na zapade*, ed. B. G. Dansky, I (1st ed., St. Petersburg, 1913); A. Vishnevitsky, *Razvitie zakonodatel'stva o sotsial'nom strakhovanii v*

Under the weight of more pressing problems, the Provisional Government did not give much attention to income-maintenance programs. During its eight months of existence, it did, however, issue three laws on social insurance which added about 250,000 new workers to those already covered, returned the payment of benefits during the first thirteen weeks following a work-connected accident to the insurance societies, and lowered workers' contributions into the *kassy* so that they supplied half instead of three fifths of the total. The *prisutstviia*, while retaining their old functions, were changed in composition by a reduction in the number of official representatives and an increase, equally distributed, in workers' and employers' delegates. Women workers were permitted to vote for candidates. Although employers were excluded from the management of *kassy*, they continued to wield an important influence as members of control commissions. No reforms in poor relief appear to have been attempted.

II

During the period 1917–1957, three types of income-maintenance and status programs have been available in the Soviet Union: social insurance for the wage and salaried workers; children's allowances for the entire population; and mutual aid for those paid in kind or in labor-days (*trudodni*).[7]

Having taken the position that the best form of insurance for workers was state insurance, Lenin and other leaders in the Russian Social Democratic Labor Party carefully studied provisions in the more advanced countries and gave considerable thought to the major substantive and administrative problems involved. They concluded that a sound social-insurance program must embody four principles: (1) it must cover all risks that interrupt income; (2) it must cover everyone working for hire and members of his family; (3) benefits must replace total earnings and must be financed entirely by employers and government; and (4) the scheme must be administered by unified organs, of a territorial type, in which the insured exercise complete control.[8] The party used this program as one of the major rallying points in 1904, and after the 1905 Revolution

Rossii (2nd ed., 1926); and V. S. Gokhman, *Ocherki po strakhovaniiu ot neschastnykh sluchaev* (Moscow, 1928).

[7] Provisions for war veterans, governed by special legislation, have always been administered by the Commissariat of Social Welfare and, after the reorganization of welfare services in 1921, took three forms: support for the severely disabled (pensions or placement in homes for invalids), accompanied by training or retraining; help in finding suitable work for the partially disabled; helping the veterans to make full use of services in kind provided at community expense. Essentially, these provisions, integrated into those for all invalids, have remained unchanged: currently, they comprise the payment of pensions, assistance in kind, and assistance in the form of work. What has changed is the quantity and quality of these services. There has taken place a substantial improvement and expansion, as a result especially of the impetus given to this work by the Second World War.

[8] Lenin, *Sochineniia* (4th ed., 1948), XXIV, 427.

continued an active campaign which exposed the shortcomings of the proposed Health and Accident Act. After its passage, the party was directed
to utilize the *kassy* to enlighten workers about its inadequacies and the
principles and demands of the party in this area. Thus, under tsarism,
Lenin's party used social insurance not as a resource for improving the
economic position of the proletariat, but as one of the weapons in developing their class consciousness and strengthening organization among
them.

On November 13, 1917, with the zeal that characterized the immediate
postrevolutionary period, the government announced its intention to
create a social-insurance system based on principles developed by the
Social Democrats, but going beyond them in one important respect: coverage would be broadened to include the city and village poor as well as
those working for hire. In this way the party hoped to outstrip the capitalist countries almost overnight, in their slow progress from outworn
systems of poor relief to modern social-insurance provisions built on the
proposition that security from want is a fundamental right.

A series of decrees implementing this position culminated in the general act of October 31, 1918 which extended coverage to all persons supporting themselves by their own work, added nonwork-connected disability and unemployment to the risks included in the 1912 law, and placed
the entire burden of financing on employers. The prerevolutionary administrative structure was radically changed: the *kassy* were retained and,
with their functions enlarged, became the unified local administrative
organs for all types of social insurance; all other agencies were liquidated.
From the *kassy* the hierarchy led to social-insurance management boards,
attached to the Commissariats of Labor in the republics and at the
center.

In practice, the new arrangements encountered numerous and often
insurmountable difficulties. The insurance of peasants, artisans, and home
workers never materialized at all. Even for the wage earners it was impossible to institute social insurance in the period of War Communism. As the
sole employer, the state alone contributed toward social insurance; since
all workers had to remain at the disposal of the state, they acquired the
right to be maintained by the state when unemployed; nonproletarian
elements, however clear their rights to benefits, were denied them. In
short, everyone who received support got it from the state, either in wages
or in "benefits." This system resulted in heavy burdens for the employing
establishments, which were forced to pay contributions averaging as high
as 21–28 per cent of payroll. These inordinate rates, as well as inefficient
administration, in some cases led to a failure to collect as much as 70 per
cent of the payments due. Obviously, the sweeping objectives enunciated
in the ardor of the revolution could not be reached; the government found
it impossible to meet even minimum obligations. With the introduction of

the New Economic Policy, there occurred a drastic reorganization of the whole system of social welfare, including social insurance.

The legal basis for the social-insurance scheme is found in the 1936 Constitution which, in article 120, declares that "citizens of the USSR have the right to material security in old age as well as in the event of sickness and loss of capacity to work. This right is ensured by the wide development of social insurance of workers and employees at the expense of the state, free medical aid, and the provision of a wide network of health resorts for the use of the toilers." Additional benefits stem from provisions in the constitution implementing the equality of rights of women.

The chief value of available social-insurance expenditure figures lies in indicating the trend rather than in showing strictly comparable absolute amounts. From this point of view, it appears that during the thirty-year period from 1925 to 1955 these disbursements increased fifty-three times, while the sums spent during the Fifth Five Year Plan were ten times the sums spent during the First Five Year Plan. These increases are less imposing, however, when related to the fact that the cost of living increased by more than fourteen times during the years 1928–1952. The latest major legislation, the pension law of July 14, 1956, by broadening coverage and materially increasing benefits, raised the annual social-insurance bill by 13 billion rubles. While these developments do not necessarily mean that the government assigns high priority to social insurance as a method of meeting human-welfare needs, they do seem to indicate that the trend upward has been consistent and progressive.

As for the division of outlays among the various insurances and services provided, pensions and benefits absorb by far the largest share: almost 77 per cent. The remaining funds are used for health, child welfare and "other," in that order of importance, with only 1 per cent said to be spent for administration. An examination of the voluminous social-insurance legislation on the Soviet statute books reveals that the whole scheme has been pretty consistently attuned to certain basic principles which have undergone relatively little modification over the years. Abandoning the short-lived attempt at universal coverage in 1921, the social-insurance system narrowed the availability of its benefits to those working for hire. No deviation from this limitation has taken place, although coverage has been broadened by liberalizing the conditions governing the receipt of benefits, and presumably by no longer having to exclude the "social origin" disfranchised. Other members of the working population are covered by the so-called "socialist mutual aid."

By 1955, the overwhelming majority of the 48.4 million persons counted as workers and employees were within the social-insurance scheme. The only exclusions of significance were those who performed temporary and casual work for private employers, members of nomadic tribes, and some individual hunters and fishermen. By adding to the primary insured their entitled dependents, it can be deduced that the social-insurance system currently reaches about 40–45 per cent of the total population.

The risks to interruption of income for which social insurance accepts responsibility have been added to steadily. By now almost all the major hazards to human life that result in loss or lowering of earning power or exceptional expenditures are dealt with: old age, disability (both work- and nonwork-connected), death, and sickness (including pregnancy). In addition, long service pensions are paid to certain officeholders such as educators, agronomists, and veterinarians. Funeral benefits are available for all the insured, and special benefits for layettes and infant feeding are given in appropriate circumstances. Furthermore, children's allowances, introduced on a limited scale in 1936 and substantially liberalized in 1944, strengthen the social-security system in the creation of a national minimum. In contrast to other benefits, these allowances are paid to *all* mothers (not only to those who are workers and employees) who qualify; that is, to married women and widows with three or more children, and in part to unmarried mothers whatever the number of their children.

Low temporary-unemployment benefits — for only a few of the unemployed and limited by a stringent means test to those without any income whatsoever — existed up to October 1930. At that time they ceased to be payable, unemployment having dropped to its lowest point. To what extent this drop was due to the demand for labor generated by the First Five Year Plan, on the one hand, and to the great increase in population of the corrective labor camps in 1930, on the other, it is difficult to say. That both these factors influenced the employment situation is undoubtedly true. Unemployment insurance has never been reintroduced. Presumably the trade unions (in supersession of the former labor exchanges) have been able to find employment promptly in occupations within the capacity of any able-bodied man or woman, although not necessarily in his own trade or at his place of residence. For those needing to acquire certain kinds and degrees of skill, training is provided free, accompanied by allowances for maintenance. Anyone incapable of work must be medically certified and is then dealt with under the heading of sickness or disability.

With the exception of a few lump-sum payments, benefits in the Soviet scheme are related to previous earnings rather than to need or contributions. In almost no case, however, do benefits equal the amount the beneficiary earned when he was an active member of the labor force. In this respect the Soviets seem to adhere to the famous principle of "less eligibility" enunciated by the English Poor Law commissioners in 1834 (and since then applied to the social-security systems of all capitalist countries) which expressed the view that publicly assured income should never exceed the earnings of the lowest category of independent worker.

Behind it was the fear that a too liberal publicly assured income would, by reducing the economic penalty for not working, discourage initiative and thereby cause a drop in national output. At the same time, attainment of the security objective requires the assurance of a minimum adequacy in relation to the level of consumption to which the beneficiary had been accustomed by the level of his earnings.

Various devices are used in the attempt to achieve such adequacy. To begin with, the benefit formula is weighted in favor of the low wage earners and those who have lost the greatest degree of working ability. Secondly, statutory minimum money benefits — set in 1956 at 300 rubles per month for old age pensioners from the lowest-paid categories — are established. That the 1956 adjustment in the minimum benefit was long overdue is underscored by the fact that it was the first since 1932 when the monthly *maximum* on which pensions could be calculated was set at 300 rubles. How inadequate pensions were during most of the period between 1932 and 1956 may be surmised from the official statement that the modifications introduced in the latter year raised the former minimum pension for old age by six times, and the former minimum for all invalids and for survivors by six to seven times. Thirdly, dependents' benefits and supplements for the service of an attendant in the case of the totally disabled are added. And a fourth device is the partial pension, granted irrespective of the work record and never permitted to be less than one fourth of what the full pension would have been.

The principle of differentiation is the reverse of egalitarianism (*uravnilovka*, denounced by Stalin as a left heresy as early as 1931), which made it possible, according to Soviet leaders, for floaters, malingerers, and habitual absentees to receive benefits on an equal footing with *udarniks* and outstanding workers with long and uninterrupted work records. Differentiation was introduced to correct this situation by applying less stringent eligibility conditions and a more advantageous benefit formula in calculating benefits for "best" workers, trade-union members, and those in "leading" industries and unhealthy occupations. Although immediately following its introduction there was some resistance to differentiation, it is now universal. Thus, social insurance is subordinated to broader objectives and is used by the government for strengthening labor discipline, encouraging socialist competition, and increasing the productivity of labor.

Social-insurance benefits are financed entirely from contributions by the employing establishments. Contributions are made as a percentage of payroll: a certain per cent of the wages, but not from the wages, is added by the enterprise for social-insurance purposes. The percentage of payroll is graded between different enterprises according to the degree of risk which employment in them entails, the range being from 3.7 to 10.7 per cent. Private employers make similar contributions. In this context, the payroll includes various types of payments — regular pay, over-time pay, cost of payment in kind, commissions, and so on. The main characteristic is that all of these sums are paid in connection with worker-employer relationships. The rates for individual enterprises and employers are established by the All-Union Central Committee of Trade Unions together with the interested bureau and the Ministry of Finance.

Since 1938 the resources of the social-insurance system have been collected and spent in accordance with a single, centralized plan which is established on the basis of the five-year-plan figures on number of workers and employers and amount of wages and salaries. Centralized budgeting is apparently used for equalization, made necessary by the un-equal rates of premiums in the different industries. In this way the central organization makes certain that every insured person, regardless of the industry or locale in which he is employed, enjoys equal oppor-tunity for benefits. In the past some local insurance organs opposed this procedure, feeling that it led to surrendering "their" money to the central administration. This attitude arose in part from a deep-seated conviction that complete self-government is impossible under central direction.

It will be recalled that almost a fifth of the social-insurance budget is spent on health and child-welfare activities. In relation to the major pension and benefit program, these are supplemental undertakings. The unions appear to be seriously interested in them, however, because of their positive effect on lowering morbidity, shortening the periods of ill-ness, cutting down absenteeism, and so forth, all of which, in turn, pro-longs working ability, raises productivity, and lowers insurance costs.

As a result of the merger of the Commissariat of Labor with the Central Council of Trade Unions in 1933, the unions passed over from control of social insurance to its direct administration. Since that time, there has been manifest a trend toward decentralization, strengthened by the establishment of local paying centers, one for each union. At the same time, policy determination has been further centralized by the abolition of the several Commissars of Labor in the republics and the transfer of their social-insurance functions to the All-Union Central Congress of Trade Unions. The detailed, daily work is done by the factory commit-tees, together with their subordinate insurance councils, elected by the trade unionists of individual establishments.[9]

Undoubtedly, administration by trade unions has given a broad base

[9] A voluminous literature is available. Among the most helpful works were the following: A. S. Krasnopolsky, *Osnovnye printsipy sovetskogo gosudarstvennogo sot-sial'nogo strakhovaniia* (Moscow, 1951); A. Barit and B. Miliutin, *Osnovy sotsial'nogo strakhovaniia* (Moscow, 1934); V. M. Pototsky, *Strakhovoe ustroistvo v SSSR* (1927); G. K. Iniutin, *Chto daet trudiashchimsia novyi pensionnyi zakon* (1956); Studenkin, Vlasov, and Evtikhiev, *Sovetskoe administrativnoe pravo* (Moscow, 1950); V. V. Karavaev, *Posobiia po vremennoi netrudosposobnosti* (Moscow, 1950); A. A. Abra-mova, *Okhrana trudovykh prav zhenshchin v SSSR* (1954).

to the system, lowered costs, and brought insurance activities closer to
the working masses. On the negative side, however, there is ground for
thinking that in some instances — especially when procedure is not minutely spelled out in the law but is rather determined by discretion —
the practical and the ideal are a step or two apart. For example, access to
sanatoriums is sometimes more dependent upon one's "connections" in
the trade union than upon one's state of health. The same is true when
children are selected for summer camps or for day-nursery care.

Many questions might be raised concerning the Soviet social-insurance
system. Among the most pertinent seem to be those in regard to coverage,
benefit adequacy, and the approach to children's allowances. It will be
recalled that by limiting its benefits to workers and employees and their
dependents, the social-insurance system extends to possibly 40–45 per
cent of the population. This would, indeed, be a serious limitation if no
provision were made for the remaining 55–60 per cent. Since, however,
this is not the case, the real question revolves around the relative merits
of securing against income loss through one rather than another of several
possible methods. In arriving at a decision concerning the choice of
method, many arguments, economic and social, might be marshaled
against the Soviet choices. On the other hand, equally strong arguments
might be adduced to support their position.

The question of benefit adequacy must take account of the fact that
adequacy is a relative concept varying in relation to the standard against
which it is measured. Thus, if the standard is the replacement of previous
earnings, then it can be flatly asserted that Soviet provision is inadequate:
at present, pensions equal 50 to 100 per cent of former earnings. Once
this standard is abandoned, adequacy becomes a matter of arbitrary decision as to the precise differential between benefits and earnings that
will constitute adequate protection and at the same time carry out other
objectives of the program: the narrower the differential, the more "adequate" the benefits since they are more likely to buy for the beneficiary
the standard of living his wages bought. As stated earlier, the current
minimum pension is 300 rubles per month; the maximum in some instances
may go up to 1,200 rubles per month. The scope of the differential may
be deduced from the estimate that places the current average monthly
wage at 600–800 rubles.

Introduction of children's allowances indicates that the Soviet concept
of income security has extended beyond the mere assurance of continuity
of income, to include a concern about the adequacy of any given average
level of income to meet the needs of families with children. The Soviets
have also apparently resolved the conflict between cash benefits versus
benefits in kind by providing both: cash payments are made to families
in proportion to the number of children in each, and services and benefits
in kind, of a nature which is peculiarly appropriate to the needs of chil-

dren, are also available (day nurseries and such). What is not clear, however, is why no allowances are paid for the first two children and why they stop when the child reaches age five (except for children of unmarried mothers). The only sound reasons for these limitations would be the presence of an income in Russian families so high that parents could raise two children at an accepted level without any outside economic help; and the presence of such varied and adequate benefits in kind for the child from five to legal working age that cash benefits would be superfluous. It is not likely that both of these conditions exist for the majority of Russian children. As for the flat amounts paid as allowances (flat sums are paid because allowances are status grants), their adequacy is again a relative concept. It depends on the decision that has been made as to whether allowances are to furnish full support for the child or only partial support which serves to help parents carry out their responsibilities, but is not designed to relieve them entirely of these responsibilities. In settling for the second alternative, the Soviets have brought themselves in line with the thirty-four capitalist countries that have this type of protection and have reaffirmed the pivotal position of the family in bringing up the future generation.

In postrevolutionary Russia, two characteristics distinguish mutual aid from what it was like in Tsarist Russia: its spread among large groups previously not involved and its encouragement by the government (through subsidies and supervision), amounting in most instances to compulsion. Like other social institutions, mutual aid is used to fulfill functions that further the entire plan laid out by the leaders.

During the early postrevolutionary period, trade-union mutual-aid societies were voluntary organizations which did quite a bit to ease the lot of the workers at times of severest need, when neither social insurance nor other types of aid were adequate or certain. Wishing to use the societies as the "elementary schools of communism," the new regime required that each one register with a trade union. In 1928 a model act was issued which permitted some voluntary activity, but slanted the main purpose toward encouraging *udarnichestvo* and social competition. While belonging to such societies is mentioned as one of the advantages of union membership, little else has been said about them since 1935.

In 1931 mutual-aid societies of a special type were authorized in twelve heavy industries and in rail transportation. Financed entirely by government and supervised directly by the factory committees, these societies soon became indistinguishable from the over-all social-insurance organs.[10]

Mutual-aid societies in producers' cooperatives and in the kolkhozy

[10] Information on early developments was found in N. Antipov, *Finansovaia praktika professional'nykh soiuzov* (Moscow, 1923), and V. A. Palepa, *Kassy vzaimopomoshchi: sbornik materialov* (Kharkov, 1935).

are supervised by the Commissariat of Social Welfare. When the Soviet government came into power, this commissariat was given the huge three-fold job of reshaping the Tsarist welfare institutions; creating new programs and services; and securing the active participation of local organs in the whole gigantic undertaking. It quickly became big and unwieldy.[11] Gradually, some of its functions were turned over to other ministries; by now its special province, in addition to directing mutual aid, is the management of assistance to all those unable to work, the needy, and war invalids. Clarification and contraction of function did not, however, alter the original purpose or the operating philosophy of the commissariat: it implements the principle of public responsibility in accordance with eligibility conditions clearly defined in the law, and its objective is to rehabilitate as many as possible, and offer care and services to those who cannot work, either in institutions or through money payments. Charity and indiscriminate giving are ruled out, and a determined struggle is waged against all parasites and idlers, with useful work as the most potent rehabilitative tool.

In the republics, the minister at the head of social welfare is directly responsible to the Council of People's Commissariats. The next stage is formed by the social-welfare sections of the regional administrative bodies which direct the work of the social-welfare institutions within their local competence. Lastly, the primary authorities are the town social-welfare sections, the local inspectors, and the town and village soviets' social-welfare boards. All activities are financed by moneys earmarked for them in the national and republic budgets.

The model act regulating the activity of mutual-aid societies in producers' cooperatives was promulgated in 1929. Its provisions created benefits similar to those in the social-insurance system, financed by the members themselves, however, with some subsidy from the government.

Mutual-aid societies in the kolkhozy (KOV) were first organized in 1921 for the relief of needy peasants and war invalids. In addition, KOV were expected to protect the interests of agricultural workers and small peasant households against the "kulaks." With collectivization, the societies became the mutual-aid organs for kolkhozy, their operations having been regulated by the model act of 1931. A society — serving either

[11] During November–December 1917, this ministry was called Narkomat Prizreniia; that is, the Ministry of Philanthropy. This designation, it was felt, was inappropriate to the concept of social welfare from a socialist point of view. It was, therefore, changed to Narkomat Sotsial'nogo Obespecheniia early in 1918, a name retained to date. *Obespechenie* has been variously translated by those writing in English as social assistance, social aid, social security, and social welfare. While none of these expresses exactly the meaning of the Russian word, social welfare is used in this paper because it conveys more correctly than the others the range of functions carried out by this commissariat in a frame of reference familiar to American social scientists. For a few months in 1920 the commissariat and the Ministry of Labor were merged into a single ministry, but this union was artificial and short-lived.

one collective farm or several farms in a given area — may be established by a two-thirds majority of the membership. It must be registered and is run by elective officers who are supervised by the village soviets and the social-welfare authorities.

Finances are derived from members' contributions, proportionate to individual earnings and fixed annually by the general meeting at not more than 2 per cent of earnings; payments from the common funds which cannot exceed 2 per cent of gross output; sums received from the social-welfare authorities, and fines levied by decision of the courts. A reserve fund must be set up. KOV are required to assist survivors and members who are incapable of working because of old age, disability, sickness, and maternity, and to improve conditions by organizing health and welfare services. They also make loans to members in case of serious misfortunes and for basic improvements such as the construction and repair of buildings.[12]

Thus, for about 55–60 per cent of the population income maintenance takes the form of self-help. Since members of kolkhozy and producers' cooperatives technically are not "employed" but are, rather, self-employed, they themselves make contributions to finance the program. Although only scattered and infrequent references to this program appear in the literature, it seems clear that for kolkhoz members at any rate benefits are lower than those provided by social insurance. What proportion exactly of *trudodni* earnings they represent, it is not possible to say. There is some indication, too, that the duration of benefits is less generous. As far as the handling of funds is concerned, apparently there is no centralized budgeting; rather, individual kolkhozy manage their own funds. This may mean that kolkhozy which do not do too well economically have less available for benefits than the more prosperous ones, and yet it is likely that the former include proportionately more members who need assistance than the latter. It is possible, of course, that government subsidies may be used to offset at least partly the inequality of resources that probably exists, but nothing has been found in the literature that would confirm this supposition. From references to standard rules governing eligibility, it is clear that the principle of differentiation operates here as in the insurance system.

There exist in the Soviet Union social-welfare programs which emphasize services for socially handicapped groups in contrast to centering attention on income maintenance. Of particular interest from a welfare point of view are the mutual-aid societies operating in the disabled persons' cooperatives. These came into being soon after the revolution and, in spite of insufficient means and lack of acceptance by local authorities, succeeded in raising morale among the disabled and in preventing their

[12] In addition to sources already cited, see Narkomat Sotsial'nogo Obespecheniia, *Sotsial'noe obespechenie za piat' let, Aprel' 30, 1918–Aprel' 30, 1923* (Moscow, 1923).

isolation from the general population. By 1927, they were recognized by statute and in 1932 were required to join the mutual-aid societies in producers' cooperatives. They increased in size and importance during World War II, by 1945 employing 200,000 invalids of war and labor in the RSFSR alone.

While not closely comparable to sheltered workshops in other countries, the disabled persons' cooperatives appear to serve a somewhat similar purpose. Supervised by the social-welfare department, they form an independent system, with all administrators and controllers elected by the membership. Financial resources come from members' entrance fees, subsidies from the department, and so on. The All-Russian Union of Disabled Persons' Mutual Aid Societies is the central administrative body. While the major objective of the cooperatives is to improve the economic position of the disabled, this purpose is in itself a service that makes life for the handicapped more normal and richer from the psychological and social points of view.

Services for the handicapped are centered in the All-Russian Blind and Deaf and Mute Societies. The activities of both were regulated by special decrees in 1931 and 1932, respectively, which placed them under the supervision of the social welfare department. Finances come from entrance fees, government subsidies, income from workshops, enterprises, dramatic entertainments, concerts, and so on.

The responsibility for children needing care outside their own homes — dependent, neglected, and emotionally disturbed children — is not lodged with social welfare but with the local soviets which have special commissions in charge of this work. These commissions coordinate the activities of the Ministries of Health, Education, and Internal Affairs and of various social organizations in the child-welfare field. In line with a decree of August 21, 1943, special Suvorov and Nakhimov military and naval schools were established for children whose parents were killed by German occupationists.

From institutions children may be sent to their own, *patronat,* or adoptive homes, or may remain at the institution until age sixteen. *Patronat* appears to be a more formal arrangement than foster care, but not as final as adoption. It is based on a voluntary agreement whereby children between the ages of five months and fourteen years are placed in families where they remain until age sixteen. The placement is carried out by the appropriate ministry, depending on the age of the child; in country districts it is made by the president of the village soviet through the kolkhoz mutual-aid societies (and thus, under the direction of the social-welfare authorities). A contract, describing the responsibilities of both parties, is signed by the placing agency and the family offering its home. The head of the family becomes the child's guardian; the agency pays a set monthly sum for the child's support and supervises the home to make sure that the guardian carries out his responsibilities as agreed upon.

Adoption was reintroduced by the Family Code of 1926 because there appeared no valid grounds for rejecting sincere applications from families wanting to welcome a child; and it was known that a form of *de facto* adoption was practiced on a large scale by peasants. The court has the power to order a total break of all legal ties with the natural family so as to protect the child from intrusion on his adoptive relationship. Adoptive placements are made only by statutory agencies, and granted only if all the circumstances of the adoptive family are found on investigation to be normal for the upbringing of the child.

Little material is available on the treatment of juvenile delinquents. One early document and a number of novels seem to indicate, however, that the persons in charge have a good grasp of child psychology and that they make a thorough study of each child's background — social, economic, physical, emotional, and intellectual — on which treatment plans are based. It also seems clear that the punitive approach is not employed, but rather that the therapist seeks out and builds on the positive qualities of each child.

Bureaus of legal aid for mothers and children, first organized in 1933, are part of the public-health system. In them women receive free counseling and services to help them with problems arising out of living conditions, employment, and marital relationships.[13]

Judicial counseling on marital problems is carried on by the courts, one of whose functions is to prevent the dissolution of marriages, if at all possible, by means of persuasion. Court procedure is apparently informal, allowing the bench to discuss the situation in a permissive atmosphere and "to urge a common sense, practical approach to the spouses." Agencies for formal marriage counseling that would employ the psychiatric approach do not seem to exist.[14]

III

There has taken place a profound and fundamental change in the concept of social welfare between pre- and postrevolutionary Russia, with elements of continuity so faint by this time as to be almost indiscernible. In Tsarist times, in spite of stipulations in the poor law that want must be relieved, the poor person had no enforceable right to relief.

[13] Good sources include: U. S. Children's Bureau, *Health and Welfare Services for Mothers and Children in the USSR*, by Anna Kalet Smith; United Nations, *Study of Adoption of Children* (1953), and *Problem Children and Juvenile Delinquents and their Care in the Children's Institutions* (after materials of the Moscow Regional Conference of Directors of Children's Homes, December 15–19, 1933), O. L. Bem and V. I. Kufaev, eds.

[14] Mark Field, "Social Services for the Family in the Soviet Union," *Marriage and Family Living*, XVII (August 1955), 244–245.

Whether he was helped or not depended on a series of fortuitous circumstances beyond his control. And if he were not helped, he had no way of appealing to higher authority, no power to force the responsible organs to give him assistance. As a final resort, he could beg — and he did, in many instances, in spite of the cruel punishment that this frequently entailed. The only exception was the group of workers, about a fifth of those employed for hire, who had a right to economic help under the social-insurance laws. In their case, however, the risks for which compensation was available were limited to sickness and work-connected injuries; they themselves had to contribute a substantial part of the benefits paid them; the sums they received were low in relation to wages; and they had only a minority voice in administration.

Because public provision was spotty, inadequate, and uncertain, many needy people sought material aid from private charitable societies which, as a consequence, were unwilling to devote sizable resources for developing preventive and treatment-oriented programs. As is always true of private charitable organizations, however, they could not offer universal protection, either to all the people who needed assistance or for all the contingencies that made it necessary for people to seek help. Their boards determined intake policies, eligibility requirements, and the kinds and amounts of help that they would provide. It is not surprising, therefore, that a considerable proportion of privately supported charitable facilities were available only to the "deserving" poor, the definition of "deserving" depending on the philosophy and objectives of the donors rather than on an unprejudiced or uniform concept. In the public sector, as well, discretion ruled. With no fair-hearings machinery available, the individual decisions of local officials were supreme, however capricious or injurious some of them might be. As a rule, the assistance provided, both under public and private auspices, was in kind, for the most part as support in institutions and occasionally as commodities to be used at home. Traditionally, assistance in kind is unpopular with the recipients. It is used by the donors when they wish aid to be deterrent and when their basic assumption is that those who seek aid are almost by definition persons incapable of efficiently managing their own affairs.

In postrevolutionary Russia, the right to economic assistance is enunciated in the 1936 Constitution. If the citizen is a worker or employee, or a dependent of a worker or employee, his economic aid will come from the social-insurance system and will be paid by his employer; if he is a member of a producers' cooperative or a kolkhoz, it will come from the mutual-aid society formed by him and his fellow workers who will pay for it themselves (with some subsidy from the government) because, technically, they are their own employers; if he falls outside of both of these, his assistance will come from the Commissariat of Social Welfare and will be financed out of general taxation. The first two of these systems will aid him during most contingencies that occur in industrial societies to diminish or cut off income. Furthermore, he will also be helped when the number of children for whose support he is responsible is deemed too large for him to do a good job of raising them unaided. The third system (comparable to the public-assistance system in the United States in this context) is apparently a residual program, the catchall underpinning the entire income-maintenance scheme but gradually contracting as the main line of defense against income failure — social insurance and mutual aid — grows stronger and more extensive. Throughout, assistance for the most part is given in money or work so that the beneficiaries retain the decision-making power over their affairs and are not set apart and below the rest of the population by being deprived of the universal medium of exchange. Institutional care is available when the interests of the beneficiary are best served by it. Rehabilitative services, vocationally directed, are stressed, while preventive efforts appear to be continuous and consistent. Thus, private charity has been abolished altogether, as inimical to the principles governing human relationships in a socialist state, while the old poor law has been replaced by a modern scheme of social security. Philanthropy and charity have yielded to social welfare; social insurance, carried over in the form of mutual aid to those not working for hire, has remained, but coverage of people and of risks is so extended that it bears only a distant resemblance to its 1912 predecessor.

That this transformation represents substantial progress is obvious. That this progress is largely the Soviet counterpart of the changes in welfare services occurring throughout the world is likewise clear. That the benefits of modernization have not been and are not now available to those opposing the regime, however indirectly, is well known: sorely needed help was denied to the "socially inimical," pensions were taken away from those who received them under the tsar, the hundreds of thousands now in corrective labor camps are excluded from the social-security system. The question arises, too, of whether the right to assistance is fully, partially, or not at all implemented, in the latter case remaining a mere slogan. It would be most difficult to answer this question even if field research were possible; without it, only cautious deductions may be hazarded. There is little doubt that the resources allocated to social insurance during the first ten or twelve years following the revolution were too meager to make effective implementation possible. This was even more true of mutual aid and social welfare. Since the First Five Year Plan, there is apparent a more consistent and significant effort to implement paper commitments, which, however, continued to produce only partial results and necessitated arrangements such as the trade-union mutual-aid societies. In the postwar era, and especially with the passage of the pension law of July 1956, implementation has gradually become more real in the sense of reaching the security objective for most of the population to a meaningful extent.

Degree of implementation depends, too, on administrative procedure, and especially on the availability of fair-hearings machinery. The social-insurance system does provide for appeal from lower to higher authorities in the trade-union hierarchy. Those receiving pensions from social-welfare authorities may take their complaints to the executive committee of the municipal soviet; no information has been found, however, about appeal avenues in the mutual-aid societies. Presumably, a dissatisfied member may carry his grievance to the total membership; perhaps he may also take his complaint to the social-welfare authorities or to the village soviet. Both of these courses may be difficult or even impossible, nor is it certain that reconsideration can be forced, after all. Nothing has been learned about the methods used by social-welfare authorities in determining eligibility for aid of those who are excluded from the social-insurance and mutual-aid systems and of those who, although included, receive benefits insufficient to fulfill even minimum needs. That such individuals and families exist seems to be indicated by the official statement which, after enumerating the covered groups, adds: "other invalids and *needy* persons, not included in the enumerated groups, are 'made secure' within the limits of resources at the disposal of social-welfare organs." [15] How is need determined? Probably through some form of a means test. If so, how much of the deterrent poor law — discretion, relatives' responsibility, and such — is still lurking in the procedure? To whom and how do these people appeal if they are not helped? The pervasive silence on this aspect of welfare administration may mean that the new society has neither eliminated need nor created a magic formula for meeting the problems that it breeds: want and begging still exist.

Far-reaching changes have also taken place in the welfare administrative structure. Under the tsars, the Ministry of Interior was responsible for supervising public and private poor relief in its various forms. Its influence on day-to-day administration was negligible, however, because the central government made no grants-in-aid to the local authorities, set no standards, and used its licensing power in a formal and inflexible manner. In relation to pauperism, begging, and vagrancy, the police rather than the welfare authorities had jurisdiction, with their repressive and often cruel methods which precluded rehabilitation and individualization. Locally, relief administration was in the hands of a multitude of organizations, public and private, with the great variation in kind and amount of aid available to any applicant that always follows from local responsibility. Community cooperation and participation were rarely mentioned. In social insurance, the power of the central council, from the point of view of encouraging a uniform interpretation of the law, was

[15] Emphasis mine. *Bol'shaia sovetskaia entsiklopediia* (1st ed.), LII (1947), 299.

perhaps more tangibly felt, especially through its right to conduct fair hearings on appeal. Nevertheless, inequality of opportunity to receive benefits probably existed at the local level because the resources of the sickness funds and the *tovarishchestva* were circumscribed by the financial position of individual establishments from which they were derived and in which they were paid out.

In the Soviet scheme, the different types of provision are related to one of three central organs: to the AUCCTU in the case of social insurance; to the Commissariat of Social Welfare in the case of mutual-aid societies and assistance outside the scope of either social insurance or mutual aid; and to the Commissariat of Finance in the case of children's allowances. Close and continuous cooperation among the three, at national, republic, and local levels, seems to exist. The central organs, with policy-making and supervisory powers, apparently make their position tangibly felt throughout the administrative hierarchy, not only by requiring reports and conducting studies and inspections on the spot, but also through the centralized budgets which must have their approval. The question rises, of course, as to whether this centralization is oppressive and crushing to the local initiative, flexibility, and speed with which decisions that affect people when they may be helpless and overwhelmed can be made. That it is oppressive is undoubtedly true. On the other hand, there is some evidence that intervention by higher authorities at times wields a benign influence by protecting individuals against local inefficiencies, contributing toward consistency of policy and toward greater certainty that similar treatment will be afforded persons in similar circumstances. In addition, at the local level, administration by unions, mutual-aid societies, social-welfare authorities, and soviets, who work closely with groups drawn from a variety of local citizens, may give more room than other areas of Soviet life for the "localism" and "familism" which are known to act as defenses against the pressures of the center. Social-insurance councils — modernized vestiges of Tsarist sickness funds — and all of the other local organs involved theoretically can make their thinking known to the central authorities. To what extent they actually do is problematic.

Very little, indeed, can be said about the qualitative aspects of welfare administration in prerevolutionary Russia. The literature is devoid of any specific discussion of this subject. From the general tone of the materials studied, however, it is clear that no professional training — in fact, no training of any kind — was required or available for welfare work. All activity was permeated by the charitable approach, with the benevolence of those who carried it on being the only characteristic constantly extolled, frequently in servile and exaggerated terms. There is no mistaking, too, the condescension, sometimes genuinely kind but often coldly indifferent, on the part of the givers and officials toward those who received. At best, these attitudes frequently assumed that poor people were so weak or simple that they could hardly be helped to escape perpetual dependency; at worst, they showered cruelty and humiliation on those who could not defend themselves. It is also obvious that the rehabilitative possibilities in work with the poor and the socially handicapped remained largely unexplored, with the major effort directed toward relieving stark poverty. Rigid in attitudes, many officials were loath to experiment or to introduce already tested innovations. As far as almshouses went, the only mention of such possibilities was the sporadic attempt to provide work and conduct Bible readings in a few places. In organizing work relief in famine-stricken areas, occasional effort was made to devote part of the sums to training some of the needy in occupations they could practice after the emergency had passed. Even in children's institutions, low standards marked not only the physical care but also the meager education offered. In its empire-wide study of children's orphanages, the Romanovsky Komitet found only two that even remotely came up to the standards which this organization, modeling itself on Swiss experience, considered desirable.[16] From the sums spent on the education of children from socially higher classes, it may be assumed that its quality was somewhat better than for the rest of the children brought up in institutions.

Some idea of the quality of welfare services in Soviet Russia may be pieced together from scattered and infrequent statements in the literature. Thus, in 1949, we are told, "In the active cadres [in the trade unions] we have about one million group organizers, over 1.2 million insurance delegates and social inspectors for workers' protection, over 1 million members in wage commissions, and over 2 million voluntary social workers occupying themselves with welfare matters." [17] Apparently, the tasks of many of these 5.7 million persons were, in some respects at least, similar to those of American social workers. Thus, group organizers conducted cultural activities in clubs attached to employing establishments, at first endeavoring to attract the more outstanding individuals who were interested in some specific activity, but gradually shifting to a broad propaganda approach which sought to "reach the masses" and to develop the abilities of the membership for self-determination and initiative. As volunteer "social workers," social-insurance delegates visit sick members in their homes; investigate and report on the home and employment conditions of invalids, the aged, patients in psychiatric clinics and hospitals, and alco-

[16] G. I. Shcherbinin, K voprosu ob organizatsii zemledel'cheskikh priiutov dlia sel'skikh sirot (Petrograd, 1915).

[17] Statement by Kuznetsov at the All-Union Trade Union Congress in April 1949, quoted in Leif Bjork, Wages, Prices and Social Legislation in the Soviet Union (London, 1953), 22.

holics; give advice to spouses experiencing marital conflict — and intervene in many other situations created by "life." What preparation, if any, they have for this type of work is not clear. The general impression gained is that there is much use of group work and community organization techniques, but little recourse to therapy through the one-to-one relationship. It appears, too, that the services given by these "social workers" are for the most part of an environmental type and occasionally of a simple emotionally supportive type, when the "worker" gets to know his "client" well and develops a friendly relationship with him. Nor has it been possible to ascertain what training workers in the Commissariat of Social Welfare receive for carrying on their jobs which in some instances, at least, demand a great deal of varied knowledge and skill — for example, in making and carrying through plans for the rehabilitation of the disabled and the handicapped within the framework of an interdisciplinary approach. Again, group work and community organization methods, with the object of providing environmental and emotionally supportive help, seem to be heavily relied on. Psychotherapy, when used, is evidently carried out by medical personnel only; there is no evidence that "social workers" are proficient in this area. As for welfare services to children living outside their own homes and to mothers and children who come to bureaus of legal aid, they are offered by workers trained primarily for functioning in educational and medical, rather than welfare, settings. It appears that these workers have a good grasp of the major treatment tools known to modern psychology. Treatment plans appear to be based on a thorough study of each child's background — social, economic, physical, emotional, and intellectual. When dealing with emotionally disturbed children, the punitive approach is not used. Rather, the process is conceived to be in essence educational, with the most constructive results expected from individualizing each child and building on the strong and healthy elements of his personality.

One common trait seems to characterize all of the welfare activities discussed: the consistent reliance on useful work, adapted to the varied needs of receivers of benefits and services, as the major therapeutic tool. Helping people to enter or re-enter productive life, even on a partial basis, seems to be the main driving force behind all welfare endeavor and the measure of its success. So insistent and pervasive is this objective that one cannot help wondering whether those human needs which can be met only by relationship and pursuits that are nonproductive in a conventional sense are neglected. One also wonders how much genuine appreciation there exists for the plight of those who, through no fault of their own but because of the imperfect knowledge and skill of their therapists, cannot become productive, and to what extent, therefore, welfare services in Soviet society are available for those "who only stand and wait" — the ultimate test of man's humanity to man.

MEDICAL ORGANIZATION
AND THE MEDICAL PROFESSION

MARK G. FIELD

I

Interest in the medical system is, generally speaking, apt to turn to the twin aspects of availability and quality. Yet there are broader social issues or factors that underlie the dispensation of medical services to the members of a society and that determine, to a significant degree, what kind of medical philosophy and medical practitioner a society will produce, maintain, tolerate, or encourage. Thus, while it might be possible to trace the numerical growth of medical practitioners in Russia over the last hundred years, or study changes in the incidence, prevalence, and treatment of pneumonia, typhus, or St. Vitus's dance, or even analyze the movement of infant mortality since the Soviets took power, and while such studies would undoubtedly yield data of great significance, I would prefer here to concentrate on some more historically and sociologically relevant, though less known, aspects of the Russian medical system. In particular, I should like to focus on medical organization, the medical profession as an organized corporate group, and briefly on some of the sociological functions of the medical system in Soviet society over the last hundred years.

Historically, the Bolshevik revolution profoundly affected the organization of medical services by bringing about their centralization and bureaucratization, and the medical profession through a reorganization of its associational bases. The revolution thus marks, in medicine as in so many other fields, a pivotal point in the development of medical services in Russia and serves as a good vantage point to cast a retrospective look at Tsarist, and an appraising glance at Soviet, medicine.

It is a characteristic trait of the Bolshevik mentality (perhaps a reaction against the Oblomovism of Tsarist Russia) not to leave anything to chance, even in areas as distant from the political scene as medicine and public health. Almost from the day they seized power, the Bolsheviks proceeded to reshape medical services along lines calculated to bring maximum benefits to the regime and its supporters, and to be used as an instrument against their opponents and detractors. This entailed a well-defined, two-pronged enveloping movement aimed at medical *facilities* and medical *personnel*. Control over facilities was relatively easy to achieve, involving only changes of ownership and legal manipulations, and could be accomplished with a stroke of the pen. Control over medical personnel was somewhat more difficult to achieve, since the Bolsheviks were facing medical practitioners and medical associations that were anything but receptive to any type of political control over medicine and, least of all, Bolshevik dictation. The lack of enthusiasm on the part of medical circles to embrace the Bolshevik cause led the regime to assume about the prerevolutionary medical profession certain motivations which it then explained in terms of its own political position. The Bolsheviks maintained, for example, that medicine was not, never had been, and never could be "apolitical." Just like any other science it had served the interests of the bourgeoisie and had helped the "exploited classes" only insofar as this would benefit the bourgeoisie.

The task of the Bolsheviks, as they saw it, was to involve medicine and the physicians in the service of the proletariat, the new ruling class: "Toward this goal, workers and peasants must take into their hands the protection of health in the same way as they have seized all the political and economic power in the rupblic." [1] The fact of having "served the interests of the bourgeoisie" under the old regime was one that the Bolsheviks could easily understand in terms of their own political theories; what they condemned, on the other hand, was the understandable reluctance of the medical profession to side politically with the Bolsheviks (that is, its alleged refusal to serve the new ruling classes) which they promptly labeled as "medical sabotage," an expression that was to be heard again in the thirties, the purge trials of 1937 and 1938, and as recently as the "Doctors' Plot" of 1953. Barsukov, for example, in his book "The Great October Socialist Revolution and the Organization of Soviet Public Health," [2] gives many examples which purport to show that physicians actually refused to give medical care to the Bolsheviks while, at the same time, treating White Guardists and using medical installations to hide and protect the "counterrevolutionaries." He quotes, for example, A. Okhapkina who wrote as follows about events in the Khamovnik District in Moscow (now Frunze):

they brought the wounded to the secondary school on the Krymsky Ploshchad. The old gate-keeper under a series of pretexts did not open the door. I ordered to beat on the window panes. After the first blow, a key was found, and the door was opened. In the school there were White wounded. I myself, with difficulty, found the doctor in another room; he started to beat around the bush and to bare his teeth; knowing that we were Reds, he found a pretext to refuse to operate. I called some of our own people, ordered the doctor to go to the operation room, forced him to boil the instruments, asked the attendants to look

---

[1] Statement by Khirin, at the First Ural Regional Congress, 1918, in G. E. Gurevich, "Istoricheskii s"ezd," *Sovetskoe zdravookhranenie*, VI (1947), 39.

[2] M. I. Barsukov, *Velikaia oktiabr'skaia sotsialisticheskaia revoliutsiia i organizatsiia sovetskogo zdravookhraneniia: X.1917–VII.1918* (Moscow, 1951).

after the wounded, put someone on duty, and then brought in the rest of the wounded.[3]

It is difficult, of course, to determine whether or not physicians actually refused to treat "Red" patients in the early days of the revolution. Enough is known, however, of Soviet methods of rewriting history, including medical history, to throw some doubts on these assertions.[4] Yet this alleged sabotage was justification enough for the gradual elimination of the Russian medical profession as a corporate group, with its traditions, its strong code of ethics (which makes the refusal to give help to wounded men difficult to believe), and its relative freedom from political dictation even under Tsarism.

II

The medical profession under Tsarism, in the latter part of the nineteenth century and in the early part of the twentieth, had achieved a considerable degree of autonomy and political influence. Particularly prominent in this respect was the Society of Russian Physicians in Memory of N. I. Pirogov. The society, founded in 1885 to commemorate one of Russia's ablest military surgeons, actively campaigned not only for medical but also for political, social, and economic reforms, and was identified with the liberal intelligentsia. Confronted as they were in their everyday activities with illness and poverty, the Pirogovists had come to the conclusion that medical reforms could accomplish little unless paralleled by an improvement in the living standards of the population. The significant aspect of the existence and the activities of the Pirogovists, under the conditions of Tsarist autocracy, was their ability to band together and maintain an organization of professionals with a corporate identity, able to act in a concerted manner and to take and support a political stance. Moreover, this ability to act independently, particularly in professional matters, was the guarantee of high standards of medical practice, free from dictation from outside sources, and also of high social status. This was true even in those cases when physicians were on salaries, as in zemstvo medicine which played such a critical role in the unfolding of Russian medical organization in the nineteenth century and which helped to establish certain operational principles which later were to be adopted, adapted, and amplified by the Soviets in setting up their own medical system.

In public health and medicine, Russia lagged far behind Europe in

[3] *Fevral'-oktiabr' v Khamovnikakh 1917: sbornik statei i vospominanii* (Moscow, 1927), 129, as cited in Barsukov, 74.
[4] Thus, for example, the famous Doctors' Plot (1953), in which outstanding physicians were accused of having hastened the death of important Soviet personalities, was revealed after Stalin's death to have been a complete fabrication. The same could undoubtedly be said of such famous doctors as Levin and Pletniev who were accused of "medical sabotage" during the purge trials of the late thirties.

1861. Particularly neglected were the majority of the population who lived on the land. Zemstvo medicine inherited from the Bureaus of Assistance a small and inadequate network of medical installations, the majority of which were in a dilapidated condition, particularly since the bureaus had known for some time that their installations were to be transferred to zemstvo jurisdiction and thus did not keep them in good repair. According to Alabin, who was at that time chairman of the Samara Province administration:

One knows in what sad shape are the hospitals in the town of the provinces when they are placed under the direction of the Bureaus of Assistance. The minimum salaries which the physicians received, the paucity of resources assigned to the hospitals for their upkeep . . . the abuses of all types which existed in the domestic economy of these establishments, all this made the hospital an institution that was supported only by the apathy of society at that time . . . as to the persons whom fate brought within the walls of these establishments, most of them regarded the necessity to enter a hospital as a punishment from God.[5]

The zemstvo medical program developed unevenly since there was no over-all, nation-wide, coordinated program or plan applicable to the whole of Russia, as there would be later in the Soviet Union, nor was the zemstvo system to be found in every province of Imperial Russia (there were zemstvo assemblies in only fifty-four of the eighty-nine provinces). And yet zemstvo medicine, in addition to making medical care available to segments of the population that had never had it before, made an even more significant contribution: it encouraged the development of a new social and professional type in the zemstvo physician, combining traditional medical ethics with the humanitarianisms of some of the great Russian thinkers and writers of the nineteenth century and the progressivism and missionary quality of the Populist movement. In addition, zemstvo medicine was *public* medicine, financed from taxes and with the physician cast in the role of a public servant. According to some thinkers of the time, this was a higher type of medicine, since it had been shorn of "commercialism." As Professor Kapustin described it:

medical care has been dealt with as a *personal* transaction between the patient and the doctor, established on the same basis as commerce or a trade. Zemstvo medicine is essentially a public institution. Here the ministration which the physician gives the patient is not a personal service, nor is it an act of charity, it is a public function which he fulfills. In European towns competition among doctors is general; it is a question as to who will have the largest practice; this competition does not exist among Zemstvo physicians in the countryside, because the doctor is a public servant. Whether the doctor has noble or mean sentiments, the goal he seeks to reach is always to decrease the number of patients and shorten the course of the illness.[6]

[5] Cited in E. Ossipow, I. Popow, and P. Kourkine, *La Médecine du zemstwo en Russie* (Moscow, 1900), 62.

[6] M. Kapustin, "Questions fondamentales de la médecine du zemstwo," *Travaux de l'Assemblée de Kharkow* (1889), cited in *La Médecine*, 89–90.

This conception of medical services and of the patient-doctor relationship was, to a large extent, the one the Soviet Union was to adopt as its blueprint of socialized medicine. Thus the cash nexus (symbol of "capitalistic" or "commercial" medicine) was to be removed from the medical relationship and the costs were to be borne by the community or society through tax funds. This conception, furthermore, removed, at least officially, the stigma of charity from medical care, and gave everyone a claim for medical attention as a service society "owes" the individual. Thus the principle of "public practice" was already favorably regarded by the medical profession as part of a cultural tradition upheld by some of the most respected members of the prerevolutionary medical profession. The hitch, however, came in the public-servant aspect of the doctor's role under Soviet conditions, which meant subjugation to the dictates of the party in a manner unacceptable to the profession and particularly to the Pirogovists.

Prior to the Bolshevik revolution, in the period of democratic ferment that followed the February Revolution, there were two other significant developments:

1. The medical profession undertook to reform and improve the medical system along the lines elaborated in the half century preceding the revolution. It sponsored the formation of a Central Medical-Sanitary Council which was the embodiment of this movement and a clear indication of the principle that medical care, and particularly public health, should have central government backing and financing, and yet should be supervised and controlled by the medical profession in its capacity as a corporate group. The Pirogovists, naturally, played a crucial role in the creation of the Council. Thus, if anything, the February Revolution strengthened the power of the medical corporation.

2. Parallel to the growth of unionization in the labor movement, there arose in medicine several medical unions based primarily on the physicians' specialties and particularly place of employment (hospital, city, army, navy, means of communications, and factory).[7] This movement originated in Petrograd where these associations amalgamated, in May 1917, into the Council of the Petrograd Union of Physicians. From Petrograd the movement rapidly spread to other cities, culminating later in the creation of a central organization, the Pan-Russian Union of Professional Associations of Physicians. Thus while the Medical-Sanitary Council was more of an official body (concerned with medical organization), working in close cooperation and liaison with the political organs, the Pan-Russian Union represented the organized (we might even call it unionized) medical profession attempting to define its place, its role, and its status vis-à-vis other occupational groups in the new society that

[7] Henry E. Sigerist, *Medicine and Health in the Soviet Union* (New York, 1947), 77–78.

was to emerge from the February Revolution. It should be clear, further-more, that none of these organizations or associations looked favorably upon the Bolshevik bid for power. As members of the "bourgeois-liberal" intelligentsia, they tended generally to support the Provisional Govern-ment and to oppose the Bolsheviks.

III

Another element of the Bolshevik *Weltanschauung* is a certain blind-ness to shades of nuances, an inability to be satisfied with compromises or to regard society as a balance of competing groups. Politically this trans-lates itself into the old adage: "If you are not with us, then you must be against us." [8]

By definition, the typical prerevolutionary medical doctor was a "bourgeois." Politically he was seen by the Bolsheviks as an ineffectual liberal, content with reforms, and not interested in or convinced of the need for a complete overhaul of the political and social structure. As such it would be unthinkable, in the eyes of the handful of doctors who had joined the Bolshevik side before the revolution, to leave medical and public-health leadership in his hands or in the hands of the associations that spoke for him, particularly the Pirogov Society. Moreover, the Bolshe-viks knew that their ideas on the role of medicine in the new society would be opposed, generally speaking, by the prerevolutionary medical corps. Its existence as a corporate body would thus be cumbersome to the new regime. What the Bolshevik medical and lay leaders wanted was a new type of medical organization and association, completely responsive to party wishes and dictates and dispensing medical care on a "class basis." Medically this meant differential treatment in accord with the individual's class position, a principle that clearly ran against the ethical universalism of medicine. This universalism sees the patient as someone to help, regardless of *any* other considerations, including of course class position. Another point of friction was the regime's policy, in line with the egalitarian notions of the times, of reducing the status of the physician from a professional to a medical "worker." He was to be con-sidered the social equal of nurses, feldshers, orderlies, morgue attendants, and other such "medical workers," and his authority over auxiliary medical personnel would be correspondingly diminished.

It is perhaps the medical profession's lack of acceptance of these conceptions of medical care and the status of the physician which Bolshe-

[8] "The value of a man depended exclusively upon the value of his class. If he were a bourgeois his value was not the same as that of a working class man . . . the two cannot be equated . . . there cannot exist any tolerance or consideration, nor any humane feeling toward any 'enemy' of the working class. . . . One of the basic qualities of a party member, according to Stalin, is that of pitilessness, irreconcilability, and ruthlessness toward enemies of the working class." D. A. Tomasic, *National Com-munism and Soviet Strategy* (Washington, 1957), 160–161.

vik medical leaders defined as "sabotage," since disagreement, in Bolshevik terms, meant hostility and hence such hostility was bound to come out in "medical sabotage." The period that followed the revolution was characterized, in medical affairs, by the simultaneous neutralization of the medical corporation and the creation of a Soviet medical administration as an instrument of control over medical affairs.

In the days immediately following the seizure of power, a Medical-Sanitary Section (*Otdel*) of the Petrograd Military-Revolutionary Committee was formed to organize medical services for the "workers and soldiers." This was a Bolshevik organization with no ties to previous medical organizations in the capital. Furthermore, it was destined within a short period of time to become the nucleus of the Soviet system of administrative controls over medical services. The formation of similar sections to serve the other soviets of workers, soldiers, and peasant deputies at all levels of the Soviet structure and wherever they existed was urged by the Petrograd Section. These sections were to become the medical arm of the new society, dedicated to serving the interests of the toilers and watching over the medical profession to make sure they did not commit acts of sabotage. In addition, special medical boards, *collegia*, were either instituted or taken over in the Commissariats of Internal Affairs, Transportation, and Welfare in November 1917. Two months later, early in January, Lenin signed a decree instituting a Soviet of Medical Collegia to unite, supervise, and coordinate their activities. This soviet, called the "highest medical organization of the workers' and peasants' government," also took over the functions of the Medical-Sanitary Section of the Petrograd Committee. One more link had been forged in the direction of centralizing and controlling medical services under the new regime.

The next step might have been anticipated: a decree (in February) abolished the Central Medical-Sanitary Council established, as seen earlier, by the Provisional Government. It was eliminated on the now familiar ground that it was counterrevolutionary, although Barsukov informs us that many attempts were made by the Bolsheviks to reach an understanding with the council.[9] The refusal of the medical profession to cooperate with the Soviet medical authorities was interpreted by the Soviets as deriving naturally from its class composition, and this left no alternative but the formation of Soviet medical institutions "which could be trusted, and which would work honestly and without refusals."[10] Finally, on July 11, 1918, a decree over Lenin's signature raised the Soviet of Medical Collegia to the status of a commissariat (*Narodnii kommissariat zdravookhraneniia* — literally, People's Commissariat of Health Protection). This decree, which must be regarded as the basic charter of

[9] Barsukov, 148.
[10] Barsukov, 64.

Soviet medical organization, defined the primary task of the commissariat as the "unification of all medical and public health work in the Russian Soviet Federated Socialist Republic." [11]

Thus was accomplished, on Soviet terms and in less than a year, the reorganization and centralization of medical services in the Soviet Union.

In medical circles, opposition to the regime's medical policies lay mainly in the Pirogov Society. The society therefore constituted an independent locus of power which the regime was not willing to tolerate, in medicine any more than in other areas. Eliminating the medical corporation was thus consistent with Inkeles' statement: "Totalitarianism does not merely subordinate the *individual* to the 'state,' but it also, indeed preëminently, subordinates human *associations*, the organizations and institutions which man creates to meet his social needs." [12] Undoubtedly, in the light of the amount of energy to be expended, the regime would have preferred to seize control over the medical corporation and run it as it saw fit. Unable to do so, the next step was simply its elimination as a social organization. At the time the Central Medical-Sanitary Council was dissolved, the Pirogovists suffered the same fate. It is interesting to note, for the record, how a Bolshevik physician interpreted the purging of the Pirogovists:

Soviet public health historically was built and grew in the struggle against reactionary bourgeois medicine, among whom were the reactionary ideologists from the "Pirogovist" camp and the debris of the bourgeois Mensheviks and Socialist Revolutionaries.

The ideologists of bourgeois medicine, emanating chiefly from the reactionary part of the Pirogovists, were hostile to the Soviet regime, not only rejected the term "Soviet medicine," but also rejected the very possibility of its existence.

The Pirogovists rejected the class character of medicine, endowing it with above-class [*nadklassnii*] elements. Standing on the idea of the solidity of the bourgeois order in society, not recognizing the dictatorship of the proletariat as a new world-historical type of proletarian democracy, Pirogovists opposed the idea that public health should be a state matter in the conditions of Soviet society. They felt that medicine should be autonomous, independent from the Soviet state, and that it must be turned in its entirety to the community, i.e., to the bourgeois zemstvo self-government with the leading role given to the medical corporation. [13]

And so was silenced the most influential voice of the prerevolutionary medical profession. [14] It remained for the regime to clear one more hurdle: this was the Pan-Russian Union of Professional Associations of Physicians.

[11] Text of the decree; see G. A. Miterev, *XXV let sovetskogo zdravookhraneniia* (Moscow, 1944).

[12] Alex Inkeles, "The Totalitarian Mystique," in Carl J. Friedrich, ed., *Totalitarianism* (Cambridge, Mass., 1954), 90.

[13] Barsukov, 27.

[14] For more details, see the review of Barsukov's book by Dr. G. Schulz in *Vestnik Instituta po Izucheniiu Istorii i Kultury SSSR*, no. 1 (1951), 170–73.

Unable to capture the leadership of the association, it was more successful in obtaining control of unions of junior medical personnel, whose
position as having been formerly "exploited" by the physicians put them
in a favorable political position. A Pan-Russian Federated Union of
Medical Workers (known now as *Medsantrud*) was founded in 1918 and
began its work in 1919, without the formal participation of associations
of doctors (as well as pharmacists and veterinarians). The few physicians who had joined the union constituted less than 10 per cent of the
nine-hundred members at the time. At the end of 1919, the pharmacists
and veterinarians withdrew their objections and, at the beginning of
1920, they joined the union, though in special sections. Only the physicians
remained outside.

Then followed a familiar step: the Pan-Russian Union of Professional
Associations of Physicians was ruled out of its corporate existence through
a decree of the All-Russian Central Council of Trade Unions with which
the Medical Workers' Union was affiliated. In 1920 an agreement was
reached whereby physicians could join the union but in nonpartisan sections not committed to its political aims. By 1924, the nonpartisanship
clause was dropped.[15] With the emasculation of the Soviet trade unions
after 1930 they became, even more than previously, agencies of the state
and a further means to control workers (including medical workers,
among whom were the physicians). No trace was left of the medical profession as an organized, self-governing, social group and social force.
Indeed, if we accept the definition of Carr-Saunders and Wilson, the medical profession no longer exists in the USSR because: "A profession can
only be said to exist where there are bonds between the practitioners, and
these bonds can take but one shape — that of formal association." [16] It
might perhaps be wiser to use Lewis and Maude's expression "a body of
expert officials," instead of a profession, particularly when it is the state
that organizes, trains, and employs all members of a profession.[17]

IV

Early in this chapter the idea was put forward that an examination
of the medical services in any society would reveal certain basic factors
underlying them, the role and status of the medical practitioner, and medical philosophy in general. In Soviet society the important factors in this
respect are the mobilized and politically monolithic nature of the system.
It is a system in which most social processes are harnessed toward the
achievement of certain goals defined by the leaders of the regime who

[15] *A Short History of the Pan-Russian Union of Medical Workers*, 20, as cited in
Anna J. Haines, *Health Work in Soviet Russia* (New York, 1928), 32.

[16] A. M. Carr-Saunders and P. A. Wilson, *The Professions* (Oxford, 1933), 298.

[17] Roy Lewis and Angus Maude, *Professional People in England* (Cambridge,
Eng., 1953), 70.

have a monopoly on the use of force and means of communication. These goals, given the limited resources of the society in manpower and facilities, necessitate the adoption of two important operational principles: (1) a strict order of priorities dictating the manner in which resources will be invested for maximizing the chances of reaching the goals or subgoals; and (2) a system of bureaucratic controls to ensure that the decisions reached are implemented.

One can follow the impact of these principles on medicine: in the light of contemporary commitments to such first-priority goals as industrialization, an adequate agricultural system, and militarization, the medical area can receive only secondary or even residual priority. This may help to explain such phenomena as a medical profession made up so predominantly of women (76 per cent), or the extremely low salaries that most physicians can command when compared to other technical specialists or even Stakhanovites. The need for control helps to explain the elemination of the medical associations of prerevolutionary vintage and their replacement by structures such as the Medical Workers' Union which ensures constant supervision over the professional actions of physicians. Areas of conflict between the physician and the state (for example, in the problem of delivering sickness excuses to industrial and agricultural workers) are usually resolved in favor of the state; this means, of course, that the state (or its representatives) are never uninterested in decisions the professional man reaches in the clinical situation because of the possibilities of abuses that might interfere with production or with security. Control over professional actions goes hand in hand with state control of medical facilities through state ownership of these facilities, and their administration through a heavily centralized and bureaucratized agency, the Health Ministry. This agency moreover permits an effective mobilization of medical resources and personnel to a degree unthinkable in a more atomized and unregulated medical system.

This system functions according to the conception of the physician as a public servant, with little autonomy left to him in professional matters, rather than as a free professional (free in the sense of not being employed, remunerated, and disciplined by an organization). It is thus a scheme in which the voluntary nature of the zemstvo physician's role, for example, does not find a receptive ground because such a role relies on the individual's motivation and sense of dedication, qualities which are too erratic and unreliable for the regime to depend upon. Thus, for instance, the Soviet physician (in contrast to his zemstvo colleague) can be driven out to the countryside by administrative decisions, an assignment which, if we are to believe the Soviet medical press, many strive by all possible means to escape.[18]

[18] See Mark G. Field, *Doctor and Patient in Soviet Russia* (Cambridge, Mass., 1957), 78–101.

It is also undoubtedly true that the status change from professional to state functionary has meant a definite drop in status for the physician. Private practice, which to some extent has helped to preserve this status, appears to be reserved to only a small segment of the medical profession, though it has never been officially forbidden during the years of the Soviet regime. Ideologically, of course, private practice remains a "remnant of capitalistic consciousness," eventually bound to disappear under Communism.

v

One point, finally, might be pondered: in the totalitarian sea of Soviet society the medical system stands in certain respects as an island of refuge or a sanctuary from the demands the regime makes of the individual. I have reported elsewhere the role the Soviet physician plays in manipulating the medical excuse to provide some kind of relief to the population,[19] and the shock-absorbing function which the physician fills in such a system. From brief personal observations in the Soviet Union of the manner in which hospital personnel handled patients and behaved toward them, it appeared that the hospital played a similar role by providing a temporary spatial refuge to which the person could retreat. Indeed, there was in many hospital wards that I visited an extraordinary amount of kindness, gentleness, and what appeared to be genuine affection displayed by the staff toward the patients.

It was as if the staff said to the patient: "Now that you are here, you must trust us entirely and we will take care of you entirely; we will love you." Here perhaps one might find intact the humanitarianism of the Russian writers, philosophers, and doctors of the nineteenth century, which has survived the years of Soviet totalitarianism and has been preserved in the medical enclave. There is of course evidence that this arrangement has not been to the regime's liking, such as the April 1939 resolution of the Central Council of the Trade Unions on taking steps "against doctors who admit idlers and malingerers to hospitals." [20]

At the same time, the sociological significance of the medical sanctuary in Soviet society may well reside in the fact that it provides that society with a certain amount of sorely needed resilience by permitting the individual to retreat, temporarily at least, into an area where pressures are absent.

VI

Societies are dynamic entities, always in a state of flux, and the present description of medical organization and the status of the medical profession may well have to be revised in the near future, as the industrializa-

[19] *Doctor and Patient,* 146–180.
[20] Cited in *Doctor and Patient,* 167.

tion drive reaches a plateau. Should the regime at that point decide to change its priorities commitments in the direction of higher consumption and human welfare, it may well begin to put a heavier emphasis on medicine. This may even become imperative, in terms of the functioning of the whole society, if the birth rate continues to fall and the relative cost of maintaining human beings begins to rise (compared to materials). Coupled with this is the fact that, as an industrialized society becomes more dependent on highly trained personnel, the relative replaceability of such personnel will correspondingly decrease and it will be necessary to maximize returns on education and training by keeping more individuals healthy and alive longer. One might then look forward to a gradual decentralization of medical services, with more emphasis on local autonomy and quality rather than quantity (indeed, some steps have already been taken in this direction[21]). Some answer will also have to be found to the complaint of the Health Minister of the USSR that the attitude shown toward medical personnel in the USSR is one of general indifference.[22] At the same time, it is now quite difficult to conceive of the abandonment of the general principles of socialized medicine, although there may well be important adjustments, such as giving greater scope to private practice and, as the Health Minister of the Latvian SSR recently pointed out in Moscow, in creating "a system of medical care whereby the patient could choose his own physician." [23] It is also quite possible that, as medicine acquires a higher status and better rewards, the percentage of men who will choose it as a career will correspondingly increase. But as long as Soviet society remains a mobilized system, the basic features of its medical organization and the status of the medical doctor are likely to remain essentially unchanged.

SUMMARY AND REVIEW

RAYMOND A. BAUER

Any attempt to summarize the essays in this section poses the problem of selecting from among the large number of rich themes that run through them. Let us begin with those themes which are generally common to all.

Perhaps the most important motif is that of the crucial role played

[21] Speech by Maria D. Kovrigina, Minister of Health for the USSR, in *Review of Eastern Medical Sciences* (January–June 1957), 64.

[22] Kovrigina, 63.

[23] Kovrigina, 67.

by the fact of industrialization in determining the shape of Soviet life and the nature of Soviet policies. It is fairly well taken for granted that the Soviet Union must be regarded politically as a totalitarian state and economically as an industrial society. Because totalitarianism and industrialism have developed simultaneously in the USSR, and because totalitarian methods were employed in the forced-draft growth of Soviet industry, the two are often seen tacitly as almost identical, or at least highly compatible. This takes perhaps its most grotesque form in the writings of students of Western society who contend that industrialization will lead to totalitarianism in Western countries.

Unquestionably there has to this point been a great deal of compatibility between totalitarianism and industrialization in the Soviet Union. Yet this statement is perhaps tautological because, of the various possible roads to industrialization, Stalin chose the totalitarian one. It does not follow, however, that this compatibility will continue into the future — a point which Mark Field makes well in speculating on the prospects for Soviet medicine.

I

Klaus Mehnert in his study of the changing attitudes of Soviet youth comments that all the attitudinal areas with which he was concerned exhibited a common pattern in being experimental and revolutionary in the middle 1920's to the early 1930's, and then retreating to a more conservative position. The retreat in education is especially illuminating. It is true that the experimentally progressive educational policy of the early Soviet period was in many respects inimical to Stalin's general ideological orientation, or to Lenin's own ideas for that matter. However, as Mehnert points out, it was essentially the demands of industrialization that brought about the changes in educational policy. The youth themselves realized that they needed to acquire useful knowledge to succeed in the new industrial order. Perhaps it is more pertinent that the regime itself realized that educational policy had to be revised if the appropriate "cadres" were to be trained. But the youth were receptive to this change for the reason mentioned.

Of course the influence of industrialization becomes intertwined with other influences. The loss of functions of the Soviet family, discussed by Kent Geiger, is largely interpretable in terms of industrialization. But, while industrialization may explain the fact that the *urban* family is no longer a productive unit, this has little direct bearing on the fact that the rural family has also ceased to be a productive unit. While collectivization of Soviet farms did have a relation to the First Five Year Plan, there is no necessary connection between these two economic forms. The relation occurred in the Soviet Union because of the particular totalitarian methods of economic development employed.

Other functions which the family has lost, such as a large measure of responsibility for the education and training of the young, occur inevitably in developed economies. In this connection, Vera Dunham's highly original and distinctive essay on the strong-woman motif throughout Russian literature shows the influence that a modern stabilized social order can have on the changing functions of and attitudes toward the "new Soviet woman." Yet — although Russian literature has traditionally idealized the woman — the emphasis on the achievements of the new woman in the socialist-realism manner is part of the regime's constant effort at self-rationalization. It is one necessary function of totalitarianism. Similarly, the Soviet regime's taking over of the training of the young — considered in both Geiger's and Allen Kassoff's papers — is as much a function of totalitarianism as of industrialization. Even if there had not been rapid urbanization and industrialization of Soviet life, it was part of the Communist blueprint for the state to become more involved in the rearing of the young.

With respect to the family's loss of the function of caring for the sick and the incompetent, the picture becomes increasingly complex. The gradual disappearance of the rural extended family has meant that the family as a unit is less able to carry on this task. But it was and is also part of the image of the Communist welfare state that such functions *should* be taken over by society. Here we must begin to look at the distinction between the "totalitarian state" and the "welfare state." This distinction may turn out to be highly abstract but, as I shall point out later, it is essential for anticipating the future of Soviet society. It is characteristic of the totalitarian aspect of Soviet society that centralized control is maintained virtually for its own sake. Voluntary associations for welfare services would be frowned on because this would constitute a dispersal of power that preferably belongs in the hands of the state. Power is a prerogative of the state. On the other hand, welfare is a prerogative of the citizen, and the service of the citizen's welfare is the state's responsibility.

While the concentration of welfare services in the hands of the state is currently more explicable in terms of the totalitarian nature of Soviet society, we must not forget that this concentration is wholly consonant with the model of the welfare state developed in idealistic versions of communism, and present in the minds of most Soviet citizens. We may grant that the Soviet leaders wanted to cut back on the powers of the family and the independence of such self-governing bodies as the medical profession. Yet the development of the social services described by Bernice Madison and the medical services described by Field can be explained only in part by the self-interest of the leaders of a totalitarian state. It is true that even in a totalitarian state morale and health cannot be permitted to fall below a minimal level lest the efficiency of the economy suffer. But

Soviet leaders have been under pressure to keep services well above this minimum because of the welfare expectations which the citizens derive from their idealized image of the communist (or socialist) state.

From all the evidence we have — including the testimony of the émigrés interviewed by the Harvard Project on the Soviet Social System — the *forms* of welfare institutions are approved of by the vast majority of Soviet citizens. They accept wholeheartedly the principles of social insurance and socialized medicine. They complain only when such institutions do not function in the way they have learned to expect them to — at least until recent years this happened so often that the conflict between expectation and realization has become one of the real sore points of the Soviet order. Certainly until the time of Stalin's death the welfare functions of the state were kept firmly subordinate to the development of the state's industrial base. Madison indicates that the granting of welfare benefits was handled so as to favor "leading" workers and thereby to stimulate production. Field tells of how the granting of sick absences was coordinated to the needs of the economy. But more important is the secondary priority given in the allocation of resources to welfare services. The disparity in salaries between Soviet doctors and Soviet engineers has been pointed out often. Until 1956 pensions were so inadequate as to be a hollow mockery.

Quite obviously the regime is aware of the fact that its own propaganda has created a desire for adequate welfare services. The sharp increase in pensions in 1956 is evidence of this — and the reaction of Soviet citizens with whom I have talked indicates that this move was well received. Field tells of efforts to improve the medical service, and he makes a point much more interesting for anticipating future developments. Not only have Soviet citizens come to expect these services, but the very course of industrialization will make it imperative that they be granted. With the falling birth rate that ordinarily accompanies industrialization, and with the increasing demand for specialized, more highly trained personnel, it will be necessary to maximize returns on education and training by keeping people healthy, alive, and in a high state of morale.

II

Thus we may anticipate that some of the knottiest problems facing Soviet leaders will involve the interaction of these three components of Soviet society: the industrial system, the welfare state, and the totalitarian regime. As the industrial system grows it will become increasingly apparent to the citizenry that the promise of the welfare state is feasible. Furthermore, the leadership will be under increasing pressures of self-interest to attend to the welfare demands of the citizen. It is almost inconceivable that no concessions will be made to these demands. It is equally inconceivable that the regime will hurriedly and eagerly place the "welfare state" ahead of totalitarian control and economic progress. Clearly the problem involves what particular form of compromise will result from the interaction of these components.

I have spoken of the promise of the welfare state almost as though it constituted exclusively a liability for the Soviet leaders. This is far from true, and some elaboration is demanded. My impression jibes with that of Mehnert, namely that this is no "youthful revolt" against established institutional forms, either political or economic. If the promise of present institutions, and particularly the welfare aspects of Soviet society, can be fulfilled, it will be a powerful advantage to the Soviet leaders in solidifying popular support for the regime and the system.

Furthermore, any semblance of realization of the welfare state will give the Soviet Union a powerful propaganda advantage in the world arena. Even the forms themselves have a powerful attraction to the peoples of many countries. It did not fall within the scope of either Madison's or Field's chapters to compare the adequacy of welfare services and medical care in the Soviet Union with that of comparable services in the United States. Such a comparison would inevitably be problematic and perhaps should not even be attempted. However, it may very well be that in these areas of life, in relation to others such as political freedom, real income of employed workers, and such, the Soviet citizen fares proportionately well. In other words, it will be a long time before the real income of the average worker in the Soviet Union is up to that of the average American worker; it will be still longer before there is comparable political freedom in the Soviet Union; but it may well be less long before the welfare and medical services of the Soviet citizen match those of the American. In certain respects they already exceed those of the American citizen — at least insofar as they are on paper and are managed by the state or public organizations.

PART SIX

PERSONAL AND SOCIAL VALUES

RUSSIAN ETHNIC VALUES

JOHN S. RESHETAR, JR.

I

This attempt to identify Russian ethnic values as they have developed and changed in the course of nearly a century is based on an analysis of various beliefs and reasoned convictions regarding the Russians as expressed by representative members of that ethnic group. It is an essay in defining the self-image of the Russian in terms of popularly held or consequential views regarding common virtues and vices which have served to distinguish the Russians, in their own eyes, from other ethnic groups. It must include, at least implicitly, some consideration of the reasons why various Russians have expressed intense self-love and pride when speaking of their own kind and have also on occasion indicated contrary views. Such an effort is obviously fraught with difficulties since any composite self-portrait necessarily reflects much ambivalence and a certain number of apparent contradictory characteristics.

In a sense it is even incorrect to speak of many ethnic values common to all classes, and this is particularly true of the postemancipation Russia of Alexander II in which the gaps among landowners, intellectuals, the merchant class, and the peasantry were very marked and significant. Since the peasantry constituted the overwhelming mass of the population — more than forty million were emancipated from serfdom in February 1861 — the proverbs of the period constitute an important source for popular attitudes and ethnic values.

They indicate a strong sense of attachment to the native land: "The native country is a mother, the alien land a stepmother" (*Rodimaia storona — mat', chuzhaia machikha*); "Sweet is the land in which one's umbilicus is cut" (*Mila ta storona gde pupok rezan*); "One's own sorrow is dearer than alien joy" (*Svoia pechal' chuzhoi radosti dorozhe*); "Praise what is beyond the seas but sit home" (*Khvali zamor'e, a sidi doma*).[1] However,

---

[1] Vladimir Ivanovich Dal', *Poslovitsy russkago naroda* (Moscow, 1862), 338ff. This selection of proverbs from the 1860's has been employed in lieu of better data for that period. No attempt has been made here to quantify the themes of Russian proverbs since proverbs constitute but a small portion of the data utilized in this chapter. For a quantitative analysis of proverbs from three areas in prerevolutionary Russia, see D. B. Shimkin and Pedro Sanjuan, "Culture and World View: A Method of Analysis Applied to Rural Russia," *American Anthropologist*, LV (August 1953), 329–348. For all its quantification and undoubted value, this effort does not convey great precision and many of its conclusions are highly qualified. Of some significance, by way of contrast to the proverbs presented here, is a collection of Russian proverbs pub-

this sense of attachment is tempered by other proverbs: "Great is the Holy Russian land, and there is no room for truth" (*Velika Sviatorusskaia zemlia, a pravde nigde net mesta*); "The Russian people are a stupid people" (*Russki narod — glupy narod*); "In Russia, thank God, there is a hundred-year supply of fools" (*Na Rusi, slava Bogu, durakov let na sto pripaseno*).[2] There is also a rather definite awareness of sin, guilt, and temptation: "Only God is without sin" (*Odin Bog bez grekha*); "Who is not sinful before God, who is not his grandmother's grandson?" (*Kto Bogu ne greshen, kto babke ne vnuk?*); "It is a sin to steal, but how to avoid it?" (*Grekh vorovat' — da nel'zia minovat'*).[3]

The quality of patience and a recognition of fate are also evident in the proverbs of the 1860's: "Our happiness is water in a net" (*Nashe shchast'e — voda v bredne*); "Misfortune comes in poods [a forty-pound weight] — fortune comes in zolotniks [the ninety-sixth part of a Russian pound]" (*Nedolia pudami, dolia zolotnikami*); "This pineapple is not for us" (*Etot ananas ne dlia nas*); "Don't argue with misfortune — suffer" (*S bedoi ne perekoriaisia, terpi*).[4] This sense of resignation and suffering is combined with a high degree of resourcefulness based upon practical worldly wisdom, suspicion, and caution. These characteristics have found expression in the following proverbs: "Pray to God, and don't anger the devil" (*Bogu molis', a chorta ne gnevi*); "Politics is a rotten egg" (*Politika — tukhloe iaitso*) that is, avoid accidents so as not to break it; "The more friends, the more enemies. Fear your friend as you would an enemy" (*Bol'she druzei, bol'she i vragov. Boisia druga, kak vraga*); "Be friendly with the bear, but hang on to your ax" (*S medvedem druzhis', a za topor derzhis'*).[5] The Russian predilection for bluntness and for mutually exclusive extremes is seen in the expression "to receive someone in a Russian manner — either frankly and coarsely or with bread and salt," the traditional symbols of hospitality.[6]

The picture of Russian values as derived from these popular expressions of the period of emancipation is reinforced in part by the decision to grant title to the land to the peasant communes rather than to the individual peasants. The commune was held responsible for the payment of taxes and redemption payments (in return for land received), and this served as a reflection of group responsibility for the individual. Yet the

---

lished in the Soviet Union: *Izbrannye poslovitsy i pogovorki russkogo naroda* (Moscow, 1957). It contains a section dealing with the "birthland" (*rodina*) and includes the old proverb which refers to the native land as a mother and to the alien country as a stepmother. Yet it is no accident that none of the earlier proverbs containing anything derogatory to Russia or to Russians as a people are to be found in this Soviet collection.

[2] Dal', 343, 469.
[3] Dal', 207f.
[4] Dal', 27, 30f.
[5] Dal', 723, 725, 857.
[6] Dal', 344.

emancipation was an important initial step in the protracted process of breaking down barriers between classes and in transforming the nation into a more homogeneous mass as a result of its leavening effect. Thus the first step was taken to qualify Lermontov's apt reference to "unwashed Russia, land of slaves and land of lords." The 1860's also saw the beginning of the advent of a sense of self-respect on the part of the peasantry. At the same time it facilitated the beginning of mass patriotism which made itself felt at the time of the suppression of the Polish revolt of 1863. When the European powers, who had entered into an alliance against Russia in the Crimean War, threatened to intervene on Poland's behalf, patriotic feeling common to all classes manifested itself.

The introduction of universal military service on January 1, 1874, made all classes equally subject to service for a term of six years, for men aged twenty, as compared with the previous twenty-five-year term. However, the more education one had, the shorter was his period of service: university graduates served only six months and persons with secondary education served two years. Thus the peasant served the full six-year term unless he had a primary education, in which case he served four years. When War Minister D. A. Miliutin introduced literacy courses for conscripts in 1875, recruits could return home able to read and write. In addition, the army became a vehicle for propagating patriotic feeling among the masses.

Patriotic sentiment found expression in Nikolai S. Leskov's amusing tale *Levsha* (1881) which deals with the exploits of a left-handed, cross-eyed Tula craftsman. The tale commences with a visit of Alexander I to England following the Congress of Vienna. Leskov has the Western-oriented emperor accompanied by a Cossack, Platov, who in contrast to the ruler's respect for English achievements always states that Russia has the equivalent. Alexander takes Platov to a British museum and tells him that what he will see there will cause him to cease "disputing that we, Russians, with our importance are good for nothing." [7] However, when various gadgets and inventions are exhibited Platov persists in his opinion that it all matters little and notes that his Don Cossacks were able to wage war without these articles and had repelled "twelve tongues" (nations). Upon conclusion of the visit, following various outbursts of national pride on Platov's part which embarrass Alexander, the British give the emperor a microscopic steel flea which would jump and dance upon being wound with a small key. Alexander, according to the tale, is enchanted by this achievement and tells the English: "You are the leading craftsmen in the world and my people, in comparison, are capable of nothing." [8] The steel flea is taken to Russia, and when Alexander I ceased to be emperor becomes the property of Nicholas I.

[7] N. S. Leskov, *Izbrannye sochineniia* (Moscow, 1945), 203.
[8] Leskov, 206.

The new emperor is unable to make much of the microscopic flea until Platov recounts to him the story of how it was acquired on the visit to England. Platov ventures to suggest that the Russian craftsmen of Tula be consulted in an effort to surpass the English in this matter. The nationalistic emperor readily agrees and commissions Platov to look after the work. The steel flea is left at Tula, and in two weeks Platov returns it to the capital. The picture which Leskov paints of the Tula craftsmen is of a very resourceful breed. When the flea is examined by the emperor he is told to note the legs closely, and it becomes apparent that the Tula craftsmen have succeeded in shoeing the steel flea with steel horseshoes made to scale. In addition, each shoe bears the name of the craftsman who had made it, and the cross-eyed, left-handed craftsman, when questioned, states that this work had been carried on without the benefit of a microscope.

Nicholas I kisses the left-handed craftsman and sends him to London. The British are duly impressed by this Russian feat with the flea but point out to the Russian craftsman that if the Russians had had some knowledge of arithmetic they would have known that a shod steel flea would no longer be able to dance, since the shoes would upset the precisely calculated balance. The craftsman from Tula does not dispute this and declares that "we are not very advanced in sciences but are only faithfully devoted to the fatherland." [9] He declines the invitation to remain in England and take a wife there and in doing so makes an invidious comparison between the Anglican and Orthodox faiths by stating that the latter had miraculous icons, sacred relics, and many additional holy days. The left-handed craftsman is particularly interested in the muzzles of English weapons and notes that they were not cleaned in the Russian manner and that the bore remained undamaged.

On the return journey to Russia the cross-eyed craftsman from Tula becomes very seasick and drinks excessively as a result of a wager made with an Englishman. Upon arriving in St. Petersburg the Englishman is taken to his embassy and recovers while the craftsman, having arrived in his native land after enhancing its reputation abroad, is cast about from one hospital to another since his documents are not in order. His last act before expiring is to request that the emperor be informed of the English method of cleaning arms since in the event of war Russian weapons could not be fired with accuracy. The physician conveys this information to a responsible official who shouts at him that it was none of his business and there are generals in Russia responsible for such matters. The barrels of the weapons continued to be cleaned in the old manner, and firing allegedly became inaccurate. Leskov notes that if the craftsman's words had reached the emperor the Crimean War might have taken an altogether different turn.

[9] Leskov, 213f.

Thus the Russian hero and patriot went unrewarded in his homeland. Inertia held sway although the vain emperor had found momentary satisfaction in the fact that the Russians had presumably outdone the English. This tale has remained popular in Soviet Russia, and the image of the shod flea is unforgettable. It is significant that Khrushchev, in an interview granted to William Randolph Hearst, Jr., in November of 1957, cited Leskov's steel flea in connection with an assertion that Soviet methods and achievements are superior to those of foreign lands.[10] However, the analogy was not an entirely appropriate one since Khrushchev omitted the remainder of Leskov's tale bearing on the lack of appreciation of the Tula craftsman and the failure to heed his warning.

The ironic contradictoriness of so much of Russian life is a theme which has been expressed in many ways. Pride and shame, arrogance and professions of humility, sensitivity and coarseness are all present. This is well illustrated in Nekrasov's poem "Who Is Happy in Russia?" which was written in the seventies and makes it clear that there is little happiness in the country. The peasant is "working himself to death and half-killing himself with drink." Nekrasov refers to the words "scratched" on Mother Russia "as the stigma on the criminal, as the brand on the horse": *Na vynos i raspivochno* (For consumption off and on the premises)[11] — a reference to the all too prominent role of the tavern in Russian life. Yet the peasant in Nekrasov's poem is also tough and in one instance is likened to the *bogatyr'*, the enduring and valiant hero of Russian folklore. The lot of women is not easy, and Nekrasov depicts the unhappy daughter-in-law who is oppressed by her husband's hard-bitten parents with whom she must live. The popular attitude toward the clergy is also depicted in terms of the peasant's fear of meeting the priest on the street and the "jesting tales and indecent songs and every kind of obloquy"[12] uttered at the priest's expense.

Thus it is a mixed picture of the Russians which Nekrasov presents in this famous poem. At the end, the brief verses entitled *Rus'* contain the oft-quoted: "Thou art wretched, Thou art bountiful, Thou art mighty, Thou art impotent, Mother Russia!"[13] Yet Nekrasov saw the Russian heart of gold as having been saved by slavery and the people empowered by their "tranquil conscience and living truth." Sacrifice of the kind made by the Russians is not elicited by falsehood, according to Nekrasov, and a concealed spark has been kindled within Russia: "An innumerable armed host arises. An invincible force becomes manifest! Thou art miser-

---

[10] International News Service dispatch from Moscow dated November 25, 1957. Khrushchev made this statement shortly after the Soviet launching of Sputnik II.

[11] *Polnoe sobranie stikhotvorenii N. A. Nekrasova v dvukh tomakh* (St. Petersburg, 1886), 100.

[12] Nekrasov, 21.

[13] Nekrasov, 287.

able, Thou art bountiful, Thou art downtrodden, Thou art omnipotent, Mother Russia!" [14]

II

The juxtaposition of this note of triumphant confidence in Russia's future along with much that does not corroborate it, serves to underline a fundamental split in the Russian self-image. Numerous vices are conceded, and at the same time the Russians are said to be the possessors of Truth. This is a theme which probably finds its fullest expression in Dostoevsky and will be returned to later.

Populism, the favorite Russian doctrine of the 1870's, was based upon the assumption that Russia's salvation lay in the people (*narod*), actually the peasantry, which supposedly embodied all virtues. Such a creed facilitated the further development of Russian nationalism, but it could lead only to disillusionment as a result of the ill-fated effort on the part of the young intellectuals to go "to the people." Many of these crusaders, who desired to enlighten and aid "the people," had studied abroad under the influence of the Populist leader, Peter Lavrov. These youths, so far removed from the peasant masses, had their illusions shattered when they received a cold reception and were often even arrested in the rural areas into which they had gone under the guise of teachers, medical workers, midwives, nurses, and even as ordinary laborers.

The failure of Populism was accompanied not only by disillusionment with the peasantry but also with the results of the emancipation. Few writers, if any, reflected this reaction as well as did Gleb Uspensky. In *The Power of the Soil* (1882) Uspensky describes the fate of a former serf, Ivan Petrov (Bosykh), employed as a railroad worker. He has become a chronic drunkard and cardplayer, squandering his earnings and only occasionally experiencing remorse. When asked how this had come about, he attributes it to the fact of freedom (*volia*) and willfulness (*svoevol'stvo*).[15] Thus money, leisure, and freedom are viewed as leading not to a better life but to personal disintegration and corruption. The great error, according to Uspensky, was to have torn the peasant from the land, making it impossible for him to remain a peasant. Left to his own resources, he had to make his way in a changing Russian world.

The meaning of this world was the subject of much of Dostoevsky's thought. Dostoevsky was convinced of the superiority of the Russian over the European. He saw in the Russian character an instinctive ability to reconcile everything and to become an exponent of human universality (*obshchechelovechnost'*). In the Russian there was none of the "European stiffness, imperviousness, intractability." According to Dostoevsky, the Russian "gets along with everyone and adjusts to everything" since

---

[14] Nekrasov, 288.
[15] G. I. Uspensky, *Rasskazy i ocherki* (Moscow, 1944), 181.

he "sympathizes with everything human irrespective of nationality, blood, and soil." At the same time the Russian is supposedly capable of "the most healthy self-criticism, the most sober view of himself, and the absence of any self-exaltation harmful to freedom of action." He is said to be able "to speak all languages and master the spirit of every foreign tongue in all subtleties as if it were his own Russian tongue — something which is not to be found in the European peoples." [16]

However, there is another side to Dostoevsky's characterization of the Russians. He saw in them a propensity to lie, and in his *Diary of a Writer* in 1873 he posed the question: "Why does everyone in Russia lie and without exception?" Dostoevsky hastened to point out that the overwhelming majority of Russians "lie out of hospitality" and with "the most honorable purposes" and that whereas in other countries lies are uttered by scoundrels for criminal purposes, in Russia it is done "for the purpose of creating an aesthetic impression upon the hearer." [17] This is done by means of exaggeration. The Russians "fear the truth, that is, we do not fear it, if you wish, but constantly regard the truth as something far too tedious and prosaic, insufficiently poetic, too commonplace, and in this way, by constantly avoiding it, we finally made it one of the most unusual and rare things in our Russian world." [18] Thus in Russia, according to Dostoevsky, "the truth almost always has an entirely fantastic character." [19] Implied in the commonplace nature of lying in Russia was the shame which Russians have felt for themselves along with their need to "adopt an entirely different visage."

For Dostoevsky, the notion of shared guilt is a peculiarly Russian belief as a result of which crime has been equated with misfortune:

No, the people do not deny crime and know that the criminal is guilty. The people know that they are also guilty along with each criminal. But, in accusing themselves, they also prove that they do not believe in environment [*sreda*]; they believe in the opposite, that the environment depends completely upon them, upon their uninterrupted repentance and self-perfection.[20]

Related to this is Dostoevsky's belief that the "most fundamental spiritual need of the Russian people is the need for suffering, perpetual and insatiable, everywhere and in everything." He saw the Russians as being dominated by the "stream of suffering" throughout their history not merely as a result of "external misfortunes and disasters but [because] it wells up from the popular heart itself." [21] Thus Dostoevsky saw the Russian as experiencing suffering even when he is happy, "otherwise his happiness

[16] F. M. Dostoevsky, *Polnoe sobranie sochinenii* (St. Petersburg, 1895), IX, 23.
[17] Dostoevsky, IX, 320.
[18] Dostoevsky, IX, 327.
[19] Dostoevsky, IX, 328.
[20] Dostoevsky, IX, 182.
[21] Dostoevsky, IX, 206.

is not complete." Even the Russian drunkard suffers, according to Dosto-evsky. In contrasting the Russian drunkard with his German counterpart, Dostoevsky noted that the German is more amusing, happier, proud of himself, and does not cry, while "the Russian drunkard loves to drink from grief and to cry." [22]

No one was seemingly more aware of the Russian's shortcomings than was Dostoevsky. In his *Diary* for May 1876, he noted that "the Russian man in the past decades has strongly yielded to the corruption of acquisi-tiveness, cynicism, materialism" while he saw the Russian woman still faithful to ideas, manifesting great "seriousness, patience, and setting an example of the greatest courage." [23] This view was undoubtedly related to the successful struggle for higher education for women which was being waged in Russia at that time. In February of the same year Dostoevsky observed that "due to the circumstances of almost all of Russian history" the Russians had given themselves to corruption and debauchery (*raz-vrat*) and that it was remarkable that they had succeeded in retaining the human manner and form. He asked that the Russian be judged "not by those abominations which he so often commits but by those great and sacred things for which he constantly sighs even in his loathsomeness."[24]

Thus the Russian has a proclivity to manifest contradictory tendencies and to change rapidly. Dostoevsky saw the best of persons suddenly be-coming a loathsome evildoer and a criminal "if he but falls into that whirl-wind, that fateful circular motion of convulsive and sudden self-renuncia-tion and self-destruction." [25] Conversely, the Russian is supposedly in-capable of protracted and serious hatred "not only of people but of vices, the darkness of ignorance, despotism, obscurantism, and all of these other retrogressive things." [26] Dostoevsky thus made more understandable the old Russian proverb: "Reprove sin but make peace with the sinner" (*S grekhom branis', a s greshnikom miris'*).[27] The forbearance of the Russian supposedly makes him incapable of sustained hatred, and this is certainly at the basis of Dostoevsky's notion that the Russian is the bearer of the doctrine of human universality. Yet this is also the Russian's source of tragic weakness since it makes him incapable of sustained hatred of vari-ous vices and of despotism.

Dostoevsky, in stressing the forbearance of the Russians, contended that they were a great people, a truth-bearing people capable of embrac-ing other peoples and passionately wanting to do this. The goal of *ob-shchechelovechnost'* Dostoevsky defined in terms of the collapse, at some time "in the light of wisdom and consciousness," of the "natural barriers

[22] Dostoevsky, IX, 207.
[23] Dostoevsky, X, 202.
[24] Dostoevsky, X, 51.
[25] Dostoevsky, IX, 206.
[26] Dostoevsky, X, 47.
[27] Dal', 208.

and prejudices" which up to now have divided nations. Only then will "peoples live under the same spirit and order as brothers, sensibly and lovingly striving for general harmony." [28] For Dostoevsky, the achievement of this "Russian national idea of *obshchechelovechnost'* " required that Russians, first of all, be themselves:

To become a Russian means to cease despising one's own people. As soon as the European sees that we have commenced to respect our people and our nationality he will immediately commence to respect us. And, truly, the stronger and more independent the development of our national spirit, the stronger and closer would be our response to the European soul, and having become related to it, we would become more understandable to it. . . . Having become ourselves, we will at last acquire the human countenance in place of that of the [imitative] ape.[29]

In asking the Russians not to imitate Europe Dostoevsky also expressed his view that, to the Russian, Europe was a "second fatherland," almost as dear to him as Russia itself: "In it [Europe] is the Japhetic tribe, and our idea — is the unity of all nations of this tribe and even more, much more, [those] of Shem and Ham." [30]

III

It is ironic that, in a sense, the Soviet regime can be said to have adopted Dostoevsky's goal in terms of what it has expected from the Russian people, even though he and Lenin commenced from entirely different premises. Both men lived abroad and were not very happy in Western Europe. While Lenin was not the chauvinist that Dostoevsky was, they both had great faith in Russia. Although both men were aware of the shortcomings of the Russians, each preferred to concentrate on the great potential of his people: Dostoevsky seeing them as a truth-bearing people and Lenin hoping that they would embrace socialism.

However, Lenin had certain reservations regarding Russia's abilities — at least until her ruling class would be replaced by his Bolsheviks. He frequently drew invidious comparisons between Russia and Europe, as when he noted that "such a savage [*dikaia*] country in which the mass of the people are *pillaged* in terms of education, enlightenment, and knowledge — not a single such country remains in Europe other than Russia." [31]

---

[28] Dostoevsky, XI, 21. In the same article, written in January of 1877, he noted that Europeans, who speak only their own languages, had completely misunderstood the Russians and regarded them as "enemies and future destroyers of European civilization" (XI, 25).

[29] Dostoevsky, XI, 26.

[30] Dostoevsky, XI, 26.

[31] V. I. Lenin, *Sochineniia* (4th ed.), XIX, 115. Stalin, in his essay on "Marxism and the National Question" published at about the same time, declared that "Russia is a semi-Asiatic country and therefore the policy of 'attempted assassinations' not infrequently assumes the coarsest forms, the forms of the pogrom." (*Sochineniia*, II, 338).

In an article published in the July 18 (31), 1913, issue of *Rabochaia
pravda* he praised the newly opened New York Public Library and its
many branches, and contrasted it with the little being done in Russia
for "popular education." [32] In a letter written to his sister on April 22, 1914,
from Cracow, Lenin noted that "here, of course, one cannot even speak
of culture; it is almost like Russia. . . ." [33] Lenin was most critical of
the dominant role of the Russians in the Russian Empire even though
they constituted only 43 per cent of its population. Writing in the summer
and autumn of 1913 and in the spring of 1914, Lenin repeated this statistic
on a number of occasions.[34] Declaring war on the "ruling Black Hundreds
and bourgeois national culture of the Great Russians," Lenin preached a
doctrine of internationalism which the Soviet regime was to make some
attempt to put into effect.

Although he denounced his own people as oppressors of other nationalities, Lenin remained a Russian at heart. Krupskaia recounted the
following to Lenin's mother regarding his homesickness in Cracow: "And
he [Lenin] is a terrible nationalist. He would not go to see the works of
Polish painters for anything. But one day he picked up a catalogue of the
Tretiakov Galleries at the home of one of our friends and frequently
becomes absorbed in it." [35] On the issue of the privileged position of the
Russian language, Lenin in January of 1914 took the position that it was
a language which did not need to be "learned under a stick." He expressed
the view that all non-Russians within Russia should be able to learn
Russian of their own volition and would do so since "hundreds of thousands of people are moving from one end of Russia to the other" and the
"growth of capitalism . . . leads to the drawing together of all nations."
Declaring the "language of Turgenev, Tolstoy, Dobroliubov, and Chernyshevsky [to be] great and strong" [36] Lenin expressed his confidence in
its ability to triumph without enjoying the privileged status of being the
exclusive official language of the Russian Empire.

At the end of 1914 Lenin further developed his views on the Russian
people and their goals. In his article, "On the National Pride of the Great
Russians," he denied that the "Russian conscious proletarian" was devoid
of this sentiment. As proof he quoted Chernyshevsky's words of com-
miseration — "a woeful nation, a nation of slaves, from top to bottom" —
and indicated that now a "revolutionary class" had arisen in Russia:

We are full of the feeling of national pride and precisely because we *especially*
hate *our* slavish past (when the landowning nobles led the peasants to war for
the purpose of stifling the freedom of Hungary, Poland, Persia, and China) and

[32] Lenin (2nd ed.), XVI, 529f.
[33] *The Letters of Lenin*, trans. and ed. by Elizabeth Hill and Doris Mudie (New
York, 1937), 326.
[34] Lenin (2nd ed.), XVI, 553, and XVII, 120, 134, 321, 324.
[35] N. K. Krupskaia, *Memories of Lenin, 1893–1917* (London, 1942), 201.
[36] Lenin (2nd ed.), XVII, 180.

our present slavery when these same landowners, aided by the capitalists, lead us to war in order to stifle Poland and Ukraine, in order to smash the democratic movement in Persia and in China." [37]

Thus Lenin had mixed feelings regarding his own people: on the one hand, he was too well aware of their past, their propensity for despotism, their expansionism, their backwardness; on the other hand, he desperately hoped that they could overcome this past and contribute significantly to an international socialist movement which had been born and centered in Western Europe.

And so it came to pass that what had been considered unlikely actually occurred, and Russia made "socialism" her monopoly just as she had accepted Orthodox Christianity from Byzantium and then at the time of the reforms of Patriarch Nikon claimed that her religious forms were superior to those of the people from whom she had originally received them. This process occurred in Lenin's time, between 1918 and 1920. During the debate on a peace treaty with the Central Powers at the Seventh Party Congress in March 1918, Lenin declared that the war had given a "bitter, acutely painful but serious lesson to the Russian people — to organize themselves, to discipline themselves, to subordinate themselves and create a discipline which would serve as a model. Learn from the German his discipline; otherwise we are a lost people and shall forever remain in slavery." [38] Two years later, on April 23, 1920, Lenin utilized the occasion of his fiftieth birthday to observe that Russia's position had changed and quoted the earlier Kautsky to the effect that after having "received so much revolutionary initiative from the West, now, it may be, [Russia] is itself prepared to serve as a source of revolutionary energy." [39] Something of this was foreseen by Alexander Blok when he wrote his macabre poem, "The Scythians," in January of 1918 following the Bolshevik seizure of power but prior to the conclusion of the Brest-Litovsk Treaty. Calling upon the world to take heed, Blok wrote:

> There are millions of you. There are great multitudes of us.
>   Try to engage us in combat!
> Yes, we are Scythians! Yes, we are Asiatics
>   With slanted and craving eyes! . . .
>
> Russia is a Sphinx. Exulting and mourning,
>   And drenched in black blood,
> She looks and peers into you,
>   With hatred and with love! . . .
>
> We love the flesh, its flavor and its color,
>   But also the suffocating and mortal odor of flesh.
> Are we to be blamed if your skeleton cracks
>   In our heavy and tender paws? [40]

[37] Lenin (2nd ed.), XVIII, 81.
[38] Lenin (2nd ed.), XXII 328.
[39] *50-letie Vladimira Ilicha Ulianova-Lenina* (Moscow, 1920), 29.
[40] Alexander Blok, *Sochineniia v odnom tome* (Moscow-Leningrad, 1946), 262.

In playing the role of truth-possessor, the Russians have undoubtedly modified their self-image. In many ways, the Soviet regime, by assiduously and cleverly cultivating Russian national consciousness, has made itself more acceptable to the population, and the term *Rossiia* is today commonly employed by Russians to refer to the entire Soviet Union. Russian operas from the Tsarist period, such as *Eugene Onegin, Boris Godunov, Prince Igor, A Life for the Tsar* (now renamed *Ivan Susanin,* after the principal role), enjoy the greatest popularity and, significantly, are on purely Russian themes. One has only to visit the Kremlin museums, particularly the Oruzheinaia Palata, and the Novodevichy Monastery to appreciate the extent to which a calculated preoccupation with Russia's past is both permitted and utilized.[41] The Soviet regime is committed to the propagation of atheism, and yet it does not remove the gold-covered crosses from St. Basil's or from the numerous churches and chapels within the Kremlin. It has converted the more prominent old monasteries into national monuments and has permitted monastic communities to function in certain of them.

IV

Yet it would be incorrect to identify the Russians as a past-oriented people. Actually an ambivalence persists — there is an identification with much of the past along with the claim that the Russians have transcended this past in moving along the road to Communism. Time and again the Soviet leaders have insisted upon the need to look forward and to sacrifice and exchange old ways for a great and limitless future. Stalin, in the last of his series of articles on "Foundations of Leninism" published in *Pravda* on May 18, 1924, denounced "inertia, routine, conservatism, stagnation of thought, slavish regard for ancestral traditions." He warned that the "Russian revolutionary sweep [*razmakh*]" would be ineffective unless it were combined with the "American businesslike approach to work." [42] Stalin also insisted that it would go badly with the country if heavy industry were not developed. On February 4, 1932, he quoted Nekrasov on Mother Russia's wealth and impotence without mentioning the poet by name. On that occasion he declared that "Old Russia" was beaten "uninterruptedly for her backwardness" by the Mongol khans, Turkish beys, Swedish feudal lords, the Polish-Lithuanian gentry, Anglo-French capitalists, and Japanese barons — "for military backwardness, for cultural backwardness, for political backwardness, for agricultural backwardness." [43] It can be said that in many ways this backwardness — particu-

---

[41] The most thorough study of this complex problem concerning the nature and significance of the Soviet regime's use of Russian national consciousness and its impact upon the non-Russian population is Frederick C. Barghoorn's *Soviet Russian Nationalism* (New York, 1956).
[42] Stalin, VI, 186.
[43] Stalin, XIII, 38.

larly in the industrial and technological spheres — has been overcome by the Soviet regime.

This has involved a revision of the self-image in several significant respects. First of all, the regime has attempted to modify the popular attitude toward fate by preaching that man's ability to acquire knowledge is limitless, that man can control his environment and determine his destiny. It has opposed the fatalism and pessimism that were so much a part of the Russian past and of Russian literature, which Gorky characterized as the "most pessimistic literature of Europe." Gorky had noted that:

with us all books are written on one and the same theme, on our sufferings — in youth and at a mature age: from lack of wisdom, from the yoke of autocracy, from women, from love of dear ones, from the unsuccessful ordering of the universe; in old age: from consciousness of errors of life, lack of teeth, indigestion, and from the necessity of dying.[44]

Soviet literature has attempted to depict man as imbued with buoyant optimism and capable of determining his own fate. The regime has endeavored to combat the remnants of Oneginism, Oblomovism, and the indecision and aimlessness of certain of Chekhov's characters, as well as the boredom and escapism of Lermontov's Pechorin in A Hero of Our Times.[45] It has sought to root out any remnants of the Alyosha Karamazov type, the waverer and truth-seeker, or the type of Prince Myshkin, who cannot escape his fate. However, a curious inconsistency persists in this matter because the Soviet regime itself has in many ways become the embodiment of fate, and its decisions must be acquiesced in with enthusiasm.

A new "religion" has made inroads on the traditional fate, and the two belief systems coexist side by side. Atheism has been propagated with such fervor that it has taken on certain of the attributes of faith. The traditional values of the peasantry have suffered a decline as the Soviet Union has ceased to be an overwhelmingly peasant country. Greater emphasis upon technology and industrial civilization has brought with it the curse of specialization and the doom of the man who comprehends the dimensions of his own world and its meaning. The stereotyped forms of an in-

[44] M. Gorky, V. I. Lenin (Moscow, 1931), 24.
[45] Stalin told the German writer Emil Ludwig, in an interview granted on December 13, 1931, that the European image of the Russian was out-of-date: "In Europe many imagine the people of the USSR in the old-fashioned manner, thinking that in Russia there live people who are, first of all, submissive, and secondly, lazy. This is an out-of-date and radically incorrect presentation. It emerged in Europe from the time when Russian landowners began to visit Paris, squandered plundered money there and loafed. These were really idle and worthless people. From this conclusions were drawn regarding 'Russian laziness.' But this cannot in any way relate to the Russian workers and peasants who strive for the means of life with their own labor" (XIII, 110f).

dustrialized, "socialized," and urbanized society have been adopted in large part.

However, one trait which has persisted despite the change in regimes is the Russian capacity to assimilate aliens. The Italian architect, Francesco Bartolomeo Rastrelli, General Barclay de Tolly (who was of Scottish descent), the Germans Anton Delvig and Denis Fonvizin — all regarded as Russians — testify to the effectiveness of this Russian quality. Pushkin's African ancestry did not prevent him from becoming the greatest Russian poet. Vladimir Ivanovich Dal', of Danish descent, ironically was Russia's first great lexicographer. The Swedish background of the poet and novelist, Zinaida Gippius, the German origin of the poet, Blok, and the Ukrainian-Polish ancestry of the writer, Vladimir Korolenko, all bear testimony to the willingness of the Russians to confer their nationality upon non-Russians who acquire the language and demonstrate respect for Russia's cultural achievements and way of life. This assimilatory capacity has, if anything, been enhanced under the Soviet regime, especially as a result of its policy toward its non-Russian subjects.

A nominal but not ineffective Soviet "internationalism" has served as a cover for the Russian self-image expressed in an intense but not exclusive nationalism. This Soviet Russian self-image stresses the vigor and the promise of the "great Russian people" served by its "junior brothers" and by "progressives" throughout the world. However, the self-exaltation has also been tempered by a sense of guilt. It played an important role in the Populist movement, since the conscious-striken members of the intelligentsia who went to the people in the 1870's were motivated largely by guilt for the condition of the peasantry. Guilt also manifested itself in the earlier period as a result of Russia's having been regarded by many as a backward and flea-ridden country in comparison with Western Europe. The sense of inferiority and inadequacy was also reflected in Russia's adherence to the Julian calendar with its thirteen-day differential in the twentieth century; it made the Russians appear to be out of step with the rest of the world, but at the same time it served to reinforce a sense of uniqueness and the conviction of possessing true religious faith.

While the gap between the Soviet Union and the West has been narrowed by the Soviet regime in many ways, the factor of guilt may still be present in the Russian to some extent, although it is now probably not motivated by the inferiority from which it resulted in the Tsarist period. Yet a parallel of sorts may exist between Alexandrine Russia of the 1870's and 1880's and Soviet Russia to the extent that in both periods there are observable similarities in the conditions which have provoked at least a muffled defiance of the regime. Guilt has remained in the Soviet period as a result of the fear of deviating from the "truth" as expressed in the party line. This process may commence with deviation in the form of unexpressed thought, which may never be given verbal form, but its role as a source of individual guilt feeling is nonetheless significant. At the same time, the Soviet regime has dulled the edge of much of the desire to challenge established authority by harnessing popular energy in the fulfillment of grandiose construction projects and by attempting to grant the more able elements in the society a greater stake in the system.

Since the Soviet regime has promised its subjects far greater rewards in this world than the Tsarist government ever dared to promise, it has also created a climate somewhat conducive to individual disillusionment. The fate of great hopes and expectations on the part of Russians in the past promoted a series of profound disappointments, some of which facilitated subsequent upheavals. To begin with, the emancipation proved to be something less than a panacea and was soon tarnished by the burdensome redemption payments. Populism also failed to provide a solution and led to disillusionment with the peasantry. The terrorism which emerged from Populism in the late 1870's proved that there was no key to a better Russian future in assassinating the emperor. The humiliating Russo-Japanese War was followed by the revolution of 1905 which, in turn, led to a period of reaction and further disappointment. Three and one half years of participation in World War I only led to a civil war of three years' duration. The democratic experiment in the Russia of 1917 proved itself a miserable failure. The relatively relaxed period of the New Economic Policy in the twenties led to the costly period of collectivization and industrialization. The establishment of "socialism" in the Soviet Union by proclamation in 1936 was followed by mass arrests and purges on an unprecedented scale. A brief breathing space was interrupted by the Soviet Union's participation in World War II at tremendous human and material cost. The resultant craving for peace was then periodically shaken by a fear of another world war — a fear deliberately cultivated and utilized but also controlled by the Soviet regime.

It is not to be wondered at, then, that the Soviet citizen has learned, on the basis of a disparate past, to temper his hopes — and even his fears — with a healthy skepticism. In this not uncommon virtue may lie the hope for greater and higher fulfillment.

SOME RUSSIAN IMAGES OF THE WEST

FREDERICK C. BARGHOORN

I

It might be easier to deal with the theme of this essay in a three-hundred-page book than in a six-thousand-word chapter, and the study could benefit by several years of research. Fortunately, the problem of the West has been of the liveliest interest to Russians not only since the 1860's but indeed since the sixteenth century, and a wealth of material is available. The term "image," as it is used in contemporary political studies, involves both beliefs and attitudes. We use the term broadly, to include opinions, judgments, and stereotypes. The term "Russian," as used here, refers both to the period of the Russian Empire and to the Soviet Union. "West" here refers to Western Europe, including Great Britain, and also to the English-speaking countries of the British Commonwealth and the United States. I restrict my analysis to Russia and the West partly to simplify my problem and partly because for prerevolutionary Russia and to a preponderant degree for Soviet Russia relations with the West have been by far the most important external relations.

There are striking similarities and significant continuities between the two periods; there are also essential differences and discontinuities. For the most part I shall let the facts speak for themselves, subject of course to the guidance of selection. The pattern of selection should be indicated. Prerevolutionary Russia was, on the whole, an importer of foreign cultural influences. Soviet Russia has vigorously exported influence and vigorously restricted cultural imports. Prerevolutionary Russia looked to the West for standards and models in every field. Soviet Russia, until the sputniks, has imitated the West's technology and science but has officially rejected Western civilization, embodied in "capitalism" and parliamentary democracy. According to the official Soviet creed, the Bolshevik revolution in 1917 opened a new era of human history. Since then, the Soviet "socialist" system has allegedly furnished inspiration for progressive people everywhere.

The elite strata of Tsarist Russia wanted almost desperately to be considered "European." The Soviet leadership characterizes "bourgeois" Europe and America as "decadent." The policy makers of the Russian Empire accepted membership in the European system of states. They sought to maximize the position of Russia in this system, but few Russians wanted to abolish it. In contrast, the Soviet leaders predict and advocate the ultimate fusion of all nations into one unit and the establishment of a universal but Russianized culture.

Other introductory generalizations need to be made. Tsarist Russia was not monolithic. There was an official ideology, formulated by Uvarov, for example, in the 1830's, but its claim to a monopoly position was not enforced effectively. Even the combined efforts of Alexander III and Pobedonostsev in the 1880's could not achieve "integral nationalism" or "integral Christianity."[1] The partially westernized Russian imperial regime lacked the power and the will to achieve total control of thought. It permitted much freer access to foreign political and philosophical concepts and greater freedom of foreign travel by its own subjects and access to Russia by foreigners than does the Soviet Union, even since the death of Stalin. Under Nicholas I, the young Chernyshevsky could sit in St. Petersburg tea houses and read the *Journal des débats* and other Western publications.[2]

II

Prerevolutionary Russian images of the West may be roughly classified in terms of their holders' attitudes toward the Russian *ancien regime*. Terrified or indignant defenders of throne and altar against the specter of revolution tended to hate and fear the West. Moderate, reformist conservatives and the thin stratum of gradualist liberals produced by old Russia looked for inspiration to Western European monarchical or constitutional traditions, particularly those of Germany and England. Dynastic ties with Germany, Denmark, and England, travel and study in Western Europe by Russian aristocrats and bureaucrats, and Russian borrowing of Western European administrative and legal concepts, for example, in the reforms of Peter the Great or Alexander II, facilitated the identification of the Russian educated and cosmopolitan classes with their counterparts in the West. A fairly good case could be made for Chaadaev's assertion that "only Russia's government is Western."[3]

With the development of something approaching Western European middle-class liberalism in the last two decades of the empire there came the most enthusiastic and unqualified Westernism in Russia's history.[4] Russian revolutionaries, who wanted to eradicate the nobility and the bourgeoisie, such as it was in Russia, and to install Utopia, were more

[1] See Robert F. Byrnes, "Pobedonostsev On the Instruments of Russian Government," in *Continuity and Change in Russian and Soviet Thought*, Ernest J. Simmons, ed. (Cambridge, Mass., 1955), 113–128.

[2] See N. A. Alekseev, *Dnevnik N. G. Chernyshevskogo*, part 1 (Moscow, 1931), 101ff. In 1848, Chernyshevsky hoped for a German-French attack on Russia.

[3] Alexander von Schelting, *Russland und Europa* (Berne, 1948), 14.

[4] This development is spelled out for the first time in English in George Fischer's valuable study, *Russian Liberalism* (Cambridge, Mass., 1958).

selective in their perception of the West than liberals, conservatives, or even reactionaries. Russian radicals and revolutionaries saw, or wanted to see, in the West blueprints for the earthly paradise. As P. V. Annenkov observed in his memoirs, published in 1880, discontented Russians of the 1840's had admired France, but their image of France was "an ideal, imaginary" France.[5]

Since it was more the imaginary West than the actual West that they admired, Russian radicals were impatient with the failure of the West to put into practice the revolutionary theories created by its radical thinkers. It was relatively easy for Russian radicals to become disillusioned with the West, particularly if they came into close contact with it. One thinks of Herzen's partial turn to Slavophilism after 1847 or even, perhaps, of Lenin's anathematizing of the leaders of European social democracy during and after World War I.

Russian nationalists of the type of Nicholas Danilevsky, as well as some Russian radicals, regarded the West as an ideological threat to Russian culture. Some reactionaries and conservatives feared the West as a military and diplomatic rival. On the whole, Russia was not strong enough in the second half of the nineteenth century or, indeed, in the twentieth century before 1945, to regard itself as a competitor for world leadership against the major powers of Western Europe or the United States. Extreme anti-Westernism such as that of Danilevsky, Dostoevsky, and Strakhov was not representative either of official policy or of Russian public opinion. However, it is interesting and instructive to examine Danilevsky's image of the West because in some ways it resembles that of Stalin. It is one of the paradoxes of this study that the "internationalist" Bolsheviks, at least after 1930 or 1934, perceived the West in terms which might have shocked Marx and Engels, or, for that matter, Herzen, Chernyshevsky, or the younger Lenin. The relationship between Stalinist attitudes and those of nineteenth-century Russian reactionaries reflects a certain similarity of Russian-Western relationships in the two periods. In both, Western condescension and sophistication irritated and baffled a Russia torn between admiration and envy of richer, more highly developed countries. Tsars and commissars alike have deemed it wise to shield their people from the seductive influence of Western ways, mores, and concepts. In his famous, although little read, book, "Russia and Europe," Danilevsky criticized the "hostility" of Europe to Russia, an attitude which he considered reprehensible since in his opinion Russia had in 1813 "saved France from the vengeance of Europe and Europe from the oppression of France."[6] Danilevsky complained that "Europe

---

[5] *Literaturnye vospominaniia* (Leningrad, 1928), 291.

[6] N. I. Danilevsky, *Rossiia i Evropa* (4th ed., St. Petersburg, 1889), 20. The work was first published in the form of articles in the magazine *Zaria* in 1869 and as a book in 1872.

does not recognize us as its own." [7] Like the Soviet leaders after World War II, Danilevsky contrasted the good fortune of wealthy America with the harsh fate of Russia, which had been forced in its struggle for national survival to develop a powerful, centralized state.[8]

He advanced an imperialist program for Russian domination of Turkey, the Balkans, and Eastern Europe. Of course, in contrast to Stalin, Danilevsky did not urge the Slavs to conquer the world, but he maintained that they were "a special cultural-historical type" which could coexist with other cultural "types." Thus Danilevsky lacked Stalin's imperialistic messianism. However, he shared with other Russian reactionaries, such as Pobedonostsev, and with the Stalinists, the fear of infection by allegedly pernicious Western ideas. According to Danilevsky, Europeanization was Russia's "sickness." In some ways this attitude resembles that of A. N. Shelepin, current chairman of the State Committee on Security and former head of the Soviet Youth League, who after the Sixth World Congress of Youth and Students in Moscow, in July and August 1957, urged in *Komsomol'skaia pravda* that Soviet youth fight the "alien" ideas expressed by "some delegations from capitalist countries." [9]

There was a basic contradiction in the policies of most of even the ablest Russian statesmen after the great reforms of the 1860's. They attempted to reconcile medieval patriarchal absolutism with modern industrial capitalism. The spirit of Pobedonostsev dominated the Russian monarchy until it was, perhaps, too late to make a change. Despite his sympathy for Nicholas II, Sir Bernard Pares demonstrated the truth of this judgment.[10] As Pares noted, even during the crisis of 1905, the tsar was thinking in terms of partiarchal Russia but the educated public was thinking of British and French constitutions.[11]

The court and upper bureaucracy failed to take measures which could have won effective support for official policy from the Russian educated classes. As Pares observed on the basis of personal experience, in 1907, "the Russian government hampers the intellectual development of the student in the name of morality, but it does not provide for him any moral training at all." [12] Florinsky is of the opinion that in the last years of the monarchy the vast majority of educated Russians were probably to some extent in sympathy with opposition to the existing order.[13] Most

[7] Danilevsky, 50–53.
[8] Danilevsky, 545–557.
[9] *Komsomol'skaia pravda*, August 17, 1957.
[10] Sir Bernard Pares, *The Fall of the Russian Monarchy* (London, 1939). Pares called Pobedonostsev an "inverted nihilist."
[11] Pares, 81.
[12] Quoted in William H. E. Johnson, *Russia's Educational Heritage* (Pittsburgh, 1950), 224.
[13] Michael T. Florinsky, *Russia: A History and an Interpretation* (2 vols.; New York, 1953), II, 1255.

students would probably agree with Florinsky and Pares that the upper and educated classes, even in the last decades of the empire, were still separated by a deep cultural gulf from the peasant masses. As Florinsky puts it, the population of the rural areas was "as untouched by any cultural influence as though they dwelt on another planet." [14] A new elite drawn in large part from these naive but suspicious peasants rules today a Russia which in 1917 declared an ideological war on the West.

In such a situation as that of Tsarist Russia or of many contemporary underdeveloped countries, it is difficult to steer a middle course between reaction and revolution. Russian liberals such as Ivan Petrunkevich, Basil Maklakov, Peter Struve, or Paul Miliukov thought that Russia could adopt the British pattern of constitutional monarchy. During the period from about 1895 to 1905, or perhaps even up to 1914, social and economic trends fostered faith in Russian liberalism. Writing in 1910, Miliukov expressed confidence that Russia was following in the footsteps of England, France, and other advanced countries. The Russian intelligentsia was emerging from a period in which it had been frustrated and isolated from society and had consequently developed attitudes of alienation and sectarianism. With industrial and technical progress and the development of specialization, a more practical spirit as well as liberalism and a sense of law were developing. Miliukov optimistically asserted that the political ideas of patriarchalism, xenophobia, and nationalism had completely died out in the consciousness of the Russian people.[15]

Russian radicalism before 1914, or at least before 1905, was almost as synonymous with Westernism as was Russian liberalism. From Belinsky and Chernyshevsky to Lenin, modernization of Russia in terms of theories originated by Western radicals was the main aspiration of Russian radicals. The radicals fought against the "Asiaticism" of old Russia in the name of Western science, both natural and social. As Dimitri Pisarev put it, all of the representatives of Russian "realism" received their knowledge "in prepared form" from Western writers and applied it to Russian conditions.[16] Until the early 1930's, when Stalin instituted his neo-Slavophile revival, Soviet scholars were free to publish the truth regarding the Western origins of Russian radical thought.[17] Since the death of Stalin there has been a partial return to good sense in this, as in some

[14] Florinsky, II, 1256.

[15] See, for example, Miliukov's contribution to *Intelligentsiia v Rossii* (St. Petersburg, 1910), 89–191.

[16] D. I. Pisarev, *Sochineniia* (6 vols. in 2; St. Petersburg, 1897), V, 147.

[17] As recently as 1930 a Russian translation of the Marquis de Custine's famous *La Russie en 1839*, once praised by Herzen, was published in Moscow. The 1940 and 1954 editions of M. V. Nechkina's standard *Istoriia SSSR* include bibliographical references to the 1930 Soviet translation of Custine. In the 1940 edition see II, 203; in the 1954 edition, II, 151. This indicates a certain access to attitudes toward old Russia capable in some instances, perhaps, of stimulating critical thought about Soviet institutions.

other, fields. It has not, however, proceeded very far. The Soviet intellectual of 1953–1960 probably has less access to Western thought, at least in politics, social science, and philosophy, than his counterpart of 1927, 1907, or 1847. Even under Stalin, of course, a substratum of objectivity regarding Western civilization persisted among Soviet intellectuals. In both Tsarist and Soviet Russia a good deal of forbidden material seeped through the ideological barriers, sometimes with the connivance of officials.

The Westernism of pre-Soviet Russian radicals was qualified in many ways. At least two of these should be noted. One concerns the spirit in which the Russians borrowed from Western thought, and the other concerns the content of their borrowings. The Russian radicals were for the most part angry, disturbed, and alienated individuals. To them, Western social theories were not subjects of academic study. Ideas for them were weapons. The radicals lost faith in autocracy, orthodoxy, and nationality, but they adopted utilitarianism, positivism, or Marxism in a combative spirit. Unselfish utilitarians, altruistic atheists, patriotic defeatists, and idealistic materialists were numerous in nineteenth-century Russia. Most Russian radicals, at least until the beginnings of a more sophisticated outlook toward the end of the nineteenth century, took a highly uncritical attitude toward Western theories. They tended to substitute new fanaticisms for old ones. As Berdiaev wrote before the downfall of the old order, the attitude of the Russian intelligentsia toward science had been traditionally one of "idol worship." In the West, the spheres of science and religion were quite properly kept in separate compartments, but the Russian intelligentsia condemned a scientist, or a scientific theory, if the scientist and his theory were not politically "correct." [18] Later Berdiaev, in his well-known work, *The Origin of Russian Communism*, sought an explanation of the fanaticism of pro-Western Russian radicals, which could so easily turn into fanatical anti-Westernism, in patterns of belief derived from Russian Orthodox theology.[19] Many works of Berdiaev, Simon Frank, George Fedotov, and some of the modern "psychocultural" interpreters perform a useful function by calling attention to the emotional aspects of Russian radicalism. Sociologically, however, Miliukov's view that Russia was in an earlier stage of a sociocultural development through which Western Europe had already passed seems to be a sound one.[20]

[18] Nikolai Berdiaev in *Vekhi* (4th ed., Moscow, 1909), 6, 11, 17.

[19] A recent attempt to apply Berdiaev's concepts has been made by Emanuel Sarkisyanz in his study *Russland und der Messianismus des Orients* (Tuebingen, 1955).

[20] Thomas G. Masaryk, in his famous work, *The Spirit of Russia* (2 vols.; London, 1919), reached conclusions somewhat similar to the authors already mentioned in stressing the "uncritical objectivism" of most Russian thought, including that of the Russian radicals. A somewhat similar, but less tolerant, view is taken by Peter Scheibert in the first volume of his projected three-volume study, *Von Bakunin zu Lenin* (Leiden, 1956).

Almost by definition, Russian radicals were anticapitalist. Until the coming of Marx, the majority were probably also anti-industrialist. Even the "realist" Chernyshevsky hoped that Fourierist producers' cooperatives and a modernized version of the Russian village commune could solve the social problems of Russia and protect her from the evils of Western capitalism. Among the big names of pre-Marxist Russian radicalism only Vissarion Belinsky and D. I. Pisarev, and they only to a very limited degree, saw hope for Russia in the transplantation to their country of industrialism, factory production, and even, with serious reservations, of the European bourgeoisie.[21]

Pisarev's flirtation with the ideology of industrial capitalism — as presented, for example, in the works of American economist Henry Charles Carey — and his tendency to regard rationality as a more useful tool for social betterment than the class struggle help to account for the fact that the Populists of the 1860's, 1870's, and 1880's denounced him bitterly, accusing him of selfish individualism and "epicureanism." In a sense, Russian Populism resembled Indian Gandhiism. With its failure to achieve decisive results in the 1870's, either through the "propaganda" preached by Lavrov or the revolutionary terrorism which culminated in the assassination of Alexander II in 1881, some of the Russian radicals turned to the potent mixture of scientism, industrialism, and historicism which they found in the writings of Karl Marx and Friedrich Engels.[22] The Nihilism of Pisarev and the Populism of Chernyshevsky, together with certain other elements, such as the conspiratorial tactics advocated by Bakunin, Nechaev, and Tkachev, helped to shape and modify the thought of Russian Marxists, particularly those who followed Lenin rather than the more orthodox, European-oriented adherents of Martov. For Russians disillusioned with Populism, Marxism represented the last word in European social science. N. Valentinov, who was a young revolutionary during the years when Marxism was capturing the minds of Russian radicals, has written:

What attracted us in Marxism was . . . its Europeanism. It came from Europe and it smacked not of domestic rusticity but of something new and fresh and attractive. Marxism was a messenger promising that we would not remain a semi-Asiatic country but from an Eastern country would be turned into a Western one, with Western culture and Western institutions and attributes, representing a free political system.[23]

The Russian Marxists, including the Bolsheviks, were, or thought that they were, Westernizers. It can, of course, be argued that Lenin "Rus-

[21] F. C. Barghoorn, "The Russian Radicals of the 1860's and the Problem of the Industrial Proletariat," *Slavonic and East European Review* (American Series, II, Part 1), XXI (March 1943), 57–69.

[22] The word "historicism" is used here in the sense in which it is employed in Karl R. Popper, *The Open Society and Its Enemies* (Princeton, 1950).

[23] N. Valentinov, *Vstrechi s Leninym* (New York, 1953), 50.

sianized" Maxism.[24] Lenin and other Russian Social Democrats, however, were loyal members of international social democracy until the latter's leaders committed the "treason" of supporting participation, in accordance with nationality affiliation, in the "imperialist" war of 1914–1918. Thus it can be argued that Lenin did not turn against the West but that the proclaimed leaders of the Western working-class movement betrayed their own principles and left true Marxists only one alternative, that of founding the new, Third International as the victorious Bolsheviks did in Soviet Russia in 1919.

If Lenin was a Westernizer and a Marxist, he was an exceptionally impatient, intolerant, and autocratic one who helped make it impossible for the westernization of Russia to continue along the lines on which it was proceeding before the Bolshevik seizure of power. Eager to exploit the revolution of 1905, and still more so that of 1917, Lenin laid the foundations of a doctrine and a practice which is in many ways a flat contradiction of Marxism. According to this conception, which was perfected by Stalin and has not been repudiated by Stalin's successors, the Communist Party first makes the revolution and then creates the proletariat. Stalin's major works, such as *Foundations of Leninism* (1924), *Problems of Leninism* (1926), his report to the Eighteenth Party Congress in 1939, and his pronouncements on linguistics in 1950, set forth the essentials of this voluntaristic doctrine, which in some ways has more in common with the outlook of Peter the Great than with that of Marx.[25] The "revolution from above" became, in many ways, a counterrevolution.

III

After the consolidation of Soviet power, the capitalistic world was confronted by backward but "socialist" Russia, armed with the self-righteous dogma of Marxism-Leninism. In the name of this intolerant state religion the Bolsheviks passed sentence of death upon the "feudal" and "capitalist" elites of East and West. However, they themselves behaved like a strange combination of feudal lords, religious fanatics, and monopoly capitalists. Gradually the new society developed into a kind of Russian national socialism. One should not underestimate the complexity of this new society. In it there are elements of patriarchal old Russia as well as of revolutionary, imperialistic totalitarianism and yet also, in the minds of many, survivals of nineteenth-century Populist equalitarianism and Marxist social democracy. There is also a technocratic component in this pattern, which, together with what has been called "the Marxist

[24] A recent stimulating presentation of this point of view is given in Robert V. Daniels, "Lenin and the Russian Revolutionary Tradition," in *Russian Thought and Politics*, Harvard Slavic Studies, IV (The Hague, 1957), 339–354.

[25] Ample confirmation of the above assertion can be found in the historical and biographical works of Bertram D. Wolfe, Isaac Deutscher, E. H. Carr, and other scholars.

tradition in its true 'Leninist' and social democratic varieties," may lead in the future to the development of a more liberal order in the Soviet Union.[26]

Realism compels us to be concerned more with the actual than with the potential. The official Soviet Russian image of the West has been and still is that of a system of enemy states, each divided by "contradictions" both domestic and foreign but identical in their capitalist essence and in their determination to do everything in their power to destroy the Soviet Union. This "Manichean" vision of the world, as Raymond Aron has described it, has pervaded the Kremlin's view of the West for forty years. Within this framework important changes have, of course, taken place. The Soviet conception of the relationship between the Soviet Communist Party and the world Communist movement, on the one hand, and political parties and social classes within countries not ruled by Communists, on the other, underwent development and revision. Until 1953, Moscow stressed increasingly that even the proletariat of the West must play the role of pupil rather than partner of Russia in the world revolution.[27] Slogans and symbols have changed in adaptation to movements in the international arena.[28] Since 1948, and especially since 1953, there have been conflicting interpretations and reinterpretations in Moscow, Belgrade, and to a certain extent even in other Communist capitals of the right of Communist-ruled countries to choose "different paths to socialism." These developments are significant, but concern with them should not distract our attention from the fact that Moscow since 1917, and particularly since Stalin's "revolution from above" in the 1930's, has regarded non-Communist governments in the West, and indeed in the whole world, as enemies to be removed, after which the "Masses" were to be re-educated under Communist supervision.

It is possible that the balance of terror created by nuclear weapons has ushered in a new and, paradoxically, potentially hopeful era in the relations between the Soviet and the non-Soviet worlds. If further major expansion by either group is impossible, both sides may gain time to work for an ultimate solution of outstanding issues or at least for a measure of accommodation. The forces which are transforming Soviet society may work their own way. The very scientists and administrators who, both in Russia and the West, produce instruments of annihilation may eventually turn the Kremlin politicians to the paths of peace.

[26] For the above quotation, see S. V. and P. Utechin, "Patterns of Non-Conformity," *Problems of Communism*, VI (May–June 1957), 29.

[27] For a stimulating discussion of three fundamental strategies of Communism, culminating in the "Neo-Maoist" strategy, see John H. Kautsky, *Moscow and the Communist Party of India* (New York, 1956), particularly the first and last chapters.

[28] See, for example, Kermit E. McKenzie, "The Messianic Concept in the Third International, 1935–1939," in Simmons, 516–530, and F. C. Barghoorn, *The Soviet Image of the United States* (New York, 1950).

Instead of traversing well-worn paths, it might be interesting to suggest some reasons for the extremely negative images of the West which have been held and proclaimed by the rulers of Soviet Russia. One major category is made up of "objective" facts of Western hostility and aggression against Tsarist and the Soviet Russia. The ancient Russian image of the foreigner as the invader who lays waste the native land, established in struggles with Tatar, Pole, Swede, and Frenchman, was revived by the conflict with Germany and Austria during World War I. It was intensified by British, French, United States, and Japanese military intervention during the revolutionary and civil war period. The menace of imperialist Japan and Nazi Germany in the 1930's spurred Stalin's revival of traditional Russian patriotism.[29] From 1932 or 1933 to the present, the image of the Russian motherland (*rodina*) in danger of attack by Germans, Japanese, English, French, or Americans — Americans since 1945 — has been forced upon the attention of the Soviet people by every device of an energetic and insistent propaganda.

The message has been reinforced by the words and deeds of foreigners. Whatever the military needs of the United States, for example, may be, we cannot discuss them here. It is pertinent, however, to point out that Russians can hardly fail to be impressed by the apparent menace to their country inherent in American military policy. Americans who have discussed this question with Soviet Russians since the death of Stalin — and a sensible change of Soviet policy made it possible for non-Communists to visit Russia once more — have sometimes found that they could make an impression by pointing out that American bases in Europe, the Near East, Africa, Formosa, Japan, and elsewhere were established in self-defense against the policies pursued by Stalin from 1944 on. Nevertheless, realism requires us to recognize that Russians, as well as Americans, are inclined to mistrust the intentions of potential enemies.

At least two other factors probably contribute to the persistence of negative Soviet images of Western intention and Western culture. One is the Leninist doctrine of the implacable hostility of "imperialist" states toward the Soviet Union. The other is the Kremlin's fear that what it regards as the still immature Soviet people might be unsettled and corrupted if they were given full and free access to knowledge of life in the capitalist West. Khrushchev revealed this fear when he accused the French socialist André Philip of slyness for advocating exchanges of workers' delegations.

The teachings of Marxism-Leninism, as presented by authorized persons in the Soviet Union, may in the last analysis represent only a rationalization for Kremlin policy. Certainly the available evidence indicates that the Soviet people are allowed to read only those works of Marx, Engels,

[29] I have dealt with various aspects of these developments in *The Soviet Image of the United States* and in *Soviet Russian Nationalism* (New York, 1956).

Lenin, and Stalin prescribed by the Kremlin at any given time. The major writings of Marx do not bulk large in the Soviet program of political education.[30] But even if Marx and Lenin today serve only the purpose of providing sacred texts by means of which the Soviet leadership seeks to assure homogeneity and conformity of thought, the ideas contained in these texts have a life of their own. The theories of Lenin, in particular, especially those concerned with modern "imperialism," are plausible enough to create in the minds of readers who have no opportunity to acquaint themselves with opposing arguments, a very negative, menacing image of Western intentions toward the Soviet Union, and of the corruption and injustice of bourgeois society.

The frustrations and deprivations of Soviet life, particularly among the lower-income groups and, in general, among those members of society who have not achieved elite status, might lead to discontent which could be a threat to the Soviet social order if it were not shifted to foreign targets. The familiar phenomenon of scapegoating is more important in dictatorships, particularly in underdeveloped, rapidly industrializing countries, than it is in prosperous democracies. Like the tsars, the Soviet rulers fear the effects of comparison. The government is such an obvious target for criticism in a dictatorship that it is impelled to put the blame for domestic evils on foreign demons. The strategy of scapegoating involves control and manipulation of information.

Perhaps one can thus explain the fact that condemnation of Western culture for its alleged decadence was intensified after the First Five Year Plan and Stalin's collectivization of agriculture had inflicted unprecedented hardships on the peoples of the Soviet Union. The intensification of antiforeign propaganda in the 1930's was accompanied by the imposition of drastic travel controls, regimentation of the arts, and other efforts to inculcate images of the outside world desired by Stalin. Similarly, the anti-Western campaign led by Andrei Zhdanov in 1946–1948 and the even more virulent drive apparently directed by Stalin himself against "cosmopolitanism" in 1949–1953 can, in part, be traced to a desire to distract the attention of the population from hardships due to World War II and postwar Soviet policy, and to overcome the effects of contact with "bourgeois" Europe.

Of course, the concept of the "standard of living" is in many ways relative and subjective. Present Russian standards of consumption, particu-

---

[30] See, for example, *Programma kursa dialekticheski i istoricheski materializm*, approved in 1955 by the Department of Dialectical and Historical Materialism of the Higher Party School attached to the Central Committee of the Communist Party of the Soviet Union, for use in "evening universities of Marxism-Leninism" of party city committees (Moscow, 1955), and numerous other such programs. See also the selection of works by Marx and Engels collected by Paul W. Blackstock and Bert F. Hoselitz under the title *The Russian Menace to Europe* (Glencoe, 1952). The editors state that the materials contained in this book were not available to Soviet readers.

larly if displayed skillfully, probably look much better to a native of Ghana, for example, than to a Belgian. As the Soviet Union recovered from the effects of World War II, a few foreigners were allowed to visit Russia. The door was opened slightly even in the last year or two of Stalin's life, and since his death there has been a considerable reopening of Russia. In fact, on occasion Soviet behavior in international cultural exchanges after 1953 compares favorably with the policy of the United States, for example. Probably it may be called more flexible and astute. Obviously this does not mean that Soviet citizens have begun to enjoy intellectual freedom and civil liberties even remotely comparable to those available in the Western democracies. For the most part, the change in Soviet behavior in this field reflected the confident outlook of the leaders of a recovered and rapidly developing economy. They are free from some of Stalin's more neurotic fears. They are also in a position to adjust their foreign policy more flexibly to changing circumstances.

Let me conclude this chapter with a brief survey of post-Stalin Soviet images of the West, particularly of the United States. There has been a trend toward a more empirical point of view in the Kremlin. This is indicated by the new Soviet estimate of the "foreign threat." G. M. Malenkov even went so far as to state, in 1954, that a new war would cause the destruction of "world civilization" and not merely of capitalism, as Soviet doctrine had previously maintained. It seems likely that a coalition of Khrushchev and of top Soviet military leaders overruled what they regarded as Malenkov's somewhat optimistic estimate of the international situation. However, even the belligerent and ebullient Khrushchev made an important revision of the Lenin thesis that as long as imperialism existed wars were "inevitable." [31] At the same time, however, Khrushchev reaffirmed the necessity of "a revolutionary transformation of capitalist society into a socialist one." He asserted that under favorable circumstances, where the capitalists were weak, the revolutionary transfer of power could take place without a civil war.[32]

There have been indications recently of a revival of Stalin's expectation of the 1930's, that Russia can eventually defeat the West in the "battle of production." This, combined with scientific and technical leadership, could bring a preponderance of Soviet influence throughout the world within the foreseeable future, and without all-out war. In this perspective, the West is viewed as a still formidable but weakened competitor in the world struggle for men's minds. Khrushchev, in his speech of November 6, 1957, asserted that within the next fifteen years the Soviet

[31] *XX S"ezd kommunisticheskoi partii sovetskogo soyuza,* I (Moscow, 1956), 37. On the apparent disagreement between the Khrushchev and Malenkov elements in 1954–1955, see the perceptive article by Herbert Dinerstein, "The Revolution in Soviet Strategic Thinking," *Foreign Affairs,* XXXVI (January 1958), 241–252.
[32] *XX S"ezd,* 39–40.

Union would be able to surpass the United States' 1957 output of the "most important types of products." Although the United States would not stand still, it was reasonable to believe, according to Khrushchev, that the USSR could, within "an historically short period" defeat the United States in "peaceful competition." [33] A. N. Nesmeianov, president of the Academy of Sciences of the USSR, in his speech at the Twentieth Party Congress asserted that the pace of scientific training and development in the Soviet Union had surpassed that of England or the United States.[34]

What is the Soviet image of the destiny of the United States? Very confident expectations were revealed by A. Sobolev in an article in the authoritative Central Committee magazine *Kommunist* in 1956. According to Sobolev, the United States will eventually be "surrounded" by "a friendly socialist environment." It will then be easy to elect a "government of a new type." [35] Other authoritative Soviet sources have indicated that the present Soviet policy of cultural diplomacy and economic assistance is designed to eliminate Western influence from such countries as Egypt, India, and Indonesia, and eventually to bring about the adoption of the Soviet social system by the underdeveloped countries.[36]

Of course, the vision of a Moscow-dominated Communist world in which the Western nations will no longer represent a threat to Soviet Russia but will be beneficiaries of socialism and eventually of Communism has been suggested in many of Khrushchev's statements, at least once in the menacing form of his assertion that "we will bury you." Perhaps Khrushchev was speaking figuratively, as a "gravedigger of capitalism," but his remark was nonetheless disturbing. According to an important Soviet book published since the death of Stalin, after the establishment by violent revolution of the "universal dictatorship of the proletariat" a "single universal human culture" will take shape.[37] This is a vision more grandiose than any dreamed of by Danilevsky or Dostoevsky or even by any of the Muscovite theologians of the sixteenth century. It differs from other universalistic doctrines, such as Western democracy, in its reliance on force and violence and in its emphasis on centralized political control of cultural processes.

Evidence is increasingly available that while Soviet youth and intellectuals on the whole share the socialist values professed but not practiced

[33] *Pravda* (November 7, 1957), 4.

[34] *XX S"ezd*, 373–374.

[35] A. Sobolev, "O parlamentskoi forme perekhoda k sotsializmu," *Kommunist*, no. 14 (1956), 14–32. On the United States, see especially 21–24 and 31–32.

[36] On Soviet intentions toward the underdeveloped countries, E. Zhukov, "Raspad kolonialnoi sistemy imperializma," *Partiinaia zhizn'*, no. 16 (1956), 41–48, is illuminating.

[37] G. G. Karpov, *O sovetskoi kulture i kulturnoi revoliutsii v SSSR* (Moscow, 1954), 76–77.

by the present dictatorship in Russia, most of them have no active desire to conquer the world or to crusade for Communism. Moreover, some admire much in Western culture, and many resent the Kremlin's efforts to restrict freedom of contact and communication. In an age in which nationalism and individualism are still on the march, even if often in distorted form, especially in the awakening underdeveloped countries, it does not seem likely that the Kremlin will be indefinitely successful in its international missionary endeavor. The age of empires is over, and the sooner Moscow realizes it the better. On the other hand, Western arrogance has become anachronistic in the extreme. In the era of the hydrogen bomb all nations will live in some sort of peace or they will not live at all. How soon can the Soviet ruling class produce a culture that will not need to defend itself by means of censorship, radio jamming, and archaic dogmas about the wicked and decadent West? How soon can the United States overcome its own cultural provincialism? Perhaps it is not inappropriate to ask such a question, at least as a partial offset to the imbalance inevitable when one examines only one side of an argument, even if it is the "other" side's image of one's own civilization.

The Soviet image of the West is one of the indexes of Kremlin intentions which repays analysis. Perhaps in some small degree we may influence it. Certainly we must constantly compare it with all available facts, historical and contemporary. It would be idle to expect an early or easy change in attitudes deeply rooted in Russian experience, Leninist doctrine, and the structure of international politics. The attitudes discussed herein may be viewed in part as defensive reactions of an underdeveloped society in rapid transition, the compensatory reactions of which, however, represent an urgent, complex, and competitive challenge to a once-complacent West.

THE IMAGE OF DUAL RUSSIA

ROBERT C. TUCKER

I

When Ilia Ehrenburg hopefully put the word "thaw" into currency soon after Stalin's death by making it the title of a novel, he may or may not have known that it had a previous history in Russia. According to some prerevolutionary sources, Russians began to talk of a "thaw" at the close of the reign of Iron Tsar Nicholas I, who died in 1855. The thaw was manifested in a change of atmosphere, a relaxation of censorship, and other signs of softening of the bureaucratic regimentation of society which marked Nicholas' long reign, especially in the so-called years of official terror after 1848. The image of the thaw projected the period lived through as a gray interminable Russian winter of despotism above and paralysis of society below. The incipient relaxation of state controls was seen as the harbinger of a coming "spring" of liberalization.[1] The comparison between the official terror of the last years of Stalin's reign and the atmosphere in Russia as felt in the early months after his death in 1953 is very striking. No knowledge of obscure history books was needed for the word "thaw" to come back into circulation. For Russia had just lived through another long gray winter of despotism and paralysis and was now, once again, awakening to hope for change.

The symbolism of the thaw is particularly revealing in its implicit comparison of the Russian state with a bleak elemental force which holds the land in its grasp and is a blight on the life of society. This points to an element of Russian thought and feeling about the state which has been relatively constant in its core through a large part of the history of the country, relatively independent of the shift of political seasons. I propose to call this the image of dual Russia. It embraces, first, a consciousness, which remained more or less inarticulate for a long time, of Russia as a double entity: Russian state and Russian society. On the one hand, there is *vlast'* or *gosudarstvo*, the centralized autocratic state power, embodied in the person of the tsar and operating through a hierarchy of bureaucratic institutions and their local agents. In the nineteenth century, everything pertaining to *vlast'*, including the autocrat, the court, the bureaucratic officialdom, the official customs, official uniforms, official truth or ideology, and so on, came to be subsumed under the concept of "official Russia." On the other hand, there is the population at large, the society, nation or people (*obshchestvo, narod*). It came to be conceived as a separate and distinct Russia with a life and truth of its own. This we may call unofficial or "popular" Russia.

The image of dual Russia is not simply a conception of the state and people as two different Russias. It also comprises an evaluative attitude or, rather, a range of such attitudes. Their common denominator is the apprehension of the autocratic state power as an alien power in the Russian land. The relation between the state and the society is seen as one between conqueror and conquered. The state is in control, but in the manner of an occupying power dealing with a conquered populace. It is the active party, the organizing and energizing force, in the drama of dual Russia, whereas the population at large is the passive and subordinate party, the tool and victim of the state's designs. An alien power is, of course, one toward which a great many different positions may be taken,

---

[1] L. Barrive, *Osvoboditel'noe dvizhenie v tsarstvovanie Aleksandra Vtorogo: istoricheskie ocherki* (Moscow, 1909), 11.

ranging from active collaboration through resignation and passive resistance to outright rebelliousness. However, there is a unifying thread
in this whole range of responses. The liberal scholar and statesman Miliukov, writing in exile after the 1917 Revolution, summed it up by saying
that the state power had always remained in Russia "an outsider to whom
allegiance was won only in the measure of his utility. The people were
not willing to assimilate themselves to the state, to feel a part of it, responsible for the whole. The country continued to feel and to live independently of the state authorities." [2] In what follows I wish to examine
the background of this attitude and to outline the view that the story
of the Soviet period in Russian history is partly a tale of how the state
became an outsider again in the consciousness of the Russian people.

The image of dual Russia is grounded in the actualities of Russian
historical experience with the state. The consciousness of the state as an
alien power grew out of a real separation of the state from the nation.
According to Miliukov again, the two foundations of the Russian system
as it evolved in Muscovy from the sixteenth century onward were the
"autocratic power" on the one hand and the "population" on the other,
the two "more or less imperfectly linked by a system of mediating governmental organs." [3] Far from developing as a dependent political superstructure over the socioeconomic base, the Russian state organism took shape
as an autonomous force acting to create or recreate its own social base,
to shape and reshape the institutional pattern of society, in a series of
revolutions from above. The state showed itself in what might, broadly
speaking, be called a totalitarianizing role in relation to society. It brought
the society under its centralized control and direction. The fastening
down of serfdom upon the peasants in the seventeenth century was only
one great phase in the historical process of the "binding of all classes"
in compulsory service to the autocracy. A system arose whose guiding
principle was the idea of the servitude of all sections of society to the
state. Claiming ownership of the land, the state power destroyed the
boyars as a class and created a controlled nobility of "serving men" whose
landed estates were allotted on condition of military service to the state.
This was the foundation of the growth in later times of the Russian system
of an "aristocracy of rank" (chin), under which bureaucratic distinction
rather than birth became the high road of entry into the nobility.

The mainspring of the whole "binding" process was the drive of the
autocratic power to aggrandize the national territory, its "gathering of
lands," through which Muscovy expanded from an original area of a few
thousand square miles to one fifth of the earth's surface in 1917. The
expansionist drive placed a great premium upon military strength. With
the country's being economically backward and technologically inferior

[2] P. N. Miliukov, *Russia Today and Tomorrow* (New York, 1922), 10.
[3] P. N. Miliukov, *Ocherki po istorii russkoi kul'tury* (St. Petersburg, 1904), I, 206.

to its Western neighbors, the government sought to mobilize the resources for war by enlisting the population directly in its service. The exploitative relation of the state to society brought an extension of coercive controls and the hypertrophy of the centralized governmental system. In his summation of modern Russian history from the sixteenth to the mid-nineteenth centuries, the historian Kliuchevsky writes that "the expansion of the state territory, straining beyond measure and exhausting the resources of the people, only bolstered the power of the state without elevating the self-consciousness of the people. . . . The state swelled up; the people grew lean." [4]

The image of dual Russia was an outgrowth of this entire process. But it was one particular episode in the process, Peter the Great's revolution from above, which did most to make the people conscious of the state as a separate and alien power in their midst. Peter particularly aspired to borrow technology from the West, and not civilization in the wider sense, but in the process he reorganized the state administration along new centralized lines, set up the governmental bureaucracy in a new capital separate from the rest of the country, and proceeded by forcible means to carry through a cultural revolution designed to change the old Russian way of life. The group most immediately affected by the cultural revolution was the bureaucratic serving class itself, so that the rift between the state and the people became a visible fact of manners, language, dress, and so on. Consequently, later writers tend to date the division of Russia into two entities from Peter's time. Alexander Herzen, for example, wrote in 1853: "Two Russias came into hostile opposition from the beginning of the eighteenth century." He explained:

On the one hand, there was governmental, imperial, aristocratic Russia, rich in money, armed not only with bayonets but with all the bureaucratic and police techniques taken from Germany. On the other hand, there was the Russia of the dark people, poor, agricultural, communal, democratic, helpless, taken by surprise, conquered, as it were, without battle.[5]

So foreign did the Russian government become in the eyes of its own peasant people, wrote Herzen elsewhere, that Russian officials in uniform seemed to the peasant to be representatives of the German government. In the military officer, he saw a policeman; in the judge, an enemy; in the landowner, who was invested with the authority of the state, a mighty force with which he was unable to cope.[6]

Thus, *gosudarstvo* came to appear, in the eyes of a majority of the people, as a kind of occupying power in the Russian land. Summing up this development, Sir Donald MacKenzie Wallace wrote at the close of the nineteenth century:

[4] V. O. Kliuchevsky, *Kurs russkoi istorii* (Moscow, 1937), III, 11.
[5] A. I. Herzen, *Izbrannie filosofskie proizvedeniia* (Moscow, 1946), II, 253.
[6] A. I. Herzen, **Dvizhenie obshchestvennoi mysli v Rossii** (Moscow, 1907), 181.

It was in the nature of things that the Government, aiming at the realization of designs which its subjects neither sympathized with nor clearly understood, should have become separated from the nation. . . . A considerable section of the people looked on the reforming Tsars as incarnations of the spirit of evil, and the Tsars in their turn looked upon the people as raw material for the realization of their politcial designs. . . . The officials have naturally acted in the same spirit. Looking for direction and approbation merely to their superiors, they have systematically treated those over whom they were placed as a conquered or inferior race. *The state has thus come to be regarded as an abstract entity,* with interests entirely different from those of the human beings composing it; and in all matters in which state interests are supposed to be involved, the rights of individuals are ruthlessly sacrificed.[7]

The fact that the state, by virtue of its role in Russian historical experience, had come to be widely regarded as an alien and "abstract entity" is of great importance for an understanding of the turbulent course of events in Russia between 1855 and 1917. It helps to explain the paradox that liberalizing reform from above in the 1860's coincided with the rise of an organized revolutionary movement from below, and also the circumstance that in February 1917, "A few days of street disorders in St. Peterburg, and the refusal of the soldiers of the city garrison to put them down, were enough to topple the Tsarist regime. It made no real attempt to defend itself, for *it proved to have no supporters.*" [8]

II

The thaw at the close of Nicholas I's reign marked the beginning of a new period in the life of Russia, in which the direction of the earlier Russian historical process was decisively reversed. It was the time of "unbinding." The government itself remained autocratic; the system of administration, centralized and bureaucratic. However, the reforms of the sixties, beginning with the abolition of serfdom, inaugurated the emancipation of Russian society from the all-encompassing tutelage of the bureaucratic state. Official Russia, so to speak, contracted, permitting unofficial Russia to emerge into the open from behind the "shroud" with which, as Herzen expressed it, the government had covered up the life of the country. Forces in Russian society acquired a certain scope for independent self-expression. The monologue of the state with its agents gave way to a dialogue between the state and society — above all, between the state and that element of society which called itself the "intelligentsia."

Peter Struve, writing in the early twentieth century, suggested that the spiritual hallmark of the Russian intelligentsia was "its estrangement from the state and hostility toward it." [9] This statement may have been made in a spirit of polemical exaggeration; yet it is certainly true that

[7] Donald MacKenzie Wallace, *Russia* (London, 1912), 379; italics added.
[8] Michael Karpovich, "Russia's Revolution in Focus," *The New Leader* (November 4, 1957), 15; italics added.
[9] Quoted by S. G. Pushkarev, *Rossiia v XIX veke* (New York, 1956), 379.

a sense of apartness from the official world, and of closeness to the world of the Russian people — or to what that world was imagined to be — was characteristic of this group. A consciousness of the fundamental duality of Russia typified the mind of the intelligentsia, and its heart was with the people and against the state, with the muzhik and against the chinovnik. This educated minority, drawn from different strata of society, formed an image of itself as the "self-conscious people," the thinking organ of the *narod*. That image underlay its major movement in the second half of the nineteenth century, the *narodnichestvo* or Populism, and in particular the crusade of "going to the people" in the 1870's. The intense Russian national feeling characteristic of the intelligentsia was a feeling which tended to delete *gosudarstvo*, the whole official world, from the concept of the nation. It was a peculiar form of antistate nationalism which inspired Herzen, for example, to say: "The Russian government is not Russian. Its usual direction is despotism and reaction. It is more German than Russian, as the Slavophiles say. This explains the sympathy and love of other governments for it." [10]

One of the most original and influential creations of the mind of the Russian intelligentsia was Slavophilism, a philosophy of life which revolved in great measure around the image of dual Russia. Konstantin Aksakov provided a classic statement of this philosophy in a memorandum of 1855 to Alexander II, "On the Internal Condition of Russia." This memorandum was one of the results of the nineteenth-century thaw. In it Aksakov argued that the Russian people, being probably the only truly Christian people on earth, were "nonpolitical" (*negosudarstvennyi*), that is, fundamentally disinterested in politics, constitutions, revolutions, representative government, and so forth. The un-Christian power principle embodied in the state as an institution was foreign to this people's nature. They were essentially a "social people," concerned with spiritual, moral, cultural, and economic freedom in a Christian communal society, of which the Russian village commune was the nucleus. Accordingly, it had originally invited the northern Vikings to come and exercise the governmental function in Russia, and there had taken shape in ancient Russia a peculiarly Russian system, a marriage of convenience between "state" and "land" founded on the principle of "mutual noninterference." The state authority was freely accorded the right to govern autocratically, while for its part the "land" — that is, the people — was left free and undisturbed in the practice of its Christian communal way of life and culture, and also enjoyed the opportunity to voice its opinions on national affairs to the state authority at periodically convened "gatherings of the land." Later this system of alliance broke down. In the person of Peter the Great, the state invaded the land, assaulted the customs, infringed upon the religion, suppressed all freedom. As a result of this revolution

[10] Herzen, *Dvizhenie obshchestvennoi mysli v Rossii*, 170.

from above, "the previous alliance was replaced by the *yoke* of the state over the land, and the Russian land became, as it were, the conquered party and the state the conqueror." [11]

The present condition of Russia, Aksakov continued, could be traced to the Petrine aggression of the state against the land and to the refusal of Peter's successors to admit and rectify the wrong. What was the present condition? Russia was sick, and the cause was the unnatural relation of the state to society, the repression of spiritual and social freedom. The imposing external position of the Russian Empire contrasted with the profound and pervasive moral crisis within. The bloated bureaucratic organism of official Russia was shot through with venality and corruption. There was no spontaneity of social self-expression. In this stifling atmosphere no one dared to speak the truth aloud, and nothing was heard but official lies and fulsome adulation of the tsar. Above all, the government and the people were mutually estranged:

The present condition of Russia is a condition of internal division covered up with shameless lies. The government and with it the upper classes have separated themselves from the people and become alien to it. . . . The government and the people do not understand each other, and their relations are not friendly.[12]

What was the remedy for the internal crisis? In the long run, it was for the state to undo the historic wrong done to the land, to withdraw to its proper governmental sphere and stop encroaching upon the nonpolitical life of the people. Meanwhile, the urgent immediate need was to let the fresh air and light of free speech exert a medicinal effect. The liberation of public opinion was the means by which the government could cleanse the bureaucratic corruption and repair the moral estrangement between itself and the people: "To the government unlimited state power; to the people complete moral freedom, freedom of life and spirit. To the government the right of action and so of law; to the people the right of opinion and so of speech." [13] Putting it in contemporary terms, the Slavophile program for Russia was in essence antitotalitarian, aspired to roll back the encroachments of the state on the territory of society, and looked to establishment of a system of peaceful coexistence between an absolutistic Russian government and an apolitical Russian people.

[11] N. L. Brodsky, ed., *Rannie slavianofily* (Moscow, 1910), 72, 80, 86. The Slavophile aversion to the idea of the state was a powerful contribution to the development of anarchist thought in Russia. The Slavophile doctrine was a quietistic anarchism. It accepted the state as a necessary evil. But it was in no doubt about the evilness of it. Aksakov said: "The state is evil in principle; the lie is not in this or that form of the state, but in the state itself as an idea or principle; it is not a question of which form is better and which worse, which true and which false, but of the fact that the state *qua* state is a lie." Mikhail Bakunin, who was to become the leading philosopher of revolutionary anarchism, highly commended Aksakov for this view.

[12] Brodsky, 89.

[13] Brodsky, 98–99.

According to an old saying in Russia, the Populists were Slavophiles in rebellion. The foundations of the philosophy of Russian Populism were laid by Herzen. He had been a leader of the Slavophiles' opponents, the Westerners. As they saw it, the Slavophiles' idealized image of ancient Russia as a voluntary alliance of the state and the land was but a "retrospective utopia," and Russian Orthodoxy had never been anything but "apathetic Catholicism." [14] But Herzen, after taking up voluntary exile in Western Europe, discovered deep Slavophile affinities in his thinking. The Slavophile conception of the Russian people as essentially a "social people" became the cornerstone of Herzen's "Russian socialism." It pictured the muzhik as the man of the future in Russia and the mir as the foundation of a socialist society. Herzen also, as already noted, accepted the Slavophile image of dual Russia.

But Populism wrought a far-reaching change in the picture of the relation between the two Russias. The Slavophile program of peaceful coexistence between the state and the land by courtesy of a repentent Tsarist authority was discarded, as was the conception of the Russian people as nonpolitical. Popular Russia became "revolutionary Russia" (Herzen's phrase), and the image of dual Russia became an image of *two Russias at war*. Revolutionary Populism called the land to arms against the state. Herzen, writing in his London paper *Kolokol* in 1861, issued a declaration of war against official Russia on behalf of the Russian people. The occasion was the suppression by troops under the command of General Bistrom of student disturbances at the University of St. Petersburg over the peasant question. Addressing the imprisoned students, Herzen wrote: "Where shall you go, youths from whom knowledge has been shut off? . . . To the people! . . . Prove to these Bistroms that from you will emerge not clerks but soldiers, not mercenaries but soldiers of the Russian people!" [15] The declaration of war evoked a powerful response among the Russian student youth, and the following year saw the rise of the secret society, "Land and Freedom." Revolutionary Populism had come into being as an organized movement. At this time there appeared in Russia a manifesto, "Young Russia," which expressed a philosophy of revolutionary terrorism against the state. Dividing all Russia into two parts — the party of the people and the party of the emperor — it called for the physical extermination of all those who stood or even sympathized with the party of the emperor. Inscribed on the banners of the Russian revolutionary movement was the image of dual Russia.

But popular Russia was not then the revolutionary Russia imagined by Herzen and the revolutionary Populists. The conception of two Russias at war was not realistic, and the would-be soldiers of the people found

[14] Herzen, *Dvizhenie obshchestvennoi mysli v Rossii*, 137.
[15] Quoted by Alexander Kornilov, *Modern Russian History* (New York, 1943), II, 208.

themselves more or less in the position of generals without an army. The failure of the movement of "going to the people" in the seventies showed what a chasm existed between the peasantry and the revolutionary intellectuals. Although there were many isolated instances of local peasant disorders in the latter half of the nineteenth century, the peasantry in general proved politically inert. Here it should be noted that the peasant mind did not equate official Russia and the tsar. On the contrary, it tended to look to the tsar — as distinguished from his bureaucracy — for help in satisfying its claim to the land which still remained in the possession of the nobles after 1861. On the whole, as Miliukov later observed, the rural population, while always remaining in a sense "natural anarchists," tended to render passive obedience to a state authority which did not get too much "under the skin," and this peculiar combination of peasant characteristics explains to a large extent the events of the Russian revolution.[16] That is, the anarchist tendency got the upper hand in the special conditions prevailing in 1917, and the tendency to render passive obedience made for acceptance of the new dictatorial state authority which emerged from the storm.

Decline of faith in the peasantry as a revolutionary force, and in terrorism as the prime revolutionary weapon, led some Populists to turn to Marxism as the ideology of revolution. The 1890's witnessed a contest between populists and Marxists for hegemony in the revolutionary movement, followed by the rise of Leninism or Bolshevism as claimant to the role of sole authentic voice and organ of Russian Marxism. The relative success with which Marxism took hold among the radical intelligentsia of Russia may seem surprising in view of Marx's vision of history as turning on the axis of class struggle. The basic realities of mankind, according to Marx, are social-economic classes at war, and the war is now culminating in a final battle between bourgeoisie and proletariat. Not only were these latter two forces still only nascent in Russia; its history, as noted earlier, turned not on class struggle but on the issue of relations between the state and society.[17] Despite this, the Russian revolutionary mentality found no difficulty in assimilating itself to Marxism, or Marxism to itself.

Part of the explanation lies in the fact that this mentality was, even in pre-Marxist days, hostile to capitalism. But the chief facilitating circum-

---

[16] Miliukov, *Russia Today and Tomorrow*, 11.

[17] Wallace, *Russia*, 368–369, has this to say on the matter of classes and class conflict in Russian history: "Certain social groups were, indeed, formed in the course of time but they were never allowed to fight out their own battles. The irresistible Autocratic Power kept them always in check and fashioned them into whatever form it thought proper, defining minutely and carefully their obligations, their rights, their mutual relations, and their respective positions in the political organization. Hence we find in the history of Russia almost no trace of those class hatreds which appear so conspicuously in the history of Western Europe."

stance was the fact that Marx pictures the class struggle in political terms. He argues, that is, that the war between class and class has to be decided in the final analysis by overthrowing the existing *state*. Further, his doctrine appealed to the anarchist streak in the Russian revolutionary mentality, for it visualizes the withering away of the institution of the state after the final revolution. Hence it was entirely possible for a Russian revolutionary whose mind was obsessed with the image of dual Russia to become a Marxist and continue in that capacity the indigenous revolutionary tradition of warfare against official Russia. He could march to battle against the state with the war cry of "class struggle" on his lips. He could talk as a Marxist while thinking and feeling as a Russian revolutionary Populist. As Ivanov-Razumnik points out, "the Russian Marxists of the nineties identified the social with the political by contending that 'every class struggle is a political struggle'; this was an expression in new form of the old People's Will [i.e., Populist] thesis, 'To the social through the political.' " [18]

All this applies particularly to Lenin and his political creation, Russian Bolshevism. He came to the fore during the nineties as one of the leaders in the Marxist polemic against the Populists. Against them he contended that not the muzhik — who still comprised nearly nine tenths of the Russian population — but the industrial worker was the man of the future in Russia, and that the rise of Russian capitalism was to be seen as a hopeful and not a deplorable phenomenon from the revolutionary standpoint. However, the political personality of Lenin was shaped in very significant degree by the tradition of the Russian revolutionary Populists of the 1860's, especially Chernyshevsky. The principal motivating force was a consuming hate for *gosudarstvo*, for official Russia and everything it connoted.

He married the old image of two Russias at war to Marxism. His theory of the Marxist party as a small, disciplined body of revolutionaries drawn from the intelligentsia and acting as the politically conscious "vanguard" of the working class revived in a new form the old image of the intelligentsia as the "self-conscious people." Finally, in his *State and Revolution* and other writings, he accentuated the anarchist theme in Marxism. "The proletariat needs the state only temporarily," he wrote. "We do not at all disagree with the anarchists on the question of the abolition of the state as an *aim*." The immediate purpose of the revolution would be to smash *gosudarstvo* to pieces, to raze the old state apparatus to the ground and to replace it with a system of direct rule by the armed people *without* bureaucrats ("privileged persons divorced from the masses and standing *above* the masses"), preparatory to the

[18] R. V. Ivanov-Razumnik, *Istoriia russkoi obshchestvennoi mysli* (St. Petersburg, 1914), II, 109.

withering away of all statehood.[19] Lenin thought of the revolution as the rising of popular Russia against official Russia. In his mind, the Marxist concept of the dictatorship of the proletariat took concrete shape as a vision of *popular Russia in power*. Thus Leninism was a subtly Russified Marxism, a fusion of Marxist symbols and concepts with much of the content of thought and feeling characteristic of the old Russian revolutionary Populism. Lenin conceived his mission in the international Marxist movement as that of resurrecting its "revolutionary soul." But it was a very Russian spirit of revolution which he breathed into Marxism.

III

If the February Revolution of 1917 culminated the process of "unbinding" of Russian society, the Bolshevik seizure of power in October and the establishment of a new centralized and dictatorial state authority laid the foundation for a reversion of Russia to the past. The results of sixty years of Russian history in the way of emancipation of society from the aegis of the state were nullified. In practice, the dictatorship of popular Russia meant the dictatorship of popular Russia's self-appointed organ of consciousness, the Bolshevik Party. This, along with the nationalization of the economy, made *gosudarstvo* again the dominating factor in the situation. "The most pressing and topical question for politics today," wrote Lenin in September 1917, "is the transformation of all citizens into workers and employees of one big 'syndicate,' namely, the state as a whole." In his wildly utopian imagination, he thought that this could be done without recreating a governmental bureaucracy standing above society. Before he died, however, he is reported to have remarked ruefully: "We have become a bureaucratic Utopia."

Lenin's legacy was the one-party dictatorship and the New Economic Policy, under which the state retained only the "commanding heights" of the economy and permitted twenty-five million private peasant farms to exist and contribute to economic revival. During this transitional period, the situation in Russia fell once again into the historic pattern of duality. In Miliukov's formula for the system in Muscovy, there was the "autocratic power" on the one hand and the "population" on the other, the two "more or less imperfectly linked by a system of mediating governmental organs." This was reflected in the concept of the soviets, cooperatives, and other mass organizations as "levers" of the party's influence and authority among the population. Thus the outcome of the revolution, politically speaking, was that Russia had reverted to a situation with strong parallels to the remote past. Since, however, the new dictatorial state authority permitted the population or very large sections of it to carry on many nonpolitical pursuits more or less without hindrance, the state, at the height of the

[19] V. I. Lenin, *Selected Works* (Moscow, 1947), II, 181, 221.

NEP, was not on the whole experienced by the Russian people as a highly oppressive power. The NEP was, in a way, a period of peaceful coexistence between the state and the land. That, at any rate, is the way it tends to be remembered. It has become a kind of "restrospective utopia" for many among the present generation. Just as the Slavophiles once pictured the pre-Petrine past as a satisfactory time in the relations between the government and the people, so now the NEP is recalled by many Russians as the golden age of Soviet Russia, when the state, dictatorial though it was, did not trespass too much upon the popular domain, the way of life of the people. In both instances, the past is evaluated in relation to what was experienced in the historical aftermath.

In Soviet Russia, the aftermath was Stalinism, the essential meaning of which was the dynamic resurgence of *gosudarstvo*. Lenin and the Bolshevik Party had, by the seizure of power and establishment of a centralized dictatorial state structure, created a medium in which this movement could arise and flourish. But it was Stalin, a man in whom the spiritual affinities with the revolutionary antistate Russian intelligentsia were quite tenuous, who became its conscious instrument and architect. In the peculiarly Russian terms whose meaning has been considered above, Stalinism meant, to begin with, the invasion of the land by the state. Reviving the historic pattern of revolutionism from above, Stalin moved to bring every element of society under coercive state regimentation and control. He re-enacted the "binding" of all strata in servitude to the state authority. The outstanding single manifestation of this totalitarianizing process was the terroristic collectivization of the peasantry and the reimposition of serfdom within the framework of the kolkhoz. Here the state acted quite literally in the role of *conqueror* of rural Russia. As Stalin observed to Churchill during World War II, his conquest of the Russian peasantry was the hardest of all his campaigns, the casualty list totaling ten millions. As before in Russian history, the totalitarianizing process was actuated in large part by the central authority's overriding concern for external defense and aggrandizement, which dictated a policy of direct exploitation of the human resources of the economically backward country for amassing military power through industrialization. Total exploitation necessitated total control. There took place, therefore, an enormous hypertrophy of state functions of command and control of society, an immense expansion of bureaucracy. One of Stalin's Bolshevik opponents, Bukharin, caught the historic implications of this whole pattern of policy when he labeled it "military-feudal exploitation." [20] Russian history in the Stalin period retraced the course which Kliuchevsky epitomized in his phrase cited earlier: "The state swelled up; the people grew lean."

[20] *Kommunisticheskaia partiia v rezoliutsiiakh i resheniiakh s"ezdov, konferentsii i plenumov Ts.K.* (Moscow, 1954), II, 555.

Stalinism meant the resurgence of *gosudarstvo* not only in fact but also in idea. The new Stalinist order became an order of statism in the fullest sense of the word: *gosudarstvo* was its supreme symbol and object of glorification. Its philosophy was succinctly summed up by Malenkov in a speech in 1941: "We are all servants of the state." [21] Otherwise expressed, the motto read: "Place the interests of the state above all else!" In the new conception, the whole of society was regarded as a single great "interest group" identified with the goal of the unlimited expansion of the power and glory of the Russian Soviet state. The old Leninist Bolshevik idea of the party as popular Russia's authoritative organ of consciousness and rule gave way, in practice if not entirely in theory, to the concept of the party as the apostle and agent of the interests of the totalitarian state. One of the probable sources of Stalin's murderous fury against the surviving Bolshevik old guard, whom he exterminated wholesale in his purges of the 1930's, was the ingrained inability of many of these men, schooled as they were in the *Weltanschauung* of the revolutionary antistate Russian intelligentsia, to see things in the "state way" and assimilate fully the ideal, very new and very old, of the "state-oriented man" (*gosudarstennyi chelovek*). As Russian Marxists of the Leninist-Bolshevik school, they could not easily adopt the historic Russian standpoint of *gosudarstvo*. In exterminating them, Stalin saw himself as acting after the manner of his chosen model, Ivan Grozny, who had undertaken, as it were, to liquidate the boyars as a class; the old Bolsheviks were Stalin's boyars. Using his NKVD as Ivan had used his *oprichnina*, he broke the back of the party, eliminated it as a living political organism and ruling class, and refashioned it as a lever of the absolute autocracy, the first of the mass organizations in the system of totalitarian statism. Toward the end of his life he even expunged the word "Bolshevism" from the official state vocabulary.

The change of regime from Bolshevism to Stalinist statism was registered in various changes in the ideological system. The Marxist reading of Russian history had to be condemned and radically revised in order to permit the official glorification of *gosudarstvo* to be projected upon the Russian past. Stalin corrected Marx and Engels — not to mention Lenin — on the embarrassing point about the desirability of the earliest possible withering away of the state. Despite all this, however, he performed the phenomenal mental feat of continuing to regard himself as a Marxist. How he did this is suggested by his papers of 1950 on Marxism and linguistics, in which he frowned upon the notion of revolutionary "explosions" from below and recommended as the good kind of revolutionary process the "revolution from above" carried out "at the initiative

[21] G. M. Malenkov, *O zadachakh partiinykh organizatsii v oblasti promyshlennosti i transporta* (Moscow, 1941), 39.

of the existing regime." [22] Having identified himself with the historic pattern of revolution from above, he mentally assimilated Marxist revolutionism to this pattern. He thus became, in his own self-image, a kind of Marxist tsar. It was a standpoint from which he could see himself as the legitimate successor of *both* Ivan Grozny and Lenin.[23] If Lenin fused Marxism with antistate revolutionary Populism, Stalin fused it with prostate revolutionary Tsarism. If the one mixed Marx with Chernyshevsky, the other mixed Marx with Ivan Grozny.

IV

The full implications of the recapitulation of the earlier Russian historical process under Stalin emerged into clear view only in the final period of his reign, the years following World War II. This was the heyday of Stalinist statism, and also the time when it became plain in innumerable ways that Stalinist statism meant the resurrection of official Russia. This new official Russia found its visible incarnation in the huge hierarchy of officialdom, the privileged stratum of bureaucratic serving men, many of them dressed in uniforms similar to those of the old *chinovniki*, and organized according to a new "table of ranks" which was analogous in substance if not nomenclature to that which Peter created. This bureaucracy itself was the only approximation to a ruling class, but it was not really that; its mission was to serve the goals, needs, and whims of the absolute autocrat. It did, however, consist (to use Lenin's phrase) of "privileged persons divorced from the masses and standing *above* the masses." The separation of this stratum from the people was reflected in an image of the government which Stalin drew in 1945. In a toast proposed at a victory banquet in the Kremlin, he spoke of the great mass of "ordinary" people in Russia, the workers, peasants, and lower employees who held no ranks or titles, as "cogs in the wheels of the great State apparatus" and, again, as "cogs who keep our great State machine going in all branches of science, national economy, and military affairs." "They are the people who support us," he told the assembled dignitaries, "as the base supports the summit." [24] The Iron Tsar might have spoken in a similar vein.

This was the view from the summit looking down. What was the view from the base looking upward? What picture did the millions of "cogs" form of the "great State machine"? Broadly speaking, the processes which had led to the resurrection of official Russia had led also to the resurrection of popular Russia as something separate from the official

[22] *Pravda* (June 20, 1950).
[23] This thought was certainly in his mind. For instance, in 1947 he commented privately that of all the leaders in Russian history, Ivan and Lenin were the only two who had introduced a state monopoly of foreign trade. See S. M. Dubrovsky, "Protiv idealizatsii deiatel'nosti Ivana IV," *Voprosy istorii*, no. 8 (1956), 128.
[24] *Pravda* (June 27, 1945).

world. They had produced a revival of the popular consciousness of the duality of Russia, of estrangement from *gosudarstvo*. This is particularly the case if we consider the situation as it stood at the climax of Stalin's reign, the years from 1945 to 1953, when the people discovered that the hopes for liberalization which the regime had covertly encouraged during the war years were not to be fulfilled, and that life in Russia, far from becoming more tolerable, was in fact much less so than in the period before 1941. By now the "great State machine" had become, in the minds of millions of ordinary Russians, a great alien "It" which commanded their fear or even their awe but did not inspire any affection or sense of identification. When one spoke to them in private, one found that they referred to the government as *Oni* — "They." Very many of them spiritually seceded from the life of the Russian state, inwardly "emigrated." They felt themselves in it but not of it. It was an attitude of resignation rather than rebelliousness. The state was seen as an alien oppressive force, but as a force in firm control, a force to which the individual must adapt himself somehow while hoping secretly for change.

The popular mind dimly sensed that this hope was bound up with the death of the autocrat. This thought was reflected in an anecdote which circulated in Russia in 1947. It concerned a citizen who, in a letter to a relative in America, remarked: "He is getting old now. I wonder when he will die." The censor marked this passage and forwarded the letter to the secret police, to whose offices the citizen was summoned. A police officer asked him: "Whom were you thinking of when you wrote that passage?" "Churchill," replied the citizen after a moment's deliberation. He was then excused, but as he departed he turned and asked the officer: "And whom were *you* thinking of?" The implication, of course, was that the death of Stalin was secretly on everybody's mind in Russia, from bottom to top.

The revival of the consciousness of the state as an alien power was governed by the basic facts of the historical situation: the invasion of the land by the state, the mercilessly exploitative relation of the state to the people, the politicalizing and regimentation of all public pursuits, the punitive attitude of the central authority toward those guilty of any infraction of its impossible rules, the presence of a bureaucratic officialdom whose behavior was increasingly characterized by a soulless formalism, a worship of red tape, a servility to superiors and arrogance to inferiors, and so on. The fact that the new bureaucracy had largely been recruited from the common people made no essential difference. To the ordinary person, the "great State machine" was a force which was constantly mobilizing him, calling upon him for fresh sacrifices, taking all and giving nothing, breaking its promises to him, lecturing, scolding and indoctrinating him, constricting his choice of occupation, his ability to employ his talents profitably and productively, his opportunity to travel and move around, his freedom to speak his mind above a whisper. It was a force whose institutions had become "bureaucratic fortresses," to use Dudintsev's phrase, whose system of administration forced one to bribe his way through life, whose press and radio were a mass of boring harangues, whose economic policies compelled a rich country to live miserably, whose secret agents were everywhere in society, listening to hear what he might say in an unguarded moment. This, roughly, was the Stalinist Russian state as experienced by millions of its subjects in the period from 1945 to 1953. It suggests why the idea of a thaw carried so much meaning in the period just following Stalin's death, when the tension broke and the atmosphere changed.

The press of official Russia propagated the image of the country as a monolithic unity of state and people. It maintained the pretense that the people lived the life of the state, that its goals and interests and values were theirs too, that the millions at the base were willing and eager cogs in the great machine. In effect, it continued to propagate the myth of the revolution, according to which the new state system was the political incarnation of popular Russia. At the same time, it revealed in many indirect ways how far the monolithic picture was from the truth. When Malenkov, for example, spoke at the Nineteenth Party Congress in 1952 of the need for "Soviet Gogols and Shchedrins," he implied, whether wittingly or not, that there had arisen a new official Russia similar in basic ways to the one which Gogol and Shchedrin had satirized. Again, internal propaganda constantly complained that "some" citizens were attempting to get what they could from the state and give as little as possible to it. This showed that the exploitative attitude of the government toward the people was being reciprocated insofar as conditions permitted, that the ordinary person had developed an opportunistic code of behavior in his relations with the governmental apparatus. Finally and most revealingly, the leaders and their press began, approximately from 1946 onward, to castigate regularly what was called *apolitichnost'* — the "apolitical attitude." This went along with *bezideinost'* — the "non-ideological attitude." Taken together, they signified a failure of response, an alienation from the official world, and a tendency among the people to live, as best they could, a life apart.

Russia had again become a dual entity. Despite the spread of literacy and education in the Soviet period, there was a revival of the cleavage of cultures in the country. The culture of official Russia, with its apotheosized autocrat in the Kremlin, aristocracy of rank, all-powerful bureaucracy, pervasive atmosphere of police terror, regimentation of all activities, rituals of prevarication, grandiose "construction projects of Communism," great new foreign empire, official friendships and enmities, cold and hot wars — this was one thing. There was also a suppressed and little known unofficial Russia with a life of its own. In the late Stalin period, this was largely an underground life. For many it meant a life of underground private enterprise in various forms. For the peasant, it typically meant the effort to evade work in the State fields and concentrate his concern on the family's private garden plot. For the artist, thinker, and writer, it often meant an underground creative life over which the state had no control, an escape from the dreary official culture to real self-expression in secret.[25] Among some youthful elements, there was a revival of evangelical religion, carried on in underground ways, and the old Populist tradition came alive again when university students at Moscow, Leningrad, and elsewhere formed secret circles to preach among themselves tendencies of oppositional political thought with an anarchist tinge. Unofficial Russia also developed other forms of expression, in which the life apart from the state was a life of crime or centered in the consolations of vodka.

This picture finds considerable confirmation in the works of post-Stalin imaginative literature which have stirred up interest in Russia and abroad. Some of these writings are in fact representative of the underground literature of the late Stalin period, and many of them are concerned with the life of the country during that time. From Ehrenburg's *Thaw* and Pomerantsev's powerful tract *On Sincerity in Literature* down to Dudintsev's *Not By Bread Alone*, the theme which emerges is that of a duality in Russian life and consciousness, of division between the official and unofficial Russias. Ehrenburg's hero is an underground artist who severs himself completely from the official art world in order to be able to work creatively. Dudintsev gives a portrait of the underground life of invention. His hero does battle with the state bureaucracy, for which Dudintsev has created a significant literary symbol in the figure of Drozdov, and serves a term in a concentration camp for his pains. The wide interested response which these writings have aroused among the reading public in Russia is closely related to the fact that they raise, between as well as in the lines, the deeply meaningful question of the two Russias and their relations.

One of the significant themes of this recent literature is that the line of division between the two Russias may run through the individual person. The image of dual Russia becomes here an image of the Russian

[25] A young painter with whom I spoke in Russia in 1946 said: "All the good work in the arts here is being done underground." Once in a great while, some hint of this situation penetrated the press. For example, during the so-called philosophical discussion of 1947 one speaker referred to the "dualization" of philosophy. It resulted from the fact, he said, that the philosophical bureaucrats were afraid to clear for publication any article or book containing a trace of originality. As a consequence of their "protectionism and "mystical fear of mistakes," there had come into existence a "second" and "hidden" social science and philosophy in Russia: "There exists a manuscript and typescript literature on philosophy and the history of philosophy which is richer, fuller and deeper than the one we know." *Voprosy filosofii*, no. 1 (1947), 375, 376, 377.

functionary as a dual personality. He has a role and self-identity in official Russia, but also a hidden unofficial existence and identity. He is "two persons in one man," as a character of Dudintsev's expresses it. There are "two sides — the hidden one and the visible one." [26] Alexander Ianshin's story "The Levers," published in the almanac "Literary Moscow" for 1956, is constructed around this theme. It introduces a group of persons conversing informally in a room of the administration building of a collective farm. Out of their quiet uninhibited talk unfolds a picture of the farm as an utterly run-down institution where the peasants earn only a mere pittance, where there are no more cows, where the planning of crops remains a jealously guarded prerogative of district officials. They comment acidly about the district party boss who, while knowing all this, pretends that it is not so and repeats catch-phrases about "animal husbandry growing from year to year," the steady upsurge of the peasants' "welfare," and so on. Then, suddenly, a meeting is called to order, and it happens that this group of persons composes the collective farm's party organization. A metamorphosis of personality occurs: "Their faces all became concentrated, tense and dull, as though they were preparing for something which was long familiar to them but nevertheless ceremonial and important. Everything earthly and natural vanished, and the action shifted to another world. . . ." The action has shifted to the world of official Russia. The individuals have changed selves. Now they are acting and speaking in the capacity of representatives of official Russia, its "levers" in the countryside. They proceed to repeat the official catch-phrases of the district party boss, those very phrases which they have just been ridiculing. They pass the requisite official "resolution," and the meeting ends.

The question arises: Who actually are the people? Ianshin leaves us in no doubt that the real selves are the unofficial ones: "They quickly departed, and it seemed that each had in his soul a sense of duty done, but at the same time of uneasiness, of dissatisfaction with himself." [27] In the tradition of his predecessors in the Russian intelligentsia a century ago, Ianshin feels the existence of a rift between the state and society, between official and popular Russia, and takes his moral stand with the latter. As might be expected, the official press has denounced this point of view. It strikes at the heart of the myth of the Soviet regime as the political incarnation of popular Russia.

The death of Stalin, like the death of Nicholas I a century earlier, brought a whole period of history to an end and posed the problem of internal change and reform. In both instances, the autocratic system revolved around the autocratic personality, and the situation toward the

[26] Vladimir Dudintsev, *Ne khlebom edinym* (New York, 1957), 196.

[27] M. E. Aliger, ed., *Literaturno-khudozhestvennyi sbornik II* (Moscow, 1956), 510, 513.

end of the reign assumed the aspect of a profound national crisis, a crisis of paralysis and compulsion. Pent-up forces for change and reform were released in the aftermath. In the period since Stalin's death, however, the limits of the official conception of reform have become abundantly clear. The regime would not go forward to 1861 but back to about 1930. The reform idea with which it has been operating under the leadership of Khrushchev does not envisage the new period as one of a new "unbinding" of society; it would unbind, at most, the provincial party secretaries. It sees the solution in terms of reorganizational schemes, the decentralization of the bureaucracy, the restoration of party rule, the relaxation of police terror. It attacks the agrarian crisis by the cultivation of virgin lands and corn rather than by the abolition of serfdom in the kolkhoz. More recently, in the person of Khrushchev, it has been emphasizing material things, adumbrating, as the new formula for "Communism," the soviets plus supermarkets. The regime, it would appear, looks to a rise in the material standard of consumption as a means of reconciling the Russian people to unfreedom in perpetuity.

But it is very doubtful that a policy of reform operating within these narrow limits can repair the rupture between the state and society which is reflected in the revival of the image of dual Russia. A moral renovation of the national life, a fundamental reordering of relations, a process of genuine "unbinding," or in other words an alteration in the nature of the system, would be needed. The state cannot resolve the situation satisfactorily as long as it clings to the positions won in its reconquest of the Russian land, just as it cannot work out firm relations with the peoples of Eastern Europe as long as it holds on to the structure and idea of empire. But of reforms on this major scale the present leadership appears to be, for various reasons, incapable. So it goes on attempting to square the circle, to make the system function well by merely tinkering with it rather than by fundamentally altering it. This is the dilemma of Russia today.

In 1857, when the post-Nicholaean reform period was still in the incipient stage, Herzen wrote in his paper *Kolokol:* "The government corrects this or that particular situation, but the principle, the idea out of which all our radical abuses spring, remains untouched. . . . It is still the same old Nicholaean period, but diluted with molasses." [28] There is reason to believe that large numbers of people in contemporary Soviet Russia view the situation in a manner rather similar to this. They will not be satisfied with a Stalin period diluted with molasses. If, as has been suggested, there is a "silence" in Russian culture today, it is in part an enforced silence and in part the pregnant silence of intensive thought in the face of this problem.

[28] Nestor Kotliarevsky, *Kanun osvobozhdeniia: 1855–1861* (Petrograd, 1916), 127.

CHANGING ATTITUDES
TOWARD THE INDIVIDUAL

GEORGE L. KLINE

Russian thinkers have long been intensely concerned with the problem of the individual (*lichnost'* — also translatable as "individual person" or "personality"). During the first half of the period in question (and beginning as early as 1840 in the work of Belinsky and Herzen) — that is, until about 1906 or 1907 — a central theme of Russian ethical and social theorizing was the defense of the freedom, the rights, and the *dostoinstvo* (dignity and worth) of the individual person. There were repeated attempts to outline a theoretical (and, to a lesser extent, institutional) framework within which such rights and freedoms might be preserved and extended. This concern was shared by thinkers who ranged politically from conservative to liberal and radical; by theists, agnostics, and atheists; by *Narodniki* (Populists) and even a few of the early Russian Marxists (the "Kantian" and the "individualistic Nietzschean" groups). But, beginning about 1907 or 1908, a countervailing tendency began to gain momentum, particularly in the group of Marxists whom I call "collectivistic Nietzscheans," which carried to its logical conclusion the impersonalism or anti-individualism implicit in Hegel and Marx. Somewhat earlier, hints of such a position were put forward (in a religious context) by Vladimir Solov'ev and Leo Tolstoy, under both Hegelian and Schopenhauerian influence. This collectivistic anti-individualism was sharply stated by certain early Soviet theorists, particularly Trotsky. Its penetration into Soviet policy and practice was early and complete.

I

Despite the almost unanimous nineteenth-century Russian emphasis upon what might be called "ethical individualism" or, alternatively, "democratic liberalism," there is virtually no tradition in Russia to compare with that in the West which we associate with the names of Locke, Montesquieu, and John Stuart Mill. The difference is not simply that Russia lacked a history of liberal and democratic institutions, the "rule of law," constitutional safeguards, division of powers, checks and balances (whether in the American or European form). It is also that in Russia the primary burden of defense of the individual fell to the *radical* rather than the liberal or reformist tradition.

If we take Mill's *On Liberty* (1859) as a paradigm of ethical individualism or democratic liberalism — a classic defense of the freedom, worth, and dignity of the human individual — the contrast between the West European and the Russian tradition becomes clear. Mill was a "reformist"; he accepted and worked within and through the existing sociopolitical institutions of nineteenth-century England. To be sure, he protested and was alert to violations of individual freedom as he conceived it. But he did not repudiate the existing order as such or advocate its violent overthrow.

In contrast, Russian intellectuals of Mill's generation, who were equally concerned to defend and enlarge the freedom and dignity of the individual, found the existing sociopolitical order in Russia so oppressive and unjust, so restrictive of individual rights and freedoms, that they could think only of abolishing it, drastically and by violence. Some of them argued convincingly that nonviolent, merely reformist, changes were either impossible or ineffectual. Liberalism of the moderate, constitutional variety was never very strong in Russia; it lacked articulate spokesmen until the late nineteenth century, and the few who emerged then were relatively uninfluential. Thus by default political radicals assumed much of the defense of individualism which fell to liberals in the West.

Against what were they defending the individual? The answer, as most of them saw it, was twofold. (1) First, against the facts of Russian history, against, as these thinkers liked to call it, "Russian reality." Radicals and liberals alike viewed dominant and persistent institutional patterns of Russian history as a threat to be overcome. Some of them traced to the Tatar occupation practices and institutions which had served to restrict and repress the individual. Indeed, one widely discussed socioeconomic institution, the peasant village commune (the obshchina as its economic and social side, the mir as its political and administrative side) was criticized for submerging individual freedom and initiative in an amorphous social collectivity. (2) Less well known, but equally important, many Russian thinkers, especially among the radicals, regarded themselves as defending the individual person against the *theories* of Western thinkers, in particular the impersonalism and anti-individualism of Hegel and Marx. This was true both of "revisionist" Marxists of the 1890's and early 1900's and of such men as Belinsky and Herzen. Detailed discussion of the views of Belinsky and Herzen falls outside the scope of this essay, since the former died in 1848 and the latter left Russia permanently in 1847.[1] I will say only that in about

---

[1] Bakunin and Kropotkin are omitted for similar reasons: they were in European Russia only briefly and sporadically after 1861. Moreover, their anarchist-socialist defense of the individual, though impassioned, was doctrinaire and incoherent.

For a stimulating discussion of Herzen's views on individual freedom, in contrast

1840 they both came to interpret Hegel as reducing the individual person to a mere instrument or means for the self-realization of absolute Spirit, through the rationally determined processes of the historical dialectic. They came to feel — with passion — that Hegel left no room for the individual's autonomy, freedom, or creativity. Somewhat later, two major Western thinkers — Kierkegaard (in the 1840's) and Nietzsche (in the 1870's) — gave powerful expression to a similarly motivated revolt.

When, in the early 1900's, some of the early Russian Marxists (especially Lunacharsky and Vol'sky) became dissatisfied with the impersonalism and anti-individualism of Marxian historical materialism (a lineal descendant, in this respect, of Hegelianism), they turned explicitly to Nietzsche for support in their "deviation." Other Russian Marxists (especially Struve and Berdiaev) had turned in the 1890's to Kant, whose ethical and social philosophy also stands in sharp opposition to Hegel's.

One of the most passionate defenders of the autonomy of the individual during the period immediately after 1861 was the "nihilist," D. I. Pisarev (1840–1868). His central emphasis fell, negatively, upon the "emancipation of the individual person" from social, intellectual, and political constraints; and, positively, upon the preservation of the wholeness of human personality in the face of the fragmenting influence of specialization and division of labor.[2]

Historically, Pisarev insists, "the necessity of respecting the human person has not been recognized in its full scope either by the thinkers, from Plato to Hegel, nor by men of action, from Cyrus to Napoleon III."[3] The present and pressing task, as he sees it, is "to emancipate the human individual from the manifold constraints which are laid upon him by the timidity of his thought, caste prejudices, the authority of tradition, the aspiration toward a common ideal, and all such obsolete rubbish — which prevent the living human being from breathing freely and developing himself fully."[4] This is a highly original catalogue of constraints; but Pisarev is serious about all of them. In writings centered around 1861 he stressed systematically the individual's liberation from traditional moral codes, ideals, and values, developing an extreme moral relativism and sketching the position that is now referred to as "non-cognitivism" or "emotivism" in ethics. Morality, in this view, is a matter of individual taste, like the preference for port or sherry. However,

---

to those of Bakunin, see Isaiah Berlin, "Herzen and Bakunin on Individual Liberty," in E. J. Simmons, ed., *Continuity and Change in Russian and Soviet Thought* (Cambridge, Mass., 1955), 473–499.

[2] The notion of the "critically thinking individual" was put forward by Pisarev and by Lavrov at about the same time (early 1860's), but received a more systematic theoretical development in the works of the latter.

[3] D. I. Pisarev, *Sochineniia* (St. Petersburg, 1894), I, 349.

[4] Pisarev, I, 339.

"when it is a matter of judging port or sherry, we remain calm and cool, we reason simply and soundly . . . but when it is a question of lofty matters, we immediately put on a Lenten countenance, get up on our stilts and begin speaking in a pompous style. . . . We let our neighbor indulge his taste in hors d'oeuvres and desserts, but woe unto him if he expresses an independent opinion about morals, and even greater woe, not to say stoning . . . if he translates his ideas into life." [5]

Sounding very much like Mill, Pisarev writes, "Do not suppress your originality and autonomy for the sake of the established order or the taste of the mob." He goes on to attack the "intellectual and moral bondage" of conventional morality and "generally accepted" standards. "A common ideal," Pisarev declares, "has just as little *raison d'être* as common eyeglasses or common boots, made on the same last and to the same measure." [6] Eyes differ, feet differ, individuals differ; hence glasses, boots, and ideals (for "every ideal has its author") should be individually fitted. No single ideal can possibly be appropriate to all men.

The emancipated individual, Pisarev goes on, must be a whole man, an "integral personality, developed in a completely unartificial and independent way, not constrained by the service of various ideals, not wasting energy in struggle with himself." [7] This is an echo of Khomiakov's doctrine of the *tsel'naia lichnost'*, but with a naturalistic and social-psychological emphasis which was to be carried further by Nozhin and Mikhailovsky.

The integrity or wholeness of the individual person is threatened from three sides: by socioeconomic specialization of function, by psychological splintering (under the pressure of artificial moral codes), and by esoteric art and science. The first threat is symbolized by the functional hierarchy of Plato's *Republic*, in which, as Pisarev points out, "there are civil servants, soldiers, artisans, merchants, slaves, and females, but there are not and cannot be any human beings. Each individual person is a screw, pinion, or wheel of a given size and shape in the mechanism of the state; and apart from this function, he has no significance." [8]

The second threat is described in these terms: "We deliberately split ourselves in two, look upon ourselves as a dangerous enemy, try to fool ourselves, and catch ourselves in the act, struggle with ourselves, conquer ourselves, find animal instincts in ourselves and take up arms against them with the force of reason." [9]

Pisarev warns his readers against art that can be enjoyed "only by a

[5] Pisarev, I, 267.
[6] Pisarev, I, 358, 266.
[7] Pisarev, I, 369.
[8] Pisarev, I, 277–278.
[9] Pisarev, I, 360.

few specialists" and science that is "in its very essence inaccessible to the masses" and only "vaguely understood by an insignificant number of one-sidedly developed people, who spend their whole lives buried in abstractions." [10] Pisarev generalizes his rejection of esoteric art and abstruse science to include abstract theorizing and "ideologizing," with its dangerous tendency to merge into fanaticism. He develops an idea formulated by Schiller in such plays as "Don Carlos," and by Belinsky in his criticism of Bakunin — that the ideologue, the man passionately committed to large ideals, readily becomes the fanatic, to whom individual men are less important than the furthering of an abstract principle. Advocating "a good dose of skepticism" as an antidote to fanaticism, Pisarev vigorously condemns the "revolting vulgarity of intolerance." [11]

N. G. Chernyshevsky (1828–1889), whose political commitment Pisarev shared during the mid-1860's, was less articulate (not to say flamboyant) in his defense of the freedom and dignity of the individual person. He did criticize conventional morality and, in particular, corrupt institutions — economic, social, and political — as constraints upon the individual. "Justice, respect for the dignity of man," he wrote in 1859, "are ideas which are irreconcilable with serfdom." [12] And, more passionately: "We hold nothing on earth higher than the human individual." [13] After 1861 his characteristic emphasis fell upon the distinction (also stressed by Marx) between merely "formal" and truly "effective" individual rights and freedoms. "Legal rights have no value for a man until he possesses material means to benefit by them." Chernyshevesky criticizes liberals for concerning themselves solely with abstract rights and neglecting the poverty and ignorance which shuts men off from the enjoyment of such rights. "Man," he declares, "is not an abstract juridical person, but a living creature; . . . a man who is dependent for his material means of existence cannot be an independent human being in fact, even though his independence is proclaimed by the letter of the law." [14]

N. A. Dobroliubov (1836–1861) was less gifted as a theorist than either Chernyshvesky or Pisarev, but he had a flair for concrete social criticism and pungent statement. [15] His characteristic insight is a curiously modern one: he sees the individual human being as overwhelmed by

---

[10] Pisarev, I, 366.

[11] Pisarev, I, 356; IV, 25.

[12] N. G. Chernyshevsky, *Sochineniia* (St. Petersburg, 1906), IV, 52.

[13] Chernyshevsky, IV, 440.

[14] N. G. Chernyshevsky, *Sochineniia* (Moscow, 1948), IV, 740.

[15] He is included here, even though he died in 1861 (at the age of twenty-five), because certain of his ideas entered into the mainstream of nineteenth-century Russian individualism.

the vast, impersonal machinery of society. Dobroliubov sees the "depersonalization of man, the degradation of his moral dignity" as inevitable in feudal Russia, where every manifestation of the individual's free and rational activity is blocked and his inherent demands for justice stifled. "The wilful stupidity [of the rulers] depersonalizes, and depersonalization is wholly opposed to all free rational activity." [16] The environment, says Dobroliubov, "devours" the individual; the "common malady" of the time is a lack of individual autonomy and independence.

Dobroliubov calls repeatedly for the "natural, vital, free development" of the individual person and deplores the loss of "respect for one's own worth and dignity." [17] He has only scorn for "idealistic moralists" who harp on "self-abnegation, the destruction of the individual, the subjugation of individual natural impulses to an abstract, dead principle." [18] And he adds, with charming inconsistency, that it is the duty of every honest man to persecute anyone who stifles free impulse or independent growth in himself or others. As a radical, he calls for the violent overthrow of an order which deprives the individual of his rights. "Become fully aware of the rights of your own person to injustice and happiness and you will become a mortal enemy of social injustice." [19]

Professor K. D. Kavelin (1818–1885), a somewhat right-of-center liberal, was much concerned — though rather Platonically — with the preservation of the rights of the individual person.[20] He insisted (with Leo Tolstoy and the Christians, against the radicals and reformers) that institutional change alone is insufficient to guarantee individual rights. The problem lies in individual men, and the solution will be achieved by "directing all the best forces of knowledge and practical experience toward the moral growth of the individual person." Individualism, respect for the individual, he wrote in 1884, is barely beginning in Russia. "The more individualism develops among us the more strongly will the demand for moral ideals be felt." [21] Kavelin insisted that science cannot grasp individuality, since it is impersonal, dealing with the general and abstract. Yet individuality is precious; and, where science fails, the way is left open for morality and religion. In the end, Kavelin embraces the morality if not the theology — as a positivist he rejected all metaphysics — of New Testament Christianity.

F. M. Dostoevsky (1821–1881) was acutely tormented, especially in

[16] N. A. Dobroliubov, *Sochineniia* (Moscow, 1934–1940), II, 402; V. Poliansky, N. A. *Dobroliubov* (Moscow, 1926), 92.

[17] Dobroliubov, II, 331; Poliansky, 94.

[18] Dobroliubov, I, 440.

[19] Dobroliubov, IV, 103.

[20] In 1862 Kavelin defended the harsh sentence passed upon Chernyshevsky, thus alienating not only radical but also liberal opinion.

[21] K. D. Kavelin, "Zadachi etiki," *Sochineniia* (St. Petersburg, 1899), III, 951, 903,

the period after 1861, by the fate of the individual. As a Christian, he was a passionate defender of human personality, which remained for him, even in the most insignificant human being, an absolute value. Yet he brutally unmasked the "man from the underground." There is an echo of both Pisarev and Dobroliubov in Dostoevsky's statement (in *Notes from the Underground*) that "the whole human enterprise consists exclusively in man's proving to himself every moment that he is a human being and not a cog."

Dostoevsky's novels show the fateful consequences of a failure to respect the human person as an absolute value, of using individuals as means to some further end. Ivan Karamazov passionately rejects the utilitarian criterion of morality — the "ultimate general welfare" or "the greatest good of the greatest number" — casting across this abstract calculus the absolute value of the life of a little child. He declares, blazingly in earnest, that if he were offered the certain choice of making all mankind happy forever under the condition that one innocent child should suffer briefly now, he would repudiate it.[22] Dostoevsky himself formulated the assumption underlying Raskolnikov's "utilitarian murder" in these words: "A highly developed person, who feels more keenly than one who is undeveloped the suffering of unfulfilled needs, must have money to satisfy these needs — why should he not kill the undeveloped person, if there is no other way to get money?"[23] Dostoevsky's own answer, of course, is simple and direct: the life of even the most "undeveloped" human being represents an absolute and inviolable value.

Dostoevsky was sharply critical of "self-enclosed atomistic individualism" — the live-and-let-live laissez-fairism of the European middle classes. To the bourgeois individualist's rhetorically self-righteous question, "But am I my brother's keeper?," he answers, out of the fullness of a mystical, almost Buddhistic, compassion: "All are guilty for all." This sense of individual guilt and responsibility is close to the social conscience which earlier had impelled Dostoevsky toward Belinsky's utopian socialism, and as late as 1876 brought from him a passionate rejection of "the idea that only one tenth of all human beings should receive a higher development, and the remaining nine tenths should merely serve as material and means to make this possible, themselves remaining in darkness."[24]

Close to Dostoevsky, yet with a highly individual accent, was K. N. Leont'ev (1831–1891). He is sometimes called, with reason, "the Russian Nietzsche." However, his "Nietzschean" views were developed independently; Leont'ev's own major writings antedate Nietzsche's by more

---

[22] F. M. Dostoevsky, *The Brothers Karamazov*, bk. V, ch. iv.
[23] F. M. Dostoevsky, *Diary of a Writer* (1873), III.
[24] *Diary*, January 1876.

than a decade, and he died before Nietzsche's fame had spread to Russia. Leont'ev held that the self-complacent, vulgar, liberal individualism of Western Europe was "destroying contemporary societies." [25] He vigorously repudiated "the new faith in the earthly man and earthly mankind, in the ideal, independent, autonomous dignity of the individual" as an expression of the "deification of the rights and dignities of man which became dominant in Europe at the end of the eighteenth century." "European thought," he adds, "now worships man simply because he is man." [26]

As opposed to this view, Leont'ev puts forward a Nietzschean individualism which glorifies the individual who is strong, creative, daring, "beautiful" — the source of the variety, complexity, and richness in the historical process. Such an individual, he wrote in 1864, "is higher than his works. The many-sided strength or the one-sided heroism of the individual is, more than anything else, the clear goal of history. . . . The important thing is not that there should be no violation of law, no suffering, but that the suffering should be of high quality, that the violation of law should result not from sluggishness or dirty bribery, but from the passionate demands of the individual person." [27]

An important defense of the freedom and dignity of the individual is to be found in P. L. Lavrov (1823–1900), who is sometimes unfairly dismissed as a mere revolutionary propagandist or intellectual historian. He was both, in his later years; but in the 1860's he produced major works in ethical and social theory. Individuals, Lavrov maintains, are the only reality in history; society elaborates individuals, and an elite of "critically thinking individuals" reconstructs society, under the pressure of individual needs — including, in the first instance, moral norms and ideals. The individual has a duty to repay society for his own development by perfecting its institutions through intellectual criticism — "a seeing of possibilities and weighing of alternatives" — and society has a *right* to demand such critical activity on the part of the individual. "Society is threatened with . . . stagnation if it smothers its critically thinking individuals." [28]

Respect for one's own person, according to Lavrov, is "the basis of human morality." The point of departure in history is "the individual's setting of goals for himself as if he were autonomous." [29] "The ideal of the individual moral personality," he wrote in 1870, "is that of a personality which has developed its powers and capacities to the extreme limit, on the basis of the most rigorous and consistent criticism, apply-

[25] K. N. Leont'ev, *Sochineniia* (Moscow, 1913), VI, 21.
[26] Leont'ev, VIII, 160; VII, 132.
[27] Leont'ev, I, 414, 415.
[28] P. L. Lavrov, *Istoricheskie pis'ma* (St. Petersburg, 1870), 26f, 65.
[29] P. L. Lavrov, *Zadachi ponimanii istorii* (Moscow, 1898), 103.

ing these powers and capacities to further growth on the basis of the most rational and unswerving conviction." [30]

"Moral criticism" discovers an equal potentiality for moral growth in all men. Hence, "we must recognize the equal worth and dignity of all men." And we have a moral obligation to further the growth of other individuals as much as our own. "An injury to the worth and dignity of another is an injury to our own. Failure to act in the face of the suppression of another's growth is immoral." [31] It was this moral imperative of action to combat injustice which impelled Lavrov, after 1870, along the path of violent revolution.

B. N. Chicherin (1828–1904), a devout Christian and cautious liberal, was close to Kant in his ethical individualism. This generated a certain tension in his thought, since he was an orthodox Hegelian in logic, metaphysics, and philosophy of history. Chicherin opposes the "monstrous notion" that society is a "physical organism," an all-devouring Moloch, whose function is "to make mankind happy by putting it in chains." He resists sociopolitical invasion of the private and personal, stressing the individual person as the "foundation-stone of the entire social edifice." Recognition of the human person is basic to both law and morality. "Not society, but individuals, think, feel, and desire." The human individual is a single, spiritual substance, possessed of free will and reason and, in consequence, of a worth and dignity which demand respect. Man as a rational creature and "bearer of the Absolute" must "always be regarded as an end, and must never be degraded to the level of a mere means." [32] We shall presently consider an eloquent restatement of this Kantian dictum by two early Russian Marxists.

Chicherin's individualistic liberalism found more formal expression in the Muromtsev memorandum of 1880, which urged a guaranty for "personal rights, freedom of thought, and freedom of speech," and in the draft resolution adopted by the Zemstvo Congress of 1904, which sought to establish the principle of the "inviolability of the individual," as well as the traditional civil liberties.[33] Unfortunately, the *institutional* impact of such resolutions was severely limited.

The tension between Kant and Hegel persists without clear resolution in Chicherin's thought; he himself seems to have been only dimly aware of its existence. Thus, we find him saying that, under favorable conditions, a national collective (*narodnost'*) "may become an individual per-

[30] P. L. Lavrov, *Sovremennie ucheniia o nravstvennosti* . . . (St. Petersburg, 1903), 56.
[31] Lavrov, *Sovremennie* . . . , 69, 70.
[32] B. N. Chicherin, *Polozhitel'naia filosofiia i edinstvo nauki* (Moscow, 1892), 332f; *Filosofiia prava* (Moscow, 1900), 26, 25, 54f; *Sobstvennost' i gosudarstvo* (Moscow, 1882), v.
[33] Cf. George Fischer, *Russian Liberalism: From Gentry to Intelligentsia* (Cambridge, Mass., 1958), 67, 183f.

son," or that great men are merely "organs and instruments of a universal spirit [Hegel's *Weltgeist*]." [34] Chicherin's characteristic emphasis, however, remains libertarian and individualistic.

A similar tension marks the (rather meagre) utterances of K. P. Pobedonostsev (1827–1907) on the problem of the individual and society. On the one hand, as lay administrator of the Russian Orthodox Church (1880–1905), he finds ample occasion to glorify church and state at the expense of the individual, and to speak of a religious people (*narod*) as a "living organism." On the other hand, he joins Chicherin in accusing socialists of a readiness to "sacrifice the most sacred interests of individual freedom," and castigates the "socialist" view that "private life should be swallowed up by social life, and social life . . . controlled by the state." The human individual, Pobedonostsev adds, is immortal and of absolute value; he "is not to be crushed as one crushes an insect." [35]

"The Struggle for Individuality," the title of a major essay by N. K. Mikhailovsky (1842–1904), well symbolizes the latter's life-long concern. The chief threat to the freedom and integrity of the individual person, in his eyes, is posed by increasing socioeconomic specialization and division of labor. Primitive man was "an integral individual, an individual in whom the intellectual and physical aspects existed in mutual harmony." [36] His group activities took the form of "simple cooperation," in which several nonspecialized individuals assisted each other in carrying out a common task. Civilization brought "complex cooperation," based upon specialization of function, and the individual lost his wholeness. In opposition to the fragmented contemporary individual, Mikhailovsky sets up the ideal of the "layman," the nonspecialist, who still retains his integrity as an individual. "The layman," he writes, "is man par excellence." [37]

At the present time, says Mikhailovsky, "it may be that society is progressing, but . . . the individual is retrogressing. . . . Society, by the very process of its development, strives to split up the individual, to give him some special function and to distribute the remaining functions to others, transforming the individual into an organ." [38] The full development of the individual is incompatible with the full development of society, conceived on the Hegelian or Spencerian model of organic growth. The individual human being "must not be sacrificed to the development of an ideal [abstract] whole such as society." [39] If he is, Mikhailovsky declares, echoing the gifted young biologist N. D. Nozhin (1841–1866),

[34] Chicherin, *Filosofiia prava*, 75, 78.
[35] K. P. Pobedonostsev, *Moskovskii sbornik* (Moscow, 1896), 13, 181.
[36] N. K. Mikhailovsky, *Sochineniia* (St. Petersburg, 1909), I, 34.
[37] Mikhailovsky, III, 354.
[38] Mikhailovsky, I, 477.
[39] Mikhailovsky, 41.

his progressive depersonalization is paralleled by "pathological" social development. (Nozhin had said in 1866 that division of labor among individuals of the same species is "pathological," producing "disintegrated individuals.")

Mikhailovsky also echoes Belinsky's and Herzen's revolt against the subordination of the individual to an abstract social or historical entity. Even the passion of the revolt is reminiscent of Belinsky: "I declare," writes Mikhailovsky, "that I shall struggle with the higher individuality which threatens to swallow me up. . . . Let anyone who wants look upon me as part of something greater than I am . . . I do not cease to regard myself as a whole man, an integral personality." [40] He defined progress (in 1869) as "a gradual approximation to the wholeness of individuals, and to the fullest . . . possible division of labor among various organs, with the least possible division of labor among human beings." [41] It is clear that, despite his professed positivism, Mikhailovsky regards the individual person, in the achieved wholeness of a full life, as an absolute value. "The individual must never be sacrificed," he once wrote; "he is sacred and inviolable, and all [our] efforts should be directed toward . . . establishing him at the point where he may triumph." [42]

N. I. Kareev (1850–1931), a political liberal, was close to Lavrov in his ethical individualism (his own term); he devoted a sympathetic monograph to Lavrov's theory of the individual. [43] But his formulation of Lavrovian views — which is closer to Kant than Lavrov was — is original enough to warrant brief consideration. "I wish to maintain," Kareev wrote, ". . . the concept of the autonomous individual." This was in opposition to three influential contemporary tendencies: (1) the tendency which breaks the self down into a series of psychic events (Hume), (2) that which turns it into an expression of the *Zeitgeist* or *Volksgeist* (Hegel), and (3) that which reduces it to a product of socio-economic relations (Marx). [44] Kareev's "autonomy" explicitly includes sociopolitical freedom: "From the point of view of the human dignity and worth of the individual person . . . external freedom is a necessary condition for the spiritual growth and happiness of all the members of society." [45]

From the moral standpoint, Kareev writes, "the utilitarian attitude toward the person, which treats him as an object, is inadmissible." The individual rightly resists being treated as a mere means. "The principle

[40] Mikhailovsky, III, 423, 336.
[41] Mikhailovsky, I, 40.
[42] Mikhailovsky, IV, 451.
[43] N. I. Kareev, *Teorii lichnosti P. L. Lavrova: k istorii sotsiologii v Rossii* (St. Petersburg, 1907).
[44] Kareev, "K voprosu o svobode voli," *Voprosy filosofii i psikhologii*, no. 4 (1890), 119.
[45] Kareev, *Mysli ob osnovakh nravstvennosti* (St. Petersburg, 1895), 135.

of individuality is not a mere ascription to man of the right not to be an instrument or means for another, but also a respect for this right." [46] In the name of the absolute value of the human person, Kareev opposes killing of any kind, including euthanasia, capital punishment, and political assassination. He insists that the individual has a right to choose his own life profession; society should not force his choice. The individual is not to be considered an organ of a social "organism." Man has a right not only to life and the satisfaction of essential needs, but also to unhindered growth. This doctrine is not *egoism*, according to Kareev, for egoism is an attack upon other individuals; it is *individualism*, which is a defense against attack on the part of other egoisms.

Individualism and moral autonomy are correlative concepts. "Individualism is the autonomy of the individual person, his freedom in the sphere of thought and life, and only in the sphere of life is this freedom limited by demands flowing from the existence of other individuals, who have an equal right to freedom of thought and life." [47] We have moral obligations, says Kareev, only toward persons because "we attribute to them a certain inner worth, from which flows their moral right to demand of me, as a matter of obligation, that I should respect their human dignity." [48] In attributing absolute value to individuals as such, we respect both their "natural" rights and the present possibility of their future moral growth.

From Kareev, whose ethical individualism is very close to Kant's, the leap to the early "Kantian Marxists" is not great. P. B. Struve (1870–1944), during his brief Marxian period (*ca.* 1895–1902), laid central stress upon the Kantian dictum that the individual person (as a rational creature and a member of the "realm of ends") must always be treated as an end and never as a means only. Like Berdiaev during the same period, Struve regarded this as an essential supplement to the Marxian theory of history and society. But both of them rejected Kant's "ethical formalism" and emphasis on "abstract obligation."

"The idea of the equal [moral] value of men, as a fully thought-out philosophic conviction," Struve writes, "rests upon the idea of the substantial being of the spirit . . . in this sense the term 'Christian-democratic morality' is perfectly correct. Men have equal value not as empirical and contingent 'bundles of impressions' (as Hume called the self or soul), not as animal organisms, but as spiritual substances." [49] Such equality must include: "First, the *samotsel'nost'* [end-in-himself-ness] of man — man must never be regarded as anyone's instrument; and second,

---

[46] Kareev, *Mysli* . . . , 138.

[47] Kareev, *Mysli* . . . , 151. This is essentially Mill's position on intellectual freedom.

[48] Kareev, *Mysli* . . . , 152.

[49] P. B. Struve, foreword to N. A. Berdiaev, *Individualizm i sub'ektivizm v obshchestvennoi filosofii* (St. Petersburg, 1901), lxviii.

the embodiment in *every* man of the *summum bonum* in the human form of individuality. . . . Equality without individuality is a reactionary ideal." [50] The "morality of absolute good," says Struve, accords highest moral value to the "ideal" personality. But to the "empirical" personality it grants full freedom (autonomy) and equality of value and rights with other "bearers of the human form." [51]

N. A. Berdiaev (1874–1948) was, while a Kantian Marxist (*ca.* 1894–1902), more sensitive than Struve to the influence of earlier Russian thinkers, particularly Herzen, Mikhailovsky, and Leont'ev. "Few Russians," he wrote in his autobiography, "have felt personal freedom as keenly as Mikhailovsky, although Alexander Herzen is, perhaps, even more important in this connection." But Berdiaev's chief indebtedness is to Kant: "Human consciousness," he wrote in 1901, "has never risen higher than Kant's thought concerning man and mankind as an end in itself [*samotsel'*], which gives moral sanction to all else and does not itself require sanction." [52] Berdiaev vigorously denies that Kant sacrifices the individual to an abstract norm, as some critics have charged. On the contrary, he declares, no one valued the moral autonomy of the individual more highly than Kant did. "Man cannot suffer from the fact that we subordinate him to an abstract norm; rather, this norm deifies man." [53]

The Marxist social ideal, in Berdiaev's view, finds its sanction in the notion of man as an intrinsic end. "The historically progressive vanguard of society works constantly to raise the value of man and to bring him to a consciousness of absolute justice." [54] But by 1902 Berdiaev had rejected Marxist doctrine, and by 1905 he had repudiated the Marxist political program. (Lunacharsky had predicted such a break in 1899, charging Berdiaev with "dangerous individualism.") "The attempt to attain freedom by means of denying freedom to oneself or to others," Berdiaev wrote later of the revolution of 1905, "is doomed to failure." [55]

II

Four young Russian Marxists turned in the early 1900's to Friedrich Nietzsche for an ethical and social theory to supplement historical materialism; their position involved an explicit rejection of the category of moral obligation and a central emphasis upon the individual as free creator of values and ideals. Of this group, Lunacharsky and Volsky are most "individualistic," hence closest to Nietzsche himself. Bazarov and Bogdanov, while sharing their comrades' rejection of moral norms and

[50] Struve in Berdiaev, lxxiii, lxxiv.
[51] Struve in Berdiaev, lxxiii.
[52] Berdiaev, 74.
[53] Berdiaev, 75n.
[54] Berdiaev, 79.
[55] N. A. Berdyaev, *Dream and Reality* (New York, 1951), 137.

obligation, are more social-minded and "collectivistic" in their interpretation of creativity, hence less concerned with the freedom and dignity of the individual per se.

We turn first to A. V. Lunacharsky (1875–1933). "Nietzsche," he wrote in 1903, "and all the other critics of the morality of duty, have defended the autonomy of the individual person, the individual's right to be guided in his life solely by his own desires." [56] Sounding very much like Pisarev, he goes on to reject laws, norms, and "universally human ideals" as constraints upon the free individual. Moral indoctrination, according to Lunacharsky, can generate only slaves. The goal is, as in Nietzsche, an enlargement or expansion of human personality, a total emancipation of man.[57] Individual and social interests, he admits, may clash, but they are identical in one sense, "for the species has no existence apart from its individual members. What is a living, powerful species if not an aggregate of living, powerful individuals?" [58] However, "only in the splendid future will we construct a social order in which the interests of the individual and those of society will be in complete harmony." [59]

Lunacharsky opposes the attempt to "transform the individual into a cell of the social organism," [60] and speaks of a future social order which will provide "the broadest foundation for an infinitely luxurious growth of the most varied individualities." Yet his own preference for "macropsychic" (broad-souled) over "micropsychic" (narrow-souled) individualism seems to impel him toward a "collectivist" view. The *I* of the macropsychic individual, he writes, "is identified with some broad and enduring 'we.' " [61] This raises the macropsychic individualist to a level of aesthetic perfection which is unattainable for the micropsychic individualist.

Lunacharsky also accepts humanistic "religious feeling" as a "supreme ecstasy, an enthusiasm, in which the individual is dissolved and transcended, in which he enters into joyous communion with a higher principle." [62] He even goes so far as to assert that "the individual will learn to regard his life as a "component [*moment*] with respect to the life of the species." [63] This theme was much emphasized by Bogdanov and Bazarov.

A more consistent, and no less eloquent, defender of the individual person was Stanislav Vol'sky (his real name was A. V. Sokolov, 1880–

[56] A. V. Lunacharsky, " 'Problemy idealizma s tochki zreniia kriticheskogo realizma," *Obrazovanie,* no. 2 (1903), 133.

[57] "Osnovy positivnoi estetiki" (1904) in *Ocherki realisticheskogo mirovozzreniia* (St. Petersburg, 1905), 180.

[58] "Osnovy . . . ," 137.

[59] "Osnovy . . . ," 142.

[60] "Voprosy morali i M. Meterlink" (1904) in *Etiudy* (Moscow, 1922), 255.

[61] "Voprosy . . . ," 240, 256.

[62] "Budushchee religii," *Obrazovanie,* no. 11 (1907), 30.

[63] "Osnovy . . . ," 138.

1936?). His major work, "The Philosophy of Struggle," subtitled "An Essay in Marxist Ethics," [64] he characterizes as an investigation of the various forms in which the individual's struggle with the natural and social environment expresses itself. His position might be called a "pluralistic individualism."

Class solidarity and discipline, the renunciation of individuality, says Vol'sky, is tactically (and temporarily) necessary for victory in the class struggle. But obligatory norms will disappear with the defeat of capitalism. Then the individual, "freed from the numbing pattern of coercive norms" and from the "idea of duty" — which is "the inevitable companion of bourgeois society" — will make himself "an integral, harmonious personality." [65] "The class," Vol'sky writes, "sees in itself something to be eliminated, the individual something to be asserted." [66] The bourgeoisie, Vol'sky declares, freed the individual in the hour of revolution only to enslave him in the hour of triumph; the proletariat commands the individual in the hour of revolution only to free him in the hour of triumph. Man's ultimate moral ideal is a system of values created by free individuals in a classless society, and thus wholly exempt from class sanction.

According to Vol'sky, societies belong to individuals, serving them as weapons in the struggle with the natural environment. In a society based on *fixed* division of labor (the analogue of Mikhailovsky's "complex cooperation") functional groups are closely connected in the labor process, but at the same time are separated by a deep psychological abyss; there is mutual aid among individuals, but it is devoid of personal sympathy. In the case of *variable* division of labor (which corresponds to Mikhailovsky's "simple cooperation") there is a correlation and supplementation of organs, psychic flexibility, and individual adaptation. Individuals regard each other as persons, exhibit personal sympathy and antipathy. Class conditions, Vol'sky explains, may halt the development of the individual at any of three stages: that of (1) "physiological complex," (2) "character," and (3) "end in himself."

Typically, in bourgeois society (based on fixed division of labor) the individual is free to develop only within the narrow confines of a specialty, and he understands other specialists less and less. The resulting self-alienated human individual is petty, myopic, and narrow. The bourgeoisie as a class attempts to root out any originality which its individual members might attain. Classless society (based on variable division of labor) will be made up of differentiated, self-determining individuals, each of whom, growing into unique, unrepeatable selfhood, will be an end in himself. This *samotsel'nost'* is not, as with the Kantian Marxists, a

[64] *Filosofiia bor'by: opyt postroeniia etiki marksizma* (Moscow, 1909).
[65] *Filosofiia bor'by*, 272, 37.
[66] *Filosofiia bor'by*, 282.

formal postulate or imperative; for Vol'sky it is a goal to be achieved by struggle and creativity. In sharp opposition to the bourgeois, the proletarian will be unafraid of selfhood hospitable to originality.

Sounding very much like Nietzsche, Vol'sky writes, to paraphrase him: I grant full freedom to the individual whose ideal is inimical to mine; I strive to make him an "integral personality" and work with him to remove external obstacles to our sharp and clear collision. In struggling with me he enriches me. He enlivens my highest value, pressing it eternally forward. "Of all those who surround me . . . the most precious, most essential is he with whom I struggle for life and death." [67] He is both friend and enemy; I want both to vanquish and to preserve him. To strengthen myself I must strengthen him and those like him. "Such," Vol'sky concludes, "is the morality of 'friend-enemies' — the morality of the future." [68] The future, in fact, was to be quite otherwise. Vol'sky's book was one of the last defenses of naturalistic ethical individualism to appear in Russia. The position taken by the collectivist Nietzscheans, and by later Leninists and Stalinists, was diametrically opposed.

A. A. Bogdanov (real name Malinovsky, 1873–1928) and V. A. Bazarov (real name Rudnev, 1874–1936?), the major "collectivists" among the Nietzschean Marxists, exhibit a common doctrinal tension. They are genuinely concerned to free the individual from the constraints of coercive norms and abstract obligations; yet they proceed to dissolve the "emancipated" individual in an impersonal social collective.

Bogdanov is close not only to Nietzsche, in his rejection of norms and obligations, but also to Mikhailovsky, in his emphasis upon the "integration of man." [69] Bogdanov's professed ideal is the maximum of life for society as a whole, coinciding with the maximum of life for its individual members. Future societies will know a "harmonious and whole man, freed from contradictions and coercion." [70] We have a vague presentiment of such a harmony, Bogdanov wrote in 1905, "in ecstatic moments . . . when it seems to us that our tiny being disappears, is fused with the infinite." [71]

Bogdanov distinguished systematically between "coercive norms" and "expediency norms," [72] concepts which correspond roughly to the Kantian categorical and hypothetical imperatives. Social progress, he maintains, results in a supplanting of the former by the latter. In a classless society

[67] *Filosofiia bor'by*, 310.
[68] *Filosofiia bor'by*, 311.
[69] The two influences are fused in his essay, "The Integration of Man" (1906), which bears an epigraph from Nietzsche: "Man is a bridge to the superman" ("Sobiranie cheloveka," in *Novyi mir* [Moscow, 1920], 5).
[70] "Prokliatye voprosy filosofii" in *Novyi mir* (Moscow, 1920), 125.
[71] "Tseli i normy zhizni" (1905), *Novyi mir* (1920), 64.
[72] The latter should perhaps be called "instrumental" norms.

freed from competition the individual will no longer oppose his interests to those of society.[73] "Being conscious of himself as an integral part of a greater whole, living a life continuous with its life, man will lose the very idea of egoistic, narrowly individualistic ends. At the same time, the coercive norms which regulate the conflict of those ends will become superfluous." [74] The situation will resemble that under primitive communism where, according to Bogdanov, "individual interest was not separated from collective interest . . . man was organically fused with the whole, with the group or commune, as cells are fused together in living tissue." [75]

Volsky, as one might expect, took vigorous issue with Bogdanov's view that "the mass, society as a whole, is destined to become the god of socialist mankind, that the good of the collective is the ideal, the ultimate goal for each of its members." [76] Bogdanov himself qualified his collectivism somewhat, asserting that individual *differences* will not disappear. "In the collective each [individual] supplements the others. . . . But he can supplement them only to the extent that he differs from them, to the extent that he is unique . . . independent." [77] However, independence does not mean defense of individual interests. The latter must be consciously subordinated to the interests of the collective.

Bazarov, even more sharply than Bogdanov, repudiates "sodden, dull, self-satisfied moral systems. . . . Life . . . appears a hopelessly vulgar thing precisely because it is viewed through the dim glass of moral norms. . . . One must revolt against norms as such." [78] Like Volsky and Bogdanov, Bazarov reduces the function of norms to a purely instrumental one; they are "means for attaining the joys of life." Every individual, he maintains, is a creator and can realize, in some degree, the "infinitely joyous possibilities" which life presents.

Individualism, for Bazarov (as for Bogdanov), is reactionary, although in earlier periods it was a source of social change and progress. In bourgeois society the individual is formally supreme, but factually empty and impotent. Individualism cannot be overcome in the present social order, in which "a man with a powerfully developed sense of the objective value of creativity and . . . a lowered sense of the 'I' cuts a most miserable, ridiculous figure." [79] In the new society, emphasis will fall

[73] Individualism, according to Bogdanov, was a liberating movement in its conflict with authoritarianism. But today its struggle against the authoritarian past is eclipsed by its struggle against the socialist future.

[74] "Tseli i normy zhizni," 90.

[75] "Tseli i normy zhizni," 90.

[76] Volsky, 30n.

[77] Bogdanov, "Ideal vospitaniia" (1918), in *Novy mir* (1920), 135.

[78] V. A. Bazarov, *Na dva fronta* (St. Petersburg, 1910), 105.

[79] "Bogoiskatel'stvo i 'bogostroitel'stvo'," *Vershiny* (St. Petersburg, 1909), 362.

upon *sobornost'*,[80] upon "objective, immediately social creativity, in which the very notion of 'the individual' and his interests will be extinguished. . . . Only socialism is forging the sword with which, at last, the multifarious 'I's,' those 'money-changers in the temple' of universally human impersonal creativity" will be driven out.[81] The socialist world of "collective life-building" will not be "walled off into the miserable little cells of self-sufficient individualities." The intimacy of lovers gives only "a faint hint of that fusion of all human souls which will be the inevitable result of the communist order." [82] Collective creativity, says Bazarov, will extend to art as well; the new society will favor not "artists of disorderly individual searching, but artists in schools which move by plan toward their goal." [83] The relevance of this remark to Soviet conditions scarcely requires emphasis.

Similarly relevant to Soviet developments, and notable as the first such statement by a Russian Marxist, is Bazarov's sharp rejection of the Kantian dictum that the individual must always be treated as an end, never as a means only. In opposition to this principle, vigorously defended by Berdiaev and Struve, Bazarov writes: "It really is an astonishing thing: because, for purposes of zoological and certain other classifications, it is convenient to refer to me and to another given individual by the same term 'man' . . . that 'man' as such should become the highest task of my life, that I should be obliged to recognize a practical [moral] universal validity between myself and every empirically given human being." [84] "The free man," Bazarov insists, "not only regards his neighbor as a means; he demands that his neighbor should see in him only a means . . . for the neighbor's own ends." [85] In a political context the point becomes even more explicit: "The recognition of the 'individual person' as an absolute principle has always been, and will always be, alien to the proletariat." [86]

From such a position it is only a step to Trotsky's scornful repudiation, a decade later, of "Kantian-clerical, vegetarian-Quaker chatter about the 'sanctity of human life.' " [87] The Kantian dictum, says Trotsky, is "meta-

[80] Bazarov here uses a Slavophile term meaning, literally, "conciliarity," that is, "organic (religious) togetherness."

[81] Bazarov, 141, 61.

[82] Bazarov, 140.

[83] Bazarov, 164. Bogdanov, intoxicated with the notion of collective creation, went so far as to deny that Goethe produced *Faust* or Darwin the theory of evolution. Both men merely put the finishing touches to an extended collective effort! *Padenie velikogo fetishizma* (Moscow, 1910), 46.

[84] Bazarov, "Avtoritarnaia metafizika i avtonomnaia lichnost'," in *Ocherki realisticheskogo mirovozzreniia* (St. Petersburg, 1905), 269.

[85] Bazarov, "Avtoritarnaia . . . ," 271.

[86] Bazarov, *Na dva fronta*, 141.

[87] L. D. Trotsky, *Terrorizm i kommunizm* (Petrograd, 1920), 61.

physical" and "bourgeois." Where necessary (for revolutionary expediency), individuals are and should be treated merely as means. A. B. Zalkind, a prominent party theorist of the 1920's, reiterated this view: "For the proletariat, human life does not have metaphysical, self-sufficient value. The proletariat recognizes only the interests of the . . . revolution." [88] And these interests justify the suspension of individual rights and freedoms wherever necessary.

III

After Stalin came to power, such forthright public attacks upon the rights of the individual came to an abrupt halt. The utterances (as opposed to the policies and practices) of Soviet leaders began to stress — particularly after 1936 — the "infinite value of the individual person." Only in the Soviet Union, we are told, is concern for the individual's freedom and dignity other than hypocritical and sentimental. Yet the classical principle of individual responsibility was explicitly repudiated by Lenin in theory and practice as early as 1918, and thus far little has been done to "rehabilitate" it. Lenin introduced "collective criminal responsibility" and the principle of "guilt by association," based on kinship or even sheer contiguity, reviving the nineteenth-century doctrine of *krugovaia poruka* (responsibility of the group as a whole, and of *each* of its members, for the actions of *any* member). [89]

A statement of anti-individualistic collectivism more extreme than even those of Bogdanov and Bazarov appeared in a brochure published anonymously in 1906 and reissued under Soviet auspices in 1918 and 1923. The author asserts that an "individual," so called, is merely a "synthetic element in a general organic process." "The individual organism," he writes, "is only a physiological product of the physiological activity of the universal organism. . . . Conception, birth, nourishment, and upbringing are all phases of *social* creativity." [90] Official Soviet spokesmen avoid such rhetorical extremes, but their anti-individualism is no less pervasive. In socialist society, they uniformly insist, the "flowering of the individual . . . is possible only on the basis of the leading role of social interest." [91] Personal, moral, and religious values and attitudes in the Soviet Union have been increasingly subject not only to "socialization" but also to "politicalization."

[88] A. B. Zalkind, *Revoliutsiia i molodezh* (Moscow, 1925), 54.

[89] As Marc Raeff has pointed out, *krugovaia poruka*, in the sense of "communal responsibility [of peasants] for taxation" goes back at least to the 1860's, the term having appeared in print in 1864 (in *Den'*, no. 10 [1864]). See his unpublished dissertation on "The Peasant Commune in the Political Thinking of Russian Publicists" (Harvard University, 1950), 50. Herzen had used the term in the general sense of "group responsibility" a decade earlier. See the section entitled *Zapadnye arabeski* (1855) in his *Byloe i dumy* (Moscow, 1946), 415.

[90] *O proletarskoi etike* (Moscow, 1918), 37; italics added.

[91] A. I. Zis, *O kommunisticheskoi morali* (Moscow, 1948), 30.

IV

We have seen a continuing defense of the individual person by Russian thinkers who span a broad political spectrum: radicals like Pisarev, Chernyshevsky, and Dobroliubov; leftward-moving liberals like Lavrov; moderate liberals like Kavelin, Chicherin, and Kareev; revisionist Marxists like Lunacharsky and Vol'sky; rightward-moving Marxists like Struve and Berdiaev; conservatives like Dostoevsky, Leont'ev, and, to a degree, Pobedonostsev. In opposition stand the collectivist tendencies of Tolstoy, Solov'ev, and such Marxists as Bogdanov and Bazarov — tendencies carried further by such early Soviet theorists as Trotsky and Zalkind.

Ethical individualism in Russia has drawn support from Kant and Nietzsche, as well as from John Stuart Mill. Anti-individualistic collectivism has drawn support (directly or indirectly) from Hegel and Marx. It is no accident that Kant, Nietzsche, and Mill stand high on the Soviet ideological blacklist, while Hegel and Marx (in a Leninist reading) remain ideologically obligatory. Yet one ventures to hope that ethical individualism is not a dead issue for Soviet intellectuals. The existence of an active "cultural underground" in the major cities of the Soviet Union lends support to such a hope. Perhaps the next (post-Khrushchev) generation will witness a sufficient relaxing of doctrinal and institutional constraints to permit the emergence of a new Pisarev or Lavrov, a new Leont'ev or Berd'aev. And just possibly the generation after that may see the beginnings of an institutional structure which will provide at least minimal safeguards for the freedom and dignity of the Soviet individual.

THE SOVIET MODEL OF THE IDEAL YOUTH

RALPH T. FISHER, JR.

In this essay, "youth" refers to those between the ages of fifteen and the middle or late twenties — that is, those roughly within the age group of the Communist League of Youth, or Komsomol. The "Soviet model" is that constructed by the top Soviet leaders in their public expressions and actions. This abstraction combines the ideal images appropriate to the countless social roles demanded of Soviet young people. It is a model that is important because it has been propagated by the immense educational and coercive resources of the Soviet state. This model bears no necessary similarity to those that have actuated the leaders in their own lives. Nor is it the only model that has influenced Soviet youth. Certainly there are widely differing models of youth in operation for many of the subcultures within the conglomerate of Soviet society. The coexistence of other models must be kept in mind as we study the most conspicuous ones.

There have obviously been changes, through forty years of the Soviet regime, in what might be called the external appearance and functions of the Soviet model of the ideal youth. Some of these changes reflect shifts in the composition of the Soviet population. For example, the composite model youth of today is better educated and less "proletarian" than his counterpart in the early postrevolutionary years.[1] Other changes reflect the major stages in the development of the Soviet regime. Whereas the model of the Civil War years had a military cast, the model youth of the NEP was waging mainly ideological battles, and each succeeding period left its distinctive imprint. Within each area of Soviet life the detailed functions associated with the model have changed. If in the countryside the ideal youth of 1918–1920 was confiscating grain and recruiting soldiers; under the early five-year plans he was collectivizing the farms and wiping out the kulaks. If in the educational realm the ideal youth of the early 1920's sneered at conventional schools and tried to combine education with factory work, the ideal youth of the 1940's was actively reinforcing discipline under the command of the authorities within the regular school system. But a survey of these changes in the multiple roles of youth in each area of Soviet life would involve the whole history of Soviet youth since 1917, and cannot be undertaken here.[2]

I

Granting these changes in the shell of the model, we must focus our attention on the central core of traits demanded. We want to see what kind of personal character the regime has been trying to produce in its youth and whether the kind of character has changed significantly in the course of the past forty years. To learn this we may first examine the model that characterized the full bloom of postwar Stalinism, after the "abnormal" eras of the Great Purge and World War II, and then proceed

[1] For relevant statistics from the congresses of the Komsomol, see *S"ezd IV*, 325–331; *S"ezd VI*, 299–302; *S"ezd VII*, 489–491; *S"ezd VIII*, 546–547; *S"ezd IX*, 405–406; *S"ezd X*, II, 399–404; *Komsomol'skaia pravda* (hereafter abbreviated *KP*) (April 1, 1949), 2; (March 23, 1954), 2. (Note that in 1949 and 1954 the proportion of "workers" was no longer given at all.) The abbreviation *S"ezd* followed by a Roman numeral will be used here to designate the stenographic report, in book form, of one of the first ten Komsomol congresses (held in 1918, 1919, 1920, 1921, 1922, 1924, 1926, 1928, 1931, and 1936). All were published in Moscow, and the dates of editions used here are as follows: I (3rd ed.) — 1926; II (3rd ed.) — 1926; III — 1926; IV — 1925; V — 1927; VI — 1924; VII — 1926; VIII — 1928; IX — 1931; X (2 vols.) — 1936.
[2] For further details on the specific functions demanded of young people at various periods see Ralph Talcott Fisher, Jr., *Pattern for Soviet Youth: A Study of the Congresses of the Komsomol, 1918–1954* (New York, 1959).

to determine how far this model differed from that of the early years of the Soviet regime and that of the post-Stalin era.

The essential features of the ideal youth of postwar Stalinism emerge from the authoritative proceedings of the Komsomol congress of 1949, published at length in the Soviet press for the guidance of those who were training Soviet youth. For example, the letter sent to the Komsomol congress from the Central Committee of the Communist Party declared:

The Komsomol must bring up, among our youth, fighters who are fearless, cheerful, buoyant, confident in their strength, ready to overcome any difficulties — fighters for the freedom and honor of our Homeland, for the cause of the Party of Lenin and Stalin, for the victory of Communism.[3]

This passage was often repeated during the congress and and was incorporated with little change into the revised regulations of the Komsomol.[4] Another typical characterization appeared in the letter sent by the Komsomol congress to Stalin:

We vow to you, dear Comrade Stalin, warmly to love our socialist Homeland, mortally to hate her enemies, not to know fear in the struggle, patiently to endure hardships and misfortunes, to display determination and persistence in reaching the goal that has been set. The young generation of our country is ready to carry out all your instructions and all the instructions of the Communist Party and the Soviet Government. We promise you always to be watchful, ready to deliver a crushing rebuff to the imperialist aggressors, ready to give all our strength and, if necessary, our lives in the defense of our socialist Fatherland.

You teach Soviet youth perseveringly to master knowledge, culture, science, and technology.

We vow to you, Comrade Stalin, to carry out with honor these instructions of yours. . . .

Love of you and loyalty to the Fatherland is the life and the spirit of the youth of our country![5]

From those statements and many others like them, one could draw up a list of traits sought in youth — patriotism, loyalty, courage, vigilance, honesty, persistence, industriousness, optimism, initiative, cheerfulness, idealism, obedience, militancy, ideological purity, and many others.

The central theme that gave the above traits their meaning was that of absolute devotion, respect, and subservience to the leadership represented in the trinity — Stalin, party, and government.[6] Although the worship of Stalin was then near the peak of its extravagance, even the

---

[3] *KP* (April 1, 1949), 1.

[4] *Rezoliutsii i dokumenty XI s"ezda VLKSM* (Moscow, 1949) [hereafter abbreviated *Rez. i dok.*], 50.

[5] *KP* (April 10, 1949), 1.

[6] For some of the many possible illustrative statements, see *Rez. i dok.*, 3–5, 13, 50, 51, 55; *KP* (March 30, 1949), 1, 2; (March 31, 1949), 3; April 1, 1949), 1, 2; Tamara I. Ershova, *O rabote komsomola v shkole* . . . (Moscow, 1949), 31.

gaudiest panegyric[7] illustrated that the cult was of Stalin as the leader of the party and, hence, of the people and their government; when the ideal youth was told to regard Stalin as the incarnation of everything good, the recipient of vows, and the source of inspiration and strength, these demands only reinforced the demand for loyalty, respect, and obedience to the party leadership.[8] Komsomol orders were an extension of party orders for the young. The Komsomol regulations declared that "the strictest observance of Komsomol discipline is the first obligation of all members of the Komsomol" and went on to say that each member "must faultlessly carry out the decisions of party, soviet, and Komsomol bodies." [9] Not only the reference to discipline[10] and to unity and solidarity,[11] but the whole conduct of the congress, including the nature of the discussion and the always miraculously unanimous votes, made it clear that the party leadership was exercising very tight control and that eager acceptance of this "guidance" was a distinguishing feature of the ideal youth.

It was in that context alone that all the other traits demanded in the ideal youth could be interpreted. Words like patriotism, courage, daring, heroism, self-sacrifice — these were applicable only to those who fought for the party's cause.[12] "Vigilance" concerned the security of the party and the Soviet state; "honesty" concerned the observance of principles laid down by the leadership.[13] Persistence, industriousness, all-out effort, the constant striving for perfectionist goals, the refusal to be satisfied with what one has attained — such qualities were of course related to the "building of Communism," that is, the tasks enunciated by the party leaders.[14] Virtuous conduct in personal life was inseparable from political life.[15] "Initiative" must follow strictly the commands of the party.[16] The cheerfulness that was part of the ideal did not preclude some satisfaction with the present, but was essentially based upon optimism regarding the

[7] See the chant of praise at the end of the above-mentioned letter in *KP* (April 10, 1949), 1.

[8] For illustrative statements, see *KP* (March 30, 1949), 1, 2; (March 31, 1949), 3; (April 1, 1949), 2, 4; (April 2, 1949), 3; (April 3, 1949), 1; (April 6, 1949), 2; (April 7, 1949), 2; *Rez. i dok.*, 6, 8.

[9] *Rez. i dok.*, 62.

[10] *Rez. i dok.*, 27–28, 31; Ershova, 8; *KP* (March 30, 1949), 2, 3; (March 31, 1949), 3.

[11] For example, *KP* (April 1, 1949), 3; *Rez. i dok.*, 5; V. N. Ivanov, *Izmeneniia v ustave VLKSM* . . . (Moscow, 1949), 3. For sample references to party guidance, see *Rez. i dok.*, 13, 51; *KP* (March 31, 1949), 3.

[12] *KP* (March 30, 1949), 2; (March 31, 1949), 1, 2, 3; (April 1, 1949), 2; *Rez. i dok.*, 9.

[13] For example, see *Rez. i dok.*, 51–53.

[14] For illustrative passages, see *KP* (March 30, 1949), 2, 3; (April 1, 1949), 2; April 3, p. 4; April 8, p. 2; April 10, p. 1; *Rez. i dok.*, p. 7; Ershova, 13; Ivanov, 19.

[15] *KP* (March 31, 1949), 2 (Mikhailov speaking).

[16] *Rez. i dok.*, 7; *KP* (March 30, 1949), 2; (March 31, 1949), 4.

promised future.[17] One might conceivably argue that it was that future — the long-range goal, Communism — to which the ideal youth was subordinating himself, rather than to the leadership of the party. When, however, one takes into account the persistent vagueness of all descriptions of that ultimate goal,[18] as well as the leaders' assumption that only they knew how to reach it, then one is bound to conclude that, while references to the goal were used to justify the immediate demands of the leadership, those demands themselves were the essential guideposts for the ideal youth.

The Soviet model of the ideal youth in 1949 was, in short, the "eager robot" — inwardly so complete a tool of party leadership as to be devoid of a genuine self, yet outwardly seeming to possess such human attributes as will and judgment and enthusiasm.

II

With this ideal youth of postwar Stalinism in mind, we can now return to the early Soviet period when Stalin had not yet added his impress to the mold. Although there was in those days very little glorification of any leader, including even Lenin,[19] subservience could nevertheless be demanded. How subservient was the ideal youth?

When the Komsomol, which ostensibly embraced the best young people, held its first congress, in October 1918, the assembled delegates agreed virtually unanimously that while the League was to be "solidary" with the Bolshevik Party it was at the same time to be "independent." [20] It was to safeguard "the principle of the spontaneous activity of youth." [21] In April 1919, however, a plenary session of the Komsomol's central committee "requested" that the Komsomol be brought more closely under the party's direction,[22] and soon (August 1919) the two central committees jointly declared that the Komsomol must be "directly subordinate" to the party from top to bottom.[23] While the Komsomol continued to be called "autonomous" (as well as *samostoiatel'nyi* or "self-standing"), the word "independent" dropped out of use and by 1920 was already stigmatized as typical of the dangerous "counterrevolution of the left." [24]

[17] *Rez. i dok.*, 8; *KP* (March 31, 1949), 4; (April 2, 1949), 2; (April 3, 1949), 2, 3; (April 8, 1949), 3, 4.
[18] The nearest approach to a description at the congress of 1949 was by Mikhailov, in *KP* (March 30, 1949), 2.
[19] For illustrations of the treatment of top party leaders at the Komsomol congresses of 1918, 1919, and 1920, see *S"ezd I*, 38–39, 62, 95; *S"ezd II*, 33, 67, 121–125, 154–155; *S"ezd III*, 26, 236–237. For a discussion of this point, see Fisher, 36–37.
[20] *S"ezd I*, 75, 97, 98.
[21] *S"ezd I*, 74.
[22] *S"ezd II*, 183–184; *Bol'shaia sovetskaia entsiklopediia*, supplementary volume SSSR (1948), cols. 645–646 (hereafter abbreviated *BSE, SSSR* (1948).
[23] *S"ezd II*, 45–47, 168, 183–184; *VKP(b) o komsomole i molodezhi: sbornik reshenii i postanovlenii partii o molodezhi, 1903–1938* (Moscow, 1938), 77–78.
[24] *S"ezd III*, 101.

The direct subordination of the League to the party was evident in deed as well as in word. Some of those whom the first and second congresses elected to the League's central committee were unceremoniously removed from their posts by the party.[25] Already by 1920 the top officials of the League, although ostensibly still elected by the Komsomol congress, were in fact designated by a "Communist faction" operating behind the scenes and subject to party orders.[26] Pronounced tendencies toward authoritarian rule from the side of the party were evident in the conditions of deliberation and criticism in the early Komsomol congresses, in the admission and expulsion of members, and in the organizational structure.[27] When some especially zealous Komsomolites launched satellite groups designed to influence and guide the broad masses of Soviet youth, the party stopped them, evidently fearing to let Komsomolites gain too much influence over auxiliary youth groups until the Komsomol itself was more firmly under party domination.[28]

In that early institutional setting the personal quality most insistently demanded in youth was discipline. This discipline was to spring from acknowledgment of the Communist goal and was to be conscious, self-willed, and self-enforced, rather than imposed from without in an "authoritarian spirit."[29] Thus it was theoretically not in conflict with the parallel demands for initiative and spontaneity. But it must produce unity and solidarity — in Lenin's words, "a single will" for all the millions of workers and peasants.[30] It must be manifested in strict obedience to higher authority.[31] Said Shatskin at the Komsomol congress of 1920:

There are some comrades among us who say that there is one discipline in the party and another in the League. They say that since our organization is an educational one, we can somewhat loosen the reins with which the leading bodies must hold their subordinate Komsomol organizations in check. This opinion must be refuted root and branch. . . . We must finally establish the most unconditional unquestioning subordination of all active workers to the leading bodies of our organization, and the personal responsibility of each responsible

[25] S"ezd II, 57; VKP(b) o komsomole, 80–82; S"ezd III, 34ff.
[26] For significant episodes, see S"ezd I, 43, 89–91; S"ezd II, 112, 117–118; S"ezd III, 102, 235.
[27] For amplification of these points, see Fisher 28–39.
[28] Relevant to this generalization are the issues of the "Young Proletarian Homes," the "Youth sections affiliated with the trade unions," the Dunaevsky dispute, and the "Ukrainian Opposition." For sample passages from the sources, see S"ezd I, 48–49, 70, 75, 77–78, 90–91, 94–95; S"ezd II, 34–38, 56, 60, 74, 108–110, 141–147, 179–181, 188, 195; S"ezd III, 98, 186, 195, 198–200, 212–240, 247–248, 257–276, 300, 302; VKP(b) o komsomole, 80–82. For an account and analysis of these issues, see Fisher 17–28.
[29] See S"ezd I, 64; S"ezd II, 123, 171–173; S"ezd III, 31, 37, 242, 243, 305.
[30] S"ezd III, 11. Preobrazhensky and Bukharin echoed the same thoughts (III, 31, 37). See also S"ezd II, 125; S"ezd III, 33–37.
[31] See, for example, S"ezd I, 99; S"ezd II, 55–56; S"ezd III, 100, 242–243.

official for each member of our League, for that work which these members are performing.[32]

The same congress in closing issued to all members "an appeal for the greatest self-control and discipline." After describing the perils they faced, it proclaimed that

> In such conditions, there stands before the whole proletariat and also before proletarian youth first of all the task of preserving, developing, and strengthening iron discipline in the ranks of their organizations. Only with such discipline, consolidating the proletariat into an impregnable granite rock, can it resist the crowd of enemies and the loose petit-bourgeois element.
>
> The Third Congress appeals for the preservation of such iron discipline in our ranks. May the ranks of our League be invincible battalions of young proletarians storming the old world.
>
> Long live our militant front!
> Long live the victorious proletariat!
> Long live revolutionary proletarian discipline! [33]

Other traits much in demand included self-sacrificing bravery for the Communist cause,[34] alertness and vigilance against hostile forces,[35] confidence in the victory of Communism,[36] a sense of responsibility, and such qualities as toughness, dexterity, precision, and industriousness.[37] Those and other demands — to learn Marxism, to set an example, and to avoid dogmatism and pride[38] — were expressed in harmony with the overriding insistence on conscious discipline and strict obedience. The Soviet ideal youth in 1918–1920 was above all a good follower.

Thus the models of 1949 and 1918–1920 appear highly similar. Although in the early Soviet ideal there was probably a shade more independence than in the Stalinist version, the characteristics of the eager robot were already predominant.[39]

III

One might protest, quite logically, that the conditions of the Civil War would have produced the eager-robot ideal, no matter what had

[32] *S"ezd III*, 242–243. Lazar' Shatskin was one of the top Komsomolites of the League's first decade.

[33] *S"ezd III*, 305.

[34] For a few of the many references to bravery and self-sacrifice, see *S"ezd I*, 62, 68; *S"ezd II*, 16, 19 (an especially colorful passage by Trotsky), 20–21, 30–31, 66; *S"ezd III*, 29, 31.

[35] *S"ezd I*, 40, 62; *S"ezd III*, 18, 277, 306–307.

[36] *S"ezd I*, 39–40, 97; *S"ezd II*, 14, 28, 65–67; *S"ezd III*, 61–63.

[37] *S"ezd II*, 12–13, 103, 146, 171; *S"ezd III*, 6–22, 139, 141.

[38] *S"ezd II*, 157; *S"ezd III*, 7, 18, 20, 29–30, 36–37, 244–245, 300.

[39] In the light of this predominance, steps were soon taken to ensure that the deterministic side of Marxism could not furnish an excuse and refuge for the nonconformist. See Raymond A. Bauer, *The New Man in Soviet Psychology* (Cambridge, Mass., 1952).

been the Communists' original intent. It is therefore pertinent to examine briefly the prerevolutionary Bolshevik model of the ideal youth, as revealed in the writings of the chief prophet of Bolshevism.

Lenin left no finished portrait of his ideal Bolshevik, young or old, even though his program called for remaking man and society. But as a revolutionary leader he demanded and appreciated certain traits in his followers. He especially prized worker and student youth for their turbulence, daring, and revolutionary potentialities,[40] and considered young people suited to play the semisacrificial role of a vanguard or skirmishing force which could be sent into battle without committing the main body of the party.[41] Apart from such notions, however, Lenin's image of the ideal youth was roughly equivalent to his image of the ideal Bolshevik, for he considered his party to be the party of youth.[42]

Lenin conveniently divorced his model from customary ethical standards by labeling those standards either "feudal" or "bourgeois"[43] and by asserting that the proletariat — whose will he considered himself uniquely fitted to interpret — would establish the moral code of the future.[44] Proletarian ethics admitted all methods. Lenin declared that "Social Democracy does not tie its hands . . . it recognizes all means of struggle so long as they are suited to the available forces of the party and afford the possibility of gaining the greatest results attainable under the given circumstances.[45]

Lenin insisted that his followers exhibit "partyness," by which he meant allegiance to his Bolshevik faction of the Russian Social Democratic Workers' Party and observance of party discipline.[46] In his view a truly nonpartisan approach was impossible.[47] When some of his disciples intimated that partyness was a negation of freedom within their own group, Lenin retorted that partyness constituted "freedom from bourgeois-anarchist individualism." The principle of freedom of organization, he declared, gave the party the right to exclude those who insisted on being individualistic.[48] Lenin was not above declaring support of his own tactics to be a criterion of partyness.[49] But when he was accused of using

[40] V. I. Lenin, *Sochineniia* (2d ed., Moscow, 1927–1932), V, 79 (March 10, 1902), 347 (August 15, 1903); XXI, 319–320 (October 21 [8], 1917).

[41] Lenin, VIII, 294 (October 17 [4], 1905), 325–326 (October 16, 1905); XII, 336–341 (October 16 [3], 1908).

[42] Lenin, X, 188 (December 20 [7], 1906).

[43] Lenin, I, 261–262, 292 (late in 1894).

[44] Lenin, I, 94 (1894).

[45] Lenin, IV, 58–59 (December 1900).

[46] The Russian word is *partiinost'*. See Lenin, IX, 390 (July 14 [1], 1906), and XX, 419 (June 6 [May 24], 1917).

[47] Lenin, VIII, 400–401 (December 1 [November 18], 1905), and VIII, 302 (October 17 [4], 1905).

[48] Lenin, VIII, 386–390 (November 26 [13], 1905).

[49] Lenin, XV, 202 (1911).

partyness as a mere cloak for his own political demands, he argued that his policy was that of "the majority of class-conscious Marxist workers participating in political life." [50]

He did not always sound completely authoritarian. For example, he could say:

Precisely in order not to become too outspoken and . . . harsh regarding "anarchistic individualism" we must, in our opinion, do everything possible — even to the point of some retreats from the pretty diagrams of centralism and from an unconditional submission to discipline — in order to grant these little groups freedom to express themselves, in order to give the whole party the possibility of weighing the profundity or insignificance of disagreements, and to determine just where, in what, and *on just whose side* there is *inconsistency*. . . . We must have more faith in the independent judgment of all the masses of party workers. They, and only they, can soften the excessive vehemence of schismatically inclined groupings; can, with their gradual, imperceptible, but all the more persistent influence, inspire these groups with "good will" toward the observance of party discipline; can cool the ardor of anarchistic individualism.[51]

But this semi-tolerance toward "little groups" within the party was exhibited late in 1903, after the party had split and Lenin had lost his fight to control the party organ, *Iskra*. In other words, it was at a moment when he had reason to fear that he and his followers might for a time be one of those "little groups" — that is, until they could fight back to a position of power.[52]

Lenin's view of personal relationships fit into the framework of partyness and centralism. He condemned clannish or cliquish relations — which included personal loyalties to individuals other than himself — on the ground that they obstructed party discipline.[53] Comradeliness had for him a special meaning: "We acknowledge the duty of comradeship, the duty of supporting all comrades, the duty of tolerating the opinions of comrades." "But," he went on, *"for us the duty of comradeship stems from the duty to Russian and to international Social Democracy, and not vice versa."* Comrades were comrades, he said, "only because and insofar as they toil in the ranks of Russian (and, consequently, also international) Social Democracy." [54] While Lenin appealed for initiative,[55] this merely complemented his demand for discipline. A reminder on discipline could be used to bring into line comrades who did something

[50] Lenin, XVII, 25–26 (October 30 [17], 1913).

[51] Lenin, VI, 120–121 (December 8 [November 25], 1903).

[52] For a fuller account of this period in Lenin's life, see Bertram D. Wolfe, *Three Who Made a Revolution* (New York, 1948), chaps. 14 and 15, especially 255. For the colorful conclusion to Lenin's article, see Lenin, VI, 122–123.

[53] Lenin, VI, 354 (August 1904).

[54] Lenin, II, 541–542 (1899).

[55] Lenin, IV, 383 (1902), and VII, 149 (March 8 [February 23], 1905).

wrong, while a request for more initiative could stimulate those who were merely not doing enough of what was right.

Plainly underlying Lenin's concept of the ideal Bolshevik was his preoccupation with fight and struggle. For him there was no possibility of a peaceful compromise. "The question," he said, "can be posed *only this way:* bourgeois or socialist ideology. There is no middle ground." "Therefore," he went on — in a phrase that has since become a Communist slogan — "*any* belittling of socialist ideology, *any deviation* from it means the same thing as a strengthening of bourgeois ideology." [56]

This by no means exhaustive survey of Lenin's prerevolutionary desiderata suggests strongly that the eager-robot ideal of 1949 and 1918–1920 was already well developed early in the twentieth century.

IV

The ideal did not die with Stalin. In 1954, at the first Komsomol congress after Stalin's death, the leadership called for a revival of "criticism from below," observance of the collective principle in leadership, and wider democracy within the League.[57] But the congress itself, in its discussion, criticism, and voting, gave no hint of genuine relaxation.[58] Soviet literature was still said to be failing to depict lifelike heroes who could serve as models for the young.[59] Although the Stalin cult was gone, the cult of the party and its Central Committee provided ample occasion for the same extravagant expressions of devotion. In their letter to the party's Central Committee the delegates said:

> The young men and women of the land of the Soviets have boundless love and loyalty for the Communist Party. Their most cherished thoughts and hopes are bound up with the party; they are obligated to it for all the happiness and joy of their lives. . . . In all its activities the Leninist Komsomol senses the daily, fatherly care of the Communist Party and its Central Committee. . . .
> The Communist Party is the wise teacher and mentor of youth. For the Komsomol, the word and deed of the party come before all else.[60]

And when that letter was read at the final session, all delegates reportedly rose "in a united transport of boundless love for their own Communist Party" and gave a "tumultuous ovation," shouting "Glory to the Communist Party!" [61]

Since 1954 there has been no clear sign of change. The Komsomol central committee in February 1957, while calling for more democracy in

      [56] Lenin, IV, 391–392 (1902).
      [57] *KP* (March 20, 1954), 3, 4; (March 24, 1954), 1; (March 26, 1954), 2; (March 27, 1954), 3; (March 30, 1954), 2.
      [58] *KP* (March 20–30, 1954), *passim.*
      [59] *KP* (March 20, 1954), 3; (March 24, 1954), 2; (March 25, 1954), 3; (March 26, 1954), 4.
      [60] *KP* (March 27, 1954), 1.
      [61] *KP* (March 27, 1954), 2.

the League, insisted also, in the very same sentence, on the need for stronger discipline, and the attitude toward the party leadership was just as subservient as ever.[62] In July, when Khrushchev's victory over Malenkov, Kaganovich, and Molotov was announced, the accompanying editorial — studded with references to monolithic unity, discipline, and obedience to party directives — was in the Stalinist tradition.[63]

V

The Soviet model of the ideal youth — the model expressed by the party leadership — has had, then, an almost unvarying core. Changes have occurred in the external appearance and functions of the model, but these have not significantly affected the continuity of the eager-robot ideal — the ideal of utter loyalty to the party chiefs, iron discipline, self-sacrificing bravery, incessant vigilance, burning enthusiasm, unshakable conviction, and uncompromising militancy. While many of those qualities suggest a military figure, the ideal youth, unlike a soldier, is never off duty. There are no areas of human knowledge, appreciation, or action in which he can exercise full freedom and imagination.

The persistence of the eager-robot ideal reflects the continuing importance of doctrine for the Soviet regime, the regime's reliance upon an atmosphere of crisis, and the regime's totalitarian and authoritarian character. The official ideal as treated here could not change significantly without considerable changes in the nature of the regime.

But the answer to the question of continuity and change in the Soviet model of the ideal youth must be termed incomplete. We are driven back to the difficulties suggested earlier, which stem in large part from our lack of free access to Soviet society. We lack the means of penetrating very far beyond the formal or official or external model, but we can perceive that it does not monopolize the scene. To the extent that it appears too harsh and uncompromising, to the extent that it fails to *live* for Soviet citizens, it encourages other models to flourish. The Soviet system, never completely authoritarian or totalitarian despite its aims and its dictatorial excesses, can inspire models of careerism, of apathy, of compromise, of opposition. The cynicism of the leaders vitiates the official model, while beyond the circle of political chiefs there are other model makers who play significant but not easily appraisable roles in establishing operating images of the ideal. Thus there is the possibility that, while "the Soviet model" remained the same, other models, without being formal or official, nevertheless could alter significantly the orientation of Soviet youth.

[62] *KP* (February 28, 1957), 1, trans. in *Current Digest of the Soviet Press* (April 17, 1957), 16–18.

[63] *Pravda* (July 3, 1957), 1, trans. in *CDSP*, (July 17, 1957), 7–8.

SOME NOTES ON THE RUSSIAN NATIONAL CHARACTER

HENRY V. DICKS

I

This chapter is a condensed restatement of some conclusions arrived at by the writer on the strength of intensive interviews with Soviet defectors, published in 1952 [1] and revised in the light of later work by others and of reading some relevant Russian authors of the period under review. Since there has to be some pruning in such a large theme, this essay is almost entirely about the peasantry. Bearers of power in the Soviet Union are largely the children of Great Russian peasants, or the urban working class, many of whom have retained a close connection with their peasant background.

It may be desirable first to summarize the general conceptual framework within which I approached the interviews with Russian defectors in 1950. Some familiarity of the reader with psychoanalytic terms will be assumed.

(1) Personal data and literary products can be used by a skilled psychiatric observer and interviewer working with psychoanalytic concepts for making inferences about deeper attitudes and motivations. For present purposes the analyst has only to vary his focus from what is idiosyncratic for individuals to what is *recurrent* in material from his sources.

(2) By such means there can be defined a *modal character* which is shared by representatives of a given national cultural group over and above subgroup differences. It is this modal configuration of traits of behavior which I mean when speaking of "national character." Within the context of this volume's theme of transformation, I shall be interested in exploring what variation this basic configuration has undergone, and where it shows itself as still a live factor in my interpretation of the contemporary Russian scene.

So far the psychiatrist is in his own field — the motivations of individual behavior. Some extrapolations will also be made from personality study into the sphere of sociopolitical behavior, and these rest on more debatable conceptual ground. The writer is aware that the description of the functioning of a society demands not only insight into the per-

---

[1] H. V. Dicks, "Observations on Contemporary Russian Behaviour," *Human Relations,* V (1952), 111–176.

sonalities of an adequate sample of members of that society, but also needs to consider historical, economic, and similar factors. To this extent this paper is only *one* strand in a canvas woven by several disciplines, and it should not be assigned more status than its modest title of "some notes." There is, however, one crucial aspect of personality psychology inseparable from the interpretation of social behavior. This is the area of attitude to authority.

(3) It is here assumed that the kind of experience a child has in authority relations within his primary family group will be internalized to form the basis of his later expectations as to how the role of power-bearer and of subordinate, of leader and of led, will be played in his wider social group. I assume further that a given culture rests on an internalized and more or less unconscious system of mental images or models for the regulation and channeling of psychological needs of individuals and for signaling what is sanctioned and approved, or forbidden and punished. The way authority roles are exercised within a society sharing such an internalized unconscious system will be conditioned by the qualities of this system — including its rigidities and irrationalities based on the culture "myth" concerning human nature. The main mental mechanisms involved in transferring the internal system of the members to the interpretation of their external world are those of displacement and substitution, and of projection and identification. It is precisely this shared regulation of biopsychological need systems and authority relations which imparts to a culture its distinctive modal characteristics.

Though some of my earlier conclusions have changed while thinking about the question at hand, my main concepts about the source of the authority problem in Russians do not seem controverted by any subsequent observations or reading. I have been gratified by the amount of support which my ideas received from the Harvard University Project led by Clyde Kluckhohn and his associates, and from the Columbia Studies under the leadership of Margaret Mead, sponsored by RAND. To both of these I owe a great debt.

The procedure will be followed of describing first some of the more fundamental characteristics of Russian behavior and relating them to the primary family group. This is the psychiatrist's proper sphere. Next there will be included some interpretations about the motivations of wider social behavior by reference to primary object relations. It is hoped that by stressing the nature of the primary processes we may be able to form estimates as to the depth and degree of irrationality behind some of the secondary social processes.

II

In 1952 my account of the modal Russian personality stressed ambivalence as the outstanding trait. Ambivalence as such is a universal characteristic of human beings. It is the manner in which this ambivalence is manifested and countered or disposed of which provides a key to the interpretation of Russian character. It is seen to oscillate in large swings of mood in relation to self, to primary love objects, and to outgroups. The quality of these swings is most readily understood in terms of oral need satisfactions or deprivations. At one end there is the "omnivorousness," the lusty greed and zest for life, the tendency to rush at things and "swallow them whole"; the need for quick and full gratification; the spells of manic omnipotence feeling and optimistic belief in unlimited achievement; the overflowing vitality, spontaneity, and anarchic demand for abolition of all bounds and limitations to giving and receiving.

At the other end of the spectrum there is melancholy, dreary apathy; frugality; meanness and suspicion of universal hostility; anxious and sullen submissiveness; self-depreciation and moral masochism, together with a grudging admission of the necessity for a depriving and arbitrary authority, thought of as the only safeguard against the excesses of Russian nature. In this mood we find a diffuse guilt feeling, a capacity for subtle empathy, and a ruminative self-doubt and self-torment. Outward servility and secret obstinacy coexist, as if one could bend the knee to Ceasar in outward conformity and yet inwardly remain wholly on the side of God before whom all men are equally small and fallible. Nothing is so persistent in the Russian as a sense of moral outrage (*izdevatel'stvo*) — that ubiquitous feeling of guilt and shame at injustice and a sensitiveness about whom to trust not to hurt one. The Russian can vary between feeling that he is no good and that he is superior to all the rest of mankind. He can concede a man's social status and at the same time be consumed with envy of superior wealth.

Whether in his Bacchanalian mood or in his depression, he always needs direct, spontaneous, heart-to-heart contact and communication, a sense of being loved and belonging, and he respects that need in others. He loves the fun of teamwork which goes with a swing and a song, and a total investment of strength and feeling. He understands commands and obedience. But he is distressed by distant hauteur, formalism, and bureaucratic protocol and hierarchy, preferring direct informal leadership and spontaneous improvisation to methodical procedure in tackling difficulties. Elaborate hierarchy troubles him, as does any kind of rigidly and uniformly controlled activity.

A word should be added about what is connoted by unconscious oral needs and fantasies which to the writer appear to play such a large part in Russian character. It is at primitive oral levels of human development (at the stage of the baby up to a year or so in age) that objects can be only partly distinguished in terms of self and not-self, and ego is not yet clearly demarcated. The contrast between objects felt to be "good" and "bad" is extreme, according to whether they gratify or deprive. At the oral level also there is an almost total separation between the attribution of loving and destructive powers to the self and to the external objects to whom this primitive dichotomy is projected. This concept helps us to understand the deeply embedded feeling that there are inscrutable, remote, and uncontrollable powers who can do what they like, which is part of the tacit assumption of Russians about the world. To this type of feeling we give the name "paranoid" because of its domination of the mind in mental disorders of that category. This ties in with Margaret Mead's statement that "friends could behave like enemies" and then like friends again (see below). As examples of the "break-in" of oral level fantasy from my interviews, the following may suffice: grandmothers threaten children that they must keep their mouths shut because the devil who is ever lurking near will get in through the mouth, or smash the child's teeth and gain possession; "blood-sucker," "man-eater," hyaena, and such, are standard epithets to call capitalist enemies as well as Soviet oppressors. Here the bad objects are *outside* the self.

We also begin to understand the frequent appearance in Russian myth and self-appraisal of feelings of omnipotence, of a giantlike strength — even of infants — against which strong measures of constraint and control have to be taken. As Gorer and Rickman pointed out,[2] Russian women swaddle their children because they believe that, left unconstrained, the child with his uncontrolled strength will injure himself. The peasant Khor's personality moved Turgenev to write about Peter the Great that he was a typical Russian, "so confident in his strength and power that he is not averse to breaking[3] himself." Here the dangerous powers are located *inside*. This is the other side of paranoid feeling, more often experienced as a sense of anxiety or guilt.

About the same time as my study, but independently, Margaret Mead wrote:

> In this traditional [Russian] character, thought and action were so interchangeable, that there was a tendency for all effort to dissipate itself in talk or in symbolic behavior. While there was a strong emphasis on the need for certain kinds of control . . . this control was seen as imposed from without; lacking it, the individual would revert to an original impulsive and uncontrolled state. Those forms of behavior which involved self-control rather than endurance, measurement rather than unstinted giving or taking, or calculation rather than immediate response to a situation, were extremely undeveloped. The distinctions between the individual and the group and between the self and others were also less emphasized than in the West, while the organization of the *mir*, the large, extended families and religious and social rituals stressed confession

---

[2] G. Gorer, and J. Rickman, *The People of Great Russia* (London, 1949).

[3] Author's translation of the text culled from *Zapiski* (see note 15). *Lomat'* is to break, and this carries the meaning of extreme exertion, as in the English "breaking one's neck" (to achieve a goal).

and complete revelation of self to others and the merging of the individual in the group. . . .

Traditional Russian character assumed the co-existence of both good and evil in all individuals, and, in attitudes towards individuals, an expectation that friends could behave like enemies was combined with an expectation that this behavior could also be reversed — by confession, repentance and restoration of the former state. . . . Little distinction was made between thought and deed, between the desire to murder and the murder itself. All men were held to be guilty, in some degree, of all human crimes. Against this lack of distinction between thought and deed there was a strong emphasis upon distinction among persons, on a purely social basis, an intolerance of any ambiguity between superiors and subordinates. This rigidity in matters of deference and precedence, however, was relieved by a strong countertendency to establish complete equality among all human souls and to wipe out all social distinctions.[4]

While this may be said to outline one end of the spectrum of the Russian modal personality as it is revealed in both literature and by my interviews, the behavioral characteristics here described are in great contrast to the other end of the scale — the expected role behavior of the elite. Although this is particularly true of the Communist Party elite, it may also be said to have been the role of pre-Communist authorities since Peter I, at least, to educate and force this modal-character structure toward a higher level of mastery over primitive impulses, "to catch up with the West." The Communist revolution is sometimes compared to Russia's passing through the Puritan phase of development, and there are grounds for making this comparison. The germs of Puritan attitudes were discernible in Russia despite all that was stated above. Religious asceticism existed in Russia for centuries, for example, among the Old Believers. There was also a rather uncritical "swallowing" of Western scientific rationalism once it penetrated to the intelligentsia — typical of the Russians' immoderation in what they do. The "New Man" in Soviet psychology is he who overcomes his anarchic spontaneity in favor of leaderlike abstinence from immediate impulse gratification; he who suppresses sentiment and private feeling through systematic thought and planned purposeful activity in wholehearted pusuit of the party line. Virtue and charisma are attached by the culture to those who show this rational mastery over impulse and greed as against mere passive capacity to endure deprivation. This contrast between the modal mass character and the "Puritan" prescription for elite behavior has been one of the abiding tensions in Russian society, part of that sense of the alien and remote character of elites which forms at once their claim to veneration and their incurring of highly ambivalent resentment. Dudintsev, in *Not by Bread Alone*, has a cynical party bureaucrat, Drozdov, say this to his wife: "Touch me where you like, you will always find a living, tender,

[4] M. Mead, *Soviet Attitudes towards Authority* (New York, 1951).

sensitive spot. That's why I need armour, like a snail . . . my strong will . . . not a bad thing for a man . . . holds him in check."

This is the sacrifice of modal Russian character which a man who climbs the party ladder to success has to make. This, indeed, is what I have called in psychoanalytic terms the oral-anal conflict in the Russian character.[5] It need not be assumed from my emphasis on this polarization that there are not, or will not be, intermediate positions; nor that the educational efforts and the economic changes in the Soviet Union will not produce an approximation to personalities more typical of an industrial society. The conflict, however, goes on both within the culture and within individuals who share in it. Such a conflict is much less settled than in Western European society.

III

It is in the context of these basic traits, including beliefs about the deeper nature of the child, about what is hidden in mankind, that we should look at the relationships in the primary social and economic unit of rural Russia — the peasant family as it existed on countless small-holdings and, from available evidence, as it still exists today. It is typically a patriarchal family of grandfather and grandmother with their sons, wives, and children, as well as any unmarried daughters and sons, living incredibly close together, farming the holding by joint labor. There is little privacy and the children participate in all that goes on in this living space. At the head of the household the child perceives a composite authority figure, a blend of both grandparents, of which one is the almost wholly awe-inspiring and arbitrary father-figure, shouting commands from his seat of power on the stove or at the head of the table. The other is an equally unpredictable, on the whole indulgent but also nagging and dominant, mother-figure, who inculcates prayer and demonology. Both claim divine sanction for their right to rule and chastise all their dependents, adults and children alike, and they are also the prescribed objects of love and pious duty. (One cannot help making the analogies: tsar and church; state and party.)

The typical prevailing feeling of terrified reverence for authority is best denoted by the Russian word *strakh*. In the family setting its presence leads to the phenomenon of marked duplicity in behavior. On the one hand, there is an astonishing degree of priggish, dutiful lip service and subjection to the grandfather; on the other hand, in his absence, something not far short of conspiracy of the adult sons against their father. This ambivalence is well described by Gladkov in the following words, speaking of his father's relation during his childhood to the grand-

---

[5] H. V. Dicks, "Observations on Contemporary Russian Behaviour."

father: "He nourished in himself a constant resentment against grandfather. . . . He bore himself with contempt toward grandfather in his
absence, but to his face he expressed devotion and unconditional subordination." [6]

Periodically there occur violent outbursts against the authority of the
grandfather by the grown-up sons in fits of sudden desperation, more
often than not terminated by remorseful and self-humiliating contrition
(such as prostration at his feet) and begging for forgiveness. The motive
ascribed to these revolts is the sons' wish for freedom to leave home because the old man will not make over to them their independent plot of
land, their inheritance. But it is also moral outrage and hurt dignity as
a result of his tyranny. It is no accident that parricide forms such a
prominent theme in Russian literature.[7] The child's own image of immediate adults is of people subject to higher authority and filled with
ambivalent resentment and submissive love for the authority figure. A
little later he learns that even grandfather is but a serf and can be bullied
and humiliated by his *barin* (landowner, lord) or the police. There is
indeed a series of infinite regress, leading via grandfather to the barin
and so to the tsar and to God.

A correlate of this situation is the frequency with which the sons
identify themselves with grandfather's arbitrary power and play their
own role in due course in a like manner. Aggression passes down the
echelon of the family structure: the grandmother, herself under her husband's heel, coerces and torments her daughters-in-law; the adult sons
assert their status and dignity by beating or bullying their wives,
children, or younger brothers. Lowest in rank order is the daughter-in-
law, as a "stranger." At all levels of this group, obedience is exacted by
beating, threats of expulsion from the homestead, and invocation of terrible sanctions based on a near-medieval religious and demonological
system of beliefs, followed by contrition, tears, and forgiveness. Emotion
of every kind flows fully and unrestrainedly in comparison to, say, a
nineteenth-century English family.

In sum, then, the typical childhood of a Russian peasant, including
many a prominent Russian now in his prime, was spent in a helpless participation in scenes of his elders' crude emotional oscillations between
tenderness and brutality. He received an ambivalent perception of his
own father as strong and good as well as cowardly and weak, his mother
(grandparents' daughter-in-law) as lovable but despised, and himself as
powerless and dependent. A rich if chaotic inner world of emotional po-
tentials is thus created. The experience also develops a capacity to
tolerate silently the most contradictory and powerful emotions. The

---

[6] F. Gladkov, *Povest' o detstve* (Moscow, 1949).
[7] For example, *The Brothers Karamazov*, and Bunin's "Gervasii," in *Rasskazy*
(Moscow, 1955).

nature of the identifications made is highly paradoxical. The little boy will tend to idealize and to identify himself in part with the victim position — with the tender, persecuted, suffering mother. There is evidence that this theme is later elaborated into the hero fantasy of rescuing the oppressed, suffering mother-figure.[8] But it makes for a kind of despair about weak, tender emotions which can never lead to happy endings. These are covered over by a defensive identification with the power and cruelty of the male line, by repression of the inner "mother's boy" in favor of rugged, swaggering "masculine" behavior. The mother-figure is treated with sadistic contempt in fantasy — for instance, the unprintable standard oath of Russian men — and also revered, pitied, and idealized. Girls will harbor much hostility toward men and rebellion against the marital role as a fate not much worse than death. Love is always tragic in Russia. The strong, independent woman is admired.[9]

The young child receives a good deal of spoiling, praise, and love from the *babushka*, from aunts and neighboring women, and a special kind of intimate, almost forbidden, love from his own mother who scarcely dares show she is human. All these female figures, except perhaps the tragic mother, convey a sense of support and shield the child from the excess of paternal wrath. The child's emotional reward comes when he feels he is considered strong, a good little helper, an eager student, and above all obedient and quiet. From this source we may visualize arising some typical attitudes toward good citizenship behavior in present Russian society.

Lastly there is also a strongly marked motive to escape from the tyranny and oppression toward a distant beckoning land of freedom, equality, and opportunity, where one can be his own master and lead his own life. This may have its sources in the oedipal feelings about the mother. The tight control of the kinship group by the patriarch, no less than the experience of swaddling in infancy, may be more reasons for the need for "more space," more elbowroom (*prostor*), by which the Russians are driven despite the size of their territory. Qualities which may be expected to persist, and are indeed seen to be modal, are a high degree of *strakh*;[10] a duplicity of behavior which combines a certain priggish eager-beaver subordination with a capacity for impassive absorption of humiliation and indignity, together with a smoldering sensitiveness and

[8] For example, the fairy tale of the prince who delivers the maiden from the evil sorcerer, Koshchei "The Immortal" (cf. "Firebird"). Such motivations are also one source of fervent love of the mother-country. It was remarkable how often my interviewees expressed the postwar state of Russia in terms of their "starving, neglected mother."

[9] See Vera S. Dunham's "The Strong-Woman Motif" above.

[10] This *strakh* has nothing to do with cowardice in external danger, but with a kind of awe given to authority-bearers. An example is the poor fellow Suchok, in Turgenev, who was more afraid of the barin than of drowning when his boat sank.

vindictive revolt in quick sympathy with the underdog against the authority that perpetuates these insults.

The economic situation of most peasants ensured that the Russian learned to live on very little. But this itself, together with the fitful indulgences by the mother-figures of childhood, may partly account for the undoubted longing for softness and tenderness and "fat" living as a basic motif. This is very directly expressed at the most typical end of the scale, and is strongly counteracted in the authoritarian leader sort of person. Periods of joy and happiness occur when the child sees his elders in merry harmonious teamwork at harvest time for the common purpose; and at festival times when, relaxed and all status forgotten, they feast and dance together, full of warmth and generosity. At the peasant level, it is this nature-imposed rhythm and economic necessity which exacts the discipline, not any principle or consistent handling by humans, which modally is fitful and arbitrary as well as contradictory.

IV

The March 1917 revolution was made by the heirs of the epoch just sketched against authorities essentially unchanged for centuries. It was a revolt against intolerable conditions as were all the desperate anarchic spontaneous mass risings which ineffectively preceded it. There followed a brief honeymoon *à la Russe* — a spate of egalitarian sentiment and talking in town and village meetings, and of possession of land taken from the murdered father-figures. The authorities whom the Russians had thrown off had been weak and ineffective, men, though remote in status, too much like themselves: unorganized, lazy, greedy. Into the power vacuum stepped Lenin and his coterie of exiles, with an appeal which was thoroughly culture-congenial: a father speaking in angry peasant tones yet in the terms of Western "science," promising bread and land and revenge on oppressors, a severe order, and a material plenty. It would be interesting to attempt, however imperfectly, an analysis of the psychological vicissitudes of authority relations with this peasant character, of their mutual interaction, during the last eighty or ninety years.

During Turgenev's time the established order was a unity and could be taken for granted by both him and his characters. As a barin himself, he could naively describe his wonderment at the human qualities he discovers among his peasants: how wise and shrewd the old men; how tender the muzhik in his friendship and how like the barins in his veneration of order. In brief, during the Victorian era there is no difficulty in transposing our concepts from the family to the social scene, except for that tiny top crust — the French-speaking upper aristocracy, almost entirely alien to their own lower orders. The peasants viewed the "infinite regress of authorities," to which allusion was made above, much as sons viewed fathers and grandfathers, with *strakh* and duplicity, but with an understanding of their authoritarian ferocities and a use of the same methods of propitiation and self-abasement toward them that they expected to receive from their own dependents. These traits were so ingrained that they persisted into the writer's own recollection of peasant behavior in the early nineteen-hundreds. Serfdom seemed like a safe order, a knowing where one stood. The barin, the village mayor (*starosta*), and the county police were near to their "children." Their impact was personal and their *izdevatel'stvo* was often linked with tenderness and paternalism. The bad object that deprived could be projected into a blurred distant "They," but was also attributed to one's own sinfulness.

As serfdom is abolished there always comes a loosening of the bonds of pious tradition, felt by the older peasants as a dangerous loss of security. For what happened to the barin begins to happen to the elder's own authority over his sons. The predicament is touchingly presented by Gladkov. In a scene in which the eldest son tells his father that "times have changed" and he feels free to leave home where there is no land, the old man, in an effort to preserve his hold over his son, bursts out:

We are the servants of God. We are *krest'iane* [peasants; *krest* means cross]. From olden times we bear the labor of the cross; but never the slaves of Anti-Christ and his angels, of priests or of German [the Russian is *nemetskii*, meaning "foreigner" in general and German in particular] authority, of heretics who smoke tobacco, of shaven men with their tinsel and badges. You young have no freedom nor sense but what comes from the elders. In them alone is order and firmness of life.[11]

This quotation illuminates the complex feelings of the peasant in the 1890's. There is his own identification with due authority and fear of anarchy of the young. At the same time, there is total hostility to what are felt to be *alien*, bureaucratic, newfangled secular authorities and their hirelings — the clergy.[12] Long suffering and hard fate are transfigured by the sanction of the Cross which gives the dignity of moral principle both to humility and to obstinacy.

After the reforms of the 1860's, secularization evolved along with industrialization and social mobility. The almost mythical freedom and opportunity of factory work lures the emancipated landless sons to the cities. They take with them their ambivalent expectations of oppression and of boundless hope. They already have a conviction that the urban dweller (*fabrichnyi chelovek*) is a smarter fellow than they. They find

---

[11] Gladkov, *Povest' o detstve*. Gladkov's grandfather's family were Old Believers and anticlerical.

[12] Gladkov's book, published in 1949, might have been satirizing the incursion of the Communists into the life of the village. Equally, that plea could have belonged to the era of Peter the Great.

nothing reassuring in labor conditions which exploit and deprive, without the compensation of paternal affection. Gorky was the finest painter of these conditions. Crafty townsmen and kulaks multiply in the countryside and batten on the average peasant no less than on his barin. They are hated as "man-eaters" and "fat men." We still read of religious resignation, in Gladkov, for instance, as a valued form of defense against mounting despair and envious resentment. Peasant-saints, ambivalently preaching love and self-surrender, but also calling for the repentance of the oppressors, seem ubiquitous and revered by the population just as the people of India revere their holy men.

Another attitude is so typical that it requires mention. Gladkov describes the scene of arrival of the police inspector in his native village for the supervision of rent and debt collection. When his carriage appears, the whole population berates its children, pushes the wives around, and flogs its horses — even the chickens scatter. This behavior means: "look, we are calling our dependents to order to show due reverence." But it also means: "scatter, for the Antichrist is riding among us. *We*, the heads of families, show *strakh*, but see how we can control all this undisciplined rabble." In miniature, here is the quintessence of modal Russian authority feelings as felt by the underlings: hate of the policemen who come to support and protect the exploiters — the barin and his bailiff; eagerness to show one's siding with authority by displacing the resentment down to "stupid, unruly women and children," who must be made to toe the line and punished. Scenes with similar meaning were reported to me by the defectors I interviewed, and I have also witnessed such things personally. The police or the mayor could not be seen instrumentally — only as total enemies. Some of this is, doubtless, more of a feudal than a specific Russian trait.

Closely related is the culturally prevalent mechanism of self-undoing. Caught in hopeless impotent revolt against the all-powerful creditor or oppressor, resignation and passivity fail, and smoldering hate turns against the self and its good objects. This well-documented behavior pattern of Russian life, widespread in all classes, usually takes the form of depressive apathy, neglect or desertion of work and family, wife-and-child beating, bouts of desperate, reckless drinking. Both observer and subject usually have insight that this is a symbolic attack on the authorities. In my more recent interview material there were many examples of this "throwing up the sponge," of "making of one's own ruin a stick to beat the authorities with." It is like Dostoevsky's Raskolnikov, who makes a total mad protest by murder, equivalent to suicide, accusing and expiating at one and the same time the guilt of the evil dominating persecutor with whom he also feels at one.

Scenes like those reported during the collectivization of farms under Stalin, when peasants destroyed crops and livestock rather than hand them over, knowing they would be shot or deported, occurred often during prerevolutionary days at impoundings of property for debt. Behavior under MVD interrogation as described by my interviewees followed the same pattern: "Do what you like — I am through." "Alright — kill me then," and so on.

The Soviet masters of Russia with Lenin at their head have given convincing evidence of both their Russian-ness and their hate of Russian-ness in the above sense. Psychologically we may think of them as a conspiratorial band of determined parricides who were able to catalyze the release of endless paranoid hate of Russians for the bad inner authority figure; to sanction cathartic revenge against ever-present scapegoats, and so to free also the lusty, constructive omnipotence feelings. It was a psycho-catharsis on the grand scale. But how to ride this storm of anarchic, savage hate that accompanied the constructive energy? The Bolsheviks' Russian-ness was demonstrated by their wholesale, uncompromising acceptance of Western patterns of socialism but with their paranoid lack of discrimination of finer shades between black and white, by their belief that nothing was impossible, by their magical faith in the entirely "scientific," rational nature of their "system," supplanting the sense of mission of orthodox Russian Christianity, ever watchful of the least error which would enable "the devil to get in." It was thus consonant with the deepest modal fantasies that before long they re-established the persistent authority model inherent in the Russian mind: an absolute power which is the sole repository of Truth and which cannot be questioned or deviated from. This "restoration" was well on its way by 1928 and completed during the purges and by the reintroduction of officer status with Tsarist-like accouterments and ranks during World War II. People's commissars became ministers. It is true that they still called one "comrade," a relic of the days of equality, and that some Bolsheviks were friendly fatherly persons who pitied one.

The new elite bases its goal values on the doctrine of the will — the doctrine that man can master his own nature as well as the environment. This is culture-congenial where it stresses maximum effort, achievement, and surpassing the foreigners. It is resented when it means the exercise of authority in that impersonally implacable, *nemetskii*, alien way which has been the most hated feature of Communist rule. Not only was increasing instrumentalism and decreasing expressiveness bound to come because of the growing complexity of industrialization and bureaucratization. It came also because of the internal conflict of the rapidly promoted men who implemented the plan. Though they came, except in the earliest days, chiefly from the people, these men had made the closest identifications with the Western-thinking Leninist group, with its proclaimed goals of mastering the backward muzhik and turning him into a disciplined Communist paragon — the ideal industrial man. This has meant incessant war by the party against the Russian peasant character in themselves and in the "masses." I believe this is what all the current trouble is about in Russia.

For Bolshevik fantasies, greed, hate, and apathy no less than unpolitical, human relations were a threat to the efforts to build, change, and control. This cursed anarchic human material was the only obstacle to a wonderful scheme. Hence, people must not be allowed to have doubts, guilt, ambivalence, or personal wishes. The mechanisms of displacement and projection which are by nature designed to buffer the personality against excessive guilt feelings are massively mobilized at all levels by the party elite to a degree which constitutes a qualitative change from prerevolutionary patterns. The compulsive, inhuman tempo to industrialize and build up an invulnerable military-technological empire is due, I suspect, to this paranoid dynamic. Sadistic dominance needs are projected to foreign out-groups, creating an "encirclement" situation and a siege mentality. This externalizes the "enemy" and deflects hate with its attendant guilt from the in-group authority to the "blood-sucking" imperialists, symbols of themselves, who enact the role of everyone's oppressive father-image but also of one's own anarchic greed and hate. Internal deviation can also be projected in this way as the work of "agents" of the external enemy. Leites and Bernaut, in a notably subtle analysis of Bolshevik mentality, have shown the fantasy-thought process by which the inner split of "total submission — total hostility" can create this recurring public myth of the party leader turned enemy.[13] A succession of these figures can then be "unmasked" as scapegoats drawing upon themselves the wrath and execration of the group and thus purging collective guilt feelings in the people for having felt traitorous toward the government as a whole.

This mechanism is still to some extent in line with modal behavior: it demonstrates the power of supreme authority, the all-seeing eye, to level even the strong. It increases *strakh* with its bracing and reassuring aspects. What is uncertain is the degree to which the rulers consciously use such mechanisms, and to what extent they are impelled by unconscious forces to rely on such myths and ritual expiations. We now know that the top Nazi leaders were as much the victims as the cold-blooded exploiters of their own paranoid fantasies, not unlike some of the more fanciful Soviet ideological propaganda themes. This behavior makes the most sense when we interpret it as the secondary elaboration of that early oral conflict in the Russian, that war in the mind against the bogy of anarchic strength and destructive power which has to be counteracted by all the forces available to a primitive ego.

Another, more readily understandable, mechanism of defense against

[13] N. Leites and E. Bernaut, *Ritual of Liquidation* (Glencoe, 1954).

typical conflicts is that of *manic denial*, observed also in tense managerial personalities of the West. This akin to the compulsive drive, seeking escape from doubt and guilt feelings by the restless urge for achievement and organizing activity. Here we find motivations for coercing the "backward masses" (symbols of the subject's id) to higher tempo and norms; for the need of more and more technical mastery over nature and machines in an effort to convince oneself that "everything is under control." The practice as well as the terminology of Bolshevism are replete with this pseudo-objective technological scientism. The all-pervading secret police, for example, are dignified by the term "apparatus."

The effect of this war by paranoid pseudo-rationality against the depressive, insightful, sensitive side of the Russian character, is clearly discernible. We do not know how deep this effect is, for the Russian is adept at lip-service conformity and dissimulation. We know something of the attitudes of men who deserted during and after World War II — and of those who refused to be repatriated from German captivity, most of them peasants, or "rural intelligentsia" in the case of my own sample, and under age thirty-five. They felt ethically betrayed by the falsity of their masters' descriptions of Western conditions. They also had put into practice what the dispossessed sons had always done — to walk away when possible as a gesture of defiance. The chief recurring reason given was the revolt against the party's *izdevatel'stvo* against the people — their own poor hungry mothers symbolizing their motherland and people. These men — and they could not all have been atypical — felt morally insulted because after a war in which they felt they had saved the country they were again mistrusted, coerced, and terrified into total compliance. Theirs was the groan of Russians through the ages. That part of them which sought love and nurturance from "their own government" felt enraged — not with what had been done but by the manner. It has been typically Russian for this situation to recur from generation to generation.

The chief changes after 1917 were: (1) the regression in thinking and feeling toward the least mature and most psychotic layer of Russian fantasy — from the humane, broad tolerance of good and evil toward an acceptance of "black and white" mythology, a need to betray and become a turncoat, to deny friends and one's real feelings; (2) impoverishment of free communication, and suspicion of one's neighbor as a possible informer; (3) limitation of privacy; (4) lack of security from terror; and (5) the conscious awareness of disappointed expectations that the government would speed a higher standard of living and of the amenities of life.

Defectors in the younger age group showed a significantly greater acceptance than the older ones of "Soviet reality," and their defection was motivated less by principle than by their chance exposure to the West and by material dissatisfactions.[14] They seemed to demand more from their regime. This in itself is perhaps a significant achievement of the Soviets — the truly downtrodden do not aspire to rising standards.

For a time after Stalin's death, Khrushchev not only permitted execration of the archtyrant as the supreme scapegoat, but himself wept before his comrades when he reported being forced by Stalin to dance the gopak.[15] He thus not only expressed his identification with the insulted and oppressed, but on this and other occasions staked his claim as heir to idealized Little Father Lenin and displayed his own need to deny guilt as one of Stalin's leading henchmen. Since then, as we know, he has shown more tyrannical features, tempered with the gruff, jovial "oral" behavior he typifies. His standing in the popular mind appears not to have been improved by the latter: it is reported that he is "not respected because he is too close to the people." This *panebratstvo* (hail-fellow-well-met) is not the modern Soviet-conditioned people's idea of a top leader any more than it would have been respected by the generations that preceded them. Such is the Russian ambivalence. Now, as ever, the Russians value sincerity and real warmth, and are quick at spotting false cordiality in a calculating confidence-trickster. A leader ought to be distant and dignified, and severe like an angry father. It remains to be seen which Khrushchev is.

v

In trying to strike a balance between change and persistence of the old, we must try and look at the available phenomena from the Russian point of view.

The Communist leaders have known how to use to the breaking point, but always stopping short of it, that contradiction in Russians which wants omnipotently to possess and achieve everything preferably by spurts of group effort, but which also counts abstinence and postponement of gratification a virtue. Within limits, they have given immense opportunities for able people to traverse the whole gamut of social mobility and economic success. They have created a literate population whose education has made them aware not only of their own history but of economic standards, of the fun of machine-mindedness into which so much dominance need has been channeled. They have used xenophobia and envy of the rich neighbor to divert hate from themselves to the West, weaving healthy Russian love of country into this parricidal

[14] R. A. Bauer, A. Inkeles, and C. Kluckhohn, *How the Soviet System Works* (Cambridge, Mass., 1956).

[15] See the story of the peasant Ovsianikov whose barin made him dance (just as Stalin did Khrushchev) as part of his sense of possession of the serf, and then praised the humiliated man; in I. S. Turgenev, *Zapiski Okhotnika* (St. Petersburg, 1883).

and near-demonological theme, and thereby adding a persecutory paranoid urgency to their people's effort.

The leadership has also played the role of authority according to the modal stereotype. Utter devotion is demanded but really not expected — that is, there is reliance on external sanctions and controls on the tacit Russian assumption that there is a totally hostile traitor in every man. This leads one to ask: can a society be said to be maturing if it continues to treat *all* its citizens as potential traitors and saboteurs, not fit to have mental freedom? This deep "fault" in Russian unconscious imagery moreover has fostered the rise to power mainly of the most sado-masochistic, authority-identified, and insecure among the citizens, who have for lack of other inner models aped the hate-invested, rigid, and status-conscious authority models of Russian culture, minus their easygoing tolerance and laxity. These soulless party men have made a hollow mockery of the longing for spiritual freedom, justice, and equality. Perhaps they have killed the revolution. We have seen that the young generation, especially in the cities, have so far accepted and "adapted" to the cruelty and unprincipledness of this production-machine. With them lies the future. Will they, who know no other system and whose chief value seems to be, according to reliable studies, the expectancy of bigger and better careers and rewards from it, be content with this hedging in of their freedom, especially in the sphere of contact with the West, of criticism and discussion of men and policies and priorities?

There has been a great concretization of thought and action as the result of technical education. Can the strengthening of realistic thinking in the technical sphere for long be kept out of the political sphere which is still dominated by poorly disguised modal fantasies and myths? Again, we do not know what millions of fathers and mothers and babushkas are transmitting to their children in private. My guess is that it is not very different from Gorky's or Gladkov's nursery experiences. A young simple cowherd from Viatka oblast said this to me: "In the USSR May 1 and November 7 are great feast days. But we in our village have a holiday called Easter . . . have you heard of it?"

It is thus not easy to guess how and in what direction this great society will develop its values and guiding goal aspirations. Perhaps with the lessening of their ancient sense of underprivilegedness through technical achievement, together with the enduring religious values still transmitted by Russian mothers — with the passing in a few years of the last remnants of the original Leninists and Stalinists and the emergence of a solid, educated middle layer of professional and managerial personalities — one can hope for a reduction in the primitive defensive, paranoid features of Soviet attitudes. They are, with us, heirs of the same deep currents of civilization and ideas. But they have yet to show that they can tolerate doubt and uncertainty of feeling and thought without excessive anxiety, which is revealed in the aggressive dogmatism of their recent behavior toward all those not in complete agreement with their notion of truth.

SUMMARY AND REVIEW

HANS SPEIER

I

The preceding six chapters on personal and social values in Russia differ considerably in scope and method. They contain discussions of stated and inferred Russian feelings; of traits of behavior; of Russian opinions about the self and others, social and political organizations, history, and fate; of Russian ethical theories and of stated or inferred Soviet estimates as to what the political intentions of Western governments are.

The data which have been used in these six essays are similarly varied in nature. They include statements by well-known persons, official resolutions, and responses by unnamed individuals to questions that they were asked in interviews. Evidence has been adduced also from proverbs, poems, short stories, novels, and philosophical works. The prevailing emphasis has been upon writings by professional writers. Occasionally certain important political and social events have been treated as decisions which reflect values of interest to the inquiry. Finally, personal observations of life in the Soviet Union have yielded some insight into the values held by contemporary Russians.

Each author has felt free to proceed on the basis of his own personal understanding of the terms of reference, and each has examined the data which he judged to be most relevant to his task. In these circumstances it is not to be expected that the chapters in this section are well-fitting parts of a clearly delineated whole. They are loosely connected essays, each of which discusses certain selected problems of Russian history and psychology.

For evident reasons, the chapters by John S. Reshetar, Jr., and Henry V. Dicks, which are primarily concerned with the peasants, put more stress on the continuity of Russian culture than do the essays by Frederick C. Barghoorn and George L. Kline, in which attention has been focused on the upper classes and the intelligentsia. Robert C. Tucker, too, puts heavy stress on elements of continuity in Russian history.

Ralph T. Fisher, Jr.'s essay does not offer comparisons of prerevolutionary and Communist values in Russia. It deals with the ideals of Soviet youth as they have been defined by the Communist political authorities.

With the exception of Reshetar's essay, there are very few references in all these discussions of values to religion, to the bearing religion has upon attitudes toward other, worldly, matters, and to the transformation or survival of religious attitudes after the rise of the Bolsheviks to power. Similarly, there is little if any explicit discussion of the impact of industrialization upon the values in Russian society.

II

Ralph Fisher's is one of the few chapters in the whole volume which deals with Communist ideology. His analysis is carried through four periods: the prerevolutionary era of Bolshevism, the early years of Soviet rule, the Stalinist period, and the most recent past. Despite minor changes in emphasis, the model of ideal youth has had "an almost unvarying core" for the last forty years: Fisher calls it "the eager-robot ideal." Loyalty to the party chiefs, discipline, bravery, vigilance, and militancy are extolled. Self-sacrifice is demanded for the sake of the party, and enthusiasm is enjoined upon those who at the same time are told to follow their leaders blindly. Fisher is aware of, but does not discuss, other, nonofficial ideals of conduct. Nor does he deal with conduct itself; his essay presents only official ideology.

Robert Tucker sees Russia as a double entity, consisting of an autocratic state and a passive society, the former working as an alien, energizing force upon a victimized population. He stresses that this exploitative relation between official and popular Russia has existed ever since the sixteenth century. After the October Revolution, he says, Russia "reverted to a situation with strong parallels to the remote past"; Stalin resembled Ivan Grozny, and the Communist purges under Stalin are likened to the liquidation of the boyars. Tucker insists that the image of dual Russia has been a fairly constant core of Russian thought and feeling about the state, "relatively independent of the shift of political seasons."

The distinction between state and society — familiar from eighteenth- and nineteenth-century Western social theory, perhaps especially from Hegel's philosophy of law — seems indeed to fit the Russian case very well. The empirical task, of course, is to study the specific images of the state which have been held by various classes of the population at various times. Tucker could do no more than make a few preliminary remarks on this subject; he paid special attention to the images current among the intelligentsia.

In Tucker's essay as well as in those by Kline and Barghoorn, it is made clear that Slavophiles, Populists, and Marxists respectively held, of course, very different views of what Tucker calls the image of dual Russia. The picture would become even more complex if the specific attitudes of the peasants and workers, and indeed of the ruling classes themselves, could be ascertained as easily as those of the intellectuals, who left a readily accessible record of their views. Thus, Tucker's account may be taken not so much as proof of the proposition that the image of dual Russia has been constant over a long period of time, but rather as an essay focusing on the analytical distinction between state and society. Tucker sets forth both the dissimilarities among various political ideologies in which the distinction plays a role and — perhaps too sweepingly — the similarity between Soviet totalitarianism and Tsarism.

Tucker's stress on the sharp and rigid compartmentalization of official and popular Russia points the way to a sociological explanation of the weakness of moderate liberalism in nineteenth-century Russian political thought. Such an explanation would be compatible with Miliukov's sharper observation (to which Barghoorn subscribes in his chapter) that nineteenth-century radicalism in Russia must be seen with reference to the fact that the sociocultural development of Russia lagged behind that of the West.

Examining the changing attitudes toward the individual as expressed by Russian authors of ethical and social theories, Kline points out that these theories gave little support to ideas of political reform which flourished in the West. There is no Russian tradition comparable with that which in the West we associate with Locke, Montesquieu, and John Stuart Mill. In Russia many of the influential philosophers who fought for freedom were political radicals who attacked the political, social, and economic institutions of their country and often advocated the overthrow of these institutions rather than their reform.

Kline points out that in exploring the conditions of individual freedom some Russian critics also turned against the Western theories of Hegel and Marx, because of their impersonalism and anti-individualism. Partly anticipating Nietzsche, partly citing him in support of their views, and partly turning to Kant, writers like Belinsky and Herzen, and among the early Russian Marxists, Struve and Berdiaev, Lunacharsky and Vol'sky, set forth views on ethics and social philosophy which were sharply critical of Hegel.

In this connection it may be observed that Hegel's political philosophy, of course, contained important liberal elements that were lacking in the romantic and traditionalist political philosophies which his system superseded, just as this system was designed to supersede the philosophies of Kant and Fichte. This dual aspect of Hegel's philosophy led to the subsequent development of two antagonistic schools, the so-called "old" and "young" Hegelians, conservative and liberal, respectively. Marx himself started out as a "young Hegelian," turning first against certain aspects of Hegel's philosophy itself, but soon also against other left-wing critics of Hegel like Arnold Ruge, Max Stirner, and Ludwig Feuerbach, and later against the Fichtean Lassalle. Like the anti-Hegelianism of Kierkegaard, the other important nineteenth-century critic of Hegel, Marx's anti-Hegelianism was inspired by concern for human freedom and self-determination. Marx inherited this concern from German classical philosophy. Many of the Russian social critics of the nineteenth century were well informed about the conflicting schools of thought that were inspired by Hegel. The understanding of the Russian theories of freedom will be advanced if these theories are closely examined in relation to the views of the "young Hegelians" as well as to the liberal aspects of Hegel's system itself.

Barghoorn, in his essay on "Some Russian Images of the West," is concerned primarily with the opinions of the intelligentsia and of the ruling classes both in prerevolutionary Russia and in the Soviet Union. The educated and cosmopolitan groups in Tsarist Russia were on the whole pro-Western, identifying with their counterparts in Europe. By contrast, the ruling groups of the Soviet Union adopted attitudes of hostility toward Europe and America and feared the West. As for the intellectuals in the Soviet Union, they are not permitted to express publicly any views that deviate from those held by the ruling political class, whereas the opinions of intellectuals in Tsarist Russia covered a wide range on the political spectrum. Barghoorn classifies these opinions in terms of their holders' attitudes toward the Russian *ancien regime,* a classification which can be applied with the obvious adjustments to nineteenth-century West European thought as well.

In Russia there were those who defended throne and altar and thus hated and feared the West. The extreme anti-Westernism of men like Dostoevsky, Strakhov, and Danilevsky — the latter incidentally, a forerunner of Spengler in some respects — was an expression of individual views rather than of public opinion. Danilevsky's nationalism and anti-Westernism resembled in some ways Stalin's attitude. Like other reactionaries of his period and like Stalin, Danilevsky feared the infection of Russia by "Europeanization." There were others, however, reformist conservatives and the small group of gradualist liberals, who looked to Germany or England for models of constitutionalism. Finally, there were the radicals, who turned against old Russia and expected a brighter future from the adoption of Western natural and social sciences. Some of the radicals criticized the West for its failure to put into practice its own revolutionary theories.

Barghoorn suggests some reasons for the hostility of the Soviet rulers toward the West, and all these reasons are defensive or self-righteous from the Soviet point of view. Barghoorn mentions the long history of actual Western aggressions, a record forced upon the attention of the Soviet people by official propaganda; the apparent menace to the Soviet Union inherent in more recent American military policy; the persistence of the Leninist doctrine that the imperialist states are implacable enemies of the Soviet Union; and the fear of the Soviet rulers that contact with the West might corrupt the Soviet people. Barghoorn believes that under conditions of a nuclear balance of terror the scientists and administrators who have created that balance may eventually turn Kremlin policy to the paths of peace. It may be noted, however, that, as the views of the Kremlin have become blatantly optimistic, the Soviet rulers have claimed not only that the capitalist encirclement of the Soviet Union will be broken in time but also that the Soviet ICBM has rendered manned aircraft obsolete. One may well wonder whether such claims are altogether reassuring to those who hope for a more stable peace.

III

Reshetar's and Dicks's chapters contain less controversial matter than does Barghoorn's essay, at least politically speaking. Reshetar's inquiry begins with an account of the self-image of Russian peasants. To a large extent their notions of virtue and vice are inferred from proverbs, a particularly important source of information on common beliefs in preindustrial, peasant cultures. The findings are drawn in part also from analyses of popular tales, poems, and other writings, with Dostoevsky playing a fairly large role in the account. The Soviet rulers, of course, have tried to combat this self-image and to replace it by an activist one which extols man's self-determination and ability to control his environment.

It is interesting to note that Dicks's interpretations of the modal traits of the Russian peasant, based on interviews with Soviet defectors in 1950, are on the whole consistent with Reshetar's findings on the pre-Soviet period. Many, but by no means all of them, I should think, hold for peasants in other countries as well as in Russia. The Russian peasant is attached to his native land, is aware of sin, temptation, and, strongly, of guilt. His patience, sense of resignation, and passive acceptance of fate are combined with a practical, worldly attitude of caution and suspicion. At the same time, however, he has a predilection for bluntness and is aware of the fact that he is given to "mutually exclusive extremes" of behavior. According to Reshetar, there is evidence of "a fundamental split in the Russian self-image." Numerous vices are conceded, and yet the Russians are said to be possessors of truth, a theme prominent in Dostoevsky's writings. In a similar vein, Dicks points out that "the Russian can vary between feeling that he is no good and that he is superior to all the rest of mankind."

To be sure, Dicks's psychological portrait of the Russian peasant contains more detail, especially in respect to attitudes toward authority, than Reshetar's account because this portrait is drawn from both empirical data and psychoanalytic theory. According to Dicks, the performance of authority roles by the adult members of society depends on the way in which they internalized their experiences of dependency as infants. In the primary peasant family the Russian child is exposed to arbitrary exercise of power by an "almost wholly awe-inspiring father-figure" and an "equally unpredictable mother-figure." The later "paranoid" feeling of grown-up men and women that there are inscrutably remote and uncontrollable powers — according to Dicks, a "tacit assumption of Russian psychology and culture" — is traceable to the experiences of babies up to the age of a year or more. As adults they are given to "unconscious oral fantasies" swinging between satisfaction and deprivation, which lend a specifically Russian form to the universal human characteristics of ambivalence. If a man succeeds, however, in acquiring authority himself, not by becoming a father but by reaching a position of political power, he enters in Russia the realm of a contradictory, puritan morality. He will then display what Dicks calls "the oral-anal conflict in the Russian character."

Occasionally Dicks suggests certain analogies between individual psychology and governmental political behavior. For example, he says, "The tight control of the kinship group by the patriarch, no less than the experience of swaddling in infancy, may be more reasons for the need for 'more space' . . . by which the Russians are driven despite the size of their territory." Such analogies will sound daring to historians and social scientists who maintain that psychoanalysts tend to attribute little importance to the institutions of adult society and to their power to shape the attitudes, conduct, and perhaps even the character of its members. Such psychoanalysts treat grown-ups as eternal children.

This is a wide field, and if we enter upon it it is by Dicks's invitation. Let me illustrate, in conclusion, the kind of problem which the psychoanalytical interpretation of national character encounters. Dicks refers to the observation made by Margaret Mead that Russian peasants regard their friends as though they may become their enemies. As Reshetar points out, there is indeed a Russian proverb to that effect. Now, is it true that this attitude is indicative of the oral fantasies of Russian peasants, as Dicks suggests? Perhaps so. But adages recommending precisely the same attitude toward friends can be found in the writings of sixteenth-century Spanish Jesuits and in virtually all the conduct books for aspiring courtiers in seventeenth-century Western Europe and England. Perhaps it is necessary to consider that distrust of friends is likely to develop in situations in which personal security is a matter of great uncertainty and depends on uncontrollable power. And it should be noted that sometimes such power is not only believed to be uncontrollable but indeed cannot be controlled by the person who lives in fear of it. It is possible that friendship becomes "unreliable" not because of any oral fantasies but simply because in certain trying circumstances the temptation is great to enhance one's own security at the expense of the fortunes of one's friend.

PART SEVEN

CONCLUSION

THE MODERNIZATION OF RUSSIAN SOCIETY

CYRIL E. BLACK

I

In interpreting the transformation of Russian society since 1861, it is useful to think in terms of the broad pattern of social change which is now commonly known as "modernization." Modernization is the process of change from an agrarian to an industrial way of life that has resulted from the dramatic increase in man's knowledge of and control over his environment in recent centuries. In Europe this process has been evolving for half a millennium or more, and in modern times the influence of European knowledge and institutions has spread to most other parts of the world.

Modernization in this general sense has come to be accepted as a desirable, if not indeed inevitable, change in human affairs. Yet it must be recognized that the transformation of traditional societies has been in many ways a vastly destructive process. Not only have governments, ruling classes, and systems of knowledge and belief been destroyed, but social institutions, personal values, and not infrequently the psychological security of the individual have been undermined. Even in the societies which were the first to modernize, where change took place gradually over a period of many generations, the destructive aspects of modernization have been apparent. In societies that have modernized more recently, under great pressure to compete with the earlier modernizers, one frequently has the impression that traditional institutions and values have been destroyed before their modern replacements were available. Now that mankind has discovered the means to destroy itself, many will no doubt question to what extent modernization can be equated with progress. In any event, it is clear that what is involved is a vastly complex and universally pervasive process of change.

What concerns us here, however, is not the destiny of mankind but the much more limited question of social change in Russia in the century since the emancipation of the serfs in 1861. It is significant that Russia was not one of the early modernizers, and that the new ideas and institutions came to Russia from Central and Western Europe in forms which the Russian government believed to be as much a threat to its security as an opportunity for the development of the peoples under its rule. The influence of the more modern societies was felt in Russia with rapidly increasing force from the seventeenth century on, and to the extent that their institutions were adopted it was rather for the purpose of protecting the traditional Russian way of life against foreign intrusions than for undertaking a fundamental modernization of Russian society. Indeed, in Russia as elsewhere, modernization seems to have come in two phases: the first defensive and superficial, and the second aggressive and more thoroughgoing.

Insofar as borrowings from the West could contribute to strengthening the autocracy and increasing state power, they were accepted with alacrity. The armed forces and bureaucracy were reconstructed, mines and factories were established, an academy of sciences was created, and the nobility was transformed into a class of higher civil servants. But care was taken not to disturb the condition of the great mass of the peasants, who lived in some form of service to the state or bondage to the nobility — and on whose labor, directly or indirectly, the welfare of their owners was based. Even the emancipation in 1861 was not intended to inaugurate an era of thoroughgoing modernization, although it very soon became clear that this would be its effect. The significance of 1861 for Russia, as far as such comparisons are valid, was thus somewhat similar to the change of pace which took place in Central Europe in the first half of the nineteenth century, in France and the United States at the end of the eighteenth century, and in England somewhat earlier. To the extent that one can construct a general pattern of modernization as a yardstick for social change in Russia, it must be based primarily on the European and American experience. Something can doubtless also be learned by comparing Russian developments with those in Japan and Turkey, which modernized at about the same time and under somewhat similar circumstances, the former at first more rapidly and the latter more slowly.

Although any generalizations about the course of social change in Russia must be regarded as highly tentative at this stage, in view of the shortcomings both of our knowledge about Russia and of the theoretical bases available for the interpretation of such knowledge, it nevertheless seems worthwhile to attempt answers to three rather general questions. To what extent has the course of social change in Russia since 1861 followed more or less universal trends, as far as these can be established on the basis of what we know about other societies? To what extent can Russian deviations from such universal trends be explained by certain historically formed traditions of Russian society? And, finally, to what extent can the course of modernization in Russia be attributed to contingent circumstances, and more specifically to individual leaders, political parties, and state policy?

Any attempt to suggest brief answers to sweeping questions must of necessity omit much of the detail which provides the richness and variety of history. Such an attempt also runs the risk of neglecting important distinctions of degree and emphasis which may account for significant contrasts within superficially consistent trends. This risk is particularly great when one is discussing general trends in a very controversial period of Russian history. Indeed, some maintain that Tsarist autocracy and Soviet totalitarianism are so different that any attempt to find continuities will meet with insuperable obstacles, whereas others see them as essentially similar. In any event, a particular burden is placed on the reader to distinguish between the secular trends under consideration here and the short-term developments which are equally important and were no doubt much more real to the participants. For these essential distinctions one must look to the more detailed discussion of individual aspects of social change. The reader will also recognize that "Russia" is used here as a general term embracing the wide variety of nationalities and cultures within the changing boundaries of the Russian Empire and the USSR. It is a measure of the shortcomings of our understanding of this country that it is so difficult to give due weight to the differences which characterize its many peoples.

II

In measuring social change in Russia by the yardstick of universal trends, it is useful to start with the area of government, since so many of the changes characteristic of modernization have taken place within a framework of political action.[1] In this realm, the most characteristic feature of modernization has no doubt been the growth of the functions and scope of authority of governments. Governments which once performed no more than a few political and military functions are now engaged in a vast number of activities involving not only the maintenance of order on the provincial and local levels, but also the education and welfare of the individual, the administration of communications, and

[1] These concluding remarks, not presented at the conference where the papers in this volume were discussed, have drawn so extensively on these papers that it is hardly possible to make separate reference to each obligation. At the same time, the views set forth here differ in some instances from those expressed above and on occasion enter into fields not treated in detail in this volume. Among the wide range of studies one could cite, the following general interpretations are of particular relevance: K. Kocharovsky, *Sotsialnyi stroi Rossii* (Prague, 1926); Nicholas S. Timasheff, *The Great Retreat: The Growth and Decline of Communism in Russia* (New York, 1946); Barrington Moore, Jr., *Soviet Politics — The Dilemma of Power: The Role of Ideas in Social Change* (Cambridge, Mass., 1950); Dinko Tomasic, *The Impact of Russian Culture on Soviet Communism* (Glencoe, 1953); Alex Inkeles, "Social Change in Soviet Russia," in *Freedom and Control in Modern Society*, Morroe Berger, Theodore Abel, and Charles H. Page, eds. (New York, 1954), 242–264; Otto Brunner, *Neue Wege zur Sozialgeschichte* (Göttingen, 1956); Werner Markert, "Marxismus und russisches Erbe im Sowjetsystem," *Tübinger Studien zur Geschichte und Politik*, no. 8 (1956), 53–71; *Soviet Society Today*, A Symposium of the Institute for the Study of the U.S.S.R. (Munich, 1958); and Alex Inkeles and Raymond A. Bauer, *The Soviet Citizen: Daily Life in a Totalitarian Society* (Cambridge, Mass., 1959), especially ch. 16.

the regulation of commerce and industry, wages and prices. If it were possible to construct a table showing the proportion of the gross national product that has been administered more or less directly in recent centuries by governments, it would no doubt reflect the growth in the functions which they perform. Even in the United States, which started out with a very decentralized federal structure, a main theme of its political and legal history has been the accumulation by the federal government of a wide variety of functions. Although the American political system is still relatively decentralized, the federal budget is now equivalent to about one fifth of the gross national product.

This growth in the role of government has been accompanied by an increasing identification of the government with the people, and this has been reflected in the development of political democracy in those societies where the prerogatives of the government traditionally have been limited and the dignity of the individual has been held in high respect. In these countries the rule of law, equality before the law, and representative government have been accepted as the goal of political development. This identification of government with the people has been accompanied by sentiment favoring national self-determination, particularly in the dynastic empires, and movements for national independence and unification have been a dominant theme of modern history.

Russia had a long tradition of autocracy at the time the serfs were emancipated, but there also the functions of the government grew rapidly after 1861. The areas of local administration which had been left to the landowning nobility under serfdom were now assumed in part by the government, and in addition it soon became involved in general education, the regulation of labor, economic development, and many other activities. Until 1917 important aspects of local affairs were left to the zemstvos, the local government organizations created in 1864. The central government kept a sharp and jealous eye on the zemstvos, but the latter expanded their activities steadily until 1917 when local authority was swept away in all but name. What had been an autocracy, in considerable degree restrained by custom and by circumstance, now became a totalitarian government concerned at least in theory with every aspect of Russian life. With the inauguration of the five-year plans and the increasing urbanization of Russian life, theory has been converted into practice. The Soviet government has now achieved a more total control over society than has any other modern government and in fact administers more or less directly some three quarters of the gross national product of the USSR.

In Russia also there has been an increasing identification of the government with the people and a growth of nationalism in these years, although to a much lesser degree than in Europe. Contemporary Western observers expected Russia to follow the European example fairly promptly once the serfs were emancipated, and indeed in a moment of exuberance the *New York Times* assured its readers that "Russia is on a sure, steady career of progress and reform. With the new provincial bodies, and the spread of common schools and newspapers (of which we hear such encouraging accounts), she will soon educate a mass of intelligent and orderly citizens who will be fully capable of governing themselves." [2] In actual fact, the zemstvos were representative only to a limited extent, and the Constitution of 1906 and the accompanying electoral law made reluctant provision for only a modest degree of representative government at the national level. A system of almost universal representation was prepared in 1917 by the Provisional Government for the elections to the Constituent Assembly, but this proved to be an end rather than a new beginning for representative government in Russia.

The struggle of the national minorities of the Russian empire for autonomy and independence followed a course somewhat parallel to that in the West, and after the revolution of 1905 substantial gains were made in the recognition of local rights. The First World War brought the liberation of some of the principal minorities, although at the end of the Second World War all these except the Poles and the Finns — along with some new territories — were once more annexed. The identification of government and people in the Soviet Union is reflected in the attention devoted to the forms and symbols, as distinct from the substance, of representative government and minorities' rights.

In the economic realm, modernization has meant a rapid increase in production as a result of technical improvements, a parallel growth in capital investments, the division of labor, expansion of trade, and a greater mobility of the factors of production. In general terms Russian economic development fits this pattern, although it has been interrupted by formidable changes in policy. In the periods of most rapid expansion — 1890–1900, 1906–1917, and since 1928 — the rate of growth of industry has equaled or surpassed that of Russia's rivals. Agriculture and domestic trade, on the other hand, have been relatively neglected. Also, throughout the period the state has played a much more active role in economic life than has been the case in most other societies.

Similarly, in the intellectual sphere Russian developments in the past century have in significant respects followed the course pioneered by the societies that modernized earlier. Scholarship in the humanities and social sciences expanded rapidly in the latter half of the nineteenth century, and Russia became part of the community of Western scholarship. There was an active interchange of ideas with the rest of the learned world, and Russian thought made numerous original contributions. In many aspects of literature and the arts, Russian achievements were unsurpassed. In the natural sciences, applied research was held

[2] *New York Times* (March 9, 1865), 4.

back by the relatively low level of technology, but in theoretical work Russian scientists were productive. Intellectual activity was to a considerable degree interrupted by the revolution, and after the inauguration of the five-year plans it was increasingly harnessed to the needs of the state as interpreted by the Communist Party. Under this policy selected branches of science and technology flourished, and the performing arts were generously provided for; but creative thought in the humanities, in the social sciences, and in some of the natural sciences worked under ever-tighter restrictions and in significant measure lapsed into silence.

Primary and secondary education were less immediately sensitive to changes in policy and grew steadily throughout the period when not interrupted by war or civil strife. Under the empire the government was slow to take up the idea of universal education, and much of the initiative was left to the zemstvos. Very substantial progress was made after 1905, however, and this was continued by the Soviet regime. By 1960, the literacy rate was rapidly approaching that of the most advanced countries, and educational facilities were available for universal primary and secondary education. The content of education was throughout the century subject to political control. Neither Tsarist nor Soviet educational policy favored freedom of thought, although the controls exercised by the latter were immeasurably tighter. With the exception of a decade of experimentation in the immediate postrevolutionary period, since 1861 emphasis has been placed on languages, literature (carefully screened), mathematics, and the natural sciences — the latter particularly stressed in the Soviet period — and on political orthodoxy based largely on the official version of history and on the approved religious or social doctrine. The content of political orthodoxy has of course changed radically as a result of the revolution, but the relationship of state to education, while greatly intensified since 1917, has been a constant theme. To this extent Russian educational policy has resembled in form, but with far greater intensity, that of the Continental European states.

The social structure of Russia has in the past century also evolved in a manner that is in many ways similar to that of the societies which modernized earlier. During the past century what may loosely be called Russia's elite, for want of a better term, has grown in size from perhaps two or three million to some fifteen million and has changed substantially in composition. These changes began in the latter part of the nineteenth century, when a rising generation of professional men and technicians was added to the traditional elite of noble landowners and state officials. This process was greatly accelerated in the first decades of the twentieth century, and at the same time the influence of the nobles declined even though they retained most of their formal privileges. The revolution of

1917 brought an end to these privileges, and perhaps as many as several hundred thousand members of the elite went into exile in the course of the civil wars. The Bolsheviks and their followers were now catapulted into a position of leadership, but many members of the prerevolutionary elite at the level of the bureaucracy and the professions continued to work in their old positions. It took another generation before an essentially new elite, educated under the Soviet regime and greatly enlarged to meet the needs of industrialization, was created. In the meantime the urban population has grown from 12 per cent of the population in 1861 to almost 50 per cent today, reflecting the fundamental impact of industrialization on the way of life of the mass of the population.

The family was much affected by these changes, in Russia as elsewhere. In size it has tended to shrink to the nuclear family, authority within the family has been more equally distributed, and women have gained greater freedom to work outside the home. The family has become more mobile, less bound by traditional social customs, and more closely reflects the values of the state and the developing mass society. There has also been an increasing social mobility as the requirements of industrialization have drawn more and more people into urban and professional life, as well as a gradual reduction in the differences among social strata as to opportunities for general education and technical training.

In the realm of values there has been in Russia, as in other modernizing societies, a gradual adjustment to the new knowledge and to the urban and industrial way of life. A traditional fatalism has given way to the belief that life can be mastered and society transformed. Perhaps because the Russian Orthodox Church was a state institution until 1917, it was slower than most Western churches to adjust to the challenge of modern ideas. In the last decades of the empire this challenge took the form within the church of support on the part of some priests of political liberalism and of reform of the church administration. The Provisional Government, during its brief existence, took the first steps toward separating church and state and curtailing the influence of the church on education. The Soviet government, for its part, has followed a policy of thoroughgoing secularization, undermining the church through a wide variety of indirect attacks and doing its best to win over the younger generation to atheism. At the same time, the Communist Party has recognized the continuing influence of the Russian Orthodox Church and, since its establishment as an autonomous institution in 1943, has employed it increasingly as an instrument of policy at home and abroad. The church has thus regained its formal status to a considerable degree. The government has also been relatively lenient with the Moslem religious bodies, although it has been less compromising in its treatment

of the other minority faiths. It seems likely that popular religious feeling
has declined somewhat more rapidly in Russia than in other modernizing
societies, although it still retains a significant influence even among
members of the younger generation.

There has likewise been an increasing attention paid to the welfare
of the individual in Russia since 1861. This has been reflected not only
in the steady growth of educational facilities, but also in the provisions
for public medicine, economic assistance to the poor, and various types
of social insurance. Since the latter part of the nineteenth century the
Russian state has also been active in regulating the pay and working
conditions of industrial labor. Under the empire these measures were
taken in part by a paternalistic government and in part by the zemstvos
which reflected local needs; in the Soviet period they have been expanded to meet the requirements of the continued growth of industry
and adapted to the needs of the Communist Party. There has also been
a growing recognition at the level of official policy of the desirability
of greater cosmopolitanism in the treatment of national, political, and
religious minorities. This trend was reflected especially after 1905 in the
easing of the restrictions on public activities on the part of the minorities,
and under the Provisional Government and in the Soviet period in the
formal legal provisions for civil liberties. At the level of practice, on
the other hand, in Russia as elsewhere, the strains of social change have
brought to the surface deep-seated tensions — as evidenced by the
pogroms under the empire and the extreme forms of political persecution
in the Soviet period.

Scarcely less impressive than the development of Russia along the
lines suggested above has been the destruction accompanying it. Not
only have many customs and techniques become outmoded and left
behind, but values and traditions that had stood the test of centuries
have been cast aside. Indeed, it is in the realm of human values that
the destructiveness of modernization has been most striking. In a manner
parallel to that in other societies undergoing social change, but in a
more extreme form, material values were deified at the expense of the
dignity of the individual. The impulse of the nihilists in the 1860's to
reject traditional values in the name of reason proved to be only the
beginning of a growing tendency to believe that the goal of building a
new world was important enough to justify any sacrifice. This phenomenon of people committing crimes in the name of ideals was one of the
central preoccupations of Dostoevsky's thought, and he recognized that
Russia was sharing in a widespread occurrence. "This . . . happens
not only in our midst but throughout the world," he wrote in 1873; "it
has been so from time immemorial, during transitional epochs, at times
of violent commotions in people's lives — doubts, negations, scepticism
and vacillation regarding the fundamental social convictions. But in

our midst it is more possible than elsewhere, and precisely in our day. . . ."[3]

The belief that the end justifies the means formed an important element in the Leninist version of Marxism, which regarded the allegedly inexorable laws of a historically determined destiny as the only guides to action. This attitude had its natural culmination in a political system which did not balk at destroying millions of human lives in the name of "building socialism." As Dostoevsky noted, this attitude is by no means a uniquely Russian phenomenon. "There has been a slipping off of ancient restraints; a real *decivilization* of men's minds," wrote H. G. Wells in 1920,[4] and this is no doubt one of the fateful consequences of modernization. The examples of Nazi Germany and Communist China illustrate the extent to which the deification of a historically rationalized ideology can result in the destruction of human values.

These various ways in which social change in Russia during the past century has paralleled developments in countries that modernized earlier or at about the same time are trends of such a general character that they could hardly have been avoided by any regime in Russia, although they might have been delayed or accelerated in one respect or another. They deserve consideration, however, as the setting for a discussion of the more interesting question of the ways in which the course of Russian modernization has been unique.

III

The question of the role of Russian historical traditions in the course that social change has taken in that country is both simpler and more controversial than that of the relationship of Russian to general modernization. It is simpler because Russian historical traditions differ from those of the West in certain major respects on which there is fairly general agreement; more controversial because it involves seeking out continuities between the Tsarist and Soviet eras which the adherents of both find odious. It is nevertheless an essential exercise, for it is clear that the form a modern society takes is in a substantial measure dependent on the nature of its traditional values and institutions. The things that a society does may change very rapidly, but the way in which they are done continues to bear the imprint of age-old beliefs.

The special character of Russian modernization, which sets it somewhat apart from the Western pattern, can perhaps best be discussed in terms of three interrelated circumstances, not in themselves unique yet scarcely matched elsewhere in this particular combination: the predominant role of the state, Russia's backwardness and defensiveness in

---

[3] *The Diary of a Writer,* trans. Boris Brasol (2 vols.; New York, 1949), I, 149.
[4] *The Outline of History* (New York, 1930), 1089; italics in original.

relation to the more modern societies, and certain characteristic attitudes and values.

The role of the state is no doubt the most obvious continuing trait of Russian society, and in the century since 1861 it has manifested itself in many ways. Throughout this period the state has had a virtual monopoly of political power, except for brief transitional phases of anarchy. The state has made provision for the organization and regulation of social groups. Through the instrumentality of legal institutions and of the political police it has kept a close control over all social, intellectual, and spiritual activities that might challenge its position. It has taken the primary initiative in economic growth through investment, ownership, supervision, and fiscal policy. Under its auspices, education, scholarship, and the performing arts have been developed. Indeed, it is difficult to point to a significant area of human activity in which the state has not participated throughout the century. The quality and purposes of this participation have of course varied significantly with policy and circumstance, but its existence and acceptance has been a continuing reality.

This dominant role of the state in modern Russia has deep roots and may be explained by a variety of historical circumstances. Geography played its role in giving Russia a land without natural frontiers — at least in its populated areas — and without significant mountains or other internal barriers. External influences also had some effects, for Byzantine autocracy was the principal political model for Russian statesmanship in its formative years, and for over two centuries Mongol rule exerted pressures both direct and indirect which tended to weaken resistance to central authority. In more modern times the poverty of Russia's land and the strength of her neighbors to the West have also played a role, for through the centuries Russian statesmanship has learned that domestic division can only lead to defeat and control by foreigners. After periods of profound civil strife, Vasily II, Ivan IV, and finally the Romanov dynasty emerged with successively increased authority, and a formula of statesmanship was hammered out which gave the tsar and his government authority over all in the realm. While Europe was moving from feudalism through various forms of limited monarchy and enlightened despotism to constitutional and representative government, Russia was evolving a form of autocracy which was in some degree limited only in the turbulent years from 1905 to 1917.

It is not difficult to describe the role that the state has played in Russian affairs, but to explore this role in all of its ramifications would go beyond the limits of this essay. One aspect, and it may indeed be one of the most important, is nevertheless pertinent to our problem. This is the role of the state in protecting a Russia that was backward by comparison with its principal neighbors, and in trying to redress the balance by means of a disproportionate exertion of national effort.

As a relative latecomer, Russia was confronted with the problem of modernizing on the basis of institutions and ideas borrowed from the very Western states with which it was competing and under circumstances in which failure might mean national defeat. Serfdom was one answer, for it served to mobilize the principal source of national wealth on terms considered at the time to be most favorable to the state. Reform of the army, bureaucracy, and nobility was another, for it provided the state with the technical means of playing a successful role in European affairs. Although Russia had one of the lowest per-capita national incomes in Europe, the size of the population and the manner in which its resources were concentrated in the hands of the state provided a solution to Russia's problem during the era in which agriculture and commerce were still the major sources of wealth. The turning point came in the first half of the nineteenth century, and the Russia which had turned back Napoleon was unable forty-three years later to prevent Anglo-French force from seizing Sevastopol. European industrialization is by no means the only explanation of this change in fortune, but from this defeat the conclusion was drawn that serfdom was no longer a sound basis for the autocracy.

Throughout the period since 1861, Russia has been under the pressure of competition felt by all the later modernizers, and the fact that it had a long tradition of national greatness only served to make this pressure more urgent. This position as a latecomer was not an unmitigated disadvantage, for it permitted Russia to import techniques and institutions which had been developed elsewhere as a result of many years of experimentation and at great expense. With the aid of massive infusions of state support, Russia was able to make rapid progress and in isolated fields of endeavor has surpassed its tutors. At the same time, the necessity of borrowing from its rivals has presented the state with a continuing challenge to its security. Alexander II is reported to have remarked that to wait until the serfs liberated themselves from below was the only alternative to liberating them from above, and throughout the century since emancipation the Russian state has felt the hot breath of history upon its neck. The tsar and his bureaucracy themselves undertook to serve as the modernizing elite and up to a point succeeded in maintaining their initiative. But the burden of tradition and of vested interests was too heavy to sustain this initiative, and neither Alexander III nor Nicholas II was capable of playing the role of autocrat-modernizer. Even such conservative and loyal modernizers as Witte and Stolypin came to be regarded as a threat to the autocracy, and the relations between ruler and ruled were strained to the breaking point during the First World War. The various potential heirs of the Tsarist system in 1917 all regarded themselves as modernizers, and after a brief struggle the succession was seized by the leaders best able to harness the popular desire for peace and land reform.

The course of social change in Russia has also been marked by certain characteristic attitudes and values, stemming in part from tradition and in part from the circumstances of modernization itself. Of the traditional attitudes, no doubt the most persistent has been the messianic belief, which can be traced back to the doctrine of the Third Rome formulated in the sixteenth century, in the rightness of Russian values. The belief that the Russians are a "God-bearing" people with attributes of human universality was perhaps most vigorously expressed by Dostoevsky, but it has been shared in one form or another by many Russians of whom the Bolsheviks are only the most recent. No doubt all peoples tend in some measure to become convinced of the universal validity of their views, but the Russian version of messianism has had deeper roots and more powerful political support than most.

Equally deep-rooted and no doubt much more widely held in Russia are the attitudes which seem to spring from the traditional way of life of the Russian peasant patriarchal family. In an era in which many millions of Russians have been transferred within a generation or two from the countryside to all levels of urban life, it can hardly be doubted that the attitudes and values characteristic of the former peasantry continue to have a powerful impact. Their patience and patriotism, their ambivalence with regard to neighbors and foreigners, their submissiveness when confronted by authority despite their frequent hostility to it — elements such as these give the Russian national character its distinctive features. It is indeed as though there were two Russias: the official Russia, powerful and implacable, and the popular Russia, submissive but frequently resentful. When studies have been made of the attitudes characteristic of a wider range of national groups, it will no doubt be possible to identify with greater accuracy the qualities that are peculiarly Russian.

Other attitudes may be traced more directly to Russia's position vis à vis the West in modern times, although in some instances these also have a traditional basis. The fear of foreign encirclement, a recurrent theme in Russian official thought, can be found in the writings of Ivan the Terrible. The assertion by Khrushchev that encirclement is a thing of the past, and that the Soviet Union is now becoming the encircler, may properly be regarded as a milestone in the Russian outlook if it proves to be genuine and lasting. The desire to match the West, in technology and productivity if not necessarily in values and institutions, is also a recurrent theme. If the victory over Napoleon gave the Russian government a certain complacency in the era of Nicholas I, his successors turned again to the West with almost the same unrelenting vigor as did the Russia of Peter the Great. This is particularly true of the Communists, who have systematically drawn on the experience of the West and have made "overtake and surpass" a major national slogan. This desire to borrow the technology of the more modern societies while rejecting their political and social values is by no means a purely Russian phenomenon, and indeed the virulently anti-Western modernizer is one of the more common types of leader in the newer states. With the exception of the short-lived Provisional Government, no Russian regime has given serious consideration to reproducing on Russian soil a political culture of a West European type.

Equally characteristic of Russia has been the position of the intelligentsia — deeply attached to their country, profoundly concerned with social problems, and yet in considerable measure alienated from the state. The intelligentsia was in fact defined as that group of intellectuals, the most productive in terms of the public discussion of Russia's problems, who did not have responsible official positions. They relied for their living on their literary and critical skills, if they did not have an inherited income, and not infrequently they lived in Siberian exile or abroad. As is so commonly the case with intellectuals in societies relatively late to modernize, they were torn between the European standards which they had set as their model and the reality which they saw around them. To follow uncomprisingly in the Western path meant in some degree to abandon Russia, and indeed not a few went to Europe to live as distinguished citizens of the world, returning to Russia only occasionally if at all and then usually under police surveillance. To accept Russian reality and to enter public service, on the other hand, meant to become an accomplice in some measure to the policing and censorship of free intellectual inquiry and to work within the relatively narrow framework of officially approved ideas.

If one defines intellectuals as those with higher education — as distinct from the special category of intellectuals known in Russia as the intelligentsia — it must be recognized that many intellectuals achieved distinction and influence in public service in the period of the empire. They also were keen students of the West and, while they did not leave a comparable treasure of creative writing, their memoirs and public documents frequently reflect a profound and responsible concern for the modernization of Russia.

In the Soviet era this dichotomy between the large number of university-educated officials and the small group of independent thinkers has persisted, although the issues are somewhat confused by the Soviet use of the term "intelligentsia" to describe the entire white-collar class which now numbers perhaps fifteen million. If one adheres to the earlier definitions, however, one can distinguish a continuing if limited intelli-

gentsia of free-thinking individuals, critical of officially approved doctrines and standards, irked by the constant harassment of party hacks
and security officers, and on occasion willing to take the risk of expressing
their views in a variety of ways. The members of this intelligentsia are
primarily writers and artists, but there is also evidence of unorthodoxy
among natural scientists and other scholars. In many cases they are
direct survivors or descendants of the prerevolutionary intelligentsia, but
the group is also being replenished from new sources. In the 1920's they
had a modicum of freedom, but in the 1930's many ended their days in
labor camps. The Communist Party nevertheless values their prestige
and skills, and is engaged in a continuous battle of wits and of numerous
more or less subtle pressures to keep at least their publicized works
within the narrow channel of orthodoxy.

The members of this small intelligentsia appear to have worked out a
variety of viable compromises with the state authorities, by whom they
are of necessity employed since there is no other source of livelihood
except for the few who can be supported by friends and relatives. Their
attitudes are not easy to evaluate, however, because little is known of
their writings except as they are by chance published abroad or occasionally seen in unpublished form. To this group of free-thinking intellectuals must be added the many distinguished Russians who have sought
freedom in exile, in some respects an equally difficult compromise, and
who in the course of forty years have stimulated the intellectual life of
the Western world with their acute appreciation of both Western and
Russian attitudes. These, like their prerevolutionary forerunners, can
trace their ancestry back to Prince Kurbsky, who in 1578 from his self-
exile in Poland taunted Ivan the Terrible with having "shut up the kingdom of Russia — in other words, free human nature — as in a fortress of
hell." [5]

Of the many controversies that have engaged Russian thought in
modern times, the one that most concerns us here is the debate over the
relationship of Russia to Europe. Was Russia bound to follow in the footsteps of Europe, as the reforms of Peter the Great seemed to imply, or
did she have a parallel but distinct destiny? While the arguments in this
prolonged debate, which has lasted in one form or another for some four
centuries, are too intricate to be summarized here, it is of interest to
touch briefly on the main themes as they have developed since 1861.

Of the principal participants in this debate, only the various branches
of the liberal movement and the Menshevik wing of the Social Democratic Party can be said to have looked to Europe more or less uncondi-
tionally as the model for Russia to follow, although they differed in the
theoretical basis of their reasoning. The other participants, again for a

[5] *The Correspondence Between A. M. Kurbsky and Tsar Ivan IV of Russia, 1564–
1579*, ed. and trans. J. L. I. Fennell (Cambridge, Eng., 1955), 215.

variety of reasons, saw Russia developing along its own distinct lines. The Tsarist government expected that the autocracy, supported by a modernizing bureaucratic elite, would continue to rule the masses in a paternalistic fashion. Conservative modernizers regarded Prussia and Japan as possible models. The Populists, and their successors in the Socialist Revolutionary Party, envisaged a modern society arising from a socialized peasantry without an intervening period of free-enterprise industrialization. The Bolsheviks, finally, employed the methods of the extremist wing of the Russian revolutionary movement in implementing what they considered to be a Marxist program. The Soviet state has worked out a formula for modernization that is in many respects quite distinct from European precedents, although it employs in a more drastic form some of the methods of exploiting labor which were characteristic of early capitalism.

In these various ways Russian traditions and attitudes have differed from those of the earlier modernizers and have confounded those who persist in interpreting Russian developments in terms of West European political and social values. These are no doubt only differences of degree, but they nevertheless comprise a distinctive political and social culture. Seen in a world-wide spectrum of modernizing societies, the Russian pattern resembles somewhat that of Turkey, Iran, Japan, and China. As societies with a tradition of vigorous, independent, and relatively centralized governments; modernizing at first defensively but in due course aggressively, and to a marked degree at the initiative of the state; borrowing wholesale from the West, but with a characteristically ambivalent attitude toward Western values and influences — they bear a certain resemblance to each other. This pattern of modernization is distinct not only from that of the West but also from that of the newer states of Asia and Africa.

IV

To say that the modernization of Russia has in very important respects followed the same course as in other societies, but that its style and manner have been significantly affected by certain characteristic Russian institutions and values, does not account for the many specific policies that have marked the course of social change since 1861. These must be explained rather by interests, points of view, and circumstances expressed ultimately through the medium of political leaders, and they may be regarded as contingent influences in the sense that the particular direction and emphasis of policy was the outcome of unpredictable human choices.

That the system of serfdom would at some point have to be changed, for instance, was generally recognized; but the timing and terms of the emancipation were the result of negotiations and decisions not immediately related to broader historical trends. Emancipation had been under discussion for half a century and was given serious consideration by Nicholas I; and the possibility existed of a variety of compromises between landowner and peasant interests. Once the decision was taken, it set the course of social change for a generation or more. The serfs were emancipated, but they were left poorer than before and confined within the communal framework of the mir under circumstances which gave them little mobility. Indeed, the decision to emancipate was not a decision to modernize, although the government soon found it necessary to take further measures which had unforeseen consequences for social change. Once the noble landowners were removed from their traditional responsibilities, new institutions had to be established to take their place, and there ensued a chain reaction of reforms. Organs of local administration were created, the judiciary was reformed, the representative basis of municipal government was broadened, and universal military service was introduced. Public opinion was infused with a new spirit, and most educated Russians felt that their country was finally moving along the trail blazed by Western Europe.

The exhilarating atmosphere of reform was nevertheless deceptive, for thoroughgoing modernization was as yet scarcely under way. The hopes aroused by Alexander II were of West European dimensions, but his performance was quite modest insofar as it affected the mass of the population. Under these circumstances the extremists became increasingly disaffected, and the reign that ushered in a new era was terminated by an assassin's hand. The successors of Alexander II did not have his vision, but they reaped some of the benefits of his reforms and were advised by abler statesmen. The personality of Witte dominates this period, and his skill in using the Ministry of Finance to prime the pump of industrialization marked a new phase in the economic development of the country. The rate of growth of Russian industry was among the highest in the world in the 1890's, and the social consequences of this rapid expansion soon made themselves felt. This dynamic industrial growth, however, was not matched in other spheres. Self-government institutions were increasingly restricted in this period, and harsh censorship stifled public opinion. The decade or two which culminated in the revolution of 1905 were thus marked by a combination of economic boldness and political caution which has few parallels among the societies that modernized earlier, although it resembles rather closely the policies of Japan, Turkey, and perhaps also China in their earlier phases. Here again, the origins of these specific policies must be sought in men rather than in trends and forces.

When the government's authority collapsed as a result of the Japanese victory in 1905, it had to make concessions on a wide front. Once the government regained its equilibrium, however, it worked out a modification of the earlier formula which again sought to provide for economic growth within a traditional framework of autocracy and censorship. The plan of Stolypin to make the transition from communal to independent agriculture was comparable in its implications to the economic measures of Alexander II and Witte, and had it not been for the war it would have had a profound effect on Russian society. The rapid change since the late 1880's was continued in those aspects of society that reflected more or less directly the introduction of modern technology — intellectual ferment, education, industrialization, urbanization, and the erosion of the social traditions based on the peasant patriarchal family — but not in other aspects. In particular, political power remained very largely in the hands of the autocracy, which drew upon itself all the blame for the inequities that seem inevitably to result from rapid social change.

Another emperor, or other advisers, working with the same materials, could have evolved a very different policy. As it is, the political collapse of the empire during the First World War has cast a shadow over all of its policies and has led many to neglect the rapid social change that occurred in Russia in the generation or two before 1917. Indeed, a good case can be made for the proposition that if the rate of change experienced in the later years of the empire had been continued for a generation or so without the burdens of war, revolution, and civil strife, the results might not have differed very greatly from what was actually achieved after 1917. Since no such calculation can be tested, one must satisfy oneself with the realization that Russia was a dynamic society after the 1860's, however different the pattern of change may have been from that of European societies.

The tenure of office of the Provisional Government in 1917 was so brief and stormy, and under such insistent pressure from the Petrograd Soviet, that it is difficult to evaluate its impact on social change. Such influence as it exerted must in fact be judged more as an indication of already existing trends which had been suppressed by the autocracy, or of goals which liberal Russians hoped to achieve, than in terms of its actual accomplishments. The abolition of discrimination on legal and religious grounds, the separation of church and state, and the establishment of electoral procedures for the Constituent Assembly stand as its principal achievements, and its general outlook probably fitted the West European pattern more closely than that of any other Russian government. The measures which the Provisional Government adopted were nevertheless not concerned with the most urgent problems of the moment — peace, land reform, and vigorous administration. It favored a continuation of the war and postponement of land reform until after the war; and it recognized rather helplessly that it had little control over what was going on in the country.

To many, Lenin's victory in 1917 seems to be as much a result of the shortsightedness of his rivals as of his own perspicacity, but few will deny his skill in manipulating the mood of the masses and his grasp of the essentials of politics. As a political event, the Bolshevik seizure of power was as decisive a revolution as has occurred in modern times. In terms of social change, however, it had few immediate results. It was not until 1928 that the 1913 level of production in agriculture and industry was regained, and the trend toward urbanization and a growing working class was in fact temporarily reversed. Modernizing experiments were carried on in education and the arts, but their influence did not extend far beyond a few major urban centers. While efforts were made to educate groups of the population which had hitherto been underprivileged, the quality of general education suffered. The family, youth, public health, intellectual work — all suffered during the first decade after the revolution and recovered only gradually.

By contrast with 1917, 1928 is the dramatic turning point in the Communist program to modernize Russia. The inauguration of the five-year plans, and the use of the vast power at the disposal of the government to mobilize the resources of the country in the drive for industrialization, produced social consequences out of all proportion to those of the political revolution in 1917. No aspect of society was left untouched by this great effort, and in technology and in the aspects of social change directly affected by industrialization Russia again began to move rapidly along the course set by the more modern societies. In many respects the social scene resembled that of the 1890's, although change was now more rapid and more all-embracing. It may seem paradoxical that, in the realm of technology and related matters which were his principal concern, Stalin rather than Lenin should appear as the initiator of the Soviet phase of Russian modernization. This is no doubt more for reasons of circumstance than of policy, for the five-year plans would not have been possible without the preparatory work of the preceding decade. At the same time, it is from 1928 that one must date the purposeful and thoroughgoing totalitarian methods which today characterize the Soviet pattern of social change.

Whether a change of similar significance has occurred since Stalin's death is problematical. As striking as many of the innovations undertaken by Khrushchev are, they are in fact little more than variants of the pattern set a generation earlier. The essentials of the Stalinist formula — emphasis on heavy industry and on those aspects of social change directly related to industrialization, at the expense of almost everything else — have not been altered. The somewhat easier way of life and the relatively relaxed methods of government that have marked Khrushchev's administration seem to be more the result of a need for greater efficiency and of differences in the personalities of the two leaders than of any fundamental change in the philosophy of modernization.

V

In reviewing the ways in which the course of social change in Russia has run parallel to that of societies that modernized earlier or at about the same time, the extent to which traditional social institutions and values peculiar to Russia have influenced its development, and the impact of specific leaders and policies, one is struck by the complexity of this process and impressed by the caution that must be exercised in drawing conclusions and making generalizations.

The comparative study of modernization is still in its infancy, and it will be a long time before an understanding of social change in Russia can overtake (let alone surpass) the level it has reached with regard to West European societies, for instance. Yet even now it seems reasonably safe to make two rather elementary generalizations. The first is that Russian social traditions and values are different from those of Western Europe — certainly only in degree, but in sufficient degree to be significant — and are likely to remain different for the foreseeable future. The pattern of social change set by the early modernizers in the West has had such a powerful influence on men's minds that it has become the standard by which all modernization is judged. Many believe that modernization will have a universally homogenizing effect in creating a more or less uniform world society. Yet the evidence would seem to point in a different direction, toward a uniformity of scientifically verifiable knowledge and of its technological applications but a continued diversity of social institutions and values. Just as a language may become modernized without losing its distinctive features, so also other aspects of group behavior — in varying ways and degrees — are likely to preserve their unique styles and characteristics for some time to come. Apart from the countries of Europe and those settled primarily by Europeans, Russia and Japan are the only ones where social change has gone as far as in the societies that have modernized earlier, and it will therefore be a long time before this generalization can be tested. In any event, the evaluation of social change in Russia must be based on a careful consideration of what is universal and what is relative, and a recognition that there is likely to be significant distortion when one judges Russia (or other societies) only by European standards.

The second generalization is that within the framework of traditional Russian social institutions and values there is a wide range of choice available to the individuals and groups involved in the myriad of decisions that make up social change. The state, for example, is likely to play a predominant role in social change in Russia for a long time to come, but it need not be a totalitarian state. The state is likely to be purposeful and task-oriented, but there is no historical necessity that requires it to place the real income of the average citizen near the bottom of its scale of values. The differences between the policies of Stalin and Khrushchev provide evidence of the range of choice inherent in the Soviet system, and one can imagine many other concessions that could be made to the desire for an easier way of life without significantly affecting the party and state as the source of authority.

CONTRIBUTORS

Contributors

FREDERICK C. BARGHOORN — Professor of political science, Yale University. Author of *The Soviet Image of the United States* (1950), *Soviet Russian Nationalism* (1956), and *Soviet Cultural Diplomacy* (1960). Coauthor of *Modern Political Parties*, ed. by Sigmund Neumann (1956).

RAYMOND A. BAUER — Professor of business administration, School of Business Administration, Harvard University. Author of *The New Man in Soviet Psychology* (1952), *Nine Soviet Portraits* (1955), (with Alex Inkeles and Clyde Kluckhohn) *How the Soviet System Works* (1957), and (with Alex Inkeles) *The Soviet Citizen: Daily Life in a Totalitarian Society* (1959).

GEORGE Z. F. BEREDAY — Professor of comparative education, Teachers College, Columbia University, joint editor of *The Yearbook of Education*, and editor of *The Comparative Education Review*. He has edited *Liberal Traditions in Education* (1958), (with Luigi Volpicelli) *Public Education in America* (1958), (with Jaan Pennar) *The Politics of Soviet Education* (1960), and (with W. W. Brickman and G. H. Read) *The Changing Soviet School* (1960).

CYRIL E. BLACK — Professor of history, Princeton University, and editor of *World Politics*. His publications include (with E. C. Helmreich) *Twentieth Century Europe: A History* (2nd ed., 1959), (ed.) *Rewriting Russian History: Soviet Interpretations of Russia's Past* (1956), and (with John M. Thompson) *American Teaching About Russia* (1959).

HERBERT E. BOWMAN — Associate professor of Russian literature, University of Oregon. Author of *Vissarion Belinski, 1811–1848: A Study in the Origins of Social Criticism in Russia* (1954).

ZBIGNIEW K. BRZEZINSKI — Associate professor of public law and government, Russian Institute, Columbia University. His publications include (with Carl J. Friedrich) *Totalitarian Dictatorship and Autocracy* (1956), *The Permanent Purge: Politics in Soviet Totalitarianism* (1958), *Political Controls in the Soviet Army* (1959), and *The Soviet Bloc: Unity and Conflict* (1960).

JOHN S. CURTISS — Professor of history, Duke University. Author of *Church and State in Russia: The Last Years of the Empire, 1900–1917* (1940), *The Russian Church and the Soviet State, 1917–1950* (1953), and *The Russian Revolutions of 1917* (1957).

NICHOLAS DeWITT — Associate of the Russian Research Center, Harvard University, and research associate of the Office of Scientific Personnel of the National Academy of Sciences, National Research Council. Author of *Soviet Professional Manpower: Its Education, Training, and Supply* (1955).

HENRY V. DICKS — Consulting psychiatrist, Tavistock Clinic, London. Author of *Clinical Studies in Psychopathology* (2nd ed., 1947), (with others) *The Case of Rudolf Hess: A Problem in Diagnosis and Forensic Psychiatry* (1947), and "Observations on Contemporary Russian Behaviour," *Human Relations*, V (1952).

VERA SANDOMIRSKY DUNHAM — Assistant professor of Russian literature, Wayne State University. Author of many articles on Russian literature and society.

WARREN W. EASON — Assistant professor of economics, Princeton University. Author of articles on Soviet manpower and labor problems, and contributor to *Soviet Economic Growth*, ed. by Abram Bergson (1953).

ALF EDEEN — Graduate of the University of Stockholm. Author of *Rysslands Nya Medelklass* (1954).

MERLE FAINSOD — Professor of government and director of the Russian Research Center, Harvard University. Publications include *How Russia Is Ruled* (1953) and *Smolensk Under Soviet Rule* (1958).

ROBERT A. FELDMESSER — Assistant professor of sociology, Brandeis University, and author of articles in the field of social stratification.

MARK G. FIELD — Lecturer in social relations and research associate of the Russian Research Center, Harvard University. Author of *Doctor and Patient in Soviet Russia* (1957), and joint author of *New Perspectives on Mental Patient Care* (1960).

GEORGE FISCHER — Associate professor of history, Brandeis University. Author of *Soviet Opposition to Stalin: A Case Study in World War II* (1952) and *Russian Liberalism: From Gentry to Intelligentsia* (1958).

RALPH T. FISHER, JR. — Associate professor of history and program director for Russian area studies, University of Illinois. Author of *Pattern for Soviet Youth: A Study of the Congresses of the Komsomol, 1918–1954* (1959).

RAYMOND L. GARTHOFF — U. S. Department of Defense. Author of *Soviet Military Doctrine* (1953), *Soviet Strategy in the Nuclear Age* (1958), *The Soviet Image of Future War* (1959), and (ed. and trans.) General Pokrovsky, *Science and Technology in Contemporary War* (1959).

KENT GEIGER — Assistant professor of sociology, Tufts University, and author of articles on the Soviet family.

ALEXANDER GERSCHENKRON — Professor of economics, Harvard University. His publications include *Bread and Democracy in Germany* (1943), *Economic Relations With the U.S.S.R.* (1945), and *A Dollar Index of Soviet Machinery Output* (1951).

JERZY G. GLIKSMAN — Member of the social-science division of the RAND Corporation at the time of his death in September 1958. He was author of *La Structure professionelle et sociale de la population juive en Pologne* (1929; Polish ed., 1931), *L'Aspect économique de la question juive en Pologne* (1929), and *Tell the West* (1948). He also edited *Coercion of the Worker in the Soviet Union* (1953) and *Police-State Methods in the Soviet Union* (1953), and contributed numerous articles to learned journals on problems of Soviet labor.

LEOPOLD H. HAIMSON — Assistant professor of history, University of Chicago, and director of the Project on the History of Menshevism. Author of *The Russian Marxists and the Origins of Bolshevism* (1955) and (with others) *Contemporary Civilization* (1959); contributor to Margaret Mead, *Soviet Attitudes Toward Authority* (1951) and Margaret Mead and Rhoda Metraux, *The Study of Culture at a Distance* (1953).

SIDNEY HARCAVE — Professor of history, Harpur College, State University of New York. Author of *Structure and Functioning of Lower Party Organizations in the Soviet Union* (1954) and *Russia: A History* (4th ed., 1959).

JOHN N. HAZARD — Professor of public law and government, Russian Institute, Columbia University, and editor of *The American Slavic and East European Review*. His publications include *Soviet Housing Law* (1939), *Law and Social Change in the U.S.S.R.* (1953), and *The Soviet System of Government* (1957).

ALEX INKELES — Professor of social relations, Harvard University, and director of the Harvard Project on the Soviet Social System. Author of *Public Opinion in Soviet Russia* (rev. ed., 1958), (with Raymond A. Bauer and Clyde Kluckhohn) *How the Soviet System Works* (1957), and (with Raymond A. Bauer) *The Soviet Citizen: Daily Life in a Totalitarian Society* (1959).

ALLEN KASSOF — Assistant professor of sociology, Smith College, and author of articles on problems of Soviet youth.

GEORGE L. KLINE — Associate professor of philosophy and Russian, Bryn Mawr College. In addition to publishing numerous articles in scholarly journals, he has translated V. V. Zenkovsky, *A History of Russian Philosophy* (2 vols., 1953) and edited *Spinoza in Soviet Philosophy* (1952).

BERNICE MADISON — Professor of social work, San Francisco State College. Author of *The Public Assistance Job and the Undergraduate*

Social Work Curriculum (1954) and of numerous articles in the field of social welfare.

KLAUS MEHNERT — Editor of *Osteuropa* and executive director of the Deutsche Gesellschaft für Osteuropakunde. His publications include *Youth in Soviet Russia* (1933) and *Der Sowjetmensch* (1958).

SIDNEY MONAS — Assistant professor of history, Smith College, and author of a forthcoming book, *The Third Section: Police and Society in Russia under Nicholas I.*

TALCOTT PARSONS — Professor of sociology, Harvard University. His publications in the field of social theory include *The Structure of Social Action* (1937), (with others) *Toward a General Theory of Action* (1951), *The Social System* (1951), *Essays in Sociological Theory* (rev. ed., 1954), and *Structure and Process in Modern Societies* (1960).

JOHN S. RESHETAR, JR. — Associate professor of political science, University of Washington. He is the author of *The Ukrainian Revolution, 1917–1920* (1952), *Problems of Analyzing and Predicting Soviet Behavior* (1955), (with Gerhard Niemeyer) *An Inquiry Into Soviet Mentality* (1956), and *A Concise History of the Communist Party of the Soviet Union* (1960).

HANS SPEIER — Head of the Social Science Division of RAND Corporation. His publications include *Social Order and the Risks of War* (1952), *German Rearmament and Atomic War* (1957), and (with others) *West German Leadership and Foreign Policy* (1957).

NICHOLAS S. TIMASHEFF — Professor emeritus of sociology, Fordham University. His publications include *Religion in Soviet Russia, 1917–1942* (1942) and *The Great Retreat: The Growth and Decline of Communism in Russia* (1946).

ROBERT C. TUCKER — Associate professor of political science, Indiana University. He has published numerous articles in the field of Soviet affairs.

LAZAR VOLIN — Specialist on the Soviet Union in the Foreign Agricultural Service, U.S. Department of Agriculture. He is the author of *A Survey of Soviet Russian Agriculture* (1951) and is a frequent contributor to learned journals.

THEODORE H. VON LAUE — Associate professor of history, University of California at Riverside. Author of *Leopold Ranke; The Formative Years* (1950) and of articles on the policies of Witte.

ALEXANDER VUCINICH — Professor of sociology and anthropology, San Jose State College, and research associate of the Hoover Institution, Stanford University. Author of *Soviet Economic Institutions: The Social Structure of Production Units* (1952) and *The Soviet Academy of Sciences* (1956).

INDEX